The Study of Anglicanism

Edited by
Stephen Sykes and John Booty

SPCK/FORTRESS PRESS

First published in Great Britain 1988
SPCK
Holy Trinity Church
Marylebone Road
London NW1 4DU

First published in the USA 1988
Fortress Press
2900 Queen Lane
Philadelphia
Pennsylvania 19129

British Library Cataloguing in Publication Data

The Study of Anglicanism.
1. Anglican Communion
I. Sykes S. W.   II. Booty, John E.
283 BX5005

ISBN   0 281 04330 2

Library of Congress Cataloging in Publication Data

The Study of Anglicanism.
1. Anglian Communion. I. Sykes, Stephen.
II. Booty, John.
BX5005.S78 1988   283   87–45906

ISBN 0–8006–2087–9

Typeset, printed and bound in Great Britain by
William Clowes Limited, Beccles and London

CONTENTS

CONTRIBUTORS

The Revd Canon A. M. Allchin is Director of The St Theosevia Centre for Christian Spirituality, Oxford, UK.

The Revd Dr Paul Avis is Vicar of Stoke Canon, nr. Exeter, UK.

The Revd Dr John E. Booty is Professor of Anglican Studies in the University of the South, Tennessee, USA.

The Revd Dr Paul F. Bradshaw is Professor of Liturgics in the University of Notre Dame, Indiana, USA.

The Revd Dr Perry Butler is Vicar of St Michael and All Angels, Bedford Park, London, UK.

The Very Revd Dr Henry Chadwick is Master of Peterhouse, Cambridge, UK.

The Revd Dr William R. Crockett is Professor of Dogmatic Theology in the Vancouver School of Theology, British Columbia, Canada.

The Revd Dr O. C. Edwards JR is Professor of Homiletics in Seabury-Western Theological Seminary, Illinois, USA.

The Revd Dr Paul Elmen, now retired, was Professor of Moral Theology in Seabury-Western Theological Seminary, Illinois, USA.

The Revd Dr Reginald H. Fuller, now retired, was Professor of New Testament in Virginia Theological Seminary, Alexandria, USA.

The Revd Dr W. J. Hankey is Associate Professor of Classics at King's College and Dalhousie University, Halifax, Nova Scotia, Canada.

The Revd Canon James Hartin is Professor of Pastoral Theology in Trinity College, Dublin, Republic of Ireland.

The Revd Dr Marion J. Hatchett is Professor of Liturgics in the University of the South, Tennessee, USA.

The Revd Dr William P. Haugaard is Professor of Church History in Seabury-Western Theological Seminary, Illinois, USA.

The Revd Dr Peter B. Hinchliff is Fellow of Balliol College, Oxford, UK.

The Revd Dr David R. Holeton is Associate Professor of Liturgics in Trinity College, Toronto, Canada.

Dr A. S. McGrade is Professor of Philosophy in the University of Connecticut, Storrs, USA.

The Revd Dr Richard A. Norris is Professor of Church History in Union Theological Seminary, New York, USA.

The Revd Dr W. S. F. Pickering, now retired, was Lecturer in Sociology in the University of Newcastle-upon-Tyne, UK.

The Revd Dr John S. Pobee is Director of the Programme on Theological Education for the World Council of Churches, Geneva, Switzerland.

The Revd Dr Frederick H. Shriver is Professor of Church History in The General Theological Seminary, New York, USA.

The Revd Dr W. Taylor Stevenson is Professor of Philosophical Theology in Seabury-Western Theological Seminary, Illinois, USA.

The Revd Canon Stephen W. Sykes is Regius Professor of Divinity in the University of Cambridge, UK.

Mrs Mary Tanner is Theological Secretary for the Board for Mission and Unity of the General Synod of the Church of England, London, UK.

The Revd Dr Peter Toon is priest-in-charge of Boxford parish, Suffolk.

The Revd Dr Philip H. E. Thomas is Rector of Heighington, nr. Darlington, UK.

Dr Fredrica Harris Thompsett is Academic Dean and Professor of Church History in the Episcopal Divinity School, Cambridge, Massachusetts, USA.

The Revd Dr John B. Webster is Associate Professor of Theology in Wycliffe College, Toronto, Canada.

The Revd Dr Louis Weil is Professor of Liturgics in the Church Divinity School of the Pacific, Berkeley, California, USA.

The Revd Dr J. Robert Wright is Professor of Church History in The General Theological Seminary, New York, USA.

The Revd Dr Timothy E. Yates is Rector of Darley Dale, nr. Matlock, UK.

PREFACE

The purpose of this collection of essays is to provide the reader with an introduction to the history and ethos of the Churches which constitute the Anglican Communion. This is at once a difficult and controversial undertaking. It is difficult because of the sheer number and variety of aspects which ought to be taken into account; and it is controversial because of the well-known breadth of conviction which Anglicanism has traditionally embraced.

In planning this work, the editors tried to cover as much of the substance of Anglicanism as can be reasonably contained in the pages of one volume. A glance at the table of contents will quickly show the reader what has been included, and what has had to be left on one side. The book begins with a survey of Anglican history from the Reformation onwards—a starting-point which is admittedly controversial and is discussed below. After the two historical chapters, a long contribution, the longest in the volume, considers the way in which the Churches of the Anglican Communion have understood and borne witness to the Gospel which Christ has entrusted to his Church. These two Parts together are foundational for all that follows. First, in Part Three, comes the consideration of Scripture, Tradition and Reason as traditionally constitutive of the Anglican understanding of authority and theological method. These chapters are succeeded by a section which deals with specific Anglican standards (Part Four). Here we treat not merely Prayer Books, The Thirty-nine Articles, and the Ordinals of Anglicanism, but also standard divines—those whom experience has shown to be eloquent interpreters of the faith—councils, conferences and synods, and canon law. Here too we find place for a theological treatment of a theme of great importance to Anglicans, the relation between prayer and belief.

The Churches of the Anglican communion teach and embody both a theory and a practice, which are examined in Parts Five and Six of the book. The doctrines of the Church, the sacraments and the ministry include in their perspective the whole people of God in their vocation and ministry, and the doctrine of the fundamentals of Christianity, beloved of Anglicans, as well as the equally foundational sacraments of baptism and Eucharist and the specific questions of priesthood and the episcopate. The section on Anglicanism in practice (not that what precedes it is 'mere theory') deals with spirituality, moral teaching, the pastoral tradition and Church-State relations. It is also eminently part of the practice of Anglicanism that its contemporary configuration is subjected to sociological scrutiny. The final section of the book, Part Seven, deals with some prospective issues, ecumenism, the growth of Anglicanism in its newer dioceses, the complex matter of Anglican coherence, and, finally, its attitude to mission.

From this outline it will be apparent that we have not attempted to offer a description of the contemporary Anglican Communion, Province by Province. This has been done in the past,[1] and Bishop John Howe has provided an illuminating picture of aspects of contemporary world Anglicanism;[2] but a general survey of the whole Communion would have been another undertaking altogether and has not been attempted in this volume.

The focus of this work is, rather, upon the sort of 'ism' which Anglicanism constitutes; and that is nothing if not controversial, for a number of obvious reasons. It is notorious that general terms for complex movements in human history (terms like Platonism, Buddhism, Existentialism and so forth) tend to suggest to the reader that a definition is going to be offered which will place the phenomenon in some secure location on the map of human thought. This is always an illusion, and it is one of the advantages of a collected work from many hands that it cannot be presented as though it offered a single perspective on a complex phenomenon. Any bias in our choice of authors, who, we believe, amount to a reasonable cross-section of current Anglican opinion, will have been unconscious.

At the same time it will be obvious that all of us have written from contexts in which there is the leisure to pursue the demanding task of historical enquiry, and these are mostly coterminous with those places in which what is sometimes called 'classic Anglicanism' has taken shape and has flourished.[3] But this sort of account of, and apology for, Anglicanism is unquestionably English in character, accent and idiom. Constructed in seventeenth-century England and strongly revived in the nineteenth century by the Tractarians, it was disseminated throughout the world by the rapid growth of the Anglican Communion. 'Classic Anglicanism' is what many people believe Anglicanism to be; and in giving an account of that phenomenon, we plainly run the risk of lending weight to its ossification, of freezing Anglicanism in its Anglo-Saxon past, or at least of assuming its normativeness.[4]

No one, however, who has considered the massive shifts taking place in world Christianity today, especially the numerical shift from the predominance of the Churches of the northern hemisphere to those of the south, can fail to ask whether the days of 'classic Anglicanism' are not numbered. This, indeed, was one of the questions faced by the Inter-Anglican Theological and Doctrinal Commission (of which three of our authors were members), and the mature and sensitive clarification of the issue in their first report is relevant to what we have attempted here.[5] They argue that for centuries Anglicanism has been marked by two characteristics; a readiness to be 'located' in a particular culture, place and time, and an acceptance of internal pluralism. They conclude:

It is natural and appropriate, therefore, that the Anglican communion today should take the form of a fellowship that encourages local and regional initiative and nourishes styles of church life which fit—and address—particular societies and cultures.

This book is compiled in the same conviction. It is intended to assist, not to frustrate, that process of 'location' or 'relocation', by making it easier for Anglicans in all parts of the world to understand how they came to be where they are.

We should not overlook the fact that adaptation of 'classical Anglicanism' has already been taking place in such places as North America, the West Indies and Australasia. Here much of the Englishness of Anglicanism has been qualified by cultures which are in important respects unlike those of the British Isles. But even in those parts of the world experience shows that it is a matter of some difficulty to distinguish between what is Christianly essential and what is accidental, or merely cultural colouring. If the future of the Anglican Communion is to contain still more pluralism than we have already experienced, we are going to have to be equipped and prepared for a lot of frank and informed argument with one another. It is the editors' hope that this book may contribute usefully to that discussion.

But why start a historical account of Anglicanism at the Reformation? Is this not to rule out by editorial fiat any consideration of an issue which many Anglican writers have insisted is central to the identity of Anglicanism, namely its claim to continuity with the whole history of the Church and its special fidelity to the early Church? Did not the see of Canterbury come into existence in the sixth, not the sixteenth century?[6]

In order to do some justice to the issue which is at stake we have to distinguish between claims and observations. It is indeed true that the Anglican reformers of the sixteenth century and the apologists of the seventeenth went to great lengths to *claim* that the Church of England lived in continuity with the undivided Church of the early centuries. It is also the case that many modern Anglicans *claim* that their Church does not constitute or cultivate a separate denominational identity. Despite these claims, one is bound to *observe* that the *de facto* distinctness of Anglicanism begins in the sixteenth century, and that the seventeenth-century apologists devoted the most strenuous efforts to distinguish their Church from both Roman Catholicism and non-conformist Churches.

What we have tried to do as editors is not to prejudge a verdict on the claim, and to ensure that the views of those inclined to stress the continuities are represented together with the opinions of those who affirm the importance of the reforms. At the same time we are keen to embody another proposal, namely that as an 'ism' Anglicanism looks to the future, precisely because it has *not* decided the question whether the Church must always be what it was in the sixteenth *or* in the fourth centuries. We agree that Anglicanism, even if we could successfully define it, could not be a definitive form of Christianity. While in the providence of God the Churches of the Anglican Communion may at present still have a witness to bear among the Churches of the Christian world, we can be certain that they must continue to reform themselves in the future, as they have repeatedly done in the past. In that sense we do not have to insist on the perpetuation of 'classic Anglicanism' of the sixteenth, seventeenth or any other century. We are provisional Churches; and in asserting that we do not find ourselves to be distinctive in world Christianity.[7]

The last word, however, must concern a trend which we believe we detect in some Anglican writing of the recent past. This has to do with an apparent willingness to allow Anglicanism to be isolated from the central traditions of world Christianity. It seems as if Anglicans have become rather unwilling to expose their understanding of the Church to the comment of other Christians; and it would be in complete contradiction to the intention of this volume were the result of it to be increased self-satisfaction and isolation.

The book was planned because we perceived a need to bring together in a single volume authoritative essays on the many aspects of the history and ethos of Anglicanism. We were conscious that teachers who prepare students for ministry in the Anglican Church cannot presume on much familiarity with Anglican traditions. We realized too that nowadays many Anglicans find themselves in ecumenical contexts in which they are under pressure to supply explanations for their *de facto* distinctiveness.

A sense of all these pressures has sustained the editors during the not inconsiderable labour of assembling and editing the volume. But we acknowledge a danger in its outcome, namely a further encouragement to the already detrimental isolation of Anglicanism. As editors we would by no means deplore the existence of courses (and even chairs!) in Anglican studies, but they need to be integrated with all other aspects of the study of the Christian tradition. A careful reader of the footnotes of 'classical' Anglican writers will discover to what an extent those authors were engaged in dialogue with the Fathers of the early Church, with the scholastics of the Middle Ages, with the leading Protestant Reformers on the continent, and with contemporaries, both Roman Catholic and Protestant, from many countries. It would be a complete negation of the catholicity of that tradition were we now to content ourselves with knowledge of our own great writers, or with the celebration of our own modes of thought in isolation from the concerns of contemporary theology.

What Anglicanism has become in the twentieth century needs to be submitted to the friendly appraisal of many other Christians. Our sense of living in a 'single communion and fellowship' of Christ's religion requires that we give an account of our stewardship of the nurture of those fifty million of today's disciples who live their Christian lives enriched, or impoverished, by our structures and disciplines.

It is in that spirit that we offer this collection of studies to friends in our own and in other traditions, with a prayer

for the good estate of the Catholic Church; that it may be so guided and governed by [God's] good Spirit, that all who profess and call themselves Christians may be led into the way of truth, and hold the faith in unity of spirit, in the bond of peace, and in righteousness of life.   *(From The 1662 Book of Common Prayer)* [8]

STEPHEN SYKES
JOHN BOOTY
November 1987

NOTES TO PREFACE

1 See J. W. C. Wand, *The Anglican Communion: A Survey* (OUP 1948), and G. F. S. Gray, *The Anglican Communion: A Brief Sketch* (SPCK 1958).

2 In *Highways and Hedges: Anglicanism and the Universal Church* (London, CIO Publishing, 1985).

3 The implicit claim to classical status is contained in the well-known work edited by P. E. More and F. L. Cross entitled *Anglicanism: The Thought and Practice of the Church of England, Illustrated from the Religious Literature of the Seventeenth Century* (first published SPCK 1935).

4 In his contribution to this volume Professor John Pobee discusses what he calls 'the Anglo-Saxon captivity of the Anglican Church'; see below, pp. 395–8.

5 See *For the Sake of the Kingdom: God's Church and the New Creation* (published for the Anglican Consultative Council, London 1986).

6 See the discussion of the origins of the term 'Anglican' by Professor Robert Wright, below, pp. 424–8.

7 See, for example, the argument of Christian Duquoc OP, in *Des Églises Provisoires* (Paris, Éditions du Cerf 1985); ET, *Provisional Churches* (SCM 1986).

8 The collect is thought to have been drafted by a former Regius Professor of Divinity (from 1661) and Master of St John's College Cambridge, Peter Gunning, later Bishop of Ely.

ACKNOWLEDGEMENTS

The Editors acknowledge with gratitude the substantial contributions of Dr Perry Butler, author of the second essay in Part One, in the preparation of the outline of the present volume, and of David Porter, who drafted the Glossary and laboured to splendid effect to bring order and consistency to thirty-one separate manuscripts.

ABBREVIATIONS

AC   Alcuin Club.

ACC   Anglican Consultative Council.

ARCIC   Anglican–Roman Catholic International Commission.

ASB   Alternative Service Book.

BAS   Book of Alternative Services (Canada).

BCP   Book of Common Prayer.

BEM   World Council of Churches, Faith and Order Commission, *Baptism, Eucharist, and Ministry*, 1982.

CIO   Church Information Office.

CMS   Church Missionary Society.

COPEC   Conference on Politics, Economy, and Citizenship (1924).

CTS   Catholic Truth Society.

CUP   Cambridge University Press.

DLT   Darton, Longman & Todd.

ET   English translation.

FE   The Folger Library Edition of the Works of Richard Hooker. Cambridge, MA, 1977–81.

GB   Grove Books. Bramcote.

GLS   Grove Liturgical Studies. Bramcote.

IATDC   Inter-Anglican Theological and Doctrinal Commission.

JTS   *Journal of Theological Studies*, vols. 1–50, new series vol. 1–. Oxford and New York.

LCC   Library of Christian Classics. Philadelphia and London 1953–66.

OED   Oxford English Dictionary. Oxford, 1884–1928.

OSB   Order of St Benedict.

OUP	Oxford University Press.
(P)ECUSA	(Protestant) Episcopal Church of the United States of America.
PEER	R. C. D. Jasper and G. J. Cuming (eds.), *Prayers of the Eucharist: Early and Reformed*. 2nd edn., New York 1980.
SBT	Society for Biblical Theology.
SCM	Student Christian Movement.
SL	*Studia Liturgica*. Rotterdam 1962–.
SPCK	The Society for Promoting Christian Knowledge.
SPG	Society for the Propagation of the Gospel.
USPG	USPG Association of Missionary Candidates; in 1975 name changed to Christians Aware.
WA	Weimar Ausgabe.
WCC	World Council of Churches.

PART ONE

The History of Anglicanism

1 From the Reformation to the Eighteenth Century

WILLIAM P. HAUGAARD

Booty, J., *John Jewel as Apologist of the Church of England*. SPCK 1963.

Collinson, P., *Archbishop Grindal: The Struggle for a Reformed Church*. Cape 1979.

Collinson, P., *The Religion of Protestants: The Church in English Society 1559–1625*. Oxford, Clarendon Press 1982.

Cragg, G. L., *Freedom and Authority: A Study of English Thought In the Early Seventeenth Century*. Philadelphia, Westminster Press, 1975.

Dickens, A. G., *The English Reformation*. Batsford 1964.

Green, I., *The Reestablishment of the Church of England 1660–1663*. OUP 1978.

Haugaard, W. P., *Elizabeth and the English Reformation*. CUP 1968.

Haigh, C., ed., *The English Reformation Revised*. Cambridge CUP 1987.

Higham, F., *Catholic and Reformed: A Study of the Anglican Church 1559–1662*. SPCK 1962.

Jones, N. L., *Faith by Statute: Parliament and the Settlement of Religion*. London, Royal Historical Society, 1982.

Lake, P., *Moderate Puritans and the Elizabethan Church*. CUP 1982.

McAdoo, H. R., *The Spirit of Anglicanism: A Survey of Anglican Theological Method in the Seventeenth Century*. A. & C. Black 1965.

Scarisbrick, J. J., *The Reformation and the English People*. Oxford, Blackwell, 1984.

Sykes, N., *From Sheldon to Secker, Aspects of English Church History 1660–1768*. CUP 1959.

Tyacke, N., *The Anti-Calvinists*. OUP 1986.

A THE FIRST AND FORMATIVE CENTURY OF ANGLICANISM: 1509 TO 1611

The Church of England emerged from its first century as an autonomously governed body with a character that distinguished it from other European Churches. 'Anglicanism', as a term for a particular way of understanding and practising Christianity (see pp. 406f., 424–8), appeared only in the nineteenth century; but distinctive forms of Anglican faith and practice were initially shaped 300 years earlier. Anglicanism began to evolve as English people shared in those movements of reformation and counter-reformation which divided the Church of Western Christendom into denominational divisions that have persisted to our own day.

1. THE ENGLISH CHURCH IN THE FIRST YEARS OF HENRY VIII

Religion in England at the beginning of the sixteenth century was typical of the Christian West. Foreign visitors observing well-attended churches commented

3

favourably on English piety, and this impression was echoed in the popularity of both Latin and English devotional books that flowed from the newly invented printing presses. Deficiencies in religious life which were to evoke drastic change in the Western Church were endemic in England as elsewhere: inadequate instruction of most lay persons, the related low level of the education of most clergy, prevalent satisfaction with minimal conformity and with mechanical participation in liturgical and sacramental life, failure to emphasize the principal themes of Christian faith, widespread sub-Christian superstition especially in the cult of the saints, preoccupation with manipulation of conditions of life after death to ensure a graceful passage through purgatory, and relative decline in the spiritual quality of life in most monastic and other religious orders. Interwoven with explicitly religious shortcomings were abuses accompanying the political role of many clergy and their control of a significant portion of national wealth in the income-producing property which supported them and the religious orders.

Two Movements of Protest: Lollardy and Renaissance Humanism

Before the thunder of the continental Reformation began to resound on English shores, prevailing religion was called in question by two movements: one local, covert, and comprised largely of humble men and women; the other international, manifest, and patronized by the highest levels of ecclesiastical and lay society. Lollardy, owing its origin to the fourteenth-century John Wyclif, embraced scattered loosely related coteries of sectarian believers in English towns who read their Bible in English from forbidden manuscripts and denied the priestly authority of the clergy. Such groups were to provide ready seed-beds for Reformation teachings from Saxony and Switzerland that would differ much in substance from that of the Lollards, but would share a common concern for Bible reading, preaching, and a repudiation of much of medieval theology. Renaissance humanism had struck as deep roots in English as in any European soil. Before the turn of the century, John Colet, soon to be Dean of St Paul's in London, returned from studies in Italy with a zeal for biblical studies which he conveyed to the young lawyer Thomas More and to his Dutch visitor Desiderius Erasmus. At the invitation of the newly crowned Henry VIII, Erasmus returned to England where he prepared the text for his influential Greek New Testament. Court and the universities had their circles of scholars and dilettantes who discussed the 'new learning' and its implications for introducing reforms in the teaching and life of the Church. Lollardy and humanism both fostered dissatisfaction with the religious status quo in England.

England as a Part of Western Christendom

Geography has encouraged ambivalence in the relations of England with the rest of Europe, an ambivalence reflected in the life of the English Church. When

Henry VIII ascended the throne in 1509, England was immersed—as it had been since the Norman conquest—in European secular and ecclesiastical politics; even though English continental territories, once half of France, had been reduced to a tiny enclave around Calais. In spite of growing nationalism and the ineffectiveness of the unifying role of the Western Empire, the medieval ideal of Christendom or the *corpus Christianorum*, comprising western and central Europe and most effectively symbolized by the papal office, persisted: one society, politically and religiously united, ruled by dual hierarchies of civil and ecclesiastical governments. The hierarchies could meld with one another; Thomas Wolsey was unique only in the extent of his power when, in Henry's second decade, he combined the highest offices of Church and state, serving as Lord Chancellor as well as Archbishop of York and special papal legate. As elsewhere, royal and priestly authorities had often clashed, and neither in conflicting theories nor pragmatic resolutions had England differed substantially from continental nations. In part motivated by a pervasive lay anti-clericalism, England's Parliament had been, among nascent European legislatures, uniquely active in championing the royal cause against a Church hierarchy whose upper reaches belonged to a foreign papacy. Strains had appeared periodically between the ideal of a united Western Christendom and that of the English kingdom whose identity was effectually expressed when ecclesiastics, nobility, and commons joined the sovereign to form the governing 'King-in-Parliament', the corporation of the English nation. The strains might have been contained, had not increasing discontent with prevailing religion provided the impetus for writing the medieval ideal small within the confines of one nation (see pp. 352–7).

English Responses to the Opening of the Continental Reformation

At the beginning of the second decade of Henry's reign, Pope Leo X excommunicated Martin Luther who, in turn, publicly burnt not only the offensive papal bull, but also a copy of the canon law that united the western Church under papal leadership. Gutenberg's movable type, still only three-quarters of a century old, made possible the flow of Lutheran literature throughout Europe, and some inevitably found its way across the North Sea. Before the end of the decade, these reformation publications were augmented by the works emanating from Zurich and Basle where a 'Reformed' theology, distinctive from Lutheranism, was developing. The audacious challenges to established religious authority were read with mixtures of relish and horror by those authorities, by university circles, and by literate persons either drawn to reforming convictions or merely intellectually curious. English merchants and reform-minded clerics living and travelling abroad drank the heady wine of the new teachings. Most notably, in 1524, William Tyndale sought the freedom of the continent expressly in order to prepare a vernacular English Bible. The trumpet calls of the continental Reformers evoked scattered but augural

5

resounding chords among English Christians in the second decade of Henry's reign. Lollards, as they became aware of these new religious currents, judged they had found powerful religious allies. Humanists divided: between those like More—and Erasmus—who read in their Bibles a message of Christian unity and opposed the sundering of the Western Church, and those convinced that scriptural teachings demanded reform even at the cost of Western unity.

The initial official responses of the English Church to the rumblings of the continental Reformation were all negative. The Bishop of London publicly burned Tyndale's New Testament when copies appeared in England, and the Archbishop of Canterbury made a futile attempt to buy up all surviving copies. Charges of heresy were pressed against those suspected of propagating the new continental teachings, which merged in officials' judgements with native Lollardy. The anti-Lutheran work *Assertio Septum Sacramentorum* bore Henry's name as author, and, in appreciation, Leo X granted Henry and his successors the title 'Defender of the Faith'. Thomas More, who had risen in royal service while Wolsey was Henry's chief minister and had aided the King in composing the book, took an increasingly active role in suppressing the continental 'heresies'. He insisted that Tyndale had translated the New Testament in accordance with 'the heresies that himself teacheth and abideth by.'[1] The first two priests to die in England for their Reformation convictions, one primarily as a consequence of More's initiative, went to the stake at the very time More's own conscience was struggling with Henry's anticipated break with Rome.

2. CONTINUITY AND CHANGE IN CHURCH LIFE FROM 1529 TO 1611

In a thirty-year period from the latter portion of Henry's reign to the opening of Elizabeth's, no less than six varieties of Christian faith and practice successively prevailed in the English Church. Under Elizabeth and James, pressures for further alterations were to be contained by official policies that would brook no major modification in the norms established. In Anglicanism's formative century, the two periods, one of fluctuating change and the other of tension-laden stability, provided the successive crucibles from which a recognizably distinctive form of Christianity emerged.

Ecclesiastical Independence: Henry VIII

Although concern for religious reform and national interests underlay the motivations for an independent English Church, it was Henry's well-known desire to shed Catherine of Aragon in order to marry Anne Boleyn that precipitated the break with Rome. The Pope's canonical doubts about a possible annulment were strengthened by the presence in Rome of the soldiers of Catherine's nephew. The papal predicament, Henry's infatuation with Anne, his rationalized troubled conscience, and national concern for a male heir all combined to motivate the King to press for an exclusively English solution.

Thomas Wolsey had shown Henry how ecclesiastical and civil authority might be effectively combined. From Wolsey's protégé Thomas Cromwell, Henry learned to manipulate Parliament to achieve royal goals. A four-year series of parliamentary Acts culminated in 1534 with the declaration that England's king is 'the only supreme head in earth of the Church of England, called *Anglicana Ecclesia*'. The concurrent clerical convocations affirmed that, according to the Scriptures, the Bishop of Rome had no 'greater jurisdiction in England than any other foreign bishop'. In some English eyes, the Church had returned to its ancient pristine condition when it had been 'sufficient and meet of itself, without the intermeddling of any exterior person' to manage its own affairs.[2] The judgement of others, that England had betrayed the unity of Christendom, was reflected in the witness of Thomas More and the respected Bishop John Fisher who were executed for their resistance to the implementation of the parliamentary decisions.

Parliament expressly declared that ecclesiastical independence did not imply any intention 'to decline or vary from ... Christ's Church' concerning 'the Catholic faith of Christendom'.[3] Yet Henry designated Thomas Cranmer to be Archbishop of Canterbury, a priest touched by Lutheranism through his reading at Cambridge and his experience in Germany where he had married a niece of Andreas Osiander, a prominent reformer. By 1540 English monasteries, fixtures of society since the sixth century, disappeared, their wealth to be employed for the public good as the King might define it. If the dissolution of the monasteries was the most significant direct social consequence of the break with Rome, the provision of the vernacular 'Great' Bible which first appeared in 1539 was the most significant religious consequence. The few other changes in church life were minor, and official stances on Christian faith and practice remained much as they had been when Henry came to the throne.

Programme of Coherent Protestant reform: Edward VI

When the nine-year-old Edward VI ascended the throne in 1547, the ruling Privy Council designated by Henry included a majority who favoured reformation. The new king's uncle, the soon-to-be Earl of Somerset, successfully gained control of the Council, and in tandem with Archbishop Cranmer and other fellow councillors began to encourage policies for religious change. Two and a half years later, Somerset was replaced by the more unscrupulous Earl of Northumberland, and the pace of reforming measures accelerated until they were abruptly halted by Edward's death in 1553.

Initially the Council prescribed homilies and ordered a greater use of English in parish worship. By abolishing chantries for requiem Masses and other church endowments, Parliament transferred a second block of properties into royal and private treasuries. Within two years, Parliament authorized the fully-fledged English liturgy of the 1549 Book of Common Prayer. Three years later, just as the country was becoming accustomed to the new vernacular forms, they were replaced by those of a second Prayer Book, more markedly identifiable with the continental Reformation. Convocation and Parliament formally sanctioned clerical marriage. Reform-minded bishops were appointed to replace those unable to support the changing norms. A new doctrinal stance was underscored in 1553 by forty-two *Articles of Religion* (see pp. 133–7) and an accompanying catechism (see pp. 156–9). In six years the Church of England had moved from traditional patterns through two sequential stages of religious reform.

Return to Roman Obedience : Mary

Mary Tudor interpreted the widespread rejoicing that greeted her accession to the throne, and the consequent fall of the unpopular Northumberland, as a mandate to return to the 'old religion' which 'God and the world' knew she had 'ever professed from her infancy'.[4] Within a year and a half, successive Parliaments repealed in stages the legislation of Henry and Edward, and Cardinal Reginald Pole absolved the nation from its sin of schism from the Roman see.

Married clergy, the Prayer Book, 'heretical' teachings, even the vernacular Bibles disappeared from public view, and only the largely untouched transfers of property remained of the reforms of the two preceding reigns. The revival of heresy laws brought nearly 300 martyrs to the stake. Other English men and women practised their religion in secret as Lollards had once done, and some 800 fled abroad to Protestant havens. Outwardly, Mary's five-year reign restored the forms of the English Church to those of the earlier years of her father's reign. Contrary to Mary's deepest hopes, however, many came to identify the Roman obedience with the stench of burning flesh, with her unpopular marriage to Philip of Spain, and, near the end of the reign, with the loss of Calais. When she died in 1558 Mary, like her brother, had not reigned long enough to stabilize the religion she would have replanted in English society and in English hearts.

A Stable Settlement of Religion : Elizabeth I

Six months after Mary's death, Paul IV received a report that Elizabeth was torn in religious matters between 'her pernicious learning on the one hand and her fear of losing the State on the other'.[5] The 'pernicious learning' from the reigns of her father and brother had already carried the day, for, from her first weeks as Queen, the records evidence a consistent determination to repudiate papal authority once again. After the Queen's death, Francis Bacon commented that 'within the compass of one year she did so establish and settle all matters belonging to the church, as she departed not one hair's breadth from them to the end of her life'.[6] Parliament passed legislation that recognized the sovereign as 'supreme governor' of the Church and prescribed a third Prayer Book largely based on Edward's second book. Elizabeth issued a set of injunctions governing various details of church life, and these, together with the 1559 Prayer Book (see p. 129) and royal supremacy, undergirded religious policy throughout her reign.

The Council of Trent held its final sessions during the first decade of Elizabeth's reign, and Roman Catholicism, fortified by the vigour of Counter-Reformation spirituality, proved a formidable opponent to the established Church of England. However, English men and women who clung to the 'old ways', and priests who attempted to minister to them, were caught in the dilemma posed by international politics. When in 1570 Pius V excommunicated and formally deposed Elizabeth, he identified English papal adherents as potential traitors. The fanatics who sought to force a return to Roman obedience by foreign invasion or by the assassination of Elizabeth never gained popular support among their coreligionists. Nevertheless, their plots brought the savage forms of torture and execution reserved for traitors down upon missionary priests who sought, for the cause of religion, to maintain and expand the Roman Catholic community in England.

Even in Elizabeth's first year, it became clear that there were, among reform-minded lay persons and clerics, determined militants who viewed the 1559 Settlement as an interim measure, leading to fuller reform modelled by the continental Churches that some of them had known in exile. Militants looked forward hopefully to the 1563 clerical Convocations, but all that emerged was a conservative revision of the Edwardian *Articles of Religion*. Disputes initially centred upon vestments and outward clerical dress. But from 1572 on, a well-organized minority among those who became known as 'Puritans' worked to replace the established episcopal ministry with presbyterian structures, in order to implement the discipline and godly order in behaviour and worship that they professed to find in the New Testament. Failing in Convocations, Puritans turned to Parliament where, although they could muster significant support, the Queen repeatedly frustrated their proposals. Elizabeth's death in 1603 left an English Church whose character had been shaped by the 1559 Settlement, by the external struggle with Roman Catholics, and by the internal tensions between supporters of that Settlement and those who judged the Reformation still unfinished in England.

Continued Struggle and Collaboration : First Years of James I

As James VI of Scotland travelled south to assume additional responsibilities as James I of England, he was met by Puritan representatives who hoped that he, raised in the Reformed Scottish Kirk, would bring in the 'due and godly reformation' that Elizabeth had so often blocked. Implementing his initial genial response, James brought bishops and Puritan divines together for a conference in Hampton Court Palace that concluded with the King's ringing support of the bishops and led to the promulgation of the 1604 Prayer Book (see p. 129), which

9

included only minor concessions to Puritan consciences. From the ensuing Convocation, a *Book of Canons* (see pp. 200–202) emerged which largely reaffirmed established norms and left little legal room for Puritan nonconformity.

The conference produced one major fruit: a new translation of the Scriptures. Marian exiles had prepared the Genevan Bible, and the Elizabethan bishops had produced their own revision in 1568. The bishops and James objected to doctrinally-biased explanatory notes in the Genevan work, and Puritans protested at inaccuracies in the authorized Bishops' Bible. When Puritans spontaneously broached the idea of a new translation, James became enthusiastic and entrusted the project to Bishop Richard Bancroft, soon named to the see of Canterbury. Bancroft organized a series of scholarly committees to undertake the work, and staunch upholders of the establishment worked hand in hand with fellow churchmen who longed for further reformation. In 1611, the Authorized or 'King James' Bible appeared, to become *the* Bible for three and a half centuries for all English-speaking Christians except Roman Catholics—perhaps a unique instance in human history in which a committee has produced a literary masterpiece.

The century from Henry VIII's accession to the publication of the King James Bible had been formative in shaping the outlines of a distinctive way of believing and practising the Christian faith.

3. WORSHIP AND TEACHING IN THE ENGLISH CHURCH

Although Anglicanism has never been easily defined, the weight of most descriptions rests upon the historical ancestry of Anglican Churches through the English Reformation. This merely shifts the question: how can the English Reformation be interpreted? No single dominating personality, no single coherent theological principle, no single developed theological system, no single distinctive vision of community discipline predominated in directing the course of events in England. The English Reformation may be best understood as a *political* occurrence—provided that 'political' be understood to refer not only to civil matters, but to wider human relations as they reflect the varied aspects of community life, including religious practices, convictions, and church structures. Continental Reformations were also political in this sense. But the political processes for Lutherans, Reformed, and Anabaptists were subordinated to, and/ or rationalized by, more clearly articulated and more sharply focused religious grounds that carried wide acceptance by members of these particular Church communities. In continental terms, the process (but not the content) was most akin to that of the Roman Catholic 'Counter-Reformation'.

The two sixteenth-century English leaders with the greatest influence on the eventual character of Anglicanism were the martyred cleric Thomas Cranmer, the primary architect of the Book of Common Prayer, and his god-daughter, the royal laywoman Elizabeth Tudor, whose consistent policies during her long reign allowed the Settlement to shape religious attitudes and convictions. Neither expressly laid out for contemporaries—or for later scholars—full expositions of their understandings of Christian faith and practice. Whereas, in continental Reformation communities, the theological giants of the respective traditions appeared as the communities were initially formed, the sixteenth-century English theologian most widely read in succeeding centuries was Richard Hooker, who did not publish until the 1590s (see pp. 164–6, 319–20). Hooker, born in Mary's reign, grew to maturity within the Elizabethan Church, and he wrote to defend and to explain the Church in which he had experienced the gospel and learned theology. An articulation of the stance of the English Church came toward the end, rather than at the beginning, of its reformation.

Foundations of New Religious Understandings: Bible and Prayer Book

When Henry VIII in 1538 ordered the English Bible to be placed in parish churches where 'parishioners may most commodiously resort to the same and read it', the theologically conservative monarch supplied the foundation for doctrinal change and a new piety. Initial royal injunctions of Edward's reign built on the foundation by ordering English lections to be read at certain Latin rites and by instructing clergy not to discourage private reading, but to 'exhort every person to read [the Bible], as the very lively word of God' that Christians must 'embrace, believe, and follow, if they look to be saved'.[7] In two years vernacular Prayer Books included English eucharistic lessons and a lectionary for daily offices in which most of the Old Testament was read once, and most of the New three times, yearly. Editions of English Bibles appeared in increasing numbers, and, by the time the King James' version (the Authorized version) was undertaken, the vernacular Scriptures had secured a dominant place in the cultural, educational and political, as well as the religious, life of the nation (see pp. 247–50).

The new ordination rites required priests to teach nothing as 'required of necessity to eternal salvation', but that which might be 'proved by the scripture'.[8] In Elizabeth's reign, disagreement concerning the application of biblical authority to those things not 'required' for eternal salvation underlay the conflict between reformers pressing for further change and upholders of the Settlement. The Cambridge Puritan William Perkins expressed the conviction of English militants and continental Reformed that Scripture 'must be our rule and square whereby we are to frame and fashion all our actions'.[9] Like Lutherans who judged that the Bible permitted what it did not expressly prohibit, Hooker argued that 'it is no more disgrace for scripture to have left a number of . . . things free to be ordered at the discretion of the Church, than for nature to have left it unto the wit of man to devise his own attire'.[10]

With the exception of a 1544 English Litany, Latin rites remained in place under Henry, but Thomas Cranmer's genius for vernacular liturgy immediately found free rein under his son's government. Royal injunctions and orders accompanying a parliamentary Act for communion in two kinds inserted English lections and devotions in the Latin services, including a general confession which encouraged communions by circumventing preparatory private confession. The Uniformity Act authorizing the 1549 Prayer Book replaced Latin services entirely with English rites allowing fuller congregational participation, reducing the eight monastic offices to public Morning and Evening Prayer, and reforming the eucharistic rite to emphasize communion and to minimize the sacrificial character of the Mass (see pp. 285–290).

Critiques of continental Reformers Martin Bucer and Peter Martyr Vermigli from English university posts, the example of John à Lasco's London strangers' church, and conservative interpretations of the new services combined to encourage reformers to seek further change. When the 1552 Prayer Book emerged, its rubrics confirmed the replacement of altars with a wooden holy table in the midst of choir or nave, eliminated traditional vestments except for the surplice and the bishops' choir dress, added a penitential tone to the daily offices, and severely reformed the Eucharist, leaving a drastically shorn, but still precatory, canon of consecration (see pp. 272–6).

After the eclipse of liturgical reform under Mary, the 1559 Prayer Book and Elizabeth's orders in the first years of her reign established norms of worship slightly more traditional than those of Edward's final year. Puritan consciences were offended by 'popish' remnants still present in Prayer Book rites: the required vestments, now including the cope; clerical street dress; the draped holy table placed, out of communion, as an altar; unleavened communion bread; crossing of the forehead in baptism; and the ring in marriage. Conscientious nonconformity was common and led to bitter battles in church courts and pamphlet polemics. Puritan-endowed lectureships in some towns provided additional sermons, but, in spite of the dramatic increase of educated preaching clergy from 1559 to 1611, militant reformers continued to bewail clerical 'dumb dogs' who could only read homilies. Congregational reluctance to depart from the customary medieval yearly communion meant that Eucharists were commonly celebrated only quarterly or monthly. Lengthy liturgies of Morning Prayer, Litany, Antecommunion, and sermon or read homily comprised the normal Sunday worship of English congregations. By 1611, a third generation of English men and women were learning and practising their religion within the context of the Prayer Book which, together with the Bible, provided the foundation of religious teachings and piety.

Doctrinal Definitions and Postures

The English Church under Henry alternately entertained and rejected Protestant teachings, and the reign ended with doctrinal norms encapsulated in the 1539

12

Six Articles Act and the 1543 *King's Book*, which affirmed only slightly modified medieval teachings. At the beginning of Edward's reign, Parliament voided the two conservative standards, and the Council issued the *Homilies* (see pp. 137–40) which were to be read by non-preaching clergy and included Cranmer's unequivocal assertion of justification by grace through faith (see pp. 64–71). The Prayer Book reflected these new emphases, and also confirmed traditional doctrine in the use of the Apostles', Nicene, and Athanasian creeds and in the brief childrens' catechism (see p. 158). The forty-two *Articles of Religion* with an appended catechism, published just before Edward's death, reflected common protestant convictions. Echoing phrases from Lutheran formularies, the *Articles* were closer to Reformed understandings of predestination and the eucharistic presence.

John Jewel published *An Apology of the Church of England* in 1562, seating the Church firmly with continental Lutherans and Reformed in opposition to Roman Catholic and Anabaptist extremes. Dean Nowell of St Paul's produced a catechism more heavily indebted to Calvin's Genevan catechism than to the 1553 English catechism. Although militants failed to gain confessional status for it in the 1563 Convocation, the bishops later authorized schoolmasters to employ the catechism in both Latin and English to instruct their charges. The same Convocation remoulded the 1553 Articles into the durable Thirty-nine Articles, to which clergy were to be required to subscribe at times of vocational transitions. The new version emphasized rejection of current Roman Catholicism, weakened the article on predestination, and, in concert with Prayer Book changes, strengthened the affirmation of eucharistic presence. Many Calvinists, increasingly concerned to emphasize the decrees of double predestination, found the revised article too ambiguous. Substantially compatible with views on the eucharistic presence ranging from those of Bullinger to Melanchthon, the Articles excluded both transubstantiation and minimalist Zwinglianism, and the Lutheranism of the 1577 Formula of Concord would judge them inadequate. Parliament's 1571 act requiring clerical subscription was claimed by some Puritans to apply 'only' to doctrinal Articles, excusing them from those concerning polity and order; but bishops, with unambiguous canons, insisted on the full thirty-nine.

The latitude of English theological standards was well established during the half-century after the Settlement. William Perkins developed a well-formed 'Calvinist' theological system that was influential throughout the Reformed world. At the same time in the same Church Richard Hooker provided a theological framework that eschewed systems and grounded its judgements in the authority of Scripture and reason illumined by tradition (see Part Three).

An Articulated Anglicanism: Ecumenical Implications of a non-Confessional Church

The political and social processes of the formative century of Anglicanism established a national Church unique in the Reformation era. Incorporating the fundamental insights of the continental Reformers, the Church of England grounded its religious unity, not in a confessional statement, but in (1) the supremacy of Scripture, allowing for varying interpretations of its application to contemporary morals and church life, and (2) an agreed liturgy which, with many *implicit* theological perspectives, contained as *explicit* doctrinal standards only the ancient creeds and a brief children's catechism. The Articles provided teaching standards for the clergy. Laity were directly exposed to the Book of Common Prayer and its scriptural lections; only indirectly did official doctrinal standards touch them as they listened to the official Homilies or to preachers expected to conform to the Articles.

The medieval emphasis on 'sacrament' over 'word' shifted radically in the Reformation; and identifying 'word' as sermon, all English Reformers regretted—and militants violently condemned—non-preaching priests (see pp. 185–8). Archbishop Grindal, who shared many Puritan concerns, termed sermons the 'ordinary mean and instrument of the salvation of mankind'.[11] Yet Richard Hooker, who could warmly commend sermons as 'keyes to the kingdom of heaven', insisted that scriptural readings, catechetical exercises, and the homilies also qualified as 'preaching'. Hooker wedged his discussion of preaching in between discussions of church buildings and liturgical minutiae; when he turned to the sacraments, he drew back to discuss fundamental Christological doctrines: 'It seemeth requisite that we first consider how God is in Christ, then how Christ is in us, and how the sacraments do serve to make us partakers of Christ. . . . They which by baptism have laid the foundation and attained the first beginning of a new life have [in the Eucharist] their nourishment and food prescribed for continuance of [that] life in them.'[12] Hooker's balance of word and sacrament is quite different from Grindal's. In spite of the infrequency of eucharistic celebrations in the Elizabethan Church and doctrinal standards held in common with English Puritans, Hooker's understanding of the *role* of sacraments in the Christian life is far closer to their place in traditional Catholicism.

In a period in which most Western Churches were narrowing standards of orthodox belief and practice, the official policies of the Church of England remained remarkably open to wider understandings. The devout and the indifferent, traditionalists and Puritans, learned and illiterate lived out their faith within one framework. Both Roman Catholics without and militants within the communion of the national Church might dissent, but increasing numbers of English clerics and lay persons had become convinced that, in words Elizabeth had written to Emperor Ferdinand, they followed 'no novel and strange religions, but that very religion which is ordained by Christ, sanctioned by the primitive and Catholic Church and approved by the consentient mind and voice of the most early Fathers'.[13] In this context, Richard Hooker could suggest that the bloodshed and waste of the divisions of 'Christendom' might induce Churches 'on all sides' to enter into 'such consultation as may tend to the best reestablishment of the whole Church of Jesus Christ'. He was confident that the 'calm and moderate' course of the English Reformation would 'serve as a profitable direction' for that ecumenical endeavour.[14]

4. Visions of a Unitive Society: Temporal and Spiritual Government

The medieval vision of a unitive society continued in various forms among the established separated Churches of Western Christendom. With political theories grounded in theology, various configurations of coercive authority linked the spiritual and the temporal within societies that constituted both political and religious units. Royal supremacy and traditional episcopal church government characterized the distinctive English configuration.

Royal Supremacy and Parliament

Parliament established royal supremacy even though, in theory, the legislators had only recognized what they believed 'justly and rightfully is and ought to be'.[15] English legislative authority lay with the vaguely defined 'King-in-Parliament', and although bishops already represented the spiritual estate in the House of Lords, the clerical Convocations came to be regarded as adjuncts to Parliament. According to Hooker, 'the very essence of all government' depended upon Parliament 'together with the Convocation annexed', a body consisting of the king and all his subjects, present either in person or by representation. The Henrician laws provided the king with the same legislative initiative and veto over canons of Convocation that he held over statutory legislation in Parliament. Hooker denied that 'the clergy only' ought to be able to legislate laws for laity; rather only the Crown and temporal lords and commons, together with the spiritual estate, could provide the 'general consent' of the whole Church necessary 'to define [its] regiment'[16] (see pp. 353–5).

Parliamentary statutes introduced the major structural changes of the English Reformation. Historians are still debating how the balance contained in the phrase 'King-in-Parliament' changed in favour of the representatives in the course of the sixteenth and seventeenth centuries. The degree of an actual power shift in Elizabethan days was probably minimal, but, on occasion, Protestant militants in Commons under Elizabeth acted as though their right of free speech included a right to initiate religious legislation. Privy councillors at times encouraged legislative proposals that would have modified the religious settlement. The Queen repeatedly employed her royal prerogative to block consideration of Puritan proposals as the causes of Puritanism and parliamentary democracy began to converge.[17] Elizabeth, forbidding Parliament to modify the terms of the 1559 Settlement, looked to Convocation as the proper arena for religious initiatives.

Royal Supremacy: Limits and Exercise

In spite of centuries of royal direction of church affairs and theories of imperial authority stretching back to Constantine, when the king was declared 'supreme head', no clear precedent dictated either the limits of royal supremacy or the means by which it might be exercised. The reigns of Henry and Edward produced experimental models, but only in the long rule of Elizabeth did a workable pattern emerge that was, with varying degrees of skill, exercised by her Stuart successors.

Henry VIII's insatiable vanity encouraged grandiose images of royal supremacy that lacked definition of limits. The exercise of supremacy by Edward's Council and its theoretical repudiation by Mary made extravagant claims less tenable. When Elizabeth substituted 'governor' for 'head', she cleared the title of implications stemming from its Pauline imagery. Her Injunctions repudiated any claim to 'the authority and power of ministry of divine offices', and the Supremacy Act denied the Crown's right to define any heresy but that determined by plain scriptural words or the first four ecumenical councils, assigning more subtle distinctions to lay and clerical orders in Parliament and Convocation. What the Queen held was, as the *Articles* put it, 'the chief government of all estates', ecclesiastical and civil.[18] Whereas continental Lutheran and Reformed deprecated what they judged an erroneous sacerdotalism in the distinction between estates spiritual and temporal, English royal supremacy was based on that distinction. Throughout Europe, religion was expected to be enforced by police powers; in England, as Hooker described it, the Monarch exercised that coercive authority 'over all both persons and causes', but she did so by law whose 'bounds and limits' were known.[19] The limits might be fuzzier than Hooker's statement suggests, but the fact of limits was clearly acknowledged.

Until the demise of Thomas Cromwell, Henry delegated his new authority to his chief minister. Appropriating the monasteries, issuing royal injunctions, or supervising the English Bible, Cromwell acted as a lay 'vicegerent' for the king's jurisdiction ecclesiastical. In Edward's reign, the Privy Council wielded royal supremacy on the boy's behalf, making day-to-day decisions on church matters alongside their other business. Cranmer held a key voice in religious affairs, but the net effect tended to reduce the Church to a governmental ministry of religion. Elizabeth avoided the indiscriminate mingling of ecclesiastical and civil affairs by exercising her supreme governorship primarily through commissions authorized by the 1559 Act. Her chief instrument was the central Ecclesiastical Commission at London, which always included the Archbishop of Canterbury, the Bishop of London, other higher clerics, and a clutch of prominent lay persons. The governmental instruments of the Church maintained, apart from civil authorities, an identity which is not obscured by the many conjunctures at national and local levels. Archbishop Whitgift might serve on the Council and privy councillors on church commissions as 'convenient and meet' interlocking directorates, but when the Queen formally exercised her governorship of the Church, the channels remained distinct from those of the state.[20]

Structures of Church Ministry and Government

Those Puritans who looked to Geneva sought 'an equality of ministers' instead of 'an archbishop or lord bishop', a 'godly signory' in every congregation instead of 'chancellors, archdeacons, officials, commissaries, proctors, summoners, churchwardens, and such like'; and a 'deaconship' which was not 'confounded with the ministry'.[21] Puritan dismay at the structures of their national Church eloquently testifies to the continuity of medieval forms of ministry and government through the English Reformation. The organizational life of provinces, dioceses, cathedrals, and parishes with their varied officials, courts, and procedures remained as they had been before 1534. Canon law, although drastically modified by repudiation of the papacy, remained in force except as cancelled by specific statutory and canonical legislation or by exercise or royal supremacy.

The medieval system of patronage prevailed. The dissolution of monasteries significantly increased the proportion of lay patrons as parish livings passed to them from the Crown. Crown, nobility, bishops, various collegial bodies, and local gentry appointed clergy to posts whose income often bore little relation to the responsibilities of the cure. The Crown continued to name the candidates whom cathedral chapters were expected to elect to the episcopate, but no longer could appeals to Rome frustrate the royal will. Edwardian legislation, by which bishops were named by simple letters patent, proved short-lived, and the Elizabethan laws returned to the traditional procedures.

The English Church, in dropping the subdiaconate and minor orders, gave prominence to the threefold ministry of bishops, priests, and deacons. The Ordinal insisted that a diligent reading of 'holy scripture and ancient authors' would testify to the continuity of these orders from the Apostles' times, but neither it nor the relevant Articles defined the degree to which such continuity might be essential to the Catholic integrity of the Church.[22] Initial responses to presbyterian militants argued only that episcopal polity was permissible; towards the end of the century, an increasing number of voices insisted that episcopacy had a clearer scriptural as well as a traditional mandate. Hooker regarded episcopal ordination 'the ordinary institution of God', but acknowledged that examples of occasional 'exigence of necessity' made it impossible to urge that 'without exception' ordinations required 'a lineal descent of power from the Apostles by continued succession of Bishops'[23] (see pp. 296–308).

The Vision of Coherent Christian Faith and Practise in a Unitive Society

Non-confessional teaching and prescribed liturgical practice, with their implications for future ecumenical outreach, were contained within an intensely national Church community which did not easily separate loyal citizenship from communicant membership in the Church of England. Significant numbers of committed clerical and lay persons who sought tighter doctrinal and disciplinary standards and looser liturgical strictures, nonetheless, urged their reforms from within. Only a handful of Protestant separatists and a somewhat larger scattered Roman Catholic community attempted loyally to support their sovereign while they rejected the communion of the national Church.

Royal supremacy provided the capstone of interlinking structures of civil government and traditional Catholic order. Crown and Parliament provided a means for laity to participate in religious decisions bearing upon the whole Church. The future constitutional struggle between Crown and Parliament, deeply involving religion, had begun to emerge in the initial formative century of Anglicanism. The momentum of Elizabeth's skilful use of royal supremacy and handling of parliamentary dissent carried over into James' reign. A coherent Anglicanism, centred on Bible and Prayer Book, had emerged within the national Church. The King James Bible, reflecting scriptural authority, royal patronage, national cultural achievement, wide collaborative execution, and episcopal leadership symbolizes the evanescent vision of a coherent Christian faith and practice capturing the whole-hearted allegiance of a people in a unitive society.

B MAINTENANCE OF AN ARTICULATED FAITH AS THE VISION FADES IN THE SECOND CENTURY OF ANGLICANISM: 1611–1738

Religion and church life have shared in the radical changes that have touched human life on this globe since 1611. In the years between the appearance of the King James Bible and the conversion of John Wesley, not only was the vision of an all-inclusive national Church shattered, but public repudiation of Christian faith became a viable possibility for educated English as for other Europeans. Whether the survival of a distinctive recognizable Anglicanism through this period better testifies to the integrity of its Christianity or to the tenacious persistence of entrenched institutions, is not a question of historical investigation; but the process of Anglicanism's adaptation to a changing environment required courage and searchings of heart on the part of many committed to its vision of the Christian gospel.

1. CONTINUITY AND CHANGE IN CHURCH LIFE FROM 1611 TO 1740

The struggle between the militants and supporters of the establishment overshadowed English religious history from the middle of the reign of James I until the 1689 Toleration Act. Religion provided the focus for the constitutional battles between King and Parliament, dramatically marked by the execution of Charles I, Oliver Cromwell's Commonwealth, and the Glorious Revolution that brought William and Mary to share England's throne. Gentry and mercantile classes, growing in political and economic strength, were changing the social texture of the nation. By Queen Anne's 1702 accession and under her Hanover successors, party politics dominated an ascendent Parliament, Deism of the 'Age of Reason' informed and challenged theologians, the industrial revolution had begun to change the national economy and demography, and religious pluralism, although neither warmly embraced nor justly implemented, had become a legalized reality in the national scene.

Increasing Polarization: James I (later years) and Charles I

James I, until his death in 1625, maintained the alliance of crown and mitre firmly forged at the opening of his reign. Clashes between the royal will and the endemically Puritan House of Commons occurred sporadically in matters of conscience, most notably over James' opposition to sabbatarian prohibitions of 'lawful recreations and honest exercises' on Sunday.[24] His intermittent easing of penalties against Roman Catholics also aroused militant anger, which peaked as he negotiated to marry Prince Charles to continental Catholic princesses. In his first years Charles I sought to quell an inherited theological dispute with a declaration, subsequently prefixed to the *Articles of Religion*, ordering that they be taken 'in the literal and grammatical sense' prohibiting any public claim which insisted that one's 'own sense' constituted their meaning.[25] Three months later a Commons committee endorsed a strict Calvinist interpretation of predestination to be *the* 'orthodox doctrine of our Church'. In response to this and other signs of Parliament's independence, Charles determined to rule without the legislative assembly.

He avoided assembling Parliament until 1640, when his attempt to impose an Anglican-like liturgy on Scotland had led to war requiring taxes that only legislators could authorize. Bonds that had made 'King-in-Parliament' a workable governing principle were stretched too far, and within two years civil war engulfed the land. From the beginning of Charles' reign, William Laud had been his principal ecclesiastical adviser and, from 1633, Archbishop of Canterbury. Puritans bitterly resented Laud and the increasingly dominant faction of clerics who, in Puritan eyes, promoted 'popish' doctrines and ceremonies and enforced conformity with relentless severity. Gentry, resentful of government strictures on land enclosures for grazing, and common lawyers, protesting the civil law procedures of prerogative courts, proved significant allies of Puritans and parliamentarians who together struggled against 'tyranny' in Church and state.

Anglicanism Disestablished and Restored

The executions of Laud in 1645 and of the King four years later punctuated the successive religious changes imposed by new authorities. By Laud's death, episcopacy, the Book of Common Prayer, and the *Articles of Religion* had been replaced under parliamentary ordinances by a Presbyterian ministry, a reformed *Directory of Public Worship*, and the majestic Calvinist *Westminster Confession of Faith*. By Charles' death, the dedicated General Oliver Cromwell had repudiated the rigid imposition of Presbyterianism in favour of the policies of the 'Independents'. In Cromwell's Commonwealth, congregations might determine their forms of Christian teaching and worship, provided that 'this liberty be not extended to popery or prelacy', to neither Roman Catholicism nor Anglicanism.[26]

Continental observers might conclude that Anglicanism no longer existed. Prayer Book religion, however, lived on both openly at the exile court of Charles II and more furtively in England as approximately a quarter of beneficed English clerics refused to conform. Many wrote in its defence and served as tutors or chaplains in royalist households. They and conforming sympathizers held Prayer Book services wherever they might elude governmental zeal.

The Convention Parliament which recalled Charles II in 1660 was dominated by Presbyterians disillusioned by the religious and political chaos of the Commonwealth, but the new 'Cavalier' Commons, elected the following year, contained a solid majority nurtured by Anglican loyalists. Together with solidly Anglican Convocations, the legislators followed the lead of Lord Clarendon, architect of Charles' return, and assured by appropriate legislation that both Prayer Book liturgies and episcopal leadership and ordination would be restored to the Church in a manner that effectively separated many conscientious Puritans from the national Church. The statutes provided severe penalties for public nonconforming worship and ministry.

The Church of England in a Pluralistic Society

Charles II's 1685 death-bed reception into the Roman Church and, much more, his brother James II's open espousal of Roman Catholicism alarmed all English Protestants. Although James promised that his private religion would not compromise his duties as 'supreme governor', increasingly Romanizing measures reached a pinnacle in 1688 when he ordered the clergy to read a declaration suspending 'all manner of penal laws' against Roman Catholics and other Nonconformists.[27] The defiance of Archbishop Sancroft and six other bishops won them imprisonment in the Tower of London and overwhelming popular support. Their acquittal led inexorably to the flight of James and the welcoming of his daughter Mary and her Dutch husband William. Parliament declared them joint monarchs; the legislature had won senior status in the corporate sovereignty of England's 'King-in-Parliament'.

As an ironic consequence of the Glorious Revolution, some 400 clergy, including Archbishop Sancroft and four other bishops who had defied James in the Tower, were separated from the ministry of the national Church. These 'Non-jurors', regarding their earlier oaths to James as a personal obligation, refused to swear allegiance to the new sovereigns. Schism was perpetuated with the consecration of new bishops, and the Non-juring clerics, with a tiny group of lay adherents, continued for a hundred years as a curious non-established Anglican aberration.

The substantial national consensus against James' policies, together with William's Reformed allegiance, created a favourable climate for the Toleration Act granting freedom of worship to all dissenting Trinitarians except Roman Catholics. As England moved into the eighteenth century, religious issues no longer remained central concerns of national politics. Mary's sister Anne, who acceded to the throne in 1702, was consistently solicitious of the Church, but her succeeding Hanover cousins, the Lutherans George I and George II, fulfilled their church responsibilities in a more perfunctory manner. The civil rights of dissenters to hold public office were still restricted, but the English 'constitution' now incorporated religious toleration, increasingly extended *de facto* to Roman Catholics and nascent Unitarians. The Church of England remained uniquely established, but in an acknowledged religiously pluralistic society.

Beginnings of Anglicanism Outside England

Anglicanism was present beyond England in the rest of the British Isles and some overseas territories. The four Welsh dioceses were integrally part of the English province of Canterbury, but the Welsh translations of the Bible and Prayer Book and Elizabeth's appointment of Welsh-speaking bishops had given a cultural identity to Wales which subsequent sovereigns failed to nurture.

The episcopal office had not been totally eliminated from the Reformed Church of Scotland until Charles I's anglicizing policy firmly linked nationalism and Presbyterian discipline. Although Charles II reintroduced bishops into Scottish polity, the bishops were Non-jurors in 1689, separated from the national Church with a small band of followers. Links forged with English Non-jurors encouraged the development of a recognizable Anglicanism in the Episcopal Church of Scotland.

Ireland's subservient Parliaments in the sixteenth century dutifully followed English Reformation precedents, but local struggles against England firmly linked the Reformation 'Church of Ireland' with foreign rule. A Gaelic Bible and Prayer Book were not forthcoming until the seventeenth century. Retaining all the ancient churches and foundations, the Church of Ireland retained only a small minority of Irish people, augmented by Protestant immigrants given land in the wake of the ruthless suppression of Irish support for James II in 1690.

As English explorers, traders, and colonists travelled abroad from the sixteenth

21

century onwards, they carried their Church with them. By the early eighteenth century, Church of England congregations were dotted around the Caribbean islands and the north Atlantic coast from Newfoundland to Georgia, and were formed in territories of the East India Company on the subcontinent. The Bishop of London, with nominal jurisdiction over these congregations, exercised little supervision. A beginning of support and oversight was made through the societies for 'the Promotion of Christian Knowledge' and 'the Propagation of the Gospel', founded about 1700 by Thomas Bray, who had briefly served as bishop's commissary in Maryland. The royal charters of both mentioned evangelization of the inhabitants of the far-flung regions; but, apart from sporadic beginnings of missions to Native Americans and African slaves in the western hemisphere and support of the Royal Danish Lutheran missions in southern India, most of the efforts of the societies were directed toward settling 'the state of religion . . . among our own people' abroad.[28] Anglicanism was still almost exclusively English.

2. Worship and Teaching in the English Church

Throughout the turbulence of the second century of Anglicanism, the King James Bible and the Prayer Book remained the foundations of worship and doctrine in the English Church, and the Thirty-nine Articles provided the clergy with teaching guidelines. Church leaders under Charles I continued to block Puritan attempts to 'complete' the Reformation, and militants, noting what they judged fresh doses of 'popery', redoubled their efforts to reshape the national Church. Their short-lived victory only exacerbated tensions within the restored Church. In addition to depriving it of dedicated clergy and laity, the subsequent departure of many Puritans to form dissenting denominations ended efforts to conform the Church of England to continental Reformed patterns. The doctrinal breadth of the English formularies, however, continued to encourage theological variety within the national Church, as Anglicans entered the eighteenth century as the established—but not exclusive—representative of the Church of Jesus Christ in England.

Varieties of Prayer Book Worship

Although the Prayer Book rites fixed the words of worship and specified some of its ceremonial, its setting and performance could vary considerably. In the early seventeenth century, elaboration of ceremonial became more common. Laud first encouraged and then ordered Holy Tables to be left for communion in the traditional place of the altar, fenced off by rails. The use of candles and incense, care for existing crucifixes and paintings and refurbishment with new ones, more elaborate vocal music and organs, bowing towards the altar and clergy vested in richly ornamented copes more frequently characterized Anglican worship, to the dismay of Puritans. The Eucharist became celebrated not only more solemnly, but more frequently as 'the principal office of God's service', as one scholarly priest put it.[29]

Two opposing liturgical patterns of Prayer Book revision were urged at the Restoration. Charles II sponsored a conference to attempt to design a Prayer Book acceptable to both Presbyterans and Anglicans, while an *ad-hoc* Catholic-minded group prepared a liturgy which looked something like the first 1549 Prayer Book. A few modest revisions in both directions were granted, but these and the many uncontroversial minor changes left the 1662 Prayer Book solidly in the Elizabethan tradition, 'the mean between two extremes' as the preface put it.

The 1661 *ad-hoc* proposal, more fully reflecting pre-Reformation patterns, drew from the 1637 liturgy that Charles I had attempted to impose on the Scots. Non-jurors, both in Scotland and England, employed these and other sources in scholarly liturgical experimentation. In the established Church, eighteenth-century worship would be judged 'dull' by most moderns. A small minority of clerics, known as 'High Church', kept up weekly Eucharists and public daily Morning and Evening Prayer, but ceremonial enrichments of like-minded predecessors a century earlier had ceased to distinguish them from other clerics. In most English parishes, the Eucharist was celebrated quarterly, and parishoners attended lengthy Sunday morning services of Morning Prayer, Litany, Antecommunion, and sermon.

Doctrinal Debate and Latitude

Official doctrinal formularies, grounded in Scripture and the agreed liturgy, remained unchanged. Clergy and others with teaching responsibilities subscribed to the Thirty-nine Articles, and, in spite of Puritan demands, Charles I's insistence on the 'literal and grammatical sense' eventually carried the day.

As clerical educational norms rose, Puritans no longer protested at the 'dumb dogs' who could not preach, but those who would 'vent what errors they will and neglect preaching at their pleasures'.[30] Such 'errors' often touched predestination, which had become increasingly central to the international Reformed community. The 1618 Dutch Synod of Dort condemned 'Arminians' who sought to modify the developed Calvinist doctrine of election, and Puritans used the heretical label to mark those who strayed from Calvinist orthodoxy and whose liturgics smacked of 'popery'. 'Caroline divines' has come to designate seventeenth-century English church leaders, who might adhere or not to much of Calvin's theology, but who would have agreed with Laud that an unqualified doctrine of eternal reprobation makes 'the God of all mercies to be the most fierce and unreasonable tyrant in the world'.[31] Like Cranmer, Jewel, and Hooker before them, in the interpretation of Scripture the Carolines gave special but not unqualified authority to the writers of early Christian centuries, and cited them more frequently than continental Reformation theologians (see pp. 101–103).

Fifteen centuries of Catholic tradition and sixteenth-century Reformation emphases were easily identifiable strains in early seventeenth-century English theology, but the third strain, reason, historically related to the Renaissance, became increasingly visible (see pp. 105–111).

Great Tew, an estate near Oxford, was the scene of informal discussions in pre-civil war years by a group of intellectually acute clerics and lay persons, some of whom became leaders in the Restoration Church. Repudiating Calvinist dogmatism, members of the circle also distanced themselves in varying degrees from Laud's ecclesiastical policies. During and after the Civil War, reason found other champions in a group of Cambridge dons who, nurtured in Puritan colleges, had found the doctrine of the decrees of election 'the most mischievous' news ever 'communicated to the world'.[32] Deeply attached to neo-Platonic philosophy and mysticism, these 'Cambridge Platonists', repelled by whatever they judged superstition or unreasoned dogmatism, insisted that 'in the use of reason and the exercise of virtue, we enjoy God'.[33]

Increasingly attractive to men and women wearied by killing and strife in the name of the Prince of Peace, these 'Latitudinarian' teachings drew many younger clerics in the Restoration Church. When Non-juring consciences cleared the episcopal bench of its most stalwartly Catholic-minded bishops, William filled the gap with Latitudinarians. The Church of England entered the eighteenth century with a leadership sympathetic to the intellectual climate of the 'Age of Reason'. Deism challenged traditional Christianity, arguing for a God known only through creation, not by revelation. Bishop Joseph Butler in his *Analogy of Religion, Natural and Revealed* (1736), turned the Deists' weapons against them by arguing the fundamental reasonableness of Christian claims, an apologetic *tour de force* unsurpassed in the European scene of the times.

Comprehension and its Limits

Key decisions made in Anglicanism's second century included its affirmation of its liturgy and its consistent refusal to become a 'confessional' Church by narrowing doctrinal boundaries. Until the heightened bitterness under Charles I, the English Church kept most Protestants within its communion including many unhappy with much of its official stance. In these protesters' eyes, insistence on Catholic traditions embedded in the liturgy and form of ministry eventually brought about the schismatic separations. Yet these very elements helped to preserve possibilities of ecumenical outreach in other directions. In the bitterness of Catholic/Protestant relations of these centuries, when Puritans identified Rome with 'Antichrist', Hooker and the Carolines maintained that although not a 'right' Church in all her teaching and practice, the Roman Church was nonetheless a part of the 'true' Catholic Church. As the limits of comprehension, drawn tighter by the complex strains in English society, were reached, Anglicanism lost an important and vigorous sector of its constituency, but its trajectory for the future was firmly established in the direction on which the Elizabethan Settlement had launched it and for which Hooker had provided a theological foundation.

3. FALTERING VISIONS OF A UNITIVE SOCIETY

The unitive society assumed by sixteenth-century Reformers was proved to be illusory in the second century of Anglicanism. The vision, however, did not easily fade, and the Church which had embraced the vision groped toward a foundation resting instead on its understanding and practice of Christianity. Even though committed Anglicans linked religion with hopes for royal restoration during the Commonwealth, they practised Anglicanism apart from the structures of national government. Non-jurors, in spite of their schismatic status, provided a later example of non-established Anglicanism. As constitutional and societal changes took place, Anglicans began to develop an understanding of their religious identity not wholly dependent upon their cultural and national identity.

Royal Supremacy and Parliament

By 1738, English sovereignty had shifted from the Crown's side of 'King-in-Parliament' to the legislators, a major advance in a process eventually leading to Parliament's investment with almost all real power. Royal supremacy could not remain as it had been theoretically envisaged and practically exercised under Elizabeth. With the most recent supreme governors a Roman Catholic, a Dutch Calvinist, and two German Lutherans, thoughtful Anglicans could not but judge a relatively modest role appropriate for royal supremacy in the life of the Church. The central Ecclesiastical Commission of Elizabeth's reign had increasingly functioned as a judicial body known as the 'Court of High Commission' whose reputation for penal severity reached its apex under Charles I. This agency of royal supremacy was not revived at the Restoration. The staunchly Anglican Cavalier Parliament, in fact, effectively sheared the supremacy of much of its authority by placing most of the enforcement of religious legislation in the hands of government authorities.

The monarch's need to convoke the Convocations at the times of Parliament evaporated when, by tacit agreement in the wake of the Restoration, clergy began to pay ordinary parliamentary taxes in place of the Convocation subsidies. After rancorous disputes between a lower house dominated by 'High Church' clerics and Latitudinarian bishops, George I, in 1717, ended the meetings of Convocations, effectively silencing the clerical appendage to Parliament envisaged in Tudor theory. Bishops continued to sit in the House of Lords, still an equal partner of Commons, and with the advent of organized parties of Whigs and Tories in effective control of Parliament and the Crown's ministries, the episcopal block of votes became increasingly crucial. Not only were bishops absent from their dioceses for longer periods at frequent parliamentary sessions, but party advice increasingly determined royal choices for the episcopal bench. With royal supremacy reduced, Convocations dormant, and bishops immersed in party politics, the machinery of church government was more subservient than at any other time to the established civil government.

Structures of Church Government and Ministry

The medieval systems of church courts, patronage, and provincial and diocesan organization maintained their place in English church life. Queen Anne directed clerical taxes, transferred by Henry from papacy to crown, to her 'Bounty', a fund to alleviate the grosser inequities in the inherited medieval system of clerical incomes. The eclipse of the Convocations eliminated effective clerical consideration of church needs in a time of the turbulent economic and social changes of the industrial revolution.

Episcopal polity was rapidly reasserted at the Restoration, and, in spite of presbyterian expectations and royal promises, there was no compromise on the requirement of episcopal ordination. With the departure of Protestant dissenters, protests against episcopal government within the Church ceased. However, in spite of confident assertions of the importance of 'apostolic succession' in the episcopal office, nearly all seventeenth-century Anglicans qualified their claims for episcopacy, as Hooker had done, by a recognition that circumstantial necessity might dictate another course. One such writer did so by distinguishing 'the true nature and essence of the Church' which non-episcopal Churches might claim, and 'the integrity or perfection of a Church' which demanded traditional Catholic order.[34] Many Latitudinarians, while thoroughly supporting episcopacy, would have rated it of much less importance for the 'integrity' of a Christian community.

NOTES

1 *The Complete Works of St. Thomas More* (New Haven, Yale University Press 1963–), vol. 8.i, p. 177. The spelling of all quotations in this chapter has been modernized.

2 These quotations come from the 1534 Act of Supremacy [26 Henry VIII, cap. 1], the 1534 meeting of the Convocation of York [register of Archbishop Lee], and the 1533 Act in Restraint of Appeals [24 Henry VIII, cap. 12]. Most of the relevant legislation is reproduced in H. Gee and W. J. Hardy, *Documents Illustrative of English Church History* (New York, Kraus, 1966), pp. 145–256.

3 From the 1533 Act in Restraint of Appeals [24 Henry VII, cap. 12].

4 From Mary's initial proclamation of 6 July 1553; Gee and Hardy, *Documents*, pp. 373–6.

5 An observer, Canobio, in Brussels with reports from the Spanish ambassador in England, to Paul IV, 10 May 1559; J. M. Rigg, ed., *Calendar of State Papers, ... Rome*, vol. i (London 1916), p. 10.

6 *The Works of Francis Bacon, Lord Chancellor of England*, ed. Basil Montagu (London 1825–1834), vol. iii, p. 477.

7 The second Injunction of 1538 and the seventh of 1547; Walter Howard Frere and William M. Kennedy, *Visitation Articles and Injunctions of the Period of the Reformation*, 3 vols. (London 1910), vol. ii, pp. 35–6, 118.

8 *The First and Second Prayer Books of Edward VI* (New York, E. P. Dutton, 1949), pp. 309, 455.

9 *The Works of William Perkins*, ed. I. Breward (Appleford, Sutton Courtenay Press, 1970), p. 454.

10 *Of the Lawes of Eclesiasticall Politie*, III.iv.1; FE vol. i, p. 213.

11 Edmund Grindal's December 1576 letter to Elizabeth refusing to obey her order to suppress the 'exercises' and to limit preaching licenses: in William Nicholson, ed., *The Remains of Edmund Grindal* (Cambridge 1843), pp. 376–90.

12 *Lawes*, V.xxii.1 (FE, vol. ii, p. 87); V.xviii.1 (vol. ii, p. 65); V.xviii–xxii (vol. ii, pp. 65–110); V.li–lvii (vol. ii, pp. 209–48); V.l.3 (vol. ii, pp. 208–9); and V.lxvi.1 (vol. ii, pp. 330–1).

13. *Calendar of State Papers, relating to English Affairs, preserved principally at Rome*, vol. i, ed J M Rigg (London 1916), pp. 154–5.

14 *Lawes*, IV.xiv.6 (FE vol. i, p. 342).

15 The Supremacy Act, 26 Henry VIII, cap. 1; Gee and Hardy, *Documents*, p. 243.

16 *Lawes*, VIII.vi.11; 6.vii [viii] (FE vol. iii, pp. 401–4, 393–4).

17 John E. Neale, *Elizabeth I and her Parliaments*, 2 vols. (London 1953–7), vol. ii, p. 435. However subsequent work may modify details of Neale's magisterial work, both volumes document the many instances of Elizabeth's consistent interference in Puritan parliamentary plans. See G. R. Elton, *The Parliament of England: 1559–1581* (Cambridge 1986).

18 Walter Howard Frere and William McClure Kennedy, *Visitation Articles and Injunctions of the Period of the Reformation*, vol. iii (AC 1910), pp. 8–29; this statement is among the provisions added after the numbered injunctions; Article 37; *Statutes of the Realm*, vol. iv (London 1819), p. 350, I° Elizabeth, cap. I.

19 Richard Hooker, *Lawes*, VIII.vi.1, viii.9 (FE vol. iii, pp. 357, 434).

20 Hooker describes the 'conjunction of power ecclesiastical and civil' in one person as 'convenient and meet' in the circumstances of his day; *Lawes*, VII.xv.14 (FE vol. iii, p. 240).

21 The 1572 *Admonition to the Parliament* (2nd edn) as included in W. H. Frere and C. E. Douglas, *Puritan Manifestoes* (SPCK 1907), p. 16.

22 Preface to the 1550 and subsequent English Ordinals; *The First and Second Prayer Books of Edward VI* (J. M. Dent 1949), pp. 292, 438.

23 *Lawes*, VII.xiv.11 (FE vol. iii, p. 227); see also III.ii.16 (vol. i, p. 264) and VII.v.10 (vol. iii, p. 170).

24 From the 'Book of Sports', issued by James in 1618 and reissued by Charles in 1633; Gee and Hardy, *Documents*, p. 529.

25 November, 1928; Gee and Hardy, *Documents*, p. 520.

26 From the 1653 Instrument of Government defining the powers of the 'Lord Protector'; Gee and Hardy, *Documents*, p. 576.

27 First issued by James in 1687, the King revived the Declaration of Indulgence with the order to announce it from pulpits of the national Church in April 1688; Gee and Hardy, *Documents*, p. 641.

28 First anniversary sermon of the SPG, 1702; C. F. Pascoe, *Two Hundred Years of the Society for the Propagation of the Gospel* (London 1901), p. 7.

29 Isaac Barrow in a treatise published posthumously in 1681; Paul Elmer More and Frank Leslie Cross, *Anglicanism* (SPCK 1951), p. 504.

30 From the Root and Branch Petition of 1640, item 6; Gee and Hardy, *Documents*, p. 539.

31 William Laud, *Works*, Library of Anglo-Catholic Theology (Oxford 1847–60), vol. vi, p. 133.

32 Henry More, *Immortality of the Soul*. London 1659.

33 Benjamin Whichcote, *Moral and Religious Aphorisms* (London 1753), No. 40.

34 John Bramhall in a 1660 writing, summarizing the views of Launcelot Andrewes, *A vindication of Himself and the Episcopal Clergy from the Presbyterian Charge of Popery*, in his *Works* (Oxford 1842–1845), vol. iii, p. 518.

2 From the Early Eighteenth Century to the Present Day

PERRY BUTLER

Balleine, G. R., *A History of the Evangelical Party in the Church of England*. Longmans 1908.

Bradley, I. B., *The Call to Seriousness*. Cape 1976.

Brilioth, Y., *The Anglican Revival: Studies in the Oxford Movement*. Longmans 1925.

Chadwick, O., ed., *The Mind of the Oxford Movement*. A. & C. Black 1960.

Cragg, G. R., *Reason and Authority in the Eighteenth Century*. CUP 1964.

Davies, H., *Worship and Theology in England*, vols. iii, iv, v. OUP 1961.

Herklots, H. G. G., *Frontiers of the Church: The Making of the Anglican Communion.* Ernest Benn 1961.

Howe, J., *Highways and Hedges: Anglicanism and the Universal Church.* Anglican Consultative Council 1985.

Page, R. J., *New Directions in Anglican Theology: a Survey from Temple to Robinson.* Mowbrays 1967.

Ramsey, A. M., *From Gore to Temple: the Development of Anglican Theology between Lux Mundi and the Second World War 1889–1939.* Longmans 1960.

Reardon, B. M. G., *From Coleridge to Gore: A Century of Religious Thought in Britain.* Longmans 1971.

Rowell, G., *The Vision Glorious: Themes and Personalities of the Catholic Revival in Anglicanism.* OUP 1983.

Stephenson, A. M. G., *Anglicanism and the Lambeth Conferences.* SPCK 1978.

Wand, J. W. C., ed., *The Anglican Communion: A Survey.* OUP 1948.

INTRODUCTION

Since the early eighteenth century, Anglicanism has undergone a remarkable transformation. The national Churches of England and Ireland, together with the disestablished Episcopal remnant in Scotland, have become the 'mother' of a world-wide family of self-governing Churches in communion with the see of Canterbury. This expansion has largely, though not entirely, paralleled the expansion of British interests; and although Anglicans are now found on all continents their numerical strength is greatest in countries which are parts of the British Commonwealth. Over 90% live in countries in which English is the official language (see pp. 364–70, 393–5).

The development of the Anglican Communion has, therefore, been shaped more by historical circumstance than by deliberate design. While this has contributed to its particular ethos, it creates difficulties when locating it among the various groupings of Christendom.

The Anglican Communion is not a federation, nor in the strict sense a confessional family. It is held together more by common loyalties than organizational structures, and by the participation of its bishops in the Lambeth Conference, convened by the Archbishop of Canterbury and held at roughly ten-year intervals since 1867.

Movements within the Church of England and the internal conflict they have aroused also make a definition of Anglicanism problematic. The Evangelical Revival in the eighteenth century gave an important stimulus to the Reformation tradition. The Oxford Movement in the nineteenth century, with its stress on the historic continuity of the Church signified by the apostolic succession of bishops and its sacramental doctrine, effectively distanced Anglicanism from the Reformation, emphasizing its Catholic rather than Protestant heritage. Latitudinarian churchmanship in the eighteenth century, and the impact of biblical criticism and theological liberalism since the nineteenth century, have raised fundamental questions regarding the nature of belief and the traditional understanding of authority. To the outsider the development of this tri-party conflict between Evangelical, Catholic and Liberal might seem the most characteristic development in modern Anglicanism.

Anglicanism has also experienced a profound liturgical transformation resulting mainly from the Oxford Movement. Public worship has greatly altered in style and ceremonial. To the layperson this would probably seem the most significant change since the early eighteenth century. In the twentieth century especially, liturgical change has included Prayer Book revision. This has had theological consequences, since changes have modified doctrinal emphases and may thereby have, unwittingly, weakened the cohesion of the Anglican Communion.

In one area, however, modern Anglicanism has changed less than may have been anticipated. At his enthronement in 1942 Archbishop William Temple described the Ecumenical Movement as 'the great new fact of our era'. The Anglican Churches have played an important role in that movement from the beginning, not least in providing leadership. Some have seen Anglican Churches as the ecumenical Churches *par excellence*, comprehending both Catholic and Protestant elements. Yet despite developments in the Indian sub-continent, there have been fewer successful attempts at forming united Churches including Anglicans than would have seemed probable. Indeed the last thirty years have seen the development of a greater Anglican self-consciousness in many parts of the Communion, and a desire for greater centralization which has partly been fulfilled.

THE EIGHTEENTH-CENTURY CHURCH

The eighteenth-century Church was once a byword for pastoral neglect and worldliness. Modern historians, less partisan than their nineteenth-century predecessors, have taken a kinder view. Perhaps its chief faults sprang from a too easy accommodation to the temper of the age, political subservience to the Whig government and an inability to respond effectively to the social changes of the later part of the century.

After the religious upheavals of the preceding century the prevailing desire was for stability. There was a distrust of 'enthusiasm'. The Church stood for moderation. Morality was exalted above dogma, a sober practical piety over mysticism or emotion. This was exemplified in the sermons of Archbishop John Tillotson (1630–94) which became the model for much eighteenth-century preaching.

Acute controversy arose when the mostly Tory lower clergy attempted to condemn the Bishop of Bangor for a sermon in which he denied that the visible Church had any divinely bestowed authority (the 'Bangorian Controversy'). To stop political bickering Convocation was silenced by the King in 1717. Preferment went to bishops happy to toe the party line; a necessity, because in the House of Lords the bishops provided a bloc of votes crucial for successive administrations. Prior to 1736 episcopal appointments were managed by Edmund Gibson (1669–1748), Bishop of London and Walpole's 'Pope'. For the next thirty years they were in the hands of the Duke of Newcastle.

Benjamin Hoadly (1676–1761), whose notoriously Erastian views provoked the 'Bangorian Controversy', is often taken as the archetype of the Low Church Whig prelate. Successively Bishop of Bangor, Hereford, Salisbury and Winchester, he seldom visited his diocese. Most of the bench, however, were less ambitious and strove to do their duty in large ramshackle dioceses, with poor communications and pastoral work restricted to the months Parliament was not sitting.

The publication of journals and diaries, notably James Woodforde's *Diary of a Country Parson*, has allowed a rehabilitation of the lower clergy. If unheroic, they too were dutiful and benevolent. As the majority of parishes were rural and poor, pluralism and non-residence were almost a necessity. As a result of the Enclosure movement towards the end of the century, however, the social and economic position of the clergy improved. New rectories were built, many clergy became magistrates and took their place in county society. It was the age of the 'Squarson', a clerical caste which was both squire and parson.

Yet as an institution the Church remained antiquated and cumbrous, and this hindered its effectiveness. Whatever latent strengths it possessed it was simply unprepared for the changes that were being unleashed on English society. Faced with the growth and shift of population, urbanization and the onset of the Industrial Revolution, it could not respond.

Despite the strongly rationalist tone of intellectual life, eighteenth-century Anglicanism was not without theological achievement. Perhaps its greatest was the response to the Deist challenge.

Deism's roots lay in the seventeenth century, but it enjoyed considerable vogue in the early eighteenth. It was an attempt to produce a purely rational religion. Belief in God was accepted but all possibility of special revelation rejected. Miracles, the Trinity and the incarnation were ridiculed; Christianity was reduced to a code of moral precepts. One of the ablest and most influential Deist works was Matthew Tindal's *Christianity as Old as Creation* (1730).

The challenge was met most effectively by the Non-juror William Law (1686–1761) and the future Bishop of Durham Joseph Butler (1692–1752). Law, better known as the author of a *Serious Call to a Devout and Holy Life* (1729) was an able controversialist. His reply to Tindal, *The Case of Reason* (1731) was followed in

31

1736 by Butler's *Analogy of Religion*. Butler's *Analogy* considered natural and revealed religion analogically to the world and argued for probability as the basis of action. It became one of the seminal works of Anglican divinity (see pp. 110–111).

Another outstanding exponent of classical orthodoxy was Daniel Waterland (1683–1740). A prolific theologian, his writings on the Eucharist, notably *A Review of the Doctrine of the Eucharist* (1737), were particularly influential.

THE EVANGELICAL REVIVAL

The spiritual deficiencies of the Hanoverian Church left a vacuum that was largely filled by the Evangelical Revival. An international phenomenon embracing German Pietism and the American 'Great Awakening', in England it had three strands: Arminian Methodists following John Wesley, Calvinistic Methodists following George Whitefield, and those who remained within the Church of England. Anglican Evangelicalism was, therefore, no 'off-shoot' as has often been asserted. With its own origins, doctrinal emphases and methods it was a parallel movement. Its leaders looked neither to Wesley nor Whitefield, and were often critical of them.

Its origins can be traced to those 'gospel' or 'awakened' clergy who, between 1730 and 1760 underwent a conversion experience which drew them together in common cause to revitalize the Church and evangelize the nation. At first unorganized and thinly spread, they tended to coalesce notably in Cornwall and Yorkshire. Pioneers included Thomas Walker (1719–60) of Truro (Cornwall), Thomas Adam (1701–81) of Winteringham (Lincolnshire), John Fletcher (1729–85) of Madeley (Shropshire), William Grimshaw (1708–63) of Haworth (Yorkshire) and John Berridge (1716–93) of Everton (Bedfordshire).

The Evangelical Revival recovered the Protestant emphases on conversion, the supremacy of Scripture, and gospel preaching in reaction to the prevailing rationalism. Anglican, in common with other Evangelicals, sought to reassert the doctrine of justification by faith and to revive the Augustinian strain in theology.

While they appealed to experience rather than to the intellect, Anglican Evangelicals nevertheless possessed a simple and practical theology usually called 'moderate Calvinism'. Its foundation was the doctrine of total depravity, from which followed the necessity of conversion, justification by saving faith, the centrality of the atonement and sanctification by the Holy Spirit. Most refused to make predestination a central tenet or to teach predestined reprobation. Grace was for all. For the source of their doctrine they looked to Scripture and the Anglican formularies rather than the less accommodating logic of Calvin's *Institutes*.

Anglican Evangelicals differed from Wesley on a number of theological issues; notably his doctrine of Christian perfection and his understanding of assurance, which they regarded as too subjective. Many were uneasy about his stress on instantaneous conversion. Church order, however, provided the main stumbling block. Some early Evangelicals like Berridge had practised itinerant preaching; Walker, Adam and other 'regulars' vigorously attacked this undermining of the parochial system as an unwarranted attack on clerical authority.

Adherence to church order was fundamental if Evangelicals were to gain a firm foothold within the established Church. As it was, their views provoked hostility: bishops were disinclined to ordain them and livings were difficult to procure. For mutual support they banded together in clerical societies such as the Elland Society in Yorkshire.

By the late eighteenth century, the situation was changing. Evangelicals could be found in Oxford and Cambridge colleges and in the metropolis, and had sufficiently increased in numbers to make their presence felt. By the turn of the century they had become a definite and confident Church party, perhaps 300–500 strong.

The first three decades of the nineteenth century were the Evangelicals' 'golden age'. Vital religion began to permeate the upper middle classes. William Wilberforce (1759–1833) was converted in 1786 and published his influential *A Practical View*, contrasting the conventional religion of the time with committed Christianity, in 1797. Dedicated to the abolition of the Slave Trade and the reformation of morals, Wilberforce was at the centre of the 'Clapham Sect', a group of wealthy Evangelical laymen. Wilberforce also co-ordinated an Evangelical lobby in Parliament whose members were nicknamed 'the Saints'.

The Christian Observer (founded 1802) became the official organ of the party, and Evangelical causes were advanced by voluntary societies—some interdenominational like the Religious Tract Society and some not, like the Church Missionary Society (see pp. 432–4). To secure adequate patronage for Evangelicals, the Simeon Trustees were established in 1836 and advowsons (the right of presenting a clergyman to a particular parish, subject to the bishop's consent) purchased. The Trust was named after Charles Simeon (1759–1836), the foremost Evangelical clergyman of his age. For forty-four years he was Vicar of Holy Trinity Cambridge, where he had enormous influence on generations of undergraduates, and exercised a remarkable preaching ministry.

The progress of the Oxford Movement from the late 1830s pushed Evangelicals on to the defensive. Continuing to be a significant force within the Victorian Church, they tended to become part of a wider undenominational Evangelicalism hostile to popery and ritualism. Lord Shaftesbury (1801–85) was a prominent leader and, while Palmerston was Prime Minister (1855–65), exercised considerable influence over ecclesiastical patronage.

HIGH CHURCHMANSHIP AND THE OXFORD MOVEMENT

High Churchmanship was in abeyance for much of the eighteenth century. With the Whig Ascendancy it ceased to be an influential Church party, and as a religious tradition it survived largely among individual clergy and laity. Broadly speaking, High Churchmen stressed the apostolic order and authority of the visible Church and valued obedience to its ordinances and liturgy. As the century progressed, however, High Churchmen tended to become stiff and unemotional, hence the description 'high and dry' applied to them by the Tractarians.

A significant group of eighteenth-century High Churchmen were the 'Hutchinsonians'. These included George Horne (1730–92), Bishop of Norwich, his biographer William Jones 'of Nayland' (1726–1800) and Jones' biographer William Stevens (1732–1807). Stevens was a devout London businessman and treasurer of Queen Anne's Bounty. 'Nobody's Friends', the club that perpetuated his memory, became the centre for the later revival of the High Church party.

The French Revolution gave an impetus to High Churchmanship. Confronted with the threat of radicalism and irreligion, there was renewed emphasis on order and authority. Samuel Horsley (1733–1806) successively Bishop of St David's, Rochester and St Asaph was an able champion of High Church views.

The real leadership, however, lay with the 'Hackney Phalanx'. Stevens' protégé Joshua Watson, a wealthy London wine merchant, retired to Hackney where his elder brother Archdeacon Watson was rector and H. H. Norris a neighbouring incumbent. In 1811 they founded the National Society for the Education of the Poor in the Principles of the Established Church (which promoted church schools among the poor), and in 1812 acquired the *British Critic* as a platform for their views. Associated with the group were Archdeacon Charles Daubeny (1745–1827) whose *A Guide to the Church* (1798) summed up their position, Thomas Sikes of Guilsborough (1757–1834) and a future Bishop of Durham, William Van Mildert (1765–1836). During Lord Liverpool's administration (1812–27) the 'Phalanx' exercised considerable influence on ecclesiastical appointments, and in 1818 secured the Church Building Act which provided £1,000,000 for Church extension.

Although High Churchmanship was reviving in the early nineteenth century, it was transformed by the Oxford Movement. This originated as a response to the weakening of the Church-state relationship through the constitutional revolution of 1828–32. Catholic Emancipation in 1829 alarmed churchmen; and when the Whig government suppressed ten Irish bishoprics, John Keble the Oxford Professor of Poetry (1792–1866), described it as 'National Apostasy' in the Assize Sermon of 14 July 1833.

Keble's disciples included the Vicar of the University Church, John Henry Newman (1801–90) and Richard Hurrell Froude (1803–36). Their views were disseminated in a series of Tracts. In 1835 the Tractarians, as they were called, gained intellectual prestige when they were joined by the Regius Professor of Hebrew, Edward Bouverie Pusey (1800–82).

The movement was at its height in 1839, but in that year Newman began to experience doubts regarding the validity of the Anglican position. The hostile reaction to his *Tract XC* and the attempt to establish a joint Anglican-Lutheran bishopric in Jerusalem added to his anxieties. In 1843 he resigned his living. Further difficulties arose from the development of an aggressively pro-Roman faction within the movement associated with W. G. Ward (1812–82) and F. Oakeley (1802–80). Ward's *Ideal of a Christian Church* was condemned at Oxford in February 1845. Ward and others were received into the Roman Catholic Church, and Newman followed in 1845. His loss marked the end of the Oxford Movement in the narrower sense, but the Catholic revival continued as those who had been influenced by it went into the parishes.

After 1845 it seemed possible that the leadership would fall to Henry Edward Manning (1808–92); but he also seceded to Rome in 1851, after the Gorham Judgement on baptismal regeneration which symbolized for many the intrinsic Erastianism of the Church of England. Pusey therefore became the effective leader of the Catholic Movement until his death in 1882.

The Tractarians reasserted the spiritual independence of the Church of England at a time when it was under attack from the reforming tendencies of liberalism in the Church and state. They took their stand on episcopacy in historic succession as the *esse* of the Church. Where they differed from most of their High Church predecessors was in using this to 'unchurch' other Protestants and their explicit revaluation of the Reformation. Froude's vilification of the Reformers in his *Remains* is notorious. The Tractarians judged the Reformation by the Primitive Church in preference to accepting the Reformation Settlement as the norm for Anglican belief and practice.

The ramifications of the Catholic Revival within Anglicanism have been enormous. From it have come the restoration of liturgical practices and sacramental teaching associated with Roman Catholicism, the revival of the religious life and greater emphasis on the priestly office. The second half of the nineteenth century saw bitter conflict, particularly over 'ritualism'.

In the longer term the Catholic Revival opened Anglicanism to a wider understanding of catholicity and sacramental spirituality, but its doctrine of the ministry has proved a stumbling block in reunion with non-episcopal Churches.

LATITUDINARIANISM AND LIBERAL THEOLOGY

The term 'Latitudinarian' was coined in the mid-seventeenth century to describe those who favoured latitude of opinion in religious matters and an end to religious controversy. Forms of church government, liturgy and controversial doctrines were regarded as 'things indifferent'. John Locke's *The Reasonableness of Christianity* (1695) popularized the view that Christianity consisted of a few simple fundamental truths accessible to reason (see pp. 232–41).

In the eighteenth century Latitudinarianism often veered towards anti-Trinitarianism. Samuel Clark (1675–1729) publicly espoused a position akin to Arianism, as did Bishop Clayton of Clogher. The desire for a liturgy broad enough to accommodate these views led to attacks on the Athanasian and Nicene Creeds.

In the 1750s an Anti-Subscription Movement developed under the leadership of Archdeacon Blackburne. In 1771 he and his supporters drew up the 'Feathers Tavern Petition' requesting Parliament to abolish clerical subscription to the Articles and Liturgy. Some 250 names were attached, but it was rejected by the House of Commons.

The conservative reaction to the French Revolution checked the progress of liberal theology. Mention should be made, however, of William Paley (1743–1805) whose *Evidences of Christianity* (1794) had remarkable success as a work of popular apologetics.

In the early nineteenth century the most distinguished group of liberal churchmen were the 'Noetics' of Oriel College Oxford. Edward Copleston (1776–1849), Provost of the College from 1827, Richard Whately (1787–1863), later Archbishop of Dublin, and Thomas Arnold (1795–1842), later Headmaster of Rugby, were prominent in this group. All were staunch supporters of the union of Church and state, and Arnold's *Principles of Church Reform* (1833) was an influential plea to Christianize the nation by comprehending all Christians (except Quakers and Roman Catholics) into one national Church.

Although Arnold was an historian the 'Noetics' were mainly interested in Aristotelian logic and political economy. Their views on Church and society may have had some influence on the Whig government in the 1830s. Cambridge liberal theology tended to have a more historical and literary cast, and to be influenced by Plato. Connop Thirlwall (1797–1875), afterwards Bishop of St Davids, translated Schleiermacher's *Treatise on St Luke* and with Julius Hare (1795–1855) translated Niebuhr's *History of Rome*. Both were Fellows of Trinity. Attempts to open the universities to dissenters were made by liberal churchmen in the 1830s but proved abortive. University reform was delayed until the 1850s.

The term 'Broad Church' came into use around 1850. It is found in an article in the *Edinburgh Review* of that year by A. P. Stanley, later Dean of Westminster. The biographer of Arnold, Stanley was the archetypal Victorian Broad Churchman who gloried in the Church of England as an expression of national Christianity and opposed all efforts to narrow its comprehensiveness.

S. T. Coleridge (1772–1834) and F. D. Maurice (1805–72) are often discussed in the context of liberal theology, but both drew on the earlier tradition of the Greek Fathers and seventeenth-century Platonism. Coleridge was one of the seminal minds of the nineteenth century, not least in his repudiation of the determinist mechanistic philosophy of Locke with its reductionist implications concerning human understanding. Lacking the ability to produce a *magnum opus*, he nevertheless pointed to new directions in such works as *Aids to Reflection* (1825) exploring the relationship of reason and understanding, *Confessions of an Enquiring Spirit* (published posthumously in 1840) dealing with the question of biblical inspiration, and his *Constitution of the Church and State* (1829).

F. D. Maurice, the son of a Unitarian minister, was baptized into the Church of England in 1831. His greatest work, *The Kingdom of Christ* (1838), saw the denominational identities of English Christianity as polarities held together in a Church which witnessed to the Divine Order grounded in the Trinity. He understood this to be the particular vocation of the Church of England.

The publication of *Essays and Reviews* in 1860 was a landmark in Anglican liberal theology. It provoked an acrimonious controversy in which its seven authors were described as *septem contra Christum*. Benjamin Jowett's essay *On the Interpretation of Scripture* attracted the greatest criticism for its wholehearted acceptance of biblical criticism and its rejection of traditional views of the authority and inspiration of Scripture. Although the controversy died down it showed that liberal theology was firmly rooted in the Church of England. This liberal theology differed markedly from earlier Latitudinarianism, however, for by extending the critical method to the Bible and Creeds liberal churchmen made impossible the continued acceptance of the distinction between fundamental and non-essential doctrines which the original Latitudinarians had held, and so undermined an essential element in classical Anglicanism (see pp. 419–22).

THE EXPANSION OF ANGLICANISM

The initial expansion of Anglicanism was prompted by English commercial interests. Anglican Chaplaincies were established in European ports in the seventeenth century and further afield as the Levant and East India Companies flourished. From the time of Laud, Anglicans abroad were under the theoretical jurisdiction of the Bishop of London.

With the foundation, respectively in 1698 and 1701, of the Society for the Promotion of Christian Knowledge (SPCK) and the Society for the Propagation of the Gospel (SPG) a new era opened. Initially SPCK funded Danish missionaries in South India, but eventually appointed its own. SPG was concerned mainly with North America. Both societies owed much to the creative energy of Thomas Bray (1656–1730), commissary for the Bishop of London for the American colonies; and although they were voluntary organizations, each was incorporated by royal charter (see pp. 432–4).

The creation of an overseas episcopate was impeded; an Act of Parliament was required to create a new bishopric, and new bishops had to be consecrated in London under royal mandate. Schemes for a bishop in the American colonies came to nothing, though this was as much the result of American fears of prelacy as political difficulties in England.

American Independence created further problems. In 1783 the clergy of Connecticut chose Samuel Seabury (1729–96) and sent him to London for consecration. Law forbade the Archbishop to consecrate a 'foreigner', so Seabury turned to the bishops of the disestablished Episcopal Church in Scotland. He was consecrated there in 1784 and returned to America promising to adopt the distinctive Scottish Communion Office in his Church.

In 1786 an Act was passed allowing the Archbishop to consecrate those not subject to the Crown. In the following year two other Americans were consecrated at Lambeth. In that year also, Charles Inglis was consecrated for Nova Scotia and in 1793 Jacob Mountain became Bishop of Quebec. Calcutta received a bishop in 1814. In 1824 two bishops were appointed for the West Indies, and in 1836 a bishop was consecrated for Australia.

In 1841, the Colonial Bishoprics Fund was created, inspired by Charles James Blomfield (1776–1857), Bishop of London. This greatly speeded the expansion of the overseas episcopate, so that by the first Lambeth Conference in 1867 there were nearly fifty bishops in the British colonies and thirty-five dioceses in the USA. Three years earlier Samuel Adjar Crowther (1806–91) had become the first African bishop, consecrated for Nigeria.

Anglicanism could exist independently of a state connection, as the Episcopal Church in Scotland and the United States showed. But the relationship between the Church in the colonies and the mother Church was complicated by establishment. As at home, dissenters in the colonies were hostile to the pretensions of an established Church, and it proved very difficult to make establishment abroad effective. The legal difficulties were complex and came to a head in 1857 in the so-called 'Eton College Case' when it was judged that the *established* Church of England could not exist in those colonies where there was a local legislature (see pp. 359–63).

Colonial Churches were now beginning to evolve forms of synodical government (see pp. 183–4). G. A. Selwyn (1809–78), the first Bishop of New Zealand, summoned an informal synod of his clergy in 1844. The granting of a measure of self-government to New Zealand in 1852 was followed five years later by a Constitution of the Church of New Zealand. This became the model for many subsequent constitutions. The Constitution of the Province of South Africa was adopted in 1876. The West Indies province promulgated its first canons in 1883. In 1893 the General Synod of the Canadian Church was formed. The organization of the Australian Church dates from the early twentieth century.

The missionary impulse was an important feature of nineteenth-century

Anglicanism. For instance the CMS arrived in Sierra Leone in 1804 to bring the gospel to the freed slaves of the colony, and in 1858 the Universities' Mission to Central Africa, the most Anglo-Catholic of the missionary societies, answered David Livingstone's call to evangelize up the Zambezi. An interesting aspect of UMCA strategy was the use of the bishop as missionary pioneer. C. F. Mackenzie (1825–62) was consecrated in Cape Town in 1861 to lead a missionary party to Lake Nyassa.

By the beginning of the twentieth century Anglicanism was rooted in all continents and the Anglican Communion was slowly losing its purely English character, becoming a genuinely world-wide fellowship. The century has witnessed not only further expansion, but has also seen Churches with a missionary origin become both more indigenous and more autonomous.

THE LAMBETH CONFERENCE AND THE LAMBETH QUADRILATERAL

The growth of the Anglican Communion (the term first appeared in 1851) stimulated a desire for closer links between its parts. From the 1850s a growing Pan-Anglican consciousness was becoming apparent. American bishops shared in the celebrations for the 150th anniversary of SPG. The 1866 Church Congress at York was the first to include colonial and American bishops.

The attempt by Archbishop Gray of Cape Town to depose Bishop Colenso for heresy, and the latter's subsequent appeal to the Privy Council, raised questions as to the relationship between Colonial Churches and the Crown. The revival of Convocation in the Church of England in 1852 raised the further question of whether its actions had any bearing on the Overseas Churches which, in any case, were developing their own synods. There was anxiety about *Essays and Reviews* (see pp. 112–13). To some the time seemed ripe for an Anglican gathering.

Inspired by Bishop Lewis of Ontario, the Provincial Synod of the Canadian Church formally requested that members of the Anglican Communion meet in a 'General Council of her members gathered from every land'. In a letter to Archbishop Charles Longley (1794–1868) in 1865, it asked that he convene a Synod of bishops from home and abroad (see pp. 194–7).

Such was the origin of the first Lambeth Conference. Longley was sympathetic to the request but cautious. Some English bishops doubted the wisdom or even the legality of such a gathering, and before invitations were sent Longley made it clear that the proposed meeting could neither enact canons nor make any decision binding the Church. Invitations were extended to 150 bishops; 67 attended, though the Archbishop of York, hostile from the first, refused. The gathering, therefore, was not a Synod and attempts to make it one were resisted.

It met from 24–27 September 1867 and considered intercommunion between the Anglican Churches, the Colonial Church, and co-operation in Mission. An encyclical was issued.

Ten years later a second conference was held; subsequent conferences have taken place at roughly ten-year intervals with increasing episcopal participation. They have become, in Bishop G. K. A. Bell's words, 'a special opportunity for knitting the various provinces and dioceses of the Anglican Church together in mutual counsel'. The Lambeth Conference has remained a deliberative body convened solely at the invitation of the Archbishop of Canterbury. Whatever the respect accorded to its deliberations, it has no canonical nor constitutional status. It has, however, probably enhanced the Archbishop's primacy within the Communion.

At the 1888 Conference what has become known as the Chicago-Lambeth Quadrilateral was adopted (see pp. 219–220). This had its origins in 1870 in *The Church Idea, An Essay toward Unity* by William Reed Huntington (1838–1909), an American Episcopalian priest. The Lambeth form of the quadrilateral contains four elements held to be 'a basis on which approach may be by God's blessing, made toward Home Reunion': the holy Scriptures as containing all things necessary for salvation; the Creeds as the sufficient statement of the Christian faith; the sacraments of baptism and holy communion; and the 'Historic Episcopate, locally adapted in the methods of its administration to the varying needs of the nations and peoples called of God, into the Unity of His Church'. The precise implications of this last element, which was deliberately used to embrace the differing interpretations of episcopacy within Anglicanism, have consumed much Anglican theological energy.

The Quadrilateral has played an important role in ecumenical discussion, but it has been pointed out that although it was originally intended as a basis for discussion with a view to reunion, it has usually been treated as a non-negotiable basis for reunion.

ANGLICAN THEOLOGY FROM THE LATER NINETEENTH CENTURY

The later nineteenth century was a period of theological reconstruction as the Church painfully adjusted to the new scientific and historical discoveries. The 'Cambridge Triumvirate' of J. B. Lightfoot (1829–89), B. F. Westcott (1825–1901) and F. J. A. Hort (1828–92) showed that critical study of the New Testament need not result in the scepticism of earlier critics, thereby giving biblical criticism greater respectability within the Church. Lightfoot became Bishop of Durham, and Westcott succeeded him in 1890. Hort's Hulsean lectures *The Way, the Truth and the Life* remain an impressive example of the Anglican theological temper.

The publication of *Lux Mundi : A series of studies in the Religion of the Incarnation* in 1889 inaugurated a new era in Anglican theology. The book was by a group of young Oxford scholars who aimed to unite the theology of the Tractarians with modern critical scholarship. Significant elements in the *Lux Mundi* synthesis were the stress of God's immanence, the use of evolutionary ideas, a critical attitude to the Old Testament and acceptance of some limitation of our Lord's knowledge by way of a 'Kenotic' Christology. To older Tractarians like H. P. Liddon (1829–90), the book represented a capitulation to German rationalism.

Charles Gore (1853–1932), the group's leader, described this incarnational theology as 'Liberal Catholicism', arguing that its combination of Catholic doctrine and devotion, critical method and social concern represented the authentic Anglican vocation. It is often seen as the fusion of the Tractarian inheritance with the theology of F. D. Maurice. 'Liberal Catholicism' had an important influence on the Church during the archiepiscopate of Randall Davidson (1903–28), since three of the book's contributors, including Gore, became bishops.

But Gore found himself at odds with a new generation of Liberal Catholics more influenced by the theology of experience of some Roman Catholic Modernists and prepared to allow a critical approach to the Creed. *Essays Catholic and Critical*, edited by E. G. Selwyn in 1926, was the manifesto of this later school.

Anglican Modernism flourished in the 1920s. Heir to the 'Broad Church' tradition and influenced by continental liberal Protestantism, their forum was the Modern Churchmans Union under H. D. A. Major. At their conference in Girton College Cambridge in 1921, some speakers appeared to deny Christ's divinity. The ensuing controversy led to the appointment of an Archbishops' Commission on Christian Doctrine in 1922.

The Commission's Report *Doctrine in the Church of England* was eventually published in 1938. Since it surveyed rather than defined the doctrine of the Church it did little to delineate the permitted limits of theological diversity. The recognition it accorded liberal interpretations of credal statements was ambiguous and the Church never officially accepted it. The Commission's Chairman, William Temple, Archbishop of Canterbury 1942–4, commented in his introduction that were the Commission to begin again it would make the theology of redemption central. The era of incarnational theology begun with *Lux Mundi* had reached its end.

This theological shift was evident in the return to 'biblical orthodoxy' in many quarters. It had been foreshadowed in the work of E. C. Hoskyns (1884–1937). He had translated Karl Barth's commentary on *Romans* in 1933 and had been a contributor to *Essays Catholic and Critical*. Other Anglican exponents of 'Biblical Theology' such as A. G. Hebert and Lionel Thornton also had a Liberal Catholic background.

'Biblical Theology' was not a revival of fundamentalism; however it emphasized the unity of the Bible and the distinctiveness of biblical revelation. Its weakness lay in occasionally over-simplifying critical issues and concentrating on the biblical revelation to the exclusion of God's wider activity in the world.

The 1960s saw an extraordinary explosion of 'radical theology'. Two contributions by Anglicans were the American Paul Van Buren's *The Secular Meaning of the Gospel* and J. A. T. Robinson's *Honest to God*, both published in 1963. Robinson's views, being those of a bishop, provoked particular controversy. Both wrote with an avowedly missionary purpose, attempting to make Christianity more accessible to 'modern man'. Robinson drew heavily on continental Protestant theologians like Bultmann, Tillich and Bonhoeffer, combining them in a not always justified synthesis.

In reaction, presumably, recent theological trends show a resurgence of conservatism, most clearly manifest in the revival of Conservative Evangelicalism within the Church of England. This newer Evangelicalism is, however, more sacramental and scholarly than its late-nineteenth-century equivalent. Radical theology is not entirely eclipsed; and the existence of Anglican theologians who seem explicitly to repudiate the incarnation bewilders those in Churches with a firmer ecclesiastical discipline.

LITURGICAL DEVELOPMENTS

The eighteenth century was not a period of liturgical innovation except among a few Non-jurors. Sunday worship in the Church of England consisted of a morning service comprising Matins, Litany and Antecommunion read from the pulpit with the responses led by the parish clerk. Metrical psalms were sometimes sung, accompanied by a village band. Holy Communion was celebrated at the north end of the altar, but its frequency tended to decline during the century. In country districts quarterly celebrations were usual with a monthly celebration in towns. The Evangelical Revival, however, prompted more frequent communion and more extensive hymn singing.

The Romantic Movement had an important effect on religious sensibility with its emphasis on 'feeling' and its idealization of the Middle Ages. In architecture Neo-classical gave way to Gothic Revival. The Cambridge Camden Society, later known as the Ecclesiological Society, of which J. M. Neale (1818–1886) was a leading member, promoted the cause of Gothic and had enormous influence on church buildings and fittings. Neale also translated many patristic and medieval hymns, thus communicating their sacramental doctrine to ordinary congregations.

Ritualism formed no part of the original Tractarian programme, though the Tractarians did promote daily services, weekly communion and the keeping of the liturgical year. Ritualism became an important element in the 1850s and 60s as Tractarianism became Anglo-Catholicism. It attempted to teach the Tractarian understanding of sacraments and priesthood through the eye by the introduction of the eastward position, candles, eucharistic vestments and even incense. Some priests in slum areas saw it as a way of evangelizing the unlettered. It did, however, destroy liturgical uniformity within the Church and met with open hostility from Protestant-minded Anglicans.

A Royal Commission on Ritual reported inconclusively in 1867 and the Public Worship Regulation Act of 1874 aimed to destroy what Disraeli the Prime Minister called the 'Mass in masquerade'. But the subsequent imprisonment of four ritualist priests helped change opinion, and in the late 1880s the trial of the saintly Bishop Edward King of Lincoln for ritual irregularities added to public disquiet. Another Royal Commission reported in 1906 that the 'law of public worship is too narrow for the religious life of the present generation'.

Ritualism provoked similar strife in other parts of the Anglican Communion but it flourished in missionary areas under Anglo-Catholic influence, notably Southern Africa and the West Indies. Disestablishment in 1869 allowed the Church of Ireland to introduce canons expressly forbidding ritual innovation. In England the interpretation of the Prayer Book ornaments rubric was always the source of much legal wrangling, and episcopal injunctions were largely ignored.

Unofficial amplification of the Prayer Book and reservation of the sacrament which had started in the 1870s became more common in the early twentieth century. A revision of the Prayer Book was attempted in 1928 to contain these developments. Most factions found it unsatisfactory and its provisions stirred the latent Protestantism of the House of Commons who rejected it.

The influence of the Liturgical Movement enabled subsequent liturgical reform to be undertaken for its own sake, rather than as a means of curbing Anglo-Catholic lawlessness. Originating in continental Roman Catholicism its ideas were mediated to Anglicans in two seminal works: A. G. Hebert's *Liturgy and Society* (1935) and the symposium Hebert edited entitled *The Parish Communion* (1937). The latter gave theological underpinning to the growing practice of making the Eucharist the main Sunday service. This idea was enthusiastically promoted after the Second World War by the 'Parish and People' movement in England and the 'Associated Parishes' in the United States. In *The Shape of Liturgy* (1945) Dom Gregory Dix presented the scholarly case for liturgical revision; his subsequent influence, especially on the structure of the eucharistic rite, has been enormous (see pp. 279–83).

In the last twenty years there has been a proliferation of revised liturgical texts in modern Anglicanism, as elsewhere. This process has involved considerable experiment and ecumenical cross-fertilization, particularly in regard to common modern language liturgical texts.

A new prayer book was produced by ECUSA in 1979. In England the established Church could only venture on the path of liturgical reform with Parliamentary approval. The 1662 Book of Common Prayer remains normative and the book produced in 1980 is therefore called the Alternative Service Book. Unlike other Provinces of the Anglican Communion (e.g. Ireland, Canada and the USA) the Church of England has never had an official hymn book.

ANGLICANISM AND ECUMENISM

Many Anglicans have felt a concern for Christian unity, and in modern times an ecumenical vocation has become part of Anglican self-understanding.

Cranmer and James I both had ecumenical ideals of a sort. In the early eighteenth century Archbishop William Wake (1651–1737) corresponded on Christian unity with Reformed theologians such as Jablonski and Turretini as well as with Roman Catholic Gallicans such as Du Pin and Girardin. The Anglican claim to continuity in faith and order with the primitive Church and the distinction between fundamentals and non-essential matters of faith were seen as a possible basis for fruitful ecumenical endeavour (see pp. 232–43).

The Oxford Movement's understanding of the Church led its followers to seek reunion with other episcopal Churches. The Association for Promoting the Unity of Christendom was founded in 1857 by the Roman Catholic Ambrose Phillipps de Lisle and the Anglican F. G. Lee but the venture ended with condemnation by Rome in 1864. The Eastern Churches Association was founded in 1863. Pusey published three *Eirenicons* between 1865 and 1870 appealing for unity, and Anglicans took a sympathetic interest in the Old Catholic Congresses of the 1870s.

The beginning of modern ecumenism is usually traced to the 1910 Edinburgh Missionary Conference. Charles Henry Brent (1863–1929), Canadian-born Bishop of the Philippines, returned from Edinburgh with the vision of an international conference at which doctrinal issues would be faced squarely. Delayed by the war, the first World Conference on Faith and Order was held at Lausanne in 1927. For seventeen years this movement was led and funded largely by American Episcopalians. A second conference at Edinburgh in 1937 revealed Archbishop William Temple as a leading ecumenical figure. It fell to Temple's successor, Geoffrey Fisher, to inaugurate the World Council of Churches in Amsterdam in 1948. Another noted Anglican ecumenist, Bishop G. K. A. Bell (1883–1958), was the first chairman of the Central and Executive Committees. Every Anglican Province has joined the WCC.

The Anglican commitment to visible unity was expressed most prophetically in the 'Appeal to all Christian People' issued by the 1920 Lambeth Conference. A moving plea for organic union, it reaffirmed the Lambeth Quadrilateral as the basis for such a united Church. A key figure in this initiative was A. C. Headlam

(1862–1947), later Bishop of Gloucester, whose *Doctrine of the Church and Reunion* (1920) was published just before the Conference.

Some practical results followed. Anglican-Orthodox relations became more cordial, a measure of intercommunion was established with the Church of Sweden and, perhaps most significantly, full intercommunion was attained with the Old Catholic Churches as a result of the Bonn Agreement (1931).

Reunion between Anglicans and non-episcopal Churches has proved more intractable. After twenty-six years of negotiations the Church of South India came into being in 1946. This union between Anglicans, Methodists and Reformed, on the basis of future episcopal ordination but no reordination of non-episcopal ministers, was regarded by some Anglicans as a betrayal of fundamental principles; full acceptance of the United Church by the Anglican Communion has taken time. The Churches of North India and Pakistan were formed in 1970 avoiding difficulties over ministry by a service of incorporation.

In England Archbishop Fisher's Cambridge Sermon (1946) suggesting the Free Churches might 'take Episcopacy into their system' met with a promising response from Methodists. But the scheme for Methodist-Anglican unity foundered in both 1969 and 1972 because it failed to win sufficient support among Anglicans. A new initiative involving the United Reformed Church, 'Covenanting for Unity' foundered in the same way in 1982.

One reason for this was the changing stance of the Roman Catholic Church since Vatican II, and fears that concessions to 'Protestants' might jeopardize rapprochement with Rome. The friendship between Viscount Halifax and the French priest Abbé F. Portal had led to an initiative that was blighted by the condemnation of Anglican orders in 1896. The Malines Conversations in the 1920s, again involving Halifax, came to nothing though the ecumenical ideal proposed by Dom Lambert Beauduin of a Church 'united but not absorbed' remains important. In 1966, however, the visit of Archbishop Michael Ramsey (b. 1904) to Pope Paul VI resulted in a Common Declaration and the setting up in 1970 of an Anglican-Roman Catholic International Commission (ARCIC I) which published its Final Report in 1982. A commission with a revised membership (ARCIC II) held its first meeting in August 1983.

The Anglican Communion is a participant in four international bilateral dialogues. In addition to the one with Rome, there are discussions with Orthodox, Lutheran and Reformed. The scope of each dialogue is different and only with the Roman Catholic Church is visible unity the explicit goal. Regional unity schemes (e.g. in England, Nigeria, Sri Lanka, New Zealand and the Consultation on Church Union in the USA) have lost impetus. Interim eucharistic fellowship has been achieved in the United States by Episcopalians and some Lutherans since 1976. Anglican influence at the WCC appears to have decreased since the Council's early days.

At the present time the ecumenical future is far from clear. Anglicanism's doctrinal divisions have hindered its effectiveness as a so-called 'bridge Church' and put a question mark against its ecumenical vocation (see pp. 379–392).

RECENT DEVELOPMENT OF THE ANGLICAN COMMUNION

The 1930 Lambeth Conference described the Anglican Communion as 'a federation without a federal government'. With the formation of many new autonomous Provinces, beginning with West Africa in 1951, the problems this presents have become acute. The last thirty years have, therefore, seen efforts to strengthen communication and consultation within the Communion.

The appointment of the American Bishop Stephen Bayne (1908–74) as first Executive Officer of the Anglican Communion in 1960 following a recommendation from the 1958 Lambeth Conference was the first significant step in this direction. Pan-Anglican Congresses were held in Minneapolis in 1954 and Toronto in 1963. An Anglican Centre was established in Rome in 1966.

The Anglican Consultative Council was created after the 1968 Lambeth Conference and the Executive Officer replaced by a Secretary-General appointed by and responsible to the Council. The ACC is unique in that it is the only Anglican body with a constitution. It provides a continuity of consultation and guidance on policy which the Anglican Communion has hitherto lacked. Each Province appoints one to three members, and the total membership of sixty-two includes clergy and lay people. Three members are nominated by the united Churches of South and North India and Pakistan. There is a permanent Secretariat based in London, and meetings are held in different parts of the world at two- to three-year intervals. The first was held at Limuru, Kenya, in 1971. One of its recommendations resulted in the creation of an Inter-Anglican Theological Commission in 1980.

To further advance cohesion, a Primates Meeting has been held regularly since November 1979, though this is in no sense a 'higher Synod'. Such developments have nonetheless affected the role of the Archbishop of Canterbury. He has become a more significant focus of unity within the Communion and is expected to travel extensively within it. This international role fits uneasily with his position as Primate of a national and established Church.

A further problem that faces modern Anglicanism is the uncertainty surrounding its doctrinal basis and the acceptable limits of doctrinal variation. New Prayer Books, the effective 'demoting' of the Thirty-Nine Articles and theological liberalism have undermined the appeal to the classic sources of Anglican doctrine (see pp. 140–2).

The ordination of women to the priesthood in some Anglican provinces has also created difficulties. Women were ordained in Hong Kong in 1971 and Canada in 1976. In the USA the first canonical ordinations took place in 1977.

New Zealand also ordained women in that year. Whether it is acceptable, ecumenically prudent or indeed possible to ordain women as priests continues to be debated; and the 1978 Lambeth Conference was unable to do more than accept variety of practice while affirming its commitment to the preservation of Anglican unity.

Modern Anglicanism is therefore being forced both by its inner tensions and its position within Christendom to redefine its peculiar vocation. Perhaps the Anglican witness is best seen as the attempt to hold together givenness and exploration in doctrine and to unite the critical spirit with worship and spirituality. Certainly a fellowship which embraces Evangelicals, Catholics and Liberals needs to evaluate afresh its distinctive understanding of 'Reformed Catholicism', if it is to share its gifts with Christians of other traditions in the common search for unity (see pp. 405–22).

PART TWO

The Gospel in Anglicanism

The Gospel in Anglicanism

LOUIS WEIL

Anderson, H. G., Murphy, T. A., and Burgess, J. A., *Justification by Faith: Lutherans and Catholics in Dialogue VII*. Minneapolis 1985.

ARCIC II, *Salvation and the Church*. London 1987.

Avis, Paul, *Ecumenical Theology and the Elusiveness of Doctrine*. London 1986.

Bull, George, 'On Justification', in *Anglicanism*, ed. P. E. More and F. L. Cross (Milwaukee, WI, 1935), pp. 296–300.

Chadwick, Henry, 'The Context of Faith and Theology in Anglicanism', in *Theology in Anglicanism*, ed. A. A. Vogel (Wilton, CT, 1984), pp. 11–31.

Hardy, D. W., and Ford, D. F., *Jubilate: Theology in Praise*. London 1984.

Hooker, Richard, 'A Learned Discourse of Justification, Works, and How the Foundation of Faith is Overthrown', in *Works*, vol. iii. Oxford 1841.

Ramsey, A. M., *The Gospel and the Catholic Church*. London 1936.

Weil, Louis, *Gathered to Pray*. Cambridge, MA, 1986.

One of the most notable fruits of ecumenical dialogue in recent decades has been the emergence of growing evidence of convergence among separated Christians. This convergence touches fundamental areas of theological dispute which have been the apparently insuperable basis of alienation for several centuries. This convergence is multilateral, as the Lima Statement *Baptism, Eucharist and Ministry* testifies,[1] but it has been most dramatic in the particular encounters between two traditions where there have been long-standing areas of dispute. The Roman Catholic dialogue with Lutherans, for example, has demonstrated remarkable convergence on the issue of justification by faith.[2] Between Anglicans and Roman Catholics, the ARCIC statements on the Eucharist and on the ordained ministry have revealed convergence on two theological issues which have been the source of deep-rooted hostilities in the past, and some advance on the difficult issue of authority.[3]

Convergence does not, however, equate with reunion. The Lima Statement, for example, demonstrates what are for many of the participating Churches theological views now held by only a minority of members; a theological élite perhaps, but one which in recent decades has represented a growing common ground among Christians of different traditions. The New Testament teaching that there is 'one Lord, one faith, one baptism, one God and Father of all' seems to be creating a deeper imperative for that unity to come into a practical realization in Christian experience. Although that goal will not be reached in the near future, the awareness of convergence on basic questions has inevitably affected Christian consciousness, whatever the tradition, of the significant areas of common faith which Christians share (see pp. 379–92).

51

An essay on the gospel in Anglicanism which is written in the last years of the twentieth century is thus written in an atmosphere which is quite different from that which dominated, for example, a century ago, and even into comparatively recent times. Even today, many laity and clergy of Churches which are officially committed to ecumenical dialogue find this movement threatening to their own sense of identity not merely as one denomination among others, but rather as members of the Church as Jesus Christ intended it to be. Life within a particular religious tradition has a powerful formative impact upon believers, shaping their expectations of religious faith and practice in quite profound ways.

So the gospel is both a fundamental which Anglicans share with other Christian communions, and also a particular—that is, the gospel as it has been understood and practised within the Anglican tradition. What sharply distinguishes our situation today from that of a century ago is that the evidence of convergence is readily available to those who are disposed to see it. Our discussion of the gospel in Anglicanism thus involves an awareness that the fundamental tenets of the gospel are also present in the foundations of faith in other Christian traditions (see pp. 232–43).

What then, for Anglicans, is distinctive about the way the gospel is understood and lived? What particular facet of the infinitely rich gospel of God has most influenced Anglican thinking and experience? Anglicanism has never been disposed to unchurch other Christian traditions, that is, to insist that one aspect or another of its own self-understanding, if missing, would invalidate the right of another tradition to be called Christian. By way of example we might mention the episcopate. Certainly from the time of the Reformation, Anglicans have adhered to what is called 'the historic episcopate', that is, to the succession of bishops as the sign of the ordered transmission of pastoral authority in the Church from generation to generation (see pp. 296–308). In its debate with the Puritans from the time of Queen Elizabeth I, the episcopate emerged as a fundamental characteristic of the Anglican understanding of the Church. Yet Anglican reflection on the episcopate has not defined the nature of that ministry in sharply exclusive terms, and our participation in recent ecumenical dialogue has indicated an attitude toward the episcopate as a gift to be shared for the building up of the Church's unity, rather than as a basis for the exclusion of non-episcopal traditions from fellowship with us. This fellowship has extended even to the sharing of the eucharistic gifts which are the fundamental expression of our unity in Christ.

In Anglicanism, then, what is distinctive is not necessarily divisive. What is distinctive in Anglican faith and practice is seen rather in terms of gift, particular gifts of God which are part of a treasured heritage, and which Anglicans are called to bring to the shared vision of the Church which is truly one and which will encompass all the diverse gifts which the Holy Spirit has given to Christians at all times and in all places.

Those diverse gifts include the particular history which each religious tradition carries, the unfolding of its experience as a people of faith in encounter with God. These particular histories, prior to the twentieth century, were often lived in comparative isolation from each other. This made it possible to be complacent about divisions within the Church because contact was so limited; in practice, it made it easy to understand the Church in terms of the particular characteristics of one's own history. The radical changes in social structures and in human mobility that have developed in this century have brought Christians of different traditions into direct and substantial contact. This new situation has opened the door to mutual awareness and dialogue, and an awakening to the integrity of forms of the Christian life in other traditions. This has led to a recognition that differences in theological formulations or ministerial structures, or differences of forms of worship or spirituality, do not necessarily embody irreconcilable traditions among the Churches. Such differences may be seen rather as complementary, as expressive of the diversity which characterizes the Church in history, taking root in all the varied cultures of the world.

So the understanding of the gospel in Anglicanism would not claim to define all that might be said, much less all that might be experienced, of the good news that God is the creator of all that exists and that he has entered into and shared our human life in Jesus Christ so that the whole creation might come to its fulfilment. The words, images and rites used to proclaim this good news in the Christian traditions vary, and that diversity of articulation reflects the impact of history and culture spoken of above. Yet this wealth of language which has emerged within each tradition always points to the central and mysterious reality, that 'God was in Christ, reconciling the world to himself'. This is the gospel which Christianity knows as the paschal mystery. This central theme of the doctrine of redemption has been proclaimed within the Anglican liturgical tradition with dramatic power, in the anthem which Archbishop Cranmer appointed for use on Easter Day in the Prayer Book of 1552 and which has continued in use since that time. The anthem is made up of texts from St Paul, and is known by the opening words of the form it has had since the Book of 1662, 'Christ our Passover is sacrificed for us'. The focus of the text theologically is found in the second part of the anthem, where Cranmer's version began, with these words from the Epistle to the Romans:

> Christ being raised from the dead dieth no more;
>   death hath no more dominion over him.
> For in that he died, he died unto sin once:
>   but in that he liveth, he liveth unto God.
> Likewise reckon ye also yourselves to be dead indeed unto sin,
>   but alive unto God through Jesus Christ our Lord.

This is the heart of the paschal mystery, that death has been conquered by the dying and rising of Christ, and that the members of his Body share that victory.

During the recent decades of liturgical renewal and the revision of liturgical texts which has been common to all the major Christian communions, there has been a recovery of the identification which was recognized during the patristic period between faith in the paschal mystery and its ritual celebration in the liturgies of Holy Week and in Eastertide, the 'great fifty days' between Easter Day and Pentecost. Cranmer's association of Paul's paschal theology with the Church's celebration of Easter demonstrates his remarkable liturgical intuition at a time when early texts of the Holy Week rites were not available for study.

Cranmer's Easter anthem finds a rich complementarity to a medieval text which was associated with the Easter Vigil of Holy Saturday night. In that text, known as the *Exsultet*, Christ is proclaimed as 'the true Paschal Lamb, who at the feast of the Passover paid for us the debt of Adam's sin, and by his blood delivered your faithful people.'[4] Although it is a poetic elaboration of the biblical faith, the close relation of this to the verses selected by Cranmer is obvious:

> For since by man came death,
>   by man came also the resurrection of the dead.
> For as in Adam all die,
>   even so in Christ shall all be made alive.

The use of such texts in the celebration of the Easter rites offers a pastoral opportunity to renew in the awareness of the people gathered a lively sense of the gospel, not merely in words but in an experience of the celebration of that gospel which draws into the liturgical action both the story and the signs of redemption.

This emphasis on liturgical experience offers us a key to a significant aspect of the Anglican understanding of the gospel, namely, the importance of our experience of God's present action as the way in which God's work in Christ touches and is effective in successive generations of believers. For this reason, the doctrine of the Church as a visible society in history plays a major role in the way Anglicanism has understood the consequences of faith (see pp. 219–31). Faith is not seen as a private matter between God and the believer. Faith is corporate: it is the common faith of the Church into which new members are baptized and come to participate in the power of the paschal mystery. The individual enters into a dying and rising with Christ which is understood as the common experience of all the baptized, so that the Church itself is seen as an article of faith, the fellowship of all those who share a common identity in Christ. Our unity in Christ is nourished by the sharing of the Eucharist, not as an act of private piety but as the celebration of that common identity which baptism has created. The Church's outward rites, its sacraments and all those signs which give external expression of God's inward activity, are thus fundamentally related to the Anglican understanding of the gospel. The whole structuring of the

Church's common life is an instrument for God's saving action, as it signifies the abiding grace and power of the paschal mystery in the lives of those who believe.

It is in this perspective that we see why the Book of Common Prayer has played so fundamental a role (see pp. 131–3). In no other Christian tradition does the authorized liturgy take on so great a significance. The Prayer Book is first of all the basis for *corporate* prayer. In other words, the book itself supports the dimension of common experience spoken of above. In addition to this essential role, and as a kind of natural overflow from it, the Prayer Book is also a formative element in the private prayer of Anglicans. Even in solitude, the use of the collects or psalms, or the texts of the various rites, link the individual Anglican at prayer with the common prayer of the larger fellowship. Again, the Prayer Book is also turned to as a source for the teaching of the Church. Anglicanism gives forceful expression to the ancient adage, *Lex orandi legem statuat credendi*, 'the law of prayer establishes the law of faith'[5] (see pp. 174–87).

LITURGY AND DOCTRINE

If Christian worship and the doctrines of Christian faith are so closely related, what is the nature of that relationship? How is their implied mutuality realized in practice? Wherever there is a tendency to understand faith as an intellectual activity, there has been a consequent denigration of the role of worship and sacraments in the Christian life. The Enlightenment, with its exaltation of human reason, had such an effect upon the worship of seventeenth-century Anglicanism. If rites were to be tolerated at all, the rationalist would see them only as a means by which Christian truths might be taught. The purpose of liturgical rites was thus essentially didactic. Yet this is not adequate to the Church's experience of encounter with God in the liturgical action.

It was suggested earlier that Anglicanism has understood the gospel, God's work of redemption, as present to the experience of believers in every generation. That experience is not primarily a mental activity but rather one in which the whole person is involved. Authentic liturgical worship draws all that is human into its frame of reference. Reason is not put aside, but neither should it dominate. Faith in God involves the mind, but it is not a desiccated intellectual activity. In faith the mind is illuminated by the heart. Understanding does not precede belief, but is one of its fruits.

The implications of this for the liturgy are far reaching. Fundamentally it means that liturgical rites are not ceremonial clothing for doctrinal teaching. Rather than *teaching* the faith, in the usual sense of that word, the liturgy *celebrates* the faith. It lifts it up through words and signs in a corporate experience which expresses the faith which has summoned the people to gather. Yet it also nourishes that faith, and sends the people forth to live it in their daily lives. It is a transforming experience in which the people themselves are renewed as signs of the mystery which they have assembled to celebrate.

Because of the deep mutuality between what the Church believes and what it prays, the revision of liturgical rites has serious doctrinal importance. It is not merely a question of modernization of language or clarification of ritual. Our language of corporate prayer—both word and action—is expressive of our experience of God. For a people of faith, rituals hallowed through years of use in public prayer participate in our encounter with the Holy One: they are the instruments of that encounter. Since the sixteenth century, Anglicanism has acknowledged in its liturgical documents the need for revision from time to time. In the Preface to the Book of Common Prayer in 1549, the liturgy is seen as one of the human aspects of the Church which may, for appropriate and serious reasons, undergo change or correction so that it may serve its true purpose. If such revision is not undertaken, the liturgy eventually becomes alienated from the lives of Christians as an encapsulated divine activity which ultimately betrays its roots in the incarnation. Liturgy must be experienced in its connectedness to the lives of worshippers.

Yet such changes do not remain only on the external level. The need for change is itself an indication that the context in which Christians are living their lives has changed, and with that, that our understanding of our relation with God has shifted to new ground. Worship is an articulation of faith. Liturgical change is thus an indication of underlying change both in the Church's self-understanding and of the way it understands the God who is the focus of its worship.

During recent decades, the major Christian Churches have been involved in the official revision of their liturgical books. In each communion, and, indeed, in each national body of the various communions, the character of the work of revision has been shaped by a wide range of particular factors of history and culture which cannot be considered within the limitations of this essay. In spite of such differences, however, it is possible to assert that this extensive effort is itself the fruit of the Liturgical Movement whose origins may be discerned in the latter part of the nineteenth century (see pp. 42–4).

The liturgical changes of recent years bear a somewhat ironic relationship to the Romantic Movement and its idealization of the Middle Ages. The relationship is ironic because the impact of the neo-Gothic revival upon the Churches (we might note in this regard the Anglican, Lutheran and Roman Catholic Churches in particular) was to hold up certain ideals of liturgy and doctrine, of architecture and sacred music based upon the supposed standards of the High Middle Ages.[6] This initial stage of the Liturgical Movement was at least an answer to the dry rationalism of the Enlightenment, but it also set up static models for the liturgy which were recognized, as the Church moved into the twentieth century, to be pastorally unsuited to a radically different cultural framework from that of medieval times. This awareness carried the Liturgical Movement from its early goal of restoring medieval norms into a recognition that new liturgical imperatives imposed new pastoral requirements upon the official books. In that perspective, it must be acknowledged that the various newly authorized books contain not merely refurbished old rites, but rather patterns for liturgical celebration based upon a profound recovery of a sense of liturgy as the whole Church's celebration of its shared faith. In this we are offered a particular insight into the relation of the gospel to the liturgy within the Anglican tradition, for the Prayer Book tradition is nothing less than the ordered means through which the community of the baptized participate in the redemption which those rites proclaim.

When the final stages of Prayer Book revision had been reached in the United States, organizations which favoured the preservation of the 1928 Book of Common Prayer published articles and tracts which criticized the 'new theology' of the proposed revision. Some of us who are professional liturgists responded defensively that although the rites had been revised, the Prayer Book faith remained the same. We soon realized that this response was naive to say the least, and perhaps even dishonest. The criticism was, in fact, correct, but in a positive sense. The new rites reflected significant theological changes, virtually all of them related to a recovery of a more biblical understanding of the nature of the Church as this touched such basic issues as Christian initiation, the Eucharist, and the role of the ordained ministry in relation to other ministries. In other words, the sacramental and liturgical study of the past several decades had gradually shaped a new mentality, and the eventual effect was to create pressure within the Church that its liturgical rites be more honestly expressive of the faith to which they witness.

To one degree or another, the entire Anglican Communion has been involved in this process. Provinces which are located in the so-called Third World are somewhat later in this development, because of their particular histories in regard to the nations from which they were evangelized. Nineteenth-century missionary attitudes involved not only the proclamation of Christ but generally the imposition of an alien cultural framework as well. In regard to liturgical norms, this led to an uncritical assumption that liturgical practice would quite simply conform to the models which the missionaries brought from home. These were accepted as a definitive standard with little idea that the local culture might bring its own unique gifts into the richness of the Church's liturgical prayer. At best, the Book of Common Prayer was translated, where the local language was not English, but in strict conformity to the model even if this produced anomalies in the second language (see pp. 393–8).

Recent reflection on the theology of mission has brought a severe judgement upon the limited vision of this culture-biased view of liturgical worship. Deeper insight into the theology of symbol and of language, as well as a willingness to recognize the multi-cultural implications of the incarnation in Christian faith

57

and practice, have placed all these issues in a much more open field in which fresh air is bringing new life to the traditional forms and images.

In other words, the revision of liturgical rites is not a concern restricted to a small group of liturgical specialists. The pastoral need for such revision from time to time has been recognized within the Anglican tradition from the beginning, and was given explicit articulation in the Preface to the first American Book of Common Prayer in 1789, where we read that rites 'may be altered, abridged, enlarged, amended, or otherwise disposed of, as may seem most convenient for the edification of the people'. The revision of the Book of Common Prayer has to do in its most fundamental purpose with the constant reclaiming of the gospel to which the Church is called. For Anglicans, that reclaiming inevitably bears a special and intense relationship to the way the Church prays, that is, to the ways in which the Church articulates its faith in corporate prayer. In the light of this, a revision of the Prayer Book is not limited to some changes in language.

It is interesting to note how often critics of one or another of the new versions have focused upon the question of language, to the virtual exclusion of the wider complex of other, often non-verbal, aspects of liturgical prayer.[7] The newly authorised versions are expressive of theological change, especially in regard to the recovery of a sense of the Church coming into self-realization in its liturgical celebrations. This suggests a greatly expanded theological horizon in which the Church is seen as the gathering place of all cultures and peoples whose languages and symbols merit an equal place within the framework of the Church's life. Such a theological expansion is deeply challenging to the prerogatives which the 'mother Church' concept has engendered, and the full extent of this expansion is at this time far beyond our abilities to discern. It challenges us to recognize that the God to whom the traditional rites have been addressed is, if understood as the terminus of those rites, too small a God. Our rites have tended to domesticate God within the images of Western culture projected into the heavenly places. Liturgy is most authentic when it is experienced as awestruck praise, the creature standing at the threshold of the Holy. In praise God is recognized, acknowledged, and thus adored not as the *end* of our prayer but always as the One who moves beyond the grasp of our stuttered praises. The American writer Annie Dillard has summed up the point, saying, 'I often think of the set pieces of liturgy as certain words which people have successfully addressed to God without their getting killed.'[8] No 'God in a box' is at the heart of the gospel, but the Holy One who is a consuming fire.

Liturgy must follow a difficult course if it is to permit the faithful to assemble before God 'without their getting killed' and at the same time not so tame the images of God that he becomes unworthy of authentic faith. At the centre of Christian liturgical prayer we find the doctrine of God, not as a series of credal statements but in the lifting up of images which are expressive of how God is understood through Christian faith. The collects, for example, offer a rich array of such images in a succinct form of corporate prayer.[9] In the collects, God is addressed especially in reference to his mercy, grace and love; for example,

> Let thy merciful ears, O Lord, be open to the prayers of thy humble servants . . .

or

> O God, who declarest thy almighty power chiefly in showing mercy and pity; mercifully grant us such a measure of thy grace, that we, running the way of thy commandments, may obtain thy gracious promises, and be made partakers of thy heavenly treasure; through Jesus Christ our Lord.

This theme of the mercy of God occurs again and again, especially as it is manifest in his acceptance of the prayers of the Church or in the preserving of its members from harm.

The grace of God in the collects is often linked to God's forgiveness of sin or in God's enabling us to do good. The first, for example, is seen in the collect which Thomas Cranmer composed for the Book of Common Prayer of 1549 for use on the first Sunday of Advent:

> Almighty God, give us grace that we may cast away the works of darkness, and put upon us the armour of light . . .

The same theological perspective is expressed in yet another of the traditional collects:

> Grant, we beseech thee, Almighty God, that we, who for our evil deeds do worthily deserve to be punished, by the comfort of thy grace may mercifully be relieved; through our Lord and Saviour Jesus Christ.

Here God's mercy and grace are brought together in the forgiveness of sinners. Grace as God's gift enabling us to do what is good is found in a very brief example of the form:

> Lord, we pray thee that thy grace may always prevent and follow us, and make us continually to be given to all good works; through Jesus Christ our Lord.

The grace of God as articulated in these examples is expressive of the divine power to touch human life to heal or to enable. The doctrine of God articulated here is not of a distant deity unconcerned with human pain, but of a God who is near at hand, attentive to the prayers of his creatures.

The highest attribute of God is his love, as of a father or mother caring for beloved children. Here the liturgy brings us into direct encounter with the paschal mystery; since the love of God has been most clearly revealed in the sending of Jesus, through whose death and resurrection, and our participation in them through baptism, we have been made the children of God, now addressing

God as Abba–'Father'. This aspect of the Christian doctrine of God is marvellously expressed in the familiar collect for Palm Sunday:

> Almighty and everlasting God, who, of thy tender love towards mankind hast sent thy Son, our Saviour Jesus Christ, to take upon him our flesh, and to suffer death upon the cross, that all mankind should follow the example of his great humility; Mercifully grant, that we may both follow the example of his patience, and also be made partakers of his resurrection; through the same Jesus Christ our Lord.

The theological significance of a text such as this as an expression of fundamental doctrine, and in this example of a distinctively Anglican character, becomes evident when we note the changes which Cranmer made from the Latin original of this collect. In adapting it for the 1549 Prayer Book, he added the phrase 'of thy tender love', thus indicating that it was God's love which was the motivating energy behind the incarnation of Jesus Christ. Further, with again a strong doctrinal concern, Cranmer removed the petition that we might 'merit to be partakers of his resurrection' and substituted the petition that we might 'follow' Christ's example. Here we see a characteristic concern of the Reformers that there be no question of grace earned through merit. In Cranmer's version, the grace and action of God are seen as the expression of God's love, not as rewards to be earned.[10]

Given these attributes of God which recur throughout the repertory of Anglican collects, the human response to these qualities finds its appropriate expression within the liturgical context, when the children of God gather on the basis of their common identity in Christ. That response is praise and thanksgiving, not only in the specific liturgical action of the Eucharist but in the whole of life as an offering of praise to God.[11] As expressed in the words of the General Thanksgiving, 'We, thine unworthy servants, do give thee most humble and hearty thanks for all thy goodness and loving-kindness to us, and to all men.' In words which have been used in Anglican worship since 1662, the prayer brings together every aspect of life as the ground of thanksgiving. At the centre is 'the redemption of the world by our Lord Jesus Christ', but the response of praise is to be 'not only with our lips, but in our lives, by giving up ourselves to thy service'. Here within the liturgical context the critical link is made between what we believe, what we pray and how we live.

Using the texts of the Prayer Book tradition, we might similarly explore the fundamental aspects of Christian faith as expressed and celebrated in the forms of Christian prayer. Although it is not possible to consider other examples here, it should already be evident why the Prayer Book plays such a fundamental role in Anglicanism as the basis of a shared faith. What is prayed is, as the adage affirms, what is believed. Although the *Articles of Religion* hold a significant place in Anglican history as a summary of Christian doctrine, and have special importance in showing how Anglicanism found a place to stand within the polarizing debates of the sixteenth century, it is not in such documents that the spirit of Anglicanism is to be found, but rather in its worship (see pp. 133–42).

Yet the liturgy does not articulate a static norm of faith. There is an extraordinary dynamic within the liturgical act which always holds up a 'beyond', at which the Church has not yet arrived. In this regard, there is always a proleptic, or anticipatory, dimension in the liturgy. One sees this, for example, in eschatological references such as are found in the Advent Collect quoted earlier where, after speaking of the humility of Christ's birth, the prayer continues, 'that in the last day, when he shall come again in his glorious majesty to judge both the quick and the dead, we may rise to the life immortal'. The liturgy thus holds before us the not-yet-realized aspects of Christian faith. In this perspective, the liturgy always points us to God's future action, and thus works against attempts to fix the truth of the gospel in static formulas. To claim the gospel we are required to be open to dimensions of it which have not yet been revealed, or which we have failed to discern. The Church's re-examination of its liturgical rites is thus a necessity if we are not to become complacent simply because the phrases have become so familiar. A kind of discontinuity becomes a pastoral necessity if we are to be jolted into hearing the eternally new call of God which lies behind the words and rituals.

It was to this fruitful discontinuity that I alluded earlier when I spoke of the reaction to the *new* theology of the recent versions of the Prayer Book. The theology is new precisely because it is the theology of the great tradition which must be reclaimed in terms of the life and culture of each generation of the Church's members. The eternal gospel is not preserved through a rigid adherence to the familiar rites and phrases, but rather in allowing it to speak from its centre, the experience of the paschal mystery in the lives of Christians today. In this way, the Prayer Book plays a dynamic role in shaping a new liturgical mentality in which the old truths are seen afresh. Such a transition never takes place easily, because there seems to be a natural conservatism in worshippers in regard to the rituals through which faith has been articulated. An individual believer may have used certain forms of prayer for decades, and this matter must therefore be approached by the Church with great sensitivity. But at the same time, as we have seen, change must come so that we may be faithful to the gospel as it speaks to the real world in which we live. If the law of prayer establishes the law of faith, then new forms of prayer can challenge Christians to grow into a deeper understanding of the faith they profess.

There is evidence that the Book of 1979 has already begun to reshape the theological understanding of members of the Episcopal Church in the United States. Such reshaping, as we have observed, takes place slowly because theological attitudes which have been shaped through years of experience do not change easily, and for years to come there will be clergy as well as laity who will attempt to use the new Prayer Book upon the ground-plan which operated beneath the previous edition. This misuse restricts liturgy to its surface dimensions, so that what the rite is intended to say is undermined by the manner in which it is celebrated.

One example of this problem comes immediately to mind. The baptismal rite of the 1928 Book of Common Prayer took as its model the baptism of a child or infant. Adult candidates are a clearly secondary expectation. The rite further presumed that the baptism was a separate liturgical action, not connected to any important corporate celebration, such as the Sunday Eucharist. The baptismal liturgy of the 1979 Book of Common Prayer is quite different in its expectations, in regard not only to the above matters but in its whole ethos. It is not simply a matter of changes or adjustments of the texts, but, more significantly, of the theology upon which Christian initiation is based (see pp. 261–71).

The new rite, for example, establishes that an adult is the normative candidate for baptism through the way the liturgy is structured: adults and older children are presented first, thus indicating a theological priority for those who can speak for themselves. Again, the way the rite is printed indicates that the normative pattern should be the celebration of baptism in the context of the Eucharist, and this is supported by an introductory rubric to the rite. The new rite thus reverses the expectations upon which the former rite was based.

Such significant changes are not a matter of mere ritual updating, but are indicative of a major shift in the theological understanding of the rite. The new form breaks with the privatized model of baptism which had dominated in pastoral practice for centuries. We see in this shift the fruit of decades of study of the history and theology of Christian initiation as it bubbles forth at the level of pastoral practice. The rediscovered theology of initiation is directly related to the recovery of a biblical understanding of the Church as the people of God. The gospel of our participation in the paschal mystery through baptism is thus reclaimed by changes in the liturgical rite which support such a theology.

Further results have developed out of this fundamental theological change. The celebration of baptism within the Eucharist on Sunday has reawakened the Church's awareness of the essential link between the two sacraments, that baptism is entrance into the communion fellowship, and that the Eucharist is itself a sacrament of initiation, the fulfilment of the process of the making of a Christian. Yet this link had been obscured for centuries at the level of pastoral practice, which had separated Communion from the rite of baptism and attached it to a later rite associated with a certain level of intellectual understanding. Historical research in this area has again borne fruit at the pastoral level, by revealing the questionable influences which separated what had for centuries in Christian practice been understood as integrally related.[12]

These matters concerning baptism and related issues are but one example of a whole complex of critical areas in which the mutuality between liturgy and doctrine may be seen. It is not that the liturgy is a didactic tool, but rather that it inevitably articulates an underlying theology. When research leads to deepened knowledge, when historical facts turn out not to be what we thought they were, when theology has strayed from the strong lines of the great tradition, and when pastoral practice does not bear fruit in building up the common life of the Body of Christ, then ritual patterns must be critically revised so that they may more adequately fulfil their role as signs of the abiding action of God in the Church. Liturgical change is the response in the Church to the awareness of God's present imperatives within the community of faith.

The Book of Common Prayer is for Anglicans far more than a collection of rites. Within Anglicanism the Prayer Book is a living expression of the profound union between what we believe and what we pray; a doctrinal document, not because it may contain such didactic materials as a catechism, or historical materials of doctrinal significance, but because it is in corporate worship that Anglicans find the common ground for their profession of faith. In this sense, Anglicanism has never understood itself as a 'confessional Church' in the way, for example, that Lutheranism has identified its faith with certain documents which are fundamental to its identity. Anglicanism has claimed no faith of its own, but only that faith which the Church at all times and in all places has celebrated in its corporate worship. Although the Nicene Creed is a statement of faith issued by a general Council of the Church and thus accepted as authoritative for Anglicanism, its significance as a doctrinal foundation among Anglicans is probably far more the result of its liturgical use than of a preoccupation with the authority of a Council. This is but one example of the way in which corporate prayer has shaped belief through the impact of the Book of Common Prayer, not only in shaping Anglican piety but theology as well.

This experience of the reciprocity of liturgy and doctrine is reinforced as a normative relationship in a comment made by Aidan Kavanagh at a meeting of the North American Academy of Liturgy in 1983, when he noted that liturgical theology is

> the primary theological act of believing Christians, as distinct from, say, systematic theologies *about* the liturgy or whatever, which are secondary. I think that the liturgical act, so far from being related to secondary theological endeavor as matter has been said to be related to form, is in fact the primary and foundational theological act from which all subsequent theological activity arises. The liturgical assembly is a theological corporation.[13]

These words of Kavanagh are a remarkable and forceful confirmation of the Anglican experience: 'The liturgical act ... is in fact the primary and foundational theological act.' The living God is present, known and adored by a people of faith: the liturgical action is the embodiment of the response of faith. This liturgical act, Kavanagh is saying, is the primary place at which the Church *does* theology. It is the fruitful awareness of God's presence and grace and thus both expresses faith and nourishes it. Systematic reflection upon this faith experience is what we usually call 'theology', but, Kavanagh tells us, this latter is theology in a derived sense. Primary theology is what the whole Church does in its liturgical prayer.

So it is that in the Anglican tradition, faith and praise are united. The fundamental energy which sustains the liturgical action is the faith of the gathered people. That faith may be illuminated by a high level of study and reflection: theologians also go to church and share in the common prayer. But standing beside those whose vocation it is to think about the faith, there are others who are no less fully members of the family of God. They offer prayer together. The liturgy is not concerned about distinctions of intellect, but calls all the members of the Body into a common act of praise. Their presence in such an assembly is the fundamental expression of their participation in the paschal mystery of Jesus Christ through baptism, and of the continuing activity of the Holy Spirit in deepening the life of faith. That participation in the Trinity is the way the gospel is experienced through life in the Church. It is there that the saving work of God is proclaimed, believed and celebrated (see pp. 313–24).

JUSTIFICATION BY FAITH

The doctrine of justification stands above all other theological issues as the distinctive mark of the Reformation. Although the doctrine is most closely associated with Lutheranism, it is in fact a primary aspect of the Anglican tradition as well, and indeed of all the Churches shaped out of the painful confrontation within the Church in the sixteenth century. The doctrine is concerned with God's free and gracious initiative for the salvation of the human race, an initiative revealed in human history in the paschal mystery of Jesus Christ. The fruit of God's initiative in Christ is transforming grace which liberates men and women from the burden of personal guilt and alienation from God. This act of God—*salvation*—is a free gift. It cannot be bought or earned. It can only be accepted or rejected. Its acceptance is the act of faith by which, in spite of the reality of sin, the free grace of God justifies us.

The term 'salvation' is understood in different ways in the various Christian traditions. For Anglicans, it involves not only the forgiveness of sins but also the call to a holy life. The fruit of God's gift is sanctification, that is, to live in the power of God's transforming grace. Anglicanism has traditionally emphasized the life of those who are justified, a life of sanctification and of service to mankind. This emphasis on holy living is a fundamental aspect of the Anglican interpretation of the doctrine of justification, and in regard to this essay, is an essential link with the role of the liturgy in the Christian life. In the worship of the Church, in the proclamation of Scripture and preaching, and in the celebration of the sacramental signs of faith, God's gift of grace through the death and resurrection of Jesus is articulated in word and act, that is, through the senses, as God continues to touch and transform the human situation. Although each individual person is called to accept this gift in faith, the individual can never be radically isolated from the corporate life of the community of faith. From the moment a person is baptized, the whole Church is engaged as the context in which God's gift is both proclaimed and received. This proclamation through word and sign is the most basic work of the Church, calling into and sustaining within its fellowship those who perceive in Christ the sacrament, the human and historical sign, of mankind's encounter with God.

In the *Articles of Religion*, the doctrine of justification is set forth in these words:

> We are accounted righteous before God, only for the merit of our Lord and Saviour Jesus Christ by Faith, and not for our own works or deservings. Wherefore, that we are justified by Faith only, is a most wholesome Doctrine, and very full of comfort, as more largely is expressed in the Homily of Justification.[14]

The essential concern in this passage is linked to the word *merit*: it is only 'for the merit of our Lord and Saviour Jesus Christ by Faith' that mankind is justified before God, 'not for our own works or deservings'. In the latter Middle Ages until the time immediately prior to the Reformation, the idea was linked to the principle that 'those who do what is in them' will not be denied the grace of God. We can see the importance of the human response to God's gift. As noted above, Anglicanism's concern with sanctification as the fruit of salvation indicates that the acceptance of God's grace is not just an internal mental activity but is visibly manifested in the transformation of the believer's life-style. This characteristic balance on so hotly debated an issue is reflected in the Article following the one on Justification, 'Of Good Works'. The text reads:

> Albeit that Good Works, which are the fruits of Faith, and follow after Justification, cannot put away our sins, and endure the severity of God's judgment; yet are they pleasing and acceptable to God in Christ, and do spring out necessarily of a true and lively Faith; insomuch that by them a lively faith may be as evidently known as a tree discerned by the fruit.[15]

This latter Article was aimed at striking the Anglican *via media* between what was seen as the Roman overemphasis upon good works as a means of earning forgiveness and merit on the one hand, and the rejection of any significant role for good works in the life of faith, a view attributed to Luther.

The Reformation debate on justification grew out of what was generally viewed by the Reformers as the corrupt theological climate of the later medieval period. A concern had emerged about the role of human nature in the divine-human encounter which had led into a preoccupation with what it is that Christians are called to *do* in their daily lives. It was taught that if we do what is in us, God will not deny us the gift of grace. This principle flowed easily into a dangerous distortion of the gospel in which certain types of doing—good works—were seen to earn us the grace of God. It led, in pastoral practice, to clergy urging people to prove themselves worthy of acceptance by God through the doing of such good works. For the Reformers, this was a major theological error, but it was not only an intellectual concern for them. It was in the area of practical piety that the bitter fruit of the error was most evident: salvation had come to be generally viewed as something earned by such 'good works' as the fulfilment of an array of penitential disciplines, and through stipends paid for the intentions at Mass. The latter came to be identified especially with the system of requiem Masses which developed into ever more extended and elaborate patterns as the medieval period began to wane. This system was a major source of income for the Church.

The attacks levelled by the Reformers against such practices were a threat to the entire clericalized power structure of the Church, a threat which was immediately recognized by an often decadent clergy. The emphasis of the Reformers upon the doctrine of justification must be seen against this background. They were particularly concerned about countless numbers of the faithful who lived at the edge of despair because they were unable to buy or earn sufficient merit to be assured of salvation. It was to this situation that the Reformers responded that it was 'not for our own works or deservings', but only through the grace of God which we accept in faith. The gospel was reclaimed that only through the death and resurrection of Jesus, that is, through what God has done and not anything on our own part, was salvation possible at all. This was the fundamental article of faith, that Jesus Christ 'was put to death for our trespasses and raised again for our justification'.[16]

Given the impact of the medieval merit system upon the piety of Christians, it cannot surprise us that the Reformers were deeply concerned about liturgical and sacramental matters. The corruptions associated with the stipend system left their taint upon the Eucharist itself. There was a desire for radical purification of the liturgical life of the Church as a whole, the removal of abuse and superstition, and the restoration of an authentically biblical piety. Within some of the Reformed traditions, memory of the corruptions led to a disparagement of the medieval liturgical heritage. Simplification along the lines of what were believed to be the biblical standards became an imperative, and on the whole, most of the medieval tradition was swept away.

The reform did not take so radical a path in Anglicanism, however, and this seems to have been the result not only of a natural conservatism but perhaps most significantly because of the understanding of the relation of sanctification to justification: justification involves sanctification in the Christian life, and the instrumental means of that sanctification is found in the sacramental life of the Church. Behind this we see the importance of the incarnation for the Anglican understanding of both Church and sacraments. As we read in the Article 'Of the Sacraments':

> Sacraments ordained of Christ be not only badges or tokens of Christian men's profession, but rather they be certain sure witnesses, and effectual signs of grace, and God's good will towards us, by the which he doth work invisibly in us, and doth not only quicken, but also strengthen and confirm our Faith in him.[17]

We see the incarnational principle here in the reference to 'effectual signs of grace'. The whole idea behind the sacraments for Anglicans is that God acts through persons, events and things. The physical, material world is not alien to God; it is his creation. That relation of the physical world to the will and purpose of the Creator is fully exemplified in the incarnation in which, through the instrumentality of the life of Jesus, God has brought redemption to the world.

The *Articles of Religion* thus offer a sensitively balanced treatment of this question within Anglicanism, clearly sympathetic to the emphasis placed upon the doctrine of justification as interpreted by continental Reformers, yet cutting its own path between the polarized positions on both sides. The first major exponent of the Anglican view was, of course, Richard Hooker. In a sermon preached while Hooker was Master of the Temple, and later published as 'A Learned Discourse of Justification', Hooker shows how faith and works do not exclude each other although justification is itself through faith alone. He writes,

> [Our adversaries claim] that we tread all Christian virtues under our feet, and require nothing in Christians but faith; because we teach that faith alone justifieth: whereas we by this speech never meant to exclude either hope and charity from being always joined as inseparable mates with faith in the man that is justified; or works from being added to necessary duties, required at the hands of every justified man.[18]

In this passage, Hooker refuses to isolate the doctrine of justification as though it may be esteemed in separation from the other dimensions of the Christian life, including good works as a requirement of those who have been justified.

It is in this perspective that we must consider the strong emphasis which Hooker places upon the sacraments as outward signs of God's justifying grace. In *The Laws of Ecclesiastical Polity*, Hooker speaks of the necessity of sacraments in the effecting of God's purposes:

> That saving grace which Christ originally is or hath for the general good of the whole Church, by sacraments he severally deriveth into every member thereof. Sacraments serve as the instruments of God to that end and purpose, moral instruments, the use whereof is in our hands, the effect in his ... For we take not baptism nor the eucharist for bare *resemblances* or memorials of things absent, neither for *naked signs* and testimonies assuring us of grace received before, but (as they are indeed and in verity) for means effectual whereby God when we take the sacraments delivereth into our hands that grace available unto eternal life, which grace the sacraments represent or signify.[19]

For Hooker, God's gift of justification is thus effectively signified in the sacramental signs which are truly, by God's purpose and effect, instruments of grace.

Does Hooker's teaching differ significantly from the other positions taken during the debate on justification? First, let us consider the teaching of the Augsberg Confession of 1530, since Article XII of the *Articles of Religion* was at least in part intended as a contradiction of 'solifidianism', the idea that we are saved by a bare faith. The first important question is whether this was indeed the Lutheran teaching. The Article on justification in the Augsberg Confession reads as follows:

> It is also taught among us that we cannot obtain forgiveness of sin and righteousness before God by our own merits, works, or satisfactions, but that we receive forgiveness of sin and become righteous before God by grace, for Christ's sake, through faith, when we believe that Christ suffered for us and that for his sake our sin is forgiven and righteousness and eternal life are given to us. For God will regard and reckon this faith as righteousness, as Paul says in Romans 3.21–26 and 4.5.[20]

The most interesting contrast between this statement and the Anglican Article on justification is the significant emphasis given here to the forgiveness of sin, which is not even mentioned in the Anglican form. Although there is no major theological difference in the intention of the two versions, there is clearly a difference of ethos. A certain weight of responsibility for justification falls upon Christians to *believe* they are justified, an idea which also finds no place in the Anglican Article. Yet certainly the central point in both is that justification comes only through God's grace, and that the only merit involved is that of Jesus Christ.

What is the role of good works within the Lutheran system of thought? Article XX of the Confession deals with 'Faith and Good Works'. Its opening sentence is a direct response to the accusation of 'solifidianism': 'Our teachers have been falsely accused of forbidding good works.' Later in this rather long Article, the problem of the relation between faith and works is explored in detail. First, it affirms that our reconciliation with God happens only through faith, and that works cannot achieve this purpose. This view is supported with reference to St Paul's teaching in Ephesians 2.8–9; 'For by grace you have been saved through faith ... not because of works.' Reference is also made to the teaching of St Augustine on this point.

The passage then continues with an aspect of the question which seems to have been of central concern to Luther, that is, the unrest of conscience suffered by many Christians who attempted to find salvation within the merit system: 'The conscience cannot come to rest and peace through works, but only through faith, that is, when it is assured and knows that for Christ's sake it has a gracious God.' Since clergy had failed to preach justification by faith, people had been driven to rely on their own efforts.

The final part of the Article addresses the question of good works:

It is also taught among us that good works should and must be done, not that we are to rely on them to earn grace but that we may do God's will and glorify him. It is always faith alone that apprehends grace and forgiveness of sin. When through faith the Holy Spirit is given, the heart is moved to do good works.[21]

There is obviously a tension in this passage which finds no comparable parallel in the Anglican Article on good works. One senses the depth of reaction against a piety of merit, nor is there place here for the idea that good works are 'pleasing and acceptable to God in Christ', as is found in the Anglican version. The Lutheran form takes a far more polarized view on the issue, and in this regard is more characteristic of the passion which supported this teaching in the heat of the Reformation.

Similarly, there is evident contrast between the Anglican article on the sacraments and that of the Augsberg Confession. The whole thrust of the statement in the Confession is the relation of the sacraments to faith:

They are signs and testimonies of God's will toward us for the purpose of awakening and strengthening our faith. For this reason they require faith, and they are rightly used when they are received in faith and for the purpose of strengthening faith.[22]

None of this is contradicted in the Anglican Article, but in the latter we find a firm emphasis upon the instrumentality of the sacraments as 'effectual signs of grace . . . by the which he doth work invisibly in us'. The contrast suggests that underlying the Lutheran form is a conscious cautiousness resulting from abuses of pastoral practice of the sacraments, and hence a resulting hesitancy about any reference to objective grace being effected through them.

For Calvin, faith is the source of a double grace, first, 'that being reconciled to God through Christ's blamelessness, we may have in heaven instead of a Judge a gracious Father; and secondly, that sanctified by Christ's spirit we may cultivate blamelessness and purity of life'.[23] Thus, Calvin sees both justification and sanctification as the fruit of faith. The latter, sanctification, is seen by Calvin as inseparable from justification. The justified life of faith bears fruit in good works; faith and good works must cleave together. By faith, Calvin writes,

we grasp Christ's righteousness, by which alone we are reconciled to God. Yet you could not grasp this without at the same time grasping sanctification also . . . . Therefore Christ justifies no one whom he does not at the same time sanctify. These benefits are joined together by an everlasting and indissoluble bond. . . . We are justified not without works yet not through works, since in our sharing in Christ, which justifies us, sanctification is just as much included as righteousness.[24]

Justification is itself God's free gift, in no sense a reward for good works. Those who are justified by faith are justified apart from any question of merit for works, but simply as a gift of God's mercy.

When we consider Calvin's teaching on the sacraments, it is immediately evident that abuses in sacramental theology and piety exert a powerful influence upon his views. Calvin sees the purpose of the sacraments as the confirmation of faith, not in their own right but as agents of the Holy Spirit. Their value is as God's instruments, since they do not, according to Calvin, impart grace of themselves. In his discussion of this issue, we find a high level of revulsion in Calvin against magical conceptions which had become attached to a certain type of sacramental piety. What is primary for Calvin is God's gift of justification and sanctification. In a reference to the teaching of Augustine, he rejects the idea of an objective instrumentality because 'there can be invisible sanctification without a visible sign, and on the other hand a visible sign without true sanctification'.[25] This is an important contrast to what we observed above in Article XXV of the Anglican *Articles of Religion* in which God's invisible work is effectively linked to the sacraments as outward signs of grace.

Finally we may consider how the Council of Trent dealt with the doctrine of justification. The Council reaffirmed the unique role of Christ whose passion is the source of grace for those reborn in him. Without this rebirth, a person cannot be justified before God. No one comes to justification through any personal merit, whether by faith or works. We come to be justified only by the grace of God.

It is important to note that the bishops at Trent insisted upon the primacy of faith in their description of justification: 'Faith is the beginning of human salvation, without which it is impossible to please God.' Yet faith does not stand alone but is vivified in relation to hope and charity. Thus, the bishops wrote,

> In justification itself one receives through Christ, into whom one is engrafted, along with the forgiveness of sins, all these gifts infused at the same time: faith, hope and charity. For faith, unless hope and charity be added to it, neither unites one perfectly with Christ, not makes one a living member of his body.[26]

The Council then went on to speak of faith as co-operating with good works so that consequently God finally judges human beings 'not apart from' the merit which he gives them. Although Trent asserted that Christians should never trust in themselves, this approach to the merit attached to good works left the way open for what Reformers saw to be the undermining of the gospel that trust was to be placed in God alone. In its conclusion on the issue of justification, Trent says that the justified person 'by the good deeds which are done by him, through the grace of God, and the merit of Jesus Christ (of whom he is a living member) truly merits an increase of grace, eternal life, and the attainment of that eternal life (if indeed he die in grace), as well as an increase in glory'. Although Trent's reaffirmation of the primacy of grace in justification was an important response to the Pelagianism of much late medieval piety, in the end the Council's approach to good works did not deal radically enough with the central concern of the Reformation.

This overview of the justification question reveals not only the unity of the various Reformed traditions in the rejection of any concept of merit as the source of the grace of justification, but also the distinctions of approach between Lutherans, Calvinists and Anglicans. While clearly within the Reformation tradition in its understanding of justification, Anglicanism distanced itself from both Calvin and Luther in ways which have been presented here. It is particularly with regard to the role of the sacraments as instruments of grace that Anglicanism maintained its own middle way: as Hooker wrote, 'Sacraments serve as the instruments of God.' They are thus God's actions toward mankind, occasions in which through participation in the outward forms, men and women are involved in an active response to the grace of God. In this perspective, Anglicanism pursued the *via media* which permitted the Prayer Book tradition to continue many of the forms of liturgical prayer which had been the Church's heritage from centuries past; and yet, at the same time, to take a firm stand on the Reformation principle that it is only by the gift of God's grace that we are saved. This reliance upon the grace of God as affirmed and celebrated within Anglicanism fostered what we might call a 'theology of confidence', which has set Anglican piety within an ethos clearly distinct from that of either Lutheranism or Calvinism in its emphasis upon the victory of Christ. It is thus that the image of Christ the High Priest has played so significant a role for Anglican devotion. It is a theology that underlies the world-affirming incarnational character expressed in Anglican worship, which draws its orientation from the great affirmation of the Epistle to the Hebrews:

> Since we have a great high priest who has passed into the heavens, Jesus, the Son of God, let us with confidence draw near to the throne of grace, that we may receive mercy and find grace to help in time of need.[27]

SACRAMENTAL WORSHIP AND THE GOSPEL

Our consideration of the doctrine of justification has shown, among the Churches shaped by Reformation principles, the Anglicanism has seen a special importance in the sacraments as visible means of God's grace. This high claim for the sacraments can be made because of the dynamic relation between sacraments and faith. The sacraments presume faith and yet are at the same time articulations of it. Without faith, the liturgical rites are merely external forms. This was Calvin's concern, as we noted earlier, when he asserted that 'there can be invisible sanctification without a visible sign, and on the other hand a visible sign without true sanctification'. What Calvin claims here is true, and it is a fact of the Church's life that it is possible for parishioners to participate in sacramental actions without (insofar as can be judged from the outside) the fruit of sanctification being evident. It is not a question of one standard model for a holy life by which this may be judged. What seems lacking in these instances is a making of connections, a recognition that what is proclaimed in the liturgy and professed by our lips is connected to how we go out from the liturgy to live our daily lives. It is, I think, what Hooker was referring to when he called the sacraments 'moral instruments' in that they must be linked to the inner core of a Christian's life.

The living out of the connections between worship and life takes place, for Christians, in the context of the Church. It is a major part of the Church's prophetic work—its speaking for God—to enable people to make those connections so that worship is not reduced to a pious Sunday morning routine. Through baptism, the members of the Church have been incorporated into God's saving work in Christ. It is around this work that the life of the Church is structured, not around the providing of religious rites which serve as a veneer to unconverted lives. The baptized community, through participation in the paschal mystery, is nurtured for maturity in the life of faith and is enabled to go forth to proclaim that saving mystery to the world. Through faith believers are given access to an intimate union with God, sharing in the divine energy which enlivens and nourishes the whole body. That union is created through baptism and in turn signified and deepened through the shared eucharistic meal. Yet this whole participation in the presence and grace of God springs from faith. Without faith, the sacraments are like a body without breath or blood.

Reflection on the sacraments has, on the whole, not focused adequately on their relation to faith. As we observed in Article XXV on the sacraments, they are instruments of God by which faith in him is quickened, strengthened and confirmed. Through their physicality the sacraments correspond to our physical nature, so that as the expression of love involves not just an interior attitude but the whole person, so is it also with faith: faith requires an enfleshing, a response in which the whole physical being is involved.

This is the principle upon which the idea of sacrament is founded. It is reflected in the words of Tertullian, 'The flesh is the hinge of salvation.'[28] The outward, physical aspects of the sacraments are the instrumental means by which faith articulates both God's gift of grace and the human acceptance of the gift. The gathering of the baptized on the Lord's Day to celebrate the Eucharist is a recapitulation of the whole meaning of incorporation into Christ's Body. The celebration of the paschal feast is the means by which the faithful enter into the paschal mystery into which they are baptized. The whole integrity of the act depends upon the active faith of the participants which connects its meaning with all the dimensions of human life. The gospel is seen to illuminate not just a religious segment of life, but life itself. The full meaning of the act is that of a life-bearing event which lifts the whole of life in thanksgiving to God. Surface rituals do not have such power. They tend to remain encapsulated in a private world of piety. But the sacraments link us to creation as God's first act of love toward mankind, and our participation in faith links us to God's redemptive purpose as it illuminates the whole of human history.

Every sacramental action is first of all an expression of God's initiative, and the context of our response is always shaped by the cultural and historical realities of the Church's life at a particular time and in a particular place. In our earlier discussion of liturgical change, we observed how strong the tendency seems to be to set the Church's liturgical practice in stone, as a static expression of God's changelessness. Yet the liturgical rites did not descend from heaven on a cloud. They are not divinely authored, but rather divinely imbued. As Hooker wrote: 'The use (of the sacraments) ... is in our hands, the effect in his.' Our responsibility for their use as the Church expresses its faith in every time and place requires a sensitive ear to the voice of God speaking often in new ways as the act of creation goes on. The right use of the sacraments involves an intuitive insight into how the signs of faith may best express that faith in the ordinary materials of human life. The incarnation reveals God's action in the humility of the ordinary, within the common realities of human life.

Christian belief in the incarnation establishes a principle by which we may discern the signs of God's abiding presence in the whole of creation. God's grace is not limited to the sacraments, but the sacramental principle enables us to recognize God's presence and activity beyond the quite specific framework of liturgical rites. We are permitted to see the Christian sacramental system as rooted in the elements of our common humanity. To suggest that God's grace is effective only through the sacramental forms carries us into the realm of magic. That was Calvin's fear, and he was right. God is not limited to any set of forms and rituals. But to recognize in the Church's sacraments the signs of God's active gifts of grace is to discover their purpose as his instruments for building up the Body of Christ. The sacraments can never be a private means of grace, because they always unite us to the whole family of faith in a common offering of praise and thanksgiving. As Hooker taught, 'That saving grace which Christ originally is or hath for the general good of the whole Church, by sacraments he severally deriveth into every member thereof.'

PLURALISM AND THE GOSPEL

At the opening of this chapter, the question of the understanding of the gospel in Anglicanism was placed against the backdrop of the present ecumenical scene. The discussion of justification revealed how certain aspects of the Church's teaching can overlap between one tradition and another, and yet that complementarity was also paralleled by contradiction. Justification, a fundamental issue in the understanding of the gospel, was understood differently by the various participants in the Reformation debates. The identification of these various Churches with certain geographical areas made it all too easy for each tradition to go its separate way. And so there evolved those particular constellations of factors, of worship and piety, of biblical interpretation and theological method, which came to characterize, for example, Anglicanism or Lutheranism or Roman Catholicism. Denominationalism was the result of a failure within the various traditions to deal with diversity. The hostilities of debate reinforced by geographical distance made it all too easy to live as though the other traditions scarcely existed.

We cannot look at questions of Christian faith and practice in this way any longer. No characteristic is narrowly defined by a denominational line. The Book of Common Prayer has over the centuries supplied liturgical materials for the use of other traditions. But in recent years, the influence is mutual as common ecumenical forms find a home in an increasing number of national versions of the Book of Common Prayer. We are no longer defined by what separates us from other Christians, or at least we may say that the number of Christians who are ill at ease with such a basis for religious identity is growing.

My point is that the gospel is fundamental to all Christians, and that although there are inevitable differences of ethos within each tradition, the common ground is becoming ever more visible. The Lima Statement referred to at the beginning of this chapter is a powerful example of the remarkable degree of convergence which has already been achieved. If we cherish our particularity, this can no longer include a rejection of the commonality which Christians share by virtue of the one baptism.

In its document *For the Sake of the Kingdom*, the Inter-Anglican Theological and Doctrinal Commission speaks convincingly of the pluriformity of the Church. The Anglican tradition has encompassed 'differing styles of piety, differing idioms in theology, and differing agenda for Christian witness and action'. This diversity has been difficult for some Anglicans who have wanted to envision the Church in a single mould of their own design. But the document suggests that the pluralism which has characterized Anglicanism is in fact the reality in which the whole Church finds itself, and there is thus set before us a very different cultural situation from that in which denominational distinctions were nurtured. The document continues,

> If the church, because it lives 'in Christ' by the grace and power of the Holy Spirit, is a sign and agent of God's Kingdom in and for the world, it is so—always and necessarily—in a radically 'located' fashion. The church exists in particular places and at particular times, and the truth which its life and action carry is conveyed only to the extent that it too is 'located'. This means, as we have seen, that Christians in a given place and time both will and must share the cultural idiom of their geographical and social locale. It also means that their life and witness both will and must address the issues, moral and political, with which historical circumstance confronts them in that locale. The church belongs to all its many places and times, and it is in this fact that its legitimate pluriformity is, in the end, rooted.[29]

Such pluralism is not simply a situation to be endured, but is rather a stimulus to a deeper penetration into God's purposes for the Church. It is an opportunity through which Christians may come to a fuller awareness of the scope of the Gospel.

> To affirm pluralism, then, is to affirm not one but two things. On the one hand it means to assert that there is good in the existence and continuing integrity of a variety of traditions and ways of life; on the other hand, it means to assert that there is good in their interplay and dialogue. For Christians, moreover, such affirmation of pluralism has a special meaning. It embodies a recognition that every human culture has God's Kingdom as its horizon in creation and redemption. At the same time, it acknowledges that, in the dialogue between traditions, people's understanding of the meaning of God's Kingdom, and of the Christ who bears it, may be enhanced. Pluralism, when understood in this way, is a stimulus to the repentance by which believers discern and turn to God's Kingdom.[30]

The gospel in Anglicanism is, then, one facet in a vast mosaic. In its essentials, it corresponds to the gospel as it has been proclaimed and believed all over the world. Yet it is also characterized by its particularity as an experience of God's saving work in particular cultures, and is shaped by the insights and limitations of persons who were themselves seeking to live the gospel within a particular context. In Anglicanism, the gospel tradition has been closely linked to a particular understanding of worship in the Christian life. In our dialogue with Christians of other traditions, that will be no small gift to offer.

NOTES

1 *Baptism, Eucharist and Ministry.* Faith and Order Paper No. 3 (Geneva, WCC, 1982).

2 H. G. Anderson, T. A. Murphy, and J. A. Burgess, eds., *Justification by Faith: Lutherans and Catholics in Dialogue VII* (Minneapolis, Augsberg, 1985). Cf. *Anglican-Lutheran Dialogue: The Report of the European Commission* (SPCK 1983), pp. 8–10; *Lutheran-Episcopal Dialogue: Report and Recommendations* (Cincinnati, Forward Movement, 1981), pp. 22–4.

3 Anglican-Roman Catholic International Commission, *The Final Report* (SPCK 1982).

4 The Paschal Proclamation (*Exsultet*) from the Easter Vigil, *The Book of Common Prayer* (New York, Church Hymnal Corp., 1979), p. 287.

5 See Geoffrey Wainwright's discussion in *Doxology* (New York, OUP, 1980), pp. 218–83. Important related material by several authors may be found in *Worship* 57. iv (July 1983), pp. 309–32.

6 A thorough discussion of the impact of the Gothic Revival upon the liturgy is presented in *The Cambridge Movement* by James F. White (Cambridge 1979); the wider cultural context of these matters is analysed by Kenneth Clark in *The Gothic Revival* (New York 1962).

7 See Richard K. Fenn, *Liturgies and Trials* (Oxford 1982).

8 Annie Dillard, *Holy the Firm* (New York 1977), p. 59.

9 See my study of the collect-form, *Gathered to Pray* (Cambridge, Mass., 1986).

10 An interesting discussion of doctrinal aspects of the Anglican collects is found in 'Reformed Doctrine in the Collects of the First *Book of Common Prayer*', by James A. Devereux SJ, in *The Harvard Theological Review* 58. i (1965), pp. 49–68.

11 See D. W. Hardy and D. F. Ford, *Jubilate: Theology in Praise* (London 1984), for a useful exposition of the role of praise in Christian life and faith.

12 The literature on this one subject alone is vast. See especially J. D. C. Fisher, *Christian Initiation: Baptism in the Medieval West* (London 1965).

13 Aidan Kavanagh, 'Response: Primary Theology and Liturgical Act', in *Worship* 57. iv (1983), pp. 321–2.

14 XI. Of the Justification of Man, Articles of Religion, BCP.

15 XII. Of Good Works, Articles of Religion, BCP.

16 Rom. 4.25.

17 XXV. Of the Sacraments, Articles of Religion, BCP.

18 'A Learned Discourse of Justification, Works, and How the Foundation of Faith is Overthrown', in *Works* (Oxford 1841), vol iii, p. 530.

19 *The Laws of Ecclesiastical Polity*, V. lvii. 5, (FE vol. ii, p. 258).

20 Article IV, *The Augsberg Confession* (Philadelphia 1980), p. 11.

21 Article XX, *The Augsberg Confession*, pp. 19–22.

22 Article XIII, *The Augsberg Confession*, p. 15.

23 John Calvin, *Institutes of the Christian Religion* (Philadelphia 1960), 3. xi. 1, p. 725.

24 ibid., 3. xvi. 1, p. 798.

25 ibid., 4. xiv. 7–17 *passim*, pp. 1281–94.

26 *Enchiridion Symbolorum*, 33rd edn (ed. H. Denzinger and A. Schönmetzer), nn. 1530–1. My discussion of Trent's view of justification is based upon material from nn. 1523–82 *passim*.

27 Hebrews 4.14, 16.

28 *On the Resurrection*, 8. In this passage, Tertullian shows the intimate relation between the internal and external aspects of Christian initiation, and thus epitomizes the sacramental principle.

29 *For the Sake of the Kingdom* [Inter-Anglican Theological and Doctrinal Commission], (London 1986), para 94, p. 58.

30 ibid., para 98, p. 60.

PART THREE

Authority and Method

1 Scripture

REGINALD H. FULLER

Borsch, F. A., ed., *Anglicanism and the Bible*. Wilton, CT, Morehouse-Barlow, 1984.

Fuller, R. H., 'The Authority of Scriptures in Anglicanism', in *The Report of the Lutheran-Episcopal Dialogue*. Second Series 1976–1980 (Cincinnati, Ohio, Forward Movement, 1981), pp. 87–113.

Greenslade, S. L., ed., *The Cambridge History of the Bible*. Vol. iii, *The West from the Reformation to the Present Day*. CUP 1963. Esp. pp. 141–70 and 361–82.

Langford, T. A., *In Search of Foundations: English Theology 1900–1920*. Nashville, NY, Abingdon, 1969 (Ch. V, 'Authority, Anglicanism, the Bible and the Creeds').

Morgan, R., 'Non Angli Sed Angeli: Some Anglican Reactions to German Gospel Criticism', in S. W. Sykes and D. Holmes, eds., *New Studies in Theology* (London, Duckworth, 1980), pp. 1–30.

Neill, S., *The Interpretation of the New Testament, 1861–1961.* (OUP 1966).

Reventlow, Henning Graf, *The Authority of the Bible and the Rise of the Modern World* London, SCM, 1984.

THE BIBLE AS THE WORD OF GOD

In the new Anglican liturgies, the readers of the Old Testament and New Testament lessons are instructed to conclude their readings with the words: 'The Word [ASB: This is the Word] of the Lord.' Probably to many people this suggests that the Anglican Church is fundamentalist and believes that the words of the Bible are the direct oracles of God. Such people would not be surprised by the eloquent utterance of the famous Dean Burgon in the last century:

> The Bible is none other than the voice of Him that sitteth upon the throne. Every book of it, every word of it, every syllable of it [where are we to stop?], every letter of it, is the direct utterance of the Most High. The Bible is none other than the Word of God, not some part of it more, some part of it less, but all alike utterances of Him Who sitteth upon the throne, faultless, unerring, supreme.[1]

In his day, Dean Burgon was a fine apologist for the classical Anglicanism, but on the subject of Holy Scripture we can no longer follow him. There are many reasons for this. First, this claim for the inerrancy of Scripture was never made by the Church of England even at the time of the Reformation, when there was a strong emphasis on the Bible as the word of God. Article VII of the Thirty-nine Articles pointed to knowledge of the saving work of Jesus Christ as the real point of the Bible: 'In both the Old and New Testament everlasting life is offered to Mankind in Christ.' Earlier, Article II had called the Son of God 'the Word of

79

the Father', thus encouraging us to see the Word primarily in a person rather than in a book (see pp. 133–7).

There is a more modern reason for thinking that the Anglican Churches do not require us to hold that the Bible is the word of God in a literalist sense. This is the application to the Scriptures of the historical-critical method.[2] This method has shown that however much the Bible may contain the word of God in the sense that it speaks of Jesus Christ, it is nevertheless also a very human product, the work of many human authors over a period of a thousand years or more, and all of them conditioned by the cultural assumptions of their age. Biblical criticism has further shown that the Bible is a highly pluralistic work, containing the personal views of many different writers, views that are shaped by the particular situations in which they were written. In sum, the word of God is conveyed to us through the words of human beings.

This is something we should gladly embrace, for it is wholly analogous to the doctrine of the incarnation. The eternal Word of the Father became incarnate as a first-century Jew, with all his limitations. It is also analogous to the sacraments. God uses the frail elements of water, bread, and wine as the means of communicating the redemptive presence and action of his Word to us. It is also analogous to the Church, which likewise is a very human institution, constantly in need of reform ('Where in anything it is amiss, reform it', American BCP, p. 816). All the way through, with the Bible as with all the other means God uses for our salvation, the same principle is at work: God in his wondrous condescension stoops to use human and earthly means to accomplish his saving purpose.

As the incarnate Word is the sacrament of God, as the bread and wine are sacraments of Christ's body and blood, as the Church is the sacrament of God's presence in the world, so the Bible is the sacrament of God's word, his offer of salvation through his eternal Son and Word. When we call the Bible as a whole or a single pericope the word of God, we are speaking sacramentally, as we do when we call the consecrated elements 'the body and blood of Christ'. In Hooker's language they are the instruments which convey what they signify, and may therefore be said to be what they convey, like a dollar bill or a pound note.

THE INSPIRATION OF SCRIPTURE

The Christian Church inherited from Judaism the belief that its Scriptures were inspired by God. This was interpreted in different ways. To some it meant that God guided the pens of the human writers or dictated his words to their minds. More indirectly, it was held to mean that God was the ultimate, not the immediate, cause behind the writing of Scripture. This more indirect view seems to be what Cranmer asserted in the traditional Collect of the Second Sunday in

Advent (American BCP Proper 27): 'who hast caused all holy Scriptures to be written for our learning'. It was human beings who wrote them, but God was the primary cause of their writing.

Some contemporary Anglican theologians have argued that the doctrine of inspiration ought to be abandoned today.[3] This is because it is frequently associated with the concept of inerrancy (to be discussed below). But it ought to be retained for the following reasons. First, it is a doctrine found in our formularies. See for instance 'An Outline of the Faith, commonly called the Catechism' (American BCP, p. 853), which says that the Old and New Testaments were 'written under the inspiration of the Holy Spirit'. Second, its abandonment would have serious implications for ecumenical dialogue with the Roman Catholic, Orthodox and Lutheran Churches, all of which affirm the inspiration of Scripture. Third, it need not necessarily imply the doctrine of inerrancy. The primary work of the Holy Spirit is not to guarantee inerrancy, but to produce an authentic witness to the salvation event in Jesus Christ.[4] A sacramental understanding of the Bible as the word of God would seem to require a doctrine of inspiration, not in the sense that the human words came directly from God and are therefore inerrant, but in the sense that the human words proclaim the Christ event with the power to evoke faith. To produce faith is precisely the work of the Holy Spirit.

The claim to inspiration covers both Old and New Testaments, as the 'Outline of Faith' (American BCP) and Article VII assert. In both Testaments we are offered salvation through Christ. The historical criticism of the Bible would seem to have undermined that claim as far as the Old Testament is concerned. The Old Testament prophets, the critics tell us, were speaking of events in their own day. Isaiah 40 refers to the return of the exiles from Babylon, not to the coming of Christ. This is true; however, after the return it became clear that this was not the full and final event of salvation that the prophets expected it to be. The prophecies still awaited their final fulfilment. And so Luke 3.4–6 can pick up Isaiah 40.3–5 and apply these verses to the appearance of Jesus Christ.

The Old Testament texts lived on in the community of faith and eventually were seen to have a fuller meaning than that originally intended by the authors. The whole of the Old Testament pointed forward to a future saving event, and thus came to rest in Jesus Christ. Hence Article VII's claim about the Old Testament can still stand, even in the light of biblical criticism.

The inspiration of Scripture is not to be understood as a once-for-all accomplished event. When Scripture is read in the church, the Holy Spirit uses it ever anew to proclaim the living word of salvation. This proclamation requires the response of faith, and that too is the work of the Holy Spirit. The Collect about Scripture which we quoted above goes on to pray:

Grant that we may in such wise hear them, read, mark, learn and inwardly digest them;

that by patience and comfort of thy holy Word, we may embrace and ever hold fast the blessed hope of everlasting life which thou hast given us in our Savior Jesus Christ.

The work of the Holy Spirit is not confined to the original writing which produced the authoritative witness.[5] That witness has constantly to be rekindled in the community of the faithful, particularly in the context of the liturgy. The word of God is not a static, dead document: it constantly recurs as event, and has to be apprehended through the Spirit.

If the Holy Spirit continues to inspire the reading and preaching of the word and the hearing that produces faith, in what sense is the Bible unique? Not apparently because it is inspired, whereas all other Christian writing and speech are not. Wherever Christ is proclaimed and believed in, there the Spirit is at work. But the Holy Spirit's inspiration of Scripture is unique because Scripture is the normative witness to which all later witness has to conform. There is no word without Spirit and no Spirit without word. This is expressed in the Collect written by Cranmer for the feast of Saints Simon and Jude (Proper 8, American BCP):

> O almighty God, who hast built thy Church upon the foundation of the apostles and prophets, Jesus Christ himself being the chief cornerstone: Grant us so to be joined together in unity of Spirit by their doctrine, that we may be made an holy temple acceptable unto thee ...

THE SUFFICIENCY OF SCRIPTURE

Article VI of the Thirty-nine Articles is entitled, 'Of the Sufficiency of Holy Scripture for Salvation.' The body of the Article goes on to define sufficiency to mean that:

> Holy Scripture containeth all things necessary to salvation so that whatsoever is not read therein, nor may be proved thereby [i.e. tested—the question of Scripture as norm will be discussed in the next section] is not to be required by any man, that it should be believed as an article of Faith, or thought to be necessary or requisite to salvation.

In the traditional Ordinal (see BCP—USA 1928) the second question put to the candidate for ordination to the diaconate, priesthood and episcopate was: 'Are you persuaded that the Holy Scriptures contain all Doctrine required as necessary for eternal salvation through faith in Jesus Christ?' This question has been removed in the present American BCP, but the same point is made in the oath of conformity which is now printed at the beginning of the American Ordinals: 'I ... solemnly declare that I do believe the Holy Scriptures of the Old and New Testaments to be the Word of God, and to contain all things necessary to salvation.' The Bible alone (in this sense the Anglican Churches accept the Reformation principle of *sola scriptura*) contains the primary authoritative witness of the mighty acts of God in salvation history (see pp. 93–5). No other book, however primitive or inspiring, can add anything to the witness of these acts of God, however much it may contribute to our understanding of them.[6] This is because the saving acts of God took place once-for-all, and with the events there is also a once-for-all authoritative witness. This witness is the work either of those who had themselves directly witnessed those events (the eyewitnesses and ministers of the word, Luke 1.2), or of those who were in immediate contact with that witness, who, in Hoskyns' words, were 'so completely created by apostolic witness and formed by apostolic obedience that they are veritably carried across into the company of the original disciples of Jesus and invested with the authority of their mission.'[7] It is true that there are some fuzzy areas here: some sub-apostolic texts such as I Clement were not taken up into the canon, while others who according to modern criticism were seemingly at greater distance from the original witness, such as the author of 2 Peter, were further away from it. Yet there is a central core of apostolic writings.

We may be thankful that the Anglican formularies never claim that all things in Holy Scripture are necessary to salvation. There is much in the biblical books—genealogies, primitive myths, legends and sagas, primitive religious concepts (Jehovah as a vengeful deity) and the like which we can hardly accept when proposed to us as credenda. Once again, we are only concerned with what proclaims to us salvation in Jesus Christ.

We have laid considerable stress on the Christological interpretation of the Old Testament. But this is not the sole reason for its use. The gospel asserts that God was acting in Christ. The original disciples did not meet God for the first time in Jesus Christ. Rather, they *recognized* God in him as a result of their nurture in the Old Testament-Jewish tradition. Therefore the Old Testament has to read for its own sake, as well as for its Christological significance. The God who was manifest in the Christ event was the God who also created heaven and earth, who called all nations into being, and who called Israel out of Egypt and gave it the law. Therefore the Old Testament's authority extends beyond its prefiguring of the Christ event.

THE PRIMACY OF SCRIPTURE

The primacy of Scripture means that Scripture is the norm of faith and the norm by which other norms (creeds, tradition, confessions of faith) are judged. In the past the Bible was frequently used as a proof text for doctrinal systems. Commentaries on the Articles often consisted of texts supporting each statement in the Articles, and that was the diet of theological education for candidates for the ordained ministry. Today we would question the validity of this procedure for a number of reasons. First, faith is primarily not the acceptance of a series of propositions but the acceptance of the gospel as the good news of the mighty acts of God for us and our salvation. Theological propositions have only a secondary significance. They are the attempt of faith to understand itself—*fides quaerens intellectum*. There are already attempts in the Bible itself to understand faith, as in the writings of St Paul, particularly in his epistle to the Romans. Paul starts with the primary datum, the kerygma or apostolic message, and draws out its implications for controverted points of interpretation, as in 1 Corinthians 15 where he deals with the resurrection from the dead. Paul's doctrinal conclusions are inevitably coloured and limited by the world-view of his time. The Bible as norm can no longer be thought of as prescribing to us a ready-made theology for our own day and age. What the Bible offers by way of norm is a model of procedure, whereby we too in our own day and age can move from the fundamental message or kerygma to our own problems and questions. The normative function of the Bible in matters of doctrine is therefore not rigidly prescriptive, but far more like a series of guidelines along which we may proceed in formulating doctrine. If it has any prescriptive character, this can only act negatively, ruling out certain doctrinal conclusions which are clearly incompatible with Scripture. Thus, for instance, any theology which asserted that Jesus was the revelation of God only for Westerners and not for the whole world (a view which is being proposed by some Christian theologians today) must be ruled out as contrary to the scriptural norm.

The Bible, as well as being a norm for theology, is also a norm for ethical behaviour. Modern Anglicans do not regard it as a codebook of law. Rather, the specific ethical commands of the Bible are illustrations of the kind of behaviour God requires in specific situations. They are derived from what God has done for us in his saving acts. We have many situations to face today which are not covered by the specific demands of Scripture, and therefore we have to go beyond the confines of the canon. But always we have to ask, what kind of imperative does the indicative of the gospel (what God has done) imply? (see pp. 325–36).

The Old Testament has been a characteristic resource for Anglicans in the matter of ethics. For centuries it was regularly read at Morning Prayer, which was part of the main service on Sundays. From this, Anglicans have drawn the perception that politics and the state are a special arena where Christians have to work out their obedience to God (see pp. 252–63). In earlier days, this expressed itself in England through a loyal adherence to the monarchy. But as Anglicanism spread beyond the confines of England, specially after the American colonies became independent, Anglicans have had to work out a political ethic under other forms of government. On the one hand Anglicanism respects the state as the servant of God (Rom. 13.4,6), with a God-given task to promote the good of society. On the other hand the Anglican tradition, being mindful of the fact that the state can always forget that it is the servant of God and become the instrument of injustice and tyranny, can require the Church to adopt a prophetic critique of the state—as Hensley Henson did when as Canon of Westminster he denounced the Putumayo atrocities in 1912, or as a long line of Archbishops of Cape Town have done with regard to apartheid. There is no explicit command in the Bible forbidding apartheid as such, but the indicative of the gospel leads to this kind of imperative. The teaching of the prophets, such as Amos and Isaiah, has played a prominent role in Anglicanism as in other Churches. The concern for world hunger is another issue in which Anglicans have been to the fore. We may rightly claim that these concerns are biblically based.

CANON

Closely connected with the notion of Scripture as norm is the idea of the canon, the list of books recognized as belonging to the normative writings.

The canon of the New Testament was not a matter of controversy at the time of the Reformation. Article VI simply states that 'All the books of the New Testament as they are commonly received we do receive, and account them as canonical.' With regard to the Old Testament, the situation was more complicated. Like the Reformation generally, the Church of England recognized the canonicity of those books which were contained in the Hebrew Bible. It relegated the 'other books' (Article VI), i.e., the additional items in the Greek Bible which we call the Apocrypha, to an appendix of books 'read for example of life and instruction of manners'. The Article, however, continued: 'Yet doth it [the Church] not apply them to establish any doctrine.' Anglicans always made some liturgical use of the apocryphal books, and twentieth-century lectionaries have extended that use. Modern scholarship has broken down the sharp division between the Old Testament and the Apocrypha, and it might be a good thing if Anglicans were to adopt the Roman Catholic designation of the apocryphal books as 'deutero-canonical'. We read them and value them, but they have a secondary position, being used only to reinforce the doctrines of the proto-canonical books.

The shape of the New Testament canon is not often a matter of reflection on the part of Anglicans, but it deserves attention because it has, albeit unconsciously, shaped all Christian theology including our own. The New Testament canon has this structure: the four Gospels, Acts, the Epistolary writings, and Revelation. The fact that four Gospels come first means that the incarnation together with the Trinity is, for Anglicanism, fundamental to the faith (and this of course involves faith in the God of the Old Testament, which precedes the New Testament in the canon). The structure of the Thirty-nine Articles reflects this pattern, for the Articles begin with the Trinity and the incarnation (I–V) (see p. 136).

The Pauline corpus, while presuming a high Christology, employs this Christology as a basis for soteriology. The Pauline writings proclaim the doctrine of redemption under various images, of which the most important are justification and reconciliation.[8] Some strands of Anglican theology have at times been tempted to over-emphasize the doctrine of the incarnation and to treat it as though the incarnation were in itself salvific.[9] This has no sanction in Scripture or the Thirty-nine Articles, where Articles IX–XVII develop the doctrine of salvation through Christ.

The Pauline corpus contains not only Galatians and Romans, but the deutero-Pauline Colossians and Ephesians. These letters place the doctrine of salvation in an ecclesial perspective. The Colossian–Ephesian doctrine of the Church as the Body of Christ of which he is the Head is of particular significance to Anglicanism.

On the fringe of the Pauline corpus stands the so-called Letter to the Hebrews. This book has played a long and important role in Anglican doctrine, particularly the doctrine of the Eucharist. It was Hebrews' insistence on the once-for-all character of Christ's sacrifice that gave Cranmer the warrant for his exordium to the Prayer of Consecration in the Communion Service of 1549–1552: '... who made there (by his one oblation of himself once offered) a full, perfect, and sufficient sacrifice, oblation, and satisfaction, for the sins of the whole world'. Article XXXI repeats this emphasis, placing it in the context of sixteenth-century polemic against the Romish doctrine of 'the sacrifices of Masses'. Classical Anglicanism in the seventeenth century and Tractarianism in the nineteenth sought to recover a more positive doctrine of the eucharistic sacrifice along patristic lines, but always worked within the parameters set by the finality of Christ's sacrifice as expressed in Hebrews. The same is true of Anglican attempts to formulate a doctrine of ministerial priesthood. Such a doctrine must not be allowed to compromise the finality of Christ's high priesthood. These doctrines based on Hebrews received quasi-official formulation in the archbishops' reply to the 1896 papal Bull 1896 condemning Anglican orders (see p. 292).

The Church, too, has a historical mission, as is indicated by the Acts of the Apostles, which forms a bridge between the two major parts of the canon, the Gospels and the Pauline corpus. This poses a challenge to contemporary Anglican theology. It has to be not just the theology of the Church of England, but a theology of the world-wide Anglican Communion, in which South America, Africa, India, Asia, and Oceania have to make their contribution, as well as the British Isles.

It has become increasingly clear to New Testament scholars that there is a third major stratum in the New Testament. Pre-critical Anglican theology was not able consciously to draw this distinction, but it should help Anglican theology today to clarify what had, albeit unconsciously always been its position. This is the existence of a body of literature which belongs to the sub-apostolic age and which is a witness to early Catholicism (*Frühkatholizismus*). It includes those institutional features of the second and third generation of the Christian Church which were devised to perpetuate apostolic faith and practice after the death of the original witnesses. The New Testament writings in this category include: the (deutero-Pauline) Pastoral Epistles, and some of the Catholic or General Epistles, perhaps James, 1 Peter and Jude, and certainly 2 Peter. Acts and Hebrews may exhibit a few traces of early Catholic concern, though this is highly debatable, and the Johannine appendix (John 21), produced in the same period, bears witness to the institutionalization of the Johannine churches.[10] The institutional features in question include: credal forms, an incipient canon of Christian writings (cf. Peter) and an organized ministry with ordination and succession replacing the more spontaneous charismatic ministries (Acts, Pastorals). Radical Protestantism has generally deplored these developments. In the pre-critical period they were thought to have been introduced after the New Testament period in such writings as I Clement and the Epistles of Ignatius. But given a later dating for the New Testament writings in question, the initial development of early Catholic institutional features is already discernible in the New Testament. As a result, radical Protestantism at this point invokes the principle of a 'canon within the canon'. Ernst Käsemann finds this inner canon in the Pauline–Lutheran 'message of the justification of the ungodly by faith alone apart from the works of the law'.[11] He regards early Catholicism as a denial of this central message, and therefore relegates these writings to the periphery of the canon. Anglicans would react differently to this debate.[12] It is noteworthy, to begin with, that the early Catholic institutional features are precisely those elements which in a developed form are included in the Chicago-Lambeth quadrilateral (see p. 40). Accordingly, Anglicans may welcome the presence of early Catholicism in the New Testament. The canon itself calls for creeds, a canon of Scripture and a regularized ministry.

The gospel could not exist *in vacuo*. It required institutional forms to perpetuate it. The New Testament documents which attest to their initial growth are secondary to the four Gospels and the authentic Pauline Epistles; Anglicanism has perhaps been tempted at times to suppose that they are primary.[13] Rather, it is the gospel that is primary; the early Catholic institutions exist only to serve the gospel. Thus the understanding of the structure of the canon serves both to vindicate and to challenge traditional Anglican theology.

The canon of the New Testament concludes with the Book of Revelation. This can hardly be said to be a favourite book of Anglicans, and until recently it has not figured very much in the lectionaries. It is perhaps significant that those passages which have commanded most attention are those which deal with the worship of heaven (Rev. 4, 7, 21). Anglicans have always understood their liturgy to be more than just human activity initiated here on earth; it is a participation in the worship of heaven. The ultimate destiny of humanity is seen in participation in that worship.

SCRIPTURE AND TRADITION

The subject of tradition will be dealt with more fully in this volume by H. Chadwick. But a number of points about tradition in relation to Scripture need to be made here. We have already indicated that Anglicanism accepts the *sola scriptura* of the Reformation in the nuanced sense that only in Scripture do we find authoritative witness to the Christ event. We also noted that Scripture has its centre in that witness, but also that there are contingent applications of that witness to ongoing situations in the New Testament period. This resulted in developments in the understanding of the original witness, and consequently in doctrinal development or trajectories.[14] A most noticeable example of this is in the field of Christology. The earliest Christologies were functional or agent Christologies. They describe the role played by Jesus in salvation history, and what God had done through him.[15] By the time the Johannine Prologue (John 1.1–18) was composed, Christology was becoming more concerned with the person of Jesus and his relation to God's being.[16] Jesus was now seen as the incarnation of the pre-existent logos of God who was the agent of creation, of general revelation, and of the special revelation to Israel. It was this Johannine Christology (combined with the Matthaean–Lucan assertion of Jesus' virginal conception) which formed the basis for the Christology of Nicea and Chalcedon. To this developed Christology Anglicanism has traditionally adhered. Recently, however, a number of Anglican exegetes and theologians, especially in England, have advocated a return to the agent types of Christology, leaving Nicea and Chalcedon on one side.[17] Against this other Anglican theologians have protested, maintaining that it would lead to a loss of Anglican identity.[18] Today Anglicanism cannot justify its adherence to the doctrines of the Trinity and incarnation, unless it is prepared to accord an authority to the Church as 'witness and keeper of Holy Writ' (Article XX). It is on the authority of the Church of the early centuries, not of the Bible alone, that Anglicanism upholds them.[19]

Similar considerations apply to the ordained ministry. In earlier days Anglicans appealed directly to the New Testament for the institution of episcopacy.[20] Today it is commonly held by critical scholars that the Pastoral Epistles are deutero-Pauline and therefore cannot be used as evidence for the ministry in Paul's own lifetime. Rather, in Paul's churches the ministry seems to have been largely charismatic (1 Cor. 12.4–31; Rom. 12.6–8). By the time of the Pastorals, a ministry of bishop-presbyters and deacons was developing. Ignatius of Antioch (AD 110–15) is the earliest witness for 'mon-episcopacy', a single bishop in each local church presiding over a group of presbyters. Today Anglicans can justify adherence to episcopacy only by appealing to post-New Testament developments. It is noteworthy that as early as 1930 the Lambeth Fathers sought to legitimate episcopacy in terms of development:

The Episcopate occupies a position which is, in point of historic development, analogous to that of the Canon of Scripture and of the Creeds. In the first days there was no Canon of New Testament Scripture, for the books afterwards included in it were still being written. So, too, the Apostles' Creed is the result of a process of growth which we can in large measure trace. If the Episcopate, as we find it established universally by the end of the second century, was the result of a like process ... that would be no evidence that it lacked divine authority.[21]

Once again, we have here a trajectory from the New Testament to the patristic age (see pp. 296–308).

At present Anglicanism is becoming more open—as indeed classical seventeenth-century Anglicanism was in theory open—to a Petrine trajectory, which would justify a 'primacy of honour' for the Bishop of Rome.[22] At the same time Anglicanism would reject papal claims to universal jurisdiction and infallibility as a deviation from the trajectory of the Petrine office which begins in Scripture. In this way Scripture acts as a norm over subsequent developments.

CONCLUSION

Since the Reformation, Anglicanism has understood itself in terms of a reformed or scriptural Catholicism. The *modus operandi* of that appeal to Scripture has changed since the acceptance of the historical-critical method. Yet we may justly claim that the results of this change are broadly consistent with our historic formularies, the Book of Common Prayer, the *Articles of Religion* and the Catechism, as well as with our standard divines from the Reformation to the present day.

NOTES

1 Cited by A. Richardson, *Preface to Bible Study* (Philadelphia, Westminster, 1944).

2 For a brief history of the rise and reception of the historical-critical method in Anglicanism see R. H. Fuller in F. A. Borsch, ed., *Anglicanism and the Bible* (Wilton, Conn., Morehouse–Barlow, 1984), pp. 143–68.

3 R. P. C. Hanson recommended dropping the doctrine of inspiration in his inaugural lecture as Lightfoot Professor at Durham University in 1962. He has reiterated his position in a systematic theology written in collaboration with his twin brother, A. T. Hanson, *Reasonable Belief* (OUP 1980), pp. 40–42.

4 See e.g. Mark 13.11; Luke 12.12; John 15.26–7; Acts 1.8; 1 Cor. 12.4; 1 Thess. 1.5.

5 Hence the inspiration of the Holy Spirit should be seen at each stage of the biblical tradition. In the Gospels the Holy Spirit inspired the original reception of the Jesus material by the first witnesses, its transmission in the oral tradition, its first writing and subsequent redaction, its transmission as part of the canon and finally its reception today.

6 It is often asked whether any newly discovered apostolic writings could be added to the canon. Aside from the difficulty of securing ecumenical consensus, such a writing would

have to conform to the existing canon for its acceptance, and thus the present canon would in practice remain the norm.

7 E. C. Hoskyns, *The Fourth Gospel*, ed. F. N. Davey (London, Faber, 1950), p. 92.

8 'Atonement' has long been used as a comprehensive soteriological term in Anglican theology. In the OT however it is used exclusively in cultic contexts to translate words like the *kpr* root, denoting 'to cover' and hence to cleanse. In the KJV (AV) 'atonement' occurs only at Rom. 5.11, where it translates quite a different term, *katallagē* (RSV 'reconciliation'), a concept derived from inter-personal or international relationships. It would be best to use 'soteriology' for the comprehensive term, to confine 'atonement' to OT cultic contexts, and to use 'reconciliation' for *katallagē* and its cognates. Thus 'atonement' in the sense of reconciliation should be dropped, despite its alleged etymological origin as 'at-one-ment'.

9 Such tendencies are discernible in F. D. Maurice, B. F. Westcott, the Lux Mundi School and William Temple. Hoskyns redressed the balance at this point. See A. M. Ramsey, *An Era in Anglican Theology: From Gore to Temple* (New York, Scribner's, 1960). Anglican Evangelicals have sometimes tended to stress soteriology to the neglect of the incarnation. See however a more balanced treatment by an older Evangelical, W. H. Wilmer, *The Episcopal Manual* (Philadelphia, George, 1841).

10 See R. E. Brown, *The Community of the Beloved Disciple* (New York/Ramsey, NJ, Paulist, 1979), pp. 159–61; idem, *The Epistles of John* (AB 30; Garden City, NY, Doubleday, 1982), pp. 106–15.

11 E. Käsemann, *Essays on New Testament Themes* (SBT 41; London, SCM, 1964), pp. 95–107.

12 See R. H. Fuller, 'Early Catholicism: an Anglican Reaction to a German Debate' in U. Luz and H. Weder, eds., *Die Mitte des Neuen Testaments* (FS E. Schweizer; Göttingen, Vandenhoeck & Ruprecht, 1983), pp. 34–41.

13 As manifested in the negative attitude of some Episcopalians to the interim eucharistic fellowship with three Lutheran bodies in the US, Churches which have retained the canon, Creeds, the gospel sacraments, and a high doctrine of ordination though without episcopal succession. Such Episcopalians exhibit an 'all or nothing' view of episcopacy which differs from the classical Anglican position that episcopacy belongs to the perfection rather than to the being of the Church (Bramhall), to its *plene esse* rather than to its *esse*.

14 The concept of trajectories was introduced into biblical scholarship by J. M. Robinson– H. Koester, *Trajectories through Early Christianity* (Philadelphia, Fortress, 1971). I have discussed the implications of this concept for biblical authority in 'New Testament Trajectories and Biblical Authority', *Studia Evangelica* (ed. E. A. Livingstone; Berlin, Akademie-Verlag, 1982), pp. 189–99.

15 See the Bampton Lectures of A. E. Harvey, *Jesus and Constraints of History* (Philadelphia, Westminster, 1982).

16 See R. H. Fuller–P. Perkins, *Who Is this Christ?* (Philadelphia, Fortress, 1983), pp. 43–49. Martin Hengel thinks that this development took place as early as 35–50 CE. See M. Hengel, *Between Jesus and Paul* (Philadelphia, Fortress, 1983), pp. 30–47. J. D. G. Dunn, *Christology in the Making* (Philadelphia, Westminster, 1980) thinks the pre-existence

Christology proper was not developed until the Johannine Prologue, i.e., *c.* 90–100 CE. In any case, it is a development within the canon.

17 Examples are G. W. H. Lampe in the Bampton Lectures for 1976, *God as Spirit* (Oxford, Clarendon, 1977); J. A. T. Robinson, *Twelve More New Testament Studies* (SCM 1984), pp. 138–54, 171–80, and his Bampton Lectures for 1984, *The Priority of John* (SCM 1986). The Hansons in *Reasonable Belief* (see above, n. 3) adopt a mediating position. While retaining a strong doctrine of the logos and of the Trinity, they argue for dropping the Chalcedonian doctrine of the personal identity of Jesus with the logos. The human Jesus thus becomes the bearer or spokesperson of the logos.

18 See e.g. S. W. Sykes, *The Integrity of Anglicanism* (Mowbrays 1978); R. Morgan, 'Historical Criticism and Christology', in S. W. Sykes, ed., *England and Germany* (Frankfurt am Main, Lang, 1982), pp. 80–112.

19 The tradition of the first five centuries (which mean in effect the first four ecumenical councils through to Chalcedon) have always enjoyed a special authority in classical Anglicanism, which also appealed to the 'three Creeds' as a hermeneutical principle for the interpretation of Scripture.

20 Thus the traditional Preface to the Ordinal appeals both to Scripture and to 'ancient Authors' for the claim that 'from the Apostles' time there have been these orders of ministers in Christ's Church—Bishops, Priests, and Deacons'—American BCP (1928), pp. 529. Today in the light of historical criticism, we have to rely more heavily on the development attested by the 'ancient Authors'.

21 G. K. A. Bell, *Documents on Christian Unity* (Third Series, 1930–48; London/New York, OUP, 1948), p. 7.

22 See Anglican–Roman Catholic International Commission, *The Final Report* (London, SPCK/CTS; Cincinnati, Oh., Forward Movement, 1982), pp. 57–8.

2 Tradition, Fathers and Councils

HENRY CHADWICK

Chadwick, H., 'The Status of Ecumenical Councils in Anglican Thought', in D. Nieman and M. Schatkin, eds., *The Heritage of the Early Church* (Rome, Festschrift Florovsky, Orientalia Christiana Analecta 195, 1973), pp. 393–408.
Greenslade, S. L., 'The Authority of the Tradition of the Early Church in Early Anglican Thought'; G. V. Bennett, 'Patristic Tradition in Anglican Thought, 1660–1900'; and M. F. Wiles, 'The Consequences of Modern Theories of Reality for the Relevance and Authority of the Early Church in our Time', in *Tradition im Luthertum und Anglikanismus, Oecumenica*, 1971/72, pp. 9–33, 72–87, 130–145.
Lampe, G. W. H., 'The Early Church', in F. W. Dillistone *et al.*, *Scripture and Tradition* (SCM 1955), pp. 21–52.

Parker, T. M., 'The Rediscovery of the Fathers in the Seventeenth-Century Anglican Tradition', in J. Coulson and A. M. Allchin, eds., *The Rediscovery of Newman*. London 1967.

Although as Christians we do not believe by proxy, faith is always a sharing. The baptized believer is incorporated in the family of God. To adhere to God's Word in Christ is also to adhere to the fellowship of the Spirit—to the gospel in Bible, preaching, and sacraments. These are means of grace; the media entrusted to, and creative of, the community within which the Word of God is heard and the vision of his glory seen. In the life of the fellowship a special place is occupied by the sacred written records of the Bible transmitted to us by the community. Copied with varying degrees of accuracy by ancient and medieval Christian scribes, and translated (with similar variations) into many languages and even versions in the same language, this collection of books possesses a unique position in the tradition of the Church.

Since the invention of printing, Bibles have been relatively inexpensive and widely diffused. The historical-critical study of this book has greatly illuminated the circumstances within the community which produced both particular writings and the collection as a whole. It has brought out the way in which the early Christians appealed to Scripture as a witness and as a confirming illustration of what they already did and believed. The Word of God was in their hearts before it was put into books, and in any event the Graeco-Roman world into which the first missionaries went out contained a high proportion of illiterate people. Ability to read and write has never been a prerequisite for faith and baptism. In the mid-second century Papias of Hierapolis felt nearer to the authentic tradition when speaking with those who could recall the oral teaching of the apostolic and sub-apostolic age, than when reading books.

And yet—in defending the tradition of the community, the books were indispensable. In the Scriptures received or written by the apostolic generation, the ancient Church had its title-deeds, a unique witness to the revealed will of God for his people. The early Christian 'Fathers' (the term long used for orthodox writers of East and West of the first six or seven Christian centuries) claimed very much for their authority, and distinguished between Christian literature that might be read in the lectionary and books which were edifying but outside the canon. The process of forming the canon was gradual.

For the ancient and medieval Church no official document, not even a conciliar definition, was invested with authority in the same kind or degree as the original witness of Scripture. But the consensus and apostolic tradition of the Church in worship and doctrine was of profound importance. In the medieval period from at least the eleventh century in the West, disputes and controversies not only began to set reason and logic against the received doctrine of the community, but also mountingly stressed the literal meaning of the original text. Some writers over-simplified matters by setting the literal sense over against the allegorical (oversimplified, because often the intended sense of the original was allegorical), and then equating the allegorical interpretation with the ecclesiastical tradition. So diverse were the expositions that Alan of Lille remarked that the authority of the biblical text had 'a nose of wax'.

Furthermore, from about the eleventh century the Church, at least as represented by its higher officers, seemed to an increasing number of Christians (both clerical and lay) to be too involved in the secular business of property and power. Noble medieval cathedrals were not built on Hail Marys. It was not only heretics like polemical Waldensians and Lollards who contrasted the poverty and simplicity of the primitive Church with the great endowments and rent-lists of their own time.

Humanists of the fifteenth-century Renaissance were in reaction against the learning of the medieval universities and schools. There were complaints that people knew more about the logic of Boethius than about the Bible. One should return to the sources.

Against this background it becomes easy to understand that a contrast between Scripture and the contemporary practice of the Church was much in the air. Moreover, it was an axiom of the Augustinian tradition that all necessary doctrine for salvation is in the Bible. Augustine not infrequently enunciated the principle that a Bible given by God to disclose his will must be clear on anything really indispensable to salvation (or the divine will would be frustrated). He drew the conclusion that where Scripture is unclear, the doctrine taught may indeed be true, but must be less than utterly necessary. Augustine did not draw the conclusion that we need only this minimum found in Scripture alone, and can therefore dispense with the tradition of faith in the living community. That was the inference that Reformers of the sixteenth century wished to make.

The question of authority in belief was not new in the sixteenth century, but the debate was far sharper. The problem might appear simple if only one could say that 'Scripture alone' suffices, and could then decide to neglect any other medium of guidance. But mountainous difficulties arise. 'Scripture alone' is not, after all, a principle that can be derived from Scripture alone. The formula is actually a tradition; the manner in which it is deployed determines whether it is used rightly or wrongly. It cannot work if the community and Scripture are conceived as if external to one another and capable of being set in strong antithesis to one another. If the Church has authority, that depends on the Lord's commission, not upon texts, even though the texts are historical witnesses to the Lord's intention for the Church. An anti-ecclesial employment of 'Scripture alone' confronts embarrassment in the Church's role in the formation of the New Testament canon. There are also important practices such as Sunday observance which are community tradition, rather than explicitly sanctioned by Scripture.

The tradition of the fellowship, in which Scripture is certainly the most substantial element, is also a sense which determines the Christian's discernment of what is central and what is peripheral not only in the Christian past but in Scripture itself. The consequence of stressing the author's intention, as was widespread in the later Middle Ages, produces the axiom that the biblical books were never better understood than by their original writers and first readers. To say that, or even something approximating to it, is to become aware of a great distance in time and culture between our modern world and that of the Bible. To avert mere arbitrariness and individualism in interpretation we need to formulate guidelines, and these hermeneutic rules will not be unrelated to the consensus of the community. One of the side-effects of the sixteenth-century Protestant stress on the Bible over against the Church was to give far greater practical authority to the learned professor skilled in ancient languages than to the pastors of the believing community, and so to set up the deep tension between historical and dogmatic theology which has marked the history of the subject since the seventeenth century.

The question of authority in belief might appear simple if only one could say that in fact the decision about what is to be believed or done entirely rests with the individual's private judgement according to his or her best reason and conscience. That the individual reason and conscience play much more than a merely passive part seems clear. But there are problems when the individual is set up in judgement against the community and the tradition of its sacred texts. In some vehemently anti-Anglican Puritans of seventeenth-century England such as John Owen, appointed by Cromwell to be Dean of Christ Church and to purge that society of any attachment it might have to the Book of Common Prayer, the axiom of 'Scripture alone' is combined with the second axiom of private individual judgement by the believer; that is, God has given an infallibly inspired text, indeed the sole source of infallibility, but its interpretation is in no sense committed either to the community or to its pastors but is free for every believer to take in whatever way he feels to be right. The position was a kind of caricature of something St Augustine himself had said, namely, that Scripture, given by God for our illumination and therefore clear in essentials, nevertheless contained numerous obscurities and mysteries to exercise the thoughtful, and could have many justifiable interpretations. But Augustine located an ultimate control over these many interpretations in the Rule of Faith transmitted within the worshipping community, of which the bishops as proper pastors are the collective guardians.

In reality the community decisively forms (which is not to say that it wholly creates) the individual conscience, and provides the framework of principles within which and from which reason operates. Rational discourse is a communal activity, not a private soliloquy. For the believer, reason is never properly set in stark antithesis to authority as if the latter were always inscrutable and arbitrary.

Reason is neither a subordinate handmaid always submissive to its dogmatic teacher, nor a dangerous harlot ready to seduce, but rather a great gift of God for the understanding of the faith and of the proportion and coherence of its various elements. Human minds suffer the weaknesses of incomplete knowledge, bleary vision, partial understanding of the relevant considerations and facts, often a partisan self-concern, and seldom have the time and leisure to think through a complicated question. The community with its past wisdom and experience acts as a check on partiality and idiosyncrasy.

There are acute problems, however, in talking too blandly about the authority of tradition in the Church, where the legacy of history has been division and contention taken to the point of suspending eucharistic communion. The resulting rancour turns every separated communion into a distinct body with defensive fortification against rivals. 'Tradition' as a proper norm of doctrine in the Church, derived from the interpretation of Scripture, needs to be distinguished from particular and rival traditions, reluctant to listen to one another, inclined to much caricature of the other's beliefs and practices, at some times in history ready to resort to physical violence against one another. Even in a more ecumenical age, each advocate tends to begin conversation with the assumption that disunity is conquerable only when everyone else comes to be converted to his own tradition in the narrower sense of that word. It cannot of course be denied that it is hard to assert the absoluteness of one's own tradition when the particular group to which an individual happens to belong is often determined by where he was born, or by whose agency under God he came to be a believer, whether Boston Irish or Sydney Evangelical. Such differences make it more difficult for Christians to understand one another; and talk about '*our* tradition' then becomes a formula for pointing up differences and ignoring the usually larger areas of agreement. Common experience shows how rare it is for, say, a Baptist, with the best will in the world, to give an account of the essentials of Roman Catholic belief which will seem accurate and balanced to a Roman Catholic listener, or for a sympathetic Roman Catholic to delineate Anglican belief and practice in a way that Anglicans would recognize to be totally just and correct. The point has to be allowed, even when allowance is made for the fact that there are many diversities within each of these communions. On the other hand, there are also illusions in the self-portrait that each divided body nurses in regard to itself. Sixteenth-century Anglicanism, as we shall see, adopted a policy of wide formulas in the articulation of matters of faith, trying to leave legitimate options open, and of a narrow uniformity required in liturgy and devotional practice. It can surprise Anglicans of the late twentieth century to discover that despite their self-portrait of an Erasmian liberality and comprehensiveness they may look to most non-Anglicans a body quite remarkably intolerant in regard to devotional practice, and bordering on the incoherent in central matters of faith. Roman Catholics can also be astonished and embarrassed to discover that their self-portrait as a monolithic and unchanging body, without diversity of interpretation, is far from the actuality that friendly observers perceive.

Within the Anglican Communion the accepted norms of authority are located first in the faith declared in Scripture, then in the safeguard of interpretation provided by the Catholic Creeds, and finally in the liturgical tradition of Prayer Book and Ordinal, both of which are in essentials rooted in ways of worship much older than their sixteenth-century origin. The partly controversial Thirty-nine Articles of 1571 have a standing which varies in different provinces of the Anglican Communion, but have been influential on the historical shaping of Anglicanism in its middle path between Roman Catholicism and Protestantism.

In the Book of Common Prayer and the English Ordinal, Anglican theology has commonly found its most characteristic expression, seeking to include rather than to exclude. In the spectrum of Reformation service-books, they are conservative texts. Their principal author, Archbishop Thomas Cranmer, was by instinct and training a scholar, deeply read in the Greek and Latin Fathers and in the ancient church councils. He aspired to restore an ancient Catholic purity in prayer and spirituality, unencumbered by late medieval developments in theology and popular devotions, towards a number of which he was sharply critical. It was a matter of principle to him that Bible and liturgy must be in the vernacular as in the early Church; that clergy (as the holy Paphnutius had successfully urged at the Council of Nicaea in 325) should not be canonically required to be celibate; that, as had been the general practice until the later centuries of the Middle Ages, communion be offered in both kinds;[1] that the Eucharist should be a community act, not an isolated priest making a propitiatory offering on behalf of a passive non-communicating congregation (see pp. 121–9).

Most of these propositions (other than the non-obligation of celibacy) are self-evident to modern Roman Catholics, but did not seem so in 1550 when they were associated with the upheaval of the Reformation, in Catholic eyes a malicious rebellion against due authority disrupting the unity of Western Christianity. Cranmer, in practice, bequeathed a traditional pattern both of liturgy and ministerial authority. His preface to his first Prayer Book of 1549 (since 1662 printed under the title 'Concerning the Service of the Church') declared the purpose of restoring 'the godly and decent order of the ancient Fathers'. The preface to the Ordinal emphatically stated the intention of continuing the threefold ministry of bishop, priest, and deacon, transmitted since the time the Apostles passed from the scene. The deliberate retention of the name 'priest' rather than minister, as a title for the second order of ministry, did not at the time or later seem to all Protestants to express a fully reformed view of the ministry, and it is certain that Cranmer was entirely ready to accept that the presbyterate exercised a 'sacerdotal' function. Both the 1549 and 1552 Prayer

Books granted only to bishops and priests the authority to absolve, bless, and to preside at the Eucharist. That implied a strong adherence to patristic tradition. Moreover, the forms of absolution at the Eucharist and at the visitation of the sick are entirely traditional in both letter and spirit. Only there was a shift, of far-reaching consequence, in the fact that the penitent with grave sin on his conscience is invited, rather than obliged as a prerequisite for salvation, to make his confession to a discreet priest of his own choice. In the rite for the ordination of a priest, the main text, stressing the pastoral character of the ministry, was drawn from Martin Bucer's Strasburg model. But Cranmer, while omitting the commission of the medieval Latin pontifical to offer sacrifice for the living and the dead (and thereby giving conservative Catholic critics ground to assert that the distinctively priestly authority was lacking and even by implication denied),[2] abandoned Bucer at the critical point of the commission at the imposition of the bishop's hands, where the traditional words of the Latin rite in translation were kept intact (see pp. 143–52, 285–90).

The Thirty-nine Articles were finally agreed after Pope Pius V had excommunicated Queen Elizabeth I and declared her government illegitimate (1570)—thereby identifying Catholicism with treason (an event most unwelcome to the English Roman Catholic community, which came to suffer so severely that slightly more lives were lost in the Catholic cause than had been lost in the Protestant cause under Mary Tudor). Most of the substance of the Articles may be labelled Reformed Catholicism. The rejection of transubstantiation in Article XXVIII was balanced by clauses intended to protect the real presence and causing offence to the Zwinglian party. In Article XXXI there is an unqualified rejection of the notion that in the Eucharist the priest offers Christ to propitiate the Father on behalf of the living and the dead. On the other hand, the prayer of oblation in Cranmer's eucharistic liturgy includes an intercessory pleading of the merits of Christ's passion on behalf of the entire Church. There is no such positive statement in Article XXXI, but since the time of Bishop Lancelot Andrewes at the end of the sixteenth century it has been a question whether the concept of eucharistic sacrifice affirmed in the definition of the Council of Trent (1562–3) corresponds to that denied by Article XXXI. Andrewes thought not (see pp. 273–8).

The Articles contain several clauses which to Calvinistic Puritans were painful and even unacceptable. At first sight this is surprising. A rapid reading could leave the impression that so massive a stress is placed on the primacy of Scripture as to leave no room for any other authority. But on this point the wording is ambivalent and therefore hard to interpret decisively. Article VI declares that Scripture declares everything necessary to salvation, with the Augustinian inference that nothing should be prescribed as an article of faith, or necessary to salvation, which cannot be either 'read therein or proved thereby' (a phrase which has its own difficulties, notably in deciding what proof, or making explicit, would mean in this context.) The lectionary was to retain readings from the books misleadingly called by St Jerome 'Apocrypha'; that is, those admitted to the canon of the Septuagint and the Bible of the early Gentile churches, but absent from the Hebrew. The two books of largely Protestant Homilies (1547, 1571) commended in the Articles contain many citations from these books. Since Carlstadt challenged their inspired status in 1521, the left wing of the Reformation had disliked them. Article VI offers a conciliatory traditional formula (echoing Cardinal Cajetan) that one should follow St Jerome, in reading them for moral but not for dogmatic guidance (see pp. 69–89).

In Article VIII the Catholic Creeds are accepted because they can be 'proved' from Scripture. This again echoes patristic language. In the mid-fourth century, Cyril of Jerusalem explained to his catechumens that each clause in their baptismal creed could be verified from Scripture. Some clauses in the Nicene and Athanasian Creeds would admittedly be hard to 'prove' in a 'mathematical' sense if one had nothing but the Bible to do it with. Article XX is bolder, with a clause that Puritans hated: 'The Church has authority in controversies of faith'— subject of course to consonance with Scripture.

This last sentence troubled Calvinists, and some printed texts of the Articles appeared in which the clause was omitted. The sentence raises the question of by what organs the Church exercises this authority. The traditional answer of Christian antiquity, from the late second century onwards, was the episcopal synod, at which the collective mind of the Church (e.g. on the date of Easter, on disciplinary procedures, then on doctrinal issues) was articulated by an assembly of bishops, each representing his diocesan family. In AD 325 controversy extending far beyond Egypt was raised by the teaching of the Alexandrian priest Arius, that the Son was not identical in his divine being with God the Father, and a world-wide council, with representatives of many Greek provinces and delegates from Rome, was summoned. The emperor Constantine the Great took it over, transferred it to the city of Nicaea near his residence, and enforced its decisions with the secular arm. Binding authority upon the entire Church, at least within the Roman empire, thus came to be expressed through a series of 'ecumenical councils' at which both Greek East and Latin West were represented. The main decisions were ratified by the great patriarchates and by the emperor. The first seven (Nicaea 325, Constantinople 381, Ephesus 431, Chalcedon 451, Constantinople 553, Constantinople 681, Nicaea 787) were all in the Greek East. The second and the seventh were not quickly acknowledged as ecumenical in the Latin West; and the fifth provoked temporary opposition as well.

The first four councils, which Pope Gregory the Great (living after the fifth council which he also acknowledged) hailed as a canon like the four Gospels, are treated in some Anglican texts of the sixteenth and seventeenth century as having special status (see pp. 189–94). This is notably so in the Act of Uniformity of 1559, where orthodoxy is defined by the Scriptures, 'the first four general councils or some other general council' (given biblical support), or (evidently with conscious exclusion of the Pope) as what may be defined by 'Parliament with the assent of the clergy in convocation'. In fact, the fifth and sixth councils gave definitions on the refinements of Christology which the Anglicans of the sixteenth and seventeenth century happily accepted. Their handling of the seventh council condemning iconoclasm needs special treatment (see p. 103).

The Thirty-nine Articles affirm the doctrines of the Trinity and the incarnation in the language of the ancient ecumenical councils, thereby recognizing the standing of the councils responsible for the definitions. Nevertheless, the Articles are cautious about awarding absolute authority to any of the great patriarchates, including Rome, or even to gencral councils (XIX and XXI). They are far less reserved about the authority of princes (XXI and XXXVII), which is a reminder of the primary role played by Crown and government in the English Reformation. No English Reformer, recalling that all the ancient ecumenical councils were summoned by emperors, not by popes, would think that Rome had an exclusive right to summon councils, or that their authority depended essentially upon papal ratification. In any event, it was (and is) unclear that the Western councils entitled general or ecumenical, called by the popes after the eleventh century estrangement between East and West, possess the same status as the first seven. It did not pass unnoticed in sixteenth-century England that the Greek East had declined to receive the Council of Florence's affirmation of universal Roman authority throughout the Church.

There was nothing controversial in the observation that the co-operation of secular authorities is required if a general council can take place at all (though the framers of the Article may well have intended more than they actually said on this point). Nor would Cardinal Bellarmine have disagreed with the proposition that some assemblies claiming the title 'ecumenical' have made errors (classical examples cited in medieval discussions are Ariminum 359, and Ephesus 449). Their decisions were not received by due authority and by the faithful generally.[3]

On the other hand, the last sentence of Article XXI seems distinctly prickly and reserved when it says that the definitions of faith given by general councils have 'neither strength nor authority unless it may be declared that they be taken out of Holy Scripture'. Heretics condemned by ancient ecumenical councils plentifully appealed to Scripture, and the councils would not have been necessary if Scripture had been unequivocal on the matters under debate. The Councils of Nicaea (325) and Chalcedon (451) both found it indispensable to resort to terms not in Scripture, to fend off distortions of the community's faith in the divinity of Christ and the completeness of his humanity. In a broad sense, no doubt, the faith these councils defended was 'taken out' of Scripture. In practice, the Articles grant that it is only 'sometimes' that general councils have erred, and in Article VI the universal unquestioned consensus of the community is the ground for accepting the traditional biblical canon.

Article XXI, even in its last sentence, is correct if understood to be declaring that even general councils have no power to make arbitrary decisions on their own plenary authority; they always interpret dogma in obedience to a framework which is ultimately biblically based. The slightly exaggerated wording reflects Anglican reserve both towards the decree of the Council of Constance allowing communion in only one kind, and in relation to the Counter-Reformation Council at Trent (1545–63) in northern Italy, at which bishops attending were bound by oath to defend papal claims. Despite the mere handful of bishops attending Trent's early sessions, this council claimed ecumenical standing.[4] Sixteenth-century Protestants contended that Trent was no 'free' council because the pope was judge in his own cause, controlling the bishops through his legates who presided.

Nevertheless the Articles are surprisingly reticent about Roman authority. They say no more than the wholly non-controversial assertion that sometimes popes have made mistakes even on theological matters, and—much more sharply—that because of the royal supremacy over causes both ecclesiastical and civil, 'the Bishop of Rome hath no jurisdiction in this realm of England'. This reticence stands in contrast with the vehement words of the Presbyterian Westminster Confession of 1643 requiring assent not merely to the Calvinist doctrine of double predestination, but also to the proposition that by office the pope is Antichrist.[5] This totally negative view of the papacy found no place in the Articles or Prayer Book (except for a time in the form of a special service inserted by parliamentary authority to give thanks for the escape of James I and Parliament from 'Gunpowder Treason' on 5 November 1605—an alarming liturgical form that has long disappeared from all printed texts of the book). Yet it was a view which had a few Anglican supporters, including Cranmer himself, and became diffused in the seventeenth century by the exposition of the Apocalypse by Joseph Mede (1586–1638). The cabbalistic occultism of some Cambridge Platonists of that time produced in Henry More (1614–87) some of the most luridly antipapal pages one can read. More was appalled by the exegesis of the moderate Protestant Grotius (1583–1645), denying that the prophecies of Daniel, 2 Thessalonians 2, and the Apocalypse referred to the papacy at all. The presbyterian Richard Baxter conceded that the biblical texts were very obscure, but remarked that if they did not refer to the Pope, he had 'ill luck to be so like Antichrist'.

An altogether more positive view of Roman Catholicism appeared, much to Puritan distress, in Richard Hooker. He 'gladly acknowledged' the Roman Catholics to be 'of the family of Jesus Christ' and to maintain the authentic fundamentals of the faith. Similarly his close friend Richard Field (*Of the Church*, 1606) affirmed Anglican piety and polity to be continuing the old Catholic conciliar tradition before Trent had turned school opinions into articles of necessary faith, and before the unchallengeable supremacy of popes over councils (and independence of them) came to be asserted (see pp. 220–7).

Anglicans of the generation before Field and Hooker were much divided about tradition, Fathers, and councils. Heated controversy in the first stages of the English Reformation produced a negative appeal to antiquity against Roman 'innovations'. Jewel's Challenge Sermon of 1559 listed a catalogue of contemporary Roman Catholic doctrines and practices for which he defied anyone to find evidence during the first six centuries of the Church. This argument presupposed considerable researches in patristic texts; and for the argument to stand up it had to be selective. It was effective polemic to list the claims of Hildebrand, Boniface VIII, and the medieval papacy; the technical language of substance and accidents to explain the eucharistic change; the (superstitious) veneration of images; Eucharists at which only the priest received communion; the withholding of the cup from the laity. It was more difficult altogether to suggest that there was no very ancient authority for commemorating the faithful departed, a practice which hard-line Protestants felt irreconcilable with justification exclusively through the imputation of Christ's merits rather than on the ground of anything given by grace in the believer's moral life. Nervousness on this last point may explain the deletion of a censure of prayer for the dead from the original text of Article XXII. In the 1570s, Whitgift and the Puritan Cartwright engaged in sharp exchanges over whether or not prayer for the faithful departed was implied in Burial Service of the Prayer Book, in the petition 'that we with all those that are departed in the true faith of thy holy name may have our perfect consummation and bliss . . .' Cartwright thought it was.

These and similar arguments evoked a positive evaluation of the early Fathers and ancient councils. The Thirty-nine Articles frequently echo, and even directly cite, Augustine in the propositions concerning justification. In sixteenth-century controversies about e.g. the materiality of real presence and eucharistic sacrifice, about free will and predestination, about the unicity of the Church, both sides appealed on a huge scale to works by, or generally ascribed to, Augustine. Towards councils Augustine was always respectful, especially to Nicaea (325) in debate with Arians. He held a strongly conciliar doctrine of the presidency of the Roman see, the prime duty of which was to enforce the observance of conciliar canons. Augustine was aware that, for a Christian, authority does not have to be total and absolute to be real. Councils he saw to be an indispensable tool for co-ordinating policy, for keeping unity amid much natural diversity, and for defining the bishops' position in a controversial situation. He did not think a council's decisions could not be corrected or supplemented and balanced by later assemblies. On major questions, he did not think a provincial council had the authority to make its own decisions in disregard of other provinces.

This last point raised sensitive issues for the Anglicans. To what extent could the Church of England act unilaterally in making liturgical changes? Article XXXIV, 'Of the Traditions of the Church', adopts a fascinating zig-zag course. It works from the implied axiom that what has been ordained by divine authority cannot be changed, but there is freedom in particular or national churches to change 'ceremonies or rites', subject to edification. Liturgical diversity between different countries, times and customs has always been the case. But the argument for freedom suddenly turns around to attack the Puritans challenging the liturgical uniformity imposed by queen and parliament. It is intolerable for anyone 'through his private judgment' deliberately to break the traditions and ceremonies approved by common authority. (Puritans hated the popish surplice and thought kneeling for communion implied transubstantiation.)

The Puritans objected to the preface to the Ordinal with its insistence that the episcopate is the providentially intended order for the continuity, unity, and sacramental life of the Church through the ages. From the 1570s onwards, the Anglicans were confronting a Calvinist claim that presbyterianism is the only ministerial structure which has divine authority in the New Testament, and that 'antichristian' bishops obscure the Lordship of Christ over his Church. From the initial position that all matters of church order are in principle 'ceremonies and rites' left to the freedom of particular Churches, the Anglicans from the 1590s moved to the harder position that the episcopate is a gift of God to the Church for its unity and apostolic order, something no particular Church is actually free to change, though historical circumstances in some parts of Europe in the upheaval of the Reformation might have led to severe difficulties. The immensely learned James Ussher, Archbishop of Armagh, tried to commend a synodical concept of episcopacy, seeing the bishop as moderator of his presbyters and not making major decisions without their consent. But Hammond, Archbishop Bramhall, and Herbert Thorndike argued for a more rigid view, with the bishops as the keystone of the arch, the guarantee of visible continuity and assured sacramental life in the Church (see pp. 296–308).

In this debate, patristic argument loomed large. Much seemed to hang upon the epistles of Ignatius of Antioch, the authenticity of which became a heated issue. The debate was in effect settled by Ussher (1644) with a masterly vindication of the seven letters of the so-called 'middle' recension. Two years after he wrote, Voss first printed the Greek text of a manuscript with the text Ussher had defended as authentic. The no less massive learning of John Pearson (*Vindiciae Ignatianae*) annihilated the contention of Jean Daillé (1666) that all Ignatius' letters are spurious in all recensions. In passing, it is noteworthy that Pearson applied first-rate patristic learning to demonstrating the very high probability that St Peter was martyred in Rome. He noticed how easy it became for Roman Catholic controversialists when Protestants were seduced by the short cut, taken in 1324 by Marsilius of Padua, that St Peter cannot be shown from Scripture to have gone to Rome at all.

The seventh in the list of ancient ecumenical councils, the second Council of Nicaea in 787, anathematized the dishonouring of images of saints, while simultaneously forbidding worship of them. The left wing of the Reformation was largely iconoclast, and deplored Luther's conservative defence of holy pictures and statues. English Lollards of the century before the Reformation hated images and pilgrimages to them. Article XXII rejects (peremptorily and without argument) 'the Romish doctrine concerning ... worshipping and adoration as well of images as of relics, and also invocation of saints.' In fact both the seventh council and Trent distinguish the honouring of saints, as represented by their images, from the worship due only to God.

The very Protestant Homily on the Peril of Idolatry (1571) expressed fear of popular superstitions attaching to images, and painted a lurid picture of the persons and politics at the seventh council. The actual text of the Council of 787 was carefully considered by Richard Field (1606). He observed that for an Anglican the Council's definition created no difficulty, and that there was no disagreement between Anglicans and Roman Catholics that risks of superstitious abuse must exist.

Archbishop Bramhall tersely observed, in regard to the decrees of the seven ecumenical councils: 'I know of none we need to fear.'

*   *   *

Seventeenth-century theological controversy was profound in both erudition and intellectual acuteness. But soon there came a weariness with researches in folio volumes, combined with alarm at the inhuman consequences of the religious zeal that was so large an ingredient in the Thirty Years' War and the English Civil War. The disputes of scholars were acrimonious, and mutually deaf. The disagreements were in the sphere of revealed theology: could peace come by confining oneself to the fundamental truths of religion? (see pp. 232–43). Within Anglicanism, in 1650 a powerful plea for tolerance and reason came from Jeremy Taylor's book, *The Liberty of Prophesying*. He deplored excessive definition beyond the fundamentals of the Apostles' Creed, 'the unreasonableness of prescribing to other men's faith and the iniquity of persecuting differing opinions'. Learned himself in the writings of the Fathers and decrees of councils, he did not believe they could provide an absolute certainty where Scripture itself was unclear. From the wisdom of the past the living tradition draws guidance, but Fathers and councils do not present a unanimous witness with an authority before which reason can only bow in submission. Taylor had no doubt of divine assistance to synods of good bishops, like Nicaea, enabling them to articulate not indeed new doctrines, but the faith of Scripture, sound reason, and tradition.

The voice of reason and liberality also came (through William Chillingworth) to the philosopher John Locke. By 1689 patristic studies were under a cloud, though still vigorously defended by George Bull (1634–1710). Bull engaged in controversy with the French Jesuit Denys Petau, who deployed vast learning (1644–50) to argue that the 'orthodox' writers before the Council of Nicaea of 325 were in fact Arian in their opinions. Not that Petau thought Nicaea in any way mistaken. He was turning the flank of the Protestant argument that the Church of the ancient Fathers provided a model by comparison with which modern Roman Catholicism was shown to have made gross innovations. Petau proved that doctrine was not immutable, and inferred that therefore to decide between diverse developments a living teaching authority is required. Bull's *Defence of the Nicene Faith* was no less learned and acute than Petau, and delighted Bossuet in France. He was convinced that by patient historical study, one can elicit a consensus among the Fathers which is a sign of unchanging continuity.

Eighteenth-century Anglicanism was little interested in tradition, councils, and Church Fathers. Disillusionment with old dogmatic controversies either led into reasoned philosophical arguments (Joseph Butler against the Deists) or into the piety of feeling; often with the minimum of intellectual content, as in the case of the Evangelical Revival, but in William Law finding an exponent of mystical piety combined with a strong sense of tradition as an indispensable lifeline in Anglican spirituality.

The revival of appeal to tradition came with Keble and the Tractarians. In their eyes it was disastrous to rest the authority of the Church of England on its national character, or that of bishops on their nomination by the Crown, or that of the Prayer Book on its authorization by a secular Parliament. Bishops must derive authority only from their consecration in the apostolic succession, not from the secular power. Liturgy and spirituality should be fed from study of the Fathers. *The Library of the Fathers* and volumes of *Lives of the Saints* were to provide for this need.

The study of the Fathers on the assumptions of Bull or Bossuet about unchanging revelation makes it easier for Anglicans or Gallicans to ignore Petau's thesis that there has been development in the Church like a living organism, and therefore an organ of authority is needed to adjudicate between valid and invalid developments. J. H. Newman in effect abandoned Bull for Petau, and thereby converted himself to Roman Catholicism with the argument that development in doctrine is inevitable and good, and that, while no modern Christian communion now corresponds exactly to the ancient Church, at least the Roman Catholic Church has changed less than others.

In modern Anglican theology, as in modern Roman Catholicism or Orthodoxy, the appeal to the Fathers remains a living force. It is significant that Augustine is quoted more often than any other writer in the texts of Vatican II, and the discerning reader of the Final Report of ARCIC I (1982) will notice many echoes of patristic tradition.

NOTES

1 Cranmer's 1549 Prayer Book affirms that under each kind the whole Christ is received.

2 The modern Roman Catholic rite for ordaining a priest lacks any such commission. The bearing of this point on the papal Bull *Apostolicae Curae* (1896) has as yet been unconsidered.

3 Reception is a major theme in regard to the decrees of councils or popes, but one of peculiar complexity. It would be absurd to think that a council's decrees derive no authority from their framers or from the reasonableness and evidently biblical base for their decision, but entirely from the approval of posterity. If the faithful community has received a decree as true, then we believe it was not made true by that reception, but was received because it was true. The receiving is a manifestation of its truth. The reception process also takes time. Both Nicaea and Chalcedon had long struggles to gain acceptance. In the Roman Catholic Church the Council of Trent was not accepted until the seventeenth century, after long and hard argument. Moreover, the receiving process is not merely passive, but is an active interpreting and assimilation by the community.

4 In the seventeenth century the Anglican view of Trent was largely determined by the brilliant but cool history by Paolo Sarpi, the Venetian.

5 Today in the Church of Scotland presbyterian ministers accept the Confession with freedom of conscience except in matters affecting 'the substance of the Gospel'.

3 Reason

A. S. MCGRADE

Butler, Joseph, *Works*, ed. W. F. Gladstone. 2 vols., Oxford 1897.

Cosslett, Tess, ed., *Science and Religion in the Nineteenth Century*. CUP 1984.

Farrer, Austin, *Finite and Infinite*. 2nd edn, Westminster, Dacre Press, 1964.

Jenkins, D. E., *The Contradiction of Christianity*. SCM 1976.

Locke, John, *Epistola de Tolerantia: A Letter on Toleration*, ed. Raymond Klibansky, tr. J. W. Gough. Oxford, Clarendon Press, 1968.

Macquarrie, John, *In Search of Deity: An Essay in Dialectical Theism*, The Gifford Lectures, 1983. London, SCM, 1984; New York, The Crossroad Publishing Co., 1985.

Peacocke, Arthur, *Intimations of Reality: Critical Realism in Science and Religion*. Notre Dame, Indiana, published for De Pauw University Greencastle, Indiana by University of Notre Dame Press, 1983.

Prickett, Stephen, *Romanticism and Religion: The Tradition of Coleridge and Wordsworth in the Victorian Church*. CUP 1976.

No Church claims irrationality as an identifying mark, nor do Anglicans claim that they alone are reasonable. What, then, can be distinctive about 'reason' in Anglicanism? A simple if negative answer is to be found in reason's relation to the other bases of authority and method presented in this chapter, Scripture and tradition. Reason has served Anglicans, and has often been explicitly invoked by them, as a counterpoise to unthinking biblicism or unthinking conformity to historical precedent. The Reformation principle that 'Scripture containeth all things necessary to salvation' did not prevent bitter controversy under Elizabeth I about Scripture's meaning and the Church's discretionary authority in matters of liturgy and governance. In the culminating contribution to this debate, Richard Hooker's *Of the Laws of Ecclesiastical Polity*, reason is defended as not only presupposed for an accurate understanding of Scripture but as competent to determine a broad range of issues not explicitly covered in Scripture. Indeed, Hooker held that the Church could reasonably prescribe contrary to a biblical precept, if the purpose of the precept in its historical context could be understood and could be understood to be irrelevant in current circumstances. Hooker's unwillingness to have the Bible used as a source of ahistorical, unambiguous proof texts for dogmatic solutions to all problems is typical of later Anglican thought. Thus, Locke, although he leaned heavily on the Bible in expounding a 'reasonable' Christianity free of unnecessary obscurities, sought to approach revelation itself in a reasonable way. He objected to the slicing up of Scripture into separate verses, which led so easily to citation out of context for sectarian dogmatic purposes, and to the disparagement of reason in favour of revelation: he argued that taking away reason to make way for revelation was like persuading a man to put out his eyes to receive the remote light of an invisible star by telescope.

England was not in the forefront of modern scientific criticism of the Bible. Benjamin Jowett's essay 'On the Interpretation of Scripture', which had as its first principle that Scripture should be interpreted 'like any other book', shocked many when it appeared in 1860; yet there was good precedent in earlier Anglicanism for some aspects of the new approach—and there is good precedent for the respectful wariness of contemporary Anglicans towards the exclusively revelation-oriented theology of Karl Barth. The rational exegesis of Scripture in Anglicanism—the faithful acceptance of Scripture as normative witness to what is needed for salvation—has seldom purported to be simply a spelling-out of truths accessible to faith alone. From Hooker onwards, human or natural reason has also been allowed to contribute (see pp. 103–5).

With regard to tradition, too, Anglicans have felt a need for reasonable discretion to temper a positive basic attitude. Ever since Bishop Jewel's undertaking to defend the *ecclesia Anglicana* against Rome on the basis of the Fathers, there has been a strong although not unopposed tendency in Anglicanism to follow tradition unless specific reason could be given for departing from it—

but the possibility that there might be such reason has generally been recognized. Thus Jeremy Taylor in 1647, arguing that reason, proceeding upon best grounds, is the best judge:

> It is a good argument for us to follow such an opinion, because it is made sacred by the authority of councils and ecclesiastical traditions, and sometimes it is the best reason we have in a question ... but there may also be, at other times, a reason greater than it that speaks against it, and then the authority must not carry it.

Today, when some Anglican theologians propose substantial revisions in traditional credal formulations, this is not done from lack of sympathy with the patristic making of doctrine, but from a sense that the project of intelligibly articulating Christian faith must continue: 'The tradition criticizes us, but we have also to criticize the tradition, drawing upon the best intellectual and moral insights of our own day.'

If Anglican reason can be characterized negatively as a counterpoise to unreasoning biblicism or traditionalism, what can be said of it positively? For better or worse, no single specific account can be given. This is partly because Anglicans have disagreed among themselves about what counts as reason, partly because of historical change in what counts as reason in the world at large. A good example of both these sources of variation is the controversy between Locke and Bishop Stillingfleet over the purported anti-Trinitarian implications of passages in Locke's *Essay Concerning Human Understanding*. The Bishop's views concerning such metaphysical notions as nature, essence, and person have been thought to resemble those of the great scholastic, Duns Scotus. Locke found them unintelligible. Stillingfleet, in return, had difficulty comprehending Locke's 'new way of ideas', which was to set the course of British philosophy for more than a century. (Lest this dispute be taken as a sign of lay-clerical antipathy in Anglicanism, we may note that the next major figure after Locke in the empiricist tradition was an Anglican bishop, George Berkeley.)

The best access to the essence—or varieties—of Anglican reason is through the works of Anglican reasoners. Besides the separate works of major writers such as those already mentioned, Bishop Butler, the Tractarians, F. D. Maurice, Frederick and William Temple (father and son Archbishops of Canterbury), Charles Gore, and several more recent authors, much is to be learned from a number of collaborative volumes representing different, often conflicting viewpoints within Anglicanism but close to one another in their concern to address reasonably the conditions of their time: *Essays and Reviews* (1860), *Lux Mundi* (1889), *Foundations* (1913), *Essays Catholic and Critical* (1926), *Soundings* (1963), *Christ, Faith and History* (1972), and *Christian Believing* (1976). Some important figures in English literature have been Anglican clerics: Donne, Herbert, Swift, and Sterne (the last two are significant critics of their rationalist era); and Anglican lay poets and critics such as Coleridge, T. S. Eliot, and C. S.

Lewis have had great influence in their treatment of religious themes. The present survey must be drastically selective and will be limited to developments in England. Nevertheless, both the range and the problems of Anglican reason can be suggested.

COSMIC AND CORPORATE REASON: RICHARD HOOKER

Hooker based his insistence on the role of reason in church polity on an idea of reasonable law, which he took to be manifest in the workings of God and the various orders of creation. This vision of a cosmos of many levels, at once mysterious and teleologically intelligible, combined the best insights of classical and medieval speculation and was presented in Book I of the *Laws* (1594) with the grace and power of the best Renaissance style. It has served as an ideal model for many later Anglicans, even when it has been largely discarded as an image of reality in the modern world generally. The polemical thrust of Hooker's work depended also, however, on reason in another sense. Hooker defended public or corporate reason—the collective wisdom of the whole body of the church—as against the judgements of individuals who objected to the Elizabethan Settlement as not sufficiently reformed. The unfortunate textual history of Hooker's account of religious and political authority in the posthumously published concluding books of the *Laws* has obscured both its originality and its logical and moral coherence. But no matter how we construe Hooker's system, the fact remains that an important aim of his work was to show that in 'things indifferent'— matters not of the essence of Christianity—the English Church corporate had coercive authority over all English Christians (see pp. 233–8). This claim was to be successfully contested not only in the battles of the Civil War and its aftermath, but also in the next era of Anglican reason.

CONSCIENCE AND THE REASONABLENESS OF CHRISTIANITY

John Locke's first political essay appealed to Hooker to affirm the legitimacy of coercion in theologically indifferent religious matters, but Locke's later *Letter on Toleration* (1688) is a classic defence of voluntariness as essential to authentic religion. 'Whatsoever may be doubtful in religion, yet this at least is certain, that no religion, which I believe not to be true, can be either true or profitable unto me.' Locke held the mutual toleration of Christians in their different professions of religion to be 'the chief characteristical mark of the true church', and he withstood repeated critical onslaughts in trying to make it a mark of his own Church, or at least of his country's law. Indeed in the legal sphere, although he held that atheists ought not to be tolerated, he argued for the religious freedom of non-Christians: 'Neither pagan, nor Mahometan, nor Jew, ought to be excluded from the civil rights of the commonwealth because of his religion.'

It is a great mistake to interpret Locke's advocacy of toleration as secular or unchristian in motive or intent. When he wrote the first letter on toleration, he had freshly before him the savage harrying of Protestants after the revocation of the Edict of Nantes. As he wrote later, 'The horrid cruelties that in all ages, and of late in our view, have been committed under the name, and upon the account of religion, give so just an offence and abhorrence to all who have any remains, not only of religion, but humanity left, that the world is ashamed to own it.' There was a challenge here to discover a Christianity which could cease being a moral and religious scandal on the face of the earth. It is his desire to meet this challenge which explains the doctrinal minimalism and moral earnestness of Locke's major theological work, *The Reasonableness of Christianity as Delivered in the Scriptures*: if what was necessary and sufficient to be believed to attain eternal life could be reasonably established on the basis of Scripture, Christians might differ in their further professions, but (besides tolerating adherents of other religions in their civil society) they would at least be able to recognize one another as Christians.

This is to say that Locke's aim, like Hooker's, was to achieve a basic Christian consensus which any reasonable person could accept. Hooker could take doctrinal agreement for granted and defend the national Church's corporate reason as a basis for practical uniformity in things indifferent. Locke perforce (and perhaps by preference) argued for the acceptability of a plurality of Christian religious bodies within a single civil society, but employed reason in the form of common sense in seeking an over-arching Christian peace and unity. As Mark Pattison put it in one of the less dated contributions to *Essays and Reviews*, 'This popular appeal to the common reason of men, which is one characteristic of the rationalist period, was a first effort of English theology to find a new basis for doctrine which should replace the foundations which had failed it.' First the Reformation and then the reaction against Laudianism had effectively destroyed the authority of the Church, but the radical alternative of individual inner illumination had led only to extravagance and discord under the Commonwealth:

> The re-action against individual religion led to this first attempt to base revealed truth on reason. And for the purpose for which reason was now wanted, the higher, or philosophic, reason was far less fitted than that universal understanding in which all men can claim a share. The 'inner light', which had made each man the dictator of his own creed, had exploded in ecclesiastical anarchy. The appeal from the frantic discord of the enthusiasts to reason must needs be, not to an arbitrary or particular reason in each man, but to a *common* sense, a natural discernment, a reason of universal obligation. As it was to be binding, it must be generally recognisable ... Truth must be accessible to 'the bulk of mankind.' (*Essays and Reviews*, p. 291, with reference at the end to Locke, *Essay Concerning Human Understanding*, IV.19.3.)

In the beginning, then, the appeal to reason at the level of common sense had a vital religious motive.

Locke held that the existence of God could be strictly demonstrated, and that there were objective, rational grounds for accepting Jesus as the Messiah sent by God to lead those who would believe in him and obey his commandments to immortality and bliss. This positive side of Locke's sort of rationalism was pushed further by a number of eighteenth-century authors, reaching its height of confidence in Warburton, who had a proof of Christianity 'very little short of mathematical certainty, and to which nothing but a mere physical possibility of the contrary can be opposed', and its height of eloquence in William Paley, whose *View of the Evidences of Christianity* (1794) and *Natural Theology* (1802) long retained their popularity. Locke had also emphasized the limitations of human understanding, however, and had insisted on a sharp distinction between religious faith and scientific certainty. The limited scope of human knowledge in an empiricist scheme of things is maintained with great honesty in the work of Joseph Butler, successively Bishop of Bristol and Durham.

In his sermons preached at the Rolls Chapel (published in 1726), Butler challenged his age's tendency to equate rationality with egoism by arguing that self-interest and benevolence are fundamentally compatible, that the authority of reflective, impartial moral judgement is natural, and that virtue is therefore according to nature and vice unnatural. Disinterested love of God would thus be a rational and psychologically appropriate response to God's goodness. But how is God's goodness to be known? Butler considered that reason was 'the only thing we have wherewith to judge concerning any thing, even revelation itself', and that reason can and ought to judge, 'not only of the meaning, but also of the morality and the evidence, of revelation'. The distinctive thing about his own reasoning, however, is that it candidly moves on the level of probability. He is the first, in the introduction to *The Analogy of Religion Natural and Revealed to the Constitution and Course of Nature* (1736) to speak of probability as 'the great guide of life'. The analogy in the *Analogy* is between nature as a system imperfectly understood and religion as a system imperfectly understood. 'Christianity is a scheme quite beyond our comprehension', but then, too, 'every thing in nature shows us our ignorance in the constitution of nature'. Butler's conception of nature and religion as systems allowed him to adduce many features of the former as evidence for the latter—the marked differences in the life-stages of many creatures in nature, for example, lend plausibility to the idea that our earthly life is a stage on the way to an immortal afterlife—but all of this shows, not the 'reasonableness' of religion, but its credibility. The *Analogy* is conceded to be, 'by no means satisfactory; very far indeed from it', but, 'The evidence of religion then being admitted real, those who object against it, as not satisfactory, i.e. as not being what they wish it, plainly forget the very condition of our being: for satisfaction, in this sense, does not belong to such a creature as man.'

Mark Pattison had high praise for Butler's integrity, in contrast with the more assertive apologists of the age (in whom he noted 'the astonishing want of candour in their reasoning, their blindness to real difficulty, the ill-concealed predetermination to find a particular verdict, the rise of their style in passion in the same proportion as their argument fails in strength'), but like many of his contemporaries he found this phase of rationalism unsatisfactory—not for its empirical uncertainty but for its flatness. It produced a theology 'which excludes on principle not only all that is poetical in life, but all that is sublime in religious speculation'. He agreed with a German reader's response to the *Analogy*: 'We weary of a long journey on foot, especially through deep sand.'

MYSTERY AND SCIENCE IN THE NINETEENTH CENTURY

Locke had argued that Christianity was reasonable despite what was mysterious in it. A recovery of the poetical in life and the sublime in religious speculation and a changed conception of reason are all evident in Coleridge's contention that Christianity was most reasonable precisely in its mysteries: 'The Christian faith is the perfection of human intelligence ... There are indeed mysteries, in evidence of which no reasons can be brought. But it has been my endeavour to show, that the true solution of this problem is, that these mysteries are reason, reason in its highest form of self-affirmation.' Coleridge could attempt to show the rationality of articles of faith rightly classed as mysteries because of his appropriation of Kant's distinction between reason and understanding. Understanding (the reason of the empiricists) is a capacity for judging according to the senses. Reason, on the contrary, is 'the power of universal and necessary convictions, the source and substance of truths above sense and having their evidence in themselves.'

For Coleridge the relation between reason and understanding, which was mediated and focused by the creative imagination, was tense but mutually vivifying. In his most popular theological work, *Aids to Reflection* (1825), he urged upon his readers the exercise of their reasoning and reflecting powers as necessary to keep faith alive in the heart; conversely, he insisted that 'never yet did there exist a full faith in the Divine Word ... which did not multiply the aims and objects of the understanding'. Those who based their thinking about religious realities on the natural theology of earlier empiricism were subject to increasing pressures in the nineteenth century from the new theories of geology and evolutionary biology. Coleridge's theological position, not dependent on science for its rational foundation, had less to fear from religiously uncongenial scientific developments; but it could consistently take up religiously positive ones. The mistakes of scientific men, he held, had never injured Christianity, while every new truth discovered by them has either added to its evidence or prepared the mind for its reception.

Coleridge's most direct influence was on the Broad Church movement, but the shift in sensibility he helped to bring about also had effects in other quarters.[1] So far as reason is concerned all of the main positions in nineteenth-century English theology can usefully be viewed in relation to his.

The Oxford Movement was set in motion by a professor of poetry who acknowledged a profound spiritual debt to Coleridge's sometime collaborator, Wordsworth. In his own immensely popular cycle of poems, *The Christian Year*, Keble set out to exhibit the 'soothing' quality of the Book of Common Prayer, and his programme for the Church of England was avowedly to make it more poetic. (Newman, after his conversion to Roman Catholicism, commented in reviewing a book of Keble's: 'Poetry is the refuge of those who have not the Catholic Church to flee to and repose upon, for the Church herself is the most sacred and august of poets.') Here we see a full development of the view that religion moves on a level above the empirical understanding, that it is concerned with truths which have their evidence in themselves. Thus liberated from the burden of proving their theology by an accumulation of natural evidences, the Tractarians were correspondingly undisturbed by the supposedly anti-religious results of modern science. They did not, however, take the further step of trying to place science itself in a positive theological light.

The liberal theologians represented in *Essays and Reviews* were like the Tractarians in locating religion and science in different, non-competing realms of meaning or truth. Instead of finding the mark of reason in the distinctive mysteries of traditional Christianity, however, they were inclined to equate spiritual truth with morality. Also unlike the Oxford Movement, liberalism took an enthusiastic positive interest in the course of science in its own area. As to the assignment of religion and science to separate domains, Baden Powell wrote: 'The more knowledge advances, the more it has been, and will be, acknowledged that Christianity, as a real religion, must be viewed apart from connexion with physical things.' In an advanced age recourse to miracles for proof of Christianity is counter-productive: 'If miracles were in the estimation of a former age among the chief *supports* of Christianity, they are at present among the main *difficulties*, and hindrances to its acceptance.' For all the disconnection between real religion and physical things in liberal theology, the attitude towards science is strongly positive. The entire range of inductive science is based upon, and invariably confirms, the 'grand truth' of the universal order and constancy of natural causes as 'a primary law of belief'. Darwin's *The Origin of Species* must soon bring about an entire revolution of opinion in favour of the 'grand principle' of the self-evolving powers of nature. All highly cultivated minds and duly advanced intellects have now in some measure learned to appreciate 'the grand foundation conception' of universal law. It is noteworthy, however, that liberal enthusiasm for science involved no attempt to show that science provided evidence for religion. The clearest indication of this in *Essays and Reviews* is C. W. Goodwin's detailed *refutation* of all attempts to reconcile the biblical account of creation with the findings of modern science.[2]

The contributors to *Lux Mundi*, like the Tractarians, saw the Church as properly 'standing firm in her old truths', but in some ways they were more positively engaged with modern science than the *Essays and Reviews* liberals. Their ideal aim was to assimilate new material, 'to welcome and give its place to all new knowledge'. This project is in a sense frankly opportunistic. Christian faith is presented as 'an energy of basal self' which uses as materials the sum of all our faculties—hence, no one faculty, including reason, can fully vindicate an act of faith—and so 'it uses as its instrument every stage of science; but it is pledged to no one particular stage'. Christian dogmatism is itself 'devotion to truth for truth's sake', and the doctrine of the Trinity is 'an appeal to reason'. In this spirit, the theory of evolution could be explored for possible theological significance without its dictating that significance entirely on its own scientific terms. Thus Aubrey Moore argued that evolution restored 'the truth of the divine immanence', which Deism had denied—but this led to a pantheistic reaction. In relation to these extremes, orthodox theism could be presented as reasonable, as 'the safeguard of rational religion against deism and pantheism'. Another attempt to integrate evolutionary theory with previous Christian thought was made in this volume by J R. Illingworth, who argued that 'the theory of evolution has recalled our minds to the "cosmical significance" of the Incarnation', which was a prominent thought in the early and the medieval Church. The tone here is different from that of natural theology à la Paley, but also different from that of *Essays and Reviews*. There is no insistence that scientific theory or empirical findings 'prove' Christianity, but neither is there an insistence that real Christianity must be viewed 'apart from connexion with physical things'.

TWENTIETH-CENTURY EXPERIENCES

Nineteenth-century Anglo-Catholicism and liberal Anglican theology both appealed to experience, although in ways different from one another and from the empiricism of Locke's era. The recovered experience of Catholic devotion and tradition and the liberated moral experience of a theology no longer competing with natural science both found points of contact with the mind-centred idealism of philosophers like T. H. Green. Along with the development of philosophical idealism in writers like William Temple, A. E. Taylor, and R. G. Collingwood, there was from around the turn of the century also a rising consciousness that the existing human world was far from ideal. Frederick

Temple's sweeping historical optimism about 'The Education of the World' at the beginning of *Essays and Reviews* in 1860 was replaced by a somewhat sombre assessment of 'The Modern Situation' in *Foundations* (1913), a collection to which William Temple was a chief contributor. F. D. Maurice's attempts to promote Christian Socialism in the mid-nineteenth century had failed, but the efforts of Temple and others between the wars were more successful, as faith in an assured human progress driven by science or a reason immanent in history vanished. Experience has continued to serve as a starting point for much Anglican theology, but it is often the experience of God as a source of hope and meaning in an existence which is otherwise radically problematic, only seldom the experience of a natural and divine cosmic harmony. Even in these conditions, refined philosophical debate about the meaning and truth of religious discourse has continued, influenced in England by the propinquity of theology faculties to philosophy faculties in the ancient universities. Austin Farrer, E. L. Mascall, J. R. Lucas, Ian T. Ramsey, Basil Mitchell, and others have contributed ably to these discussions, with varying degrees of commitment to perennial philosophical positions and new trends of thought. A serious attempt to take account of the philosophy of Martin Heidegger is central in the theology of John Macquarrie, and an Anglican interest in non-Christian religions (present in Hooker, for example) has been maintained by such scholars as Ninian Smart. Farrer's work is a particularly attractive recent example of qualities we have encountered in earlier authors. The 'rational' theology of *Finite and Infinite* (1943) displays speculative vision, exact metaphysical analysis, and searching inquiry: the Thomistic analogy of being is affirmed, but the dialectic through which God's relation to creatures becomes evident is marked by incisive criticism of the traditional arguments at each stage. In *The Glass of Vision* (1948), poetry as well as metaphysics proves congenial to orthodox theology.

Something of the range of reason in contemporary Anglican theology can be seen in the Anglican contributions to *Christ, Faith and History: Cambridge Studies in Christology* (1972). The first of these, by Maurice Wiles, approaches Christology as something which 'has never ceased to puzzle and perplex' the minds of Christians from earliest times, and applies a distinction between 'two different kinds of story', a scientific or human story and a mythological story, to suggest the positive lines of thought which might take the place of a (possibly mistaken) traditional Christology. The last essay in the volume, by D. M. MacKinnon, suggests in contrast that the Aristotelian metaphysical categories of substance and nature underlying the patristic *homoousion* are analytically respectable, perhaps inevitable; and that the *homoousion* itself may be theologically essential for riveting attention on the person of Christ and understanding and maintaining the Church's dependence on him (as against primary involvement in its own consciousness). Intervening essays make adroit use of philosophy in, for example, showing the poverty of a general scepticism about knowledge of the past and questioning the appeal to a supposedly interpretation-free modern experience, as a foundation on which to criticize traditional theology.

MYTH AND REASON IN CONTEMPORARY ANGLICANISM

Christ, Faith and History includes in a single volume proposals for a remarkably wide range of doctrinal positions, although the range is perhaps no wider than the gulf in spirit between *Tracts for the Times* and *Essays and Reviews*. A similar range of opinion is apparent in the two appendices and eight individual essays following the joint statement in the Doctrine Commission of the Church of England's *Christian Believing* (1976) and in subsequent controversy over the 'myth' or truth of the incarnation.[3] When one Anglican theologian says with ostensible generosity towards traditional belief that we must be 'frankly mythological' in some of our religious affirmations, another is apt to take this as an attack, to fear that the affirmations in question are being demoted or rejected, and the fear is all the greater when talk of myth is accompanied by an intense concern with logical economy and coherence in the non-mythological parts of theology or by a paramount interest in removing the real but supposedly unnecessary obstacles to belief so widely felt in our materialistic modern culture. The truth of the incarnation, it may alternatively be thought, is in the persistent, historically coherent testimony of Christians to exactly those things witnessed by the first disciples, and the true adventure of Christian faith is not a struggle to reject anything that may come to seem inductively unlikely but a life of openness to something always beyond all natural possibilities. What can reasonably be said of such dissension?

Against the background of previous theological debate within Anglicanism, the present situation looks familiar in form, however radical it may seem in content. A fervent dogmatic minimalism has seemed both reasonable and Christian to many Anglicans in the past, while to many others the self-evidently highest rationality of Christian faith has been its adherence to a God mysterious alike in transcendence and in presence. The sharply differing values assigned to terms such as 'mythological', 'poetic', and 'symbolic' in current discussions recall earlier attempts to make the Church's faith poetic or imaginative—attempts which must fail if they make the object of faith imaginary. All would no doubt agree in some sense with Coleridge's aphorism: 'He who begins by loving Christianity, better than truth, will proceed by loving his own sect or church better than Christianity, and end in loving himself better than all.' The difficulty is that while this can be taken in the spirit of absolutely unrestricted free inquiry—'to know God is to be bound to question everything' (David Jenkins, *The Contradiction of Christianity*)—it need not be so taken: 'Christian dogmatism is, after all, devotion to truth for truth's sake' (R. C. Moberly in *Lux Mundi*). No one can identify equally with every candidate for reasonableness in the tradition we have surveyed, but the consideration of past diversity may lead to a clearer recognition of personal integrity and a concern for corporate integrity in those who presently take positions very different from one's own.

A reasonable Church takes account of reason in the world at large. That world today imposes no compelling decisions on current theological controversies, but it does offer resources for prosecuting the debate more thoughtfully. Much recent philosophical work tends to obliterate any hierarchical distinction in cognitive rank between science and the domain of poetry and myth. Sensitivity to the importance of creativity in science, to revolutionary shifts within science concerning its own criteria of objectivity, and to the dehumanizing potential of an essentially mythic commitment to science and technology as substitutes for religion all serve to diminish the antagonism between science and theology, even when theology proceeds on other than an empirical basis. In this atmosphere there is no loss of status in accepting H. E. Root's analogy in *Soundings*: 'Believers are in love, theologians write love-poems and metaphysicians—natural theologians—write criticisms of poetry.'

Yet other developments encourage the pursuit of natural theology along more traditional lines. A century of research has revealed the vitality and restored the intelligibility of much of medieval thought. Modern modal logic and possible worlds semantics have led to renewed interest in the ontological argument for God's existence. Cosmological speculation is no longer excluded on principle from having theological implications.[4] In this atmosphere it is not shocking to find John Macquarrie propounding a natural theology of 'dialectical theism' which has positive incarnational and Trinitarian implications and which claims as its antecedents some of the most daringly speculative thinkers of classical, medieval, and modern times, including Plotinus, Pseudo-Dionysius, Scotus Eriugena, and Nicholas of Cusa.[5]

Anglican reason has been a dialogue of various endemic conceptions of reason with one another and with various and successive rationalisms in the world at large.[6] When integrity has been maintained—when dialogue has not collapsed into diatribe and separatism—this has not been due to the dominance of any one species of reason, but to the acceptance of comprehension as a condition of life. The acceptance has sometimes been grudging, sometimes highly idealized. In any case, it is the intellectual reflection of the same commitment to corporateness expressed in this communion's peculiar attention to common prayer. In eucharistic prayers modelled on the 1549 Prayer Book, Anglicans offer God 'our selves, our souls and our bodies, as a reasonable, holy, and lively sacrifice'. The suggestion here that so repeatedly plural a subject—'selves', 'souls', 'bodies'—may in worship become one—'a' sacrifice—and a one which is reasonable, holy, and alive in devotion to God indicates a proper and concrete spiritual context for Anglican theology. It is in worship or with reference to worship that all sorts and conditions of reasoners can practice the way of handling dissension proposed by Jeremy Taylor as God's way, the way of love. (This is in contrast with various human ways, ranging from submission to an infallible guide, through compromise, to indifferentism.) 'Theology is rather a divine life than a divine knowledge. In heaven indeed we shall first see, and then love; but here on earth we must first love . . . and we shall then see and perceive and understand.'

NOTES

1 'Through Coleridge, and through the radical shift in religious sensibility that he helped to bring about, Maurice was able to create a vision of the English Church, at once spiritual and social, that Anglicans have yet to assimilate. Through Coleridge and Wordsworth the Oxford Movement was able to re-assert both the independence of the Church and its interdependence with society. Through Coleridge and Maurice, MacDonald was able to discover something in the Church wider and more spiritual than could be found among the Congregationalists of Arundel or the moral precepts of Arnold. Perhaps most ironic of all, through Newman, the Anglican tradition of Coleridge has become part of the heritage of the Roman Catholic Church itself.' Stephen Prickett, *Romanticism and Religion: The Tradition of Coleridge and Wordsworth in the Victorian Church* (CUP 1976), p. 267.

2 'The Mosaic Cosmogony', reprinted with other interesting documents and useful introductions in Tess Cosslett, ed., *Science and Religion in the Nineteenth Century* (CUP 1984).

3 John Hick, ed., *The Myth of God Incarnate* (SCM Press 1977); Michael Green, ed., *The Truth of God Incarnate* (Hodder and Stoughton 1977). Also see Michael Goulder, ed., *Incarnation and Myth: The Debate Continued* (Grand Rapids, Mich., Eerdmans, 1979), and Durstan R. McDonald, ed., *The Myth/Truth of God Incarnate* (Wilton, Con., Morehouse-Barlow, 1979).

4 Stephen Toulmin, *The Return to Cosmology: Postmodern Science and the Theology of Nature* (Berkeley, Univ. of Calif. Press, 1982). Various misuses of science as a surrogate for religion receive appropriately devastating criticism in Mary Midgley's *Evolution as a Religion: Strange Hopes and Stranger Fears* (London and New York, Methuen, 1985). See also A. R. Peacocke, ed., *The Sciences and Theology in the Twentieth Century* (Notre Dame, Indiana, University of Notre Dame Press, 1981).

5 John Macquarrie, *In Search of Deity: An Essay in Dialectical Theism*, The Gifford Lectures, 1983 (New York, The Crossroad Publishing Co., 1985).

6 'The Holy Spirit, who guides us into all truth, may be present not so much exclusively on one side of a theological dispute as in the very encounter of diverse visions held by persons or groups of persons who share faithfulness and commitment to Christ and each other.' 'Pluralism and the Norms of Christian Judgement', in the Inter-Anglican Theological and Doctrinal Commission's *For the Sake of the Kingdom: God's Church and the New Creation* (Cincinnati, Ohio, Forward Movement Publications, 1986), p. 48.

PART FOUR

Anglican Standards

1   Prayer Books

MARION J. HATCHETT

Booty, J. E., *The Book of Common Prayer 1559: The Elizabethan Prayer Book*. Charlottesville, The Folger Shakespeare Library by The University Press of Virginia, 1976.

Brightman, F. E., *The English Rite: Being a Synopsis of the Sources and Revisions of the Book of Common Prayer with an Introduction and an Appendix* 2 vols. London, Rivingtons, 1915.

Cardwell, E., *A History of Conferences and Other Proceedings Connected with the Revision of the Book of Common Prayer; from the Year 1558 to the Year 1690*. 3rd edn, Oxford, University Press, 1849.

Clarke, W. K. L., ed., *Liturgy and Worship: A Companion to the Prayer Books of the Anglican Communion*. SPCK 1932.

Cuming, G. J., *A History of Anglican Liturgy*. 2nd edn, London, Macmillan Press, 1982.

Cuming, G. J., *The Durham Book: Being the First Draft of the Revision of the Book of Common Prayer in 1661 Edited with an Introduction and Notes*. OUP 1961.

Donaldson, G., *The Making of the Scottish Prayer Book of 1637*. Edinburgh, University Press, 1954.

Hatchett, M. J., *Commentary on the American Prayer Book*. New York, Seabury Press, 1980.

Hatchett, M. J., *The Making of the First American Book of Common Prayer 1776–1789*. New York, Seabury Press, 1982.

McGarvey, W., *Liturgiae Americanae: or the Book of Common Prayer as Used in the United States of America Compared with the Proposed Book of 1786 and with the Prayer Book of the Church of England, and an Historical Account and Documents*. Philadelphia, Philadelphia Church Publishing Company, 1907.

> To know what was generally believed in all Ages, the way is to consult the Liturgies, not any private Man's writing. As if you would know how the Church of *England* serves God, go to the Common-Prayer-Book, consult not this nor that Man.
>
> John Selden (1584–1654)[1]

In other branches of Christianity the decisions of certain councils (for example, Trent) or the writings of particular leaders (for example, Luther, Calvin, or Wesley) or certain confessional statements (for example, the Book of Concord or the Westminster Confession) have possessed authority beyond that ever granted in Anglicanism to any council, individual, or confessional statement. A distinguishing mark of the Church of England at the Reformation was the establishment of one uniform liturgy. It was not long before apologists for the

Church of England would use as an argument in its defence the fact that in the Book of Common Prayer it possessed a liturgy true to the Scriptures, consonant with the practice of the early Church, unifying to the Church, and edifying to the people. As lines began to be drawn between Anglicans and Puritans, the principal distinguishing mark of the Anglican was allegiance to the Book of Common Prayer. In sermons and in the writings of theologians and apologists, the primary standard as to what an Anglican believes and as to how an Anglican is to serve God would become the Book of Common Prayer. Though it has been revised over the years and adapted for various provinces of Anglicanism, more than anything else it is the Book of Common Prayer which is a principal bond among Anglicans throughout the world (see pp. 51–64).

A push for liturgical reform gained momentum soon after Henry's break with the papacy. 'Marshall's Primer', the Ten Articles, the Royal Injunctions, the Bishops' Book, the Thirteen Articles, Hilsey's Primer, the Six Articles, the King's Book, the Rationale of Ceremonial, the reform of the Sarum Breviary, Thomas Cranmer's drafts for Daily Offices, the English Litany, Henry's Primer, the Book of Homilies, the Edwardian Injunctions, the English editions of the *Consultation* prepared by Martin Bucer and Philip Melanchthon for Archbishop Hermann von Wied of Cologne, the *Order of the Communion*, and the 'Cranmer's Catechism' would each in one way or another help prepare the way for the Act of Uniformity which required exclusive use of the Book of Common Prayer by Whitsunday 1549.

THE 1549 BOOK OF COMMON PRAYER

Some have said that the 1549 Book of Common Prayer was simply the Sarum rite simplified. Others have suggested that it was simply another German Church Order. The book does not fit either category, but has an integrity of its own. The sources covered a broad spectrum: the early Church Fathers, Eastern liturgies that had recently come into print in Latin, various uses of the medieval Roman rite, the Reformed Breviary of the Roman Cardinal Francisco Quiñones, various German Church Orders, especially the *Consultation*, various English Reformation formularies, and Cranmer's two earlier drafts for Daily Offices. Very few texts were retained from earlier sources without editing or without revision in the process of translation.

The title, *The Booke of the Common Prayer and Administracion of the Sacramentes, and Other Rites and Ceremonies of the Churche After the Use of the Churche of England*, indicates that in contrast to the various medieval uses there was to be one liturgical use throughout the realm. In place of the various books for the clergy (Missal, Breviary, Manuale, Pontifical, and Customary or 'Pie') one book, available at a reasonable price, was to serve both clergy and laity. The texts of the rites, in a language the people knew or were able to learn, were available to the laity for their instruction and edification and to enable them to participate in the public rites.

The Church year was simplified along lines common to German Church Orders. Morning and evening offices were provided for daily use; Wednesdays and Fridays were to be distinguished by the reading of the Litany and Antecommunion after Matins; and 'The Supper of the Lorde and the Holy Communion, commonly called the Masse' was to be celebrated on Sundays. The only holy days retained in the calendar, or for which propers were provided, were feasts of our Lord and the days of Apostles and Evangelists, St Stephen the protomartyr, the Holy Innocents, St Mary Magdalene, St Michael and All Angels, and All Saints.

From reading the Church Fathers, Cranmer surmised that the Daily Office of the early Church was grounded in reading 'all the whole Bible (or the greatest parte thereof)'. He eliminated non-scriptural readings. To assure that substantial portions of the Scriptures would not be omitted, he arranged the lectionary according to the civil calendar rather than the Church year. The New Testament, except for the Apocalypse, was to be read every four months, and the Old Testament every year, except for certain repetitive portions and 'certain bokes and Chapiters, which bee least edifying'. The whole Psalter was to be read every month. Clergy with cures were bound to say the Offices publicly rather than as private devotions. To simplify the offices for the people, many anthems and responses were omitted and the diet of canticles curtailed, principally to those retained in German Church Orders. The use of the Athanasian Creed was reduced to six times a year, on principal feasts.

Among the propers the Graduals, Alleluias, Sequences, Tracts, proper Offertory sentences and prayers, and proper Postcommunion sentences and prayers were all omitted. For the Introit, a short Psalm or a section of Psalm 119 was appointed, generally in course but sometimes related to the day. One collect of the day only was provided; many were fairly literal translations from the Latin, others were revised, and a number were new to the book, especially those for Saints' Days. The Epistles and Gospels were basically retained from the Sarum use.

The Litany, to be said after Matins on Wednesdays and Fridays, except for the omission of the invocation of saints, was that authorized in 1544, which was drawn largely from the Sarum Processional and from Luther's Litany.

Many of the changes in the eucharistic rite came from Cranmer's reading of the Church Fathers, others from his acquaintance with some Eastern rites and with German Church Orders (see pp. 273–4). All of the private prayers of the priest were eliminated except for the Lord's Prayer and the Collect for Purity which were to be said during the singing of the Introit. The Kyrie and Gloria in excelsis were to be sung straight through, rather than in a farced or troped form.

The Collect of the Day was to be followed by a Collect for the King. The Epistle was to be followed immediately by the Gospel and the Nicene Creed. A sermon or one of the authorized homilies, or a portion thereof, was required. An exhortation to worthy receiving of Communion, drawn largely from German sources, followed. At the Offertory the people were to place alms in the poor men's box and the bread and wine, which was to be furnished by the communicants in turn, was to be placed on the altar. The whole of the eucharistic prayer was to be said aloud. The Prayer for the Whole State of Christ's Church portion derived from both the Roman Canon and German Prayers of the People. The remainder of the prayer drew upon the Roman Canon, the Greek Liturgy of St Chrysostom (for the epiclesis), German and English Reformation formularies, and the writings of St Basil. The amplified Institution Narrative of the Roman rite was replaced by one which was a conflation but relied entirely on the scriptural accounts. The prayer is a careful theological statement about sacrifice: Christ on the cross offered once for all 'a full, perfect, and sufficient sacrifice, oblation, and satisfaction, for the sins of the whole world' and he commanded us to 'celebrate a perpetual memory of that his precious death'; we offer this 'our bounden duty and service', 'our sacrifice of praise and thanksgiving', and the 'reasonable, holy and lively sacrifice' of 'our self, our souls, and bodies'. Since in the late medieval period eucharistic piety had come to centre on the elevation of the elements at the Institution Narrative, and Cranmer wished to recover a eucharistic piety centred on the receiving of the sacrament, the elevations which had been introduced at that point in the late thirteenth and fourteenth centuries were forbidden—the only ceremonial actions to be explicitly prohibited. Communion of priest and people was preceded by an invitation, general confession, absolution, 'comfortable words', and Prayer of Humble Access from the 1548 Order of the Communion, which was principally derived from Hermann's *Consultation*. This preparation for Communion form had precedents in the late medieval devotions which preceded receiving Communion outside the Mass from the reserved sacrament immediately after private confession. For the medieval form 'Behold the Lamb of God, who takes away the sins of the world' at the showing of the elements to the people prior to Communion, Cranmer pointedly substituted a new text: 'Christ our Paschal Lamb is offered up for us, once for all, when he bare our sins on his body upon the cross, for he is the very Lamb of God that taketh away the sins of the world; wherefore let us keep a joyful and holy feast with the Lord.' The 1549 book specified that wafers be 'without all manner of print, and something more larger and thicker' and that each 'be divided in two pieces, at the least', thereby recovering the symbolism of Christ's body broken and of bread shared. The people were to receive the cup as well as the bread. The Sentences of Administration were amplified from Lutheran sources ('given for thee', 'shed for thee'). Alternative Postcommunion sentences and a fixed Postcommunion prayer were followed by a blessing from the Lutheran tradition, beginning 'The peace of God which passeth all understanding ...'

Cranmer dealt in analogous manner with the other rites. The baptismal rite is preceded by a rubric stressing that baptism is a public act, for the receiving of the child and as a reminder to the people of their baptismal profession (see pp. 261–3). The rite begins with an exhortation on the necessity and meaning of baptism, which, like the rubric, is dependent on German sources. This is followed by Luther's 'Flood Prayer', common to many German rites, and by a signation accompanied by a form which is related to Thomas Aquinas' definition of the meaning of the Western medieval rite of confirmation. A translation of a German revision of an ancient prayer preceded the exorcism. Following German precedents, Mark's account of the blessing of the children is substituted for Matthew's; and this is used not in connection with the exorcism but as scriptural precedent for the baptism of infants. The Creed and the Lord's Prayer— remnants of the ancient *redditio symboli*—follow, with a slightly modified version of a prayer first found in the *Consultation*. A series of prayers drawn from an ancient Gallican source replaces 'The Blessing of the Font' of the Sarum rite. The threefold renunciation is not the traditional one of Satan, his works, and his pomps, but of the world, the flesh, and the devil. The threefold affirmation is followed by traditional questions concerning the desire to be baptized. The child, unless 'weak', is to be immersed three times. The Sarum postbaptismal anointing which preceded the vesting is omitted, but the giving of the remnant of the vesture is followed by an anointing associated with a form which uses a phrase, 'the unction of his Holy Spirit', common to medieval theologians in relation to the confirmation anointing, commonly considered the matter of that rite.

Having provided for the perpetuation of the medieval rite called 'confirmation' in the baptismal rite, the 1549 book set forth another rite called 'confirmation' which had precedents among the Bohemian Brethren and the German and Swiss Reformers (see pp. 262–3). This rite linked together catechetical instruction, ratification of baptismal promises, and admission to Communion. The Book of Common Prayer tied it more tightly to the bishop than its continental counterparts or even the medieval rite of 'confirmation'. The prayer for the gifts of the Spirit was revised. The ceremonial action was not an anointing as in the medieval rites, but a laying on of hands as in the German Church Orders. The imposition of hands was followed by the peace, a prayer derived from the *Consultation*, and a blessing. The order of the elements and portions of some texts resembled the medieval rite but the rationale was clearly that of the German Church Orders, though the rite could be performed only by a bishop.

The marriage rite was designed for celebration at a public Eucharist. It was drawn from the Sarum and York traditions, the *Consultation* and other German Church Orders, and the exposition of marriage in the King's Book. A homily was provided for use at the Eucharist, if the sermon did not expound upon the duties of husbands and wives. The couple was required to receive Communion on that day.

The Sarum form for the visitation, anointing, and Communion of the sick had come to be used principally for the dying; that of the 1549 book is intended for use not just with the dying but with any who are seriously ill. The book provides for Communion from the reserved sacrament on the day of a public celebration or for a celebration in the sick person's home on other days. The provisions derive principally from the Sarum rite and from the Cologne and Brandenburg Church Orders. An exhortation in the eucharistic rite commended private confession for those who could not through private prayer or a general confession quiet their consciences, and the visitation rite included an absolution to be used in all private confessions.

The 1549 book provided a burial rite which had four parts: the procession to the church or to the grave, the burial, a brief Office, and the Eucharist. The sources included the Sarum Manuale, German Church Orders, and the Diriges of English Reformation Primers. Prayers contained petitions for the departed, but the rite is far less penitential and more hopeful than its Sarum ancestor.

The ordination rites were not published until 1550 (see pp. 143–52). No provision was made for minor orders, or even the subdiaconate. The medieval rites had become so lengthy and complicated that there was debate as to what constituted the essential form and matter. The model and principal source of the ordination rites was a treatise *De ordinatione legitima* by Martin Bucer of Strassburg, which was modified by some rearrangement and by the inclusion of other material, principally from the Sarum Pontifical. The rites are preceded by a preface which asserts that the three orders of bishops, priests, and deacons existed from apostolic times, that admission to these orders was by 'public prayer, with imposition of hands', that these orders were to be continued in the Church of England, and that no one not presently a bishop, priest, or deacon should function as such in the Church of England without ordination according to these forms.

THE 1552 REVISION

From early in the seventeenth century it has been popular in some Anglican circles to idolize the 1549 book, but that book was not well received at the time. It was too radical for the Devonshire rebels and for such conservative bishops as Edmund Bonner, Thomas Thirlby, and Stephen Gardiner, and for priests who continued to use the old service books or to 'counterfeit Masses'. But, on the other hand, its revisions were not radical enough for the Norfolk rebels, or for continental Reformers such as Martin Bucer and Peter Martyr who now occupied prominent positions in the universities, or for the Anabaptists, or for some of the clergy and bishops, such as John Hooper and John Knox.

Many have written about the protestantizing tendencies of the 1552 revision, and there were quite a few. A penitential introduction was appended to the Daily Offices. Psalms were included as alternatives to the Gospel canticles. The Introits for the eucharistic rite were omitted. The preparation of the table at the offertory was dropped, and the eucharistic prayer drastically abbreviated. Communion was required three times a year rather than once. Different Sentences of Administration were substituted, and the 'Black Rubric' which denied 'any real and essential presence' inserted, and the curate is to have what remains of the bread and wine 'to his own use'. The exorcism and the chrismation were dropped from the baptismal rite, and the signation from the rite of 'confirmation'. The anointing and provision for Communion from the reserved sacrament were dropped from the Visitation of the Sick. The burial rite was simplified, the eucharistic propers for burial dropped, and almost all petitions for the departed eliminated. References to the chasuble, the alb, the tunicle, and the cope, and to candles on the altar, were deleted. In fact, use of the word 'altar' was totally eliminated. The giving of other instruments in addition to the Bible (cup and bread for priests, pastoral staff for bishops) was deleted from the ordination rites.

The 1552 revision certainly represented a move to make the book more acceptable to those more favourably inclined toward the continental Reformation, but it also brought back various medieval elements in an effort to reconcile conservatives. A few Black Letter Days, for example, were restored to the calendar, and a remnant of the octaves. The obligation to say the Daily Offices was laid on all clergy, not just those holding cures. The Athanasian Creed was to be said thirteen times a year rather than six. The late medieval custom of having the Epistle read by the priest rather than a clerk was restored. The stipulation that the bread and wine be furnished by the people in turn was dropped. The growing custom of the late medieval period, that people receive Communion kneeling, was made obligatory. (The 1549 book had not specified posture, and in some places priests had begun to administer to the people seated in their pews as in some of the continental Reformed Churches.) At various points the revisions of 1552 were reactionary rather than Protestant.

The Second Act of Uniformity, which enforced the use of this new book on and after All Saints' Day 1552, spoke of the old book as a 'godly order' that needed reform only because of misinterpretations and because of doubts as to the manner of ministration. That seems to be a pretty fair statement of the attitude of the revisers. Many of the changes were aimed at tightening rubrics and at stating explicitly what was implicit in the 1549 book.

For the first time several Occasional Prayers were provided. The Introits were dropped, and the propers for St Mary Magdalene. In 'The Order for the Administration of the Lord's Supper, or Holy Communion' the Lord's Prayer and the Collect for Purity were to be said aloud. Following precedents of medieval troped Kyries and of various Reformed rites, the Decalogue with the response 'Lord, have mercy upon us, and incline our hearts to keep this law' replaced the ninefold Kyrie. The Gloria in Excelsis was moved to the end of the rite. The sermon was followed by the collection of alms and the prayer for 'the whole state of Christ's Church militant here in earth', a revised form of the intercessions from the 1549 eucharistic prayer. Next came the exhortation, the invitation, general confession, absolution, and 'comfortable words'. The Eucharistic Prayer itself was drastically revised (see pp. 273–4). The Sursum Corda, preface, and Sanctus were retained but the Benedictus Qui Venit was reduced to one line, 'Glory be to thee, O Lord, most high'. This was followed by the Prayer of Humble Access, which had been a pre-Communion devotion in the 1549 book, and by a revised version of the paragraph which concluded with the Institution Narrative in the 1549 prayer. In it a petition for worthy reception replaced the epiclesis. Immediately after the Institution Narrative, Communion was administered to the people, who were directed to kneel to receive. Different Sentences of Administration, capable of a Zwinglian interpretation, replaced those of 1549. The administration was followed immediately by the Lord's Prayer and one of two Postcommunion prayers. The first of these was a truncated version of the final paragraph of the 1549 eucharistic prayer, the second a revised form of the 1549 Postcommunion prayer. The act of receiving Communion thus occurred in the midst of the revised 1549 prayer at precisely the place occupied by the elevations in the medieval rite—a deliberate attempt to substitute a piety centred on receiving the sacrament for one based on adoration of the consecrated elements. The bread for the Eucharist may be 'such as is usual to be eaten at the table'.

The initial signation, the exorcism, the vesting, and the anointing were all dropped from the baptismal rite. The renunciation, the affirmation, and the expression of desire for baptism were all framed as single questions, and only one immersion was required. Yet the rite incorporates a new bidding and thanksgiving which express more explicitly than any text in the 1549 rite the doctrine of baptismal regeneration. The anointing is gone but its place is taken by a signation on the forehead, the site of the medieval confirmation anointing (in contrast to the baptismal anointing on the crown of the head), accompanied by a text which echoes the medieval confirmation anointing form and is related to Thomas Aquinas' definition of the medieval rite called 'confirmation'. Changes in the 'confirmation' rite of the 1552 book only make more explicit the rationale behind the 1549 rite which had been spelled out in the writings of Cranmer and other Reformers.

The 1552 book in the Visitation of the Sick omitted the provisions for anointing and for Communion from the reserved sacrament or for abbreviating the eucharistic rite when celebrating for a sick person.

In the burial rites petitions for the departed were curtailed, and no special provisions were given for an Office or Eucharist, though accounts of burials down into the nineteenth century indicate that on occasion the body was carried into the church for a Daily Office and Eucharist before the burial.

The 1552 revision of the ordination rites eliminated directions concerning the vesture of the candidates, and did away with the delivery of any instruments other than the Bible.

THE 1559 REVISION

The 1552 Book of Common Prayer was in use for less than a year when Edward VI died and Mary ascended the throne. She restored the Sarum rite, but Elizabeth in 1559 brought back the 1552 book with some revisions. Most of the changes seem to have been aimed at conciliating those of more conservative leanings. The 'Black Rubric' was deleted. The 1552 Sentences of Administration were prefaced by those of 1549. An 'Ornaments Rubric' (subject to varying interpretations) restored the vestments of 'the Second Year of the Reign of King Edward the Sixth'. In 1561 a new calendar containing more than sixty Black Letter Days was issued. In 1562 a metrical version of the Psalter with a few hymns and metrical versions of certain Prayer Book texts was authorized for use before and after services and sermons—a concession to those enthralled with the metrical psalmody of continental Reformed Churches. During Elizabeth's reign, there was growing dissatisfaction with the Book of Common Prayer among those of Puritan persuasion.

THE 1604 REVISION

When James I came to the throne Puritans presented him with the 'Millenary Petition', which consisted largely of complaints about the 1559 book. The resultant Hampton Court Conference authorized a revision that made a few concessions to the Puritans—the chief one being the limiting of the ministration of private baptism to authorized ministers. On the other hand, Puritans were not altogether happy with the content of the addition to the catechism concerning the sacraments of baptism and the Lord's Supper, and were offended by certain other minor changes such as additional Black Letter Days.

THE 1637 SCOTTISH BOOK OF COMMON PRAYER

During the reign of James I, efforts were begun to bring Scottish practice more into line with the Book of Common Prayer. Finally, in 1637, an effort was made to impose a revision of the Book of Common Prayer on the Church of Scotland.

This book, often referred to as 'Laud's Liturgy', is now known to have been principally the work of Scottish bishops John Maxwell and James Wedderburn. It incorporated a number of features valued by the Scots and missing from the 1604 Prayer Book, including a presentation of the elements, an epiclesis, a breaking of the bread, and the liturgical use of deacons. It downplayed the Apocrypha, substituted the word 'presbyter' for 'priest', used the King James Version rather than the Great Bible for Scriptural passages, and incorporated other changes designed to make the book more acceptable to the Scots. But other features (for example, an increase in the number of Black Letter Days) were offensive, and it was still entitled 'Book of Common Prayer' and retained the basic format and contents of the 1604 book. Efforts to introduce this book brought a temporary end to episcopacy in Scotland.

THE 1662 REVISION

During the Interregnum the Book of Common Prayer was outlawed. At the time of the Restoration the Puritans presented their 'Exceptions' and Baxter's alternative liturgy, but by that time people anxious to restore the Book of Common Prayer were in control both in Convocation and in Parliament. Cosin prepared a draft for revision—'The Durham Book'—which made some concessions to the Puritans but was largely based on notes he and Wren had made earlier. Relatively few changes were actually made. Some occasional prayers and thanksgivings and the 'Sea Forms' were added, and a few changes were made in texts, among which were inclusion of a petition for the blessing of baptismal water and a commemoration of the departed. The most important changes were in the rubrics rather than the texts. Many of these came from the Scottish book of 1637 and represented a heightening of eucharistic doctrine: the bread and wine were to be presented at the offertory, the eucharistic prayer was given the title 'Prayer of Consecration', a breaking of the bread was restored, a portion of the eucharistic prayer was to be repeated if additional elements were needed, and remaining consecrated elements were to be consumed by the communicants rather than being given to the curate for his own use. The ordination rites were tightened against presbyterian interpretation. On the other hand, the Black Rubric was restored, though in a form that denied not 'any real and essential presence' as in the 1552 book but 'any Corporal Presence of Christ's natural Flesh and Blood'. The 1662 revision is still the official Prayer Book of the Church of England.

REVISIONS FOR OTHER PROVINCES OF ANGLICANISM

The newly acquired independence of the United States of America made a revision of the Book of Common Prayer necessary. Developments since 1662 caused it to involve more than accommodation to the changed political situation. Many of the Puritan and Laudian proposals had not died with the Act of Uniformity. Attempts at reconciliation were made through proposals for revision in 1668 and 1689. Some Anglicans published and used with small groups revisions based on Eastern liturgies, especially the Apostolic Constitutions. Additional rites were bound with Prayer Books printed for use in Ireland. English and Scottish Non-jurors revised certain rites. Latitudinarians published proposals for revision, as did the late-eighteenth-century 'Arians'. In 1784 John Wesley published a revision for American Methodists, and in 1785 King's Chapel, Boston, adopted a revision based on that of the 'Arian' Theophilus Lindsey. A number of people involved in the first American revision were familiar with and sympathetic to these various proposals and revisions.

The first American Book of Common Prayer of 1789 updated the language slightly, simplified rules on fasting, cut back on repetitions, abbreviated somewhat various pastoral offices, and allowed for a selective use of psalmody in the Daily Offices. It omitted the Athanasian Creed, allowed the Apostles' and Nicene Creeds to be used as alternatives, and allowed the omission of the phrase 'He descended into hell' or the substitution of 'He went into the place of departed spirits'. It deleted references to private confession from the Exhortation and the Visitation of the Sick, abridged the Benedictus Dominus Deus, and omitted the Magnificat and the Nunc dimittis. The most important feature of this revision was the inclusion of a eucharistic prayer, modelled after that of the Scottish 'Wee Bookies', which was much closer in structure and content to the historic eucharistic prayers than was the prayer of the 1662 book.

The only Prayer Book revision in the nineteenth century, other than the 1892 American, was the 1877 revision for the newly disestablished Church of Ireland. This book made some concessions to Evangelicals and did some tightening against the growing 'ritualism' of the period and against certain 'advanced' interpretations of the rites. The only changes made officially in the nineteenth century related to the English Prayer Book were the withdrawal of the State Services in 1859, the new lectionary of 1871, and the 'Shortened Services' Act of 1872 (see pp. 42–4).

A committee on 'Prayer Book adaptation and enrichment' of the Fifth Lambeth Conference of 1908 adopted certain principles for Prayer Book revision: adaptation of rubrics to custom; reduction of repetitions and redundancies; provision for enrichment, alternatives, and greater elasticity; substitutions for obscure or commonly misunderstood words; revision of Calendar and Tables prefixed to the book. The Prayer Book was soon revised in Scotland (1912 and again in 1929), Canada (1922), Ireland (1927), and the United States (1928). An English revision (1928) received the approval of Convocation but not of Parliament. In all of these revisions, most of the changes were in the interest of flexibility and enrichment. The most controversial aspects had to do with prayer for the departed and with changes in the eucharistic rites (in the eucharistic prayer or in the order of the components) which were seen as affecting eucharistic doctrine. In the following decades, similar revisions were made in various other provinces of Anglicanism.

REVISIONS SINCE LAMBETH 1958

The Lambeth Conference 1958 acknowledged that the time for more drastic Prayer Book revisions had come and set forth certain guidelines which were more fully developed by the Anglican Congress 1963. Since that time, most provinces of Anglicanism have revised their Prayer Book or have authorized 'Alternative Services'. These revisions have been carried out with the aim of returning to the sources, the biblical and patristic heritage, incorporating the results of liturgical scholarship, and adapting to present conditions and missionary and pastoral needs. These revisions attempt to make the language more intelligible, to incorporate social concerns, and to allow for more flexibility to meet needs of particular worshipping communities. Various provinces have participated in ecumenical groups developing common translations of texts (International Consultation on English Texts, or its equivalent for other languages) and have adopted common lectionaries, based on either the post-Vatican II Roman lectionary or that developed by the Joint Liturgical Group.

The newer books in the Daily Offices allow more flexibility and provide a richer diet of canticles and lectionaries more closely related to the Church Year. Some of the new books provide proper liturgies for major days, such as Ash Wednesday, Palm Sunday, Maundy Thursday, Good Friday, Easter (including a vigil), and Pentecost. In the eucharistic rite the new books allow more flexibility in the entrance rite, provide for an Old Testament Lesson and Psalm as well as a New Testament Lesson and Gospel, and provide alternative forms for the Prayers of the People. The Peace is restored, and also the four-action shape of the Liturgy of the Table: preparation of the table, eucharistic thanksgiving, breaking of the Bread, and Communion of priest and people. The eucharistic prayers of the new books have recovered elements of ancient prayers, normally including thanksgiving for creation and the incarnation as well as redemption, an eschatological reference, an invocation of the Holy Spirit in some form, and a concluding doxology. The oblation and epiclesis obviously continue to be matters of controversy in some provinces.

The revised rites of initiation differ greatly, but indicate some common concerns: indiscriminate baptism, confirmation as a rite for a mature reaffirmation, admission to Communion not tied to confirmation, parents admitted as sponsors and making promises, and ceremonial enrichment, including in some cases the use of chrism.

In several of the new books a thanksgiving for the birth or adoption of a child replaces the old churching rite. Some of the new books provide a rite for the reconciliation of a penitent. Other pastoral rites are enriched and made more flexible.

Though the revisions that have followed Lambeth 1958 have been the most radical revisions in Prayer Book history, they have been based on the same principles that were said to underlie the first Book of Common Prayer of 1549: (1) 'grounded upon the holy Scriptures'; (2) 'agreeable to the order of the primitive Church'; (3) unifying to the Church; and (4) 'edifying' to the people.

NOTES

1. *The Table-Talk of John Seldon Esq.: with a Biographical Preface and Notes by S. W. Singer Esq.* (London, William Pickering, 1847), p. 115.

2 The Articles and Homilies

PETER TOON

Applegate, S. H., 'The Rise and Fall of the Thirty-Nine Articles: An Inquiry into the Identity of the Protestant Episcopal Church in the United States' (*The Historical Magazine of the Protestant Episcopal Church of the United States*, l. 4, 1981), pp. 409–21.

Archbishops' Commission on Christian Doctrine, *Subscription and Assent to the 39 Articles: Report of the Archbishops' Commission on Christian Doctrine*. SPCK 1968.

Gibson, Edgar C. S. *The Thirty-Nine Articles of the Church of England*. Methuen & Co. 1904.

Griffith Thomas, W. H. *The Principles of Theology: an Introduction to the Thirty-Nine Articles*. Longmans, Green & Co. 1930.

Griffiths, John, ed., *The Two Books of Homilies*. OUP 1858.

Hardwick, Charles, *A History of the Articles of Religion*. Cambridge 1859.

Kidd, B. J., *The Thirty-Nine Articles*. London, Rivingtons, 1911.

O'Donovan, Oliver, *On the Thirty-Nine Articles: A conversation with Tudor Christianity*. Exeter, Paternoster Press, 1986.

Packer, J. I. and Beckwith, R. T., *The Thirty-Nine Articles: their Place and Use Today*. Oxford, Latimer House, 1984.

Turner, H. E. W. (with J. C. de Satgé, J. I. Packer, H. G. G. Herklots and G. W. H. Lampe), *The Articles of the Church of England*. Mowbray, 1964.

As part of the one, holy, Catholic and apostolic Church, the reformed Church of England proclaimed its doctrine and polity in relation to holy Scripture, the ancient creeds and certain contemporary theological questions and controversies in its Thirty-nine Articles of 1563/1571. By doing so the Church also made it clear upon what theological principles it had already produced its Book of Common Prayer (see pp. 121–30). Thus the Articles and the Prayer Book belong together both in the Settlement of Elizabeth (1559) and the later one of Charles II (1660–1662) (see pp. 8–21).

To the Prayer Book and Articles must also be joined the Ordinal (which Article XXXVI authorizes (see pp. 143–52) and the *First* (1547) and *Second* (1571) *Books of Homilies* (which Articles XI and XXXV authorize). The two books (bound together from 1623) present a lively, sermonic declaration of Christianity in terms of salvation by grace and faith in the context of the vision of, and call for, a renewed Church in a just society.

It will be our task in this chapter to examine the origins and contents of the Articles and Homilies, to notice their teaching in the context of the sixteenth century, to comment upon the way in which they have been interpreted within Anglicanism, and to note their position and authority within the Anglican Communion of Churches.

THE ARTICLES

Origins[1]

To find the effective origins of the Thirty-nine Articles, we must go back through the reign of Mary Tudor (1553–1558) and the young Edward VI (1547–1553) to the latter part of the reign of Henry VIII. After the break with Rome in 1534, three statements of faith appeared in order to identify where the Church of England was in the disputes of the time: they were the Ten Articles (1536), the *Institution of a Christian Man* (1537) which was known as the 'Bishops' Book', and *A Necessary Doctrine and Erudition for any Christian Man* (1543), known as the 'King's Book'. These represent the way in which the Church of England was being pulled by the old and new religious forces in one way, then another, in the changing theological climate of western Europe. However the Thirteen Articles (1538), which were never published at that time, represent a distinctly Protestant statement of faith in the theological agreement arrived at by Lutheran and English theologians.

They had met in England with the agreement of Henry VIII because it suited his foreign policy at that time to have a concord with Lutheran princes. What they produced, which owed much to the Lutheran Augsburg Confession (1530), may be seen as the first stage of the process which culminated in the Thirty-nine Articles of thirty years later.[2]

Archbishop Cranmer had many contacts with Lutherans and he had been prominent in the agreement involving the Thirteen Articles. And he was also the major figure behind the next stage of the process, the drafting, authorizing and publication of the Forty-Two Articles (1553). In between his original drafting and the production of the final version, they were examined by various bishops and advisors to the young king. Yet they had to wait for their appearance until other Protestant publications (for example the Prayer Books and the *First Book of Homilies*) had appeared; and, when they did appear, there was little time to enforce them, due to the death of Edward and the reign of the Roman Catholic Mary. There is some debate as to whether or not they were officially approved in Convocation; but they certainly appeared on 19 June 1553, accompanied by a Royal Mandate, requiring all clergy, schoolmasters and members of the universities taking their degrees, to subscribe to them.

The Forty-two Articles are certainly Protestant, that is, Reformed Catholic, in their positive teaching concerning the orthodox doctrines of the Trinity, the person of Christ and human sinfulness and concerning their particularly Protestant emphasis upon justification by faith, the Scriptures and the two gospel sacraments. They safeguard this Reformed Catholicity by the rejection of a variety of views being propagated by the radical reformers ('Anabaptists') and by the Church of Rome and medieval, scholastic theology.[3]

With the accession of Queen Elizabeth I in 1558 and her Settlement of Religion (1559), the Church of England reverted to her Reformed Catholicity as a Protestant Church. The production of the Thirty-nine Articles is to be attributed primarily to Archbishop Parker, a disciple and admirer of Cranmer. He made use of the recently published Lutheran Confession of Württemberg (which had been presented to the Council of Trent by the ambassadors of Württemberg in 1562) and account was taken of the Calvinist ('Reformed') views of the recently returned exiles from Switzerland and Germany.[4]

Essentially, the Thirty-nine Articles are a revised form of the Forty-two Articles and the former were approved, virtually in what became their final form, by the Convocation which met in 1562–3. When they appeared in print there were two changes from the manuscript copy agreed by the bishops in Convocation in February 1563. Article XXIX, 'Of the wicked who eat not the body of Christ', was omitted, and to Article XX was added the clause 'and authority in controversies of faith' to strengthen the teaching on the authority of the Church. The Queen and her Council were responsible for these changes made in the original Latin edition which came from the royal press. However, eight years later Article XXIX was replaced by Convocation and the clause on authority was also retained. Thus in 1571 the Thirty-nine Articles in their final form were approved first by Convocation and then by Parliament. There appeared official versions in both Latin and English, and the Bill that went through Parliament required their use in English, to be signed by all candidates for ordination. The full title was *Articles Agreed upon by the Archbishops and Bishops of both Provinces, and the whole Clergy in the Convocation holden at London in the year 1562, for the avoiding of diversities of opinions and for the establishing of Consent touching true religion.* In 1628 Charles I added a preface to the *Articles*, in which he stated that they 'do contain the true doctrine of the Church of England agreeable to God's Word' and he as 'Defender of the Faith and Supreme Governor of the Church' required all his 'loving subjects to continue in the uniform profession thereof'.

Doctrine

In drawing up and imposing the Articles the purpose of Cranmer and his colleagues was fourfold. They wanted to ensure that the Church of England was an apostolic Church in the sense that it taught apostolic doctrine : they desired to ensure that the clergy would be sound in their teaching and thus not expose the laity to unorthodox (radical or Roman) teachings : they wanted to have genuine unity within the Church (as the full title of the *Articles* suggests) : and they wished to set the perimeters of a comprehensiveness based upon the gospel.

There are various ways of indicating the themes of the Articles, by breaking them down into groups. For example, it has been proposed that there are four principal groupings of Articles, as follows :

   (i) The substance of faith (I–V) ;
  (ii) The rule of faith (VI–VIII) ;
 (iii) The life of faith, or personal religion (IX–XVIII) ;
 (iv) The household of faith, or corporate religion (XIX–XXXIX).

Within the last section the subgroupings are also reasonably clear, as follows :

  (a) The Church (XIX–XXII ; though the consideration of purgatory seems out of place) ;
  (b) The ministry (XXIII–XXIV) ;
  (c) The sacraments (XXV–XXXI) ;
  (d) Church discipline (XXXII–XXXVI) ;
  (e) Church and state (XXXVII–XXXIX).[5]

We now see why, in the title of the Articles, it is claimed that they are 'for the avoiding of diversities of opinions and for the establishing of consent touching true religion'. In the effort to set forth Reformed Catholicity, the writers of the Articles set aside troublesome views being propagated by the active sectarians ('Anabaptists'), by the traditionalist Romanists and by the growing band of Puritans. But they also sought peace in their attempts to provide straightforward statements of such doctrines as predestination and the descent into hell. Therefore, from one viewpoint, they are *pacificatory*, while from another they are *denunciatory*.

The Articles are certainly not ambiguous (when interpreted historically and contextually) but they are minimal in their requirements, leaving many secondary questions open. Bishop John Pearson rightly claimed in 1660 that :

The book [of Articles] ... is not, nor is pretended to be, a complete body of divinity ...
but an enumeration of some truths, which upon, and since, the Reformation have been
denied by some persons; who upon denial are thought unfit to have any cure of souls in
this Church or realm ...[6]

The Articles only lay down, within the mid-sixteenth-century situation, as much
as was necessary to secure Catholic faith and ordered life in the Church of
England: and they do not seek to go past the minimum. On the central issues of
the gospel they are full and exact. Yet they are as broad and comprehensive as
was deemed to be consistent with theological safety.

Apart from being conscientiously minimal, the Articles are also conscientiously
eclectic. As we have noted they make use of the teaching of the patristic period
for doctrines of the Trinity, Christology and original sin; of the Augsburg and
Württemberg Confessions for the teaching on the gospel and justification; and
of the teaching from Geneva and Calvinism/Reformed theology for sacramental
understanding (Articles XXV–XXIX). As a whole they present the Reformed
Catholicity of the *ecclesia Anglicana* and are (in the title of the first commentary
upon them) *The English Creede; consenting with the True, Auncient, Catholique and
Apostolique Church in all the points and articles of Religion which everie Christian is to
knowe and beleeve that would be saved* (1585, 1587 in two parts by Thomas Rogers).

Generally speaking, expositions of the Articles from the seventeenth to the
twentieth century have fallen into four types—(1) Evangelical and Reformed (2)
Broad Church and Latitudinarian (3) High Church and generally Arminian, and
(4) Anglo-Catholic.[7] Of course some expositors have had feet in two traditions of
interpretation. That there have been different traditions of interpretation is
generally acknowledged: it ought also to be generally accepted that, 'the Articles
ought to be read in the light of the situation out of which they came, and to
which they were addressed, and ... their words must be taken in the context and
the sense they bore at the time of writing, and their statements construed in the
light of the known views, assumptions and intentions of their authors.'[8]

THE HOMILIES

Origins[9]

As with the Thirty-nine Articles, so with the Homilies: their origins are to be
sought in the reign of Henry VIII and in the reforming zeal of Cranmer. Inspired
perhaps by his knowledge of Luther's collection of sermons for reading in parish
churches, the Archbishop had conceived the plan for a book of homilies as early
as 1539. It must be remembered that the office of preaching was highly valued
by the Reformers, for they saw it as the divinely-appointed way of taking the
truth of the gospel to the minds, hearts and wills of the people. And if the men

who were supposed to preach were ignorant, then they had to be given something good to preach (read).

In the Convocation of 1542–3 Cranmer was busy explaining why a book of homilies was necessary, and inviting men to write sermons for it. Not only must the gospel be proclaimed in all parishes, but also the errors of the ignorant and heretical must be prevented from being disseminated. By the end of the Convocation some sermons were prepared but, due to the opposition of the King, the collection remained in manuscript form. It was not until 1547, following the death of Henry VIII and the beginning of the reign of Edward VI, that Cranmer was able to bring his plan to fruition by releasing what we have come to call the *First Book of Homilies* of 1547. This book contained at least a couple of sermons recently prepared, but it appears that the majority of the twelve had been produced in 1542/3. As a doctrinal statement, set against the doctrinal publications of Henry's reign (to which we referred above when discussing the Articles), the Homilies represent the first, coherent statement of the reformed doctrines of salvation to be set forth by official authority in England. In particular they present a clear, unambiguous, 'Lutheran' statement of justification by faith; and, they replaced the 'King's Book' of 1543 as authoritative doctrine.

The Homilies were published with a preface by Edward VI, whose royal Injunctions of 31 July 1547 required every parish church in England to have a copy of the whole Bible in English, the Paraphrases on the Gospels and Acts by Erasmus (translated by Nicholas Udall) and the Homilies, and to use these three as the basis for reading, studying and preaching from the Bible. Thus the Homilies were part of a larger plan to bring the message of the word of God to the people of England.

They cover these topics: Reading Scriptures; the Sinfulness of mankind; Justification by faith; Apostasy: How to die well; Obeying magistrates, and Public and private morality. Apart from Archbishop Cranmer's contribution of four sermons, other writers included John Harpsfield (d. 1578), Bishop E. Bonner (d. 1569), Thomas Becon (d. 1567) and Bishop H. Latimer (d. 1555). The third homily on Justification is the most famous, since Article XI points to it for an authoritative exposition of the subject (see pp. 64–71).

Doctrine

It would be wrong to see these twelve sermons merely as teaching basic, biblical doctrine and morality. Taking various themes from the royal preface, Dr John N. Wall Jr has suggested that the contents of the Homilies

> are, quite specifically, to be read in order, 'as they stande in the boke'; in some sense, they form a unit, a collection specifically arranged to move in a progression of argument from a beginning toward a particular end. Second, they emerge as a way to meet specific needs—'the decays of religion' and 'the desire of subjects to be delivered from al

errors'—and to achieve specific goals—'to honor GOD, and to serve their kynge and to behave them selfes'—by specific means; 'the true setting furth of GODS woorde.' The Preface also defines the ends of the work in terms of moving 'the people to honor and worshippe almightie GOD, and diligently to serve hym.' It described what this means in terms of honouring God, serving the king 'with all humilitie and subjeccion' and 'godly and honestly, [behaving] them selfes towarde all men.' What is being evoked here is the vision of the *respublica christiana*, the true Christian commonwealth, that humanist vision of national life, which goes beyond matters of religious ceremonial or devotional practice to embrace total reform of all aspects of human society.[10]

Obviously both the Christian humanist, and the Lutheran soteriological, roots of the Homilies need to be seen in order to capture their original intention.

After being widely used in the reign of Edward VI, the Homilies had no official sanction during the reign of Mary but were effectively reintroduced by the Act of Uniformity of April 1559, since the rubric in the Communion Service requiring them to be read was unaltered in the modestly revised Prayer Book. Therefore a new edition appeared in 1559 bearing the sub-title, 'By her Grace's advice perused and overseen, for the better understanding of the simple people' and with the Queen's title changed from Supreme Head to Supreme Governor in the tenth homily. There was a further edition in 1562 whose Preface declared that her Majesty commanded and straitly charged the clergy to make right use of them.

In the Second Prayer Book of Edward VI of 1552, the following rubric is found after the Creed: 'After the Crede, if there be no sermon, shal follow one of the homelies already set forth, or hereafter to be set forth by commune authoritie'. The young king was at this time looking for the 'making of more Homelies': regrettably he never lived to see them appear.

The Second Book of Homilies was approved by Convocation in early 1563 along with the Thirty-nine Articles. However, the Queen and her advisers took a few months to review the twenty sermons (divided into thirty-eight parts) and some alterations were made. The book appeared in the summer of 1563 under the title: *The Second Tome of Homilies, of such matters as were promised and intituled in the former part of Homilies: sent out by the authority of the Queen's Majesty, and to be read in every Parish Church agreeably.*

Apparently Bishop John Jewel (1522–1571), author of the important *Apologia Ecclesiae Anglicanae* (1562), was the editor of this volume of homilies. Some sermons were written solely by him while others were adapted by him from a variety of sources. Both the present and the next Archbishop of Canterbury, Parker and Grindal, made contributions. In 1571 a further 'Homily against Disobedience and wilful Rebellion' written by Archbishop Parker was added, following the rebellion in the north of England in late 1569.

The *Homilies* of 1563 provide sermons for all the major festivals as well as for the rogationtide services of an agriculturally based society (13–17). They teach a powerful doctrine of conversion to God (20), of personal spirituality (4,7) and of moral standards for personal and family life (5, 6, 18, 19). They place great emphasis upon the need not only to attend but rightly to participate in the services of the parish church (8–9). The latter is to be truly a house of worship and prayer, suitably furnished for those who hear and live by the gospel (1–3). The 'Homily against the Peril of Idolatory' is exceptionally long, being about one quarter of the total before the addition of the further long sermon on rebellion in 1571. Even as Cranmer believed that justification by faith was the primary message that must be heard in 1547, Jewel held that in 1563 the primary message was the purity and right ordering of Christian worship—free from a medieval images cult. The Homilies are clearly Protestant, but they are not Puritan.

THE ARTICLES IN THE ANGLICAN COMMUNION

There have been, in the history of Anglicanism, three kinds of dispute about the Articles. In the first place the interpretation of the Articles was a central feature of the argument which raged between Calvinist and Arminian Anglicans. As late as the early nineteenth century, a distinguished theologian, Bishop Herbert Marsh of Peterborough (1757–1839), attempted rigorously to exclude from his diocese all clergy inclined to a Calvinistic interpretation. Secondly, throughout the eighteenth century there were disputes about the propriety of scholar-clergymen being tied by an oath of assent to doctrines which, on rational investigation, they might find to be untenable. In 1772 the Feathers Tavern Petition against clerical subscription attracted the signatures of about 200 liberal-minded supporters, and was debated, and defeated, in Parliament. Thirdly, associated with the Oxford Movement was a determination to interpret all merely Reformation standards in the light of the tradition of the undivided Church. Newman's effort along these lines in Tract XC (*Remarks on Certain Passages in the Thirty-Nine Articles*, 1841) provoked such a storm that it brought the series to an end.

The precise implications of subscription to the Articles, which has never been required of any but the clergy and, until the nineteenth century, members of the universities of Oxford and Cambridge, has received various accounts. Some have held the necessity of a very precise assent. Others, among them the seventeenth-century Archbishops Laud, Ussher and Bramhall, agreed in holding that clergy were not bound to agree at every point, merely to refrain from public dissent. At the end of the century the moderate scholar-Bishop Burnet of Salisbury (1643–1715) expounded the Articles as an expression of the comprehensiveness of the Church of England. In 1865 the form of assent for clergy of the Church of England was changed in line with these understandings. In 1975 a new Declaration of Assent accompanied by a Preface was produced in the Church of

England and incorporated in Canon C15. It runs as follows:

PREFACE

The Church of England is part of the One, Holy, Catholic and Apostolic Church worshipping the one true God, Father, Son and Holy Spirit. She professes the faith uniquely revealed in the Holy Scriptures and set forth in the catholic creeds, which faith the Church is called upon to proclaim afresh in each generation. Led by the Holy Spirit, she has borne witness to Christian truth in her historic formularies, the Thirty-nine Articles of Religion, the Book of Common Prayer and the Ordering of Bishops, Priests and Deacons. In the declaration you are about to make will you affirm your loyalty to this inheritance of faith as your inspiration and guidance under God in bringing the grace and truth of Christ to this generation and making Him known to those in your care?

DECLARATION OF ASSENT

I, A B, do so affirm, and accordingly declare my belief in the faith which is revealed in the Holy Scriptures and set forth in the catholic creeds and to which the historic formularies of the Church of England bear witness; and in public prayer and administration of the sacraments, I will use only the forms of service which are authorised or allowed by Canon.

One of the points of this declaration, which was largely prepared by Bishop Ian Ramsey, though amended by the General Synod, is that it relieved clergy of the Church of England from even that relatively unspecific assent by which they had been bound since 1865. Despite this, the Articles remain one of the authorities mentioned in Canon A5 of the Church of England:

The doctrine of the Church of England is grounded in the holy Scriptures, and in such teachings of the ancient Fathers and Councils of the Church as are agreeable to the said Scriptures. In particular such doctrine is to be found in the Thirty-nine Articles of Religion, the Book of Common Prayer, and the Ordinal.

It is in some degree a reflection of the foregoing history that the Articles do not have the same position in each of the Provinces of the Anglican Communion. The Churches of Ireland, Scotland, Wales, Australia, Canada and New Zealand, along with those of Uganda, Ruanda-Burundi-Zaire, Nigeria and West Africa have retained them. The Churches of Kenya and Tanzania make them an option an individual diocese may adopt. At least in their Constitutions the rest of the Churches do not specifically refer to the Articles. However, in some cases it is possible that there is an implicit reference to them when the claim is made that the same faith is shared with the mother Church of England.[11]

A deliberate attempt to demote the Articles can be seen at the Lambeth Conference of 1930, where the Report of a committee on the Anglican Communion defined the identity of the Communion in an ecclesiastical and doctrinal sense without reference to the Articles:

... the Anglican Communion includes [irrespective of geographical location, those] whose faith has been grounded in the doctrines and ideals for which the Church of England has always stood.

What are those doctrines? We hold the Catholic faith in its entirety: that is to say, the truth of Christ, contained in Holy Scripture; stated in the Apostles' and Nicene Creeds; expressed in the Sacraments of the Gospel and the rites of the Primitive Church as set forth in the Book of Common Prayer with its various local adaptations; and safeguarded by the historic threefold Order of the Ministry.[13]

A somewhat hasty decision along the same lines was taken in the closing hours of the 1968 Lambeth Conference, when, against the advice of Bishop Ian Ramsey, the Conference bishops voted strongly for the proposal that each Province of the Communion should (a) consider whether the Articles needed to be bound up with the Prayer Book; (b) no longer require assent to the Articles from its ordinands and (c) ensure that subscription to the Articles should only be given in the context of the full range of the inheritance of faith and within their historical context.[12]

It is evident that these decisions, whatever their authority (Lambeth Conferences have, of course, no legislative power), raise the question, whether Anglican Churches are to be thought of as 'confessional' bodies in the same sense as Lutherans (with the Augsburg Confession and other documents) or Presbyterians (with their confessions, e.g. the Westminster Confession.) Certainly some Protestants in the sixteenth century thought so; hence the inclusion of the Articles in *A Harmony of the Confessions of Faith of the Orthodox and Reformed Churches* (Geneva, 1581)—and this, despite the fact that the Articles do not cover all major aspects of doctrine—for example, eschatology is omitted.

However, in the developing Anglican tradition since the sixteenth century the (orthodox) tendency has been more to view the Articles as one strategic lens of a multi-lens telescope through which to view tradition and approach Scripture, than to treat them as the single doctrinal foundation of the Anglican Household of Faith. Therefore it was recommended in *Subscription and Assent to the 39 Articles* that the Articles be always printed in the same volume as the Book of Common Prayer and the Ordinal. The other important lens, on this way of stating their place, is the Catholic Creeds. Such an approach leaves open the possibility of a further 'lens' being produced by the Churches of today or tomorrow.

NOTES

1 The best study of the origins and history of the development of the *Articles* is still Charles Hardwick, *A History of the Articles* (Rev. edn; Cambridge 1859).

2 The text of the *Thirteen Articles* was found among the papers of Archbishop Cranmer and is printed both by Hardwick, op. cit., pp. 259ff., and by B. J. Kidd, *The Thirty-Nine Articles* (5th edn; London 1911), pp. 22ff.

3 For the text of the *Forty-Two Articles* see Hardwick, op. cit., pp. 275ff; and E. C. S. Gibson, *The Thirty-Nine Articles* (4th edn; London 1904), pp. 70ff., for the text in Latin and English.

4 The Württemberg Confession is printed in *Die Bekenntnisschriften der altprotestantischen Kirche Deutschlands*, ed. H. Heppe (Cassell 1855). For the Marian Exiles see C. H. Garrett, *The Marian Exiles* (Cambridge 1938).

5 In W. H. Griffith Thomas, *The Principles of Theology* (2nd edn; London 1930), pp. lix–lx.

6 J. Pearson, *Minor Theological Works*, ed. W. Churton (1844), vol. ii, p. 215.

7 Examples would be the expositions by (1) W. H. Griffith Thomas and D. B. Knox (1967); (2) Bishop G. Burnet (1699); (3) Bishop W. Beveridge, and (4) Bishop A. P. Forbes (1867–8).

8 *Subscription and Assent to the 39 Articles* (London 1968), p. 13.

9 The most accessible studies of the origins of the *Homilies* are provided by John Griffiths in the Introduction to the *Two Books of Homilies* (1858) and by John N. Wall Jr in 'Godly and Fruitful Lessons: The English Bible, Erasmus' Paraphrases and the Book of Homilies' in *The Godly Kingdom of Tudor England*, ed. John E. Booty (Wilton, Conn., Morehouse Barlow, 1981), chap 2. I also had access to the MS on the *Homilies* by Canon John Tiller of Hereford Cathedral: regrettably this has not yet been published.

10 Wall, op. cit., p. 91.

11 I am grateful to Miss Wild at the offices of the ACC in London for helping me to examine the Constitutions.

12 *The Lambeth Conference 1968: Resolutions and Reports* (SPCK and Seabury Press 1968), pp. 40–41. See also the Addendum on 'The 39 Articles and the Anglican Tradition' on pp. 82–3.

13 *The Lambeth Conferences, 1867–1930* (SPCK 1948), p. 246. See also Resolutions 48 and 49 at p. 173f.

3 Ordinals

PAUL F. BRADSHAW

Bradshaw, P. F., *The Anglican Ordinal: its History and Development from the Reformation to the Present Day*. AC 53. London, SPCK, 1971.

Brightman, F. E., *The English Rite*, vol. ii. (London, Rivingtons, 1915), pp. 928–1017.

Echlin, E. P., *The Story of Anglican Ministry*. Slough, St Paul Publications, 1974.

Hughes, John Jay, *Absolutely Null and Utterly Void*. London, Sheed and Ward; Washington, Corpus Books, 1968.

Whitaker, E. C. *Martin Bucer and the Book of Common Prayer*, AC 55 (Great Wakering, Mayhew-McCrimmon, 1974), pp. 176–83.

HISTORY OF THE ORDINAL

The first Anglican Ordinal was published at the beginning of March 1550 under the title, *The forme and maner of making and consecratyng of Archebishoppes, Bishoppes, Priestes and Deacons*. It is generally agreed that its primary source was an ordination service drawn up by the German Reformer Martin Bucer, who had come to England in 1549. In this Bucer had directed that, since there were three orders of ministers in the Church, changes should be made so that when a bishop was ordained it should be carried out 'more solemnly and at greater length' and when a deacon was ordained it should be simplified. This was in effect what was done in the three Anglican rites, that for bishops being also intended for use at the consecration of an Archbishop. The variations between them were effected mainly by the addition of elements adapted from the medieval ordination rites.

With the publication of the second Book of Common Prayer in 1552 (see pp. 126–9), the Ordinal was bound up with the Prayer Book, although it retained its own title page. A number of changes were made to it at this revision. Whereas the first Ordinal had directed that candidates for the diaconate and the priesthood should be vested in a 'playne Albe', and candidates for the episcopate in a 'Surples and Cope', in 1552 all these directions were deleted in response to protests from extreme Protestants who regarded them as encouraging the perpetuation of a medieval concept of the nature of the ordained ministry. At the same time, and for the same reason, the delivery of the symbols of office within the rites was modified. The first Ordinal had taken from medieval practice the custom of handing over to the newly-ordained something which symbolized their new role. Thus the medieval deacon had received a book containing the liturgical Gospels which he would read, the priest a chalice and paten, and the bishop, after having had the book of the Gospels laid on his neck during the imposition of hands, then received it along with the rest of the episcopal insignia (pastoral staff, mitre, ring, and gloves). The 1550 Ordinal had provided for the New Testament to be given to deacons, the Bible along with the chalice and bread to priests, and for the Bible to be laid on a new bishop's neck after the imposition of hands and a pastoral staff to be given to him. In the 1552 revision, however, whilst deacons continued to receive the New Testament, both priests and bishops were given only the Bible.

At the 1661/2 revision of the Prayer Book, some, albeit vague, directions about vesture were restored to the Ordinal: candidates for the diaconate and priesthood were to be 'decently habited', and a candidate for the episcopate was to be 'vested in his Rochet' and was to put on 'the rest of the Episcopal habit' during the rite, after the examination. Further alterations made at this time will be treated at appropriate points below.

REQUIREMENTS FOR ORDINATION

The rites were preceded by a Preface which, among other things, required candidates for the diaconate to be at least twenty-one years of age, those for the priesthood to be twenty-four years old, and those for the episcopate to be 'fully thirty years of age'. The minimum age for the diaconate was increased to twenty-three in 1575, although the text of the Preface was not amended to take account of this until 1662. Candidates for ordination were also required to be 'first called, tried, examined and known to have such qualities as were requisite'. Such a requirement was typical of the ordination practice of all mainstream Reformation Churches at this time, as they sought, on the one hand, to put an end to what they saw as the lax conditions of the Middle Ages when little had been demanded of ordinands, and on the other hand, to oppose the position taken by some extreme sects who denied the need for any formal admission to ministry at all. Thus, by 'called' was meant not the inner vocation of God, though that was always presupposed, but the outward mandate of the Church: no one 'by his own private authority' (to quote the 1550 Preface) might presume to execute the functions of the ordained ministry.

With regard to 'trial and examination' the Preface itself prescribes only that the candidate should be 'of virtuous conversation and without crime' and 'learned in the Latin tongue and sufficiently instructed in holy Scripture', though other regulations were subsequently made in canon law. Following earlier medieval practice, at the presentation of the candidates for the diaconate and priesthood (though not the episcopate) at the beginning of the rites, the archdeacon presenting the candidates affirms that he has examined them and thinks them to be suitable in their learning and 'Godly conversation', and an opportunity is given to the congregation present to allege any crime or impediment which would constitute a bar to their ordination. All three rites also include a series of questions addressed to the candidates concerning their beliefs and intentions, drawn from Bucer's service. Such public examinations were a universal feature of Reformed rites of ordination, and were modelled on similar questions which had been put to candidates for the episcopate in the medieval rites.

The Preface also directed that the diaconate was to be conferred on a Sunday or holy day, and that this was to be done 'in the face of the Church'—both these requirements being characteristic of all Reformed ordination rites and intended to restore ordination to the public event it had been in the early Church. Presumably these directions were also meant to apply to the conferring of the priesthood. No such instructions were needed in the case of the episcopate, since it was already the medieval custom for this to be restricted to those days, although at the 1661/2 revision an explicit note to this effect was appended to the title of the rite. At the same time the statement was added to the Preface that the diaconate was to be conferred 'at the times appointed in the Canon' (i.e. during the traditional Ember seasons) and only 'on urgent occasion' on another Sunday or holy day.

THE RITES

During the Middle Ages there had been considerable diversity of opinion among theologians as to what constituted the minimum essential features of an ordination rite. According to scholastic theology all sacraments were composed of two elements, 'matter' and 'form', categories derived from Aristotelian philosophy. In this context, by 'matter' was meant the material element used in the sacramental act and by 'form' the words which must necessarily accompany it. In the case of ordination, 'matter' and 'form' were not easy to define, not least because of the large number of ceremonies which had gradually been added to the medieval ordination rites, and as little was known at the time about the relative antiquity of many of them, some strange conclusions about the essential elements were often drawn. Some theologians believed that the matter and form for all the orders had been instituted by Christ himself, others that it had been left to the Church to determine what was appropriate in each case. Many believed that the ritual handing over of the symbols of office constituted the essential 'matter' of ordination, whilst others included the anointing or the laying on of hands. They usually designated as the 'form' the imperative formulae which accompanied these actions.

The Preface to the Ordinal cut through this confusion by turning to New Testament evidence and defining the essential ceremony of admission to office as 'public prayer, with imposition of hands', a conclusion which more recent scholarship has shown to concur with the practice of the early centuries of the Christian Church. There was, however, one significant difference. Whereas in the early Church the prayer had comprised both the petitions of the whole worshipping assembly (either in silence or in the form of a litany) and also a prayer for the candidate said while hands were laid on him, this was not the case in the Anglican rites. Its compilers appear to have understood the New Testament to be speaking only of congregational prayer preceding the act of ordination, and not of an ordination prayer for the candidate in close association with the laying on of hands. Thus in the rite for the diaconate prayer is made for the ordinands in the litany near the beginning of the service by means of a special suffrage and concluding collect, but then the ministry of the word and the examination of the candidates intervene before the imposition of hands itself, which is accompanied not by prayer but by an imperative formula, following the model of common medieval practice, although the form itself is a new composition: 'Take thou authority to execute the office of a Deacon in the Church of God committed unto thee; in the name of the Father, the Son, and the Holy Ghost. Amen.'

The rite for priesthood is similar, except that in this case there is a prayer immediately before the imposition of hands, taken from Bucer's rite, but it completely leaves out the central section of the original, which was a petition that the Holy Spirit might be poured out on the candidates, and so turns it into a

146

general prayer for the congregation instead. The imposition of hands here is accompanied by an imperative formula based in part on John 20.22–3, which had been used in this way in some medieval rites: 'Receive the Holy Ghost, whose sins thou dost forgive, they are forgiven: and whose sins thou dost retain, they are retained, and be thou a faithful dispenser of the word of God and of his holy sacraments. In the name of the Father, and of the Son, and of the Holy Ghost. Amen.'

In the rite for the episcopate, the litany with its special suffrage and collect is preceded by a bidding which claims that in praying before 'we admit and send forth this person presented unto us', the congregation is following the example of Christ, who continued the whole night in prayer before he chose and sent forth the twelve apostles, and of the Christians at Antioch, who fasted and prayed before they 'laid hands upon, or sent forth Paul and Barnabas'. On the other hand, there is also in this case a prayer for the candidate immediately prior to the imposition of hands, formed by the fusion of the beginning of the prayer from Bucer's rite with a free translation of part of the medieval ordination prayers, although the imposition of hands itself is again accompanied by an imperative formula, this time using material from 2 Timothy 1.6–7: 'Take the Holy Ghost, and remember that thou stir up the grace of God, which is in thee, by imposition of hands: for God hath not given us the spirit of fear, but of power, and love, and of soberness.'

In spite of the statement concerning prayer in the Preface to the Ordinal, these imperative formulae accompanying the imposition of hands came to be thought of by many Anglicans as the essential 'form' of ordination, and in the seventeenth century those in the rites for the priesthood and episcopate came under heavy criticism from Roman Catholics for failing to name explicitly the particular order being conferred. At the revision of 1661/2, therefore, the words, 'for the office and work of a Priest/Bishop in the Church of God, now committed unto thee by the imposition of our hands', were inserted into them, in an attempt to remedy this alleged defect.

THE THREEFOLD MINISTRY: BISHOPS AND PRIESTS

In contrast to the medieval ordination rites, which had portrayed the priesthood primarily in cultic and sacrificial language, the Anglican service, although retaining the term 'priest', instead stresses the ministry of the word and of pastoral care (see pp. 285–8). Thus one of the Gospels appointed is John 10, with its reference to shepherding the sheep, and the exhortation addressed to the candidates by the bishop speaks of them as having been called to be 'the Messengers, the Watchmen, the Pastors, and Stewards of the Lord, to teach, to premonish, to feed, and to provide for the Lord's family, and to seek for Christ's sheep'. The questions in the examination refer to teaching from the Scriptures, to ministering the doctrine and sacraments, and the discipline of Christ, to being diligent in prayer and study, to being an example to the flock of Christ, and to encouraging 'quietness, peace, and love' amongst those committed to their charge. Finally, after the imposition of hands, when the bishop hands a Bible to the newly ordained (together with the chalice and bread in the first Ordinal), he says: 'Take thou authority to preach the word of God, and to minister the holy sacraments. . . .'

The Ordinal describes the bishop as appointed to 'the government of the congregation of Christ', and modifies the questions in the examination of the candidate, which are derived from the rite for the priesthood, so as to emphasize the bishops's particular functions of maintaining the purity of doctrine, correcting and punishing the disobedient, and caring for the needy (see pp. 296–300). The prayer before the laying on of hands, using language taken from the medieval rites, speaks of him spreading abroad 'the glad tidings of reconcilement to God' and of using his authority for the good of God's family, and the formulae addressed to him after the imposition of hands refer to teaching and to shepherding.

Throughout the Middle Ages there had been a considerable theological debate concerning the relationship between the priesthood and the episcopate. Some regarded the two as distinct orders of ministry, but others held the view that the episcopate was simply a hierarchical rank or 'dignity' within the one order of priesthood, and preferred to speak of a bishop being 'consecrated' rather than 'ordained' to his office. Among the theologians of the Reformation it was widely accepted that the New Testament did not distinguish between bishops and priests, a belief shared by Thomas Cranmer, Archbishop of Canterbury at the time of the composition of the Ordinal and undoubtedly its chief architect.

Thus, although the Preface begins by affirming that 'it is evident unto all men, diligently reading holy Scripture, and ancient authors, that from the Apostles' time, there hath been these orders of Ministers in Christ's Church, Bishops, Priests, and Deacons', this does not necessarily mean that those responsible for framing the Ordinal were all agreed that bishops and priests constituted two separate orders. Just as the eucharistic rite of the 1549 Prayer Book seems to have been deliberately worded in a way which would encompass different understandings of the sacrament, so too certain features of the ordination rites appear to have been intended to permit the interpretation that those being appointed as bishops were not receiving a new order or new powers of the Holy Spirit, but merely the commission of the Church for a particular function.

Firstly, whilst the rites for the diaconate and the priesthood begin with 'an exhortation, declaring the duty and office of such as come to be admitted Ministers, how necessary such Orders are in the Church of Christ', no such rubric appears in the rite for the episcopate. Secondly, whilst the titles of the rites for the diaconate and priesthood speak of 'ordering', that for the episcopate uses the word 'consecrating' instead. Thirdly, within the rite for the episcopate itself 'ordain' and 'order' are not used, and even 'office' occurs only once, but 'consecrate', 'work', and 'ministry of a bishop' are found instead. Thirdly, in the bidding preceding the litany, the prayer made by the Church at Antioch before the commissioning of Paul and Barnabas (Acts 13.3) is cited as a precedent for what the congregation is about to do. Fourthly, the identity of bishops and priests in New Testament times is further emphasized by the use of 1 Timothy 3, which speaks of the qualities required in a bishop, as the Epistle in the rite for the priesthood as well as the rite for the episcopate; and by the use of Acts 20.17–35 as the alternative Epistle in the rite for the priesthood, since in verse 28 it describes the elders of the congregation at Ephesus as 'overseers' who are to 'rule the Congregation of God'. Finally, whilst the imperative formula at the imposition of hands in the rite for the priesthood begins, 'Receive the Holy Spirit . . .', that in the rite for the episcopate has, 'Take the Holy Ghost, and remember that thou stir up the grace of God, which is in thee, by imposition of hands . . .', which is at best ambiguous about whether a new gift is being conferred at this time or whether a gift received at a previous imposition of hands is being revived.

Puritans in the Church of England later fastened on many of these points to support their contention that a distinction ought not to be made between bishops and priests, but since by the seventeenth century the supporters of episcopacy did believe that bishops constituted a separate and distinct order, it is not surprising that some changes were made in the 1661/2 revision of the Ordinal. The words 'ordaining or' were inserted before 'consecrating' in the title of the rite for the episcopate, and 'ordained and' was inserted before 'consecrated' in the words used at the presentation of the candidate. Ephesians 4.7–13 was substituted for 1 Timothy 3 in the rite for the priesthood, and the reading from Acts 20 was transferred to the rite for the episcopate. Even two of the three alternative Gospels in the rite for the priesthood, Matthew 28.18–20 and John 20.19–23, both of which contained commissions to the Apostles, were transferred to the rite for the episcopate, presumably to show that bishops and not priests were the successors of the Apostles; and another Gospel, Matthew 9.36–8, was substituted in the rite for the priesthood.

Moreover, the word 'pastors' was deleted from that rite, so that the Puritans could no longer argue that the Church of England taught that priests as well as bishops were to rule over the flock of Christ: the word made an appearance instead in a new collect at the beginning of the rite for the episcopate, which also spoke of the bishop administering 'the godly discipline'. A reference to the bishop's 'well-governing' of the Church was added to the collect after the litany, and an additional question inserted in the examination now made explicit mention of his duty of ordaining. Finally, the imperative formula at the imposition of hand was also amended so that it now read: 'Receive the Holy

Ghost, for the office and work of a Bishop in the Church of God, now committed unto thee by the imposition of our hands. In the name of the Father, and of the Son, and of the Holy Ghost. Amen. And remember that thou stir up the grace of God which is given thee by this imposition of our hands . . .'

THE THREEFOLD MINISTRY: DEACONS

The concluding collect and rubric in the rite for the diaconate expect that deacons will pass from 'this inferior office' to 'the higher ministries' of the Church after a minimum period of one year in which they are to become 'perfect and well expert in the things appertaining to the Ecclesiastical administration'. Nevertheless, the rite contains a number of other features which suggest that its compilers viewed the order as something rather different from the mere stepping-stone to the priesthood which it had become in the course of the Middle Ages and which unfortunately it would continue to be even after the composition of the Ordinal.

Firstly, there is no reference anywhere in the rite to the Holy Spirit being bestowed through it, as there is in the case of the priesthood. The hymn 'Come Holy Ghost' is not used in the service, though it is in the other two rites; the imperative formula at the imposition of hands does not mention the Holy Spirit, but merely 'authority to execute the office of a deacon'; and the concluding collect of the litany attributes the appointment of ministers to 'divine providence' instead of to the 'Holy Spirit', which is the case in the equivalent collect in the rites for the priesthood and the episcopate. Indeed, the Holy Spirit is only mentioned once in the whole rite, and that is in the opening question of the examination of the candidates, which is not found in the other two services. This asks whether the candidates trust that they are 'inwardly moved by the Holy Ghost' to take upon themselves this office, a requirement almost certainly deriving from the account of the appointment of Stephen and his companions in Acts 6.2–7, used as one of the alternative Epistles in the rite, where the Apostles direct the people to choose men 'full of the Holy Ghost'. This suggests that the diaconate was here viewed as a creation of divine providence working through the Apostles, in which the authority of the Church to minister was given to men who had already received the Holy Spirit, in contrast to the priesthood in which the Holy Spirit was given to the candidates just as it had been bestowed upon the Apostles by Christ.

Secondly, the deacon is not portrayed as having merely liturgical functions, although those referred to in the medieval rites—assisting at the Eucharist, reading the Scriptures, baptizing and preaching—are still mentioned, but also as having the duty of searching out 'the sick, poor, and impotent people of the parish', a dimension which had disappeared from the office in the course of the

150

history of the Church and which other Reformers had already suggested was of its essence. In response to Puritan criticism that baptizing was not a normal function of the diaconate, this was restricted to occasions 'in the absence of the priest' at the 1661/2 revision.

THE MINISTER OF ORDINATION

The Ordinal assumes that the presiding minister at all ordinations to both the priesthood and the diaconate in the Church of England will be a bishop, and makes no provision for any alternative. At the consecration of a bishop it directs that the presiding minister is to be the archbishop of the province 'or some other Bishop appointed'. In accordance with ancient practice, other priests present at the ordination of a priest, and other bishops present at the consecration of a bishop, are to join in the imposition of hands on the candidate. Traditionally, at least three bishops were required to participate in the ordination of a bishop, and although the Ordinal does not specify any minimum number for this, two other bishops need to be there in order to present the candidate to the archbishop. In 1559, at the beginning of the reign of Elizabeth I, four bishops were charged with the duty of consecrating Matthew Parker as Archbishop of Canterbury, and the Scottish Ordinal of 1620 included a rubric directing that at least three bishops must consecrate a bishop, and four an archbishop. Subsequent consecrations have usually involved more than that number.

Nevertheless, this does not mean that the Church of England has always regarded this as the only method of ordination which was valid. The original intention in 1550 seems to have been to continue former practice because there was no compelling reason to change it. The evidence appears to suggest that in the sixteenth and seventeenth centuries the commonly held opinion among Anglicans was that where episcopal ordination was available, then it should be retained, but that in what were viewed as cases of necessity where this had not been possible, as for example in Reformed Churches elsewhere in Europe, then presbyteral ordination might suffice. An entirely different attitude was taken, however, towards those Puritans in England who had refused to accept ordination by a bishop and were ordained instead by presbyteries or by congregations, since no plea of necessity could be made in such cases. For this reason, when episcopacy was restored to the Church of England in 1660 after the period of the Commonwealth (see pp. 18–25), the bishops insisted on reordaining all ministers who had been ordained in some other way during that time.

It is hardly surprising, therefore, that when the Ordinal was revised in 1661/ 2, changes were made in it in order to require episcopal ordination as an absolute necessity for admission to the ministry of the Church of England. Whereas previously the Preface had simply stated that no one who was not already a bishop, priest, or deacon should be permitted to execute the office unless he were admitted 'according to the form hereafter following', it was now amended to read that no one would 'be accounted or taken to be a lawful Bishop, Priest, or Deacon' unless he were admitted 'according to the form hereafter following, or hath had formerly Episcopal Consecration or Ordination'. Since this requirement applied to ministers from all non-episcopal Churches, both in England and elsewhere, it thus effectively—even if unintentionally—resulted in the Church of England adopting a position which denied the sufficiency of non-episcopal ordination.

THE ANGLICAN ORDERS CONTROVERSY

From the sixteenth century onwards, Anglican orders were continually alleged to be invalid by Roman Catholic theologians. At first such attacks tended to centre on the claim that sufficient consecrating bishops could not be found when Matthew Parker had been appointed as Archbishop of Canterbury by Queen Elizabeth I, and that therefore both his consecration and those of all subsequent Anglican bishops were invalid. Fuel was added to the fire by the invention of the 'Nag's Head Fable' in 1604, which asserted that Parker had actually been consecrated in the Nag's Head Tavern, Cheapside, by a strange, illegal, and invalid rite; the flames of controversy were later fanned by the discovery that there was no extant record of the consecration of William Barlow, Parker's chief consecrator. Anglicans attempted to answer these historical doubts and subsequently relatively little emphasis was placed on them in the polemic between members of the two denominations; but there still remained allegations that the Anglican rites themselves were defective in matter, form, or intention, although there was considerable diversity of opinion as to what constituted the essential requirements of an ordination rite in these respects.

This long-running controversy finally culminated in the issue by Pope Leo XIII in 1896 of the Bull *Apostolicae Curae*, which declared that there had been defects of both form and intention in the 1550 rites for the priesthood and the episcopate: the imperative formula at the imposition of hands in the rite for the priesthood was not sufficient as the form because it did not definitely express the order of priesthood or its grace and power, nor were other prayers in the rite able to provide a valid form because they too were insufficient for a number of reasons, and especially because all references to the Catholic concept of sacrifice and priesthood had been deliberately removed from them. The same was true of the formula and prayers in the rite for the episcopate, and since their meaning could not change in the course of time, any alterations made in 1662 were in vain. Moreover, the substitution of a new rite for that approved by the Church with the manifest intention of rejecting what the Church did and what by the institution of Christ belonged to the nature of the sacrament clearly demonstrated that 'not only is the necessary intention wanting to the Sacrament, but that the intention is adverse to and destructive of the Sacrament'. The Bull concluded, therefore, that 'Ordinations carried out according to the Anglican rite have been and are absolutely null and utterly void'.

This did not finally settle the matter, and the debate continued, with Roman Catholics attempting to interpret and clarify the meaning of the Bull, and Anglicans challenging its reasoning. However, with the development of ecumenical dialogue and the emergence of a different approach to sacramental theology, the discussion about ordination and ministry between the two Churches has now begun to be conducted on an entirely different basis. Perhaps the one positive lesson which emerges from this whole story is that the validity of orders can never be satisfactorily determined merely by appeal to technical issues concerning rites, intention, or episcopal succession, but is intimately related to the recognition of the sufficiency of the faith of the ecclesial body in which those ministries are exercised and the ordinations performed.

MORE RECENT DEVELOPMENTS

Other provinces of the Anglican Communion tended at first to adopt the 1662 Ordinal with only the minimum changes necessitated by their different circumstances, but after the appearance of the unsuccessful proposals for a revised Prayer Book in England in 1927–8, certain features of the Ordinal included in it influenced revisions taking place in other parts of the Anglican Communion, the most notable being the introduction of an ordination prayer immediately prior to the imposition of hands in the rite for the diaconate, the insertion of a petition for the candidates into the equivalent prayer in the rite for the priesthood, and a strengthening of the existing petititon for the candidate in the prayer in the rite for the episcopate. It was, however, the rites of ordination drawn up for the Church of South India in 1958 which established a new pattern for Anglican practice. These dispensed with the imperative formulae at the imposition of hands and reverted to the primitive practice of an ordination prayer said while hands were laid on the candidate, and this has since become the standard arrangement in all recent Anglican revisions, among them the 1979 Book of Common Prayer of the Episcopal Church in the USA, and the Church of England's *Alternative Service Book 1980*.

4 Catechisms

JAMES HARTIN

A Revised Catechism: Being the report of the Archbishops' Commission to revise the Church Catechism. SPCK 1961.

Siegenthaler, D., 'Religious Education for Citizenship: Primer and Catechism' in J. Booty, ed., *The Godly Kingdom of Tudor England.* Wilton, Conn., Morehouse-Barlow, 1981.

Tompsett, F. H., 'Godly Instruction in Reformation England: The Challenge of Religious Education in the Tudor Commonwealth' and Booty, J. E., 'The American Church Since the Reformation; An emphasis on the American Experience', in Westerhoff, J. H. and Edwards, O. C. eds., *A Faithful Church: Issues in the History of Catechesis.* Wilton, Conn., Morehouse-Barlow, 1981.

Wilson, W. G., *The Faith of an Anglican: a Companion to the Revised Catechism.* SPCK 1980.

In the Anglican Communion we have a continuous history of the use of catechism since a catechism 'for children' appeared in the service of Confirmation in the 1549 English Prayer Book. Even in the 1960s when many new questions were being asked about the ways of Christian education, most Churches of the Anglican Communion took on the task of revising and enlarging the traditional catechism rather than making decisions to abandon its methods and basic content. A revised Catechism set out in 1962 in the report of the Archbishops' Commission to revise the Church Catechism is a good example of this process in the English scene. An earlier attempt at revision in 1887 had come to nothing. Other efforts had been made in 1926 and 1939. The English revised catechism was in 1971/2 taken up and used in the Church of Ireland with minor alterations. A similar process is seen at that time in the Churches of North America—and in the Church of India, Pakistan, Burma and Ceylon (1960). It was a period of catechism revision and enlargement to meet new needs.

The continued presence of the catechism in Anglican Prayer Books or in documents associated with them emphasizes the strong and consistent Anglican conviction that the members of the Church are to be encouraged to grow in personal understanding of the faith, in the devout practice of worship and in godly ways of life. We continue to witness to this hope by including a form of catechism alongside our liturgical documents. Certainly we have had wide-ranging criticism of the idea of 'catechism' as a learning by rote—but there is much evidence that the Church intends the material to be used by the catechist in a personal and flexible way. The very idea of question-and-answer is capable of wide extension in practice, and suggests an effective learning experience going on between teacher and student. In the world of education, many lectures and classes lead to sessions of question-and-answer in which what has been set out earlier in principle and broad statement can be analysed in a more immediate way; and so the information is absorbed into personal understanding. The method of catechizing seems to offer a way of bringing together the Church's double responsibility of teaching as clearly as possible basic tenets of Christian faith and life, and of doing so in a way which will awaken personal response in those who are taught. The ideal of catechizing suggests steady interchange between clergy and people in the Christian learning process. It implies also the use of the comparatively small local group. It also links the personal experience of learning in the local group with what is going on in the Church as a whole, so that there is some sense of all the members of the Church being formed in basic belief in much the same way. But of course in practice not all use of the catechism has gone on in these ways nor produced these results. George Herbert in the seventeenth century set out reasons for the country parson's use of the Catechism—'He useth and preferreth the ordinary Church Catechism partly for obedience to Authority, partly for uniformity sake, that the same common truths may be everywhere professed, especially since many remove from Parish to Parish, who like Christian soldiers are to give the word, and to satisfy the Congregation by their Catholic answers.'[1]

The term 'catechism' derives from various forms of a Greek word which means to repeat, like an echo. It may have been used to describe a teacher pronouncing a sentence to his pupils and then making them repeat it back to him. It seems to have been applied at first to elementary types of teaching and later to all kinds of instruction. An important element in its meaning was that of oral instruction by one person to another. Several of these nuances flow together in our use of the term 'catechism', with its particular emphasis on teaching by question-and-answer. The word catechism comes into use in this special sense in the early sixteenth century as part of the experience and process of Protestant Reformation. The use of the word is new in that period, but the emphasis on the need to teach the faith of the Church is not new.

The practice of instruction at times by question-and-answer was a regular feature of Jewish life. From that background it could pass easily into the life of the early Christian Church. Catechizing was the regular process of preparing catechumens for baptism – this form of instruction was not confined to a question-and-answer method. An important development of the whole concept of catechizing is seen in the famous catechetical school of Alexandria flourishing from the second to the fourth century. Here the work was basically that of theological education as teachers gave courses of lectures on the elements of the Christian faith—instruction going on at a different level from the regular preparation of people for baptism. We may assume that some of these lectures would be followed by the use of question-and-answer to ensure that the content of the lectures had been assimilated and understood, just as a lecture in the

155

modern university context may turn into something more like a seminar when the lecturer tries to discover, by some careful questions, whether his class has followed some difficult argument. The term 'catechetics' and others associated with the basic concept had then, and continue to have now, the connotation of instruction carefully given on a personal basis with the aim of arousing personal understanding, acceptance and response in the hearers.

In AD 400 we find St Augustine writing to a young deacon on the subject of catechizing. His letter gives the deacon, Deogratias, some valuable practical hints about methods of teaching the basic elements of the Christian faith and life. In the preface Augustine writes:

> You have told me, brother Deogratias, that at Carthage where you are a deacon, persons are often brought to you to be instructed in the rudiments of the Christian faith, in consequence of your reputation for possessing great resource and power in catechizing, on account of your knowledge of the faith, and your happy way of expressing yourself; but that you yourself always experience a painful difficulty in deciding how to set forth with profit to your hearers that very truth by believing that we are Christians.[2]

St Augustine's understanding of the process of catechizing included the need for conviction and understanding in the catechist and for effective gifts of communication. He expected that the catechist would be personally concerned to achieve a good response to his catechizing, so that the hearers would be set forward in their faith and life.

The specific task of 'catechizing' those preparing for baptism is set in new liturgical contexts in the medieval Church, but the responsibility of instructing the faithful continues to be emphasized. In England many manuals were available for use by the clergy and some 'primers' for the laity. Bishops and synods issued injunctions requiring the clergy to teach and explain the Creed, the Lord's Prayer and the Ten Commandments in English to the children and people for whom they had spiritual responsibility. In 740 Egbert, Archbishop of York, directs 'that every priest do with great exactness instil the Lord's Prayer and the Creed into the people committed to him, and shew them to endeavour after the knowledge of the whole of religion, and the practice of Christianity'. The emphasis here is on direct teaching by the clergy; there is no suggestion of a dialogue between clergy and people, such as the sixteenth century term 'catechism' was to imply. The Council of Clovesho (747) provides that priests shall explain, in the regular tongue, the Creed, the Lord's Prayer and the meaning and words of administration of Baptism and Holy Communion.

In the sixteenth century the early days of reform created fresh efforts to teach the faithful. Henry VIII and Edward VI issued royal injunctions about the teaching of the Lord's Prayer, the Creed and the Ten Commandments in English—the clergy are to teach their parishioners and to exhort all parents and householders to teach their children and servants the same, as they are bound in conscience to do. This attempt to involve parents and householders in teaching the faith of the Church to the young is reflected in Marshall's Primer of 1534 which contained 'A Dialogue Between the Father and the Son' expounding the baptismal covenant with the Creed and Commandments. 'It was natural therefore that when the new Book of Service was prepared, a Catechism should be placed in it, as an authoritative exposition of the profession and renunciation in Holy Baptism, and in connexion with the service of Confirmation, with directions for its use as the basis of a system of catechizing to be maintained on Sunday afternoons in each parish.'[3]

The title 'catechism' is first used to describe a body or book of Christian teaching in the early sixteenth century. The Reformation emphasized religious instruction, and this emphasis led to the writing of many catechisms. Martin Luther issued his *Shorter Catechism* in 1529, set out as a dialogue between father and son—this was to be the most famous of the sixteenth-century catechisms and remains a Lutheran standard work. In the Calvinist traditions the *Heidelberg Catechism* (1563) was to be equally important. The shape of Anglican preparation for confirmation was to be set by the catechism in the 1549 Prayer Book. The Roman Catholic Church produced many catechisms, some of which are really doctrinal expositions.

John Bossy in his recent *Christianity in the West 1400–1700* regards this widespread carrying to the people of catechism versions of Christianity as having, in the long run, more considerable effects than any other innovation of the sixteenth century. In the very early stages of the use of catechism, there was the hope of parents teaching children in this way in the home—this ideal lay behind Luther's *Shorter Catechism*—but very soon the emphasis in both Protestant and Catholic reformations was placed on the catechizing duties of the clergy.

> Hence the Church of England hierarchy was not out of step with the general practice of reformed Churches in taking it for granted that catechism was a parochial activity and that parishes would be well edified if their children spent Sunday afternoons learning by rote the obligations which had been undertaken for them at their baptism. There was also no obstacle, in the state of alarm inspired by the success of Reformation catechizing, to Catholic borrowing of the outlines of Reformation catechisms as a guide to their own efforts in the field, as the Jesuits did on a large scale.

The sixteenth-century catechisms were of course intended for the instruction of children after baptism, so that they might come to a real knowledge of what baptism had meant for them and so be prepared to take religious responsibility on themselves as they approached confirmation. This was in great contrast with the practice of the early Church, where catechizing was the preparation for baptism. It reflects the effective medieval separation of the initiation rites of baptism and confirmation. John Bossy analyses the effects of the sixteenth-century catechism teaching:

Catechism was well designed to instil obedience and mark out boundaries, between versions of the Reformation as much as between Catholic and Protestant, and it could be the foundation of a reflective Christian life. It was less well adapted to inspiring a sense of the Church as a *communitas*, a feeling for the sacraments as social institutions, or simply the love of one's neighbour.

The use of catechism was becoming an effective medium of instruction about behaviour and deference to parents and civil authorities—there was in the process an element of the desire to impart 'Christian civility' as an ingredient in a quiet and well-ordered community.[4]

The Church Catechism with which we are familiar makes its first appearance in the first Prayer Book of Edward VI in 1549. We find there the service of 'Confirmation, wherein is contained a catechism for children' (see pp. 262–5). The direction given is that those who are to be confirmed must be able to say in their mother tongue the Articles of the faith, the Lord's Prayer and the Ten Commandments—they must also be able to answer 'to such questions of this short Catechism, as the Bishop shall by his discretion appose them in'. The parish clergy are directed that at least once in six weeks upon some Sunday or holy day, they shall instruct children in the Catechism for half an hour before evensong openly in the church. Parents, masters and dames are to cause their children, servants and apprentices who are not yet confirmed to come for this instruction. In the Elizabethan Prayer Book the clergy are to give this instruction diligently upon Sundays and holy days before evening prayer. The Church of England now had a definite form of instruction in the faith of the Church— available for general use in the shape of a catechism. This was an important part of the effort to create a system of Christian education for the young.

The origins of this Catechism remain uncertain. The traditional attribution of it to Nowell is almost certainly wrong—there is a lack of evidence that he had written any catechism by 1549. It seem most natural to attribute the Catechism to Cranmer. Other names which have been suggested in this context are Goodrich, Bishop of Ely, and Ponet, Bishop of Winchester, whose catechism however does not follow the same structure and order as that of 1549, exchanging the places of the Ten Commandments and the Creed.

The Catechism of the sixteenth century was set out in four sections—the privileges and profession of a Christian, the Creed, the Commandments and the Lord's prayer. In 1604 the section dealing with the sacraments was added. This section was prepared by Overall, Dean of St Paul's, and incorporated elements of the catechisms upon which Dean Nowell worked in the 1560s and 1570s. The later sixteenth century was a time of great interest in the work of religious education in England, interest created by the need to instruct the people of the Church of England in their distinctive religious attitudes in contrast to the continued claims of the Papacy and the challenge of more extreme forms of Protestantism. Plans were made to produce catechisms for use with those who were already communicants and for use in schools. The developing schools provided further opportunities for instruction in the teaching of the Church. In 1662 the Catechism was printed in the Prayer Book as a separate item between the services of Holy Baptism and Confirmation—the title is altered from that of 1549 to replace 'child' with person. Since 1662, the title in the Book of Common Prayer has been 'a catechism, that is to say an instruction to be learned of every person, before he be brought to be confirmed by the bishop'. The clergy are diligently to instruct and examine the children in this Catechism—upon Sundays and holy days after the Second Lesson at Evening Prayer he may do so openly in the church. Here would seem to be the possibility of drawing the congregation as a whole into the experience of the children.

The use of the word 'person' lies behind such statements as that of Bishop Ashton Oldham of Albany USA in his book *The Catechism today* (1929)—'Just at the outset I wish to correct the very prevalent though erroneous impression that the Catechism is meant only for children. It is equally valuable and necessary for adults . . . the principles of the Catechism are essential for all who desire to make any progress in the Christian Faith.'[5] Through the centuries the Church has created a powerful tradition of teaching based on the Catechism, in the hope that this teaching of the young may become the foundation on which the adult Christian life can be built. The Catechism appears as we know it in the Prayer Book of the Church of England, but it has been adopted and used in variant forms through the Anglican Communion. In Canada and the United States a number of revisions have been made to update the use and content of the Catechism as a teaching medium for different age groups.

The ideal place of catechism in the work of a seventeenth-century priest is set out by George Herbert in his writing on 'A priest to the temple or the country parson his character and rule of holy life.' Herbert devotes a chapter to 'The parson catechizing' and concludes it all by insisting on the use in catechizing of homely dramatic illustrations to illuminate divine truth—'Doubtless the Holy Scripture intends this much, when it condescends to the naming of a plough, a hatchet, a bushel, leaven, boys piping and dancing; showing that things of ordinary use are not only to serve in the way of drudgery, but to be washed and cleansed, and serve for lights even of heavenly truths.' Herbert is very much aware of the need of a lively, personal and down to earth approach by the parson using the catechism; he has the material and the method, but he has to create the conditions of effective communication. 'The Country Parson values catechizing highly . . . He exacts of all the Doctrine of the Catechism; of the younger sort, the very words; of the older, the substance . . . He requires all to be present at Catechizing . . . that those who are well grown in the knowledge of religion may examine their grounds, renew their vows, and by occasion of both, enlarge their meditations.' Herbert views the use of the catechism as a progressive process—different groups of the people in the parish are at different stages of religious understanding, and so require different treatment. His understanding of Christian education is clearly from the cradle to the grave, and his great source of teaching material was 'the Church catechism to which all divinity may easily be reduced.' Herbert encourages the parson in catechizing to learn to ask his own distinctive and supplementary questions:

> Helping and cherishing the Answerer, by making the Question very plain with comparisons, and making much even of a word of truth from him ... this is an admirable way of teaching wherein the Catechized will at length find delight, and by which the Catechizer, if he once get the skill of it, will draw out of ignorant and silly souls, even the deep and dark points of religion ... At sermons and prayers men may sleep and wander; but when one is asked a question, he must discover what it is. This practice exceeds even sermons in teaching.[6]

In this century, many efforts have been made in revising and enlarging the Catechism in different Churches of the Anglican Communion. Efforts were made in England in 1926 and 1939.

In May 1956 the Convocations of Canterbury and York requested the Archbishop to appoint a Commission for the Revision of the Catechism. This was done in 1958, and the Commission reported with a proposed revised Catechism in 1962.[7] The statements of the members of this Commission give us a very well-considered view of the place of the Catechism in the 1960s. 'One of the first questions faced by the Commission was whether the catechetical form of instruction remained valid in the twentieth century ... the weight of opinion was on the side of retention. The question and answer method emphasizes the moral responsibility of each person for his actions. Its increasing use in various forms of publicity indicates that it is not to be discarded because it is out of date.' The Commission would be reinforced in their approach by the present increasing popularity of many kinds of quiz programmes on radio and television in which people create enormous interest among thinkers, as well as listeners and viewers, by long series of question-and-answer sessions.

The Commission decided against the suggestion of two catechisms, one for children and one for adults. 'Behind the use of any Catechism stands the teaching Church. The catechist is a most important person. It is for him to select from the Catechism, or to enlarge and amplify it; bringing in, no doubt, much material which different people would have liked to see included in the new Catechism but for which there is no room ... The Catechism is meant to be a tool in the hands of the teacher.' In producing the revised Catechism the Commission added considerably to the teaching given, and modernized the language. They gave attention to the changed social conditions of the day in which there is less distinction between social groups and strong resentment of any kind of paternalism. The revised Catechism added to the older form new material on church worship and the ordained ministry, on the sacraments and other means of grace, on the Bible, on Christian duty and Christian hope.

In the discussions which arose after the revised Catechism was published, two main sets of issues were clear. There is great difficulty in producing any form of catechism which will be able to meet the need to supply a brief but adequate statement of the faith of the Church and the responsibility asked of the Christian, and at the same time to set these out in a form which will meet the requirements of the teachers of the young in these days.

In *The Catechism and the Order of Confirmation* (1963), Canon Frank Colquhoun set out a pattern of preparation for confirmation based on the use of the Revised Catechism.[8] 'The value of the Church Catechism is that it is concise and comprehensive, simple and scriptural. It adheres firmly to the essential facts of the Christian religion and refuses to get side-tracked by secondary issues.' He quotes the famous statement of Archbishop Benson in 1891 : 'I believe that there never has been in the hands of any Church any manual representing the doctrines, the true spirit of the Bible, to compare with the Catechism of the Church of England.'

There remains within the Anglican Communion a great affection and regard for the Catechism. It continues to represent our experience of reformation in which we emphasized strongly the need for the people of the Church to be helped towards a personal understanding of the Christian faith. The method of the Catechism begins where people are, in their immediate human experience, and encourages them to think through their place in the Church, and to keep on discovering what membership means. At the present time we are examining again what baptism means and that is where the Catechism begins. To know ourselves members of the Body of Christ requires us to move on to deeper examination of all the implications of discipleship—and that is the way set out in the Catechism. The simple direct questions raise many issues which have to be explored—what are our basic beliefs in an understanding of reality, what are the principles which should shape our human life in community, what are the sources of guidance and strength as we face the tasks of humanity. The Catechism leads us into this exploration and analysis along the path of human experiment and growth in the framework of Christian belief. It is the way towards personal maturity, set at once in the worshipping life and fellowship of the Church and in the wider world of social reality where we need all possible encouragement in living by and witnessing to Christian principles of life.

A scrutiny of three recent Prayer Books of the Anglican Communion show three different possibilities for the future of catechesis. The *Alternative Service Book 1980* of the Church of England makes no reference to catechizing in its confirmation services, and does not reproduce any version of the Catechism within its text. The *Australian Prayer Book* of 1978 includes a Catechism which is a modern language version of the Catechism of 1662, with no alteration in sense whatever. The book has two forms of confirmation, the second of which makes no reference to the Catechism, while the first form contains the words

'Our Church requires that all who are to be confirmed should know and understand the Creed, the Lord's Prayer, and the Ten Commandments, and be able to answer the other questions in the Church-Catechism.'

By contrast with both those books, the proposed Book of Common Prayer of ECUSA (1977) contains a document called 'An Outline of the Faith Commonly Called the Catechism'. This document partly reflects the common catechetical tradition, but in structure is a systematic work, beginning with the heading 'Human Nature', and working through sin, covenant, Scriptures, sacraments etc., to end at 'The Christian Hope'. The question-and answer form is used throughout. The rubric states that the Outline is 'a point of departure for the teacher' and provides 'a brief summary of the Church's teaching for an inquiring stranger who picks up a Prayer Book'. The Outline is certainly an attempt to provide an alternative to adopting simply the contents of 1662, with the risk of its being ignored, or going the way of silence as in the Alternative Service Book.

The Catechism comes to us through our history and it carries within it distinctive sixteenth-century understandings. These understandings of Christian experience arose in a period of radical and complex change in almost every area of life. The framers of the Catechism in content and method aimed to give Christians a solid base of self-knowledge, personal understanding of basic Christian principles and high aspirations for Christian life in a confusing and demanding world. They hoped to teach the members of the Church to see the Christian life as human experience lived out fully in their own times and places, and to rely upon the work of grace being wrought in them by the divine initiative of God in Christ. Twentieth-century Anglicans find themselves in an equally confusing world with the constant pressure of rapidly changing situations. The basic concept and approach of the Catechism still point us to the authentic Christian responses to be made in our own kind of language in our contemporary situations in many forms of human society, where the greatest need is for some kind of consensus about the ultimate meaning of humanity. To think, to believe, to pray and to live in the Catechism way seems to be the essence of that elusive Christian experience which we describe as 'Anglicanism'.

NOTES

1 Wall, J. N., ed., *George Herbert: The Country Parson, the Temple* (SPCK 1981), p. 83.

2 Gwynne, Walker, *Primitive Worship and the Prayer Book* (Longmans Green and Co. 1917), p. 296.

3 *A New History of the Book of Common Prayer: On the Basis of the Work by Francis Proctor, Revised and Rewritten by W. H. Frere* (Macmillan & Co. 1955), pp. 599, 600.

4 Bossy, John, *Christianity in the West 1400–1700* (OUP 1985), pp. 118–120.

5 Oldham, G. Ashton, *The Catechism Today* (Longmans Green & Co. 1929), p. 2.

6 Wall, J. N., op cit., p. 83f.

7 *A Revised Catechism: Being the Report of the Archbishops' Commission to Revise the Church Catechism* (SPCK 1961).

8 Colquhoun, F., *The Catechism and the Order of Confirmation* (Hodder and Stoughton 1963), p. 15.

5 Standard Divines

JOHN BOOTY

Hill, W. S., ed., *Studies in Richard Hooker.* Cleveland and London 1972.
McAdoo, H. R., *The Spirit of Anglicanism.* New York and London 1965.
More, P. E. and Cross, F. L., eds., *Anglicanism: the Thought and Practice of the Church of England, Illustrated From the Religious Literature of the Seventeenth Century.* Milwaukee 1935; London 1962.
Neill, S. C., *Anglicanism.* Harmondsworth 1958.
Standing Liturgical Committee of the Protestant Episcopal Church in the United States of America, *Prayer Book Studies XVI. The Calendar and the Collects, Epistles, and Gospels for the Lesser Feasts and Fasts.* New York 1963.
Sykes, Stephen W., *The Integrity of Anglicanism.* London and New York 1978.
Wolf, W. J., ed., *Anglican Spirituality.* Wilton, Conn. 1982.
Idem, ed., *The Spirit of Anglicanism.* Wilton, Conn. 1979; Edinburgh 1981.

Although Anglicanism has no theologian comparable to Thomas Aquinas for the Roman Catholics, Luther for the Lutherans, or Calvin for the Calvinists, there have been certain theological writers whose works have been widely regarded as, in some sense, standards not only for faith and doctrine but also for public worship and personal spirituality. Such persons are defined here as 'Anglican divines'. There is no authoritative list of such divines, and different people of differing theological convictions would list different theologians. Nevertheless, there are some whose names would most likely be found on most lists, divines whose names appear in calendars of lesser feasts, those whose works are most often anthologized.

What constitutes an Anglican divine? Examining some of the most prominent in the sixteenth and seventeenth centuries, when modern Anglicanism was in process of development, we may begin by observing that an Anglican divine is a bishop or priest of the Church of England, a learned theologian who has bequeathed to posterity a body of writings. That corpus customarily includes a wide range of materials: theological treatises, polemical or apologetical tracts, catechetical works intended for the instruction of communicants, books and essays designed to counsel the faithful in making moral-ethical decisions, sermons, liturgical forms, prayers and meditations for personal devotions. The Anglican divines are persons committed to the faith as conveyed by Scripture and Creeds and embodied in the Book of Common Prayer; they therefore regard theology and prayer as a whole, after the example of the ancient Greek Fathers of the Church. Anglican divines are committed to the one, holy, Catholic, and Apostolic Church as embodied in the Church of England and defend that Church and its daughters and sons against its detractors to the right and to the left. Such persons adhere to a *via media* which is not a matter of compromise but a positive position, witnessing to the mystery and the universality of God and God's kingdom working through the fallible, earthly *ecclesia Anglicana*. Anglican divines on the whole regard Scripture interpreted through tradition and reason as authoritative in matters concerning salvation. They believe that Scripture presupposes the existence and activity of tradition and reason and thus co-operation between God and nature, God and humanity, the sacred and the secular. Authority for doctrine and the Christian life is not interpreted narrowly, therefore, but rather as dispersed. The rigid doctrine of infallibility is rejected. The distinction between things essential to salvation and things not (*adiaphora*) is frequently made (see p. 264). There is a largeness in their understanding, a constant impulse to reach out to all people and all nature in the realization of God's universal rule, as Creator, Redeemer, and Sanctifier, the Alpha and Omega. A close investigation reveals a constant devotion to Christ, an emphasis upon the incarnation as viewed from the perspective of the crucifixion. Over and over again in their writings they emphasize the doctrine of sacrifice, of God's self-offering in Christ, inspiring Christians to offer themselves, their souls and bodies, as a living and a reasonable sacrifice. This profound theological doctrine is both rooted in Scripture and in the liturgy of the Prayer Book, and helps to emphasize the Eucharist, eucharistic devotion and eucharistic living, in the Church. Such are some of the elements in a definition of Anglican divines. There assuredly are others and there admittedly are other ways of defining the term.

Who were the Anglican divines? The names of Hooker, Andrewes, and Taylor come to mind most readily, but when thinking of the formative period in modern Anglicanism many would add Hall, Laud, Ussher, Cosin, and others. A case can also be made for including the metaphysical poets, especially Donne and Herbert. Richard Hooker (1554–1600) comes first. He acknowledged his debt to John Jewel and was deeply immersed in the Book of Common Prayer. By extension, many would include Cranmer and Jewel as prominent among the Anglican divines, but Hooker rightly comes first. He was pre-eminently a theologian; his major theological work, *Of the Laws of Ecclesiastical Polity* (1593 seq.), had very great influence on those who came after him, and was the theological writing most often consulted through the years by those scholars concerned to understand the nature of Anglican teaching.

The *Polity* is a defence of English church government over against those who sought to restructure that government after the example of Calvin's Geneva and that of the Book of Acts; but it was far more than that. Its first book is a philosophical treatise of considerable profundity, and its eighth book is a treatise on Church and state widely noted in histories of law and of political theory. The much-debated sixth book contains a short treatise on repentance and church discipline that seemingly influenced the development of moral theology in England, as well as the *Devotions upon Emergent Occasions* and the Holy Sonnets of John Donne. The fifth book is central to an understanding of this complex yet rationally constructed theological masterpiece. A casual perusal reveals that it is the first systematic commentary on, and defence of, the Book of Common Prayer, and contains a very important dissertation on the incarnation. But there is much more to it than that.

The fifth book is the theological heart of the *Polity*, its central chapter, 56, being linked to Hooker's *Discourse of Justification*. Taken together the two places cited indicate the intensity of Hooker's conviction that salvation comes through Jesus Christ, that it is unmerited, and that at the very moment of justification the gift of the Holy Spirit is received, and habitual sanctification begins to be actualized (see pp. 67–71). In Chapter 56 of Book V this teaching is related to the concept of participation, which further deepens and universalizes his doctrine of sanctification and prepares the way for an understanding of the sacraments in which both baptism and the Holy Communion are means of participation in Christ and thus in God, baptism being the sacrament of justification and the Eucharist the sacrament of sanctification. It is not surprising that Hooker elected to emphasize the ends and purposes for which the sacraments are given— personal and communal salvation—and disdained to discuss whether or not, and if so how, the bread and wine become the body and blood of Christ. For him as for many others the consecration was in the use, not in the magical transformation of the elements.

Doing theology was thus for Hooker far more than an academic occupation or intellectual game. Theology involved prayer and was concerned with ultimate issues. Nor was his theological focus alone on the individual yearning for salvation. He had a deep awareness of the unity of all in God and of the vital importance of the community and especially the worshipping community. He wrote, 'God hath created nothing simply for itself, but each thing in all things, and of every thing each part in other have such interest, that in the whole world nothing is found whereunto any thing created can say, "I need thee not."' Here was the foundation for political and social action in years to come, as well as a basis for such interest in the natural world as that exhibited by John Ray (1625–1705), the priest and naturalist, author of *The Wisdom of God Manifested in the Works of Creation*. Finally, it should be noted that Hooker was a parish priest who ended his days in the country living of Bishopsbourne in Kent where he shepherded his flock, feeding his sheep the bread of life and the water of life. He represents a degree of humility often, but not always, found among Anglican divines.

Hooker provides a measure, a standard, by which to judge those who came after him. Lancelot Andrewes (1555–1626), who knew Hooker, ended his days as Bishop of Winchester. Andrewes wrote no *magnum opus* such as Hooker's *Polity*, but he left behind a much larger body of works than did Hooker. There are writings involved with controversy such as the *Tortura Torti* and the *Two Answers to Cardinal Perron*, defences of the Church of England against its Roman Catholic detractors. He was best known for his *Ninety-six Sermons* and his *Preces Privatae*, published posthumously. In these works the profound piety of this Anglican divine is most apparent, influencing many from his day to the present. In addition, there are catechetical works, such as his *A Pattern of Catechistical Doctrine* and his sermons on prayer and the Lord's Prayer. There are also liturgical contributions such as *A Form for Consecrating Church Plate*, and there is *A Manual of Directions for the Sick*. His fundamental theological position is best discovered in his sermons. Andrewes was united with Hooker in regarding the universe as a universe of grace, grace which does not destroy God's creation but perfects it. 'Nature, *qua natura*, is "good", yet imperfect,' he said, 'and the Law in the rigour of it not possible, through the imperfection of it. Nature is not, the Law is not taken away—"good" both; but grace is added to both to perfect both.' Reason as a part of the created order is thus not a hindrance but an aid. Reason is the candle of the Lord and all who resist this light of nature are *rebelles lumini*. 'Howbeit this light hath caught a fall, as Mephibosheth did, and thereupon it halteth; notwithstanding, because it is of the blood royal, it is worthy to be made up.' And grace comes to do just that. Here was a fundamental teaching of Andrewes, one that remained central in his thought throughout his life.

His sermons were impressive not only for their doctrine, but also for the manner in which they conveyed God's word. T. S. Eliot, in writing his poem 'Ash Wednesday', was inspired by Andrewes' image of turning, in an Ash Wednesday sermon on Joel 2.12–13. In that sermon Andrewes dwelt on turning as the inspired dancer might turn: 'Now at this time is the turning of the year . . . Everything now turning, that we also would make our time to turn to God in.' His Good Friday sermon on Zechariah 12.10 was a meditation with Christ on the cross held high before his auditory, water and blood issuing from his pierced side. We pierce him by our sins; he pierces us by his love. And from his pierced side flow the water of baptism and the blood of the Eucharist. 'Mark it running out, and suffer it not to run waste, but receive it.' Receive the blood we shall, at the holy mysteries this day. 'There may we be partakers of the flesh of the Morning Hart, as upon this day killed. There may we be partakers of "the cup of salvation", "the precious blood" "which was shed for the remission of our sins."'

R. W. Church in the nineteenth century honoured Hooker for his 'vindication on its behalf [of] the rights of Christian and religious *reason*, that reason which is a reflection of the mind of God'. He honoured Andrewes for his vindication 'on its behalf [of] the rights of Christian *history*'. Andrewes regarded the Church of England as belonging to the Church universal and its history beginning from Jerusalem. In his *Preces Privatae* he drew inspiration and much content from the Eastern as well as the Western Church, and prayed for all Churches ('catholic, eastern, western, British') as a member of the one Church to which all belonged. So long as Andrewes' influence was felt, Anglicanism would be neither ahistorical nor insular.

Jeremy Taylor (1613–67), fellow of All Souls College, Oxford, and Bishop of Down and Connor in Ireland, followed in the way of Hooker and Andrewes. In his voluminous works there are collections of sermons, and there is a manual of daily prayers called *The Golden Grove*, with its 'Credenda; or, What is to be believed', its 'Agenda; or, Things to be done', and its 'Postulanda; or, Things to be prayed for'. There is his great work of casuistry, *Doctor Dubitantium*, and there are the spiritual classics, *The Rule and Exercise of Holy Living* and *The Rule and Exercise of Holy Dying*. There are useful treatises such as *The Doctrine and Practice of Repentance* and *The Worthy Communicant*. There are edifying works such as his *Life of our Blessed Lord and Saviour Jesus Christ* and his *Discourse of Confirmation*. And there are apologetic works such as the *Dissuasive from Popery* and *An Apology for Authorized and Set Forms of Liturgy*. Taylor reminds us of the strong practical, ethical and moral thrust in Anglicanism, not only in the seventeenth century but throughout its history.

An avid concern for correct behaviour can pave the way for obscuring the truth in the doctrine of justification through the cultivation of pelagian zeal. Taylor has been faulted for straying from Hooker's understanding of justification and sanctification, but if he did, it was in large part because he shared Joseph Hall's concern—expressed most strongly in *The Divine Arte of Meditation* (1606)—that intellect, or correct doctrine, was being emphasized while the affections, and thus the modification of human behaviour in the light of the truth, were being neglected or ignored. Hooker himself urged that attention be paid to the end or purpose of the divine law; and thus, looking at the Eucharist, he argued that grace was given to change lives, not material elements. Taylor was concerned for changed lives, for repentance, for holy living and holy dying.

Furthermore, in his *The Liberty of Prophesying* Taylor contributed to the discussion concerning the distinction between essentials or fundamentals and *adiaphora*. Hooker had outraged Calvinists by arguing that it is sufficient to believe in salvation by Christ alone in order to be saved (belief, of course, issuing in acts of love). Taylor agreed with Hooker, citing Romans 10.9, and concluded that persons may deduce other doctrine from this central one, but 'no such deduction is fit to be pressed on others as an article of faith'. Nor is the Church to be followed when it goes beyond the legitimate task of making 'belief more evident' to add to that essential belief, making it 'more large and comprehensive', but in effect, narrower and more exclusive, possibly even false and tyrannical. Then, too, Taylor maintained the same basic understanding of reason as that taught by Hooker. 'By reason,' he said, 'I do not mean a distinct topic, but a transcendent that runs through all topics; for reason, like logic, is instrument of all things else; and when revelation and philosophy, and public experience, and all other grounds of probability or demonstration have supplied us with matter, then reason does but make use of them.' Such an understanding was losing ground in Taylor's day, the realm of reason being more and more limited to quasi-mathematical reasoning such as was necessitated by modern science. But the Hookerian view was to be perpetuated by the so-called Anglican divines.

The divines we have been considering were learned men, rightly designated in the saying: *clerus Angliae stupor mundi*; but they wrote no great summas or systems of theology. Rather they drew upon Scripture and tradition, especially the tradition of the early Church, its councils and doctors, and to a lesser but still important extent upon the great theologians of the Middle Ages and of their own times, interpreting in the light of God-given reason what they received from the past in order to explain the gospel, to defend the Church, to preach and teach, to counsel and advise, their intellects ranging through the cosmos, penetrating nature's mysteries, and yet regarding the ultimate with awe and acknowledging mystery and miracle.

Who were the successors of Hooker, Andrewes and Taylor? There were the rest of the Caroline divines, of course, and the Cambridge Platonists and their successors among the great Latitudinarians. In the eighteenth century there were the Wesleys and Whitefield. There were William Law and Joseph Butler— Law justly famous for *A Serious Call to a Devout and Serious Life*, and Butler for his sermons and his *Analogy of Religion*. Some critics will regret the omission of any discussion of learned churchmen such as Tillotson, Waterland, and Warburton, but none of them have had the influence that Hooker, Andrewes, and Taylor have had on subsequent generations.

As we approach the nineteenth century there emerge prominent Anglican Evangelicals, pre-eminently Charles Simeon (1759–1836), the author of many sermons, such as *The Offices of the Holy Spirit: Four Sermons preached before the University of Cambridge*. A major work was Simeon's *Horae homileticae: or, Discourses digested into one continued series, and forming a commentary upon every book of the Old and New Testament*. Simeon, along with William Romaine and others, was devoted to the Scriptures and taught the twin doctrines of the corruption of human nature through the fall and recovery through Jesus Christ by means of conversion. But while some of his fellow Evangelicals tended to slight the public worship of the Church of England as they promoted personal piety, Simeon was a defender of and an apologist for the Church's liturgy. He taught that 'the scope and tendency of our Liturgy is to raise our minds to the holy and heavenly state, and to build us up upon the Lord Jesus Christ as the only foundation of a sinner's hope'. He revered the Prayer Book in which 'truth, the whole truth, is brought forward without fear ... but also without offence; all is temperate, all is candid; all is practical; all is peaceful and every word is spoken in love'. While Simeon did not display the range of scholarly work found in the earlier divines he was nevertheless, at least much of the time, in tune with them.

In the nineteenth-century Church of England there were many who at least to some degree followed in the tradition of Hooker, Andrewes, and Taylor. Space is limited to naming but a few, and again I am concerned chiefly with persons who have served in some sense as 'standards'. There were, for instance, John Keble (1792–1866), Edward Bouverie Pusey (1800–82), and John Henry Newman while an Anglican (1801–45)—all men of influence. They had a wide range of interests and concerns from polemics, such as Keble's Assize Sermon and the *Tracts for the Times*, to homiletics (Newman's university and parochial sermons are still read and still merit attention); from theological works such as Pusey's *The Doctrine of the Real Presence* and his edition of St Augustine's *Confessions*, to devotional works such as John Keble's *The Christian Year* and Newman's edition of Andrewes' *Preces Privatae*. It was Keble who edited the first modern edition of the *Works* of Hooker. There are others amongst the leaders of the Oxford Movement who might be mentioned, such as Robert Isaac Wilberforce with his theological trilogy, crowned by his *The Doctrine of the Incarnation*; Richard Church, the historian of the movement and widely acknowledged preacher, historian, and essayist; and in the background, hovering over all, Samuel Taylor Coleridge. But for widespread influence it would be difficult to equal men like Keble, Newman, and Pusey.

Frederick Denison Maurice (1805–72), who served for years as Chaplain of Lincoln's Inn at the Inns of Court in London and died as professor of Moral Theology and Moral Philosophy at Cambridge, was a loyal priest, a founder of the Christian Socialist movement, and author of works ranging from the theological *magnum opus*, *The Kingdom of Christ*, to articles in the weekly *Politics for the People*. It is possible that his sermons were most influential, especially his *Lincoln's Inn Sermons*, but also the sermons published as *The Doctrine of Sacrifice* and *The Prayer Book ... and the Lord's Prayer*. With his doctrine of Christ as 'the head of everyman whether that fact is acknowledged or not', with his success in thus bridging the chasm developing between the sacred and the secular, with his view of reason as 'conversant with that which is universal as well as with that which is necessary', with his devotion to Scripture and the Church of the incarnate Lord, Maurice distinguished himself and took his place with the long procession of Anglican divines, and has influenced many since his own day.

Other names come to mind when contemplating the nineteenth century, such as Richard Whately (1787–1863) among the Noetics, Thomas Arnold (1795–1842) among the Liberals, and J. C. Ryle (1816–1900) among the Calvinist

169

Evangelicals, but they cannot stand comparison with the Cambridge triumvirate of Lightfoot, Hort, and Westcott. Joseph Barber Lightfoot (1828–89), Bishop of Durham, wrote commentaries on Paul's epistles, edited the works of the Apostolic Fathers, wrote on the Christian ministry and preached sermons subsequently collected in numerous volumes. F. J. A. Hort (1828–92), Cambridge don and priest, edited the Greek text of the New Testament with Westcott, wrote commentaries on New Testament epistles, edited the works of Clement of Alexandria, and published lectures on *The Christian Ecclesia*, on the creeds, and on *The Way, The Truth, and The Life*. Brooke Foss Westcott (1825–1901), also Bishop of Durham, most clearly conforms to our early models, at least in his writings. He too was a biblical scholar, writing commentaries on New Testament epistles, publishing a survey of the history of the New Testament canon, of *The Bible in the Church*, and of the *English Bible*. He wrote major theological books such as *Christus Consummator* and *The Incarnation and Common Life*. He surveyed *The History of Religious Thought in the West* and lectured on the Apostles' Creed. He preached many sermons, subsequently published, and prepared *Common Prayer for Family Use*. In addition he applied his theological insights to the modern industrial world in books such as *Lessons from Work*, *Social Aspects of Christianity*, and *The Two Empires, the Church and the World*. As did Lightfoot and Hort, Westcott helped mediate the transition of Anglican thought as found in Hooker, Andrewes, and Taylor to the modern world of historical, biblical criticism, natural science, and industrial progress. He did this while professing belief that all people live in Christ: 'Life which Christ is and which Christ communicates, the life which fills our whole being as we realize its capacities, is active fellowship with God.' Furthermore, 'The coming of Christ, the Incarnation, binds together two worlds, and makes the earthly with all its workings a sacrament, so to speak, of the heavenly.'

Bridging the nineteenth and twentieth centuries there is Charles Gore (1853–1932), Bishop of Oxford, whose writings range from theological dissertations such as *The Reconstruction of Belief* to sermons, such as those on *The Deity of Christ*; from instructive works such as *The Church and the Ministry* to works dealing with modern problems, such as *Christ and Society*. In the twentieth century there is William Temple (1881–1944), Archbishop of Canterbury, with his theological trilogy, *Mens Creatrix*, *Christus Veritas*, and *Nature, Man, and God*, his popular *Christian Faith and Life* and his *Readings in St. John's Gospel*, his *Repton School Sermons* and his *Christianity and Social Order*. Temple was, and still is, a towering figure in Anglicanism with a spirituality that embraces the cosmos. For Temple the aim of the Christian life is fellowship with God, 'fellowship with Love—utter, self-forgetful and self-giving love'. Who else might be suggested for the twentieth century? Dare one suggest, amongst others, Austin Farrer, or Ian Ramsey, or Stephen Neill, or J. A. T. Robinson, perhaps? Only time will tell whether or not such men, prominent in their own time, will be remembered and remain persons of authority in time to come.

The designation 'Anglican divines' is not properly limited to Englishmen, however rooted it may be in the sixteenth- and seventeenth-century Church of England. Scotland may very well look back to Robert Leighton (1611–84), Professor of Divinity at Edinburgh University and Archbishop of Glasgow, author of commentaries and lectures on New Testament books, of theological and of expository lectures, of *An Exposition of the Creed, Lord's prayer, and Ten Commandments ...To which is annext a short catechism*, meditations, spiritual exercises, *Rules and Instructions for a Holy Life*, and many sermons. Leighton attempted to reconcile episcopacy with presbyterianism and thus heal the wounds dividing his country. In the process he wrote *A Modest Defence of Moderate Episcopacy*.

In Colonial America there is Samuel Johnson (1696–1772), one time teacher at nascent Yale College, Connecticut priest and pastor, the first president of King's College (later named Columbia University). Johnson was a learned man, author of a brief *Encyclopedia of Philosophy*, and defender of the Church of England in *Three Letters to Dissenters* and *Letters Concerning the Sovereignty of God*. He produced *A Short Catechism*, preached many carefully polished sermons, including *A Demonstration of the Reasonableness, Usefulness and Great Duty of Prayer* and *The Beauty of Holiness in the Worship of the Church of England*, and published *A Form of Morning and Evening Prayer*, and *Two Collects*, for private and family use. Johnson emphasized the incarnation as instrumental for our incorporation into Christ, 'so that by being united to our nature and dwelling in it, he is united to and dwells in us, and we in Him. Thus dwelling in the tabernacle of his Body he has united himself and dwells in mankind.'

In the Protestant Episcopal Church of the United States of America there is William Porcher DuBose (1836–1918), a teacher at the University of the South in Tennessee. Widely recognized as the most original and creative thinker the American Church has produced, author of numerous works, including *The Reason of Life, The Gospels in the Gospels, The Soteriology of the New Testament*, and *High Priesthood and Sacrifice*, DuBose was assuredly a learned and devout churchman of wide ranging sympathies and interests, but he is seldom read or referred to, save in passing, and as included in the American calendar. Others might be mentioned, including John Henry Hobart (1775–1830), Bishop of New York, William Meade (1789–1862), Bishop of Virginia, and others who for their times and places were learned, wrote theological treatises, gained reputations as influential preachers, provided materials for public and private devotions and (to recall the name of one of Meade's works) provided *Reasons for Loving the Episcopal Church*. Two other bishops warrant attention. One was Phillips Brooks (1835–93), Bishop of Massachusetts, a great preacher whose chief legacy has been volumes of exemplary sermons, but who also published works on *Baptism and*

Confirmation, on *Preaching*, on *Tolerance*, on *The Influence of Jesus*, and a collection of *Essays and Addresses, Religious, Literary, and Social*. As A. V. G. Allen has said, Brooks and others of Broad Church persuasion 'held with Hooker and Bishop Butler that the human reason was the God-given faculty for verifying the divine revelation'.

The second bishop worthy of note is Charles Henry Brent (1862–1929), Bishop of the Philippines and of Western New York. Brent was a Canadian born and bred, who served the Church in the distant Philippine Islands. An ecclesiastical statesman of consummate skill, Brent was also a thoughtful theologian, author of *The Commonwealth, its foundations and pillars*, *The Mount of Vision, being a study of life in terms of the whole*, and *Presence*. He was a deeply spiritual man, author of *Adventures in Prayer*, and concerned for the welfare of planet earth, as demonstrated in his *With God in the World*. And of course there are others, in the United States of America and elsewhere in the Anglican Communion. Amongst Canadians, in addition to Brent, who became a citizen of the United States, mention should be made of Philip Carrington (b. 1892), Archbishop of Quebec, author of a commentary on Mark, a history of the Church in Canada, a history of *The Early Christian Church*, and a treatise on *The Meaning of Revelation*.

Admittedly one could and perhaps should mention numerous others, prominent members of Anglican Churches around the world. But sufficient examples have been provided to point the way toward the identification of others. It should be added that the character of Anglican divinity is such that it allows for expansion and modification, as was required with the development of non-Anglo-Saxon Anglican Churches, especially in the southern hemisphere. Then too, it should be noted that this discussion of Anglican divines has been limited to men alone. With the ordination of women in member Churches of the Anglican Communion, this limitation will pass away. It is therefore appropriate to inquire who, among women in the past, future Anglican divines who happen to be women will be able to regard as predecessors.

There comes to mind Lady Ann Bacon, the translator of John Jewel's *Apology* (1564), one of the learned, devout Cooke sisters. And what of Queen Elizabeth I, her public utterances and her prayers? More seriously, there is the venerable Evangelical, Hannah More (1745–1833), with her tracts and treatises, her writings on St Paul and on *Christian Morals*, her *Practical Piety* and her *Book of Private Devotions*. However, there would be those who would justly complain that she was not very learned; and it is doubtful that she influenced many very far beyond her own time. But Evelyn Underhill (1875–1941) was certainly learned and remains influential among many Anglicans. Her major works were the scholarly classics, *Mysticism* (1911) and *Worship* (1937). She also wrote more popular books such as *The Life of the Spirit and the Life of To-day* and *The Fruits of the Spirit*. In her understanding of adoration, communion, and co-operation as representative of Trinitarian faith and life, Underhill summed up much that has been passed on and emphasized from the Anglican divines of the early generations. Theology and prayer are one in her writings, and she laboured to overcome the bifurcation of the sacred and the secular, individuality and community, and similar divisions.

Although she has not had the influence of Evelyn Underhill, the marks of the Anglican divines can be seen in the writings of Vida Scudder (1861–1954). Professor of English Literature at Wellesley College in the United States and an early member of the Society of the Companions of the Holy Cross, Scudder translated and edited the letters of Catherine of Siena and wrote a history of the Franciscans in their early years. She wrote fiction; a biography of James Huntington, the founder of the Order of the Holy Cross; *On Journey*, a spiritual autobiography; and the scholarly *The Life of the Spirit in Modern English Poets*. A socialist, she possessed a keen sense of the relevance of the Christian gospel to the social crises of her day, and wrote books on *Christian Citizenship*, *The Witness of Denial*, and *The Social Teachings of the Christian Year*. For Scudder as for Underhill and Maurice, Pusey and Simeon, for Hooker, Andrewes and Taylor, the concept of sacrifice was of central importance. 'Willingness to accept the death of God offered that we may live, to take the ever-renewed sacrifice into that ever-changing being which can otherwise not live at all, is the ultimate act of faith,' wrote Scudder. 'It is the seal on the awful mystery of interdependence, the lie forever to all attempts to live a self-sufficing life. Existence itself is a continual Communion, in which man feeds upon the universal God.'

In thinking of the expansion and modification of Anglican divinity it is important to note the prominence of certain laity, other than women, in the twentieth century. In England there are prominent, influential Anglicans such as C. S. Lewis with works ranging from the Narnia series and other novels to *The Screwtape Letters* and essays in Christian apologetics. In relation to Lewis one should also mention the barrister, Owen Barfield; the immensely creative Charles Williams; and another woman, Dorothy L. Sayers, who wrote theology, such as *The Mind of the Maker*, translated Dante, and contributed other works that were largely apologetic. T. S. Eliot, an American by birth but an Englishman by temperament, mediated Anglicanism to many people through his own devotion to and explanation of Andrewes and the metaphysical poets, as exemplary of that unified sensibility that he considered essential to the fullest humanity and found most fully in Prayer Book worship. In America during recent years there is William Stringfellow, praised by Karl Barth. Such Anglicans have exercised considerable influence, and have some claim to being considered in any list of standard divines; because, as loyal members of the Church and devout Christians, they have understood the coinherence of theology and devotion with personal and social life.

What is an Anglican divine? The answer to this question is to be found in the lives and theological writings of persons such as those mentioned in the course of this essay. There is no 'standard' or authoritative list of such theologians, there are only those people of learning and piety who have served the Church in the tradition identified with the *ecclesia Anglicana*, and whose influence has permeated the Anglican Communion in varying degrees down through the years.

6 Lex Orandi–Lex Credendi

W. TAYLOR STEVENSON

Clarke, W. K. L., ed., *Liturgy and Worship: A Companion to the Prayer Books of the Anglican Communion.* SPCK 1932.
Cross, F. L., ed., *The Oxford Dictionary of the Christian Church.* OUP 1958.
Ricoeur, P. *The Symbolism of Evil.* Boston, Beacon Press, 1967.
Stevenson, W. T., 'Is There a Characteristic Anglican Theology?' in *The Future of Anglican Theology.* New York and Toronto, Edwin Mellin Press, 1984.
Sykes, Stephen W., *The Identity of Christianity.* London, SPCK; Philadelphia, Fortress Press, 1984.
Trevelyan, G. M., *History of England.* London, Longman, Green and Co., 1945.
Wainwright, G., *Doxology: The Praise of God in Worship, Doctrine and Life.* New York, OUP, 1980; London, Epworth Press, 1982.

In Anglicanism, the worship of the people of God plays a very distinctive role, being the principal arena not only of supplication and praise but also of theological experimentation and formulation (see pp. 51–75). This relationship of worship and belief is often discussed under the Latin tag, *lex orandi, lex credendi*—'the law of praying is the law of belief'.

How did this distinctive situation emerge in Anglicanism, and what are its strengths and limitations? How is it possible to justify the process of having worship as the principal arena of theological experimentation and formulation? Are there ways in which this distinctive situation can be reappropriated, so that its strengths may be enhanced and its weaknesses diminished? If so, what difference would that make in relation to Church, sacraments, and ministry? It is the purpose of this essay to explore each of these questions in turn.

THE DISTINCTIVE ROLE OF WORSHIP IN ANGLICAN THEOLOGY AND SELF-UNDERSTANDING

There is not now, and there never has been, a distinctive Anglican theology. We have no Thomas or Luther, no Calvin or Zwingli. Nor is there any authority in Anglicanism which corresponds to the *magisterium* of the Roman Catholic

Church or the theological themes which provided the touchstones of theological inquiry of the Protestant Reformation. The pre-eminent theologian who is identifiably Anglican is Richard Hooker, whose late sixteenth-century *Laws of Ecclesiastical Polity* is respected but has never been definitive nor influential in any systematic way. *If* there is any theology which has been pervasively influential for Anglican thought, it is the conflicted, ambiguous, and largely Christologically-oriented patristic theology, which clusters around the first four ecumenical councils, culminating in Chalcedon (451) (see pp. 92–105). This theology, however, couched in the Hellenistic thought-forms foreign to the historical consciousness of the modern period, can only be one resource among many for Anglican theology.

What has been definitive for Anglicanism, from its inception in the sixteenth century until the present day, is the Book of Common Prayer in its successive editions (see pp. 121–33). The Prayer Book contains the daily offices of Morning and Evening Prayer, the forms for the administration of the Eucharist, Baptism, and the other sacraments; the litany; the Ordinal; the Psalter; and lesser rites and collections of prayers. Because the successive editions of the Prayer Book have been infrequent and conservative in spirit, it is fair to say that the first two Books of Common Prayer (1549 and 1552, respectively) together established the fundamental outline and spirit of Anglican theology and practice. The first made moderate changes in a Protestant direction; the second, reflecting the ongoing development within Anglican theology and practice during the period, continued those changes in a more thoroughgoing way. Hence, the contemporary concern to make Christian theology and Christian practice interdependent in a Christian 'praxis' was at least prefigured in the crucial liturgical experimentation which marked Anglicanism from its beginnings.

The formation of the Prayer Book of 1549 was presided over, and marked by the genius of, Thomas Cranmer (1489–1553); who, over a period of years, gathered, edited, and himself contributed to the collection of texts which eventually resulted in the formation of the first Prayer Book. Consequently, if it can be said that anyone is the definitive Anglican theologian, then that person is Thomas Cranmer. Cranmer, however, was not a theologian in the sense of somebody who produced systematic reflections upon theological topics. He was, rather, a priest and pastor; and, as Archbishop of Canterbury, an administrator and politician. In addition, he was in effect what we would call today a liturgiologist. His theology is formulated (1) in terms of the selection, arrangement, and composition of the prayers that are prayed constantly by Christian people, and (2) in terms of the rubrics which stipulate the permissible variations in the prayers and the ceremonial practice which accompanies them. In addition, the Prayer Book's 'Lectionary' stipulates, with some degree of latitude, which portions of Scripture are appropriate to be read in the worship of the Church during each week of the Church year. In these ways 'the law of worship is the law of belief': *Lex orandi, lex credendi.* The texts which are heard and prayed, according to the Book of Common Prayer, inform profoundly the Christian self-understanding and systematic theological reflection of Anglicans. This situation prevailed in Anglicanism during the Reformation in the sixteenth century, and continues to prevail to the present day.

Two aspects of the formation of the Prayer Book of 1549 need to be stressed because they are essential to the subject of this essay.

First, Cranmer's Prayer Book was an arena both for theological formulation and for theological experimentation. In formulating the 1549 Prayer Book, Cranmer drew upon Latin, Greek Orthodox, Lutheran, and other sources. During the decade prior to 1549, he had prepared certain major portions of the envisioned Prayer Book, and some of these were used experimentally in parishes in England. The theological and popular reactions to these experimental liturgies were taken into account in the formulation of the Prayer Book of 1549. The 1549 Prayer Book itself then became, in effect, the experimental text which was modified in the successive revisions of 1552, 1559, and (after a period of suspension of the use of the Prayer Book due to the ascendancy of the Puritans in England) 1662. In this process of liturgical formulation, experimentation, and reformulation, the reforming of the Church in England was effected which established a distinctive form of Christianity which was both Reformed and Catholic. In England, the 1662 Prayer Book continues as the legal Prayer Book until today, alongside recently authorized revised liturgies.

A similar process of theological formulations and experimentation has prevailed as the other Churches within the Anglican Communion have each proceeded to produce their own Prayer Book, including the first American Prayer Book (1789). Thus, the production of the American Prayer Book of 1979, the most comprehensive and theologically significant revision of any Prayer Book since 1662, was marked by this same process as successive 'trial' Prayer Books (or portions thereof) were formulated and then given to the Church for experimental use within the context of the congregational life of the American Episcopal Church. The reactions of those who prayed these 'trial' liturgies, week-in and week-out, were taken into serious account in the final formulation of the 1979 Prayer Book. It is significant that the variety of liturgical options permitted by this Prayer Book far exceeds anything that could have been imagined in previous centuries, and this flexibility in prayer both reflects and reinforces the flexibility in belief to be found in the pluralistic Church of the late twentieth century: *Lex orandi, lex credendi.*

WHENCE COMETH ANGLICANISM?: THE ENGLISH ETHOS

The Christian heritage of worship and theology available to the Church in England at the time of the Reformation was not substantially different from that available in many other areas of Western Europe. Why, therefore, did the distinctive approach to theological formulation and Christian self-understanding described above arise only in England? Historical questions of this scope do not have definitive or exhaustive answers because the issues involved are so complex. Nevertheless, there were political and social conditions present in England in the sixteenth century which were conducive to the unique way in which the process of *lex orandi, lex credendi* was manifested there. In addition, even a brief description of these conditions begins to uncover the strengths and weaknesses of this Anglican process.

These political and social conditions I will summarily denominate the 'English' or, more generally, 'Anglican' ethos. An ethos is made up of the predominant conditions and assumptions of an ethnic group; it is the underlying feelings which inform the beliefs and customs of that group. An ethos tends to be intractable because it consists of *underlying* assumptions and feelings, and because they are underlying they go unchallenged and thereby dominate the group. An ethos is a 'habit of the mind', but more importantly it is constituted by 'habits of the heart'—a way of being in the world. There are two aspects of the English ethos which are most important for the purposes of this essay, both well-known. First, there is the assumption that consensus, comprehensiveness, and contract is the normative mode for establishing and maintaining the order of society. The living-out of this assumption contributes to a prevailing absence of violent conflict, and reinforces the related assumption that the continuation of this condition is both desirable and feasible. Second, there is in the English ethos a certain pragmatism and lack of speculative interest in the approach to human affairs. These two fundamental aspects of the English ethos are interrelated and reinforce one another, and each needs some brief additional comment in order to clarify its pertinence to this essay.

Consensus, Comprehensiveness, and Contract

At least since the time of the Magna Carta (1215) the English were engaged in a halting but persistent struggle to transform their hierarchical medieval society. The strength of medieval society was that it imposed some degree of order upon its diverse economic-political components. The weakness of such a society was that the order imposed was limited, fragile, and brought with it the conditions of almost constant limited warfare.

Theologically, and notwithstanding the many accommodations which the Church made with it, this medieval ordering of society in England as elsewhere in Europe was in tension with the Christian vision of human life. That tension was expressed in such specific ways as the Church's imposition of periodic truces in warfare and in the practice of 'sanctuary', and more generally and ambiguously in the centuries-long struggle between Church and state which had, in England during the years 1162–74, reached a protracted, dramatic, and violent expression in the conflict between Archbishop of Canterbury Thomas Becket and Henry II. Pragmatically, this medieval ordering of society was less and less able to provide coherence and stability for a society in which there was the burgeoning of a sense of individual liberty (by the norms of the thirteenth century, not the twentieth), and in which self-contained local agriculture was being progressively modified by commerce and international trade.

Pragmatism

This was the context which enabled Magna Carta to be thinkable, and then to succeed. The 'Great Charter' is not only the first major document in the process of English constitutional development, but it also established the spirit of that development. The Great Charter was pragmatic. It established definite and practical remedies for temporary evils. There is very little in it which is abstract or theoretical. The barons who forced the Charter upon King John were not revolutionaries; rather, they acted to 'control the King through the Common Law, baronial assemblies, and alliances with other classes'. The barons acted with the active support of the 'freemen'. In a process of strong assertion followed by compromise, a 'middle way'—a *via media*—was found, which aimed at the most comprehensive consensus possible at the time. That consensus was established in a contract, the Great Charter, which was 'then subject to constant reissues, revisions, infringements, and reassertions'.[2]

Three centuries later, as we have seen, the first Prayer Book of 1549 was formed by a process remarkably analogous to that which produced the Great Charter. Cranmer and others built, over a period of a decade or more, not a consensus but nevertheless a pervasive climate of opinion, that the worship and belief of the Church in England needed to be changed; and this was not to be done in the spirit of revolution but rather of revision and amendment. A 'middle way' was sought between those who were inclined to look to the late medieval Church for guidance in these matters, and those who were inclined to look to the continental Reformation for that guidance. This 'middle way' was expressed in a 'contract', the Book of Common Prayer of 1549. The contract was a pragmatic one, eschewing for the most part matters of doctrinal speculation and controversy in favour of the practical matter of how the people of England were to worship week-by-week. It was understood from the beginning that this contract was 'then subject to constant reissues, revisions, infringements, and reassertions'. And so it continues to be until the present day. This continuity is the expression of the continuing English or Anglican ethos which, although it obviously finds different expressions in different historical periods and cultural situations, gives rise in analogous ways to a process of consensus, comprehensiveness, and contract.

Pragmatism and the Lack of Speculative Interest

The pragmatism of the English or Anglican ethos has already been noted in the preceding discussion. While it may be of very limited historical import, it is certainly appropriate that the only heresy associated traditionally with Britain is that of the British (or Irish) monk Pelagius (active 410–18) who argued that the individual, apart from divine grace, makes the initial and fundamental steps toward salvation. That is a practical, a 'sensible', idea. It is more significant historically, and quite in keeping with the English ethos, that English piety and theology has had an earnest Pelagian flavour extending from the Puritanism of the seventeenth century through the Evangelical movements of the eighteenth and nineteenth centuries. It was probably inevitable that the Salvation Army (1885), with its great stress on the moral side of Christianity, would arise out of this English ethos. To be English is 'to do one's duty', as the delightful lyrics of Gilbert and Sullivan's operettas make clear!

Why this pragmatic orientation arose specifically in England at least as early as the Great Charter is speculative and probably unanswerable.

What is important for our purposes, however, is that it did arise. It is embedded in the English constitutional process with its accompanying juridical system embodied in the 'common law', and it was to give rise to the British philosophical tradition of empiricism and to British leadership in the development of the natural sciences in the eighteenth and nineteenth centuries (see pp. 108–113).

THE STRENGTHS AND LIMITATIONS OF *LEX ORANDI, LEX CREDENDI* WITHIN THE ANGLICAN ETHOS

Strengths

The strengths of the process of *lex orandi, lex credendi* within the Anglican ethos are clearly manifested in the preceding discussion.

First and foremost, this process places a high value upon, and gives great respect to, the traditions which come together to form the Christian faith. More specifically, it is the liturgical expression of these traditions which is primary. This liturgy is, on the one hand, pervasively informed by the symbols, myths, and metaphors of Scripture and the traditions; but, on the other hand, Scripture and the traditions are appropriated by the believer within the context of the liturgy as it is prayed in the contemporary situation.

Second, the ongoing appropriation or ordering of the Christian traditions within the historical process can only be accomplished by the body of those persons within whom those traditions live, the Church. Third, the ordering of the traditions proceeds by means of the activity of reflection and negotiation which aims at a comprehensive consensus for the ordering of the Church and its relation to society. Fourth, the consensus reached at any given point in history is pragmatically formulated in liturgical contract, the Book of Common Prayer, which bodies forth the ordering of the Church and its relation to society in a way which is constantly available to all persons. Fifth, because the Book of Common Prayer is couched primarily in terms of the symbols and myths of the various liturgical texts, which by their nature are open to a number of interpretations, the way is left open for the development of a variety of forms of personal piety and of discursive theological systems, as long as those forms and systems do not come into open conflict with the Book of Common Prayer.

Collectively, these strengths result in the following general characteristics of Anglicanism. First there is a strong sense of tradition, continuity, and order. Second, there is a high ecclesiology (see pp. 219–231), because it is the Church which holds in trust the Book of Common Prayer upon which order is centred. Third, there is a high anthropology, because it is by means of rational human reflection, deliberation, and negotiation that the traditions of the past are brought again and again into a consensus which is adequate to the present. Fourth, because the traditions of the past necessarily are in tension with the need for a present consensus, a self-critical element is present which helps to protect Anglicanism against the idolatry of either past traditions or current reformulations. And fifth, because of its desire for consensus and its high anthropology, Anglicanism leans strongly in the direction of a critical yet positive orientation to human culture, for example, critical historical studies, the natural sciences, and the arts (see pp. 313–324).

Limitations

The limitations of Anglicanism are constituted by the reverse sides of its strengths. Thus, the proven strength of finding order and unity by means of careful respect for the liturgical texts of the Christian tradition, carries with it the tendency to expend a disproportionate amount of energy on historical and technical discussions of those texts, to the relative neglect of the contemporary restatement of those traditions which is so essential to the ongoing life of the Church. This tendency is countered in part by the positive orientation of Anglicanism toward interaction with its surrounding culture. Nevertheless, *lex orandi* tends to prevail in an unbalanced way over *lex credendi*.[3] Insofar as this happens (and there are notable exceptions) there is a betrayal of the Anglican quest for the 'middle way' which strives to achieve balance through the integration of the legitimate claims of both sides of an issue.

Another, closely related set of limitations arises out of Anglicanism's pragmatic desire to reach consensus through negotiation and to embody that consensus in a contract. This desire gives rise to the 'sweet reasonableness' inherent in Anglicanism, which is a legitimate dimension of the gospel of Christ. Its value in promoting order, unity, and stability in the Church and in society is readily demonstrable. At the same time, however, this pragmatic desire for reasonableness and order is prone to degenerate into a bargaining variety of compromise which loses sight of any vision of unity in favour of 'peace at any price' among the dominating elements of the society. The historical traditions are rehearsed and many points of view are acknowledged, but none is passionately affirmed and an evangelical stance is not assumed. When this spirit prevails it is impossible to sound the clarion call of the prophets, and those who do sound that call are *slowly* (thus preserving the semblance of 'peace') edged out of the Anglican community. The most notable instance of this process took place in relation to John Wesley's Methodist movement during the years from 1739, when Anglican churches were closed to him, to 1784, when the annual conference of Methodist lay preachers was provided with a legal constitution.

Anglican Limitations, Anglican Legitimacy, and a Way Forward

The limitations of Anglicanism's pragmatic interest in consensus, as well as its legitimate stress upon the centrality of liturgy and worship, can be placed in a wider perspective through an examination of the philosophy and implicit theology of the French Protestant, Paul Ricoeur (b. 1913). Ricoeur articulates the crucial problem for human discourse in general, and religious discourse in particular, from the eighteenth century until the present day. Technically stated, this problem is: Is the *Cogito* within being, or is it vice versa?[4] In less technical and in explicitly theological language, the problem may be stated thus: Is my life to be found within the reality of God, or is the reality of God derivative from me? This crucial problem is widely recognized, and it has been addressed also by Bernard Lonergan, Karl Rahner, Wolfhart Pannenberg, and many others. It is Ricoeur's reflections upon this central problem, however, with their great stress upon the function of symbol and myth in human discourse, which are most pertinent to the concerns of this essay. Consequently, it is to these reflections that I now turn.[5]

What Ricoeur would have us attend to is our lack of awareness of the transcendent order which is absolutely determinative for human life *as such*, that is, for human experiencing, imagining, reflection, and action. This transcendental order is referred to variously as the sacred, the holy, Being, God. However, named, the sacred addresses us and we respond to it by means of symbols and the narratives or myths which related the symbols to one another. It is this response which constitutes and informs human life in all of its dimensions.

It is easy to miss Ricoeur's point. It is not the case that the sacred is within us and therefore arises as a human construction, a product of human religious consciousness. The sacred is not first of all within us. Rather, we, together with all that we feel and think and do, are within the sacred. The sacred is indeed within every person, but only derivatively as it is mirrored or imaged there from its transcendent source. We are theomorphic; or, traditionally, we are created in the image of God.

What is the character of symbols which permits them to function in this way? Ricoeur writes:

'Symbol gives rise to thought.' This maxim that I find so appealing says two things. The symbol gives: I do not posit the meaning, the symbol gives it; but what it gives is something for thought, something to think about. First the giving, then the positing; the phrase suggests, therefore, both that all has already been said in enigma and yet that it is necessary ever to begin again and rebegin everything in the dimension of thought. It is this articulation of thought left to itself in the realm of symbols and of thought positing and thinking that I would like to intercept and understand.[6]

'Symbol gives rise to thought.' First the giving, then the positing is crucial for the concerns of this essay. *Lex orandi* has the priority, *lex credendi* is essential but logically and ontologically derivative. The dialectical relationship between the two halves is intimate and pervasive. When we first become aware of ourselves as human beings we are already engaged in thinking *about* the symbols. Nevertheless, the order is crucial: first the giving, then the positing. It is this order which situates us individually and corporately within God, and not vice versa. It is this order which is expressive of the intrinsically Anselmic character of Christian faith: faith in search of understanding, understanding in search of an adequate articulation of the faith which undergirds it, which in turn alters what is received. It is within this process that Christian preaching finds its essential and indispensable role; and this process continues throughout the life of the individual and of the Church.

For Anglicans, as for all Christians, this givenness of the sacred is manifested first and most fully in the symbols and mythic narratives which present the life, death, and resurrection of Jesus of Nazareth as he is remembered through the activity of the Holy Spirit in the Church. It is these given symbols and narratives which are enacted ritually, prayed, chanted, and sung. They constitute the icons of the Christ faith. Meaning appears *there*, just in these symbols as they are assembled in narratives. It is these symbols and narratives which are central and determinative for Christian faith.

Within the staggeringly complex world of symbols, everyone must begin from somewhere. Christians begin from the symbolic life of the ministry, death, and resurrection of Jesus as summarized in the Apostles Creed. This narrative is privileged. Other narratives and devotional practices, such as those associated with the lives of the saints, may be drawn into this privileged symbolic-narrative orbit. And, indeed, certain symbols and myths of other religions may be drawn into this orbit. In such instances, however, that which is received can only be received legitimately insofar as it is congruent with the privileged narrative of the Christ. It is from this given that positing proceeds, that the reflective articulation of faith begins.

The privileged symbols and narratives of the Christ live most fundamentally within Scripture as it is remembered and prayed within the liturgical worship of the Church. The individual's use of Scripture and prayer is dependent upon the more comprehensive experience of the Church. No Christian community or theology ever totally loses sight of the givenness of this dimension of Christian experience, and Anglicanism is most self-conscious and emphatic about it. It is this which provides the experiential and theoretical ground and thus the justification for Anglicanism's insistence upon the primacy of liturgy and the Book of Common Prayer in the life of the Church, together with its particular articulation of *lex orandi, lex credendi.*

If Anglicanism in particular has never completely lost sight of this dimension of its experience, it has too often permitted the centrality of symbol, myth, and worship to slip from the centre of its vision as it goes about articulating its theology and its life. When this happens, it is a violation of the intrinsic character of Anglicanism discussed earlier, a violation to which it is prone in part because of its tendency toward compromise, pragmatism, and order. The result, as is always the case when an individual or tradition loses its sense of identity, is a diffuseness and lack of creativity which serves itself and others poorly. Thus, while there have been significant Anglican contributions to theology in the twentieth century, particularly in the historical fields (Scripture, patristics, and liturgics), nevertheless Anglican theology in general has been marked by this loss of identity and creativity. Anglicanism's contributions to the Liberal theology of the early twentieth century were limited and modest, and its involvement in the mid-century's Neo-orthodoxy theology was almost non-existent. More recently, Anglicanism's participation in the properly dominant linguistic and hermeneutical concerns of the theology of the last thirty years or so have been restricted to the useful, but very limited, studies of Ian Ramsey and others concerned with the validity of 'God talk'.[7]

The way forward for Anglican theology, then, if it is to be true to the evangelical charge to proclaim the gospel to all the world, is not through some revolutionary new beginning but rather through an reappropriation of its lost vision of the centrality of *lex orandi, lex credendi* in the life and thought of the Church.

THE SYMBOL GIVES RISE TO THOUGHT:
THE REAPPROPRIATION OF *LEX ORANDI, LEX CREDENDI*
IN ANGLICAN THEOLOGY

A climate of opinion has emerged in Anglicanism and beyond affirming the necessity for the Church and for the Christian of an Anselmic movement of faith rooted in a participation in the process of *lex orandi, lex credendi* as described in the preceding section. The aphorism, the 'tag' if you will, which encapsulates that process is Paul Ricoeur's 'the symbol gives rise to thought.'[8] The aphorism in one sense only restates the Latin tag, but it restates it in a form which by affirmation or implication takes account in the following ways of our having moved through (not around) the great spiritual adventure which has proceeded out of the Enlightenment.

First, 'the symbol gives': we do not create symbols, rather we 'find' them. When we first become aware of ourselves as human beings we discover that we are living and thinking out of a matrix of symbols related to one another in the narrative structure of the myths embedded within our native language. These symbols give us our sense of identity, value, self-worth, and order both as a community and as individuals. In brief, the symbols give us our humanity. Thus symbols are manifestations of prevenient grace as they give us to ourselves; and in this sense we find symbols only because they first 'find' us. It is the Christian testimony that that which finds us is the sacred, is God; that the symbols are theophanies; that the privileged symbols and myths of this God are those of Scripture as these are received and lived by the worshipping Church; and that we live within this God whom we reflect or image. It is this situation which undergirds the priority which Anglicans give to prayer over belief, for the symbols around which prayer turns are theophanies.

In one sense this first affirmation pointed to by the phrase 'the symbol gives' only affirms what the Church has said from the beginning. It is now affirmed, however, in a way which recognizes explicitly the vital role of the human subject and language in forming our relationship with God. The recognition of this role has only become possible as a result of the preoccupation of Western philosophy and psychology with the human subject and with language from the latter part of the eighteenth century to the present. Further, this new way of affirming the priority of prayer is indebted to over a century of study of the history of religions (in which, significantly, Anglicans in their desire for comprehensiveness and consensus have played a prominent part) which has impressed upon us the centrality of symbols and myths in the forming of the consciousness and lives of all peoples. With the recognition of this centrality there comes a thoroughgoing recognition of the pluralistic and historically conditioned character of symbols and myths. There are different symbols and myths both within a particular religious tradition and between different traditions. The symbol gives, and it gives again and again in a historical process which is no more under our control than are the symbols themselves. Therefore, no one symbol or set of symbols, such as that of the Christian faith, can stand in isolation from the others. Nor can the symbols of any one tradition triumphantly assert its supremacy over those of another tradition. Rather, both the symbols within a single tradition and those of different traditions stand in a conversational relationship in which they criticize and complement one another. This is one manifestation of the working of the self-critical principle within the symbolic life. Consequently, while the claim for, and a commitment to, a privileged status for a particular symbolic tradition is both inevitable and essential for those who participate in that tradition, such a claim can only be made on the basis of human testimony and in the full recognition that there will be an ensuing conflict of testimonies which can only be resolved eschatologically. Stephen Sykes wisely points to this in relation to Christianity when he asserts that 'What Christianity entails [is] seen to be essentially contested', and 'Christian identity is, therefore, not a state but a process; a process, moreover, which entails the restlessness of a dialectic, impelled by criticism.'[9]

Second, 'the symbol gives rise *to thought*': if there is to be thought, there must be something to think about. What there is to be thought about are the symbols, the theophanies, which we find and thereby discover ourselves to be found. We are addressed by the symbols, and they demand our response. Our response is thought about the symbols, and this thought initially takes the form of placing the symbols in the narrative structure of ritual and myth, and then proceeds into theological speculation about the significance of these rites and symbols for every area of human activity. It is this process which constitutes religious consciousness. All human thought is rooted in this consciousness, and retains its vitality only insofar as it maintains that rootedness. As Sykes observes more concretely, 'Communal worship [in which the symbols, rites, and myths are continually rehearsed] ... is a theatre in which doctrine, ethics, myth, social embodiment, ritual and inward experience are integrally related.'[10]

All of this is a way of restating the place of *lex credendi* in its relation to *lex orandi*, but again it is restated with a difference. It is now seen that the 'law' of both prayer and belief (thought) is more aptly denominated as 'process' or 'life'. That was implied in the traditional Latin tag, but now it is explicit. It is necessary for this to have become explicit because, again, of the interrelated developments of the modern Western preoccupation with the human subject, with language, and with the emergence of critical historical consciousness. (These developments themselves are rooted in the eschatological and incarnational symbols of biblical and particularly Christian religious consciousness, although that subject cannot be pursued here.) Here all is process as the symbols give rise to thought, which modifies our perception of the practically infinite facets of meaning which inhere in the symbol, which in turn enables the symbol to give rise to new thought. And the process continues. Although it never loses its rootedness in the symbols from which it proceeds, the process is eschatologically oriented toward the new, the future. All claims to finality and completion fall under the rubric of suspicion, and the process continues.

185

IMPLICATIONS FOR CHURCH, SACRAMENTS, AND MINISTRY IN ANGLICANISM

The preceding exploration critically affirms Anglicanism's stress upon worship in general and the sacraments in particular as both a resource and a theatre for theological statement and exploration. The thought to which symbols give rise takes place first and most fundamentally within the context of worship and rite, as individuals standing within a community attempt to respond to and interiorize the presence of the holy which the symbol betokens. What are the implications of this appreciation of *lex orandi, lex credendi* for Church, sacraments, and ministry? Limitations of space will permit only the briefest of answers.

Church

On the one hand, the priority of the Church and its discipline of worship over the individual is strongly affirmed. It is the ritually-formed Church which is the bestower of the symbols which find us and bestow our humanity upon us. This is often an unpopular message in a society which careers back and forth between uncritical individualism and unthinking conformity to rapidly changing social trends. On the other hand, and for the same reasons, the Church is precluded from laying claim to final and exhaustive (idolatrous) answers to the ends of human life and the means of attaining those ends. The Church does not control, but is created by and is answerable to, the processive unfolding of the symbols, the theophanies of God. Because this is so, theology and the theological community are indispensable to the life of the Church. The symbols and myths do not change, but the doctrines, rituals, canons, and so on which proceed from the symbols and myths are continually changing and are always provisional. It is the unending task of theology to examine critically the question of the fidelity of what proceeds from the symbols to the symbols themselves. Anglicanism needs to be less restrictive in its attention to this task than it has been in the past.

Sacraments

On the one hand, the symbols, the theophanies of God together with the mythic narratives in which they are set find their most comprehensive and authoritative expression in the Scriptures of the Old and New Testaments. On the other hand, those Scriptures are only transmitted, read, and continually reappropriated by the ritually-formed community of the Church. Therefore, either the tendency to give a privileged position to sacraments over Scripture (through liturgical preoccupation, ritual preciosity, the de-emphasis or elimination of preaching) or of Scripture over sacraments (through liturgical minimalism, ritual carelessness, the intellectualization of human life) are equally unfaithful to the insights available in the phrase, *lex orandi, lex credendi*—or, 'The symbol gives rise to thought.' Anglicanism has most characteristically succumbed to the former tendency, although recent liturgical scholarship has done much to correct that imbalance. Both tendencies, however, each of which is a deformity, are perennial temptations for modern consciousness.

Ministry

Lex orandi, lex credendi yields three fundamental insights which should have a pervasive influence on Christian ministry (see pp. 338–49). First, human life in general and the Christian life in particular is symbolic life; corporately and individually we live in and through symbols, for only through them are we discovered by the fullness, courage, and joy of life. Second, symbols are the theophanies of God and presentations to every man and woman of God's prevenient grace. We live in God. Individuals may attempt to reject the symbols, but no one is excluded from the symbols. Finally, the symbolic life, the life of grace, is a processive or eschatological life. Consequently, any final, closed pronouncements as to what constitutes 'truth' and must be believed or as to what constitutes the 'good life' and must be obeyed can only be deemed idolatrous.

NOTES

1 The origin of the tag *lex orandi, lex credendi* is attributed to a lay monk, Prosper of Aquitaine, from a capitulum annexed to a letter of Pope Celestine I (422–32) between 435 and 442. The phrase originally read *legem credendi lex statuat supplicandi*, 'Let the law of prayer establish the law of belief,' and was used to argue (against semipelagianism) that the apostolic mandate to pray for all persons in 1 Timothy 2.1–4 proves that one is obligated to believe that faith is entirely a work of grace. The principle that has been established through the centuries is that worship and liturgy reflect and express doctrine. Debate has occurred throughout concerning to what extent worship and doctrine are authoritative for each other.

For a more complete discussion, see Geoffrey Wainwright, *Doxology: The Praise of God in Worship, Doctrine, and Life: A Systematic Theology* (New York, OUP, 1980; London, Epworth Press, 1982), pp. 218–50. Wainright includes the development of the principle in the thought of Augustine, Chrysostom, Ambrose, Jerome, Cyprian, Tertullian, and Irenaeus. The early history of the principle to the time of Prosper is also sketched by K. Federer, *Liturgie and Glaube: eine theologiegeschichtliche Untersuchung* (Freiburg in der Schweiz, Paulus-Verlag, 1950). *Mediator Dei* (1947; ET, *Encyclical Letter of His Holiness Pius XII on The Sacred Liturgy*, Washington DC, National Catholic Welfare Conference), an encyclical of Pius XII, restates the Roman Catholic position, particularly in paragraphs 49–67 (of the ET). A modern discussion is found in Aidan Kavanagh, OSB, *On Liturgical Theology* (New York, Pueblo, 1984); and Robert J. Taft, SJ, in 'Liturgy as Theology,' *Worship* 56 (1982), pp. 113–7.

2 G. M. Trevelyan, *History of England* (London, Longman, Green and Co., 1945), pp. 170–72.

3 W. Taylor Stevenson, 'Is There a Characteristic Anglican Theology?', in *The Future of Anglican Theology* (New York and Toronto, Edwin Mellen Press, 1984), pp. 24–5 and *passim*.

4 Paul Ricoeur, *The Symbolism of Evil* (Boston, Beacon Press, 1967), p. 356.

5 The influences upon the philosophy of Paul Ricoeur are extensive and complex. Moreover, he has unified them in a position which is distinctively his own and which defies assigning him to any 'school of thought'. If one has to place him in any one modern theological tradition, it would be that of Neo-orthodoxy with its radical stress upon the primacy of God's address and the dependent quality of our human response to that address. This relationship to Neo-orthodoxy remains unarticulated and only implicit in Ricoeur's writings. The influences upon Ricoeur which are explicit and pervasive include that of the Roman Catholic existentialist philosopher, Gabriel Marcel (d. 1973) which directed Ricoeur toward a concrete ontology and anthropology infused with the themes of freedom, finitude, and hope. Methodologically, the greatest influence was provided by the phenomological writings of Edmund Husserl. Karl Jaspers and Jean Nabert were other important influences. A good introduction to the sources and themes of Ricoeur's philosophy is found in John B. Thompson's 'Introduction' to *Paul Ricoeur: Hermeneutics and the Human Sciences* (Cambridge, CUP, 1981).

6 Paul Ricoeur, *The Conflict of Interpretations* (Evanston, Northwestern University Press, 1974), p. 288.

7 I. T. Ramsey, *Religious Language* (London, SCM, 1957); *Models and Mystery* (London and New York, OUP, 1964).

8 Paul Ricoeur, op. cit., pp. 347ff.

9 Stephen Sykes, *The Identity of Christianity* (London, SPCK; Philadelphia, Fortress Press, 1984), pp. 282, 284.

10 ibid., p. 267.

7 Councils, Conferences and Synods

FREDERICK H. SHRIVER

Anglican-Roman Catholic International Commission, *The Final Report*. London, SPCK and Catholic Truth Society, 1982.

Board for Mission and Unity, *Towards a Church of England Response to BEM and ARCIC*. London, Church House Publishing, 1985.

Greenslade, S. L., 'The English Reformers and the Councils of the Church', *Oecumenica*, 1967, pp. 95–115.

Fairweather, Eugene R., and Hardy, Edward R., *The Voice of the Church*. Greenwich, Conn., Seabury Press, 1962.

Huizing, Peter and Walf, Knut, eds., *The Ecumenical Council: Its Significance in the Constitution of the Church*. Edinburgh, T. &. T. Clark; New York, Seabury Press, 1983.

Margull, Hans, ed., *The Councils of the Church*. Philadelphia, Fortress Press, 1961.

Esp. S. Neill, 'The Anglican Communion and the Ecumenical Council', pp. 370–390.

In the life of the Church, councils are those representative gatherings which meet for the purpose of finding mutual consent or consensus in Christian belief and practice. In the Anglican tradition, as it has developed from the inheritance of the ancient and medieval Church through the reforms of the sixteenth century to the present, councils have functioned in different ways, with varied authority, purpose, and composition. First, there are the 'general' or 'ecumenical' councils which met in the fourth through to the eighth centuries, whose significance has continued to be acknowledged in the Church of England and the other Churches of the Anglican Communion.

Second, there are the national, provincial, and diocesan councils, more usually called 'synods' or 'conventions', by which the various Churches are governed and regulated. In the Church of England this includes the synods of the Provinces of York and Canterbury, known as 'convocations'; and the 'General Synod', which has in recent years, with the addition of lay delegates, taken over much of the historical authority of the two convocations. In the Protestant Episcopal Church in the United States of America the General Convention, which meets every three years, is actually a synod. Each Church or province of the Anglican Communion is governed in a similar way, with a synod, composed of clerical, and often lay, delegates, being part of an episcopal polity.

Third, there is the Lambeth Conference of Anglican bishops, which is a kind of council. Although the Lambeth Conference has no legal authority over any of the independent Anglican Churches, it does provide an opportunity for discussion of issues facing the Christian Churches in general, and the Anglican Communion in particular. And there also exists the Anglican Consultative Council, which is quite different from all of the above, being more of a representative committee, the membership reflecting the international and intercultural nature of the Anglican communion. This chapter will discuss these general topics, and conclude with some remarks concerning conciliarism and its relationship to the Anglican Churches and the ecumenical movement of the twentieth century.

THE ECUMENICAL COUNCILS

The first four ecumenical Councils of Nicaea (AD 325), Constantinople (AD 381), Ephesus (AD 431), and Chalcedon (AD 451), have a special place in Anglican theology, secondary to the Scriptures themselves, but the way in which their authority is acknowledged is complex and very important in its expression of classical Anglican theological method.

In 1559 Parliament, with the assent of Elizabeth I, passed the Act of Supremacy, restoring the sovereign authority of the English Crown over the

Church of England (see pp. 8–9, 98–9 and 353–5). In this Act, the 'first four General Councils' were the authority by which heresy was to be defined in the newly reformed Church. No 'matter or cause' was to be considered legally as heresy, except:

> such as heretofore have been determined, ordered or adjudged to be heresy by the authority of the Canonical Scriptures, or by any other General Council wherein the same was declared heresy by the express and plain words of the said Canonical Scriptures, or such as hereafter shall be ordered, judged or determined to be heresy by the High Court of Parliament of this realm, with the assent of the clergy in their Convocation; any thing in this Act contained to the contrary notwithstanding.[1]

Putting this in positive terms, the dogmatic canons of the first four councils gave, and may still be presumed to give, the Church of England and the other Churches of the Anglican Communion the basic doctrine concerning the person of Christ and the relationships of the persons of the Trinity. In common with the Lutheran and Reformed Churches of the sixteenth century, the conciliar theology of the fourth and fifth centuries was considered by the Church of England to be consonant with the doctrine of the holy Scriptures, the absolute ground of Christian doctrine. The relationship between the conciliar theology and the teaching of the Scriptures was further defined in 1563.

In 1563, the Thirty-nine *Articles of Religion*, devised by Convocation as a doctrinal standard for the clergy, clarified the relationship of the decrees of the Councils to the Scriptures (see pp. 82–3). The eighth Article, 'Of the Creeds', made it clear that the Nicene Creed and the Apostles' and Athanasian Creeds (though the latter two were not 'conciliar' creeds) were to be 'received and believed: for they may be proved by most certain warrants of Holy Scripture'. As for councils themselves, Article XXI spells out clearly the authoritative view of 1563, ratified by Parliament in 1571:

> General Councils may not be gathered together without the commandment and will of Princes. And when they be gathered together (forasmuch as they be an assembly of men, whereof all be not governed with the Spirit and Word of God,) they may err, and sometimes have erred, even in things pertaining unto God. Wherefore things ordained by them as necessary to salvation have neither strength nor authority, unless it may be declared that they be taken out of holy Scripture.

Behind these formulas lie the struggles between the reformed and Roman Churches in the sixteenth century. The Roman Catholic Council of Trent was coming to an end just as the Articles were being formulated. For the English and continental Protestants, the 'pope's council' was not a free and true general council. But the newly reformed Church of England wanted the world to know that it maintained the traditional Catholic faith of the Church as it existed before the illegitimate additions of extra-scriptural teaching. Also, the Protestants in general wished to affirm the traditional teaching of the Church on the incarnation and the Trinity, because of the radical theologians, like Servetus and Sozzini, who had called those doctrines into question. Moreover, if the doctrine of the ecumenical councils was used to define Christian orthodoxy, then the Roman insistence on later dogmas like transubstantiation, which had brought about the death of so many Protestants in England under Queen Mary, would be shown to be innovations.

But also, in the *Articles of Religion*, the Church of England made it clear that mere 'tradition', i.e. the decrees of councils (as well as of popes), no matter how venerable or true, could not establish beliefs that were 'necessary to salvation'. The Council of Trent had elevated church tradition to a level equal to the Scriptures. The English *Articles of Religion* expressly denied that assertion. The authority of the Church alone could never establish doctrine, but only the Word of God, enshrined and expressed in the holy Scriptures.

And so, in the beginning of the reform of the Church of England, it was asserted that the ecumenical councils' decrees, merely taken by themselves, did not establish the doctrine of the Church of England. The most that could be said is that the Act of Supremacy and the *Articles of Religion* recognized that the dogmatic decrees of the councils—including the 'Nicene' Creed, hallowed also by centuries of use in the liturgy—were definitive, but not absolute. Or to put it another way, the dogmas of the councils had only a derivative authority, because the dogmas truly expressed the teachings of the Scriptures on the vexing issues of the nature of the person of Christ, and the relationships between the persons of the Trinity.

This sixteenth-century attitude has largely been borne out by modern scholarship concerning the councils, the attitudes of the bishops who gathered there, and the way in which the councils' decrees were accepted by the Church. The councils were ecumenical, not because the emperor called the council, or because bishops issued the official statements. Rather, they became ecumenical, because over a period of several centuries the majority of Christians accepted the Niceno-Constantinopolitan Creed, the condemnation of the heresies of Arius, Apollinarius, Nestorius, and Eutyches, and other conciliar formulas, such as the 'Tome of Leo' and the Decree of Chalcedon. Most of the bishops at Nicaea, for instance, held a theory of tradition which looked upon it as virtually synonymous with the Scriptures, which might be thought of as 'written' tradition. And for this reason, there was considerable opposition at the Council, and for some decades, to the term '*homoousios*' (of the same substance) which was inserted into the Creed, because it was clearly not biblical. For the Fathers of the Council, and indeed, for the heretics as well, the issue that underlay the Arian controversy was the proper interpretation of the Church's whole teaching. But that teaching was in no way to be understood as separate from the Scriptures. There had not developed in the conciliar period itself a theory which would have considered the possibility of discrepancy between tradition and Scripture. As S. L. Greenslade put it: 'While the ultimate authority of Scripture was always affirmed, the notion of tradition, though very powerful, was not precise (perhaps by its very nature it cannot be) and the possibility of modifying or correcting tradition by fresh understanding of Scripture was insufficiently considered.'[2]

In the century or so which followed the Elizabethan Settlement it became necessary for Anglican theologians to clarify the meaning of the Church of England's teaching on the authority of the councils. Some Anglican theologians, and the *Book of Homilies* (see pp. 137–40), were ready to acknowledge the authority of the first six; adding to the four cited above, Constantinople (553), and Constantinople (681). But as the *Oxford Dictionary of the Christian Church* succinctly puts it, 'It appears ... that such Councils are ultimately revered in the C[hurch] of E[ngland] on the ground that their decisions are acceptable rather than vice versa.'[3] Probably the best statement of the Anglican attitude toward the general councils which has prevailed is to be found in the comment on Article XXII of Gilbert Burnet, the Bishop of Salisbury from 1689 to 1715:

> As to the strict notion of a general council, there is great reason to believe that there was never any assembly to which it will be found to agree. And for the four general councils, which this church declares she receives, they are received only because we are persuaded from the scriptures that their decisions were made according to them: that the Son is truly God, of the same substance with the Father. That the Holy Ghost is also truly God. That the divine nature was truly united to the human in Christ; and that in one person. That both natures remained distinct; and that the human nature was not swallowed up of the divine. These truths we find in the scriptures, and therefore we believe them. We reverence those councils for the sake of their doctrine; but do not believe the doctrine for the authority of the councils. There appeared too much of human frailty in some of their other proceedings, to give us such an implicit submission to them, as to believe things only because they so decided them.[4]

In the sixteenth and seventeenth centuries Richard Field and William Laud are typical examples of theologians who would have been in agreement with Burnet. Field was very 'respectful' of the councils and the bishops who sat in them:

> when there is a lawful General Council ... we are so strongly to presume that it is true and right that with unanimous consent is agreed on in such a Council, that we must not so much as profess publicly that we think otherwise, unless we do most certainly know the contrary; yet may we in the secret of our hearts remain in some doubt, carefully seeking by the Scripture and monuments of Antiquity to find out the truth. ... But concerning the General Councils ... we confess that in respect of the matter about which they were called, so nearly and essentially concerning the life and soul of the Christian Faith, and in respect of the manner and form of their proceeding, and the evidence of the proof brought in them, they are and ever were expressly to be believed by all such as perfectly understand the meaning of their determination.[5]

William Laud (see p. 237), in his 'Conversations with Mr Fisher the Jesuit' pointed out that a council, being representative, has only the authority that belongs to the Church, and nothing more. Agreeing with Augustine, he notes that though a general council may be relied on to have the assistance of the Holy Spirit, that does not mean that general councils are infallible: 'It seems it was no news with St. Augustine, that a General Council might err, and therefore [be] inferior to the Scripture.' Or, as he puts it elsewhere, 'the Scripture is absolutely and every way divine; the Church's definition is but *suo modo*, "In a sort or manner", divine. But that which is but in a sort can never be a foundation in a higher degree than that which is absolute and ever such.'[6] In this, Laud was a clear follower of the *Articles of Religion* (as indeed he was obliged to be) and points the way to Burnet.

Since the rise of modern critical historical study of the Scriptures and the history of the Church, there has been considerable discussion of the place of the councils in the development of a teaching authority in the Church. The complex way in which their authority came to be understood has led theologians to question to what degree the conciliar theology, particularly its terminology and metaphysical assumptions, must be honoured in order to be loyal to the authority of the Scriptures. Anglican theologians have differed in their opinions concerning this question. Theoretically, the question is how far the Church might go in revising the traditional language by which we speak of the person of Christ and the persons of the Trinity. On the one hand, there are those who would insist that the vocabulary of the conciliar definitions is sacrosanct and unalterable. On the other hand, there are those who believe that the vocabulary is time-bound, and does not express fully either a modern or biblical understanding of God (see pp. 113–17).

SYNODICAL GOVERNMENT

The 'Anglican Communion' may be said to have come into existence with the reformation of the Church of Ireland in the sixteenth and seventeenth centuries. The anomalous Episcopal Church of Scotland was forced into independent existence in 1689, then followed the creation of the Protestant Episcopal Church in the United States of America in 1789 as the result of the American Revolution, and the Anglican Churches in New Zealand, Australia, and Canada, and a host of others in the wake of the development of the British Empire and its dissolution. All of these Churches, whatever their different relationships to Crown or Parliament, have been governed synodically, even though they also have their individual political characteristics.

It is not possible within the scope of this chapter to discuss the history and development of the varied polities of the Anglican Churches. Looking at the global Anglican Communion from the perspective of the late twentieth century, we see the various independent Anglican Churches governed by 'councils' which recognize bishops' authority in some form as crucial and distinct, but which include not only representation from the presbyterate, but also from the laity.

This synodical character owes a great deal to the tradition of the Church going back to the second century at least (some would say to the first century, and the 'council' of the church in Jerusalem recorded in Acts 15, *c.* AD 50) and the common human experience of consulting in a body when important decisions have to be made. But the development of synodical government also reflects the spread of increasingly democratic forms of representative government in the secular governments. If England is in some sense the 'Mother of Parliaments', the Church of England is also a mother of representative government within the Church. The formation of the Episcopal Church in the United States, whose General Convention with a House of Bishops and a House of Deputies, including laymen (and laywomen since 1973), was established in the 1780s, is the first example of the interaction of inherited English secular and ecclesiastical forms producing a new Anglican polity. Since then, the representative character of synodical government in the Anglican Churches has been clearly established.

But this representative character affects only individual Churches, or independent 'Provinces'. The Anglican Communion, rather like the international fellowships of the other non-Roman Catholic Christian bodies, is not, in the Roman Catholic sense, an international 'Church'. There is no Anglican authority which stands above the Church of England, the *Nippon Sei Ko Kai*, or the Church of the Province of West Africa, for instance. There may well be doubts as to whether or not this is a good thing. The missionary movement, British and American imperialism, the dissolution of the British Empire, and serious awareness of the need for independence from assumptions of Anglo-American cultural superiority, brought about the tremendous growth of non-English Anglican Churches. An independence of spirit as well as literal independence has ensued. But, naturally enough, the younger Churches often look to the mother Churches, still richer and more influential in ecumenical dialogue, for guidance. The vestiges of imperial and colonial attitudes are not dead by any means (see pp. 395–8). But just as the nations on the planet have not devised a system of international government, neither has the Anglican Communion been able, or wanted, to create a means by which the different sister Churches might unite with some form of central authority. The tensions between a desire for unity and a desire for independence have been evident throughout the Communion, at least since the early decades of the nineteenth century.

THE LAMBETH CONFERENCES

The Anglican tradition's common experience of episcopacy, symbolized by the historical link with the see of Canterbury, as well as a common and complex liturgical tradition, has provided a measure of unity, especially as the Lambeth Conferences have developed. That conference of bishops has demonstrated the usefulness, perhaps even the necessity, of inter-Anglican cooperation, but it has also shown that an over-arching authority will not be easy to achieve. If there were to be a greater measure of formal unity within the Anglican Communion, it would have to be in some sense conciliar, because of the developments noted above.

The first conference of Anglican bishops met at the Archbishop of Canterbury's London home, Lambeth Palace, in September 1867. It was composed of bishops from England, Ireland, Canada, the United States, and various parts of the colonial British Empire. There had been interest expressed in the formation of some kind of international Anglican synod, especially in the United States and Canada, since the 1850s. The actual conference took place because of the action of the triennial Synod of the Province of Canada in requesting Archbishop Longley of Canterbury to summon 'a National Synod of the Bishops of the Anglican Church at home and abroad'.[8] It ended after only four days of meeting without any great accomplishments, but its great achievement was simply to have met.

The second Lambeth Conference, in 1878, was far more significant than the first, since it went further in establishing a precedent. The third, in 1888, was summoned by Archbishop Edward White Benson without any petition from abroad. It was in the context of this Conference that the famous 'Lambeth Quadrilateral' emerged (see pp. 209–10 and pp. 219–20). One of the items on the Archbishop's agenda had been the relationship between the Anglican Churches and the other Christian Churches. In the General Convention of the Episcopal Church in the United States in Chicago in 1885, a resolution had been passed by the House of Bishops which set out four principles which were to be the basis of discussions on church unity between the Anglican Churches and the other Churches—the holy Scriptures, the Apostles' and Nicene Creeds, the two sacraments of Baptism and the Supper of the Lord, and the historic episcopate 'locally adapted'. This resolution, without any legal or binding force, has come to be regarded by many Anglicans as an important reference point governing the relations with other Churches.

It was also at this time that Archbishop Benson enunciated what was to become the generally agreed-upon understanding of this Anglican episcopal conference (the words are taken from his diary):

> I opened the Conference by pointing out that the Conference was in no sense a Synod and not adapted, or competent, or within its powers, if it should attempt to make binding decisions on doctrines or discipline—the unsuitableness to the constitution of our church—and its relation to America—the fact that they had been foreseen and settled by Archbishop Longley and Tait in their addresses, etc.[9]

The subsequent Conferences—among them 1920, with an important appeal for Christian unity, and 1948, which helped heal the terrible disruption brought about by World War II—have reflected the tremendous growth of the Anglican Churches outside the Anglo-Saxon world. The range of topics that have been discussed, and that to some degree have been reflected in the printed reports, have developed Anglican self-consciousness in the midst of great cultural diversity. But from the beginning, Christian unity beyond the confines of Anglicanism has also been one of the leading themes. The Lambeth Conferences have become enormous, and consequently there have been serious critiques concerning their value: for instance their expense, their practical ineffectiveness, the English, or Anglo-Saxon domination in the proceedings, and their limitation to bishops only. But as the practice came into being through a desire for consultation on common problems, there has not yet been created another effective way in which mutual responsibility can be totally exercised.

There were three large international meetings or Congresses of Anglicans, open to laity, held in London in 1908, Minneapolis in 1954, and Toronto in 1963. Today it seems most unlikely that anything quite like them will occur again, but the latter two, in particular, underlined the fact that whatever the importance of the Lambeth Conferences, they could not be understood as being the sole voice of international Anglicanism. The Congresses helped many Anglicans to articulate and understand the variety and unity that were a part of the Communion. With the influence of Archbishop Arthur Michael Ramsey, and Bishop Stephen Bayne, Executive Officer of the Anglican Communion from 1960 to 1967, the Congress in Toronto was a preparation for the work of the Lambeth Conference of 1968. This Conference, reflecting the growing world-wide sense of the problems of the 'Third World' and the chasm between the rich and poor nations and Churches, established the Anglican Consultative Council. This first met in 1971, and has continued to play an important part in the cohesion of the Anglican Communion. As Bishop John Howe, the Secretary General of the Council from 1971 to 1982, has stated,

> In several respects, the Anglican Consultative Council (ACC) was, and is, unique. It remains the only international Anglican body with a Constitution. Also it was authorized by the Communion as a whole ... [It] includes clergy and lay people. Every Anglican Church has members ... The total number is comparatively small, partly to facilitate a frequency of meetings ... The ACC meets every two or three years, and its Standing Committee annually. As far as possible the Council is to meet 'in various parts of the world'.[10]

The Council is still relatively young, and its activities, to the member Churches, and individual church members, remain somewhat obscure. It suffers from the same problems that all 'executive bodies' of large institutions endure. But it is, at the very least, like its venerable parent, the episcopal conferences of Lambeth, a guarantee that the individual Anglican Churches will not be allowed utterly to remain in provincial indifference. And it may well evolve, like the Lambeth Conferences, in ways that will promote the unity of the Communion.

CONCLUSION

The 'conciliar' nature of the Anglican Communion is perhaps one of the least recognized, and yet most characteristic, features of modern Anglicanism. It is a characteristic that is shared with almost all other Christian bodies, and one that has been an important part of the Ecumenical Movement. The hope for a truly general council of Christendom has been in existence with particular poignancy ever since the Great Schism in the papacy in the fourteenth and fifteenth centuries. For the Protestants of the Reformation era, the Council of Trent was decidedly not that hoped-for Council. But, venerating the accomplishment of the first four councils as they did, both Luther and Calvin held up the conciliar ideal as a function of the Church as the *communio sanctorum*—the communion of saints.[11] The Roman Catholic Church has displayed the energizing effect of conciliar authority, within its own quite different polity, with the Second Vatican Council. The current interest among all the Christian Churches in the Lima Statement produced by the World Council of Churches, and the convergence of theological and missionary concerns in all the Churches, points to a growing atmosphere which is conducive to unity. A recognition of the function of conciliar principles working toward a Christian communion which is wider than merely Anglican, but which is obviously consonant with one of the most basic of Anglican principles, should serve the movement toward Christian unity. Conciliar principles, when recognized by Anglicans, can also serve to clarify for them, and for other Christians, the way in which the episcopal principle (often erroneously considered to be the sole distinguishing characteristic of the Anglican Communion) works.

If the function of the episcopate in the Church is to call to the individual churches' attention the fact that the Church is truly a world fellowship—i.e. ecumenical and catholic—then that function is displayed most clearly when the episcopate meets together, in council. The bishops of the Church, however, in the developing practice of the independent national or provincial Anglican Churches, are not the sole representatives of the *consensus fidelium*, the fellowship of the faithful. The clergy and laity are also part of that representative consensus. If the bishops of the great ecumenical councils of the fourth and fifth centuries saw themselves as truly representative of the faith of the Church as it had been received, and as it was understood by the presbyters and laity, then—in the absence of the imperial authority which called those councils into being—the conciliar nature of the Church must include, in some way, the representatives of the whole Church.

The recent statements of the Anglican-Roman Catholic International Commission have dealt with the issue of conciliar authority in the context of the issues of episcopal and papal authority. There, perhaps inevitably, considering that papal infallibility and primacy are the most divisive issues between the Anglican and Roman Churches, councils are assumed to be episcopal councils. Nevertheless, the 1976 Venice Statement on Authority in the Church (I), has acknowledged the place of the clergy and laity along with the bishop in the exercise of the bishops' 'special responsibility for promoting truth and discerning error'. And, furthermore that 'the interaction of bishop and people in [the] exercise of [that special responsibility] is a safeguard of Christian life and fidelity'.[12]

The Venice Statement and its 'Elucidation' in 1981 reiterate certain classical Anglican positions, returning to the *Articles of Religion*, and their interpretation by later Anglican theologians. Conciliar decrees are only binding when they 'formulate the central truths of salvation', and when 'faithful to Scripture and consistent with Tradition'. Also, it is pointed out that a balance must be maintained between 'primacy' and 'conciliarity'.[13] The Commission was discussing the immediate issue of the primatial authority of the Bishop of Rome. But the principle could be applied as well to the primacy of any of the bishops within their provincial or diocesan jurisdiction.

The International Commission also clarified the place of the 'reception' by the Church in the authenticity of binding conciliar decrees, by explaining that

> Reception does not create truth nor legitimize the decision: it is the final indication that such a decision has fulfilled the necessary conditions for it to be a true expression of the faith. In this acceptance the whole Church is involved in a continuous process of discernment and response. The Commission . . . on the one hand rejects the view that a definition has no authority until it is accepted by the whole Church or even derives its authority solely from that acceptance. Equally, the Commission denies that a council is so evidently self-sufficient that its definitions owe nothing to reception.[14]

As has been noted above, the Anglican Communion has no developed positive teaching on conciliar authority, principally because of the recognition of the splintered character of the Catholic Church since the sixteenth century (or perhaps the eleventh). But the whole drift of the history of the Anglican tradition, in the context of the development of parliamentary representation and democratic government, has been to strengthen the impression that the important decisions concerning the Church's faith and life can only be made in the context of a truly representative body. In the latter part of the twentieth century, therefore, Anglicans must articulate a new conciliar theology. On the one hand there is the energizing example of the Second Vatican Council of the Roman Catholic Church under the Pope, on the other is the encouraging example of the conciliar theological consensus developing within the structure of the World Council of Churches. Councils alone have never solved the Church's problems. Their authority is limited and temporary. But they can articulate effectively for their own time authentic Christian witness and belief. Then, like the general councils of the ancient Church, in time they may be seen to have spoken according to the Holy Spirit. The Christian Church would appear to have found no better way to strive toward unity than through the practice of holding conference in councils.

NOTES

1 Elton, G. R., *The Tudor Constitution* (Cambridge 1965), p. 368.

2 Greenslade, S. L., 'The Authorities Appealed to by the First Four General Councils' in *Councils and the Ecumenical Movement*, WCC Studies No. 5 (Geneva, WCC, 1968), p. 53.

3 *Oxford Dictionary of the Christian Church* (London 1957), p. 977.

4 Burnet, G., *An Exposition of the Thirty Nine Articles* (Oxford 1845), p. 239.

5 Field, R., *Of the Church* (Cambridge 1852), vol. iv, p. 60.

6 Laud, W., *A Relation of the Conference between William Laud [. . .] and Mr. Fisher the Jesuit* in *Works* (Oxford 1849), vol. ii, p. 276.

7 The Anglican-Roman Catholic International Commission in their 'Elucidation' of 1981 attempted to deal with this matter, in stating that the 'Scriptures are the uniquely inspired witness to divine revelation,' but recognising that also it is 'impossible' to express the truths of revelation without 'resorting to current language and thought.' The 'Elucidation' uses '*homoousios*' as an example of a word that is 'different from the original text of Scripture without being alien to its meaning.' At the end of this particular section, the Commission calls for a balance between the recognition of the definitive character of the Scriptures and the necessity of drawing 'upon everything in human experience and thought which will give to the content of the revelation its fullest expression and widest application.' Anglican-Roman Catholic International Commission, *The Final Report* (SPCK/CTS 1982), pp. 70–71.

8 Howe, J., *Highways and Hedges: Anglicanism and the Universal Church* (Anglican Consultative Council 1985), p. 62.

9 A. C. Benson, *Life of Edward White Benson* (London 1899), vol. ii, p. 214, quoted in Stephenson, A. M. G., *Anglicanism and the Lambeth Conferences* (SPCK 1978), p. 79.

10 Howe, op. cit., pp. 85–6.

11 Kantzenbach, F. W., 'The Call for a Council in the 16th Century—the Protestant View of Councils' in *Councils and the Ecumenical Movement* (Geneva, WCC, 1968), p. 109.
12 Anglican-Roman Catholic International Commission, *The Final Report* (see n. 7), pp. 61–2.

13 ibid., pp. 62, 71–2.

14 ibid., p. 72.

8 Canon Law

W. J. HANKEY

Standing Committee of the General Synod of Australia, *Canon Law in Australia, A Summary of church legislation and its sources.* Sydney 1981.

The Canon Law of the Church of England, Being the Report of the Archbishops' Commission on Canon Law, together with Proposals for a Revised Body of Canons. SPCK 1947.

Clarke, H. L., *Constitutional Church Government.* SPCK 1924.

Thomas, P. H. E., *The Lambeth Conferences and the development of Anglican Ecclesiology, 1867–1978.* Unpublished Ph.D Thesis, University of Durham 1982. (This comes closest to updating H. L. Clarke, an urgent necessity.)

Briden, T., and Moore, E. G., *Moore's Introduction to English Canon Law*, 2nd edn, Mowbray 1985.

Addleshaw, G. W. O, 'The Study of Canon Law' in H. S. Box, ed., *The Priest as Student.* (SPCK 1936), pp. 201–36.

Canon law, or the law of the Christian Church, has its origin in the freedom of Christians. This freedom derives from the fact that, through the death and resurrection of Jesus Christ, Christians have passed over into the presence and power of the Creator and Governor of the heaven and the earth. Because Christian 'life is hid with Christ in God',[1] it has passed beyond subordination to spiritual and natural powers, as well as to the laws of particular historical communities. Thus, as the Acts of the Apostles and the Pauline epistles indicate, the law which defined Israel as a particular religious, political, and social community is no longer binding on Christians and the Church is open to Jew and Gentile alike.

The liberty of the Church is a freedom and necessity to live under God's reign as established in Christ and is a freedom and necessity to make law. So this liberty is radically and directly found in subordination to sovereign power in divinely established institutions. The present reign of God is recognized in the rule of the Apostles and their successors (to whom are given the power of binding and loosing), of kings, governors and those to whom they delegate their power, of fathers and husbands, and of masters in the economic sphere.[2] Freedom from the Law of Moses requires the recognition of new legislative power, so that God may actually be the ruler of his new creation. For the early Church, obeying God meant obeying (or at least suffering under) the rulers of the state and bishops.[3] If the problems and conflicts of millenia are suggested in the existence from the beginning of conflicting divinely sanctioned sovereignties, there is also another difficulty consequent on the freedom of Christians from the law of the old Israel.

R. C. Mortimer distinguishes between invariable and unalterable canon law and that which may be altered.[4] In respect to the former, he maintains that the Church does not create law, rather that laws have the nature of 'judgements of fact'.[5] Bishop Mortimer places that law which consists of doctrinal statements or regards the validity of sacraments into this category. Without necessarily accepting his arrangement of material, it must be recognized that the logic of Christian freedom compels that canon law should have some basic division. The freedom is mediated by what God has done in Christ and the fundamental part of canon law must recognize, and maintain as authoritative in the Church, that from which Christian liberty to live by a self-made law springs.

The Church confronted very early the paradox of this mediated freedom. Being ruled by God meant submitting to the bishop and clergy, for to them were committed the knowledge and power of Christ by which Christians were free. But, so long as these were secret mysteries, there could be no certainty that the Churches were ruled by the Father of the Lord Jesus and not by the tyranny of personal private inspiration. Thus the foundation of the law of the Christian polity became the recognition of the canon of Scripture and, related to this, publicly defined and agreed doctrine. These have an inherent universality and objectivity, characteristics which came to be understood as necessary marks of an essential part of that law by which Christians were governed.[6]

There is a convergence of Scripture, doctrine, and apostolic power, to communicate both Christ's life and the conditions of participation in it, in liturgy. The law of liturgy is a law of believing, and more. It regulates also various moral and spiritual obligations of clergy and people. It is necessary that the rules governing liturgy and the sacraments, and the conditions of admission to them, will become essential and determinative features of canon law.

The canon law by which the Churches of the Anglican Communion govern themselves stems from the law of the patristic and Western medieval Church which was received with limiting conditions in the sixteenth-century English Reformation. Therefore, it embraces the laws of councils, synods and courts of diverse sorts, of bishops and other authoritative ecclesiastical persons, of kings, popes and other authorities who have successfully wielded—mediately or immediately—both secular and sacred swords, and even purely secular legislatures, so far as they determine the power of ecclesiastical authorities.[7] The determinations of theologians are also part of canon law in as much as they give the accepted meaning of formularies and indicate which doctrinal questions may be regarded as settled within an ecclesial community. Further, the canon law of the Churches of the Communion must be distinguished into laws of several degrees of necessity, variability, weight, and locus of jurisdiction. Finally, canon law is also of very diverse kinds and forms. Scripture itself is part of Anglican canon law, and partly determinative of it. (Whether the law of Church and society could be read directly from Scripture was a great question at the Reformation. Richard Hooker's treatment of this question in his *Laws of*

Ecclesiastical Polity (1594–1662) is the statement and justification of the classic Anglican position.) Liturgy and liturgical books are absolutely essential to it. Within the Communion, credal and doctrinal statements are carried into law through their presence in liturgical books, as well as in other ways. Anglican canon law governs moral and spiritual discipline, property, and administrative activity of great complexity and diversity. This range of authority, degree and kind of legislators and of law will readily appear as necessary features of the canon law of the Christian Church from the patristic period.

Any attempt to describe the characteristics and state of Anglican canon law as distinguished from the ecclesiastical law of the patristic period and of the Western medieval Church faces a number of grave obstacles. Some of these are so nearly insurmountable that it may be impossible for us to judge whether or not we have risen above them to a point from which the whole may be successfully viewed, or whether in fact the mountains have risen above our vision. The obstacles are these: the absence for more than two hundred years of a superior legislature for the Anglican Church, the radical effects on the law of a Church of the Anglican type of the fundamentally altered relations between secular and sacred since the eighteenth century, the enormous difference between the status and character of ecclesiastical law in the established Church of England and in the other Churches of the Communion, the diversity of the historical origins and geographical conditions of the several Anglican Churches (an essential matter for a Christianity which is committed to the legislative power of particular or national Churches), the speed with which Anglican Churches in Africa are growing and, hence, are being divided and created, the varying weight and importance attached to different parts of the canon law during diverse times and in diverse places, the widely varying attitudes to government by law in different temporal and geographical circumstances, and finally, the rapid and fundamental changes now taking place in some Churches of the Communion in respect to the whole range of law.

It is well known that the Lambeth Conferences, as well as more recent gatherings like the Anglican Consultative Councils and the Anglican Primates meetings, have no legislative or jurisidictional power in the Communion. But even before the constitution of independent Anglican Churches, the English Parliament had ceased to tbe the legislature for the Church outside of England. The intimate relation of Church and state established in the sixteenth century by the royal supremacy meant that the ecclesiastical law of the Anglican Churches was subject both to changes in the relations of the English Crown to its legislatures and territories and to changes in the relation of the secular and sacred spheres generally (see pp. 351–63). Changes of the first kind were powerfully evident in the eighteenth century, those of the second kind in the nineteenth. The establishment of an independent episcopate in the United States of America with the aid of the Scottish episcopate (1784), itself already operating independently of the British Crown, constituted an Anglican Church for which the English Parliament was no longer the superior legislature. Another effect of the American Revolution was to move the colonial legislatures toward greater independence from Parliament with attendant consequences for ecclesiastical law. In any case, it had already been settled that the Church could only be legally established in a colony by an act of the colonial legislature. When the Crown itself set up an overseas episcopal jurisdiction by Letters Patent to Charles Inglis (consecrated Bishop of Nova Scotia in 1787), it left unsettled many questions about the relation of his jurisdiction to that of the governors and legislatures in his territories. But it is certain that the Church of England was never established in the English sense within his jurisdiction; that is, he had legal power only over those who chose to associate themselves with the Church and could enforce the civil consequences of his acts only with the assistance of the secular courts. Although there are exceptions (especially in the West Indies) and disputed instances (especially in Australia), this is generally the situation of the Anglican ecclesiastical authorities outside the United Kingdom in the nineteenth century and, after the disestablishment of the Church in Ireland and in Wales, it is true everywhere except in England.

The nineteenth century brings changes of a different sort. The Anglican episcopate spreads outside the United Kingdom beyond North America, and for the first time into areas which were never British territories. Capetown consecrated a bishop for Zambesi in 1861.[8] Synods (or 'conventions') develop as ecclesiastical legislatures for the new Churches and the overseas episcopates. Certainly these developments require transformations in how the law of the Church is conceived and how the 'Church of the United Kingdom of England and Ireland' could have a law independent of the English Crown and Parliament. But, difficult as these conceptual shifts were for many to accept, especially where the Anglican Churches were valued for their ties to the United Kingdom, the legal principle had been conceded already in the eighteenth-century developments. What are significant are the changes consequent on the changing relations of sacred and secular in England.

On the one side, from 1832, there is the diminution of the distinct courts where ecclesiastical cases were tried. Ecclesiastical law is reduced to the less flexible statute law, a shift exemplifying the Erastianism of the nineteenth-century state. This explains the odious rigidity of the law and judgements in the ritual and doctrinal cases of the second half of the century.[9] On the other side there is the religious reaction to the secularism of the period, exemplified in the Tractarian Movement which marks its start with John Keble's sermon protesting the treatment of the Church by the government in disestablishing the Church of Ireland. The catholicity of this movement was initially its emphasis on the completeness, temporal continuity, independence and universality of the Church. That emphasis demanded from them a strong interest in canon law, but it did not provide Tractarians with a good sense of the nature of the Church of England.[10] They stressed apostolic succession, and the episcopate appeared to them to be independently the source of canon law. Consequences of this are the endeavours to begin canon law from the conception of the Church as *societas perfecta* over against the state, and sharply to divide canon law, as the law the Church makes for herself, from ecclesiastical law, as the law the state makes for the Church.[11]

The endeavour to restore to the Church a law-making capacity independent of the state leads to the re-establishment of synods in the nineteenth century. The American Church by necessity had led the way, but the Canadians followed and bishops with Tractarian principles were among the most ardent (for example, Bishop Hibbert Binney of Nova Scotia). In the beginning the synods had extremely limited conceptions of their law-making powers. The Americans are something of an exception here, but one which proves the rule. They recognized that it was in their power to change everything, and considered radically unitarian proposals, for example. In the end, however, the Americans changed the formularies most conservatively, as the Prayer Book revision of 1789, and the version of the Articles of Religion adopted by their Convention in 1801, attest.[12] In the United States, as elsewhere, the assumption was that the Anglican law of doctrine, liturgy, moral and spiritual discipline was basically fixed, and that the business of synods and their officers was adaptation to practical circumstances—promoting the interests and mission of the Church and coping with the financial and disciplinary effects of life outside the establishment. Thus, the synods outside England originally accepted, at least implicitly, that purely ecclesiastical bodies did not have sovereign power over the Church; they accepted formularies developed within a wider Christian polity.

By the end of the century, however, synods, even within the British Empire, had gained sufficient sense of the completeness of their authority to conceive of themselves as, in principle, sovereign ecclesiastical legislatures. Certainly, in some cases, they saw this power as derived from the episcopate. The constitution of the General Synod of the Canadian Church seems to proceed to such an unlimited jurisdiction from an essentially Tractarian idea of the episcopate. Thus, the legal ground was laid for the developments of the second half of the twentieth century. But, fundamental alteration of doctrine, liturgy and order is not to be found in the Anglican canon law of the nineteenth century. In Canada, as elsewhere, the new General Synod of the sovereign national Church (or, sometimes elsewhere, province) limited itself by a Solemn Declaration as the diocesan synods which preceded it had done. The Solemn Declaration of 1893 became, in 1934, part of the Declaration of Principles and therein the General Synod limited its jurisdiction to 'the definition of the doctrines of the Church in harmony with the Solemn Declaration'. This Declaration tied the Canadian Church not only to communion with the Church of England, but also to the canonical Scriptures, the creeds of the undivided Church, the divinely ordained Sacraments and Apostolic orders, and to 'the Doctrine, Sacraments and Discipline of Christ as . . . the Church of England hath received and set forth the same in "The Book of Common Prayer" . . . and in the Thirty-nine Articles of Religion . . .'[13]

The nineteenth-century developments are necessitated by the spread of the Anglican Church beyond the bounds of British territory—Letters Patent can have no power to establish jurisdiction there. Also, they are required if the Anglican Church is to continue in countries growing independent of the Imperial Parliament. Finally, they are compelled if the Church is to survive when the secular culture is hostile, or if the state is incapable of seeing in the Church more than a Department of Religious Affairs. In the West Indies, where establishment lasted a relatively long time, it was essential for the survival and growth of the Anglican Church that the Church show its independence from the corrupting unity of Church and state; the plantocracy and the establishment went together. But the development of an independent episcopate and a complete legislative power by ecclesiastical, as opposed to secular, bodies means that both the law and the attitude to it in the Anglican Churches formed in the nineteenth and twentieth centuries comes to be markedly different from that of the Church of England itself. The constitution and canon law of the Church of England maintain continuity with an earlier conception of the relation of Church and state. The General Synod functions under Crown and Parliament, and the canon law it promulgated since 1970 self-consciously carries forward the tradition.[14] Without the developments of the eighteenth and nineteenth centuries in front of us, it would be impossible to appreciate the differences in the canon law of the Communion and to arrive at some conception of what both enables and threatens an Anglican unity which is reflected in law.

The source of the differences in the canon law of the Communion is then the diversity of the legislatures of the Anglican Churches and the fundamental difference between the relation of the determinations of the synods of the established Church of England to Parliament, and those of other synods in the Communion to their respective secular legislatures (of which, paradoxically, one is the Parliament of the United Kingdom in respect to the Church in Wales, in Northern Ireland and to the Episcopal Church of Scotland). In England, synodical determinations of certain kinds must be enacted by Parliament; these then have the force of Acts of Parliament, though Parliament has exempted itself from considering matters which General Synod defines as doctrinal. The Royal Licence and Assent also allows General Synod to pass canons binding on the clergy *in re ecclesiastica* and enforceable by ecclesiastical courts. In consequence, English ecclesiastical authorities are still able to enforce at law the civil consequences of their judgements. The restoration of specifically ecclesiastical legislatures like the Convocations of Canterbury and York and the creation of

General Synod are results of the nineteenth-century shifts in the relations of Church and state. Currently difficulties in the relations of General Synod and Parliament indicate that the constitutional ambiguities in this arrangement have not been resolved. Still, in England, the canon law is continuous, so far as the constitution of the state allows, both with the law of the patristic and medieval Western Church and with the law of the Reformed Church of England—though exactly what of the pre-Reformation law applies has never been precisely delimited.[15]

The crucial judicial decisions of the nineteenth century, *Long v. Bishop of Capetown*, (1863) and the *Bishop of Natal v. Gladstone*, (1866), determined that English ecclesiastical laws and Crown ecclesiastical appointments could not be enforced abroad in their civil consequences by ecclesiastical courts acting alone, nor could they override the jurisdictions of local Churches whose status and powers were determined by the local legislatures. They had validity and power for those Churches as voluntary associations and over their adherents only so far as they were not abrogated by those Churches and legislatures. But, the judicial decisions equally determined that (so far as those Churches as voluntary associations could, by virtue of their status under their legislatures, and did, in fact, will an identity with the United Church of England and Ireland) the Churches outside England did receive the law of the Church of England.[16] This is not substantially different from the determinations of the canon lawyers of the Protestant Episcopal Church in the United States of America.[17] However, it has never been determined for any particular Anglican Church just what of the English canon law is relevant and rides within it.

Within this common but uncodified legal background, the diversity of the canon law and the attitudes toward it in the various Anglican Churches is overwhelming. Because the Churches other than the established Church of England can think themselves to be complete ecclesiastical polities over against the state, there is outside the established Church a tendency to regard canon law as if it were only the private concern of the members of a club.[18] Because of the unique relation of the English Church to its state, it has continuing need for professional canon lawyers and for legal exactness which is absent from some other Churches in the Communion. There is also a tradition of the study of canon law and care about it in the other Anglican Churches in the United Kingdom. PECUSA was necessarily conscious from the beginning of the need to consider the source of canon law, and how, and by what authority, it might be changed. Moreover, the congregational origins of that Church made it particularly aware, in the way that Americans generally are, of the problems inherent in making corporate and individual persons conform to law. So there has been in the Church in the United States a tradition of canonical scholarship and legal carefulness. In Australia, the vast distances separating the dioceses, and the relative independence of the origins of the several provinces, together with the continuing existence of strong parties in the Church mean that canon law is taken very seriously indeed. The Australian Church has produced the latest study of canon law in the Communion outside England (*Canon Law in Australia*) and, in its liturgical revisions and other acts, takes care that they do not violate the fundamental law.

In Canada, on the other hand, interest in fundamental canon law seems to have passed. Certainly there was a strong interest. In the 1960s the Primate's Commission on Canon Law proposed an eleven-volume study on canon law; one volume was published.[19] But constitutional autonomy for the Canadian Anglican Church is achieved, national episcopal and synodical government is strongly established, effective parties do not exist, and there is a sense that in the present rapidly changing circumstances, law must not restrict freedom of action. So the whole interest has shifted from fundamental to administrative law, and questions about doctrinal differences between the Book of Common Prayer (entrenched in the Declaration of Principles) and new liturgies do not seem to concern Canadian Anglicans. There is in North America generally a tendency for questions perceived by some to be at root matters of doctrine to be treated by the authorities as if they were primarily questions of procedure. It may be indicative that the so-called 'continuing' or 'traditional' Anglican Churches in North America have been preoccupied with canon law because they are convinced that deficiencies in the law of the Churches from which they have departed resulted in their perceived infidelity.

The variety in the internal constitutions of the Anglican Churches is remarkable. PECUSA had strong congregations before it had bishops, and there was no unanimity, at the time of the Revolution, that bishops were necessary. In consequence, the rights of bishops to appoint clergy and of dioceses to tax parishes are extraordinarily weak by Canadian standards. In Canada, the Church grew under the protection of bishops and the Crown, there is an un-American appearance of unanimity in the proceedings of the Church, bishops have a control over the process of clerical appointments, and dioceses a power to tax which many American Episcopalians would regard as tyrannous. The system of patronage and the strength of the parson's freehold has still remarkable strength in England. Though being eaten away by current policy and circumstance, both still are strong enough to afront the democratic spirit of American Episcopalians.[20] The episcopate is the basic element in the Scottish Episcopal Church; the Americans did not follow the Scots in this. In Australia the arrangements differ widely from place to place.

The episcopate is, however, enormously strong in the West Indies, where it enabled the Church to free itself from the establishment and its identification with slavery and the plantocracy and where congregations dependent on missionaries never acquired the habit of searching for, appointing or governing the activities of their clergy. Similar arrangements prevail in many of the African and Asian Churches where missionary societies found and paid the clergy (or still do) and where the bishop was the main mediating agent. In Australia, dioceses are strong and the national Church weak, at least so far as its power to make law for the Church is concerned. In Canada, ecclesiastical provinces still have power in respect to the election and consecration of bishops, a power residing at the national level in the USA. In North America, the primacy and the national executive structure aim to imitate the practical efficiency of a corporate business.[21] Such a model is foreign to the rest of the Communion and is not reflected in canonical arrangements.

There has been a general shift away from emphasis upon the fundamental doctrinal, moral and liturgical law of the Church to its organizational and administrative arrangements. The development of the executive primacy in the two North American Churches, a model for church and bishop imitated at the diocesan levels, is an instance. But, in general, a Church once united by fixed or very slowly evolving formularies (creeds, Articles, the Book of Common Prayer, etc.), now attempts to unite around projects and missions promoted through a synodical and consultative system, and organized with all the machinery of contemporary bureaucracies.[22] There has been a vast expansion of the law governing these councils, agencies and officers. This shift will not be evident where the resources of the Church are not sufficient to fund these consultations and agencies. Many of the same factors are at work here as those which make Churches disinterested in the tradition of canon law and which were listed above. There is a despair of theological objectivity and the possibility of real unity in doctrine and moral and spiritual discipline. There is fear of the old 'legalism' which is associated with party divisions and all uncharitableness. There is a sense of the urgency and real possibilities for the Church in the practical overcoming of un-Christian bondage and misery. Further, there is a conviction that, by constantly reshaping the agencies through which the Church carries out this mission, it can effectively adapt itself to the changing world.

If, in fact, Anglicans are united to the Catholic Church, and within that to one another by a fundamental canon law, then shifts which divert the Anglican Churches from the basic ground of their unity, or make that law ineffective within them, will threaten their communion. The evidence indicates that Anglicans are not united by similar relations of Church and state, by identical ways of conceiving the place of bishops or other authorities in the Church, by common patterns of understanding or relating national or provincial churches, dioceses, and parishes, or in the other ways in which the Church adapts itself pastorally and administratively to the cultural, political and social conditions of its particularized existence. The question as to whether there is for Anglicans a legal unity at all remains before us. If there is, then shifts which make it ineffective will present grave problems for the Communion. It is undeniable that current developments in liturgy, order, marriage discipline and ecumenical relations, all matters touching basic law, have placed strains on the Anglican Church. It is not thereby settled, however, that further developments along these lines will destroy the Communion. Indeed, many hold that they are paths along the way to greater unity within Christendom and, in consequence, with other Anglicans.

The argument of those who have this confidence has two basic aspects. On the one side, it is maintained that the unity of the Communion is analogous to that of a family, and was not and cannot be a matter of law. 'A family is essentially people, not laws or legal bodies, hence this family has a person, not a legal entity as its focus of unity'.[23] Or it may be maintained that the legal forms in which the unity was conceived are too narrow; the Thirty-nine Articles, the 1662 Prayer Book and the Lambeth Quadrilateral are criticized as past or present standards and agents of unity.[24] On the other side, efforts toward unity with non-Anglican Churches, productive of common doctrinal statements, liturgical forms and 'orthopraxis', are held to be the means of unity for Anglicans themselves. A consequence of this approach is that some ecumenical accords supplement or replace Anglican formularies.[25]

It cannot be the business of this article to judge the problems or potential for success of this way to inter-Anglican unity. We must note, however, that the adoption of ecumenical statements by legislatures of our Church has often the effect of reinterpreting our basic law, where it does not replace it by contradicting it. The adoption of ecumenically common liturgical forms in a Communion where the law of liturgy is central has the same effect. The result must be, and is, at least temporary legal confusion and disunity in the Church.

The question as to whether there is an Anglican unity at the level of fundamental canon law—despite some present interests and opinions—still remains.

The actual constitutional documents of the Churches of the Communion do, in fact, show such a legal unity; and this article will conclude by producing some of the evidence. What has united, and does unite, the Communion must be at least part of the discussion about what will, or will not, unite Anglicans in the future.

The so-called Chicago or Lambeth Quadrilateral (adopted by the House of Bishops of PECUSA in Chicago in 1886 and by the Lambeth Conference of 1888) designating the essential marks of the Catholic Church (for the purpose of reunion) as mediated through the Book of Common Prayer, with the Ordinal and Articles of Religion, provides a general statement of a common fundamental canon law for the Communion. The four points of the Quadrilateral in its Lambeth form are:

a. The Holy Scriptures of the Old and New Testament, as 'containing all things necessary to salvation' and as being the rule and ultimate standard of faith.

b. The Apostles' Creed, as the Baptismal Symbol; and the Nicene Creed, as the sufficient statement of the Christian faith.

c. The two Sacraments ordained by Christ Himself—Baptism and the Supper of the Lord—ministered with unfailing use of Christ's words of Institution, and of the elements ordained by Him.

d. The Historic Episcopate, locally adapted in the methods of its administration to the varying needs of the nations and peoples called of God into the Unity of His Church.[26]

The Quadrilateral does not itself constitute the fundamental law—except in the PECUSA where it appears in the 1979 Book of Common Prayer, with the Definition of Chalcedon, the Quicunque Vult, the Preface to the first Book of Common Prayer, the Articles of Religion and the Chicago Quadrilateral, among the 'Historical Documents of the Church'. The Nippon Seikokai has 'General Principles in common with the Holy Catholic Church throughout the world' which, influenced by the PECUSA, follow the wording of the Quadrilateral.

The fundamental law of an Anglican Church is the essential principles of the Catholic Church; and the Lambeth Quadrilateral provides a rough, generally agreed, statement of these (see pp. 39–40, pp. 219–20 and pp. 232–43). But, the principles are received as an actual living system for ordering the doctrine, sacraments, and discipline of the Church by means of the Book of Common Prayer with the Ordinal and Articles of Religion. The Solemn Declaration in the constitution of the General Synod of the Anglican Church of Canada provides a fuller statement, though with the same basic four marks. The marks themselves are abstractions from the Anglican formularies. What constitutes them as fundamental canon law is just that they have, in one form or another, been entrenched in the constitutions of so many of the Anglican Churches as fundamental principles and may be said to designate, for Anglicans, essential principles of the Catholic Church, as their formularies have transmitted them. The Catholic marks and the Anglican formularies go together.

The present canon law of the Church of England, sections A2–5, sets the Thirty-nine Articles, the Book of Common Prayer (presently 1662), the Ordinal annexed to the Book of Common Prayer, the holy Scripture 'and such teachings of the ancient Fathers and Councils of the Church as are agreeable to the said Scriptures' as fundamental law of the Church. At least some features of this fundamental law, e.g. the Book of Common Prayer, are presently protected by the overriding sovereignty of Parliament.

The Book of Common Prayer with its 'historical documents' is entrenched in the constitution of the PECUSA.[27] The force at law of the historical documents, and the coherence of the doctrine and discipline of the 1979 Book of Common

Prayer with the Anglican order as it is received in Churches which retain the legal supremacy of the more traditional forms of the Book of Common Prayer, are questions as yet undetermined.[28] The differences between the 1928 Prayer Book, which followed the eucharistic rite of the Scottish Episcopal Church, and the 1662 English Prayer Book, cannot be reasons for holding that the Prayer Book tradition is not part of our basic canon law. The Episcopal Church in Scotland itself authorized both books.[29] It is polemical to denigrate the role of the Prayer Book tradition in providing a legal unity to the Communion, after falsely narrowing that tradition to the 1662 book.

The Anglican Church of Canada has entrenched what amounts to a fuller form of the Quadrilateral's designation of the four marks of the Catholic Church in its constitution. The statement itself develops the form and language of the declarations made when diocesan synods were founded earlier, declarations which both limited the jurisdiction of the synods and provided that these legislatures would act within the principles and traditions of the Communion.[30] The Canadian Church maintains the Book of Common Prayer, Ordinal, and Articles in the entrenched part of its constitution and, like the English and Australian Church, has authorized the *Book of Alternative Services* alongside a Book of Common Prayer (1962) which stands within the tradition of Prayer Book revision. Legal questions surround the status of the BAS given its doctrinal differences from the BCP; they are questions of interest to the PECUSA, since the Canadian BAS is in considerable part derived from the 1979 American BCP. Because the Canadian Church did not alter its formularies when it ordained women to the priesthood, the question of whether there is a legal problem at this point remains open.[31] The Appeal Tribunal of the Church of the Province of New Zealand, which tried this question in November 1977, thought that the traditional Anglican formularies were not a legal obstacle to such ordinations, but this cannot be regarded as settled in England, Australia, or in some other parts of the Communion. In the Australian Church, the communion of unconfirmed children has been treated as a matter of legal concern to be considered in the light of the Book of Common Prayer and the Thirty-nine Articles. In a similar spirit, the Australian liturgical commission determined to keep their revisions within the doctrinal principles of the Prayer Book tradition.[32] It will be gathered (from the New Zealand case and the Australian instances and from the opinion of the Australian canon law commission noted above) that these Churches do regard themselves as receiving and governed by the ecclesiastical law of the Church of England and still retain the Book of Common Prayer, the Ordinal and Articles in their fundamental law.[33]

The constitution of the Church of the Province of South Africa has a Declaration of Fundamental Principles dating from 1870 basically like the Canadian form, and this has been confirmed by synods up to and including the Provincial Synod of 1968.[34] It contains important provisos allowing it to adapt the English formularies 'other than the Creeds' and, for important reasons of constitutional history, to make its own tribunals the authorities in the interpretations of its standards and formularies. The form of the constitution and provisos was, together with its exclusion of Bishop Colenso, taken to separate the Church of the Province of South Africa from the Church of England.[35] However, the constitution of the Province does conform in content to the fundamental canon law of the Anglican Communion.

If one goes on to the constitutions of other parts of the Communion, again and again a common pattern appears. Anglican Churches found themselves upon the faith of Christ as taught in holy Scripture and 'summed up in the Creeds', and they receive these, together with the sacraments and Apostolic ministry, through the Anglican formularies: Prayer Book, Ordinal and Articles. There are exceptions, but this is the rule which constitutes the Communion. It is true of the Church of Ireland.[36] It holds also for the Church in the Province of the West Indies whose constitution and canons were revised and updated in 1979. Like the Province of South Africa (in the second proviso) and other African Churches, the Province legally binds itself to altering its formularies co-ordinately with the other Churches of the Communion: adaptations, abridgements 'shall be liable to revision by any General Synod of the Anglican Communion to which this province shall be invited to send representatives'. It is the constitutional pattern for the Church of Uganda, and for the Anglican Church of Papua New Guinea. Though with a doctrinally elaborated preface, it stands for the Church of Burma.

The Church of the Province of West Africa, according to its constitution of 1963, places itself under God's Word and the English formularies (it specifies the 1662 Prayer Book, Ordinal and the Articles) and binds itself not to alter the fundamentals in ways adjudged by the Anglican metropolitans to be contrary to the terms of communion. The Church of the Province of Central Africa holds 'the Faith of Christ as taught in the Holy Scriptures, preached by the Apostles, summed up in the Creeds and confirmed by the undisputed General Councils ... as embodied in the Doctrine, Sacraments, and Discipline of Christ ... as the Church of England has received and taught the same in the Book of Common Prayer' and the Ordinal. It binds itself to refer questions of its adherence to these standards to the Anglican Consultative Council, and determines not to alter its fundamentals unless the Archbishop of Canterbury endorses the alteration. The Iglesia Anglicana Del Cono Sur, in its fundamental declaration, places itself within the Catholic Church and under the faith and order contained in holy Scripture and observed in the English Prayer Book and Ordinal (as with Central Africa, the Articles of Religion are not mentioned). The Constitution of the Church of the Province of Melanesia (1973) sets its foundation upon the faith of Christ and 'the teachings, sacraments and discipline of the One, Holy Catholic and Apostolic Church as the Anglican Communion has received them'. Its standards are the holy Scriptures and the Catholic Creeds.

Strict legal uniformity is not to be expected in the Anglican Communion, nor can it be found. But there are common legal traditions and patterns. The Communion has a unity in fundamental canon law, although it cannot be doubted that this unity is at risk.

NOTES

1 Col. 3.3.

2 Cf. Matt. 16.17–19; Matt. 18.18; John 20.23; 1 Pet. 2.13–18; Rom. 13.1–7; Luke 20.19–26; Eph. 5.20–6.9.

3 On obeying God by obeying the bishop cf. the epistles of Ignatius of Antioch.

4 R. C. Mortimer, *Western Canon Law* (Adam and Charles Black 1953), pp. 74ff.

5 ibid, p. 76.

6 *Vide* the Vincentian Canon and Irenaeus, *Adversus Haereses.*

7 The polity of the Church of England does not permit a final division between canon law and ecclesiastical law. That this is so is demonstrated by the reversal which takes place when one begins from the division and then tries to describe the relation of Church and State in England. Article XXI: 'General Councils may not be gathered together without the commandment and will of Princes' and Article XXVII: the King's Majesty rules 'all estates and degrees ... whether they be Ecclesiastical or Temporal' give the principles involved. G. W. O. Addleshaw, 'The Study of Canon Law' in H. S. Box, ed., *The Priest as Student* (SPCK 1939), pp. 201–36 begins with the Church as *societas perfecta* in contradistinction from the state and with canon law divided from ecclesiastical law, the division is abrogated when the 'Byzantine' polity of England is treated.

8 Cf. F. Makower, *The Constitutional History and Constitution of the Church of England* (London 1895), p. 146.

9 Cf. G. W. O. Addleshaw, *The High Church Tradition* (Faber 1944); R. C. Mortimer, 'Foreward', H. S. Box, *The Principles of Canon Law* (OUP 1949); *The Ecclesiastical Courts, Principles of Reconstruction, Being the Report of the Commission on Ecclesiastical Courts set up by the Archbishops of Canterbury and York in 1951 at the request of the Convocations* (SPCK 1954), pp. 24ff.

10 S. W. Sykes with S. W. Gilley, '"No Bishop, No Church": The Tractarian Impact on Anglicanism' in G. Rowell (ed.), *Tradition Renewed* (DLT 1986).

11 Cf. H. S. Box, *The Principles of Canon Law* and n. 7 above.

12 On the 1789 Prayer Book cf. Marion J. Hatchett, *The Making of the first American Book of Common Prayer, 1776–89* (Seabury Press 1982).

13 H. L. Clarke, *Constitutional Church Government* (SPCK 1924), p. 24; on the Tractarian conception of the episcopate in Canada see W. J. Hankey, art. cit., n. 22 below.

14 *The Canons of the Church of England* (Church Information Office); *The Canon Law of the Church of England, Being the Report of the Archbishops' Commission on Canon Law, together*

with Proposals for a Revised Body of Canons . . . (SPCK 1947) ; and *Canon Law Revision 1959* (SPCK 1960).

15 Cf. *The Canon Law of the Church of England*, and E. Garth Moore and Timothy Briden, *Moore's Introduction to English Canon Law*. (2nd edn ; Mowbray 1985).

16 Standing Committee of the General Synod of Australia 1981, *Canon Law in Australia, A summary of church legislation and its sources*, p. 2114.

17 Cf. F. Vinton, *A Manual Commentary on the General Canon Law and Constitution of the Protestant Episcopal Church in the United States* (Dulton 1870), pp. 32–3 ; E. A. White and J. A. Dykman, *Annoted Constitution and Canons*, 2 vols. (Seabury Press 1954) ; D. B. Stevick, *Canon Law, A Handbook* (Seabury Press 1965), pp. 67–70.

18 For example, J. Arnold, 'The Church and the Law', in *Conference Report 1984 : Church Polity and Authority*, ed. G. R. Bridge (Charlottetown, PEI, Canada, St Peter Publications, 1985), p. 3f.

19 Namely, R. V. Harris, *An Historical Introduction to the Study of the Canon Law of the Anglican Church of Canada* (General Synod Commission on Canon Law 1965) ; of the 'from colony to nation' genre.

20 On the compromise at the heart of the polity of PECUSA, cf. J. E. Booty, *The Church in History* (Seaburg Press 1979), pp. 71–2.

21 R. Foster, *The Role of the Presiding Bishop* (Forward Movement 1982).

22 On causes and consequences, cf. W. J. Hankey, 'The Ends and Limits of Spiritual Authority' in G. R. Bridge, ed., op. cit., pp. 42–51.

23 Bishop John Howe, *ACC-4, Anglican Consultative Council, Report of the Fourth Meeting 1979* (ACC 1979), p. 72 ; the person is the Archbishop of Canterbury !

24 ibid., p. 70 and *Bonds of Affection, Proceedings of ACC-6* (ACC 1984), pp. 72–5.

25 Cf., for example, the treatment of the WCC's Baptism, Eucharist and Ministry documents in *Bonds of Affection*, p. 76 ; and S. W. Sykes, 'ARCIC and the Papacy, An Examination of the Documents on Authority' in *The Modern Churchman*, xxv, 1, pp. 9–18.

26 J. Robert Wright, ed., *A Communion of Communions : One Eucharistic Fellowship* (Seabury Press 1979), pp. 231–2.

27 *Constitutions and Canons for the Government of the Protestant Episcopal Church in the United States of America otherwise known as the Episcopal Church* (Seabury Press 1982), Article X, p. 8.

28 Note that the Articles of Religion are found both in the 'historical documents' and in Article X of the Constitution ; their legal force is established.

29 *Code of Canons of the Episcopal Church of Scotland* (CUP 1973), p. xvi ; and canon xxii, p. 34.

30 W. J. Hankey, art. cit.

31 Nor is it completely resolved within PECUSA ; some maintain that the alteration was not made in proper legal form ; cf. Editorial, *The Living Church* 192. xv (13 April 1986), p.

12; J. R. Zimmerman, 'Women in the Episcopate Now?' *The Living Church*, 192. xxii (1 June 1986), pp. 8, 12.

32 *Prayer Book Revision in Australia* (Sydney 1966), p. iv and documents of the 1981 General Synod.

33 H. L. Clark, op. cit., pp. 146, 190.

34 ibid., pp. 343–4.

35 ibid., pp. 337–8

36 ibid., p. 511.

PART FIVE

Church, Sacraments and Ministry

1 Doctrine of the Church

PHILIP H. E. THOMAS

Avis, P. D. L., *The Church in the Theology of the Reformers*. John Knox Press 1981.

Hanson, A., *Church, Sacraments and Ministry*. Mowbray 1975.

Jay, E. G., *The Church* (vol i, ch. 13; vol ii, chs 17–18). SPCK 1978.

Ramsey, A. M. *The Gospel and the Catholic Church*. Longman 1936.

Ramsey, A. M. ed., *Catholicity: A Study in the Conflict of Christian Traditions in the West*. Dacre Press 1947.

Sykes, S. W. ed., *Authority in the Anglican Communion*. Toronto, Anglican Book Centre 1978.

Toon, P. *Evangelical Theology*. Marshall, Morgan and Scott 1979.

William Reed Huntington is known in Anglican history by a footnote. As Rector of an influential New York congregation he wrote in 1870 *The Church Idea*, which first put forward the formula for Christian unity eventually known as the Chicago–Lambeth Quadrilateral. His proposal—that acceptance of Scripture, Creeds, the sacraments of baptism and the Eucharist, and the episcopal ordering of ministry should provide the basis for effective union among the Churches—has stood for nearly a century as a cornerstone of Anglican ecumenical endeavour

Huntington's achievement however was much closer to the main theme of Anglican ecclesiology than that incidental footnote might suggest. His concern for unity was not confined to a defence of denominational norms, but was placed within the context of the question of what was involved in being Anglican, and in particular, being Anglican in North America. He was dismissive of the merely nostalgic appeal of Anglicanism: 'The word brings up before the eyes of some a flutter of surplices, a vision of village spires and cathedral towers, a somewhat stiff and stately company of deans, prebendaries and choristers, and that is all' (p 124). *The Church Idea* took the incarnation seriously and saw it as becoming increasingly the perspective of the Church in a changing society.

> If our whole ambition as Anglicans in America be to continue a small but eminently respectable body of Christians, and to offer a refuge to people of refinement and sensibility, who are shocked by the irreverences they are apt to encounter elsewhere; in a word, if we are to be only a countercheck and not a force in society, then let us say as much in plain terms and frankly renounce any and all claim to Catholicity. We have only, in such case, to wrap the robe of our dignity about us, and walk quietly along in a seclusion no-one will take much trouble to disturb. Thus may we be a Church in name and a sect in deed.

The nature of that charge, brought be it noted some fifty years before Troeltsch's formative church-sect typology, deserves closer attention. But Huntington did not restrict himself to criticism. In the ringing tones of pulpit oratory he continued:

219

But if we aim at something nobler than this, if we would have our communion become national in very truth—in other words, if we would bring the Church of Christ into the closest possible sympathy with the throbbing, sorrowing, sinning, repenting, aspiring heart of this great people—then let us press our reasonable claims to be the reconciler of a divided household, not in a spirit of arrogance (which ill befits those whose best possessions have come to them by inheritance), but with affectionate earnestness and intelligent zeal (p. 159).

It was in pursuit of that claim that Huntington laid down his version of the Quadrilateral, and in so doing gave an instructive example of the way in which Anglican ecclesiology is pursued.

It is no simple matter to relate Anglican thinking about the doctrine of the Church. Quite apart from well-known internal differences which make it difficult to 'read off' any ecclesiology which would be acceptable to all Anglicans, there is also a notable reluctance on their part to acknowledge any peculiarly Anglican dogma—of the Church or of anything else. Anglicans have received the faith of the Church, it is claimed; and therefore nothing more can or need be said. Whether such a position is tenable is one of the questions that must be explored in this chapter, but one thing to be noted at this stage is the fact that Anglicanism, since its beginnings, has been forged on the anvil of ecclesiological controversy. Part of the case to be presented is that while Anglican ecclesiology cannot offer any consensus on the constitution of the Church, it has been able to maintain its credibility by the way in which Anglican Churches have been forced to engage with their own history and with the theological issues raised for them by it. When Huntington addressed the situation faced by the episcopal Church in his time, and sought to draw out from its inheritance the resources to meet the demands of Christian unity and mission, he was doing something that has been characteristic of the Church of England throughout its history, and that has been carried on by the Churches of the Anglican Communion ever since. What follows will seek to suggest some of the lines of argument which have given shape to Anglican understanding of the Church, and at the same time attempt to show why most Anglicans do not believe that their lack of a normative ecclesiology is a fatal flaw but is rather the source of a distinctive theological and ecumenical opportunity.

1 THE DOCTRINE OF THE CHURCH AS RECEIVED BY THE CHURCH OF ENGLAND

The official formularies of the Church of England—the Thirty-nine Articles, the Book of Common Prayer and Ordinal, and the Canons Ecclesiastical are not 'confessional', if by that term it is meant that they provide the foundational dogmas or ideological texts upon which all later Anglican teaching was based (see pp. 121-33, pp. 133-43, pp. 143-53 and pp. 200-213). What they present are the beliefs which made it possible to change the direction of English Christianity during a decisive period of its development. The sixteenth-century reforms in England may have been occasioned by Henry VIII's marriage problems or by Elizabeth's desire for peace, but such changes were only possible because a set of theological convictions eventually persuaded a majority of Tudor churchmen that the new course set by Church and state was a proper one to follow. These convictions were threefold. First there was the belief that the Church of England had a continuous history reaching back to Augustine of Canterbury and beyond. Second, it was held that the life of the Church must be drawn into renewed conformity with the teaching of the Bible, and that this could be done without breaking the continuity of faith and history to which it was heir. Third, while abuses were to be corrected, things of value were to be retained and therefore ceremonies and ideas which were not explicitly contradicted by Scripture were simply left open to the continuing evaluation of the Christian community.

Enough has been said elsewhere about the mixed provenance of the formularies between 1548 and 1662 and the tensions that are reflected by them as a result. There is however no ambiguity about the way in which the Church of England was seen in them to be Reformed yet quite plainly still part of the universal Church. This is evident from the title of the Book of Common Prayer, when it sets forth the 'Rites and Ceremonies of the Church, according to the use of the Church of England'. The compilers of the Prayer Book intended primarily to collect and arrange liturgical resources from the historic Church and make them available for use by the English in their own language. The English liturgy, borrowing as it does from various periods of ecclesiastical history, itself expresses the conviction that the Church is one and the Church of England a part of it. At the heart of their intercessions worshippers were to beseech God to 'inspire continually the universal Church with a spirit of truth, unity and concord', and to pray that 'all they that do confess thy holy name may agree in the truth of thy holy Word, and live in unity and godly love'. At baptism the priest received candidates into 'the congregation of Christ's flock' and declared them to be sacramentally regenerate and 'grafted into Christ's Church' with the expectation that they would become 'lively members of the same'. In the ordination rite the bishop was to lay hands on those being priested with the words, 'Receive the Holy Ghost for the office and work of a priest within the Church of God'. To belong to the Church of England was to be part of Christ's Church, and it was this which gave legitimacy to Anglican liturgy, membership and ministry.

At the same time, the Church of England in the sixteenth century was also represented as being Reformed. Along with the emphasis on continuity, there was an equal stress on the constitutive power of the Word of God in the life of the Church. In the ordination formula the bishop presented the new priest with a Bible (in itself a symbolic change from the earlier practice of offering the sacramental instruments) and prayed that the Church would have grace 'to hear and receive what they shall deliver out of thy most holy Word, or agreeable to the same'. Each congregation, as part of its intercession for the whole state of Christ's Church, prayed for all God's people and 'especially this congregation here present' that 'with meek heart and due reverence, they may hear, and receive thy holy Word'. Catholic tradition was tested and proved against the reading of Scripture.

The same dual conviction concerning Anglican teaching was evident in the Articles (see pp. 134–7). Articles I to VIII reiterate that Anglicans are held to the doctrines of the Church by means of Creed and Bible, while simultaneously acknowledging the Reformers' hermeneutical concerns by clearly defining the theological limits of the biblical canon. At the heart of these opening paragraphs the typical Anglican assertion of the sufficient but not exhaustive authority of Scripture (Article VI) provides the touchstone for all other beliefs (see pp. 82–5). Even the Creeds are received precisely because 'they may be proved by most certain warrant of Holy Scripture' (Article VIII), and altogether eighteen of the Articles allude or refer to the Bible as the source of their authority. So settled was the conviction that the Church of England in the sixteenth and seventeenth centuries was simply the Church in England undergoing an internal process of renovation, that the Canons Ecclesiastical (1604) threatened excommunication to anyone who denied that the English Church was a 'true and apostolical church', or who suggested that its forms of worship 'containeth anything in it that is repugnant to the scriptures'. The apologetic was plainly directed against Roman Catholic critics on the one hand and the more radical spirits of the Reformation on the other, but the positive claim which lay behind it was equally clear: the Church of England was Reformed, but still Catholic.

What understanding of the Church could give rise to that sort of assertion? The answer is spelled out in principle by Article XXXIV. Churches are at least partly the creation of their history and culture. At different times and in different places the life of the Church will be encapsulated in different traditions and ceremonies. 'Particular and national Churches' hold the responsibility for shaping their corporate existence in accordance with the precepts of Scripture but within the context of their own local environment. The universal Church must take on a particular identity.

If the principle underlying the establishment of Reformed Catholicism in England was the concept of the national Church, then the procedure depended on the belief, already noted, that many elements of church life were 'in their own nature indifferent' and so could be arranged as matters of convenience rather than conviction. The idea of *adiaphora* or 'things indifferent' had been advanced on the continent by Melanchthon and utilized in passing by Calvin (see pp. 234–5). It received a distinctive exposition in an appendix to the 1549 Prayer Book, and this was expanded as part of the Preface to the Book of Common Prayer in

1662. Abuses and unnecessary burdens, it was explained, had to be abolished; yet in Anglican liturgy 'the main body and essentials . . . have still continued the same'. Change was not seen as an end in itself and respect for antiquity as well as good order meant that much that was familiar could still be utilized. No counsel of perfection could be invoked. The claim for Anglican ceremonial and worship was simply that it did not 'contain in it anything contrary to the Word of God, or to sound doctrine, or which a godly man may not with a good conscience use and submit unto'. What was argued for the Book of Common Prayer could also be held to apply to the structures and offices of the Church: its threefold ministry, episcopal ordination, details of vesture and ritual in worship, along with the continued existence of cathedrals and universities, the administrative hierarchy of deans, chapters and archdeacons, and it would appear, much of the old parochial system of pastoral organization.

With the benefit of hindsight, some commentators have felt able to discern a distinct national consciousness in the English Church almost from its inception; but the thinking found within the formularies of the Church of England cannot be described as nationalistic. The English Reformers certainly acted under royal patronage, but the best of them were not merely opportunist. The Sixteenth century saw no independent doctrine of the Church introduced, but it did see a new confidence on the part of the Church as 'witness and keeper of Holy Writ' (as Article XX put it) in its responsibility to judge controversies of faith. Article XIX summed up the change: it was responsiveness to the word and sacraments that should mark the Church of Christ, not the form of its outward organization or allegiances. When the circumstances of its history demanded that the English Church should mark its autonomy from the Church of Rome at one stage, or from the radical wing of the Reformation at another, it was not abandoning its sense of participation in the history of the universal Church any more than it was denying its broad sympathy with the continental movements for reform. It was simply choosing to differ over specific interpretations as to how commitments to the authority of the Bible or tradition were to be identified and expressed. It is the debates over the range of such interpretations that largely make up the course of Anglican theological history; but the central belief that makes such discussion possible is that the Church, while universal in its faith and obligation, also possesses a particular vocation and calling.

2 THE DOCTRINE OF THE CHURCH AS INTERPRETED WITHIN THE CHURCH OF ENGLAND

Most Reformed bodies acknowledged the continuing importance of Catholic norms of belief. More than one realized also the utility of allowing that some aspects of the Church's existence were matters of indifference. Where the English

Reformers had broken new ground was in retaining intact many of the traditional structures of the Church, and in allowing that certain doctrinal matters could be included among the *adiaphora*. A thoroughgoing biblical critique does impose its own limitation on doctrinal formulae, precisely because the Bible is not doctrinally precise, especially in matters of ecclesiology. The English understanding of biblical authority made it logically necessary to allow that some beliefs were open to dispute, and therefore that a diversity of interpretations had to be allowed in several areas of theological debate. The problem was of course in deciding just when the limits of biblical authorization had been reached, and just what could or could not be considered 'indifferent'.

It was in the terms of that controversy that Richard Hooker compiled *The Laws of Ecclesiastical Polity* (1593–7). Against the Puritan ideal of replicating an exact New Testament model of church organization, Hooker argued that the Church was an organic not a static institution, and that the law of God was such that methods of church government and administration would change according to circumstances. Where the Bible was silent or unclear Hooker claimed that guidance should be taken from four propositions 'such as no man of moderate judgement hath cause to think unjust or unreasonable'. These were: that anything which effectively promotes godliness, has received the approval of antiquity, or has received the support of the Church's own system government, should prove acceptable; and that conversely, no institution or ordinance which is not expressly commanded by Scripture should be made a matter of necessity for the Church, no matter how useful or profitable it may appear to be.[1]

The biblical radicalism of the first Reformers was arguably better sustained by Hooker and his younger contemporary Richard Field than by their continental counterparts, inasmuch as the former refused to tie the Church of England to particular forms of dogma or discipline, and recognize the eschatological and dialectical nature of truth and purity.[2] They were at one with the Reformers over the central question of the period: 'How can I find a gracious God?' But to the second question, 'Where can I find the true Church?', they gave a more mundane answer. Assurance with regard to the Church was to be found neither in the biblical idealism of the Puritans nor in the conservative traditionalism of the Catholics. The gospel did not come with fail-safe guarantees. The Church always exists under grace, and while truth and purity were not to be taken lightly, their full achievement was still awaited and in the meantime could only be perceived in faith. No form of discipline or safeguards on doctrine could replace that perception.

Hooker's approach to the identity of the Church had its application to church doctrine as well. The question of the visibility of the Church is a case in point. The Reformers inevitably laid emphasis on membership of the invisible Church, an inward thing known only to God, in order to counter the Roman claim that membership of the Church involved participation in the hierarchical structure which centred on the papacy. The Anglican theologians attended to the concept of the Church as the mystical body of Christ or the invisible company of the elect, but never finally at the expense of the reality of the Church in its temporal form. Their language may have been ambiguous at times, but they steadily refused to identify the visible/invisible dichotomy with the notion of truth and falsity in the Church. Hooker was clear that the Church would always contain a mixed membership and that the validity of its life could only be demonstrated by way of costly obedience to the law of God. Neither he nor Field neglected the divine origins of the Church (and that was later reinforced by John Pearson's influential *Exposition of the Creed*, 1659) but concentrated on the concrete, historical existence of the people of God and their role within the body politic. Field, in *Of the Church* (1606–10), responded to the Catholic apologist, Bellarmine, that it was a waste of time his trying to prove to Anglicans that there was and always had been a visible Church, for that fact had never been doubted by them.

Hooker's and Field's attention to the central reality of the Church and their restraint over the question of its circumference presented a theological position more pragmatic, realistic and ecumenical than that of most other second-generation leaders of the reform. One might equally say that they more clearly maintained a grasp on the graciousness of God. Doctrine was not unimportant to the defenders of Anglicanism, but they appreciated that doctrinal precision of itself could never guarantee a full measure of faith, hope or love. At its best, Anglicanism's doctrinal openness recognized that the mystery of God was not to be contained by a formula or by the victory of one biblical principle over another. Just how baptism related to faith, or bread and wine communicated the presence of Christ, or the historic episcopate mediated an apostolic ministry, was never explained in the classical period of Anglican development. Scripture and history keeps such questions alive within the Anglican consciousness and the tradition of continuing debate holds out the hope of increasing clarification of the issues involved. Ideally the Anglican understanding of the Church secures to it the full variety of biblical models and metaphors by which it is described, and attempts to work out the significance of those descriptions in everyday, historical experience.[3]

Grace, however, is not easily lived with, and the demands of ongoing theological articulation are not always welcomed by the Church. Anglicanism is at its least satisfactory when it is able to avoid facing the implications of its own internal tensions. It has often been observed that the Church of England underwent a sea-change between the seventeenth century, when it opposed Puritanism because of its narrowness, and the eighteenth, when it resisted Methodism on account of its enthusiasm. The Puritans may not have been as narrow as is commonly believed and enthusiasm was certainly more complex than it may appear, but it is the change in Anglican self-consciousness that is of importance here. In the first place, as a reaction to the excesses of the

225

Commonwealth and the sufferings of the exiles, episcopal order came to assume a normative importance for Anglicans which it had not held previously (see pp. 300–307). The Church of England became identified with the episcopate. Furthermore the deprivation of the Non-jurors lost to the Church a spiritual and devotional legacy which was more important than the actual number of priests and bishops who were involved would suggest. Not only did this diminish the bond of worship which, it was held, still unified different theological emphases within the national Church; it also left it firmly established as a guardian of self-interest. The Church of England emerged looking suspiciously like a department of state, ill-equipped to cope intellectually with the spread of Enlightenment thought, or pastorally with the effects of the Industrial Revolution, or theologically with the rise of the Evangelical Revival.

It would be idle to pretend that Anglican restraint in defining doctrine was always the result of a highly principled commitment to comprehensiveness. Equally important was the fact that at critical points of church history no one group was able to dominate for long enough to impose its ideals on the remainder of the Anglican body. The failure of the Church of England during the eighteenth century was most evident in the way it was dominated by the state to such an extent that Newman would have some justification believing that by his day it was the establishment alone which erected the Church of England to unity and individuality. Strip it of this world, he challenged, and it will be a mortal operation, for it will cease to be.[4] Accompanying this virtual Erastianism, partly as a cause and partly an effect, was the loss of any theological sense of the origin and destiny of the Church as such. Such ecclesiology as was advanced—the rights of the episcopate and the necessity of liturgical conformity—was largely used to unchurch and disenfranchise those who in any way dissented from Anglican jurisdiction. Only during the nineteenth century did renewal come, largely through a reassertion of the doctrine of the Church in Anglican thinking.

Renewal came from various sources. Churchmen influenced by the Evangelical Revival pressed the need for personal conversion as the key to effective church and social action, although for them this was often expressed in inter-church or voluntary associations of the like-minded, rather than in the mainstream of church life. Leaders like Charles Simeon (1759–1836) (see pp. 168–9), and especially those who learnt from him, ensured that biblical and pastoral preaching found its proper place in parochial ministry. However, they remained relatively unconcerned with proposals for wholesale reform like those advocated by Coleridge or Thomas Arnold in *On the Constitution of Church and State* (1830) and *Principles of Church Reform* (1833) (see pp. 358–9). The liberal or Broad Church voice within Anglican opinion could trace its accents back to the Latitudinarians or the humanist tradition of earlier generations; but the approach of men like Arnold, R. D. Hampden or Richard Whately would only ever appeal to a small if influential minority in the Church. At a time when the established Church was

226

increasingly marginalized in its influence, theirs was a serious attempt to relocate its position nearer the centre of intellectual and public life in England. The most enduring changes came from the Tractarian or Oxford Movement which in contrast to the liberal group boldly reasserted the divine origins of the Church in order to establish its spiritual autonomy from the state. The Tractarians sought to demonstrate its true character by restoring what they believed to be primitive practice in the Church and laying claim to the essential Catholicity of Anglican faith and order.

While the Evangelical emphasis on personal religion and the liberal programme for rationalizing dogma left ecclesiological questions still on the periphery of the Church's agenda, the High Churchmen placed them right at the centre. In 1838, W. Palmer's *Treatise on the Church of Christ* had put forward a so-called 'branch theory' of the Church and this was taken up enthusiastically by the Tractarians. It was postulated that there were three authentic scions of Catholic Christianity— the Roman, Eastern and Anglican Churches—which shared common historical and sacramental stock. While not in communion with each other, this common ancestry meant that these three groups of Churches alone could claim to be part of the Catholic and apostolic Church. Focusing as it did on a particular idea of apostolic succession, this theory proved too much for some critics (since it left the Reformed tradition within the Church of England exposed to an anomaly), and too little for others (as the departure of Newman and others in favour of the more self-confident claims of the Roman Catholic Communion demonstrated).

The second half of the nineteenth century certainly saw attention directed once again to the doctrine of the Church, but this was accompanied by a hardening of attitudes and an increase in dogmatically held positions. What was even more significant was the failure of the Church of England to find any means of resolving these differences. Falling back on a succession of legal tests ranging from the Gorham Case in 1847 to the Lincoln Judgement of 1890, it proved impossible to use the Articles or the other formularies to define just what were the beliefs of the Anglican Church. Each appellant claimed that his interpretation represented a legitimate line of Anglican theological development. With no means of achieving or even approaching a consensus, the different groupings within the Church of England became increasingly partisan in their attitudes; and the Anglican understanding of the Church took on the varied complexion of apparently contradictory opinion which still typifies Anglicanism in the eyes of some of its critics.

3 THE DOCTRINE OF THE CHURCH AS AMPLIFIED BY THE ANGLICAN COMMUNION

If the nineteenth century saw a failure to resolve problems of ecclesiology in the Church of England, it also witnessed a dramatic expansion of the context in which they were to be raised. Missionary activity, with commerce and colonization, led to the founding of Anglican Churches in many parts of the world. This led to new questions about status and relationship, and in fact gave rise to the situation where it was possible or indeed necessary to talk about 'Anglicanism' as such. The story of the growth of the Anglican Communion and the gathering of the first Lambeth Conferences has been told elsewhere (see pp. 194–7 and pp. 37–40), but these developments had a twofold significance for Anglican ecclesiology. Firstly, they led to a new awareness of the autonomy of the national Churches, and secondly, to a consideration of their interdependence.

The freedom of national Churches to order their own affairs was of course precisely the right claimed by the Church of England in its most formative period, and by choice or from necessity it was reiterated by the leaders of new Churches as they struggled towards their independence. When Huntington challenged Episcopalians in the United States to take their vocation more seriously, he was not only returning to the aspirations of those who had reorganized the Church there after the War of Independence, but also the convictions of those who had given the Church of England its particular identity some two centuries earlier. The North American example had in fact proved instructive, as colonial bishops, realizing their own spiritual authority, followed the American example and organized their churches under synodical compacts in order to take responsibility for their own local life and leadership (see pp. 202–209).

At the same time as asserting their independence, the new Churches affirmed a strong inclination to maintain connections with the Church of England and to take opportunities for 'brotherly counsel and encouragement' with each other. To this end the first Lambeth Conference met in 1867, and from it stemmed the network of inter-Anglican organization and ideology which gives shape to the Anglican Communion as 'a fellowship of national Churches' today. What sort of shape is it, though? From the beginning the Conferences renounced any legislative powers. The authority of each meeting was limited to the inherent wisdom of its deliberations. Any statement made possessed only the authority of those bishops who put their names to it. The Conference could make recommendations, but it was up to the member Churches to judge their worth and take whatever action they deemed appropriate. Each ten-yearly meeting 'focusses the experience and counsels of our communion' explained a statement from the 1920 Conference, 'yet it claims no power of control or command'. A committee of the 1930 Lambeth Conference underlined the conviction concerning Anglican unity: 'There are two prevailing types of ecclesiastical organization: that of a centralized government, and that of regional autonomy within one fellowship.' In common with the Church of the first centuries and with Orthodoxy to this day, it argued, the Anglican Communion was constituted on the second model. It was not always clear however just what sort of fellowship

Anglican Churches shared, nor gave cohesiveness to their Communion, nor indeed in what way that Communion was Anglican. Various solutions have been proposed. If ideas of a centralized council seemed inappropriate, unity which was based on any statement of peculiarly Anglican beliefs was even less likely to win recognition. The Thirty-nine Articles, the most likely candidate for such a confessional role, had already faded in Anglican consciousness as a result of their failure to maintain peace during the nineteenth-century controversies in England. To Churches intent upon discovering their own indigenous character they seemed remote in the extreme, and in 1968 the Lambeth Conference recommended that Churches should formally distance themselves from the Articles, honouring them for their historical significance but discarding any attempt to utilize them as a contemporary confession of faith. For some time it was held, as an alternative source of authority, that the Book of Common Prayer could act both as a bond of union and a principal source of Anglican teaching. The inevitable process of liturgical translation and revision carried out by the national bodies meant that at most, they could only share a common structure of worship. The cultural diversity of the Churches of the Communion made the idea of a common liturgical form an impossibility. At a rather different level, the Archbishop of Canterbury, as convenor of the Lambeth Conferences, has played a distinct role in giving cohesion to Anglican unity. His authority like that of the Conferences is moral, given to him by mutual consent and not exercised as of right. As a personal link the office is increasingly valued by the Churches, but the Archbishop remains a pivot not a pope, as Randall Davidson put it.[5] The role of the Archbishop, like that of the Conferences, the Anglican Consultative Council and the Primates Meeting, the Doctrine or Justice and Peace Commissions as they now exist, is a contingent and not a necessary factor in Anglican ecclesiology.

The apparent failure to find in formularies or administrative norms a focus for Anglican identity should neither alarm nor suprise an observer. It brings back into focus, amongst others, William Reed Huntington and his insistence that it was on the basis of faith, sacraments, and a shared ministry that the 'church idea' would be established.

4 THE DOCTRINE OF THE CHURCH AND THE CREDIBILITY OF ANGLICANISM

Huntington, it will be remembered, was doing two things. He was drawing out of the inheritance of the Church of England theological resources which could unite Christians in North America, and he was doing this in order that the message and reality of the incarnation of Christ might have a formative influence on the emerging life of the new nation. Enough has been said to make it apparent why that work was taken as typical of the way in which the doctrine of the Church is treated within Anglicanism. Anglicans, like the early Church, and like the Orthodox Churches to this day, have refrained from producing a standard, systematic theology of the Church, but that does not mean that they have shown no interest in ecclesiology. All the historic questions about unity, catholicity and holiness have been raised repeatedly in the course of Anglican theological development: numerous ecclesiological models have been put forward from within Anglicanism, but it remains true that Anglican self-consciousness has not been fixated upon any one of them. If it is charged that such indecision robs Anglicanism of the right to serious theological consideration, it must be countered that the Anglican system is not that of a confessional Church whose norms and standards are fixed and open to scrutiny, so much as it is that of a confessing Church which must demonstrate its credibility by the way it meets successive challenges of faith and history in its ongoing life. Two brief examples must suffice to show the sort of evidence that may count for this purpose.

It must be admitted that quite often talk of Anglicanism's doctrinal comprehensiveness is a mask to cover doctrinal indifference. However, at its best the willingness to hold open various interpretations of the Church makes Anglicanism into what Michael Ramsey has called 'a school of synthesis'. The fact that the Anglican Communion has no complete theological system keeps it aware that the Church awaits its restoration. The fact that the Lambeth Quadrilateral imposes no interpretation on how faith and order are to express the fullness of Christ's salvation is itself a witness to the present incompleteness of the Church, yet if also holds out an anticipation of its achieving eschatological wholeness. If it is true that the gospel of Christ has its Catholic and Protestant principles, that the Bible is concerned with prophetic and with priestly religion, and that the early Church was formed under both institutional and charismatic impulses, then the Anglican attempt to bring together in one fellowship such different understandings of Christian discipleship justifies itself.

Anglicans are painfully aware also that their claim to be a 'bridge Church', or the reconcilers of a divided household, has been made to look delusory when tested against the hard realities of ecumenical engagement (see pp. 379–84). Nevertheless, by the eventual achievement of intercommunion with the united Churches of South and North India, by their participation in the wider Episcopal Fellowship of Churches, and the close accord established with Lutherans in North America especially, Anglicans have shown that their commitment to the ideal of genuinely national Christianity involves more than the orchestration of denominational merger schemes. It was Michael Ramsey again who emphasized that true Catholicity is not to be found either in the adjustment of confessional differences or in the imposition of particular structures in pursuit of ecumenical agreements. The biblical metaphors of the Church—building, body, vine, ecclesia—all speak of both the given-ness of its life under God and also of the way in which it must constantly grow to become perfectly what it is.[6]

It is because the Anglican view of the Church seeks to do justice both to a vision of the Church in its universal dimension and to the reality of the Church in its local manifestations, that it is difficult to envisage a systematic treatment of its teaching. Yet to promote a dogma which resolved the Anglican dilemma at the expense of one or the other aspect of it would be to take from Anglicanism its vocation and its ecumenical and missionary opportunity.

At about the time Huntington was writing in America, E. B. Pusey was called upon to explain to a German correspondent the peculiarities of Anglican ecclesiological scholarship:

> You will doubtless have observed that few, if any, of our writings have originated in an abstract love of investigation; our greatest and some immortal works have arisen in some exigencies of the times; the writings of Chillingworth, Hooker, Butler, Bull (and so of the rest) were written not merely to solve problems of importance in themselves, but such as the good of the Church in our country at that time required.[7]

If that is granted, then it must also be acknowledged that while the Anglican view of the Church may be incomplete from a doctrinal point of view, it is not in its spirit or in its teaching unbiblical. Anglican ecclesiology claims more, but no less, than that.

NOTES

1 *The Laws of Ecclesiastical Polity*, V. vi–ix.

2 See Paul Avis, '"The True Church" in Reformation Theology', *Scottish Journal of Theology*, 30 (1977) pp. 319–45.

3 For a Roman Catholic's appreciation of this fact, see Avery Dulles, *Models of the Church* (1976), p. 10.

4 *Discourses to Mixed Congregations, XII* (1849), pp. 265–6.

5 G. K. A. Bell, *Randall Davidson* (1935), vol i, p. 444.

6 *Canterbury Pilgrim* (1974), p. 110.

7 H. P. Liddon, *Life of Pusey* (1893–7), vol i, p. 238.

2 The Fundamentals of Christianity

STEPHEN W. SYKES

Congar. Y., *Tradition and Traditions*. London 1966. Esp. Excursus B, 'Scripture and the "Truths Necessary for Salvation"', pp. 508–19.
Congar, Y., *Diversity and Communion*. London 1984. Esp. ch. 11, 'Agreement on "Fundamental Articles" or on the Positions of the Early Church', pp. 107–25.

Joest, W., 'Fundamentartikel' in *Theologische Realenzyklopädie* XI (Berlin and New York 1983), pp. 727–32.

Leclerc, J. SJ, *Toleration and Reformation*, 2 vols. New York and London 1960.

Neill, S. C. and Rouse, R. eds., *A History of the Ecumenical Movement*. London 1967. Esp. essays by M. Schmidt, 'Ecumenical Activity on the Continent of Europe in the Seventeenth and Eighteenth Centuries', and N. Sykes, 'Ecumenical Movements in Great Britain in the Seventeenth and Eighteenth Centuries'.

Rowell, G., 'Die altkirchlichen Bekenntnisse in der klassichen Anglikanischen Tradition', in *Una Sancta*.

Valeske, U., *Hierarchia Veritatum*. Munich 1968. Esp. ch. 3, 'Das Problem der Fundamentalartikel in der Theologiegeschichte der Nichtrömischen Kirchen'; and bibliography.

THE MODERN POSITION

Within Anglicanism there is a long tradition of direct appeal to the 'fundamentals of Christianity', or to 'the fundamental articles of the faith' (the two are not necessarily the same). As we shall see, it is quite mistaken to believe that such an appeal distinguishes the Anglican from other communions. What does seem to be the case, however, is that there are good reasons why the contrast between fundamentals and non-fundamentals found a ready home among Anglicans, and has been in use in various contexts and in various ways to the present day.

Examples of modern use of the distinction are to be found in both the Malta Report and the Final Report of the Anglican–Roman Catholic International Commission,[1] of which Archbishop Henry McAdoo, a distinguished contemporary exponent of this tradition, was Anglican co-chairman.[2] The connection between fundamentals and the comprehensiveness of the Church is made clear in the Report of one section of the 1968 Lambeth Conference: 'Comprehensiveness demands agreement on fundamentals, while tolerating disagreement on matters in which Christians may differ without feeling the necessity of breaking communion.'[3]

A final indication of the importance of the notion of fundamentals and a possible way of construing it is to be found in the formulation and adoption by the 1888 Lambeth Conference of what has become known as the Chicago-Lambeth Quadrilateral. The four elements of this statement (Scripture, the creeds, two sacraments and the episcopate) have received repeated endorsement up to the present, though lately with qualifications and amplification.[4]

As we shall see, there are considerable complexities hidden in the proposal that all Christians do, can or should agree on fundamentals, a proposal which on the surface appears to be self-evident, or at least highly desirable. There is no ready-made precision in the content of the fundamentals, and despite its deployment by some leading Roman Catholic theologians, among them Karl Rahner, it has been regularly dismissed as a Protestant theory, contrary to the unity of the Church as instituted by Christ and unrealizable in practice without an infallible authority to determine its content.[6] The tradition whose history we are to trace is neither redundant nor parochial; nor are all Anglicans agreed about it.

For example, in a sharp and clarifying appendix, 'On the Doctrine of Fundamentals', in his 1838 *Treatise on the Church of Christ*, the learned Tractarian, William Palmer (of Worcester College, Oxford), wrote:

> This term is capable of so many meanings as applied to Christian doctrine, and it actually is, has been, and must continue to be, used in so great a diversity of senses, that it is morally impossible to avoid perplexity while it is employed in controversy. As an ambiguous term, as conveying no one definite notion, it seems unqualified to be of any practical utility in questions of controversy.[7]

This is a challenge which must be taken seriously.

THE REFORMATION TRADITION

The reason for the Reformed Church of England's interest in 'the fundamentals' is plain enough: it derives from the charge against the Church of Rome that it has departed from the standards of the early Fathers, of the apostles and of Christ, and the corresponding claim that 'we have called home again to the original and first foundation that religion which hath been foully neglected and utterly corrupted' (Bishop Jewel's *Apology of the Church of England*, 1564).[8] The recall to fundamentals is a motif capable of being expressed in a variety of metaphors, of which 'foundation' is only one of the possibilities—but an important one, because it recalls a series of impressive biblical texts. ('If the foundations are destroyed what can the righteous do?', Ps. 11.3; 'Behold I am laying in Zion for a foundation, a stone, a tested stone', Isa. 28.16, cited in 1 Pet. 2.6; the parable of the men who built houses with and without proper foundation, Matt. 7.24–27; Luke 6.47–49; 'No other foundation can any one lay than that which is laid, which is Jesus Christ', 1 Cor. 3.11; 'So then you are ... built upon the foundation of the apostles and prophets, Jesus Christ himself being the chief cornerstone', Eph. 3.20).

At the very start of the Reformation we are introduced to a dispute which has constantly returned to complicate the recall to fundamentals. Erasmus held that it should be possible for Christians to agree upon those few and simple truths which were intimately connected with practical Christian living. Much else, including the complexities of the Reformers' view of the human condition and the terms of salvation, could be left to theological debate. Luther vehemently disagreed with such agnosticism. What he was teaching, he asserted, was simply

233

the plain content of the Scriptures, proclaimed openly to the world and taught to the heart internally by the Holy Spirit.[9] Throughout his voluminous and unsystematic writings there are scattered numerous different ways of summarizing the foundation, the chief article, the head, the heart and so forth of the gospel. For Luther the whole Christian faith hangs together, like a chain, or a ring, or a bell. No one part could be lost, if the whole is to survive.

Erasmus' proposals were ignored by the Council of Trent, but were widely influential in England. So also was another idea, closely related to that of the fundamentals, but with a long and independent history, namely the fact that there were certain matters in relation to which Christians had freedom. These *adiaphora*, or things indifferent, became of great importance to the entire Reformation tradition.[10] Luther, for example, in reply to Henry VIII's *Assertion of the Seven Sacraments* (1521), had argued that whatever went beyond the Scriptures was a matter of indifference and should not be turned into a 'necessary doctrine'.[11] The term *adiaphoron* (plural, *adiaphora*) was frequently used by William Tyndale, and certain doctrines, notably those of purgatory or transubstantiation, became tests of what was necessary and what indifferent. John Frith (*c.* 1503–1533) carefully explained, while awaiting death by burning, that he was convinced that the Christian was free to disagree with the view, held by his episcopal interrogators, that transubstantiation was 'an undoubted article of the faith, necessary to be believed under pain of damnation' ('Articles Wherefore John Frith Died', 1533).[12] Three years later, after issuing his Ten Articles, Henry VIII was instructing his bishops 'in no wise to treat of matters indifferent, which be neither necessary to our salvation ... nor yet to be in any wise contemned'.[13]

Within England, of course, power was sufficiently centralized for instructions of this kind to be enforced, and one should not underestimate the importance of political pressure for eliminating disagreement. Militating against wider Protestant concord over fundamentals was the fact that the politically separate parts of the movement of reformation accustomed themselves to different solutions of the question. The sixteenth, seventeenth and eighteenth centuries are replete with sincere and devoted persons seeking ecclesiastical agreement between the separate branches of Christendom on the basis of agreements on fundamentals. But the political forces keeping the Churches apart were stronger than good intentions. The separate political entities became accustomed to different usages, and resistence to change from outside hardened.

In the early years of the Reformation, however, matters were not so settled. From the Lutheran side, notably Philip Melanchthon (1497–1560) sought to define an area of common ground with Rome.[14] From the Roman Catholic side, solidly in the Erasmian tradition was the remarkable Georg Cassander (1513–66), a Flemish lay scholar who lived latterly in Cologne and devoted himself to the exploration of ground for restoring peace between Roman Catholics and

Protestants. In the tireless (and fruitless) work of both there is a discernible emphasis on the cognitive content of Christianity, upon fundamental *articles* of belief as supplying the only secure basis for reconciliation. Thus the Augsburg Confession of 1530, largely the work of Melanchthon, is an article-by-article distillation of Reformation teaching in its most moderate and eirenic form. And Cassander's appeal was to the Creed and the faith of the Church of the first six centuries in agreement with the formula of St Vincent of Lérins (the so-called Vincentian canon; 'What has been believed everywhere, always and by all'), as supplying the qualifying basis for a Church to be reckoned a true Church.

SEVENTEENTH-CENTURY ANGLICANISM

Stress has been laid on the non-Anglican treatment of fundamental articles in order to place the Anglican reception of this tradition in its proper context. Given Cranmer's knowledge of the Fathers and his comparative liturgical conservatism, Cassander's outline of the basis for reconciliation had obvious apologetic value. A work of the Swiss Reformer, Bullinger (1504–75), the *Decades*, was also highly esteemed in England for its demonstration that the Reformed religion was none other than that professed in the creeds and councils of the primitive Church.

But however much subsequent Anglicans owed to Roman Catholic, Lutheran and Calvinist predecessors, it is important that we observe the possibility of a *de facto* settlement of the question of fundamentals as well as a written theological apologetic. Use can determine what is held to be fundamental, as well as theory. The means by which reformation came about impinge closely on this question; these means include the authorization and imposition of Books of Common Prayer, the successive versions of the *Articles of Religion*, the issuing of authorized homilies, and in due course the provision of a Book of Canons (see pp. 6–15, pp. 121–30, pp. 133–40 and pp. 200–213)—all these were imposed with the authority of King-in-Parliament and the consent of the clergy in Convocation. Although the Thirty-nine Articles refer to Scripture as the criterion of things necessary to salvation (see pp. 82–5), in none of these instruments of settlement is there a final and authoritative formulation of the fundamentals. That too is significant, as is the eminently reformable and progressive character of the work.

From the last years of the reign of Elizabeth I onwards there developed a considerable apologetic literature to explain and justify the nature of the English Reformation. We have already referred to Bishop Jewel's *Apology*. A little later Richard Hooker himself formulated what he termed 'the essence of Christianity' (in the earliest English use of that phrase known to me) as the God-given unity of the visible Church in the profession of one Lord, one faith, and one baptism.[15]

235

The one faith is constituted by those few articles of Christian belief confessed by such early fathers as Tertullian and Irenaeus. Hooker, who was already embroiled in controversies with moderate Puritans still part of the comprehensive Church of England, is at once drawn into detailed argument about whether one complete form of church polity has been laid out in Scripture, thus forming part of what must be maintained as necessary to salvation. Against such a view, Hooker's position is clear. The articles of the Christian faith and the sacraments of the Church of Christ are absolutely necessary to salvation. The accessories are things which discretion will teach the Church how to decide, and decisions may vary from place to place and time to time without contradicting their God-given basis in natural reason.

In the seventeenth century, the appeal to the undivided Church of the first five centuries commended itself to a number of prominent persons, among them the Dutch jurist and theologian, Hugo Grotius, and the Genovese Calvinist, Isaac Casaubon (1559–1614), who immigrated to England in 1610 and contributed warmly to an apologetic for the Church of England. Georg Calixtus (1586–1656), who met Casaubon in London in 1612, was a German Lutheran likewise impressed with this argument, to which he linked the criterion provided by the Vincentian canon and a certain stress on practical Christian living deriving from Erasmus.

But the fundamental articles tradition lent itself also to the exposition of a strict Lutheran orthodoxy, which it received at the hands of Nicholaus Hunnius (1585–1643). In one of the most penetrating analyses of different kinds of fundamental, Hunnius distinguished between the *substantial* foundation, which is God and Christ, the *organic*, which is the holy Scriptures, and the *dogmatic*, the content of Christian doctrine. The last named is then subdivided between primary articles which all must confess, secondly articles which none must deny, and non-fundamentals which may be ignored or disputed. The point of this treatment is to show that though Lutherans and the Reformed might be agreed about the substantial and the organic fundamentals, there are fundamental differences in primary and secondary articles of doctrine. Here we come face to face with the fact that *per se* appeal to the notion of fundamentals is not, of itself, an ecumenically hopeful procedure. The problems are to be seen in the career of the remarkable Scottish ecumenist, John Durie (1596–1680), whose attempts to achieve European Protestant unity on the basis of agreement on fundamentals were frustrated by a combination of denominational intransigence and political rivalries.

In England the context in which the fundamentals or fundamental articles were principally deployed was that of controversy with Roman Catholic theologians. Bishop Lancelot Andrewes (1555–1626) addressed himself to the attack of the Jesuit Bellarmine on the claim of King James I to be a Catholic. Adopting the theory already advanced by Calixtus, he held that the profession of the creeds and canons of the first four Councils was a sufficient title for the Church of England. His definition of the boundaries of Anglicanism occurs in a sentence later to become famous:

> One canon reduced to writing by God himself, two testaments, three creeds, four general councils, five centuries, and the series of Fathers in that period—the centuries that is, before Constantine, and two after, determine the boundary of our faith.[16]

Andrewes was in touch with both Casaubon, to whom he showed his reply to Bellarmine, and somewhat less cordially with Grotius.

Twenty years later William Laud (1573–1645) conducted a famous controversy with a Jesuit theologian, John Fisher (1569–1641), subsequently published as *A Relation of the Conference between William Laud and Mr Fisher the Jesuit* (1639). Against the proposition advanced by Fisher that all points defined by the Church are fundamental, Laud insists that the term 'fundamental' can only apply to the articles of the Creed. There may be many true deductions from the Creed, of which simple people are unaware, but which it may be necessary for others, more learned, to believe. But nothing is fundamental merely because the Church says it is so, but only because it is of itself. Picking up Andrewes' stress on Scripture and reflecting the earlier work of Protestant controversialists, Laud asserts that the belief that Scripture is the word of God and infallible is a preceding, prime principle of faith to be held along with the Creed. That the Church of England's positive articles are grounded in Scripture, he is content to be judged by the joint and constant belief of the Fathers of the first five centuries (see pp. 101–105):

> To believe the Scripture and the Creeds, to believe these in the sense of the ancient primitive Church, to receive the four great Councils so much magnified by antiquity, to believe all points of doctrine, generally received as fundamental in the Church of Christ, is a faith in which to live and die cannot but give salvation.[17]

Others who wrote in the same sense included Archbishop James Ussher (1581–1656), and later Bishop Jeremy Taylor (1613–67) and Henry Hammond (1605–60).

But did the testimony of the Fathers cohere quite precisely as these apologists claimed? Some held that it did not. A group of scholars in England, known as the Tew Circle, believed that resort to the Fathers only produced confusion, a view which received strong support from the work of the eminent French Protestant patristic scholar, John Daillé, *On the Use of the Fathers* (French, 1632). The argument of William Chillingworth (1604–1644), who was Laud's godson, but who for a period had become a Roman Catholic influenced by the arguments of Fisher, shows a certain withdrawal from the patristic reference. In a controversial writing of 1638, *Religion of Protestants a Safe Way to Salvation*, he attempts to explain the relation between Scripture and the fundamentals. Once a person is persuaded that Scripture contains all things necessary to salvation (a quotation of Article VI), then it is enough if that person strenuously attempts to find and to believe the true sense of it. There is no final catalogue of all the truths which one must believe, because, on his argument, there is a vital moral component in all believing deriving from human autonomy. Chillingworth insisted, at the same time, upon the simplicity of the essentials of the faith.[18]

The clarification of an important point, at this time, was the work of another apologist, Edward Stillingfleet (1635–99), replying to the Jesuit account of the controversy between Laud and Fisher. In *A Rational Account of the Grounds of the Protestant Religion* (1664) Stillingfleet distinguished between things which are necessary to the salvation of persons as such, in their individual capacities, and things which are necessary to be acknowledged by Christian societies, or as the bonds and conditions of ecclesiastical communion. The discussion of fundamentals had, he held, wavered uncertainly between the two, but they should not be confused. Concentrating upon the latter of the two uses, a later defender of Stillingfleet, William Sherlock (1641–1707), undertook to define 'fundamentals' in the following way:

> A *fundamental doctrine* is such a doctrine as is in strict sense of the *essence* of Christianity, without which the whole building and superstructure must fall; the belief of which is necessary to the very being of Christianity, like the *first principles* of any *art* or *science*.[19]

REDEFINITIONS: THE EIGHTEENTH AND NINETEENTH CENTURIES

If, as suggested earlier, we must be alert to usage as well as to theory, then it must be noted that the seventeenth-century Restoration, which saw the ejection of some 1,760 incumbents from their parishes, set clear bounds to the 'comprehensiveness' of the Church of England. The fact that the Anglican Ordinal insisted that its priests be episcopally ordained must be related to its view of the fundamentals (see pp. 151–2). But how?

One learned, and ecumenically active, contributor to the discussion, Archbishop William Wake (1657–1737), was ambiguous on the point. He had read both Cassander and Grotius and was persuaded that the method of separating out the fundamental articles from the others was, for all its admitted difficulties and dangers, the only feasible way to the restoration of communion, alike with Roman Catholics and within Protestantism.[20] He corresponded extensively on this basis with friendly Roman Catholic theologians in the Sorbonne, but on the quixotic assumption that the Gallican Church would be ready to throw off papal supremacy. The Pope, Wake asserted, had wrongly claimed for himself alone the episcopate 'which Christ bequeathed in part to each several bishop to be held in common.'[21] But Wake had already committed himself enthusiastically to the view, against the Roman Catholic Bossuet's charge of incoherence in Protestantism, that Protestants are already united in whatever is fundamental in the faith (Sermon of 1689).[22] Wake stood solidly in the tradition of Hooker, Whitgift and Andrewes in holding that the kind of government of the Church was not a matter affecting the being of the Church, and that although episcopacy is a divine right, it does not follow that a non-episcopal Church is no Church (see pp. 300–308). He commended the institution of episcopacy to his Reformed and Lutheran friends; he reordained those with Presbyterian orders; but at the same time he wrote that Article XXXVI of the Thirty-nine Articles 'only asserts the validity of our Book of Ordination, but does not affirm the necessity of the three orders which we retain in our Church' (Letter of 1720).[23] Despite extensive correspondence with Swiss theologians notable for their support of the method of defining few fundamentals as a condition of union, the plans came to nothing. Wake found, as others have done since, that far from agreeing on the few Articles in common, many not of his persuasion insisted on laying the greatest emphasis on the points of difference.

A further contribution of major importance to the subject was made by a Cambridge theologian, Daniel Waterland (1683–1740), whose calm and analytic mind illuminated a number of disputes in the eighteenth century and whose works were reprinted constantly into the nineteenth century. In *A Discourse of Fundamentals* (1735), he tackles the question of what should be held to belong essentially to the 'fabric' of Christianity. His solution to the complexities is the work of a systematician. On the premise that Christianity is a covenant, it follows, he argues, that what is essential to Christianity is everything that inheres in the covenant, the two parties, the agreement, the person of the mediator, and the conditions, means and sanctions attaching to the covenant.[24] For the idea of the centrality of covenant, and for numerous features of the argument, Waterland refers to a German Lutheran and disciple of Grotius, Samuel Pufendorf (1632–94).

Following Chillingworth, Waterland asserts that no catalogue of fundamental truths is possible. It is adequate to give examples of fundamentals, which must include matters of worship and conduct as well as belief, and a rule for establishing them. If difficulties arise then it is wiser to choose the side of peace and latitude. In the case of doubt the burden of proof lies on those who would assert something to be fundamental.

Waterland acknowledges that other rules have been proposed for deciding upon what is fundamental, and undertakes to support his argument with a brief but radical refutation of alternatives. Notable among those he dismisses are: the definitions of the Church, even of the primitive Churches; the whole of Scripture or even all matters expressly taught in Scripture; the Apostles' Creed (here Waterland acknowledges his disagreement with, amongst others, Calixtus, Chillingworth, and Stillingfleet); the mere confession of Jesus as Messiah (with reference to John Locke);[25] and the universal agreement of Christians. His central theological proposal of the notion of covenant as the most comprehensive way in which to determine the terms of Church communion leaves open, he believes, the question of the terms of salvation for each individual.

In the second half of the eighteenth century a new set of ideas emerged in European Protestantism to account for the changes in successive historical forms of Christianity. For this way of thinking it became axiomatic that no one historical embodiment of the Christian faith was, or could be, normative for all time, especially no series of propositions. The reasons for this new development were complex, partly the result of investigations into biblical and patristic history which showed internal variety and disagreement, and partly the impact of a new non-cognitive theory of religion, which the Romantic Movement planted indelibly within European Christianity. The result was a need to identify, if possible, an abiding essence behind the changing forms. When Schleiermacher in his epoch-making definition of the 'essence of Christianity' (*Speeches on Religion*, 1799) spoke of Christianity as having an intuited 'principle of coherence', at the same time he denied that it could be constituted by a 'particular quantity of religious matter', a coded way of referring to the fundamental articles tradition.[26]

These European developments coincided with a period in the life of the Anglican Church when the Church of England was at its most self-preoccupied and isolated. The foundation of an independent episcopate overseas occurred through the agency of the Church in Scotland. And welcome though this *de facto* modification of what had hitherto been widely assumed to be fundamental, namely a particular relationship with the sovereign power, might be, it had the effect of intensifying Anglican efforts to explain its own distinctiveness. By the beginning of the nineteenth century, for those groups out of which the Tractarian Movement developed, it was axiomatic that an Anglican defence of its stance as a Church must be different from a commonly Protestant one. The altered state of affairs is nicely illustrated in the title of a work by the Irish bishop of Limerick, John Jebb (1775–1833), *Peculiar Character of the Church of England : as distinguished both from other branches of the Reformation, and from the modern Church of Rome*. It was this work which was given as an example of Anglican apologetic by a young friend of John Henry Newman, Benjamin Harrison, to a Frence abbé whom he had met at a dinner party in Paris in 1834. Jager engaged first with Harrison and then with Newman himself in public controversy over the claim of the Church of England.[27]

The dispute eventually came to centre upon the issue of the fundamental articles. When Newman became involved at the end of the year he had to read himself into the Anglican history we have reviewed, especially the relevant works of Laud, Stillingfleet, Chillingworth and others. In his first intervention, Newman explicitly invokes the idea of fundamentals and continued to justify it throughout the controversy. In his own mind he was merely reproducing the views of Bishop

Stillingfleet. But it is now evident, and was evident also to Harrison, that his line of defence amounted to his own theory of fundamentals, a theory which developed into a theory of development, and which eventually helped in his transfer to the Roman Catholic Church.

Jager, who had read some of the *Tracts for the Times*, was evidently astonished to discover that an Anglican was prepared to defend the distinction between fundamentals and non-fundamentals, for him a quintessentially Protestant apologetic. Newman, though his theory of religion was of a mystery lying hid in language, was still keen to insist on the existence of a central immutable core of truth, infallibly taught by the Church. But characteristically he introduced into the discussion a very considerable measure of flexibility and uncertainty about the difference between the core, which he called the apostolic tradition, and exploratory elaborations of it, which he called the prophetic tradition. The theory was indeed his own, and when he wrote it up in full as *Lectures on the Prophetical Office of the Church Viewed Relatively to Romanism and Popular Protestantism* he took pains to emphasize that what he was defending was not Protestantism.[28]

His Tractarian colleagues were more definite. W. H. Froude characteristically told a friend that he nauseated the word fundamental.[29] More seriously, as we have already seen, William Palmer offered to demonstrate the internal inconsistency of the use of the word in the works of Chillingworth, Laud, and Waterland. From the last named person's review of the varieties of opinion Palmer concluded the impossibility of arriving at any adequately agreed rule, and criticized the arbitrariness of thinking that human beings could stand in judgement on divine revelation, a criticism which Karl Barth was to echo a hundred years later.[30] Quoting Keble, Palmer concluded that the only safe way of proceeding was to insist on guarding the whole faith of Christ.

The undoubted advantage of Newman's theory of development was its capacity to absorb the impact of historical relativism. Consistency over time, he argued, required change. Newman's Anglican critics for the most part reverted to earlier static theories. The Church can only be what it has always been, and profess what it always has professed. The works of many of the theologians we have reviewed were reprinted, among them those of Andrewes, Laud, Taylor, Henry Hammond, Herbert Thorndike (1598–1672) and Bishop John Cosin (1594–1672), and were accorded a kind of normative status within Anglicanism (see pp. 164–8). Their defence of fundamental articles preserved a style of theological argument which had ceased to be current in the European context. Although, as we have seen, in its origins it was a tradition shared with a large number of Protestant theologians both Lutheran and Reformed, and a smaller group of Erasmian Roman Catholics, by the nineteenth century it had the appearance of being distinctively Anglican. Both the term 'Anglicanism' and some of the standard definition of its distinctiveness owe much to these developments (see pp. 405–22 and pp. 424–8).

With the challenge of biblical criticism to the doctrine of biblical infallibility, the scriptural basis of the fundamentals became problematic. It was an important development, therefore, when Charles Gore and the *Lux Mundi* school both accepted criticism, and yet continued to defend the truth of all the articles of the creed. Modern interpretation of the fundamentals tradition is at some pains to argue that the use of reason (as justified by, among others, Hooker and Chillingworth) is part of the method of holding to fundamentals, and that the *Lux Mundi* theologians are the natural heirs of this Anglican tradition.[31] The twentieth century, however, has seen a number of acute controversies relating to doctrines affirmed by the creeds, especially the virgin birth and the (bodily) resurrection of Christ, which raise in an acute form the adequacy of this defence.

MODERN PROBLEMS AND SOLUTIONS

At the beginning of this essay it was remarked that the fundamentals of Christianity are not necessarily to be identified with the fundamental *articles* of Christianity. In the history we have traced, distillation into articles of belief has played a very important part, and is evidently the consequence of an approach to religion which emphasizes its cognitive aspects.[32] A major objection to the fundamental articles tradition is that it is based upon an unbalanced account of what the Christian religion actually is, ignoring or relegating its experiential, ritual or cultural aspects. But there are further difficulties with the appeal to fundamentals *per se* which must also be faced.

First, as Palmer observed, there is no common agreement about what the fundamentals are. Nor is there any agreed rule for determining what they are. Waterland's proposal is ingenious, but in the face of equally plausible competitors it is, *prima facie*, arbitrary.

The charge of arbitrariness raises the question of authority, insistently posed of the fundamental article tradition by apologists for the Roman Catholic Church. Anglican responses which invoke the tradition of the undivided Church, the creeds, or the Vincentian canon bear the aspect of private judgement masquerading as tradition. On close inspection they can be found to furnish either too much or too little.[33] They all suffer alike from what has been called the 'Myth of Christian Beginnings', which were anything but homogeneous.[34]

The recitation of the history of the fundamentals also rarely enough emphasizes the repeated failure of this tradition to solve ecumenical problems. Nor, if Anglicans are honest, does it solve the problems of inner-Anglican ecumenism, the reconciliation of differences over the application of biblical criticism or hermeneutics to matters like the Gospel miracles or the patriarchalism of the Scriptures.

Nonetheless, contemporary ecumenism has shown a desire to reinvoke the notion of fundamentals and some of its inherent problems may yield to renewed thought. Anglicans have good reason to reflect on the Chicago–Lambeth Quadrilateral (see pp. 209–10). Here, after all, is not just a list of articles of belief, but a series of usages, the use of Scripture in public in the vernacular, the use of the creeds in worship, the celebration of the sacraments, and the practice of episcopal government. It is important to stress that all these presuppose the church's life of active discipleship, worship and witness, centred upon Christ. It assumes also the normal Christian activity of faith seeking understanding, attended, as it always has been, by theological argument and dispute. Agreement upon usage can, as Anglican experience testifies, be hospitable to conflict about belief. Indeed the use of the Bible as the 'prime principle of faith', to cite Laud, *provokes* disagreement, including disagreement about boundaries between acceptable and unacceptable expressions of belief. The history of enquiry in the fundamentals of Christianity contains ambiguities, confusions and errors. But it is not for that reason to be set aside.

NOTES

1 Malta Report in A. C. Clark and C. Davey, eds., *Anglican/Roman Catholic Dialogue* (London and New York 1974), pp. 107–15; ARCIC, *The Final Report* (London 1982). Esp. 'Ministry and Ordination', para. 17 (p. 38). The Malta Report is reprinted in *The Final Report*.

2 See esp. *The Spirit of Anglicanism: A Survey of Anglican Theological Method in the Seventeenth Century* (London 1965); and *The Unity of Anglicanism: Catholic and Reformed* (Wilton, Conn. 1983).

3 *The Lambeth Conference 1968* (London 1968), p. 140. It should be made clear that Reports to the Conference carry only the authority of those by whom it was approved, in this case some one-third of the assembled bishops.

4 *Bonds of Affection*, Proceedings of ACC-6 (London 1984), pp. 70–75.

5 Heinrich Fries and Karl Rahner, *Unity of the Churches* (Philadelphia 1985), pp. 7, 13–23.

6 A. Tanqueray, 'Articles fondamentaux (système des)' in *Dictionnaire de Théologie Catholique* I. iii (Paris 1923), pp. 2025–35, and the encyclical of Pius XI, *Mortalium animos* (1927), DS 3683, cited by Congar, *Diversity and Communion*, p. 118.

7 *Treatise on the Church of Christ* I (London 1838), p. 122.

8 *Apology of the Church of England* (1561), edited by J. E. Booty (University Press of Virginia, Charlottesville, 1974), p. 121.

9 From the Preface to the *Bondage of the Will* (WA 18, p. 603; American edn., 33, p. 5). In J. Dillenberger, ed., *Martin Luther: Selections from his Writings* (New York 1961), p. 170.

10 For an outline of the history of the term see B. J. Verkamp, *The Indifferent Mean: Adiaphorism in the English Reformation to 1554* (Ohio and Wayne State University Presses, Athens, Ohio, Detroit, Mich., 1977), p. 22.

11 ibid., p. 96.

12 ibid., p. 103.

13 ibid., p. 51.

14 On Melanchthon's use of fundamentals see F. Hildebrandt, *Melanchthon : Alien or Ally* (Cambridge, CUP, 1946).

15 Richard Hooker, *Of the Laws of Ecclesiastical Polity*, III. i. 4.

16 L. Andrewes, *Opuscula quedam Posthuma* (Library of Anglo-Catholic Theology; Oxford, 1852), p. 91.

17 *A Relation of the Conference between William Laud and Mr Fisher the Jesuit* (Library of Anglo-Catholic Theology; London, 1849), p. 361.

18 See R. L. Orr, *Reason and Authority, The Thought of William Chillingworth* (Oxford 1967), p. 96.

19 *Vindication of the Defence of Stillingfleet* (London 1682), p. 256.

20 Norman Sykes, *William Wake, Archbishop of Canterbury, 1657–1737* (Cambridge, CUP), vol i, p. 252.

21 ibid., vol. i, p. 271.

22 ibid., vol. ii, p. 2.

23 ibid., vol. ii, p. 19.

24 *The Works of the Rev. Daniel Waterland* (Oxford, Clarendon Press, 1823), p. 95.

25 Locke's reductionist proposals were contained in his *Second Vindication of the Reasonableness of Christianity* (London 1697).

26 F. D. E. Schleiermacher, *On Religion, Speeches to Its Cultured Despisers* (New York 1958), p. 218. On the history of essence definition see S. W. Sykes, *The Identity of Christianity* (London and Philadelphia 1984), chs. 4–8.

27 L. Allen, *John Henry Newman and the Abbé Jager*. London and NY, OUP, 1975.

28 J. H. Newman, *Lectures on the Prophetical Office*. London 1837; he reissued this work as a Roman Catholic with a new preface and notes, *The Via Media of the Church of England* (London 1877) vol. i. See Sykes, *Identity of Christianity*, ch. 5.

29 Cited by J. H. Newman in 'Palmer on Faith and Unity' (a review of Palmer's work on the Church, see n. 7), in *Essays Critical and Historical* (London 1871), p. 174.

30 Barth's discussion of the fundamental articles tradition is to be found in the *Church Dogmatics* I. ii (Edinburgh 1956), pp. 863–6.

31 See esp. the argument of P. E. More in 'The Spirit of Anglicanism' in P. E. More and F. L. Cross, *Anglicanism* (London and New York 1935), p. xxxi; also followed by McAdoo (see n. 2).

32 Note esp. G. A. Lindbeck, *The Nature of Doctrine* (London and Philadelphia 1984).

33 See H. B. Swete, *The Holy Catholic Church* (London 1915), p. 241.

34 R. L. Wilkens, *The Myth of Christian Beginnings* (London 1979).

3 The Laity

FREDRICA HARRIS THOMPSETT

All Are Called: Towards a Theology of the Laity. London, CIO Publishing, 1985.
Dozier, Verna J., *The Authority of the Laity.* Washington, DC, Alban Institute, 1982.
Gibbs, Mark, *Christians with Secular Power.* Philadelphia, Fortress Press, 1981.
Micks, Marianne H., *Our Search for Identity: Humanity in the Image of God.* Philadelphia, Fortress Press, 1982.
Schillebeeckx, Edward, *The Church With a Human Face: A New and Expanded Theology of Ministry.* New York, Crossroad, 1985.

In his January 1986 installation address the new Presiding Bishop of the Episcopal Church in the United States, the Most Rev. Edmond Lee Browning, spoke directly to laity in these strong, personal words of invitation:

> Most of all, I reach out to the faithful, the laity of this Church. I want to reach out and feel your hands in mine. For it is only with you that our mission can be authentically lived out.

Browning's vision of a compassionate future that depends 'most of all' upon lay witness, rather than upon clergy, is not entirely surprising. His theology is consistent with functional definitions of ministry and mission emphatically stated in the Catechism from the 1979 American *Book of Common Prayer*: 'The Church carries out its mission through the ministry of all its members.'[1] This is a restatement of the biblical, Pauline image of the Church as a body built up through the interdependent activities of its members. Over the past few decades, emphasis upon the work of the whole people of God, and particularly upon those 99% who are Christian laity, has increased in most denominations. Within Anglicanism there is general theological and familiar rhetorical consensus about encouraging laity to exercise their several vocations. What is at times controversial, and certainly consistently problematic, is the challenge of joining reality to rhetoric, of enfleshing the vision within the institutional Church and carrying it out into society at large.

Currently this challenge is being raised with intentional vigour. One source for data on the increased significance accorded to laity is the scholarly revision of church history. It is no longer enough (if it ever was) to dwell on scenes of clerical life. Contemporary scholarship demands that attention be paid to the

245

common folk, to what has been described as 'popular religion'. Critical scholarship has rejected the implicit two-tiered 'producer/consumer' model of supposedly articulate clergy developing doctrine for presumably inarticulate laity. Historical study of religious life presents more complex paradigms; debate is open as to what factors were and are critical in shaping, nurturing and changing religious beliefs over long periods of time. There is also a new consciousness about those whose experiences and voices have been neglected, whether for reasons of race, class, or sex. Those of us who, for example, study the history of women and Christianity bring not only new questions but also new evidence to assess the critical nature of lay witness. One implication of the debates over the ordination of women in Anglicanism and Roman Catholicism has been that church officials, whether pro or con, have come to pay more attention to professional and voluntary opportunities for lay women and lay men. The modern ecumenical movement, dating from the World Missionary Conference in Edinburgh in 1910, has also given consistent impetus to studying and extending the global mission of Christian peoples. Following the Second World War, the World Council of Churches pioneered efforts to engage institutional Churches in promoting the 'Ministry of the Laity'. The WCC continues to address this agenda as evidenced in the 1982 Faith and Order statement, *Baptism, Eucharist, and Ministry*. Finally, yet centrally in respect to Anglicanism, it is important to emphasize the role that recent liturgical renewal in several provinces of the Anglican Communion has had in both responding to and shaping new understandings of lay participation. As a result of these and other factors, there is throughout Anglicanism a heightened sensitivity to laity.

The intent of this chapter is to focus the story of Anglican laity in brief assessments of central topics. This is a compensatory, not comprehensive, perspective designed to point to and deepen understandings of Anglican laity as noted in several other chapters in this volume. Starting with the early foundations of Anglicanism, what for laity is distinctive about the Reformation? What principles of Anglican theology are called forth when we review understandings of Church, sacraments, and ministry from the perspective of the laity? What might the future character of Anglican witness look like, if it were spiritually responsive to churched and unchurched laity? This chapter in the story of Anglicanism is not a new one, though several major salient characteristics about laity have been eclipsed, underestimated or strategically ignored for long periods of the Church's history. The style of this chapter is intended to encourage the reader's own reflections, to invite further exploration, and to underscore this author's conviction that the ethical character of Christian witness depends upon giving priority to furthering the mission of laity in the world.

LAITY AND EARLY ANGLICANISM:
THE VISION OF THE ENGLISH REFORMATION

The period of massive religious change that began in the sixteenth century and is collectively called the Reformation was foundational—in both continental and English contexts and for both Roman Catholic and Protestant formulations—in underscoring the significance of faithful laity in the life of the churches. This period of reform and renewal was one of those historical epochs in which Christians laboured to reclaim the biblical power of the laity and to reform religious life in accord with their understanding of New Testament churches. The Reformation marked a religious movement of considerable strength that was similar to the Evangelical Revival heralded by John Wesley in the eighteenth century, to the awakenings and expansion of religion in nineteenth-century America, to the renewed concern for Christian discipleship among laity in Europe that followed the Second World War, to what has been called the 'Charismatic Movement' that influenced most American denominations in the 1960s, and most recently to the base communities of Latin America. In each of these and in other revival movements, emphasis has been placed on the spiritual equality of clergy and laity.

The Reformation in Europe and in England did succeed in narrowing the distance and breaking down distinctions between clergy and laity. Clergy were permitted, at times encouraged, to marry. Most also gave up late medieval clerical privileges and assumed normal responsibilities of citizenship. Throughout the Renaissance and Reformation, values shifted from elevating the contemplative to advocating the active life. The general Reformation perspective on vocations was that all were called. There were differences among vocations, but no spiritual hierarchy. This hallmark of Reformation theology is reflected in a 1985 Church of England study, *All Are Called: Toward a Theology of the Laity*: 'Though we are tainted by our sinfulness, God's wonderful grace and love offer us all this common Christian vocation. God leaves everyone free to refuse this call; but the call is there for all without exception.'[2]

There is debate about the impact and benefit of the Reformation on lay people. Recent scholarship has questioned whether most laity were actually converted to new professions of faith. One historian has suggested that laity 'acquiesced in and accepted' rather than 'promoted and initiated' the Reformation. There were aspects of lay initiative in late medieval life, for example thriving lay confraternities, that disappeared with the Reformation. Historical accounts have underestimated the difficulty of weaning the English populace away from deeply ingrained and habitual loyalties to late medieval Catholicism. Despite recent debunking of the Reformation's success, the most balanced assessment seems to be that the Reformation did witness in most, if not in all respects, 'a victory of the lay estate over the clerical'.[3] However, it will no longer do for Anglican church historians to describe the Reformation as a 'layman's revolution' or a time of pervasive 'triumph for the laity'.[4]

Extravagant estimates of lay authority were also made during the Reformation. In his 1538 play *King John*, John Bale told how Joseph of Arimathaea, the supposed founder of England's Church, had given unconditional powers to the laity of England, powers which Roman representatives had usurped and which Henry VIII was struggling to reclaim from clerical tyranny.[5] Bale's rendering of this relic of English folklore was obviously designed to win laity to the position of royal supremacy over the Church. Historians have also moderated their assessments of the practical extent of lay governance and even royal supremacy. Certainly few bishops from 1540 to 1640 would have agreed that anything like unconditional governing powers had been given to, or won by, laity. Debates over the desirability of real empowerment of laity in church governance continue in the Church of England. They were revived during the 1927–28 fiasco in which a largely non-Anglican House of Commons rejected a proposed revision of the Prayer Book, and in recent deliberations establishing a House of Laity within synodical government.

What then are more accurately modulated assessments of the early Reformation inheritance for laity? What impulses were formative in shaping Anglican expectations of laity?

A central legacy from the early years of Anglicanism was an idealistic social vision of a commonwealth in which the obligation to faithfulness connected all sorts and conditions in their practice of the faith. The Edwardian Homily on Obedience described this vision with inclusive social detail:

> Every degree of people in their vocation, call and office, hath appointed to them their duty and order; some are in high degree, some in low, some kings and princes, some inferiors and subjects, priests and laymen, masters and servants, fathers and children, husbands and wives, rich and poor; and every one have need of other . . . without the which no house, no city, no commonwealth can continue and endure.[6]

The theology of vocations in the English Reformation was not so much a simple imitation of the Lutheran doctrine of a 'priesthood of all believers' but rather an English assertion of encompassing vocations bound together in charity. In this corporate understanding of calling, each person's vocation was set within the social context of the commonwealth. This vision was central to Reformation Anglicanism. It was consistently mirrored in what have been called the 'Great Books' of that time: vernacular Bibles, biblical commentaries (particularly Erasmus's *Paraphrases*), prayer books, homilies, catechisms, primers and other devotional aids.[7]

Tudor Reformers laboured to enflesh the vision of a Christian commonwealth in Tudor England with the assistance of the epoch-making invention of printing. The Reformation, on the Continent and later in England, was the first mass movement to take advantage of the availability of relatively inexpensive printed texts. One author of popular religious tracts asserted that there was 'never so plenty of so good and playn bookes prynted, never so good cheap, the Holy Ghost as it were into mennes mouthes offyrnge hys gyftes'.[8] The advent of a print culture, along with the prescripts of Renaissance humanism, triggered a fundamental change toward vernacular education. John Foxe, the zealous Reformer and martyrologist, extolled printing as the mightiest weapon against the old religion:

> The Lord began to work for His Church not with sword and target to subdue His exalted adversary, but with printing, writing, and reading ... so that either the pope must abolish knowledge and printing or printing must at length root him out.[9]

In effect the young printing industry spread the news, shaped the methods, and traced the course of the Reformation.

The medium of print extended and deepened the possibility of a biblically informed faith and the consequent demand for a biblically literate populace. Scripture was the primary authority in the English Reformation (see pp. 11–12). It contained, as stated in the 1563 Articles of Religion, 'all things necessary to salvation; so that whatsoever is not read therein, nor may be proved thereby, is not to be required'. The Bible had been a part of the medieval world. Biblical images and stories were everywhere, for example in the statues which Thomas Cranmer disparagingly called Catholic 'laymen's books'.[10] What was new was the availability of the Bible (in whole and in part) in printed vernacular translations. Royal and ecclesiastical injunctions dating from the 1530s made it compulsory for English Bibles to be placed in every parish. The Reformers were insistent that the language of revelation was accessible to ordinary citizens. This theme was reiterated in Thomas Cranmer's 1540 preface to the second edition of the Great Bible: 'The apostles and prophets wrote their books so that their special intent and purpose might be understood and perceived of every reader which was nothing but the edification or amendment of the life of them that readeth and heareth it.'[11] The English Reformation literally returned the Bible to the people as the fundamental handbook for Christian living.

Another critical legacy was the Reformation emphasis on religious nurture and education in parishes, households, and schools. One of the Reformers' favourite words was 'edification', building up the body of the faithful through learning. Christian humanists had envisaged the reunion of piety and erudition. Erasmus of Rotterdam introduced his translation of the Bible with this optimistic proclamation, 'All can be Christian, all can be devout, and I shall boldly add—all can be theologians.'[12]

Many, though not all, Tudor citizens experienced what has collectively been described as a 'revolution' in educational facilities.[13] By the 1570s overall literacy rates had increased dramatically, though unevenly, across the social strata. There was an increase in the number of petty and grammar schools. There was a 30% increase in Elizabethans' charitable giving to educational institutions. Publishers' records indicate that printers could rely on a steady demand for printed sermons, Bibles, catechisms, primers, ABC's for adults as well as children, manuals for family and personal devotions, and a seemingly endless demand for religious polemics. Habitual use of the Prayer Book in many English parishes may present an effective index of vernacular religious education. Efforts to promote religious learning among laity were not entirely in vain. Local studies, like that of the village of Terling in Essex, provide evidence of changing cultural horizons and increased cultural differentiation based upon distinctions in education and religion. One recent historian has underscored how 'lay involvement in education paralleled the increased laicization of religion'.[14] The overall consequences of the Reformation for lay education were distinctly expansive.

Hallmarks of the English Reformation for the general populace were an inclusive social vision of the commonwealth, as well as expansive vocational, biblical and educational inheritances. All were fundamental in shaping the ongoing character of Anglicanism. Historians now believe that at least two distinct offshoots of Reformation Anglicanism were the consolidation of a clerical profession that emphasized the ministry of the 'sacramental Word', and the development of distinct lay religious consciousness exemplified in the confident ability of many (middle and upperclass) laity to contend regularly with clergy in religious debates.[15] By the eve of the English Civil War laity had joined clergy in reliance on the Word, and in debate over the future of the Church.

LAITY AND THE CHURCH:
AN ECCLESIOLOGY FOR THE PEOPLE OF GOD

The theology of the Church has often been problematic in reflecting on the lay movement. One source for dislocation is noted in the 1985 study *All Are Called*:

> *The primary location of the laity is in society at large.* It is important that the clergy and lay officials of the Church should understand and respect the truth that most laity are only *secondarily* located in the institutional Church.[16]

Given this fact, it is more accurate and helpful to emphasize that the Church is a corporate body at work in the world, and not primarily or only an institution (see pp. 219–31).

The theology of the nature and purpose of the Church, its ecclesiology, is foundational for comprehending a theology of the laity. Practical theologians from Hendrick Kraemer to Verna Dozier have repeatedly urged church officials to pay attention to ecclesiology, but without much avail in Anglicanism. Could it be that our neglect of this theological homework reflects ambiguity or reluctance within institutional Churches to live out of a theology of the Church at work in the world? No wonder those religious officials (whether lay or ordained) whose ecclesiology centres on the institutional Church, find it difficult to enable the ministry and mission of laity in the world.

The Church in biblical images and divine example is world-centred. Anglican theologians from Richard Hooker in the sixteenth century to William Temple in this century have reiterated the theme that the world is properly the Church's work place. Hooker referred to the Church as a visible, though mystical, body marked by mutual fellowship in society. For Temple the Church, though at times an 'uninspiring spectacle' was the 'means whereby Christ becomes active and carries out His purpose in the world'.[17] This assessment is repeated in inter-religious dialogues and ecumenical statements. There is remarkable agreement that the Church's purpose is to serve God in the world. As Kraemer bluntly insisted, the Church exists primarily 'on behalf of the world and not on behalf of itself'.[18]

Such statements do not resolve ongoing tensions related to dualistic separation between the Church and the world, sacred and secular, public and private. Many North American advocates of lay ministries project misleading definitions of 'Church' and 'world' as two separate but equal categories of Christian work. Much modern ecclesiology seems flawed not only by the gaps that remain between what we believe and what we practice, but also by underestimating our need to contend with the compartmentalization of Church and world.

William Temple laboured throughout his ministry to repudiate two extreme views: that Christians should have no concern for this passing world, and that Christians should be totally immersed in the earthly present. Instead he emphasized engagement on behalf of Christ:

> We are called as Christians to the service of God here and now; that on earth as in heaven His Name is to be hallowed . . . for that Christ taught us to pray; for that He has summoned us to work. *Not there but here is the sphere of our spiritual concern; not then but now is salvation to be won and made manifest.*[19]

Anglican theologians name and retain terms such as 'spiritual' and 'natural', 'sacred' and 'secular' not so much to emphasize the choice of one, but rather to point truthfully to the tension of living as Christians in this world. We are encouraged to face into this responsibility in eucharistic services, as in the post communion petition from the American Prayer Book: 'Send us out into the world in peace, and grant us strength and courage to love and serve you with gladness and singleness of heart.'[20] Resources for recalling a theology of the work of the Church in the world are dominant in our biblical inheritance, formative of our Prayer Book tradition, and strongly etched in Anglican theology.

The grounding of the Church's mission in the world is essential to Anglican theology. So too is the emphasis that this is a corporate, not an individualistic, requirement. We pray that God will send *us* out, a response that is at once singular and social. The late American theologian, Urban Holmes, described the Hebrew concept of the corporate person as informing choices about how Anglicans move and work.[21] Social responsiveness was not an option for Anglicans. Decisions should focus not on what one person should do, but on what members of the Church could do together. Holmes recognized that built into this theology of the Church was the realistic tension of living with loyalty to our particular Church's mission and remaining open to others. This implies that the Church is provisional, an earthen vessel, and not in and of itself definitive for salvation. The Canadian theologian, James Wilkes, has described how a corporate theology of the Church encourages healthier and more hopeful responsiveness. He argues that only guilt is produced when an individual is exhorted to action in isolation from others and from the social context. He sees courage as a collective social activity: 'Courage continues to live in the covenant which gives us trust in life, allows us to speak the truth, and binds us into relationships of clear and mutual expectation.[22]

A corporate, socially engaged ecclesiology is not always welcomed. Several Anglican authors acknowledge that clergy and laity are often threatened by the image or the reality of a socially engaged Church. One manifestation of this resistance that needs to be named in a chapter on Anglican laity is clericalism. Clericalism may be seen as misplaced resistance to secularism, a process of withdrawal from society into a narrowly defined and often exclusively parochial context. Clericalism is also a progenitor of mutually disabling relationships formed of devaluation of laity and exaggeration of clerical status. The authors of *All Are Called* are frank in their evaluation of the persistence of clericalism among both clergy and laity:

> Clericalism is at bottom a confusion between the status of individuals and a theological understanding of their calling. It has been historically formed and embedded in social life.[23]

They speak too of patronizing attempts to control the laity and consequently confine and restrict the mission of the Church.

Provinces in the Anglican Communion have sought not only to combat clericalism, but also to open up a wider range of understanding in the Church by urging greater inclusion of laity in church governance. This is not a remedy for clericalism, particularly if it leads to definitions of lay ministers as those who are active in the institutional Church. A clericalist spirit can continue in governing bodies, however jointly contrived. Yet from the point of view of ecclesiology, the incorporation of laity into the governing life of Churches can provide another opportunity to focus concern for the Church's mission in society at large. This perspective is consistent with the themes of early Anglicanism. Thomas Cranmer referred to the need to include lay participation in the revival of diocesan synods. Thomas Arnold in *Principles of Church Reform* (1833) advocated, as a first step, giving laity a greater share in ordinary church government. Since the 1880s, when Church of England Convocations first agreed upon establishing a House of Laymen, there has been slow but steady progress to the current form of synodical government with its House of Laity. In North America the Episcopal Church in its first informal Convention in 1784 declared 'that to make canons there be no other authority than a representative body of the clergy and laity conjointly'.[24] Canadian schemes for governance make lay participation obligatory. The serious inclusion of laity in governance is now standard throughout Anglicanism. In this respect it is important to continue to see the Lambeth Conferences as true to Archbishop C. T. Longley's initial invitation to be an informal gathering of bishops, rather than a synod with governmental authority over the Churches.

It may seem odd to conclude a discussion on the corporate theology of the Church in the world with references to synodical governments and Lambeth Conferences. Yet starting with an understanding of the Church as a people called into relationship with God and each other, Anglican ecclesiology presents a Church that is grounded in society, provisional, inclusive, and responsive. On this foundation, whether from the vantage point of Lambeth or ecumenical dialogues, Anglicanism provides theological warrants for encouraging the work of the Church in the world.

LAITY AND SACRAMENTS:
THE POWER OF COMMON PARTICIPATION

The integrity of a corporate theology of the Church is directly related to the work of the *laos*, a Greek word used in Christian theology to refer to the whole people of God (laity and clergy) assembled for worship. It is not surprising that the modern lay movement has been accompanied by, nurtured, and no doubt shaped by liturgical renewal in this century. The development, testing and implementation of the American 1979 Book of Common Prayer, the English *Alternative Service Book* 1980 and the Canadian 1985 *Book of Alternative Services* all reflect the theological and liturgical legitimacy of increased lay participation. The elucidating teaching section in the Canadian book explains this liturgical principle:

> A second difference in the Church of the present day appears in a growing sense among Christians that they constitute a complex and varied community, with many different roles and functions. This vision of the Church, as old as the New Testament, was never entirely lost but was certainly eclipsed during a long period of Christian history. A sharp line ran between the leadership role of the priest and the relative passivity of the laity. Today there is recognition that the Church not only contains but needs many roles and functions in its administration, witness, and service as well as in its liturgy.[25]

Moreover, given the intimate relationship in Anglicanism between prayer and belief conveyed in the principle *lex orandi: lex credendi*, (see pp. 174–87) these new and alternative service books will continue to ground future generations of Anglicans in liturgical expressions more consonant with a theology of the whole people of God at work in the world.

This principle of contemporary liturgical renewal corresponds with, and represents a return to, the liturgical centre of early Anglicanism. The Tudor Prayer Books were designed to encourage accessibility to, and inclusion of, all. Cranmer was clear that worship was something done by priest and people together. The principle of participation was essential for *common* prayer! In the scriptural sacraments of baptism and Holy Communion, Cranmer emphasized participation in Christ initially through the regenerating waters of baptism that signify that 'through Christ we are born anew', and through ongoing regular participation of the *laos* in Holy Communion whereby 'we be continually nourished by spiritual food: and that spiritual food is Christ also'.[26] Cranmer was confident about the ability of the people to hear and respond in faith. Thus the people's petition in the Tudor Postcommunion prayer was, 'that we may continue in that holy fellowship, and do all such good works as thou has prepared for us to walk in'.[27]

Toward the end of the sixteenth century Richard Hooker in his summative work, *Of the Laws of Ecclesiastical Polity*, provided theological exposition of this principle of participation. He believed that our sacramental participation in Christ was shaped by the incarnation, as embodied in 'that mutuall inward hold which Christ hath of us and wee of him', and that the purpose of the incarnation was to alter human nature toward conformity with divine nature.[28] It is important to understand that Hooker was referring not to making humanity godlike, but to the exercise of a mutuality that implies responsibility. Another theological emphasis that Hooker used to explicate the centrality of participation was *metanoia*, a process of ongoing conversion in the hearts of the faithful that gave courage for the amending of life. The result of *metanoia*, turning to Christ, was active charity publicly expressed by the lives of those who received the sacraments in faith. Hooker understood that the intent of the Holy Communion was to change lives, not bread and wine. Thus the prayer from the service of Holy Communion, 'that we may evermore dwell in him, and he in us', was not a pious wish but a central holy intention.

Throughout the Tudor Prayer Books and in Hooker's theological elucidation, an Anglican theology of humanity was set forth that insisted on true mutuality, the binding relational character of God and the people of God. The contemporary American liturgist, Louis Weil (who is a contributor to the present volume), has described Anglican liturgy as literally the work of the people. He maintains that worship and prayer are dependent upon the actions of participants, and carry the implication 'that we are all celebrants together'.[29]

In the latter half of the nineteenth century, Anglican theologians also underscored empowering involvement of humanity in sacramental participation. The prophet of the Christian Socialist movement, Frederick Denison Maurice, looked into the heart of the crises engendered by the Industrial Revolution and concluded, not unlike Hooker, that the incarnation was the central theological principle that benefited human nature. The underlying righteousness of humanity was derived from the indwelling Christ: 'Apart from Him, I feel that there dwells in me no good thing; but I am sure that I am not apart from Him, nor are you, nor is any man.' Maurice described the sacraments as expressing unity of God and humanity, *and* of humanity with humanity. Baptism was the sacrament of 'constant union' representing Christ's sacrifice for all people; and the Holy Communion repeatedly presented the powerful drama of God's 'continual presence with His universal family'.[30]

Young Anglo-Catholic theologians who contributed to the essays, *Lux Mundi* (1889) were even more definitive in their expression of the social significance of the sacraments. Francis Paget underlined the pervasiveness of the sacraments in the world: 'Through Sacramental elements and acts Christianity maintains its strong inclusive hold upon the whole of life.' J. R. Illingworth pointed to the incarnational centre of Christianity. 'It is impossible to read history without feeling how profoundly the religion of the Incarnation has been a religion of humanity.' Charles Gore, also in *Lux Mundi*, elucidated how the sacraments through the work of the Holy Spirit in the Church were 'social ceremonies', the means of incorporation into Christian society.[31] Gore built upon this teaching about the social nature of the sacraments in *The Reconstruction of Belief* (1926), in which he argued that the authority of the Church rests on the demonstration of the moral and social witness that is the work of the lay people.

In this century William Temple reiterated in inclusive terms and ecumenical actions the social significance of the sacraments. For Temple, baptism represented a turning away from selfishness, a concept in harmony with *metanoia*. He argued not only for the socially redemptive but also for the socially creative impact of the Eucharist in contemporary society. He suggested that we take bread and wine as symbols of our industrial and commercial life, and offer them as indications of our willingness to continue to serve humanity. For Temple, worship included all of life; sacraments, intercessions, all prayer connected humanity to the world to be won.[32]

These and other Anglican theologians have repeatedly emphasized that the sacraments, indeed the whole of Christian worship, are intended to encourage social responsiveness, whether in the Tudor Commonwealth or the post-industrial world. It is this direction that is central in the new liturgies. For example in the baptismal covenant from the American Prayer Book, the candidates promise to 'strive for justice and peace among all people, and respect the dignity of every human being'.[33] At baptism and in the Eucharist, liturgical actions are designed to empower the ministry of the people of God in the world.

LAITY AND MINISTRY:
THE SPIRIT OF CHRISTIAN MISSION

Contemporary and emerging understandings of laity reflect significant changes in traditional language. The American Prayer Book Catechism defines 'ministry' in a manner that seemingly challenges the historic threefold ministry:

Q. Who are the ministers of the Church?
A. The ministers of the Church are lay persons, bishops, priests, and deacons.[34]

In Christian Churches throughout North America and in denominational and ecumenical statements it has become common parlance to refer to 'lay ministry'. This phrase is not only redundant, it is awkward. Most laity despite well-intentioned prodding are reluctant to call themselves 'ministers'. It is probably more helpful and accurate to explore possibilities for extending Christian witness by referring, as in the title of a recent book by Norman Pittenger, to *The Ministry of All Christians*. This chapter is unusual in the genre of writing about laity because it concludes rather than begins with reference to ministry. Essentially what seems to be at stake is not the task of convincing persons that they are 'ministers'. Ministry is not our identity as people of God, Christianity is! In the global village of the twenty-first century, the exact ordering of ministry will surely not be as critical as the ethical witness of laity in a post-Christian world. This concluding section addresses present and future questions. What is the spirit, the substance of laity in mission, and what kind of everyday Christian spirituality might carry us into the future?

From the perspective of the laity, mission and ministry are interdependent. This is underscored in the American Prayer Book Catechism: 'The Church carries out its mission through the ministry of all its members.'[35] In 1965 the Second Vatican Council sounded a similar note: 'The laity, too, share in the priestly, prophetic and royal office of Christ and therefore have their own role to play in the mission of the whole People of God'.[36] Such statements continue to reflect changing use of theological terms, as well as renewed emphasis on convincing laity of their responsibility for bearing the Church's mission. However difficult this task continues to be, there is sufficient evidence in Christian history that the work of the laity has *regularly*, not just *episodically*, been that of revival, reform, and mission. The late nineteenth-century proponent of indigenous mission, Roland Allen, wrote of the Church's need to follow the New Testament model of trust in the compulsion of the Spirit, the power of spontaneous expansion.[37] There are abundant examples of this collective impetus in Anglican history: the Evangelical reform societies of the eighteenth century, organizations like the Church Missionary Society founded in 1799 (see pp. 432–7) and the interdenominational Student Christian Movement founded in 1892; the tradition of strong lay leadership, primarily that of women (though few held official positions of power), in expanding the foreign and domestic witness of the Episcopal Church in the nineteenth century; and in this century the vast indigenous expansion of Anglicanism in Africa.

The increased provision of educational resources has long been an objective of Anglican laity. The Sunday School Movement shaped both religious education and public education in America. It is difficult to underestimate the energy and commitment that this particular nineteenth-century strategy for mission attracted in the American churches. One legacy of this movement was the centrality in the 1950's of Christian Education in Episcopal parishes. The Director of Religious Education (usually a lay person) was often as influential in parochial leadership as the rector. In England, as in North America, there has been a tradition of educational philanthropy, founding and supporting schools, theological colleges and seminaries. Laity have been effective in sponsoring educational work among children, signalled in organizations such as the Boy Scouts and Girl Guides. Laity have been critical in supporting adult education, represented in the Worker's Educational Association founded in England in 1903 and in the American Settlement House movement. In Anglicanism, laity have traditionally supported the vision of an educated Church, rather than only a learned clergy.

The modern lay movement has witnessed the proliferation of adult educational resources: theological education by extension, diocesan lay training courses and schools, professional theological education degrees designed for laity as well as those seeking ordination, and the provision of training opportunities for lay pastoral care and other specialized aspects of Christian mission. In these programmes, the providers of lay education are often laity. Church officials have also increased opportunities for lay involvement in parochial and diocesan work. There are lay readers, missionaries, lay pastoral assistants, laity on local ministry teams, in all, laity engaged in a vast variety of church work. At least one study, the controversial 1983 report entitled *A Strategy for the Church's Ministry* (commonly referred to as the Tiller Report), recommends increased dependence upon lay leadership for the provision and extension of the Church's mission in England. Whether specific strategies are adopted and successfully implemented, it is clear that there is renewed urgency among denominational officials for furthering active lay engagement in mission. *All Are Called* describes this shift of emphasis: 'Adult Christian commitment means an *informed* commitment. It is not a matter of being loyal sheep.'[38] After years of paying lip service to laity in ministry, the institutional Church is at last beginning to consider serious structural provisions for supporting the ongoing mission of the laity.

The spirit and direction of mission among Anglican laity has not historically been, and should not primarily be, focused on lay ministries within institutional Church structures, or on overworked clergy parcelling out jobs for laity. Many assumptions about shared ministry still reflect patronizing and paternalistic

257

attitudes toward laity. The future integrity of the Church's mission does not depend on lay activities that imitate clerical roles, but on the spontaneous expansion of the Church's mission in society at large. In considering this present challenge, there is no need to tie increasing secularism to a decline in religious commitment. This was not true in the period of the Reformation, and it may not be true in these latter days.

However, if renewal is to continue to come from the laity, then the institutional Church needs to be more attuned to those spiritual resources that nurture persons in their everyday life. While 'spirituality' is a term of relatively recent coinage, lay mystics, poets and theological visionaries—from Julian of Norwich to Evelyn Underhill, from Walt Whitman to Annie Dillard, and from Richard Hooker to Dorothee Sölle—have for centuries inspired Christians on spiritual journeys in this world. These and other authors of spiritual 'classics' are alike in their emphasis upon humanity's 'immersion in God' in this world and upon the people of God as corporately engaged and socially responsive.[39]

In theology reminiscent of William Temple, Simone Weil wrote that 'the pursuit of truth must never be separated from the love of persons'.[40] An ethical, everyday Christian spirituality that might carry us into the future would do well to pay attention to traditional Anglican perspectives on laity. Thus, for example, the theology of humanity would be socially grounded, enlivened with the incarnational legacy of responsible belonging to God; worship and prayer would be accessible to all regardless of education or social location; educational resources would be expansive, shaped by listening to those with whom we learn; and a spirited ecumenically-minded Church in mission would be willing to explore unknown areas with persons of diverse perspectives, faiths, and nationalities. Through participation in such a Church, Anglican laity would continue to find extraordinary significance in the ordinary and know that truth reveals itself in patterns of human events, in collective testimonies old and new.

NOTES

1 *The Book of Common Prayer* (1979), p. 855.

2 *All Are Called: Toward a Theology of the Laity* (London, CIO Publishing, 1985), p. 3.

3 J. J. Scarisbrick, *The Reformation and the English People* (Oxford, Basil Blackwell, 1984), see pp. 61, 39, 165. Another Tudor-Stuart Historian, G. R. Elton, has also moderated pre-Reformation estimates of anticlericalism in *Reform and Reformation, England 1505–1558* (Cambridge, Mass., Harvard University Press, 1977), p. 57.

4 Stephen Neill, *Anglicanism* (New York, OUP, 1978), 4th edn, p. 35; and Claire Cross, *Church and People, 1450–1600: The Triumph of the Laity in the English Church* (Atlantic Highlands, NJ, Humanities Press, 1976), *passim*.

5 John Bale, *King Johan*, ed. Barry B. Adams (San Marino, Calif., Huntington Library, 1969), pp. 108–12.

6 *Certain Sermons or Homilies Appointed to be Read in Churches in the Time of Queen Elizabeth* (SPCK, 1851), p. 109–10.

7 See especially John E. Booty, ed., David Siegenthaler, and John N. Wall Jr, *The Godly Kingdom of Tudor England: Great Books of the English Reformation* (Wilton, Conn., Morehouse-Barlow, 1981).

8 Juan Heinrich Bullinger, *The Godly Boke of Christen Matrimonye* (London 1543), sig. X5.

9 *The Acts and Monuments of John Foxe*, ed. George Townsend (New York, AMS Press, 1965), vol. iii, pp. 710–20, emphasis added.

10 Thomas Cranmer, *Works*, vol. ii, Miscellaneous Writings, ed. John Edmond Cox (Cambridge, CUP, 1846), p. 179; see also Rosalind and Christopher Brooke, *Popular Religion in the Middle Ages* (Leipzig, Thames and Hudson, 1984), p. 130ff.

11 Cranmer, *Works*, vol. ii, p. 120.

12 From the *Paraclesis* printed in several editions of Erasmus' works including John C. Olin, ed., *Christian Humanism and the Reformation: Selected Writings of Erasmus* (New York, Harper and Row, 1965), p. 100.

13 Lawrence Stone, 'The Educational Revolution in England: 1560–1640', *Past and Present* 28 (1964), pp. 41–80.

14 Richard L. Greaves, *Society and Religion in Elizabethan England* (Minneapolis, University of Minnesota Press, 1981), p. 328; see also Keith Wrightson and David Levine, *Poverty and Piety in an English Village, Terling, 1525–1700* (New York, Academic Press, 1979).

15 Urban T. Holmes III, *The Future Shape of Ministry* (New York, Seabury Press, 1971), pp. 58; Marc L. Schwarz, 'Some Thoughts on the Development of Lay Religious Consciousness in Pre-Civil-War England', in *Popular Belief and Practice*, ed. G. J. Cuming and Derek Baker (Cambridge, CUP, 1972), pp. 171–8; and Rosemary O'Day, *The English Clergy: The Emergence and Consolidation of a Profession, 1558–1640* (Leicester, Leicester University Press, 1979), p. 245.

16 *All Are Called*, p. 67.

17 *Christian Faith and Life*, ed. Roger L. Robert, in *Treasures from the Spiritual Classics* (Wilton, Conn., Morehouse-Barlow, 1981), pp. 57–8.

18 Hendrick Kraemer, *A Theology of the Laity* (London, Westminster Press, 1958), p. 3; see also Verna J. Dozier, *The Authority of the Laity* (Washington DC, The Alban Institute, 1982), pp. 39–42.

19 *Fellowship with God* (London, Macmillan, 1930), pp. 207–8, emphasis added.

20 *Book of Common Prayer* (1979), p. 365.

21 *Ministry and Imagination* (New York, Seabury Press, 1976), p. 19.

22 *The Gift of Courage* (Toronto, Anglican Book Centre, 1979), pp. 42–3.

23 *All Are Called*, pp. 7–8.

24 Quoted in Neill, *Anglicanism*, p. 285.

25 *Book of Alternative Services*, p. 11.

26 Cranmer, *Works*, vol ii, 176.

27 From The Elizabethan *Book of Common Prayer*, (1559), ed. John E. Booty. (Charlottesville, University Press of Virginia, 1976), p. 265.

28 Quotations from Hooker are from FE vol. ii; see sections V. lvi.1 and V. liv.5.

29 Louis Weill, 'Anglican Understanding of the Local Church,' *Anglican Theological Review*, 64. ii (April 1982), p. 197.

30 F. D. Maurice quoted in John E. Booty, 'Christian Spirituality: From Wilberforce to Temple', *Anglican Spirituality*, ed. William J. Wolf (Wilton, Conn., Morehouse-Barlow, 1982), pp. 81–5.

31 *Lux Mundi: A Series of Studies in the Religion of the Incarnation*, ed. Charles Gore (New York, Thomas Whittaker, 1889), p. 353, 176, 269.

32 William Temple, *The Hope of New World* (New York, Macmillan, 1943), p. 70; Owen C. Thomas, 'William Temple', in *The Spirit of Anglicanism*, ed. William J. Wolf (Wilton, Conn., Morehouse-Barlow, 1979), p. 126; and Wolf, *Anglican Spirituality*, p. 87.

33 Book of Common Prayer (1979), p. 305.

34 *ibid.*, p. 855.

35 *ibid.*

36 The Decree on the Apostolate of the Laity cited in John Tiller, *A Strategy for the Church's Ministry* (London, CIO Publishing, 1983), p. 67.

37 See *The Compulsion of the Spirit: A Roland Allen Reader*, ed. David Paton and Charles H. Long (Grand Rapids, Mich., Eerdmans Publishing Co., 1983), for an expansive interpretation of the work of laity; a more limited, 'episodic' view of lay engagement is presented in *Doctrine in the Church of England* (SPCK, 1938), especially p. 116.

38 *All Are Called*, p. 23.

39 See Dorothee Sölle, *The Strength of the Weak: Toward a Christian Feminist Identity* (Philadelphia, Westminster Press, 1984), p. 102.

40 *Gateway to God*, ed. David Raper (Glasgow, William Collins and Sons, 1974), see pp. 74–102; this is a selection of the writings of Weil, who died in 1943.

4 Initiation

DAVID R. HOLETON

Buchanan, Colin O., ed., *Nurturing Children in Communion*. GLS 44, Grove Press 1985.

Cuming, G. J., *A History of Anglican Liturgy*. 2nd edn, Macmillan 1982.

Fisher, J. D. C., *Christian Initiation: The Reformation Period*. AC, SPCK 1970.

idem, Confirmation: Then and Now. AC, SPCK 1978.

Hatchett, Marion J., *Commentary on the American Prayer Book*. Seabury Press, New York, 1980.

Holeton, David R. 'Christian Initiation in Some Anglican Provinces', in *SL* 12. ii/iii (1977), pp. 129–150.

Jagger, Peter J., *Christian Initiation: 1552–1969*. AC, SPCK 1970.

Mitchell, Leonell L., *Baptismal Anointing*. AC, SPCK 1966.

The development of the pattern of Christian initiation (baptism, confirmation, first communion) within Anglicanism can only be understood if put in the context of an ongoing tension between theological opinion and popular piety. Until the last few decades popular piety has almost always emerged as victor.

SIXTEENTH-CENTURY REFORM

The medieval baptismal practice and liturgical rites which were inherited by Thomas Cranmer and the English Reformers marked a low point in the long devolution of both baptismal practice and theology. The rites, whose origins lay in the patristic period, had, at the time they were developed, assumed a long period of baptismal preparation (catechumenate) followed by a short, intense final preparation (Lent) culminating in baptism at the Easter Vigil (or Pentecost in case a candidate for some reason was unable to be baptized at the Vigil). The candidates for baptism included both infants and adults, the latter often representing the majority. The various rites which emerged in this process of preparation and baptism (exorcisms, anointings, scrutinies, the giving of the Creed and Lord's Prayer, signing with the cross, chrismation, vesting in a new garment, giving a new light) helped interpret the theologically rich and complex mystery of baptism for those involved—especially if they were adults.

The rites that the Reformers inherited, however, were a pale shadow of their former selves. Rites which had once taken place over an extended period of time, often a number of years, had come to be compressed into a single event. The triumph of Christendom, as well as an exaggerated Augustinian understanding of the fate of those who died unbaptized, had successfully eliminated adults as baptismal candidates (they had all been baptized as infants). Rites that made

261

sense when used with adults thus came to be used on infants generally less than a week old. The communal element of initiation which had been emphasized by restricting the frequency with which baptism took place (except for baptism *in extremis*) disappeared as the Church encouraged the practice of baptism as soon after birth as possible. Finally, the essential unity of Christian initiation (baptism in water, sealing/imposition of hands, reception of communion) had devolved into three rites (baptism, confirmation, first communion) celebrated over an extended period of years. The Reformers recognized some, but not all, of these historical and theological problems as they set about to effect their reforms.

Like the initial efforts of Martin Luther and Huldreich Zwingli Cranmer's first revision of the baptismal rite (1549) was relatively conservative. The shape of the rite is basically that of the Sarum Manual (*Rituale*), which had the most widespread use in medieval England. It was a rite typical of late medieval baptismal liturgies.

In revising the rite Cranmer maintained some of the Sarum prayers (in English translation) and some of the ceremonial (consignation, exorcism of the devil, chrismation and the presentation of the white baptismal garment); other prayers and ceremonies (the exorcism of salt, the *Ephphatha*, the signing of the hand, the anointing of the breast and the presentation of a lighted candle) were discarded. To this revision Cranmer added texts borrowed from Luther, the *Consultation* of Herman von Wied of Cologne and the Hispanic *Missale Mixtum*.

The resultant rite appears, on first inspection, to be very much in continuity with its late medieval predecessor with only the most obvious of the 'dark and dumb ceremonies', which were anathema to the Reformers, removed. On closer inspection there are definite signs that Cranmer was attempting much more than a cosmetic reform. The first rubric[1] indicates that Cranmer was aware of at least some of the baptismal practice of the patristic Church and that, while he conceded a replication of that period was not possible, some of its insights could well be restored. Baptism was, if possible, to take place only on Sundays and holy days, at a time when the largest number of the community could assemble, and that this public celebration of baptism was to serve as a rememorative event, reminding adults and older children present of their own baptism. Cranmer's choice of text for the chrismation may also indicate his intention to restore the primitive unity of the rite, at least as far as baptism and confirmation are concerned. This point will be discussed later.

The 1549 book provided for a separate rite entitled Confirmation (see pp. 122–6). The model for this rite was not the second post-baptismal anointing of the Roman rite found in the Sarum Manual but instead has its roots in a catechetical rite which emerged from the left-wing of the Bohemian Reformation of the previous century. This new rite was not to be administered until the candidate could recite the Creed, the Ten Commandments, and the Lord's Prayer as well as answer the questions of the catechism and 'ratify and confess' the questions answered on the child's behalf at baptism by the godparents. The administration of the rite, severely limited to bishops, was to be received by children who have 'come to that age ... [when] they begin to be in danger to fall into sin'. The effect of confirmation was to give 'strength and defence against all temptations to sin and the assaults of the world, and the devil'.

The last rubric of the rite states:

> And there shall none be admitted to the holy communion: until such time as he be confirmed.

But the last of the introductory rubrics attempts to salve the consciences of those who would not want to delay confirmation for fear that a child might die not having received the Eucharist, which was generally considered necessary for salvation.

> And that no man shall think that any detriment shall come to children by deferring of their confirmation: he shall know for truth, that it is certain by God's word, that children being Baptized (if they depart out of this life in their infancy) are undoubtedly saved.

The theological content of the 1549 baptismal rite remained basically that of the medieval West. The primary theological concern is the forgiveness of sin. The first words of the rite set the tone for what is to follow:

> Dearly beloved, forasmuch as all men be conceived and born in sin, and that no man born in sin, can enter into the kingdom of God (except he be regenerate, and born anew of water, and the Holy Ghost) ...

As in other contemporary Western baptismal rites, other baptismal images (such as baptism as gifting with the Holy Spirit, enlightenment, or sign of participation in the eschatological kingdom) are rare, if not entirely absent. Continuity, rather than change, thus characterizes Cranmer's first revision of the baptismal rite theologically as well as liturgically. Despite Cranmer's expressed preference for infrequent public baptism with as many of the community as possible gathered, private baptism, within a few days of birth, remained the common custom. The provision of a rite for private baptism in a home was a significant concession to popular practice which was not going to be changed easily in spite of the opinions of reforming bishops.

Martin Bucer in his *Censura*[2] is generally approving of Cranmer's initial reforms in the area of initiation and particularly lauds Cranmer's attempts to restore baptism to feast days in the presence of the whole church. Cranmer's new rite of confirmation is also given general approval but with the reservation that the rite not be administered in an automatic or mechanical fashion but that candidates be limited to those

> who have confirmed the confession of their mouth with a manner of life consistent with

it and from whose conduct it can be discerned that they make profession of their own faith and not another's.[3]

Bucer also suggested a series of changes and emendations to the 1549 rite. Of particular concern to him were that : (1) baptisms should take place after the sermon at the Eucharist rather than in the context of Matins or Evensong; (2) the initial part of the rite which, following the Sarum/medieval shape, had taken place at the church door, should take place in the body of the church; (3) the baptismal robe and the use of chrism should be abolished; (4) the baptismal water should not be blessed; (5) nothing should be said to infants, for they understand nothing; and (6) the exorcism is appropriate only for demoniacs and that it should therefore be turned into a prayer for protection.

Cranmer, in his revision of the baptismal rite for the second Prayer Book (1552), takes note of a number of Bucer's suggestions. The entire rite is to take place at the font but remains in the context of Matins or Evensong rather than the Eucharist. The signation, exorcism and godparents' repetition of the Lord's Prayer and Creed were suppressed. The threefold renunciation followed by a threefold profession of faith are each condensed into a single question and answer. The medieval questions: 'What dost thou desire?' ... 'Baptism', and 'Wilt thou be baptized?' ... 'I will', are condensed into a single question and answer: 'Wilt thou be baptized in this faith?' ... 'This is my desire'. The blessing of the font is reduced by a half and effectively ceases to be a blessing. The remaining prayer is to be used at every baptism rather than only monthly as permitted in 1549. The child is named and then, if healthy, immersed (now only once rather than three times) while the baptismal formula is recited. The giving of the baptismal garment (chrisome) and chrismation are omitted and, instead, the priest is instructed to make the sign of the cross on the child's forehead—the place where the second or 'confirmation' anointing had taken place in the medieval Sarum rite. The consignation was accompanied by this declaration:

> We receive this child into the congregation of Christ's flock, and do sign *him* with the sign of the cross, in token that hereafter *he* shall not be ashamed to confess the faith of Christ's crucified, and manfully to fight under his banner against sin, the world, and the devil, and to continue Christ's faithful soldier and servant unto *his* life's end. Amen.

The revision inserts a bidding that those present give thanks to God that the newly baptized are 'regenerate and grafted into the body of Christ's congregation'. The rite concludes with the Lord's Prayer, then another prayer of thanksgiving followed by an exhortation to the godparents in which they are reminded of their duties to their godchild. (Godparents were to see that their godchildren learn the Creed, Lord's Prayer and Ten Commandments in English as well as all other things Christians ought to know; that they be raised virtuously; and that they be brought to the bishop for confirmation.)

The rite of confirmation underwent several important changes in its 1552 revision. The English translation of the Sarum prayer which asked God to send the Holy Spirit on those about to be confirmed is emended so that the candidates are now to be 'strengthened' that the Spirit's 'manifold gifts of grace might daily increase in them'. The signing with the cross, together with its accompanying prayer and formula, was removed. The bishop is now instructed to lay hands upon each child and to pray.

> Defend, O Lord, this child with thy heavenly grace, that *he* may continue thine for ever, and daily increase in thy Holy Spirit more and more, until *he* come to thy everlasting kingdom. Amen.

The catechetical understanding of confirmation was underlined by an expansion of the rubric concerning admission to communion. Communicants were now required to be able to recite the Catechism as well as the Creed, Lord's Prayer and Ten Commandments to be confirmed.

The rites of initiation as they appeared in 1552 set the basic pattern of initiation within Anglicanism for the next 400 years. While the rites themselves underwent a number of minor revisions over the next century, their shape and content was but little altered.

The Prayer Book of 1604, in response to Puritan pressure, regulated the conditions under which private baptism could take place and required that emergency baptism be celebrated only by a 'lawful Minister'. The 1662 book regulated the number of godparents, provided a prayer for the sanctification of the baptismal water, and no longer required that communicants be able to recite the Catechism nor that they necessarily be confirmed, but that they 'be confirmed, or be ready and desirous to be confirmed'. The same book also provides a new rite for the 'baptism of such as are of riper years', a response to both the growing controversies with the radical (Anabaptist) reform and the missionary situation of a growing colonial empire.

Thus baptism in infancy, followed by confirmation (usually when children were in their teens), followed by first communion remained—and in many parts of the Anglican Communion remains—the normative pattern for initiation. This pattern, which implicitly assumes a biological model of the sacraments (baptism = birth, confirmation = growth, etc.), solidified both theologically and ritually under external as well as internal attack. Radical Reformers as well as Puritans attacked the rite for its retention of 'popish ceremonial' denouncing with particular vigour the retention of godparents and the consignation.

The seventeenth century saw an extended and singularly acrimonious debate over the question of infant baptism. This debate, which raged with particular ferocity just before and during the Commonwealth, caused Anglican theologians to re-examine the implicit biological model of the sacraments with which they had been working, as well as to question of the propriety of separating first communion from baptism. Jeremy Taylor, later bishop of Down and Connor, was led to remark that a name ought to be invented for those who refuse to give communion to infants that is as disparaging as is 'Anabaptist' for those who refuse to give them baptism.[4] The Restoration saw a quick end to any such radical thought.

The effect of these controversies effectively was to convince Anglicans of the rightness of their own practice. The ceremonial contested by the radical independents and the Puritans was to become entrenched as a touchstone of Anglican orthodoxy, while the theological concessions made to the arguments of Anabaptists were quickly forgotten once the Church of England was re-established with the Restoration of Charles II. Controversy had led only to a rigidity of both ceremonial practice as well as theological position.

The one piece of the pattern of initiation which suffered most over the ensuing centuries was confirmation. Until the strict churchmanship of the early nineteenth century, which grew out of the Evangelical Revival, confirmation was more often ignored than observed. In England this was, in part, the product of the vastness of many dioceses, but also of a serious problem with episcopal non-residency. Overseas it was a question of lack of bishops, there being no Anglican bishop outside the British Isles until 1785. To be confirmed one would have had to make a long and dangerous journey back to the United Kingdom. None of these difficulties, however, ever led to serious consideration being given to delegating the authority to confirm. This is as much a comment on the low view in which confirmation was held as it is on a high view of episcopal authority. Since the early nineteenth century confirmation has been observed with considerable scrupulousness, and has gained a place in Anglican piety unknown during the previous centuries.

THE TRADITIONAL MODEL IN CRISIS

The traditional pattern of initiation worked well as long as Anglicanism continued to exist in a Christendom situation. Its basic assumption, that baptism was as much into a nurturing Christian society as into a nurturing Christian community, remained viable in many parts of the world where Anglicanism existed in strength until after the Second World War. Although there had been a disparity, ever since confirmation had gained its newfound importance, between the numbers who were baptized and the number who later returned for confirmation, the disparity had not been all that great. Both baptism and confirmation were well rooted in popular or folk religion and parents or godparents would usually ensure that the baptized would later attend confirmation class, even though the children had been conspicuously absent from any sort of religious practice during the intervening thirteen years.

By the end of the Second World War this pattern had begun to undergo radical change. Not only was there an increasing disparity between the numbers baptized and the number returning for confirmation, but there was a dramatic fall in the practice rate among those confirmed. Studies indicated that this drop-out was often taking place very shortly after confirmation, and that for many children confirmation had come to serve as graduation not only from any sort of religious education, but also from church itself. The tradition pattern seemed to be failing and became the subject of considerable concern.

THE BEGINNING OF A NEW PATTERN OF INITIATION

A major report on 'The Renewal of Church in Faith' presented at the 1968 Lambeth Conference served to focus the growing concern over the traditional pattern of initiation found in Anglican Prayer Books. In a section of the report devoted to the renewal of the Church and its structures the bishops noted:

> We are concerned at the lack of any form of commissioning for laymen analogous to the ordination of the clergy, and Resolution 25 [see below] is put forward to encourage this need to be met. We commend the following alternatives as possible lines of experiment:
>
> (a) Admission to Holy Communion and confirmation would be separated. When a baptized child is of appropriate age, he or she would be admitted to Holy Communion after an adequate course of instruction. Confirmation would be deferred to an age when a young man or woman shows adult responsibility and wishes to be commissioned and confirmed for his or her task of being a Christian in society.
>
> (b) Infant baptism and confirmation would be administered together, followed by an admission to Holy Communion at an early age after appropriate instruction. In due course the bishop would commission the person for service when he or she is capable of making a responsible commitment.
>
> Experimentation along the first of the alternatives should include careful examination of the bearing of this separation in ecumenical dialogue with (a) those holding to believer's baptism and (b) the Orthodox Churches. In both instances, the intimate relationship of baptism and confirmation with admission to Holy Communion is a matter of major importance.[5]
>
> Resolution 25. The Conference recommends that each province or regional Church be asked to explore the theology of baptism and confirmation in relation to the need to commission the laity for their task in the world, and to experiment in this regard.[6]

This report, and Resolution 25 in particular, need to be appreciated as seminal in the renewal of initiation practice which has been spreading throughout the Anglican Communion for almost two decades.

Many provincial doctrine and liturgical commissions were quick to respond to the bishops' invitation to explore the theology of baptism and confirmation. For many of them the Lambeth statement had come at an important juncture; for they were already engaged in liturgical revision, a process which was to produce the most radical revision of Anglican liturgical texts since the Reformation itself.

The great corpus of liturgical scholarship in the area of Christian initiation which has been produced over the last fifty years, much of it by Anglican scholars, was to bear considerable weight in this theological and liturgical exploration. The historical unity of the rites of initiation were clearly understood in a way that Anglicans (including Cranmer) had not seen in the past. The theological implications of baptism, particularly in relation to eucharistic communion, took on a prominence previously unknown. A number of doctrinal commissions called for the restoration of baptism, confirmation and first communion as a unified rite in which all the baptized who had received the laying on of hands or chrismation would be admitted into the eucharistic fellowship. Typical of this position was that of the Church in Wales which concluded:

> Any separation of [baptism, confirmation and first communion] *either* as successively given at different stages in the initiation rite, *or* as conceivable in isolation from one another, involves grave theological confusion. This is why the disintegrated pattern of Christian Initiation, which the Western Church has inherited, is theologically unsatisfactory. Such separation leads to pseudo-problems that are insoluble theologically, if not in fact meaningless.
>
> In particular, we refer to the impossibility of giving a convincing theology of 'baptism' separated from 'confirmation', or of 'confirmation' separated from 'baptism'. ... Clear thinking, from now onwards, requires that we treat forgiveness of sin, mystical participation in the death and resurrection of the Lord, regeneration and the gift of the Spirit as alternative partial descriptions of a single ontological change of status which carries the privilege of receiving the Holy Communion as an incorporate member of the Body of Christ.[7]

Working on this new paradigm for Christian initiation, liturgical commissions began to produce single, unified, rites of initiation. These new rites encountered serious opposition around the area of episcopal involvement in initiation. While many bishops were able to accept the principles delineated by provincial theological commissions, they were not prepared to accept a pattern of initiation in which they appeared to have little or no ritual part. Few bishops were prepared to accept the argument that they were personally represented at every baptism by the priest whom they had delegated to exercise pastoral ministry in the local community; some were prepared to accept this delegation if it were to involve the mandatory use of episcopally consecrated chrism. What seemed to lie at the root of the objections was an episcopate that had for too long been forced to define its pastoral ministry in terms of confirmation as well as the understandable and laudable desire to have assurance that there would be some regular moment of pastoral contact with the faithful. A liturgical solution which both respected the conclusions of the theological commissions and took into account the bishops' objections had to be found.

A NEW PATTERN EMERGES

A number of the baptismal rites which have appeared during the recent past reflect what may be a new consensus in the pattern of initiation within Anglicanism. Cranmer's desire to restrict the celebration to Sundays and holy days, at a time when the largest number of the community can be present, is finally coming into its own. New rubrics, often re-enforced by canonical legislation, direct that the service take place during the principal celebration on a Sunday. Some provinces are even more directive and encourage the celebration be limited to five baptismal days during the year (Easter Vigil, Pentecost, All Saints' Day, the Baptism of the Lord and when the bishop visits the parish). Bucer's preference for the Eucharist as the context for initiation is also finally emerging as the norm assumed by most new initiation rites.

Thus the context in which initiation now takes place is quite different from what, despite Cranmer's expressed wish to the contrary, was the liturgical norm. Baptism has finally become a public act of the gathered church rather than a private act in the midst of a small group of family and friends. Although candidates for baptism would still normally have sponsors (who now should include the parents of infants and young children) the whole congregation is often asked a question of this sort: 'Will you who witness these vows do all in your power to support *these persons* in *their* life in Christ?' The radical shift in liturgical context reflects a post-Christendom Church where the gathered community, rather than society, provides the context in which Christian nurture is to take place. It also reflects a Church in which ministry is no longer seen in solely clerical terms, where various of the community's members are involved in baptismal preparation, and where lay Christians are beginning to demand some sign of commitment to ongoing participation in the Christian life from baptismal candidates or their presenting families.

In the new rites themselves there is a clear commitment to the integral unity of initiation itself. There is an increasing unwillingness to make age a distinguishing factor among candidates for baptism. One rite is used for all candidates and all the baptized have equal rights within the community. Baptism is increasingly seen as admission to the Eucharist regardless of age.

The richness of the biblical images which express the mystery of salvation[8] are finding a more copious expression in the new liturgical texts. These are often linked to the recovery of baptismal ceremonies which disappeared in either 1549 or 1552 (the use of chrism, the giving of a baptismal garment and a lighted candle). This again reflects a post-Christendom Church. These once 'dark and dumb ceremonies' now speak clearly not only to the community gathered but also to the baptismal candidates themselves who are, as often as not, adults.

Confirmation, as we shall see below, is emerging once again as a non-initiatory rite of reaffirmation to the covenant made in baptism. It remains an episcopal act, but is taking on a character quite different from that of the past.

The paradigm for initiation that is slowly emerging in the Anglican world is probably closer to the pattern envisioned by the Reformers than it has ever been. The vision of a public, corporate, act of worship in which the primitive unity of the rite (as the Reformers understood it) was restored was never able to prevail over the traditional forces of popular piety. The direction Christian initiation is taking today is faithful to the vision of the Reformers as well as its natural and logical consequence. It continues as a major item on the Anglican theological and liturgical agenda.

CONFIRMATION

The history and development of confirmation is one of the more complicated aspects of the history of Christian initiation. The question is no less complicated within Anglicanism. There are several questions which need some reflection apart from the earlier section on initiation.

Cranmer and Confirmation

Although Cranmer kept the outline of Western medieval confirmation there was, at the very least, a major shift in the emphasis of what he was doing. There is considerable scholarly debate over Cranmer's intentions. It is immediately evident that there was a shift in emphasis from the administration of the rite itself to the catechizing which preceded it. The extent to which Cranmer saw the new rite as remaining in continuity with the medieval rite of confirmation is much less clear, particularly since he dropped the anointing which, according to medieval theologians, was central to the sacramental nature of confirmation.

Cranmer's intentions are even less certain when put in the light of traditional 'confirmation' elements which he places within the baptismal rite itself. The anointing of the 1549 rite and the consignation of the 1552 rite both are made on the forehead as in medieval confirmation rather than on the top or crown of the head as in the medieval rite of baptism. The language Cranmer uses—'the unction of his Holy Spirit' (1549) and the declaration during the consignation (1552) (p. 265 above)—are typical of language used for confirmation rather than baptism during the Middle Ages. As Cranmer had drawn material from the Hispanic *Missale Mixtum*, where there is but one post-baptismal anointing and no separate rite of confirmation, he cannot have been unaware of a single, unified, rite of initiation.

While there is no clear answer to Cranmer's intentions when he created the rites of baptism and confirmation, it is arguable that he was being bolder than is often thought: the baptismal rite containing what he saw as the essence of medieval 'confirmation' and the confirmation rite as a novelty following in the steps of the Bohemians, Erasmus and Luther.[9] The contemporary political importance of ambiguity rather than clarity makes a final resolution to this question particularly difficult.

Various Interpretations of Confirmation

While the administration of confirmation within Anglicanism was very lax, and was often neglected altogether, during the three centuries after the Reformation the nineteenth century saw the beginnings of a strict confirmation discipline. With it this discipline brought a sacramental interpretation of confirmation unknown in earlier Anglicanism.

A literal interpretation of the confirmation rubric, which made confirmation a prerequisite to reception of the Eucharist, led to a theology which interpreted confirmation as the second and completing half of the complete sacrament of initiation. This new theology of confirmation came to have a dominant (but not absolute) influence within the Anglican Communion from about 1890.[10] Alongside this sacramental interpretation of confirmation, the older non-sacramental, catechetical, understanding of confirmation continued to exist.[11]

As long as the question 'What is confirmation?' was never forced, the two theologies were able to coexist without difficulty because the ritual practice was the same: both theologies presumed confirmation before communion. When Lambeth 1968 asked for a re-examination of confirmation theology and the process of liturgical revision began, the question once again became one of considerable debate. Confirmation, as celebrated in the new liturgical texts, is clearly emerging as a non-initiatory reaffirmation of the baptismal covenant. Confirmation as a rite of admission to communion is quickly disappearing and instead is becoming an optional rite for those who, having come to a stage of Christian maturity, wish to make a public reaffirmation of their faith in the presence of a bishop. The age at which this is taking place is becoming considerably older than the early teens, the traditional age for confirmation.

NOTES

1 It appeareth by ancient writers, that the sacrament of baptism in old time was not commonly ministered but at two times in the year, at Easter and Whitsuntide, at which times it was openly ministered in the presence of all the congregation: Which custom (now being grown out of use) although it cannot for many considerations be well restored again, yet it is thought good to follow the same as near as conveniently may be: Wherefore the people are to be admonished, that it is most convenient that Baptism should not be ministered but upon Sundays and other holy days, when the most number of people may come together. As well for the congregation there present may testify the receiving of them, that be newly baptized, into the number of Christ's Church, as also because in the Baptism of Infants, every man present may be put in remembrance of his own profession

271

made to God in his Baptism. For which cause also, it is expedient that Baptism be ministered in the English tongue. Nevertheless (if necessity so require) children ought at all times to be baptized, either at the Church or else at home.

2 E. C. Whitaker, *Martin Bucer and the Book of Common Prayer*, pp. 82–115.

3 ibid., p. 114.

4 Jeremy Taylor, *Of the Liberty of Prophesying* (London 1648), pp. 232–3.

5 The Lambeth Conference 1968, *Resolutions and Reports* (SPCK 1968), p. 99.

6 ibid., p. 37.

7 The Doctrinal Commission of the Church in Wales, *Christian Initiation* (Church in Wales Publications 1971), pp. 22–3.

8 These have been laid out before the Churches in the opening paragraphs of the Baptism section of the World Council of Churches document *Baptism, Eucharist and Ministry*. The incorporation of a greater number of these biblical images has been a conscious response to the Faith and Order process which culminated in the Lima text.

9 Marion Hatchett, *Commentary on the American Prayer Book*, pp. 260–265 has been the most lucid expositor of this position.

10 This position came to be known as the 'Mason-Dix' line from the work of two of its principal proponants, A. J. Mason, *The Relation of Confirmation to Baptism* (London 1893); and Don Gregory Dix, *The Theology of Confirmation in Relation to Baptism* (London, 1946).

11 G. W. H. Lampe defends this position in *The Seal of the Spirit* (2nd edn., London, 1967).

5 Holy Communion

WILLIAM R. CROCKETT

Cuming, G. J., *A History of Anglican Liturgy*. 2nd edn, London, Macmillan, 1982.

Brooks, Peter, *Thomas Cranmer's Doctrine of the Eucharist: An Essay in Historical Development*. New York, Seabury Press, 1965.

Buxton, Richard F, *Eucharist and Institution Narrative: A Study in the The Roman and Anglican Traditions of the Consecration of the Eucharist from the Eighth to the Twentieth Centuries*. AC 58, Great Wakering, Mayhew-McCrimmon, 1976.

Rattenbury, J. Ernest, *The Eucharistic Hymns of John and Charles Wesley*. London, Epworth Press, 1948.

Hardelin, Alf, *The Tractarian Understanding of the Eucharist*. Uppsala, Almquist & Wiksells, 1965.

Dix, Gregory, *The Shape of the Liturgy*, with additional notes by Paul V. Marshall. New York, Seabury Press, 1982.

The English Reformation was in its beginnings a political rather than a religious reformation. When religious change did eventually come it took first a liturgical rather than a doctrinal form. In 1549 the first edition of the Book of Common Prayer appeared (see pp. 122–6).[1] Its principal author was Archbishop Thomas Cranmer. As far as the eucharistic rite is concerned, it was a half-way measure which followed the traditional Roman Mass quite closely as far as order and structure are concerned.[2] The greatest departure from the doctrine of the older rite is found in the revisions made in the canon of the Mass (Prayer of Consecration or Eucharistic Prayer). The structure of the old canon was followed, but the theological emphasis was placed squarely on the sacrifice of Christ 'once offered' on the cross. All references to the Mass as a sacrifice in any other sense than that of a commemoration of the sacrifice of the cross, a sacrifice of praise and thanksgiving, or the sacrifice of 'ourselves, our souls, and bodies', were carefully excluded. The whole prayer was more clearly oriented around the theme of thanksgiving, in line with the eucharistic prayers of the early Church. The *anamnesis* (*memorial* of Christ's death and resurrection) is restored to a position of central prominence, and an *epiclesis* (invocation) is introduced which invokes both the word and the Holy Spirit on the gifts in view of their reception in communion.

In 1552 the second edition of the Prayer Book appeared. The 1552 eucharistic rite is a much more drastic revision of the old Mass than 1549.[3] Cranmer's 1549 canon had three sections. The first section contained intercessions and commemorations adapted from the Roman canon, the second section contained the thanksgiving for redemption, the epiclesis, and the words of institution, and the third section contained the anamnesis followed by the offering of 'ourselves, our souls, and bodies', and concluded with the doxology. Cranmer moved the first section to a point earlier in the service, immediately after the offertory. The third section became an optional prayer after communion. The epiclesis was removed from the middle section, so that all that remained of the Eucharistic Prayer in 1552 was the thanksgiving for redemption and the words of institution. This was followed immediately by the words for the administration of communion, which now read: 'Take and eat this, in remembrance that Christ died for thee, and feed on him in thy heart by faith, with thanksgiving', and 'Drink this in remembrance that Christ's blood was shed for thee and be thankful'. The reason for these changes is a disputed question.[4]

Anglicanism never developed a doctrine of the Eucharist bearing the distinctive stamp either of a single great Reformer or of common confessional agreement. Rather, within the broad framework of the Anglican Settlement there grew up a spectrum of doctrinal opinion which represented a *via media* between Rome and the continental reformed Churches. This *via media* was based on a broad appeal to Scripture, the early Church, reason and experience, which became characteristic of the Anglican ethos. Cranmer sought to reorient eucharistic doctrine around the act of communion, rather than around a change in the nature of the elements.[5] In doing this, he broke with the dominant medieval tradition and took up a position more in line with that of St Augustine and the Swiss Reformers. His doctrine can perhaps best be described as a doctrine of the real partaking of the body and blood of Christ in the Eucharist, rather than a doctrine of the real objective presence of Christ in the Eucharist. The sacramental signs are connected with the reality which they signify through their use rather than in an objective manner. Such a standpoint represents an attempt to retain sacramental realism in relation to the faithful believer rather than in relation to the elements:

> And therefore, in the book of the holy communion, we do not pray absolutely that the bread and wine may be made the body and blood of Christ, but that unto us in that holy mystery they may be so; that is to say, that we may so worthily receive the same, that we may be partakers of Christ's body and blood, and that therewith in spirit and in truth we may be spiritually nourished.[6]

During the Elizabethan period, Richard Hooker developed a distinctively Anglican theological method in approaching eucharistic doctrine. Like Cranmer, Hooker's doctrine can be described as a doctrine of the real partaking of the body and blood of Christ in the Eucharist, rather than a doctrine of the real presence of Christ in the Eucharist.[7] This doctrine of the Eucharist, which became characteristic of Anglican theology, is often referred to as 'receptionism'. Hooker does not deny the real presence, but he relates it primarily to the faithful communicant rather than to the elements of bread and wine:

> The real presence of Christ's most blessed body and blood is not . . . to be sought for in the sacrament, but in the worthy receiver of the sacrament.[8]

On the question of the relation of the presence to the elements of bread and wine he adopts a position of deliberate agnosticism:

> Let it therefore be sufficient for me presenting myself at the Lord's table to know what there I receive from him, without searching or inquiring of the manner how Christ performeth his promise; . . . what these elements are in themselves it skilleth not, it is enough that to me which take them they are the body and blood of Christ. . . .[9]

Hooker's agnosticism regarding the manner of the eucharistic presence reveals the emergence of a distinctively Anglican approach to the issue of authority in matters of faith. It was a cardinal principle of the emerging Anglican tradition that nothing can be proposed as a necessary article of faith which goes beyond the certain testimony of Scripture (see pp. 82–5). Beyond this, agreement with the early Church, consent among the various Christian confessions, and the testimony of reason are further tests which serve either to confirm or deny the truth of a particular doctrine. This led to a distinction in Anglican theology between those doctrines which were regarded as necessary articles of faith, and /

those matters which could be left in the realm of theological opinion (see pp. 233–8). Hooker is drawing a distinction here between theology and faith. At the level of faith, all that is necessary is that we believe that the body and blood of Christ is really received in the Eucharist by means of the sacramental signs. At the level of theology, it is legitimate to speculate about the manner of the presence, as long as it does not endanger piety.

What then, for Hooker, is the role of the elements in mediating the presence of Christ to the worthy receiver? In addressing this issue, Hooker attempts to steer a middle course between 'Zwinglianism' on the one side and the doctrine of the medieval Church on the other. To explain the relationship between divine grace and the sacraments Hooker, like Aquinas, employs the language of instrumental causality. The sacraments are not causes of grace in an absolute sense. God alone is the author of grace. The sacraments are causes only in a secondary or instrumental sense. God uses them as means of imparting grace. As means of grace, however, the sacraments do not produce their effect automatically, but only conditionally. The sacraments are 'moral instruments', not mechanical or physical instruments.[10] Hooker is employing here what we might today call a 'personalist' rather than a naturalistic or mechanical model of sacramental causality. The operation of the sacraments is analogous to the offering and acceptance of a gift between free moral agents. It is conditional both on God's free offer of grace, and upon the faithful response of the recipient. The offer of grace is unconditional, in the sense that the sacraments depend upon the divine promise. The acceptance of the gift, however, is conditional upon the free and faithful response of the recipient. The sacraments 'really exhibit', but 'they are not really nor do really contain in themselves that grace which with them or by them it pleaseth God to bestow'.[11] The bread and cup are his body and blood, therefore, 'because they are causes instrumental upon the receipt whereof the *participation* of his body and blood ensueth'.[12]

It was characteristic of seventeenth-century Anglican writers to insist on the real presence of Christ in the Eucharist, but to profess agnosticism concerning the manner of the presence in the tradition of Hooker.[13] 'Receptionism' remained the dominant theological position within the Church of England until the Oxford Movement in the early nineteenth century, with varying differences in emphasis. It is important to remember, however, that 'receptionism' is a doctrine of the real presence, but a doctrine of the real presence which relates the presence primarily to the worthy receiver rather than to the elements of bread and wine.

In true Augustinian fashion seventeenth-century Anglican writers distinguish between the *res* of the sacrament, that is, the reality or inward and spiritual grace conveyed by it, and the *sacramentum* or outward and visible sign, by means of which the grace is communicated to the faithful recipient.[14] At the same time, they maintain a 'sacramental union' between the elements and the reality signified by them. The union, however, does not abolish the distinction between the *sacramentum* and the *res*; otherwise the sacrament would cease to be a sacrament, since the nature of a sacrament always consists of two parts, a visible and an invisible, an earthly and a heavenly. While the *sacramentum* and the *res* are joined, therefore, so that the offer of grace is clearly made to all, only the faithful recipient receives the *res* of the sacrament along with the outward signs. The outward signs are received by the mouth and enter into the stomach. The inward grace of the sacrament is only eaten by faith.

The bread and wine become a sacrament by means of their consecration in the Eucharistic Prayer. However, since the purpose of the sacrament is only attained in the act of communion, the consecration is not separated from the 'use' of the elements in communion:

> It is important to remember that by consecration all the Caroline divines seem to have meant the setting apart for the sacred use of communion; this is in sharp contrast to the contemporary Roman view which regarded it as meaning the effecting of an objective change in the substance of the elements.[15]

Hooker had already thought of consecration as the 'hallowing with solemn benediction to use'.[16] This represents a recovery of the patristic notion that consecration is brought about by the recital of the Eucharistic Prayer, rather than the medieval view that consecration is effected by the recital of the words of institution.[17]

While the theme of the presence of Christ in relation to the faithful communicants predominates in seventeenth-century Anglican eucharistic thought, it is not the only eucharistic theme which appears there. With the partial receding of the sixteenth-century polemical context and the renewed study of the Church Fathers, the sacrificial aspect of the Eucharist also begins to appear again in Anglican writings. The Eucharist is described as a 'commemorative' or 'representative' sacrifice, which in no sense adds anything to the saving significance of the cross, and the ecclesial dimension of the eucharistic sacrifice stressed by Augustine comes into view again. In a sermon preached by John Buckeridge at the funeral of Lancelot Andrewes, there is a beautiful text which perfectly expresses this Augustinian emphasis:

> As Christ's cross was His altar where He offered Himself for us, so the Church hath an altar also where it offereth itself ... not Christ the Head properly but only by commemoration, but Christ the members. For Christ cannot be offered truly and properly no more but once upon the cross ... This then is the daily sacrifice of the Church in St Augustine's resolute judgment, even the Church itself, the universal body of Christ, not the natural body, whereof the Sacrament is an exemplar and memorial only, as hath been shewed ... We deny not then the daily sacrifice of the Church, that is, the Church itself, warranted by Scriptures and fathers.[18]

We have described the characteristic Anglican doctrine of the Eucharist as a doctrine of the real partaking of the body and blood of Christ by means of the sacramental signs of bread and wine. This 'receptionist' understanding of the Eucharist is a doctrine of the real presence, but a doctrine of the real presence which relates the presence primarily to the faithful communicants rather than to the elements of bread and wine. What accounts for this distinctive emphasis in Anglican eucharistic doctrine?

During the Middle Ages there developed a gradual separation between the act of consecration and the act of communion, so that the goal of the Eucharist became the production of the real presence rather than the communion of the people. This resulted in a eucharistic piety which focused on the adoration of the host, rather than on the reception of communion.[19] In medieval theology it led to a preoccupation with the question of the manner of Christ's presence in the elements. Anglican theologians from Cranmer onwards were engaged in a project of reorienting eucharistic theology away from its medieval centre and reuniting the act of consecration and the act of communion. For these theologians, the goal of the Eucharist is not the production of the real presence, but the nourishment of Christian believers. The real presence is the presupposition rather than the focus of their thought. The consecration of the elements is not regarded as an end in itself, but is oriented towards the act of communion. Christ is not present in the Eucharist as an object on the altar but as spiritual food and drink to nourish the life of faith. With regard to the manner of the presence, they saw the sacramental presence and communication of the body and blood of Christ as an event in the order of grace. It is this which accounts for their rejection of transubstantiation, which they interpreted as a naturalistic explanation of the eucharistic presence implying a local or physical presence of Christ on the altar. For these Anglican theologians, on the other hand, the presence of Christ in the Eucharist is not an event in the physical world, but a presence-in-grace which is offered to all, but which can only be received by those who receive it with a living faith. The elements play an instrumental role in communicating the presence of Christ to the faithful receiver. This does not occur in a mechanical manner, but only within the freedom of the grace-faith relationship.

In all of this, High Church Anglicans and moderate Anglicans shared a common body of teaching. While the early Anglican High Church tradition can be distinguished from moderate Anglicanism in its sacramental spirituality and its liturgical ideals, it is difficult if not impossible to establish a clear distinction in the sphere of eucharistic theology. We can agree with Richard Buxton that the differences between the two outlooks reflect 'variations of the basic early seventeenth century position',[20] which have more to do with piety than with doctrine.

Two revivals of eucharistic life and thought took place in the latter half of the eighteenth and the early nineteenth centuries. The first of these was the Evangelical Revival of John and Charles Wesley. The second was the Oxford Movement. It is not commonly known today that the Wesleyan Revival was as much a eucharistic revival as it was an Evangelical revival.[21] The genius of the Wesleys, however, lies precisely in the unity which they saw between a sacramental and an Evangelical vision of Christianity. The eucharistic theology of the Wesleys is most clearly expressed in a collection of 166 eucharistic hymns, composed by Charles and John, which combine a rich sacramentalism with joyful Evangelical experience.[22]

The theology of the hymns reflects the eucharistic doctrine of seventeenth-century Anglicanism. The hymns are introduced by an extract from Daniel Brevint's treatise *The Christian Sacrament and Sacrifice*. Brevint is a seventeenth-century Anglican writer. There is nothing in his treatise that cannot be paralleled in other seventeenth-century Anglican writers. What is remarkable about the treatise is its scope and balance, and its recovery of eucharistic themes which had not achieved as clear expression in earlier Anglican tradition.

According to Brevint there are three fundamental aspects to the Eucharist: a past, a present and a future aspect. The Eucharist is, first of all, a memorial of the saving death of Christ. Secondly, it is present grace and nourishment for worthy receivers. Thirdly, it is a pledge which assures our participation in the life of the promised kingdom of God. Brevint treats the sacrificial aspect of the Eucharist more fully than earlier Anglican writers. He is absolutely clear that the sacrifice of Christ on the cross took place once for all in the past and cannot be repeated, and that it atones completely for sin. The Eucharist, however, can be spoken of as a sacrifice in three senses. It is, first of all, a commemorative sacrifice. Secondly, in line with Augustine, it is a sacrifice of the Church in union with its Head. Thirdly, Christ as the eternal High Priest continually presents before the Father in heaven his completed sacrifice on the cross as the basis of our acceptance before him. In making the memorial of Christ's death in the Eucharist the Church not only commemorates a past action, but Christians on earth are united with Christ in the eternal pleading of his completed sacrifice in heaven. The Wesleys' collection of eucharistic hymns follow the themes in Brevint's treatise very closely, and thus mediate the principal themes of the seventeenth-century Anglican eucharistic tradition to their Evangelical followers.

In the early nineteenth century the Wesleyan Revival was followed by the Oxford Movement.[23] Whereas the Wesleys emphasized the Evangelical heritage of Anglicanism, the Tractarians stressed its Catholic heritage. Central to this Catholic heritage was an emphasis on the sacramental life and on the Eucharist as the centre of Catholic worship. In parishes influenced by the Oxford Movement there gradually developed a recovery of Catholic ceremonial and vestments in the celebration of the Eucharist. In the ritualist phase of the movement pre-Reformation ceremonial was restored or contemporary Roman Catholic practice was introduced, leading to ritual battles with the ecclesiastical authorities. The Oxford Movement has had an influence far beyond the Anglo-Catholic revival itself in bringing about a much greater emphasis throughout the Anglican Communion on the centrality of eucharistic worship.

In their theology of the Eucharist, the Tractarians saw a closer connection between the real presence of Christ in the Eucharist and the elements than did the earlier Anglican tradition. For the Tractarians, there is a strict identity between the earthly body of Christ, his risen body, and his sacramental body. The only difference is in the manner or mode of the presence. While connecting the eucharistic presence of Christ more closely to the elements than did the earlier Anglican theologians, the Tractarians were entirely at one with them in insisting that the manner of the presence is spiritual and not physical or local. It is a presence in the order of grace and not a presence in the order of nature. Christ is present in the Eucharist, however, in a specific way; namely, by means of sacramental signs.

There is nothing here which goes essentially beyond what can be found in the older seventeenth-century Anglican writers, except by way of emphasis. The Tractarians, however, went decisively beyond the earlier Anglican theology in making a clear distinction between the presence of Christ in relation to the elements and the presence of Christ in relation to the worthy communicants. According to Tractarian teaching, the presence of Christ in relation to the elements is brought about by the act of consecration and is not dependent on their reception in communion. This position was given its clearest theological expression by R T Wilberforce,[14] who distinguished not only between the *res* of the sacrament and its *sacramentum* as did the earlier Anglican writers, but also between the *res* and the *virtus* of the sacrament. The *res* of the sacrament is the reality signified by the outward signs; namely Christ himself. The *virtus* of the sacrament is the blessing, effect, or grace which Christ gives to all who receive the sacrament in faith. The union between the *res* and the *sacramentum* is brought about by the consecration. After the consecration Christ is objectively present in relation to the elements. This union between the *res* and the *sacramentum*, however, is a sacramental union, not the presence of an object in the physical world. Christ is not present in the elements in a physical or natural mode, but in a sacramental mode. The reality or *res* of the sacrament is offered to the communicants by means of the sacramental signs irrespective of their faith, but only those who receive the sacrament by faith receive the *virtus*, or grace of the sacrament. The purpose of distinguishing between the *res* and the *virtus* of the sacrament is to make it clear that Christ is objectively present in relation to the elements by means of their consecration, but present in grace only to those who receive him by faith.

In the twentieth century, the Liturgical Movement and developments in liturgical scholarship have brought about far-reaching changes in the eucharistic life and worship of Anglicanism, and have led in recent decades to extensive liturgical revision throughout the Anglican Communion (see pp. 42–4). The

Ecumenical Movement and developments in theology have also profoundly affected the Anglican understanding of the Eucharist.

The Liturgical Movement began in the nineteenth century in France as a move towards more active participation in the liturgy.[25] Its influence reached England in the 1930s and was given widespread impetus by the publication of two books by A. G. Hebert, *Liturgy and Society* (1935) and *The Parish Communion* (1937). In England the movement fostered the so-called Parish Communion as the central act of worship on Sunday morning. This was a sung celebration of the Eucharist with active participation by the people, which gained increasing popularity in parishes of different churchmanship.

Liturgical scholarship and liturgical revision in Anglicanism began with the work of Archbishop Thomas Cranmer. Cranmer himself revised the Prayer Book, and various revisions have been undertaken throughout Anglican history.[26] Anglican liturgical scholarship flourished in the seventeenth century.[27] In the late nineteenth and early twentieth centuries this tradition was continued in the work of the great Anglican liturgical scholars, W. H. Frere, F. C. Brightman, and E. C. Ratcliff. The most influential work of Anglican liturgical scholarship in the twentieth century has been *The Shape of the Liturgy* by Dom Gregory Dix (1945).[28] Dix's work had a pivotal influence on all subsequent liturgical revision in the Anglican Communion. His thesis is that the Eucharist is essentially an action which has a fourfold shape, corresponding to the actions of Jesus in 'taking', 'blessing', ('breaking'), and 'giving' the bread and the cup at the Last Supper. These four actions correspond to the Offertory, the Eucharistic Prayer, the Fraction (Breaking of the Bread), and the Communion in the eucharistic liturgy. Dix shows how this fourfold action is exemplified in the structure of the early eucharistic rites, and how it became overlaid and distorted in medieval and Reformation developments. All of the revisions of the eucharistic liturgy which have taken place in the various provinces of the Anglican Communion since the publication of Dix's book show the influence of his emphasis on the shape of the liturgy.

Along with the emphasis on the shape of the rite as a whole, a major concern in the revision of Anglican rites has been to restore the classic structure of the Eucharistic Prayer. Research into the origins and history of the Eucharistic Prayer in the present century has played a major role in Anglican liturgical revision.[29] Most scholars now hold that the Eucharistic Prayer has its origin in the *berakah* or prayer of thanksgiving said over the wine cup at the end of Jewish festal meals known as the *birkat ha-mazon*.[30] This is a prayer of thanksgiving for creation and redemption which is adapted and expanded on certain festivals. The examples of eucharistic prayers which we have from the early Church reflect this structure, adapted and expanded in a Christian direction. The oldest example of a eucharistic prayer which we have in the West is found in the *Apostolic Tradition* of Hippolytus (*c*. AD 215)[31] which has the following structure:

Thanksgiving for creation and redemption
Institution narrative
Anamnesis (*Memorial* of Christ's death and resurrection)
Epiclesis (*Invocation* of the Holy Spirit)
Doxology

An examination of the recent revisions of the eucharistic rite throughout the Anglican Communion shows that they all follow this basic structure, with variations in wording and theological emphasis and, particularly in the English rites, in the position of the epiclesis.[32]

Ecumenical scholarship and the Ecumenical Movement have also profoundly shaped the Anglican understanding of the Eucharist in the twentieth century. Two examples of this are the Anglican-Roman Catholic *Agreed Statement on Eucharistic Doctrine*,[33] the result of work by the Anglican-Roman Catholic International Commission, and the document *Baptism, Eucharist, and Ministry* of the Faith and Order Commission of the World Council of Churches (see pp. 383–92).[34]

The Anglican-Roman Catholic *Agreed Statement* tackles both the issues of real presence and eucharistic sacrifice. In language which is reminiscent of Hooker, the statement acknowledges the goal of the Eucharist as 'communion with Christ' which 'presupposes his true presence'. With regard to the elements, the real presence of Christ is 'effectively signified by the bread and wine which, in this mystery, become his body and blood'. While this presence 'does not depend on the individual's faith in order to be the Lord's real gift of himself to his Church', it is only through reception by faith that 'a lifegiving encounter results'.

The document uses the notion of the eucharistic memorial as the key to understanding the relationship between Christ's sacrifice and the Eucharist.[35] The Eucharist is seen neither as a repetition of the sacrifice of the cross, nor simply as a mental recollection of an event which took place 2,000 years ago. Rather, the eucharistic memorial is the 'effectual proclamation' in the present of the redemptive reality of events which took place once for all in the past. Through the eucharistic memorial the sacrifice of the cross is made sacramentally present, in order that we may participate in its redemptive reality in the present.[36] The statement ends with the eschatological perspective, highlighting the meaning of the Eucharist as a foretaste of the banquet in the kingdom.

The Anglican-Roman Catholic agreed statement on the Eucharist is only one of a series of ecumenical agreements on the Eucharist which have taken place during the present century. Various bilateral discussions among the Churches have led to similar ecumenical agreements. All of these statements have helped to prepare the way for the document *Baptism, Eucharist, and Ministry* formulated by the Faith and Order Commission of the World Council of Churches at its meeting held in Lima, Peru in 1982 as an expression of theological convergence on baptism, Eucharist, and ministry. Anglicans have played a major role in the theological discussions leading up to the publication of *BEM*.[37]

BEM treats the Eucharist under five headings: Thanksgiving, Memorial, Invocation of the Spirit, Communion, and Anticipation of the Meal in the Kingdom. In contemporary Anglican liturgical revision the thanksgiving character of the Eucharist is reflected in the strong emphasis on the celebration as a communal act of praise and thanksgiving for creation and redemption in contrast to the penitential note characteristic of Cranmer's rites. The central role of the eucharistic memorial for an understanding of the relationship between the sacrifice of Christ and the Eucharist, which is found in the Anglican-Roman Catholic *Agreed Statement*, is also evident in *BEM* and in recent Anglican revisions of the Eucharistic Prayer. The role of the Holy Spirit in the eucharistic celebration, which has long been emphasized by the Eastern Churches, is now reflected in the restoration of an epiclesis in modern Anglican liturgical rites. Anglicanism has long emphasized the Eucharist as 'Holy Communion', but as Dix pointed out, most often in an individualistic sense. The new emphasis in twentieth-century Anglicanism is on the Eucharist not only as an act of personal communion, but as a corporate community celebration in which all the participants are built up into communion with Christ and with one another in the Body of Christ.

The emphasis on the Eucharist as an anticipation of the meal in the kingdom of God has been a neglected aspect in Anglicanism which is beginning to appear in some Anglican revisions, particularly in new eucharistic prayers. The eschatological perspective is one of the earliest eucharistic traditions in the New Testament.[38] This theme became marginalized in later eucharistic tradition as the themes of real presence and sacrifice assumed the centre of the stage, but it is being recovered today.[39] This perspective is clearly linked to the theme of justice. A meal celebrated in prospect of the coming reign of God gives rise to a new social vision, grounded in the promise of the kingdom. Such a vision challenges the status quo in society and the prevailing set of economic and social relationships. Sharing in a community meal anticipates a just sharing of all the gifts of creation in justice and love. The Anglican-Roman Catholic *Agreed Statement* and *BEM*, therefore, both reflect changes which are taking place in the celebration and understanding of the Eucharist within Anglicanism, and offer a challenge to Anglicans to incorporate emphases which have been neglected in our tradition.

The Anglican eucharistic tradition began with liturgical change, and only subsequently developed a tradition of doctrinal and theological reflection on the Eucharist. In the twentieth century liturgical change throughout the Anglican Communion is profoundly transforming Anglican eucharistic life. The revision of Anglican liturgies which has been taking place in the various provinces of the Anglican Communion is shaping the eucharistic consciousness of Anglicans in new ways which require fresh theological reflection. The social and cultural context of Anglicanism has changed dramatically since the nineteenth century. The Anglican Communion no longer reflects English culture, but is a community of indigenous Churches which reflect a plurality of cultural and social contexts. Ecumenical developments are shaping the Anglican tradition in new ways. All of these developments present fresh challenges to Anglican eucharistic life and thought in the coming decades.

NOTES

1 For the history of Anglican liturgy see especially G. J. Cuming, *A History of Anglican Liturgy* (2nd edn, London, Macmillan 1982).

2 For the text of the rite see Colin Buchanan, *Eucharistic Liturgies of Edward VI* (GLS 34; Bramcote, Grove Press 1983), pp. 7–20. For commentary see Cuming, pp. 51–9.

3 Text in Buchanan, *Eucharistic Liturgies of Edward VI*, pp. 21–33. Commentary in Cuming, pp. 70–74, 77–81.

4 For an interpretation see Colin Buchanan, *What did Cranmer think he was doing?* (GLS 7; Bramcote, Grove Press 1976).

5 For Cranmer's eucharistic doctrine see Peter Brooks, *Thomas Cranmer's Doctrine of the Eucharist: An Essay in Historical Development* (New York, Seabury Press, 1965); Cyril C. Richardson, 'Cranmer and the Analysis of Eucharistic Doctrine', *JTS* n.s. 16 (1965), pp. 421–37.

6 Thomas Cranmer, *Writings on the Sacrament of the Lord's Supper*, ed. John Edmund Cox, The Parker Society (CUP 1846), p. 79.

7 For Hooker's sources see John E. Booty, 'Hooker's Understanding of the Presence of Christ in the Eucharist', in *The Divine Drama in History and Liturgy*, ed. John E. Booty (Allison Park, PA., Pickwick Publications, 1984), pp. 131–48; for his method see W. Speed Hill, ed., *Studies in Richard Hooker* (Cleveland, Case Western Reserve University Press, 1972); for his eucharistic theology see Olivier Loyer, *L'Anglicanisme de Richard Hooker*, 2 vols. (Paris, Librairie Honore Champion, 1979), vol. i, pp. 475–542.

8 *Laws* V. lxvii. All citations from Hooker are from *Of the Laws of Ecclesiastical Polity* in *The Works of ... Mr Richard Hooker*, ed. John Keble, 7th rev. edn (Oxford, Clarendon Press, 1888); by book, chapter, and section.

9 *Laws* V. lxvii. 12.

10 Cf. *Laws* V. lvii. 4, 5.

11 *Laws* V. lxvii. 6.

12 *Laws* V. lxvii. 5.

13 For a representative sampling of texts illustrating seventeenth-century Anglican thought on the eucharist see Paul Elmer More and Frank Leslie Cross, *The Thought and Practice of the Church of England, Illustrated from the Religious Literature of the Seventeenth Century* (London, SPCK, 1962).

14 For the Augustinian background of Anglican eucharistic theology see C. W. Dugmore, *The Mass and the English Reformers* (London, Macmillan, 1958), especially ch. 1.

15 Richard F. Buxton, *Eucharist and Institution Narrative: A Study in the The Roman and Anglican Traditions of the Consecration of the Eucharist from the Eighth to the Twentieth Centuries*, AC 58 (Great Wakering, Mayhew-McCrimmon, 1976), p. 131.

16 ibid. Cf. Hooker *Laws* V. lxvii. 12.

17 For patristic and medieval views of consecration see John H. McKenna, *Eucharist and Holy Spirit: The Eucharistic Epiclesis in Twentieth Century Theology*, AC 57 (Great Wakering, Mayhew-McCrimmon, 1975), especially ch. 2.

18 Cited in Darwell Stone, *A History of the Doctrine of the Holy Eucharist*, 2 vols. (London, Longmans, Green, & Co., 1909), vol ii, p. 266f.

19 For the history of this development see Nathan Mitchell, *Cult and Controversy: The Worship of the Eucharist Outside Mass.* (New York, Pueblo, 1982).

20 Buxton, p. 131.

21 See Paul S. Sanders, 'Wesley's Eucharistic Faith and Practice', *Anglican Theological Review* 48 (1966), pp. 157–74.

22 See J. Ernest Rattenbury, *The Eucharistic Hymns of John and Charles Wesley* (London, Epworth Press, 1948).

23 For the Tractarians see Alf Hardelin, *The Tractarian Understanding of the Eucharist* (Uppsala, Almquist & Wiksells, 1965).

24 R. I. Wilberforce, *The Doctrine of the Holy Eucharist* (London 1853).

25 For the history of the liturgical movement see *A Dictionary of Liturgy and Worship*, ed. J. G. Davies, s.v. 'The Liturgical Movement'.

26 See Cheslyn Jones, Geoffrey Wainwright, and Edward Yarnold, ed., *The Study of Liturgy* (London, SPCK; New York, OUP, 1978), pp. 263–77, 280–88.

27 See W. J. Grisbrooke, *Anglican Liturgies of the Seventeenth and Eighteeenth Centuries*, AC 40 (SPCK 1958).

28 Gregory Dix, *The Shape of the Liturgy*, with additional notes by Paul V. Marshall (New York, Seabury Press, 1982).

29 See Geoffrey Cuming, *He Gave Thanks: An Introduction to The Eucharistic Prayer*, GLS 28 (Bramcote 1981); Kenneth Stevenson, ed., *Liturgy Reshaped* (SPCK 1982). For the texts of the principal eucharistic prayers in the early and Reformation rites see R. C. D. Jasper and G. J. Cuming, ed., *Prayers of the Eucharist: Early and Reformed*, 2nd edn (New York, OUP, 1980) (hereafter cited as *PEER*).

30 *PEER*, pp. 9–10.

31 *PEER*, pp. 21–25.

32 See Colin O. Buchanan, ed., *Modern Anglican Liturgies 1958–1968* (London, OUP, 1968); *idem, Further Anglican Liturgies 1968–1975* (Bramcote, Grove Books, 1975); *idem,*

Anglican Eucharistic Liturgy 1975–1985 (Bramcote, Grove Books, 1985); *idem, Latest Anglican Liturgies 1976–1984* (SPCK 1985).

33 Anglican-Roman Catholic International Commission, *The Final Report* (SPCK 1981), pp. 12–16.

34 *Baptism, Eucharist and Ministry*, Faith and Order paper 111 (Geneva, WCC, 1982).

35 See J. M. R. Tillard, 'Roman Catholics and Anglicans: The Eucharist', *One in Christ* 9 (1973), pp. 131–93.

36 For current Anglican views on eucharistic sacrifice see the three Grove booklets, R. P. C. Hanson, *Eucharistic Offering in the Early Church*, Rowan Williams, *Eucharistic Sacrifice—The Roots of a Metaphor*, and Colin Buchanan, ed., *Essays on Eucharistic Sacrifice in the Early Church* (Bramcote, Grove Books, 1979, 1982, 1984).

37 For the history of the bilateral conversations and the background of *BEM* see John Reumann, *The Supper of the Lord: The New Testament, Ecumenical Dialogues, and Faith and Order on Eucharist* (Philadelphia, Fortress Press, 1985).

38 See Reumann, pp. 23–26.

39 See Geoffrey Wainwright, *Eucharist and Eschatology* (London, Epworth Press, 1971).

Ministry and Priesthood

JOHN B. WEBSTER

Bradshaw, P. F., *The Anglican Ordinal.* London 1981.
Church of England Board for Mission and Unity, *The Priesthood of the Ordained Ministry.* London 1986.
Echlin, E. P., *The Story of Anglican Ministry.* Slough 1974.
Hanson, A. T., *The Pioneer Ministry.* London 1964.
Holmes, U. T., *The Future Shape of Ministry.* New York 1981.
Hughes, J. J., *Absolutely Null and Utterly Void.* London 1968.
McDonald, D. R., *Towards a Theology of Priesthood.* New York 1982.
Moberly, R. C., *Ministerial Priesthood.* New edn., London 1969.
Ramsey, A. M., *The Gospel and the Catholic Church.* London 1936.
Sykes, N., *Old Priest and New Presbyter.* Cambridge 1956.

MINISTRY AND PRIESTHOOD IN THE ENGLISH REFORMATION

Like its continental counterparts, the English Reformation devoted a great part of its energies to the renewal and restructuring of the pastoral office on the basis of what it took to be a more adequate theology of ministry. '"The eye," that is to say, the preacher of God's Word, "is the light of the body", that is to say, if the curate be godly learned, "then shall all the body be full of light", that is, the Christian congregation shall have the Word of God dwell in them plenteously'.[1] Thomas Becon's allegorical reading of Christ's parable says much about the distinctive emphases of the theology of the ministry among the English Reformers, notably about the prime function of the ordained minister as one of laying Scripture before the congregation. Accordingly, for Reformers like Becon, the provision of a biblically educated clergy was a matter of considerable significance. Anglicanism emerged in a period of generally lax ministerial practice. Studies of the early Tudor period reveal that resident clergy were in general only casually educated, with university graduates usually non-resident in parishes. The revival of the pastoral ministry thus became a prime concern, not the least because of the need to establish a firm clerical base in the midst of competing confessions of faith (see pp. 338–45).

However, the early Tudor Church manifested more than simply lax practice; it also showed the long-term effects of the clericalization of the Western Church in the later medieval period. The separation of priests from laity had many roots—priestly celibacy, the decline of Latin as a popular language, the privatization of the ministry of reconciliation to a transaction between penitent and priest with power to absolve. But unlike earlier movements (notably the Lollards in the late fourteenth and earlier fifteenth centuries) the English Reformers did not focus on abuses of priestly prerogative so much as on the renewal of the theology of the ordained ministry. In particular, they sought to displace the cultic and sacrificial emphases of the medieval ordinals then in use (notably the Sarum pontifical). From the Reformed ordinals of 1550 and 1552 and from other documents of the English Reformation, a fairly consistent theology of ministry emerges, which furnished fundamental topics for debate in the century which followed (see pp. 143–52).

(1) Like other Reformed ordinals, the Anglican rites placed weight on the inseparability of ministerial office and the congregation. The point was emphasized partly by the requirement (in the Preface to the 1550 Ordinal) that no one take up office in the Church 'except he were first called, tried, examined, and known to have such qualities as were requisite for the same'; partly by the public interrogation of the candidates by the bishop after the Oath of Supremacy had been administered; partly by the requirement that ordinations should be 'upon a Sunday or holyday, in the face of the church'. In these ways office and the actual exercise of ministerial functions were held closely together.

(2) Equally, however, the significance of the mandate of the wider Church was underscored in the Preface to the 1550 Ordinal by the warning that 'no man by his own private authority might presume to execute' any of the offices of bishop, priest or deacon. And it is clear that the new Anglican ordinals did not envisage ordination as simply delegation of authority by the local congregation. In

retaining episcopal ordination (despite queries from some of the Reformers including Cranmer, and later from Hooker, about cases of necessity) Anglicanism sought to retain a ministry 'rightly, orderly and lawfully consecrated and ordered' (Article XXXVI), that is, a ministry 'chosen and called to this work by men who have public authority given unto them in [not, note, 'by'] the congregation, to call and send ministers into the Lord's vineyard' (Article XXIII).

(3) In terms of content, the ministry of the Word receives heavy emphasis in the first Anglican ordinals. '*Scala coeli* [the ladder of heaven] is a preaching matter ... and not a massing matter. God's instrument of salvation is preaching.'[2] So Latimer, and this understanding of ministry finds clear expression in the 1550 rite for the priesthood. Having outlined the work of the priest, the bishop addresses the candidates in the Exhortation: 'Seeing that ye cannot, by any other means, compass the doing of so weighty a work, pertaining to the salvation of man, but with doctrine and exhortation, taken out of holy Scripture, and with a life agreeable to the same, ye perceive how studious ye ought to be in reading and learning the holy Scriptures, and in framing the manners, both of yourselves, and of them that specially pertain unto you, according to the rule of the same scriptures.'

(4) But it is in their omission of cultic and sacrificial language that the Edwardine ordinals show themselves to have a theology of ministry quite distinct from that of the pre-Reformation rites (see pp. 143–50). In essence, the Anglican ordinals call into question the notion of a sacrificial priesthood focused in the eucharistic offering, in favour of a pastoral and didactic model of the ministry centring on public proclamation, the orderly administration of the sacraments, and private exhortation. The pre-Reformation Sarum pontifical, drawing on analogies between the levitical and the Christian priesthood, was rich in sacrificial imagery. Most particularly, that rite included the *porrectio instrumentorum*—the handing over of the chalice and/or paten as symbols of priestly office (an action considered by some medieval theologians to constitute the essential 'matter' of ordination). The action was accompanied by the words 'Receive the power to offer sacrifice to God.' The 1550 Anglican rite, somewhat curiously, retained the action but added the rubric that in addition 'the Bishop shall deliver to every one of them the Bible', and—most significantly—changed the accompanying words to 'Take thou authority to preach the Word of God, and to minister the holy sacraments in the congregation.' The 1552 revision went further by omitting the *porrectio instrumentorum* completely, retaining only the giving of the Bible with the same words as the 1550 rite.

Such moves in the ordinals were consistent with Cranmer's new eucharistic rites, in which the notion of sacrifice was not so much excluded as decisively restructured. 'Sacrifice' has a double function in Cranmer's eucharistic liturgies,

287

referring primordially to the self-offering of Christ on Calvary, and, in an altogether derivative way, to the self-offering of the people of God in praise and thanksgiving for benefits received. Crucially, however, Cranmer scrupulously separated this self-offering of the Church from any association with the symbols of bread and wine, limiting its occurrence to the post-communion prayer of the people. The Eucharist is thus shaped around the corporate memorial and participation of the redeemed in the benefits of Christ's passion, and not around the sacrificial mediation of the priest passively observed.

As a consequence, the defining activity of the priest and his relation to the congregation shifted considerably. As the first part of the 'Homily of the worthy receiving and reverent esteeming of the Body and Blood of Christ' exhorted the believer, Christ 'hath made upon his cross a full and sufficient sacrifice for thee, a perfect cleansing of thy sins; so that thou acknowledgest no other Saviour, Redeemer, Advocate, Intercessor, but Christ only ... thou needest no man's help, no other sacrifice or oblation, no sacrificing priest, no mass, no means established by man's invention.'[3] None of this is a denial of the ordained ministry as a means; rather it is an attempt to clarify in a polemical context how that means relates to its generative source and the events to which it offers public testimony. In effect, the theology of the work of Christ as the High Priest whose work is finished and completely sufficient absorbs much of what previously would have come under the rubric of the theology of ministry. The role of the priest is thus transformed from what was (however mistakenly) perceived to be mediatory sacrifice to that of ministering (or perhaps better, administering) the saving benefits of Christ's passion through word and sacrament.

In the eucharistic context, then, the mediatory role of the ordained ministry is hedged about with severe restrictions and qualifications designed to avoid any derogation of Christ's uniquely mediatory activity. Something of the same happens to the ministry of reconciliation. The new eucharistic liturgies certainly accord a place to private confession and absolution, and in the *Homilies* and elsewhere in the formularies and Reformation writings it finds a restricted role. However, the authoritative commission is conceived to be that of declaring rather than actualizing God's mercy and forgiveness towards the penitent, and the context for the exercise of that ministry is normally the public prayer of the community assembled to hear the word of God.

THE EMERGENCE OF ANGLICAN THEOLOGY OF MINISTRY

In the theological and institutional development of the English Church in the later part of the sixteenth and first half of the seventeenth centuries, it soon became clear that much clarification and consolidation remained to be done.

Cranmer's handling of eucharistic sacrifice in the liturgies did not make an end of discussion of the matter. The retention of sacrificial language is, importantly, not simply to be found amongst those Laudian divines who retained vestiges of Catholic theology and practice, but also amongst others more definitely aligned with Cranmer's eucharistic theology. William Perkins, the most intellectually acute Calvinist theologian of the English Church, concedes a sense in which the Eucharist is a sacrifice 'by way of resemblance'.[4] But here he is saying little, if anything, more than Cranmer in affirming that the Eucharist is a 'spiritual' or 'gratulatory' sacrifice as the commemoration and devoted self-offering of the assembly. Sacrifice does not entail the further notion of 'propitiatory', and so does not signify a retraction of the theology of ministry in the formularies. The seventeenth century does, however, see the growth of reflection on the continuing priesthood of the ascended Christ as the ground of the Church's pleading of Christ's sacrifice in the Eucharist (see pp. 275–7). In Tractarian theology, this affirmation was to figure large as a warrant for a particular account of the priestliness of the ordained ministry.

In terms of ministerial order, the early Reformation ideal of an institutionally ordered and hierarchical ministry, biblical, sacramental and pastoral in function, sustained criticism from two directions.

On the one side, Catholic polemic pressed the new theology to furnish some kind of account of the credentials of Anglican orders. The currency of the 'Nag's Head Fable' (a popular legend that Archbishop Parker had been consecrated at the Nag's Head Tavern in Cheapside by an irregular rite) testified to real anxieties on this score. A refutation of the legend published in 1613 by the Anglican apologist Francis Mason takes the form of an imaginary dialogue, and has the Catholic disputant argue:

> All that are called of God by the Church derive their authority by lawful succession from Christ and His apostles. If you do so, then let it appear, show us your descent, let us see your pedigree. If you cannot, then whence came you? If you tell us that God hath raised you up in extraordinary manner, you must pardon us if we be slow in believing such things ... [I]n the hatching of the Protestant brood, no ordinary vocation, nor sending extraordinary appeareth; so the ground and foundation being naught, all they which have builded upon it falleth down.[5]

Much Anglican theology of ministry has had, and continues to have, a sore conscience on just this point. The association of apostolicity so closely with 'pedigree' has been until very recently a given in Anglican-Roman Catholic polemic on ministerial validity. And Anglicanism has still not quite grown out of the attempts of a number of nineteenth- and twentieth-century writers, including R. C. Moberly and the contributors to K. E. Kirk's *Apostolic Ministry* (1946), to trace a history of descent by which Anglican orders could be certified.

On the other side, the Puritan party in England raised a number of objections to the theology of the Edwardine ordinals over the course of a debate which lasted right until the 1662 Act of Uniformity and indeed beyond, to the end of the seventeenth century. At heart, the fear of this group was that the theology of ministry envisaged in the ordinals of the newly constituted Church was not fully reformed. It went beyond the scriptural norms in its reaffirmation of the threefold order of bishops, priests and deacons, and criticized pre-Reformation models of mediatory cultic priesthood only in a half-hearted way. The continued use of the term 'priest', in view of its absence as a term for a 'special ministry' in the New Testament, became a major point of contention. In reply, Anglican apologists frequently advanced the argument that 'priest' is properly derived not from *sacerdos* but from *presbyter*. Accordingly, it is used, as Hooker suggested, both to signify eldership or leadership in the congregation, and, by way of allusion, to identify 'that which the Gospel hath *proportionable* to ancient sacrifices, namely the Communion of the blessed Body and Blood of Christ, although it have properly no new sacrifice.'[6]

Furthermore, the Puritan party raised a variety of objections to the threefold pattern envisaged in the Ordinal, sometimes to the uncertain status of the diaconate, but most especially to the distinction between bishops and priests, which they claimed to run counter to the New Testament pattern of parity of ministers. The fact that ordination was in practice a prerogative of bishops (even if the practice had no explicit warrant in either the Ordinal or the Articles) became the focus of a long-running dispute. That dispute was only resolved in 1662 by the Act of Uniformity. The Act prescribed *ex animo* consent to the revised *Book of Common Prayer* and, moreover, insisted that none could lawfully hold benefice in the Church of England 'unless he have formerly been made priest by episcopal ordination' (see pp. 296–308). The effect of the Act far exceeded that of excluding a large number from the public ministry of the restored Anglican Church, in what became recalled in Puritan memory as the 'Great Ejection' of St Bartholomew's Day 1662. Most significantly, it pushed to the margins a theology of ministry which could claim at least some basis in the Reformation formularies of the Church of England. Many attempts were made in subsequent decades to articulate a theology of ministry sufficiently comprehensive to draw in at least the more moderate of the Puritan party, notably in the work of Richard Baxter. The failure of these schemes was the first of a series of similar abortive attempts to surmount the apparently intractable obstacle of recognizing the competence and validity of the non-episcopally ordained minister. In the present century, the issue emerged in Anglican reluctance to enter into communion with the Church of South India, or in the breakdown of proposals for union with the Free Churches such as those involving the English Methodists (see pp. 379–83).

'MAGNIFY YOUR OFFICE'

From the end of the seventeenth century until the rise of the Ecumenical Movement in the earlier decades of the present century, the acceptability of Anglican theology of ministry to nonconformism was not a serious issue. Alongside a developing literature setting forth Anglican confidence in its claims to possession of an apostolic ministry, the first half of the eighteenth century witnessed a serious decline in the practice of ministry. As in the pre-Reformation era, a large fraction of incumbents was non-resident, leaving parochial duties to curates. Three separate factors combined to change the theology and practice of ministry between the mid-eighteenth and the mid-nineteenth centuries.

(1) The Methodist and Evangelical movements in the later eighteenth century did much to call into question the adequacy of established patterns of ministerial practice. In particular, they demonstrated that the deficiency of much post-Restoration theory of ministry in Anglicanism was an over-emphasis on office and a neglect of the function and context of Christian ministry. In effect, the Evangelical Revivalist movements, often tangential to the official ministry of the Church of England and often the targets of some hostility, constituted a charge that the possession of a correctly validated and ordered ministry did not guarantee effectiveness or responsiveness to the Spirit. Wesley's decision to ordain ministers for the nascent Church in America as a matter of necessity not only tabled again the seventeenth-century issue of the parity of bishops and priests, but also showed in a vivid way the frustration felt by many with the reluctance of the established order to engage with a changed context for ministry. The issue was to raise itself many times as Anglicanism became a worldwide communion in the era of missionary expansion.

(2) The work of the Ecclesiastical Commission did a great deal in the earlier part of the nineteenth century to revive the ministry of the Church of England by the establishment of more secure administrative and legal structures. And so, for example, the Plurality Acts of 1838 and 1850 did much to reduce the acute problems of non-residence and plurality of benefice, contributing in an indirect way to the revival of ministerial practice.

(3) Most significant, however, for the development of the theology of ministry in the Church of England over the course of the next hundred years was the rediscovery of a vigorous and practical sense of apostolic succession in the early days of the Oxford Movement. Eighteenth-century Anglican apologists had often appeared to use the notion of apostolic succession as a means of insuring the Church of England against serious criticism, whether from within or without its ranks. For Newman and others, however, it served both as a call to clergy to assume ministerial authority and as a means of reviving a practical sense of what Tract XVII called 'the ministerial commission' as 'a trust from Christ for the

benefit of his people'. In Newman's hands, apostolic succession was not simply about pedigree; it also constituted a call to responsibility. Certainly in the first of the *Tracts for the Times* Newman wrote with great eagerness of the grace of apostolic orders: 'There are some who rest their divine mission on their own unsupported assertion; others, who rest it upon their popularity; others, upon their success; and others, who rest upon their temporal distinctions. This last case has, perhaps, been too much our own; I fear we have neglected the real ground upon which our authority is built—OUR APOSTOLICAL DESCENT.' But the excited injunction to 'magnify your office' stands alongside that to 'act up to your professions'—to a realization, that is, of the function of the priesthood as symbolizing access to the self-giving of God in Christ. Later Tractarians, however, as well as Evangelical critics like Litton, focused more sharply on the question which had engaged Anglican apologists 150 years earlier: 'How is the ministry of the Church of England authorized?'

Two factors made an answer to that question a matter of some urgency.

First, critical historical study of the early Church had with some success proposed the theory that the patterns of ministry which were widely supposed to have been inherited intact from the Apostles were more likely to be expedients established in the second century, and could therefore claim no immediate dominical sanction. Advanced in radical dress by German historians of Christianity, or more tentatively by Anglican scholars such as Hatch, Lightfoot or Hort, the theory raised real doubts about the affirmation in the Preface to the ordinal that 'it is evident unto all men, diligently reading holy scripture, and ancient authors, that from the Apostles' time there hath been these orders of Ministers in Christ's Church: Bishops, Priests, and Deacons'. Since the last decades of the nineteenth century, Anglican theology of ministry has not been able to construct the defence of its own validity with the same kind of ease as was possible in periods with a less sophisticated historical sense.

Second, the history of Roman Catholic objections to Anglican orders came to a head with the promulgation in 1896 of the papal bull *Apostolicae Curae*, which concluded that 'ordinations carried out according to the Anglican rite have been and are absolutely null and utterly void'. The bull evoked substantial controversy in subsequent decades, much of it muddled by hasty accounts of what it had actually claimed about the prerequisites for valid ordination. Although the Second Vatican Council included the Anglican Communion among the separated Churches which 'because of the lack of the sacrament of orders ... have not preserved the genuine and total reality of the Eucharistic mystery',[7] the Council gave fresh impetus to common exploration of the theology of ministry and priesthood. From one perspective, at least, this has set Anglican-Roman Catholic dialogue on the topic in a new context, and done much to set Anglican reflection on ministry along new tracks.

A CONTEMPORARY AGENDA

The history of Anglican reflection on ministry demonstrates that until fairly recently it has been much preoccupied by polemical concerns—the propriety of a sacrificial priesthood, the authorization or 'pedigree' of Anglican orders, the retention of the episcopate. More recently, however, the debates have shifted very considerably, away from the elaboration and defence of competing theologies on generally partisan lines to the establishment of a number of areas where substantial agreement can be reached, both among Anglicans and with members of other Christian traditions.

Because contemporary Anglican theology of ministry has been articulated in a self-consciously ecumenical context, often in the form of reports of inter-Church commissions, it has come to share some of the basic common terms of recent discussion. And so, for example, the Christological context of ministry, much espoused in recent study, has found its way into Anglican documents: 'The life and self-offering of Christ perfectly express what it is to serve God and man. All Christian ministry ... flows and takes its shape from this source and model';[8] or again, 'Christ is unique: he is our one High Priest. The priesthood of the Church and the priesthood of its ministry are derived from the priesthood of Christ.'[9]

Moreover, widespread dissatisfaction with identifying 'ministry' with 'ordained ministry' has pushed Anglicanism into statements which define ordained ministry not so much in terms of the possession of special powers, cultic or otherwise, but in terms of the particular functions exercised by the ordained within the ministry of the whole people of God. For this, a variety of terms have come into common use: 'presidency', 'leadership', 'management' of the resources of the people of God and 'enabling' their use, 'focusing' the priestliness of the whole Church. The revised Anglican ordinals generally emphasize that the existence and exercise of ordained ministry cannot be divorced from the corporate ministry of the community. Thus the 1980 Ordinal in the English Alternative Service Book begins the ordination prayer with 'We praise and glorify you, almighty Father, because you have formed throughout the whole world a holy people for your own possession, a royal priesthood, a universal church'; or again, the 1979 Book of Common Prayer of the Episcopal Church of the USA has lay persons involved in the presentation of candidates for ordination to the priesthood. Nevertheless, Anglicanism continues to resist pragmatic accounts of ordination as community delegation. The Anglican-Reformed dialogue report *God's Reign and Our Unity* (London, 1984), for example, argues that 'priests' exercise 'their priestly office neither apart from the priesthood of the whole body, nor by derivation from the priesthood of the whole body;[10] and 'Ministry and Ordination' in the ARCIC *Final Report* proposes that ordained ministry 'is not an extension of the common Christian priesthood but belongs to another realm of the gifts of the Spirit'.

One of the primary effects of the rediscovery of the common priesthood of the Church has been a substantial reworking of the notion of 'apostolicity'. Apostolicity has, in effect, been generalized, to cover not simply the existence of certain patterns of ordained ministry but rather the life of the whole Church in faithfulness to the apostolic gospel, in mission, and in service to the world. The apostolicity of the ordained ministry is a function of the apostolicity of the whole body of believers. Moreover, apostolicity has been de-historicized: the apostolic character of the ordained ministry does not, that is, rest in its observable descent from Christ and his apostles so much as in its continuation of the apostolic functions. From the standpoint of most contemporary accounts of primitive Christianity, traditional defences of Anglican ministerial order (including recent classics such as Moberly's *Ministerial Priesthood* and Ramsey's *The Gospel and the Catholic Church*) have an idealist air. Contemporary Anglicans are unlikely to attempt historical validations of orders, and much more likely to favour instead arguments that are drawn from the character and needs of the Christian community.

The effect of recent work in the theology of ministry has thus been to make traditional demarcations more difficult to sustain. Significantly, the 1973 statement *Ministry and Ordination* by the Anglican-Roman Catholic International Commission explicitly shelves the judgement of *Apostolicae Curae* on Anglican orders. This it does by beginning the dialogue elsewhere—in common affirmations of a broad range of images of ordained ministry in relation to the High Priesthood of Christ and the priesthood of all the faithful. 'Agreement on the nature of ministry is prior to the consideration of the mutual recognition of ministries.'[12]

Significant divergences do, however, remain to be resolved. First, the ordination of women to the priesthood. Like debates concerning the ministry of the laity, those about the ordination of women to the priesthood have done much to alert the Church to the potential distortions introduced into Christianity by uncritical assimilation of institutional patterns derived from elsewhere. The ordination of women to the priesthood is integrally related to a larger contemporary discussion of the ideological status of paternal language and imagery about God and corresponding social arrangements. In the Anglican context, however, it has raised debates nearer home: the defining characteristics of a properly apostolic ministry, and the acceptability of Anglican orders to Rome. The 1979 *Elucidation* of the 1973 statement on ministry attempts to make agreement on 'the origin and nature of the ordained ministry' prior to 'the question of who can or cannot be ordained'.[13] Roman Catholic response has not so far endorsed the distinction, and the practice of ordaining women to the priesthood in some Anglican provinces remains a major ecumenical stumbling-block.

Second, the sacrificial nature of the Eucharist and the associated definition of the priestliness of the eucharistic president remain matters of dispute. Like that of the theology of ministry, the theology of the Eucharist has undergone major reshaping under the impact of renewed biblical and liturgical scholarship, particularly in the development of a dynamic concept of the relation between the eucharistic action of the Church and the sacrifice of Christ. On this account, the eucharistic memorial can be spoken of as a sacrifice 'in the sacramental sense, provided that it is clear that this is not a repetition of the historical sacrifice'.[14] And so 'Because the eucharist is the memorial of the sacrifice of Christ, the action of the presiding minister in reciting again the words of Christ at the last supper and distributing to the assembly the holy gifts is seen to stand in sacramental relation to what Christ himself did in offering his own sacrifice. So our two traditions commonly use priestly terms in speaking about the ordained ministry.'[15] The effect of this has been to give greater authority to the tradition in Anglicanism which has, from Laud and Andrewes onward, maintained that the eucharistic elements are offered to God by the priest as a commemorative sacrifice. The argument of the recent Church of England report, *The Priesthood of the Ordained Ministry*, places great weight on this tradition, and can show with some success that it has remained a consistent presence in Anglicanism from the Caroline period.

For all that, the relation of contemporary accounts of the theology of both priesthood and Eucharist to the Anglican formularies stands in need of clarification. However substantial the ecumenical consensus, and whatever pragmatic resolutions are reached, Anglicanism still faces a set of decisions about its theological method. In what does the normative status of the Reformation formularies consist? Some styles of Anglican theology proceed by setting the formularies in the larger context of the developing tradition of Anglican theory and practice, attempting to show that they embrace (or at least do not deny) a variety of different interpretations. Others regard the formularies as enshrining a specific theological position by which the growing tradition is to be evaluated. It thus remains an open question whether Anglican theology of ministry is to be derived simply from its canonically authoritative texts alone, or also from the history of interpretation and practice which those texts have evoked. Moreover, the polemical needs served by the Reformation formularies do not necessarily still exist or exist in the same forms: and so in what sense should those documents continue to set the terms of debate? Clearly they no longer do, and it is not immediately obvious how the Book of Common Prayer and the Articles offer resources for clarifying the task of ordained ministry in contexts which their compilers could not have imagined. On the other hand, it needs to be asked what Anglicanism would deprive itself of, if its formularies were to be treated as simply part of the developing tradition with little normative or critical role.

NOTES

1 Thomas Becon, *Works* (Cambridge 1844), vol. ii, p. 421.

2 Hugh Latimer, *Sermons and Remains* (Cambridge 1844), vol. i, p. 256.

3 *Homilies* (London 1908), p. 477.

4 William Perkins, *A Reformed Catholike* (Cambridge 1598), p. 204.

5 Francis Mason, *Of the Consecration of the Bishops in the Church of England*; in P. E. More and F. L. Cross, *Anglicanism* (London 1935), p. 379f.

6 Richard Hooker, *Of the Laws of Ecclesiastical Polity*, V. lxxiii. 2.

7 W. M. Abbott, ed., *The Documents of Vatican II* (London 1966), p. 364.

8 ARCIC *Final Report* (London 1982), p. 30.

9 Board for Mission and Unity, *The Priesthood of the Ordained Ministry* (London 1986), p. 97.

10 *God's Reign and Our Unity*, p. 79.

11 ARCIC *Final Report*, p. 36.

12 ibid., p. 38.

13 ibid., p. 44.

14 ibid., p. 20.

15 ibid., p. 35.

7 Episcopacy

RICHARD A. NORRIS

Fairweather, E. R., and Hettlinger, R. F., *Episcopacy and Reunion*. London 1953.
Kirk, K. E., ed., *The Apostolic Ministry. Essays on the History and Doctrine of Episcopacy*. London 1946.
Mason, A. J., *The Church of England and Episcopacy*. Cambridge 1914.
Moore, P., ed., *Bishops—But What Kind?* London 1982.
Stone, D., *Episcopacy Ancient and Modern*. London 1930.
Sykes, N., *Old Priest and New Presbyter*. Cambridge 1956.
Today's Church and Today's World with a Special Focus on the Ministry of Bishops (The Lambeth Conference 1978 Preparatory Articles). London 1977.

Bishops—and with them the distinction of office between bishops and presbyters—were simply a given of the English reform. Henry VIII, though he separated the Church of England from papal jurisdiction and brought it under the exclusive supervision of the Crown, altered none of its other constitutional or pastoral structures. In the days of Edward VI, accordingly, when the party that sought fundamental doctrinal, liturgical, and pastoral reform achieved ascendancy, its programme was carried out by royal authority acting through the inherited legal structures of the Church, and its leaders were bishops. As a consequence, English Reformers saw no reason to think that there was any inherent opposition between episcopacy and the cause of reformation, however much they might object to the prelatical shape assumed by the episcopal office in medieval Europe, and whatever degree of merit they might discern in the type of church order that prevailed in Reformed Churches in Switzerland or Germany. The Edwardian Ordinal regarded it as 'evident ... that from the Apostles' time there have been these Orders of Ministers in Christ's church; Bishops, Priests, and Deacons', and insisted that it was God, by the Holy Spirit, who had 'appointed divers Orders of Ministers' in the Church (see pp. 143–51). The Elizabethan Settlement of 1559 maintained these principles and the practice which they implied. Scrupulous care was taken, in the arrangements made for the consecration of Matthew Parker as Archbishop of Canterbury, to ensure that the traditional conditions for the ordination of a bishop were met.

Nevertheless it was not in episcopacy that the English Reformers saw the distinctive mark of their system of church government. What set the English Church apart was precisely the principle and the fact of royal, as opposed to papal, supremacy. The English Reformation was seen to be the work of the 'godly prince', whose supremacy in ecclesiastical as well as civil causes, in the ordering of the spiritual as well as the temporal affairs of the kingdom, the Reformers justified by appeal to the models provided by such Old Testament figures as David and Solomon. Episcopacy could indeed be—and was—supported by reference to the practice of Christian antiquity and to unvarying tradition 'from the Apostles' time', and such an appeal was entirely consistent with the general stance of a Church that sought to restore, as Jewel put it, the faith of 'the apostles and old catholic fathers'. But the ordering of the Church was the work of the prince. It was royal authority that maintained the primitive pattern of ecclesiastical government and ministry in England. Monarch and bishop stood or fell together, as James I asserted, and Charles I and his archbishop demonstrated.

For this reason among others, the earlier English Reformers were occupied less with justifying the institution of bishops or offering theoretical accounts of its place in the life of the Church than with indicating what they understood the business of bishops to be. Bishops were ministers of the Crown for the *spiritual* government of the nation. In a reformed Church, this meant that bishops were to see to it that 'the pure Word of God is preached, and the Sacraments be duly ministered according to Christ's ordinance' (Article XIX); for the defining mark of a true Church was fidelity to Scripture in preaching, teaching, and sacramental observance. The bishop, then, was not to be a feudal magnate or a court official, but a pastor in the proper sense, governing the people by the gospel word of grace and of judgement as one 'to whom is committed the office to instruct the people', as Jewel insisted.[1]

Unfortunately, neither custom, nor circumstance, nor royal policy co-operated with the Elizabethan Reformers in their desire to achieve this ideal of a ministry devoted, in all its orders, to preaching and teaching the gospel. Bishops in particular remained distant figures, garbed in the habiliments of prelacy. Inevitably, then, that party within the English Church which was most attached to reformation on the Swiss and German model became increasingly dissatisfied with what its members regarded as hesitant and half-hearted measures of reform. It called for the creation of a truly scriptural Church in England, and, to that end, for the institution of the Calvinist 'discipline'—in other words, for a presbyterian type of church government. Under the leadership of Thomas Cartwright and Walter Travers, this 'Puritan' party therefore attacked not merely the bishops themselves and the policies they represented, but the very institution of episcopacy; and it was in the ensuing controversy—which in one form or another lasted for a good deal more than a century—that Anglican understandings of the episcopal office, its status, and its function were formed.

THE OFFICE OF A BISHOP

One prominent and central issue in this controversy concerned the Puritan contention 'that between a Presbyter and a Bishop the Word of God alloweth not any inequality or difference to be made'.[2] This doctrine of the parity of ministers (that is, of pastors: deacons and such-like were not under consideration) was reinforced by appeal to Jerome's oft-cited *Epistle to Evagrius*, as well as to a scholastic tradition dating back to Peter Lombard, which held that bishops are superior to presbyters not in power of order, but only in jurisdiction. Since neither Jerome (whose principal animus was directed against deacons) nor the scholastics in question actually sought to abolish the distinction between presbyters and bishops, some Anglican authors—especially those concerned to reconcile the episcopal and presbyterian forms of church order—were content to follow a view that made the distinction one of office or dignity rather than strictly of order. The majority, however, took a sterner line. They discerned even in the New Testament clear adumbrations of imparity. The Lord himself, according to Luke, sent both the Twelve and the Seventy,[3] and with differing commissions, thus laying the basis for the later distinction of bishops and presbyters; and the office conceded by the Apostle to Timothy and Titus clearly sets them over ordinary elders. This evidence, moreover, was confirmed by the universal practice of the primitive Church. Hence Bishop Carleton of Chichester could object strenuously, at the Synod of Dort, to the introduction into the Belgic Confession of 'a strange conceit of the parity of ministers'.

If the episcopate is a distinct order, however, and not merely a job-assignment, in what does its characteristic office consist? Following, in substance, the view stated by Bishop Thomas Bilson in his treatise of 1593, *The Perpetual Government of Christ's Church*, Richard Hooker explained:

> A Bishop is a Minister of God, unto whom with permanent continuance, there is given not onely power of administring the Word and Sacraments, which power other presbyters have; but also a further power to ordain Ecclesiastical persons, and a power of Cheifty in Government over Presbyters as well as Lay men, a power to be by way of jurisdiction a Pastor even to Pastors themselves.[4]

For Hooker, then, the difference between bishop and presbyter could be expressed in terms of the derivation of authority. A presbyter is a full minister of word and sacrament, but his 'authority to do these things is derived from the Bishops which doth ordain him thereunto, so that even in those things which are common unto both, yet the power of the one, is as it were a certain light borrowed from the others lamp'.[5] On this view, which sees the distinctive marks of the episcopal office in 'latitude of the power of order' and 'in that kind of power which belongeth unto jurisdiction',[6] there is a distinction, but no separation, to be made between these two powers: the bishop's jurisdictional or supervisory authority is derived from the power of ordination. In this general account of the bishop's office Hooker is almost uniformly followed by his successors. John Cosin (Bishop of Durham 1660–72), for example, in a sermon preached in 1626 when he was Archdeacon of York, sees the authority of the episcopate to consist in the power of the keys: 'the key of order to send as Christ sent, and the key of jurisdiction to govern as he governed'.[7]

This account of the episcopal office was intended neither to minimize the role of the bishop as minister of word and sacrament nor to disallow a collegial relation of bishop and presbyters in the diocese. The difference of order that Anglican apologists insisted on was always a difference between the bishop and 'other presbyters'; and they would have agreed with Archbishop Whitgift of Canterbury (d. 1604) when he observed that 'touching the ministry' of word and sacrament 'there is an equality of all ministers of God's word ...; for ... the word preached, or the sacraments ministered, is as effectual in one ... as it is in another'.[8] Furthermore, when they spoke of the power of jurisdiction or government, what they had in mind was not, as a modern might think, the business of organizational administration, but primarily the administration of discipline under the word of God—a 'spiritual' function; and in this work the bishop had other presbyters as (subordinate) colleagues and counsellors. Hooker, following Jerome, sees 'no cause why the Bishop should disdain to consult with them, and in weighty affairs of the Church to use their advice', and indeed thinks that 'Churches Cathedral', where the bishop is associated in his work with dean and chapter, 'are as glasses wherein the face and very countenance of Apostolical antiquity remaineth even as yet to be seen'.[9] The collegial relation between bishop and presbyters in the work of a diocese was a foundation-stone of Archbishop Ussher's scheme for the reconciliation of episcopal and presbyterian church orders—though of course his proposals came to nothing, and practical adoption of his ideas had to await the day of synodical forms of diocesan government, which first appeared in Anglican Churches outside of England (see pp. 193–9).

APOSTOLICITY, DIVINE RIGHT, AND SUCCESSION

In the face of both Roman Catholic and Puritan or Nonconformist criticism— not to mention what John Cosin called the 'voluntary and transcendent impiety' that brought about the abolition of episcopacy under the Parliamentary and Cromwellian regimes—Anglican writers of the late sixteenth and seventeenth centuries addressed themselves repeatedly to questions about the relation of the episcopal to the apostolic office, about the 'divine right' (*jus divinum*) of the episcopal office, and about the importance of succession in office and continuity in ordination.

There were, needless to say, significant tracts of common ground shared by the participants in these discussions. Basic to the whole Anglican view of episcopacy was the principle that 'the office of publick preaching, or ministering the Sacraments in the congregation' was not one which any individual could assume or lay claim to in his own right. As an office in the Church and for the Church, it could belong only to 'those ... which be chosen and called to this work by men who have publick authority given unto them in the Congregation, to call and send ministers'. Framed—no doubt deliberately—in the most general terms, these words of Article XXIII make no mention of bishops; they nevertheless enunciate the principle that a necessary condition of valid ministry is its derivation through the Church considered as an ordered body. The ordering that the English Church judged normal and appropriate was then specified in the Ordinal and its preface, which made it clear that in practice the expression 'men who have publick authority' refers to bishops. Further, the reason given to justify this ordering of the Church under bishops—that it has marked the Church 'from the Apostles' time'—adds another dimension of meaning to the practice demanded by the Ordinal. To insist upon ordination by bishops who have themselves been ordained in traditional fashion by other bishops is a way of testifying that legitimate reception of authority—as distinct from mere appropriation or seizure of it—presupposes both continuity in office and orderly transmission of office. The habitual Anglican appeal to continuity and antiquity,

300

however, suggests further that, at the level of order, it is the bishop in whom the unity of the Church in one place and time with the Church in other places and times is, as a matter of fact, represented and effected.

> Ordination must be performed by those who have received authority to exercise *episcope* in the Body, and to admit others to share in that ministry. This acknowledgment by the Body of the authority of the ordaining member means that his own ordination to the ministry of *episcope* must be recognized and accepted. From this arises the principle of continuity by succession, which appears to be indispensable, at least from a human point of view.[10]

A second point on which there was general agreement among Anglican thinkers was the conviction that the office of a bishop in the Church represents a partial continuation of the office of an Apostle. John Pearson, Bishop of Chester 1673–86, explains in a neat rhetorical turn that 'an apostle is an extraordinary bishop', while 'a bishop is an ordinary apostle.'[11] No doubt by these words he intended to convey more or less what Andrewes had alleged in his statement that 'overseers' carry on 'the chief part of the apostolic function, the oversight of the church; and power of commanding, correcting, and ordaining'.[12] Hooker, as might be expected, had been more circumspect in his handling of this matter. He acknowledges that in their capacity of chosen eye-witnesses, directly commissioned by Christ as founders of the Church, the Apostles had, and could have had, no successors. He further argues that in so far as the Apostles were ministers of word and sacrament, their office is continued in that of the presbyter. He thinks, however, that a function of oversight was intrinsic to the apostolic office, and that this function was continued in the Church's bishops. 'For to succeed them is after them to have that Episcopal kind of power which was first given to them.'[13]

To say, however, that the episcopal office continues one or more distinctive functions of the apostolic office is to record a matter of fact, not of right. Yet the Puritans, by asserting that some form of presbyterian church order was prescribed by the Scriptures themselves, were appealing beyond the data of traditional practice to raise, in essence, the question what type of church order could claim divine institution. In reply, the defenders of episcopacy stated a position which was indeed calculated to claim a divine right for the office of bishop, but which at the same time rested that claim on an appeal to the continuous practice of the Church—to tradition.

The elements of this position can be found in the writings of Archbishop Whitgift. In correspondence with Theodore Beza at Geneva, Whitgift was straightforward in his assertion that episcopacy is *de jure divino*. On the other hand, he denied that any form of church government is fully or explicitly prescribed by Scripture—a denial connected, in his mind, with the distinction between matters 'necessary unto the salvation of the Church' and matters of 'government'.[14] For him it was conceivable in abstract principle that the Church should be without episcopacy, even though the institution of bishops is 'apostolical and divine'. No doubt he would have agreed with Robert Sanderson, Bishop of Lincoln 1660–3, who recognized two senses of the expression *jus divinum*: one in which it implies a positive divine precept, and a second in which it refers to something of apostolic institution and practice.

The most thorough exponent of this position was Richard Hooker. In Book III of his *Ecclesiastical Polity*, Hooker concurs with Whitgift in disputing the Puritan view that 'no form of Church Polity is . . . lawful, or of God, unless God be so the author of it that it be also set down in Scripture'.[15] He also distinguishes 'matters of faith, and in general matters necessary unto Salvation', which must be 'expressly contained in the word of God', from matters of 'government'[16] or 'external regiment'.[17] On the other hand, he does not deny that some forms of church order are more clearly consonant with Scripture than others, and asserts that 'there have ever been and ever ought to be . . . at leastwise two sorts of ecclesiastical persons, the one subordinate unto the other; as to the Apostles in the beginning, and to the Bishops always since, we find plainly both in Scripture and in all ecclesiastical records, other ministers of the word and sacraments have been.'[18] There is, then, an *analogy* between Apostles and bishops, between the church government seen in the New Testament and that seen in the later history of the Church. But is episcopacy of apostolic institution and in that sense *de jure divino*?

This question Hooker addresses only in Book VII, where, notoriously, he seems to be of two minds. On the one hand, he sets out a theory of the origins of episcopacy which is not unlike that suggested by J. B. Lightfoot in the nineteenth century. That is, he sees the bishop as emerging, so to speak, from the body of presbyter-bishops in a local church in response to the need for a single focus of authority in the community, and thus assuming, within a limited jurisdiction, the power of oversight which the Apostles had exercised without such limitation. As to the question whether it was the Apostles who were directly responsible for this development—whether episcopacy is of apostolic institution—Hooker is uncertain. He explains the view that his argument presupposes: 'that after the apostles were deceased, churches did agree amongst themselves . . . to make one presbyter in each city chief over the rest'.[19] But he also announces in the same breath that he is less persuaded than formerly of this view, and is more inclined to believe that 'the apostles themselves left bishops invested with power above other pastors'. Nevertheless Hooker declines to rest his case on this proposition— and, one suspects, not merely because of scholarly caution, but also because in argument with the Puritans he is above all concerned to deny that everything that is of God is contained in Scripture or belongs to the first Christian generation. He is confident that the Apostles had *some* hand in the emergence of episcopacy. But 'whether the apostles alone did conclude of such a regiment, or else they together with the whole church judging it a fit and needful policy did agree to receive it for a custom' is, for him, a question of little moment, since episcopacy 'had either divine appointment beforehand, or divine approbation afterwards, and is in that respect to be acknowledged the ordinance of God...'

Hooker's position—which amounts to a claim that 'divine right' can be ascribed simply on the basis of the universal practice of the Church—was not generally echoed among writers of the following generation, who were convinced of the apostolic institution of episcopacy. Lancelot Andrewes, for example, held that 'the apostles ordained overseers to have a general care over the churches instead of themselves';[20] and seventeenth-century discovery of the genuine works of Ignatius of Antioch, which seemed to show monepiscopacy as established in the immediate post-apostolic Church, encouraged this view. John Pearson— himself the most learned among the students of Ignatius—summarized the common view: 'As the Father sent Christ, so Christ [sent] the Apostles, and the Apostles, their successors.' Hence 'By this apostolic action of handing-on [*traditio*], the entire power of ordination is resident in bishops.'[21]

Nevertheless Hooker had his followers. John Cosin, for example, had no hesitation in asserting that episcopal authority was *jure divino*, but for all that affirmed that it stemmed from '*Apostolical practice* and the perpetual custom and canons of the Church' rather than from 'any absolute precept that either Christ or His Apostles gave about it'.[22] Edward Stillingfleet (Bishop of Worcester 1689– 99) in effect recorded his conversion to Hooker's view when he repudiated his youthful belief that 'the Form of *Church Government* was left at Liberty by any Law of Christ', and affirmed that 'there is as great Reason to believe, the *Apostolical Succession* to be of *Divine Institution*, as the *Canon of Scripture*, or the *Observation of the Lord's Day*'.[23] It is Stillingfleet's line, moreover, that is repeated in the report of the Committee on the Unity of the Church at the Lambeth Conference of 1930:

> The Episcopate occupies a position which is, in point of historical development, analogous to that of the Canon of Scripture and the Creeds... If the Episcopate... was the result of a... process of adaptation and growth in the organism of the Church, that would be no evidence that it lacked divine authority, but rather that the life of the Spirit within the Church had found it to be the most appropriate organ for the functions it discharged.[24]

'BEING', 'WELL-BEING', OR ...?

There are, then, certain principles which, in the controversies of the late sixteenth and seventeenth centuries, became the common property of Anglicanism. In the office of bishop the apostolic function of oversight, which includes and indeed derives from the power of ordination, is continued. Further, the institution of episcopacy, whether by reason of apostolic institution or by reason of the universal practice of the Church, is normative for the government of the Church. Finally, regular episcopal succession in office—which requires succession through the laying-on of hands of other bishops—not only guarantees the legitimacy of the Church's ministry but establishes the local church's unity, communion, and continuity with the universal Church.

From early on, however, acceptance of these principles brought the English Church—and later its daughter Churches—face to face with the issue of what they implied for the relation of a Church thus ordered to other Churches, and in particular to Churches whose ministries were not episcopally ordained. In this connection, there are three successive phases to be considered in the development of Anglican thought and practice.

First there is the question of the attitude and practice of the English Church prior to 1662. There can be no doubt that the defence of episcopacy in that period was conducted on the assumption that *foreign* Reformed Churches ordered on the presbyterian model were genuine Churches—Churches in which the word was truly preached and the sacraments rightly ministered, and hence Churches in which a real ministry existed. Furthermore, the principle on which this affirmation was made can be detected in the very terms in which episcopacy was asserted: it was a matter of 'government' or 'external regiment' not of faith, and hence, even if divinely instituted, not 'necessary to salvation'. On the other hand, this attitude was not extended to embrace presbyterian (or other) groups *within the English nation*. The reason for this apparent inconsistency becomes evident when one notes that the legitimacy of non-episcopal orders in foreign Churches was conceded on the precise ground of 'necessity', that is, on the ground that such Churches had in practice been compelled to make a choice— between reformation according to scriptural norms of doctrine and practice on the one hand, and, on the other, retention of episcopacy. The Anglican divines of the seventeenth century, with few exceptions, regarded episcopacy as normative and presbyteral ordination as anomalous; but they also realized just how fortunate the English nation had been in its possession of godly princes, whose policies had made a choice between correct faith and proper order unnecessary. Hence they commanded episcopal ordering of the Church at home (for domestic dissenters could make no claim of 'necessity') and commended it abroad, acknowledging their fellowship with Reformed Churches overseas.

Second, account must be taken of the changed situation after the restoration of Charles II. The Act of Uniformity of 1662 formally excluded clergy who had not been episcopally ordained from pastoral office in the English Church. This action was primarily directed against domestic dissenters and expressed the animus of Anglicans against those who had co-operated with the outlawing of episcopacy and of *The Book of Common Prayer* in the days of Parliamentary rule. There is little evidence that the Act of Uniformity marked a fundamental change of attitude towards Reformed Churches outside of England. These were still regarded as true Churches, whose ministries, though irregular and anomalous, were real and effective. Nevertheless it affected the English Church's practical policy with regard to clergy who had been presbyterally ordained to the ministry of foreign Churches. Prior to 1662—though with visible qualms and on rare occasion—English bishops had apparently permitted foreign clergy to hold pastoral charges without episcopal ordination. Such gestures were no longer possible.

Third, the dawning of the eighteenth century, following on the unhappy reign of James II and the 'Glorious Revolution' of 1688, brought significant change both in the circumstances of the English Church and in the attitude of stiff or 'High Church' Anglicans towards questions of church order. For one thing, this was the Age of Reason, when the very suggestion that human actions and institutions might authoritatively mediate a divine reality was received with indifference or contempt. Moreover, the position of the Church in English society had really, if subtly, changed. No longer could it count upon the 'godly prince' to maintain its traditions and identity. In their very different ways, both James II and William III had made that clear. Further, it could no longer truly claim to be a *national* Church—the 'spirituality' of England. Instead it was the *established* Church of a nation that tolerated nonconformity. Its life was openly subjected to the secular, civil authority of Parliament; and its bishops, whose votes in the House of Lords had become necessary to the continuance in office of any government, were becoming political figures, whose attention to pastoral duties, even given the best intentions, had to be severely limited.

In this situation—especially when its paradoxes and problems were brought into sharp focus by the deprivation of bishops who had refused the oath of allegiance to William III and Mary II—it is not surprising that 'High Church' clergy, to whom all these developments were distasteful, should begin to envisage the episcopal ordering of the Church not simply as a divinely approved or appointed 'external regiment', but as a divine gift that marks out the sphere of covenanted grace; or that they should seek in the apostolic office of the bishop a basis for the Church's authority and identity that was independent of Parliament. John Pearson himself had been sure that there can be no power of absolution or authority to consecrate the elements in the Lord's Supper on the part of one who has not been episcopally ordained. William Beveridge (Bishop of St Asaph 1704–8), who came to prominence in the Church during the crises attendant on the reign of James II and its aftermath, saw the succession of bishops, in traditional fashion, as perpetuating 'the Apostolical office'; yet for him the primary importance of this succession lay in its character as a sign and seal of the fact that 'Christ himself' is 'continually present at such imposition of hands; thereby transferring the same Spirit, which He had first breathed into His Apostles, upon others successively after them'. The 'Apostolical office' of the episcopate marks out the Church itself as 'truly Apostolical' and is thus a guarantee of its identity as Christ's Church; but it does this because in fact it is a mediating sign of the sanctifying presence of the Spirit in the Church.[25]

On this basis it was open to the Non-juror William Law, in his attack on the Erastian views of the Bishop of Bangor, to insist that 'Administering of a Sacrament is an Action we have no Right to perform, considered either as Men, Gentlemen, or Scholars, or Members of Civil Society', and to argue on this ground the necessity of an 'Uninterrupted Succession of Authorised Persons from Christ'; for

> If there be no *Uninterrupted Succession*, then there are no Authorised Ministers from Christ; if no such Ministers, then no Christian Sacraments; if no Christian Sacraments, then no Christian Covenant, whereof the Sacraments are the Stated and Visible Seals.[26]

The Church's constitution is independent of that of civil society; and only by maintaining that constitution—ordination by persons standing in succession to the Apostles—can the Church maintain its identity. As one Bishop of Norwich argued in 1791: 'Without this rule we are open to imposture, and can be sure of nothing; we cannot be sure that our ministry is effective, or that our sacraments are realities.'[27]

Here, then, there has taken place a significant shift of emphasis. Originally episcopacy had been defended as the normative, divinely ordained or approved ordering of the Church; but the one absolutely indispensable mark of a Church was taken to be its continuance in apostolic and scriptural teaching. Now, however, episcopacy has come to count as a factor that grounds the identity of the Church; for the Church is constituted not only by the hearing and receiving of a message, but also by the historically established order that marks it out as the covenanted sphere of God's continuous working through the Spirit—and hence as an ordered society historically independent, and indeed transcendent, of civil society. Episcopacy is therefore an institution which counts as part of the definition of 'church'. And of course it is this 'high church' tradition which was not only reasserted by the Tractarian Movement and its posterity, but encouraged by the thought of F. D. Maurice, who saw in 'the episcopal institution', as he put it, 'one of the appointed and indispensable signs of a spiritual and universal society'.[28]

In this shift of perspective and emphasis there lie the roots of the modern debate—stimulated in part by the rise of the ecumenical movement—between those who see 'the historic episcopate' as belonging to the very definition of the Church (its *esse*, as the phrase goes), and those who see it as a matter of the 'well-being' (*bene esse*), or perhaps the 'full being' (*plene esse*), of the Church. The debate has by no means ended; but the 'high' or, as it has been called, 'exclusivist' view has had a permanent influence on Anglican understandings of the importance of church order. This is attested clearly enough by the so-called 'Chicago-Lambeth Quadrilateral,' in which Catholic order takes its place alongside norms of teaching and of sacramental practice as a factor essential to 'the visible unity of the church'. This influence, however, has not meant a general commitment to the view that where there have been no bishops—or no 'Essential Ministry', to use the phrase of K. E. Kirk—there has been no Church. Rather it seems to have led to the conclusion that the divisions of the Church produce an anomalous situation in which the Body is manifested only in defective form. The Lambeth Conference of 1948 suggested that it is, for Anglicans, impossible *either* 'to declare the sacraments of non-episcopal bodies null and void,' *or* 'to treat non-episcopal ministries as identical in status and authority with the episcopal ministry.'[29] This marks a return, in effect, to the *practice* of seventeenth-century Anglicanism with regard to its relations with 'foreign' Churches, but not a return to the view that questions of order are questions of indifference to the being or identity of the Church.

PROBLEMS

This survey of the themes and issues that have dominated Anglican discussion of episcopacy indicates that from the days of Whitgift and Hooker apologetic and polemical concerns have stood at the centre of attention. By comparison, little energy has been devoted to examination of the actual workings of episcopacy, or to the sort of theological reflection on ordained ministry generally, and episcopal ministry specifically, which might support critical understanding of the role of bishops in the Church. One result of this situation has been that claims are made for episcopacy which are not, in all or even in most cases, justified by the practice of Anglican Churches. Another is that the positive lessons to be learned from that practice itself—in all its variety of cultural setting and style—have been neglected. On the subject of episcopacy, there is a set of agenda which is long overdue for systematic consideration.

First, there is the matter of the teaching office of the bishop. The English Reformers saw the bishop primarily in two roles: a role of government or oversight that stemmed from the power of ordination; and a teaching role as guardian and exponent of the Church's common faith. Almost all Anglican apologetic and polemic has been concerned with the former of these matters; yet in the classical ordinals, three of the eight questions asked of a bishop-elect at his consecration stressed the office of teaching and preaching—directed not merely to the clergy but to all the people. Behind this stress on teaching there lay, no doubt, the Reformers' vision of the bishop as pastor in the proper sense—as the principal minister of word and sacrament in his *paroikia*. Yet it is not *this* vision of episcopacy that Anglicans have normally stressed in their own practice; and certainly it is not the vision they have ordinarily conveyed in their earnest efforts to comment episcopacy in ecumenical dialogue, where all too often the bishop ends up being envisaged more as regional administrator than as local pastor. The question therefore arises of whether the Reformers' ideal is in fact justified, theologically and historically; and if it is, the further—and more controversial—question arises of the conditions under which it might be actualized.

A second matter that calls for attention is the issue of bishops' collegial relationship both to fellow presbyters within their individual jurisdictions and to fellow bishops within a Province or national Church. Episcopacy in the Anglican tradition has not infrequently been tainted by prelacy or inordinate individualism, or both; and these defects, it might be argued, stem at least in part from structures and attitudes that isolate bishops from those relationships of fellowship and communion whose maintenance is the *raison d'etre* of the episcopal office. The issue here is not merely one of polity and administration (though no doubt it is that). It also touches the bishop's role as teacher of the Church and the nature and setting of the bishop's pastoral activity. There is need, therefore, for exploration—theological and practical—of the relation between the bishop's role as one who speaks *to* the Church and his role as one who speaks *for* the Church and *with* it.

Finally—and more generally—Anglicans need to be critically aware of the cultural and social models that shape, and to some extent distort, their perception of the episcopal office. On any account of the matter a bishop is an 'authority figure'. The question of what an authority figure is and does, however, depends to a considerable degree on perceptions and expectations that are shaped by the common practice of a given society. It is easy, in modern Western societies, for the bishop's authority to be modelled on that of the expert manager who 'gets results', or on that of the political representative who is elected to forward the views and interests of a particular constituency. In other times and places, other such models offer, or have offered, themselves: that of the civil magistrate, for example, or the feudal lord, or the tribal leader. In every case, however, the issue must be raised of the extent to which the model in question runs the risk of distorting the nature of pastoral authority in the Church; and this issue in turn can only be addressed on the basis of a theological grasp of the nature and source of authority in the Church.

NOTES

1 John Jewel, *An Apologie of the Church of England*, in T. H. L. Parker, ed., *English Reformers* (LCC 26, Philadelphia 1966), p. 21.

2 Richard Hooker, *Of the Laws of Ecclesiastical Polity*, VII. x. 1.

3 Luke 9.1–3, and 10.1–12.

4 *Of the Laws of Ecclesiastical Polity*, VII. ii. 3.

5 ibid., VII. vi. 3.

6 ibid., VII. vi. 1.

7 John Cosin, *Works* (Oxford 1843–1855), vol. 1, p. 88.

8 John Whitgift, *Works*, ed. J. Ayre (Cambridge 1851), vol. ii, p. 290.

9 *Of the Laws of Ecclesiastical Polity*, VII. vii. 1.

10 *The Lambeth Conference 1958*, p. 288.

11 John Pearson, *Minor Theological Works*, ed. E. Churton. (Oxford 1844), vol. i, p. 284.

12 Lancelot Andrewes, *Works* (Oxford 1854, repr. New York 1967), vol. vi, p. 355.

13 *Of the Laws of Ecclesiastical Polity*, VII. iv. 1–4.

14 *Works*, op. cit., vol. i, p. 184.

15 *Of the Laws of Ecclesiastical Polity*, III. ii. 1.

16 ibid., III. ii. 2.

17 ibid., III. ii. 4.

18 ibid., III. xi. 20.

19 ibid., VII. xi. 8.

20 *Works*, op. cit., vol. vi, p. 355.

21 *Minor Theological Works* (Oxford 1843–55), vol. ii, pp. 73, 75.

22 *Works* (Oxford 1855), vol. iv, p. 402.

23 *Fifty Sermons* (London 1710), pp. 357, 374.

24 *The Lambeth Conferences, 1867–1948*, p. 218.

25 William Beveridge, *Works* (Oxford 1842–48), vol. i, p. 11.

26 William Law, *Works* (London 1762, repr. 1892), vol. i, p. 8f.

27 Quoted by A. J. Mason, *The Church of England and Episcopacy* (Cambridge 1914), p. 410.

28 F. D. Maurice, *The Kingdom of Christ*, ed. A. R. Vidler (London 1958), vol. ii, p. 106.

29 *The Lambeth Conferences, 1867–1948*, Part II, p. 50.

PART SIX

Anglicanism in Practice

1 Anglican Spirituality

A. M. ALLCHIN

Bouyer, L., *Orthodox Spirituality and Protestant and Anglican Spirituality*. Burns and Oates 1966.

Lossky, N., *Lancelot Andrewes, Le Predicateur (1555–1626), Aux Sources de la Théologie Mystique de l'Église d'Angleterre*. Cerf 1986.

Loyer, O., *L'Anglicanisme de Richard Hooker*. Université de Lille 1979.

Martz, L. L., *The Poetry of Meditation: A Study in English Religious Literature of the Seventeenth Century*. Yale University Press 1954.

Moorman, J. R. H., *The Anglican Spiritual Tradition*. DLT 1983.

Prickett, S., *Romanticism and Religion: The Tradition of Coleridge and Wordsworth in the Victorian Church*. CUP 1976.

Stranks, C. J., *Anglican Devotion: Studies in the Spiritual Life of the Church of England between the Reformation and the Oxford Movement*. SCM Press 1961.

Thornton, M., *English Spirituality: An Outline of Ascetical Theology according to the English Pastoral Tradition*. SPCK 1963.

I

In 1869 Matthew Arnold began the preface to his book *Culture and Anarchy*, with an appeal to the SPCK to republish Bishop Thomas Wilson's *Maxims of Piety and Christianity*. It was a book which in Arnold's judgement was even more valuable than the Bishop's better-known collection of prayers, *Sacra Privata*; 'a sample of the very best perhaps, which our nation and race can do by way of religious writing'.[1] If Wilson was little known in 1869, at the end of a period of forty years which had seen an immense activity of republishing classical works of Anglican theology and spirituality from the sixteenth to the eighteenth centuries, it is certain that he is much less known today. As we shall see, the whole field of Anglican spirituality is one where a great deal of exploration remains to be done, and where many of the basic texts are simply inaccessible.

What was it that had caught the attention of the nineteenth-century poet and literary critic in the works of the eighteenth-century Bishop of Sodor and Man? Why should he refer so insistently to a book of private thoughts on religious questions at the start of a work which has as its subtitle, *An Essay in Political and Social Criticism*? Wilson, he tells us, drew his admiration because of the way in which he combines spiritual, intellectual and human qualities which are too often separated from one another. He joins 'ardour and unction' with

'downright honesty and plain good sense. With ardour and unction religion as we all know, may still be fanatical, with honesty and good sense it may still be prosaic ... Bishop Wilson's excellence lies in a balance of the four qualities, and in a fulness and

313

perfection of them ... His unction is so perfect and in such happy balance with his good sense, that it becomes tenderness and fervent charity. His good sense is so perfect, and in such happy alliance with his unction that it becomes moderation and insight.'[2]

Here is a picture of a character, rounded and complete, in which different elements, personal and social, active and meditative, human and divine are harmoniously blended and at one.

As we read on in Arnold's essay, we find, of course, other elements in Wilson's life and writing which had won Arnold's admiration. In the first place the Bishop seemed to him to embody a combination of what he called the Hebraic and Hellenic aspects of our Western tradition; the earnest striving after righteousness is there, but there is also the contemplation of the heavenly beauty, the recognition of God's glory at work in all things. Then, he provided a much-needed corrective to the unbridled individualism of the nineteenth century. He reminds us that we are members one of another.

Individual perfection [Arnold writes] is impossible so long as the rest of mankind are not perfected along with us ... And to this effect Bishop Wilson has striking words, 'It is not, says he, so much our neighbour's interest as our own that we love him.' And again, he says, 'Our salvation does in some measure depend upon that of others.'[3]

The inner life of the Christian is evidently in no way divorced from his social and political relations with his fellow men and women. But it was above all Wilson's living testimony to the importance of the inward life of prayer, reflection and meditation, which Arnold valued, constituting as it did a rebuke to the nineteenth century's obsession with organization and machinery, machinery often seen as an end in itself, 'most absurdly disproportioned to the end which this machinery, if it is to do any good at all, is to serve'.[4]

Against this whole tendency—which, we may remark, sounds remarkably twentieth-century—Arnold set his own idea of culture, 'a study of perfection, a perfection which consists in becoming something rather than having something, in an inward condition of the mind and spirit, not in an outward set of circumstances'.[5] This ideal is clearly formulated in Arnold's words and not in Wilson's. It has been purposely cut off from the dogmatic bases on which, in the Bishop's scheme of things, it firmly rests. Yet it is clearly not unrelated to the older ideal of Christian holiness, with perfection as its aim, an aim which involves being and becoming rather than possessing, and which makes much of the often neglected potential of the human heart and mind for development and growth. In our twentieth century many have felt a need for a recovery of the contemplative dimension of human life. Arnold does not use that word, but he seems in the nineteenth century to envisage a similar need and similar operation.

II

We have started from this point not only because, as we shall find, Matthew Arnold was remarkably perceptive in his discernment of some of the salient features of the Anglican spiritual tradition, but also because the very fact of such a tribute to a venerable churchman from a distinctly agnostic poet and literary critic is a sign of the close links which have existed between poetry and faith, literature and religion in the last four centuries of the Anglican tradition. In part, of course, these links have their origin in the Bible itself and in the central place which it has taken in the prayer and devotion of all the Reformation traditions. In England the period of translation which had begun with William Tyndale culminated in the splendour of the Authorized (or King James) Version (1611), which remained for three centuries unrivalled amongst English-speaking Christians.

Within Anglicanism the influence of the Bible was channelled and reinforced by the influence of a second book, scarcely less important in the formulation of Anglican tradition: the Book of Common Prayer. It was the genius of Cranmer to bring together into a single volume many different things: the texts necessary for the Sunday Eucharist, the texts for the daily office, the services for ordination, the occasional offices which accompany the believer from birth to burial. Thus there was, in the hands of any churchman who could read, a book which linked private with public prayer, which showed the Bible as a text to be used in worship and which embraced the whole range of human life, personal as well as social. It represented a balanced and inclusive vision of Christian prayer and worship. It is a work which has had great influence on those who use it, often unconsciously, occasionally consciously, as for instance W. E. Gladstone who as a young man on holiday in Naples in 1832 found himself reading the Prayer Book with new eyes.

'It presented to me Christianity under an aspect in which I had not yet known it; its ministry of symbols, its channels of grace, its unending line of teachers joining from the Head; a sublime construction, based throughout upon historic fact, uplifting the idea of the community in which we live, and of the access which it enjoys through the new and living way to the presence of the Most High.'[6]

Here in the Book of Common Prayer was a vision of the Church as a corporate reality at once of time and eternity, the context in which the individual finds his way to God, presented in pages of memorable prose, straightforward yet solemn.

This relationship between literature and faith implicit in the liturgy becomes explicit in the tradition of Anglican poetry and prose; in the series of distinctly theological poets, from John Donne, George Herbert or Henry Vaughan in the seventeenth century to T. S. Eliot, W. H. Auden and R. S. Thomas in our own day. It can be seen in the very quality of prose-writing to be found in this tradition, whether in theology, in preaching or in prayer and meditations. One might think of Hooker, Andrewes and Taylor or Traherne in the seventeenth century, of William Law in the eighteenth, of Coleridge and John Henry Newman in the nineteenth, of C. S. Lewis and Austin Farrer in our own day. This is a tradition which by its form as well as by its content seems to speak of a particular perception of the link between grace and nature, faith and culture, divine and human, which has been characteristic of Anglican spirituality as a whole, and has had its influence more widely in the intellectual history of the English-speaking world.

In our own century this relationship is found at its most fascinating in the life and work of T. S. Eliot. If Arnold in 1867 was anxious to record a sense of indebtedness to Thomas Wilson, how much greater was the debt which Eliot revealed to another and more distinguished bishop, in the little book which he published in 1927 called *For Lancelot Andrewes*. Arnold, at times, seems to be using his quotations from Wilson as pegs to hang his own ideas on. Eliot in his essay on Andrewes makes it clear that he is writing of a man to whom he feels he owes something of his life and sanity. This, after all, was the book in which Eliot announced his adherence to the Catholic faith. He has no use for Arnold's dream of 'culture' as an autonomous reality, which can take the place of religion. For him spirituality needs to be grounded in belief, prayer needs the support of dogma. And it is the peculiar fusion of faith and prayer, of theology and experience, of feeling and thinking which for him gives to Andrewes his power and authority. In Andrewes' sermons he finds a dogmatic-ecstatic quality which enables them to convey the truths which they expound, and as it were to embody them.

> To persons whose minds are habituated to feed on the vague jargon of our time, when we have a vocabulary for everything and exact ideas about nothing ... when the language of theology itself ... tends to become a language of tergiversation—Andrewes may seem pedantic and verbal. It is only when we have saturated ourselves in his prose, followed the movement of his thought, that we find his examination of words terminating in an ecstasy of assent. Andrewes takes a word and derives a world from it, squeezing and squeezing the word until it yields a full juice of meaning which we should never have supposed any word to possess.[7]

The many-faceted words of the Bible recover their full weight of meaning. So by a way which looks pedantic, but which in fact demands a great concentration, and is itself the product of a long discipline of prayer and study and meditation, Andrewes is able to enter into his subject and expand it from within. He can speak with the authority of one who has assimilated the things which he is speaking about. He does this by way of two unifications; first the unification of his own faculties, thinking, feeling and willing, into a single movement of assent and adoration, then the unification of himself with the subject which he is considering.

> When Andrewes begins his sermon, from beginning to end you are aware that he is wholly in his subject, unaware of anything else, that his emotion grows as he penetrates

more deeply into his subject, that he is finally 'alone with the Alone', with the mystery which he is seeking to grasp more and more firmly ... Andrewes' emotion is purely contemplative; it is not personal, it is wholly evoked by the object of contemplation to which it is adequate; his emotion is wholly contained and explained by its object.[8]

Here we have an expression of the indebtedness of one of the greatest poets of our century to the man who for him had come to stand for the tradition into which he entered. Eliot and Andrewes can tell us something both of theology and mysticism. I use the words together because only together will they do justice to the nature of Andrewes' teaching and his devotion, to that vision of faith which is enshrined in the *Preces Privatae* no less than in the sermons. The word 'mysticism', in all its variations, always implies unity or union between God and humankind, between the eternal and the temporal. But for Andrewes this unity is not the unity of identity, which is at the centre of the Eastern religions, it is the unity of co-inherence and communion of which the whole Christian tradition speaks. As Nicholas Lossky writes in his recent masterly study of the preaching of Lancelot Andrewes—a work with the significant sub-title, 'To the sources of the Mystical Theology of the Church of England':

The ultimate objective of the spiritual life being union with God, we can say that the theology of Lancelot Andrewes is a mystical theology, on condition of making some precision in the meaning of this term. It is not a case of an exceptional experience reserved for some, in some way outside the traditional paths of theology. On the contrary it is a question of the interiorisation of the revealed Christian mystery, to which Andrewes summons all the baptised. This theology is mystical in the sense that it is not an abstract reflection, but a way of living the mystery in the deepening of faith through prayer and the renunciation of ones own will ... For Andrewes it is entirely evident that this is only possible in fidelity to the data of revelation, that is to say in the biblical and patristic tradition, i.e. in the catholicity of the Church.[9]

If Matthew Arnold in his praise of Thomas Wilson has drawn our attention to the Anglican desire for moderation and wholeness, to the longing for a just balance between the things of this world and the things of the world to come, Eliot in his assessment of Andrewes has made us recognize a deeply mystical element, present in the teaching of the seventeenth-century bishop, but never wholly absent from Anglican spirituality since. This is a dimension of Anglican devotion which has often been overlooked. Some of the standard works on the subject have nothing to say on it. But if one looks deeply into the writings of Charles Wesley or William Law in the eighteenth century, and E. B. Pusey, R. M. Benson or B. F. Westcott in the nineteenth, it is difficult not to recognize its presence. In our own century it may be seen in writers as different as Evelyn Underhill, Charles Williams and Michael Ramsey. It was indeed not altogether absent from Thomas Wilson himself, for all his good sense and downright honesty. Among his maxims we find 'The end of Christianity is to perfect the human nature by participation of the divine.'[10]

In the last ten or fifteen years it has become common to recognize the influence of the fourteenth-century mystics in the development of English Christianity. Perhaps it is time for us to recognize a constant vein of mystical religion in our inheritance, not only in great but relatively isolated figures like George Fox and William Blake, but in many whose lives lay much nearer to the centre of the mainstream of religious life, who like Andrewes had an intense concern for the unity and catholicity of the Church. To do this would involve a considerable alteration in our picture of ourselves and who we are.

III

We have looked at the work of two eminent poets and critics whose writings are studied wherever English language and literature are studied. We have seen their evaluation of two Anglican bishops whose works are very little known, even in Anglican centres of theological learning. We have come across one of the salient facts about the Anglican tradition of spirituality. In this century it has been much more intensively studied in departments of English literature than in departments of theology. This has been the case not only in Britain and the United States of America, but also in countries as widely separated as Canada, Australia and Japan. Indeed two of the fundamental studies for an understanding of the theological bases of Anglican spirituality have been written in the English departments of universities in France, and though published in French, have not become available in English. To one of these we have already referred, Nicolas Lossky, *Lancelot Andrewes, Le Predicateur, Aux Sources de la theologie mystique de l'Eglise d'Angleterre* (Paris 1986). To the other we shall shortly turn: Olivier Loyer, *L'Anglicanisme de Richard Hooker* (Lille/Paris 1979).

But first we must ask what it is that attracts students of English literature and civilization to the study of Anglican spirituality and theology, as it manifests itself in the work of the seventeenth-century poets, but not only there. There is evidently something in this tradition which has the effect of linking prayer and devotion with theological reflection and learning. There is something here which seems to activate and transform the human imagination. These are often learned writers steeped not only in the knowledge of the Bible, but also of the Christian tradition both in its patristic and scholastic phases. We may remark in passing that this capacity of the Anglican tradition to give rise to works of great artistic distinction, is evident also in the field of music. From the Reformation until today, there has been a constant tradition of liturgical music, centred in the English cathedrals, and spreading far beyond them. The creativity of this tradition is seen in the fact that it continued to flourish during those periods of the eighteenth and nineteenth century when the composition of secular music seemed almost dead in England. What is the root of this persistent capacity to stimulate the creation of works of art directly linked to the prayer of the Church?

There are of course many factors involved in such a cultural phenomenon, but at their heart we can surely see the primary influence of the greatest of Anglican theologians since the Reformation, Richard Hooker. In one sense Hooker is a humanist. He defends the rights of human reason, of civil laws, of the historic experience of nations, of the traditions of the churches against the criticisms of a form of Calvinism which was already tending to exalt God at the expense of man, to insist one-sidedly on the supremacy of revelation over reason. He is, as Loyer puts it, in his penetrating and detailed study of his thought, a thinker for whom the categories of conjunction and participation are vital at many different levels.

So the disjunctions which in the course of sixteenth-century controversy had become sharpened and hardened, between Scripture and tradition, between grace and nature, between the inward and the outward elements in prayer and worship, and finally between faith and religion, are consistently rejected by Hooker. Always he seeks to unite the two. Hence his high estimate of what we should call culture, his positive evaluation of human wisdom. These things are indeed the works of man, but they are the works of man inspired and sustained by God. For, in the end, Hooker's humanism is a very particular form of humanism—a theocentric humanism. As C. S. Lewis remarks, 'Few model universes are more filled—one might say, more drenched—with Deity than his. "All things that are of God," (and only sin is not) "have God in them and he them in himself likewise", yet "their substance and his wholly differeth." God is unspeakably transcendent; but also unspeakably immanent.'[11]

We must notice too how large a part of the *Laws of Ecclesiastical Polity* is devoted to the defence of the Church's tradition of prayer and worship. In this defence, Hooker is always tracing back particular points of controversy—about sacred times and sacred places for instance—to the theological principles which lie behind them. In his defence of the Book of Common Prayer, a whole understanding of human nature is implicit; it is a nature which is social as well as personal, which needs to express itself outwardly as well as inwardly. The deep roots of prayer for Hooker are to be found in the very nature of humankind; we are creatures whose end is God himself, made with a longing to go beyond ourselves into God. Loyer argues that in Book V, Hooker links the elements of preaching and doctrine in worship with the elements of prayer and sacrament, uniting them into a single movement of divine initiative and human response.

> The great texts on the divine participation and presence, that is to say on the reciprocal relations of God and man complete naturally those which define the relations between doctrine and prayer. The internal logic which prolongs the mystery of the Word and of Prayer in the mystery of the Eucharist becomes clearly evident to the reader. The progress of thought makes the eucharistic sacrament the completion of the liturgical

celebration, the theology of the incarnation, and the fulfilment of the theology of the Word and Prayer.[12]

So God's taking our nature in the incarnation of the Son, his imparting of that nature through the preaching of the word and the celebration of the sacraments which make us members of Christ, has as its consequence our humanity's return to God, the return for which our whole being longs.

Hooker insists that it is the whole man who is caught up into this activity of worship, not heart alone, nor mind and will alone, but all together in a movement in which the body and the senses have their part. This is the point of his celebrated passage in praise of music, which is more than simply an example of his style at its most eloquent and elaborate. As so often happens in his writing, Platonist and Aristotelian motifs are fused in the same paragraph, which celebrates the place of music not only in worship but in all human life.

> More than the other arts, it has this faculty to integrate contemplative reason and sensory perception; it is harmony and proportion, it speaks to the highest part of the soul, evoking the divine perfection; but first of all it speaks to man's inferior faculties and makes use of their power.[13]

It touches the heights of the spirit by touching the senses and emotions. So there is in music an analogy with the sacraments, which also stoop to our bodily nature in order to arrive at the inmost secrets of our spiritual being.

All this, it may be complained, is a tradition which is excessively elitist; a tradition of learned poets, of aristocratic devotion, of cathedral music. That there is some element of truth in such an allegation it is impossible to deny. But it is certainly nothing like the whole truth. For this tradition of faith and prayer affirms that God is to be found in all creatures. There is in it an awareness of the sacramental quality of all things, both in the sense that the sacrament of Holy Communion has universal application, and in the sense that the whole world is intended to be the vehicle of God's presence to us.

In the eighteenth century a verse from Charles Wesley's 'Hymns on the Lord's Supper' gives striking evidence of the first conviction:

> Return and with thy people sit
> Lord of the sacramental feast,
> And satiate us with heavenly meat
> And make the *world* thy happy guest.[14]

(italics original)

Christ's presence in the midst of his people is to result in the calling together of the nations into the feast of the kingdom. This conviction takes new form in the nineteenth century, in the preaching of F. D. Maurice and his successors in the Christian Socialist movement. For them, the sacrament is the sign and symbol of all human sharing.

But perhaps still more important in Anglican tradition is the conviction that all things may become sacraments to us, meeting-places between God and man. In the seventeenth century, George Herbert writes,

> All may of thee partake
> Nothing can be so mean
> That with this tincture 'For thy sake'
> Will not grow bright and clean.[15]

So the most menial daily tasks may become divine. Two centuries later, the same thought is expressed by John Keble in an even more familiar verse:

> The trivial round, the common task
> Will furnish all we ought to ask,
> Room to deny ourselves, a road
> To bring us daily nearer God.[16]

In a paradoxical way, John Keble, in Newman's judgement the true and primary author of the Oxford Movement, testifies to this sense of God's presence in all things and in all people at the very moment when he might seem to be most enmeshed in the old, literary culture of the Anglican tradition. Keble had been Professor of Poetry at Oxford, and according to the established custom he delivered his lectures in Latin, and in Latin they were published in 1844. Not till 1911 did an English translation appear. But these lectures were dedicated to one of the greatest, if not the greatest of the English romantic poets, William Wordsworth. The terms in which this dedication is phrased demand our careful attention in the context of this study.

> To William Wordsworth / True philosopher and inspired poet / Who by the special gift and calling of Almighty God / Whether he sang of man or of nature / Failed not to lift up man's heart to holy things / Nor ever ceased to champion the cause / Of the poor and simple / And so in perilous times was raised up / To be a chief minister / Not only of sweetest poetry / But also of high and sacred truth....[17]

Here the Christian priest pays tribute to the Christian poet, and recognizes how closely their callings are interwoven. Here, in particular, he celebrates the poet's gift to lift our hearts and minds to the things of eternity through the things of time, and acknowledges his calling to champion the cause of the poor and simple. The Oxford Movement began in a very academic milieu. It was a movement of the mind and spirit. But it soon had the effect of driving men and women out into the slums of nineteenth-century England and out onto the frontier of the new West in the United States, in service of their fellow human beings, because it was clearly seen, as Thomas Wilson had taught, that the salvation of each one is bound up with the salvation of all and that 'our life is with our brother'. So as Louis Bouyer commented in his study of Newman:

> The most powerful, and also the most respectable attraction of the new movement was to put forward and multiply examples of a Christianity which was at one and the same time eager for holiness and creative of it. It was the demands which this religion made,

not simply in the abstract, but immediately and in practice which gained for it such enthusiastic and effective support.[18]

All human faculties, affective as well as intellectual, active as well as contemplative were involved in this movement.

IV

In this essay we have considered some of the salient features of the Anglican spiritual tradition over the last four centuries, in particular its search for wholeness and balance, its desire at once to spread itself outwards in a concern for all human life, and at the same time to turn inwards to explore the heights and depths of the mystery of God's presence at the heart of human life. We have seen how close have been the links between spirituality and literature, not only in the century between 1590 and 1690, but in a variety of ways ever since. Throughout the centuries there has been the practice both of the inner life of prayer and meditation, and of the outward life of liturgy and service in the world, which has been reflected in manuals of devotion, commentaries on Scripture and the Prayer Book, collections of sermons and meditations, works of poetry and prose alike. In our own day too, particularly in the last twenty years, there has been a new flowering of this tradition of reflective spirituality and spiritual theology, which we can see in writers as diverse as Alan Ecclestone, W. H. Vanstone, Monica Furlong, Kenneth Leech and Rowan Williams. Much, of course, has not been said here. Whole schools of spiritual writing, the Cambridge Platonists of the seventeenth century, the Evangelicals and Methodists of the eighteenth, and the later development of Anglo-Catholicism in the nineteenth have been passed over in silence. The central place of Coleridge in the literary and religious history of the nineteenth century has only been hinted at.

We have however begun to glimpse the fact that Anglicans are heirs to a tradition of which at the present they are often almost unaware. There is here a need for a recovery of memory, which will allow for a recovery of identity. We need to make an act of *anamnesis* of the presence and power of God not only in the lives of men and women in the Old and New Testament periods, but in the subsequent history of the Church. Voices speak to us from our own past with words which we should be able to hear today. We have thought of the influence of Lancelot Andrewes in the development of T. S. Eliot's religious faith. It is no less a striking fact that it was some lines of George Herbert which marked a decisive point in the spiritual journey of Simone Weil. Such texts need to be made available for others.

We have spoken here of bishops whose names are now scarcely known. Let us conclude with another of them, Edward Reynolds, who was Bishop of Norwich from 1660 to 1676. Perhaps because during the Commonwealth period he conformed to the presbyterian arrangements then in force, perhaps for other reasons, he has been almost wholly neglected. All Anglicans owe him a debt of gratitude for two of the best-loved prayers of the 1662 Prayer Book, the General Thanksgiving and the Prayer for All Sorts and Conditions of Men—prayers which have been adapted in the new liturgical formularies. Fifty years ago, P. E. More and F. L. Cross included four extracts of his writings in their anthology, *Anglicanism*. From them one could grasp something of the beauty of his style, the depth of his insight, the extent of his learning and the clarity of his mind. These qualities become more evident when we begin to read him at length, whether in his sermons or in his more formal treatises, as for instance on *The Passions and Faculties of the Soul of Man*.

The work of such a man who can speak of the mercy of God in the sacraments as he does, is not of mere historical interest.

> It were almost a contradiction in anything save God's mercy, to be so deep that no thought can fathom it, and yet so obvious that each eye may see it . . . so humble is his mercy, that since we can not raise our understandings to the comprehension of divine mysteries, he will bring down and submit those mysteries to the apprehension of our senses.[19]

He is one who speaks of the beauty of God revealed alike in his work of creation and redemption in terms such as these:

> The sum and total of all God's works are the world and the church; the world is called *kosmos* for the beauty and comeliness of it; in which everything was very good when the Lord took a view of it. But the Lord has chosen his church upon which to bestow more abundant glory . . . In the world we have the foot-prints of his greatness; but in the church we have the image of his holiness.[20]

Above all, he is one who can speak of God's love as that living centre around which all other human loves can find their meaning and direction:

> The master-wheel or first mover in all the regular motions of this passion is the love of God, grounded on the right knowledge of him; whereby the soul being ravished with the apprehension of his infinite goodness is earnestly drawn and 'called out', as it were, to desire a union and participation of his glory and presence; yielding up itself unto him (for by love a man giveth himself to the thing he loves), and conforming all its actions and affections to his will . . . And therefore the wise man, speaking of the love and fear of God, tells us, that it is *totum hominis*, the whole of man . . . to love any creature either without God, or above God, is *cupiditas*, lust, which is the 'formale' of every sin, whereby we turn from God to other things, but to love the creatures under God, in their right order—and for God, to their right end (for he made all things for himself) this is *caritas*, true and regular love.[21]

In affirming the possibility of humankind to love and know God, the capacity of the human person for union and participation in the divine glory and presence, and in affirming that this possibility is the only true and ultimate fulfilment of the deepest longing of the human heart and mind, the Anglican spiritual tradition is asserting nothing that is not universally Christian. But in the insistence that all things created can be loved in and for God, a point which Reynolds makes in many different contexts, there is perhaps an emphasis which is peculiar to this particular way of prayer and faith, a longing to gather together the fullness of the created order in all its diversity, into the unity of the Kingdom.

> And it is the wonder of love (as St. Chrysostom speaketh) to collect and knit together in one things separated from each other. Wherein stands the mystery of the communion of the church on earth, both with itself, and in all the dispersed members of it, and with Christ the head, and with that other part of it which triumpheth in heaven.[22]

NOTES

1 Matthew Arnold. *Culture and Anarchy: An Essay in Political and Social Criticism*, ed. J. Dover Wilson (Cambridge 1932), p. 4.

2 ibid., p. 5.

3 ibid., p. 192.

4 ibid., p. 50.

5 ibid., p. 48.

6 John Morley, *The Life of William Ewart Gladstone* (1903), vol. i, pp. 87–8.

7 T. S. Eliot, *For Lancelot Andrewes* (1927), p. 16.

8 ibid., p. 17f.

9 Nicolas Lossky, *Lancelot Andrewes, Le Predicateur (1555–1626)* (Paris 1986), p. 327.

10 Thomas Wilson, *Maxims of Piety and Christianity*, ed. F. Relton (1898), p. 27.

11 C. S. Lewis, *English Literature in the Sixteenth Century excluding Drama* (Oxford 1954), pp. 459–60.

12 Olivier Loyer, *L'Anglicanisme de Richard Hooker* (Lille/Paris 1979), vol. i. p. 447.

13 ibid., p. 474.

14 J. E. Rattenbury, *The Eucharistic Hymns of John and Charles Wesley* (1948), p. 249.

15 *Hymns Ancient and Modern, New Standard* (Norwich 1983), No. 240.

16 ibid., No. 2.

17 Quoted in Stephen Prickett, *Romanticism and Religion, The Tradition of Coleridge and Wordsworth in the Victorian Church* (CUP 1976), p. 109.

18 Louis Bouyer, *Newman* (1951), p. 223.

19 P. E. More and F. L. Cross, eds., *Anglicanism* (Milwaukee 1935; repr. London 1962), p. 410.

20 ibid., p. 771.

21 Edward Reynolds, *The Whole Works* (1826), vol. vi. pp. 61–2.

22 ibid., p. 73.

2 Anglican Morality

PAUL ELMEN

Elmen, P., ed., *The Anglican Moral Choice.* Wilton, Conn., Morehouse-Barlow, 1983.

Browning, D., *The Moral Content of Pastoral Care.* Philadelphia, Westminster Press, 1976.

Kirk, K., *Conscience and its Problems. An Introduction to Casuistry.* London, Longmans, Green and Co. 1927.

McAdoo, F. R., *The Structure of Caroline Moral Theology.* London, Longmans, Green and Co., 1949.

Reckitt, M. B., *Maurice to Temple. A Century of the Social Movement in the Church of England.* London, Faber and Faber, 1947.

Temple, W., *Christianity and Social Order.* Harmondsworth, Penguin Books 1942.

To ask what kind of moral theory and what kind of moral acts are distinctly Anglican is to invite a dubious answer. There is a cluster of possible replies, each heavily dependent on the type of churchmanship of the respondent, on his theological presuppositions, and also on the prejudices buried in the period in which he speaks. There is no uniform Anglican morality in theory, much less in practice. But it is also true that moralism has been a traditional preoccupation of Anglicans, and in each century Anglicans have made a contribution towards understanding the unending ambiguities of translating the love of God into some sort of appropriate specific decision or concrete action. Some of those contributions bear recounting, if only, as Hooker said in his *Laws of Ecclesiastical Polity*, 'that posterity may know we have not loosely through silence permitted things to pass away as in a dream'.[1]

A few common threads may be detected. The goal of *via media* is the effort to establish an identity which is both Catholic and Reformed, yet in a special sense neither. In moral theology this called for a middle ground between authority and liberty. Paul Elmer More said, in the anthology *Anglicanism*, that the effort might be seen as political, resisting the claims of both Rome and Geneva; or it may have been as John Donne admitted, a convenient way of avoiding difficulties. But a more adequate account would be the one More settled for, that the aim of *via media* was 'to introduce into religion, and to base upon "the light of reason", that love of balance, restraint, moderation, measure, which from sources beyond our reckoning appear to be innate in the English temper'.[2] The hallmark of Anglican morality has been the *aurea mediocritas*, the Golden Mean, the measure of nothing too much.

Another major theme, present in Anglican moral treatises from the beginning, is the insistence on the priority of *praxis* over *theoria*. According to Paul Elmer More, 'If we are looking for a single term to denote the ultimate law of Anglicanism, I do not see that we can do better than adopt a title which offers itself as peculiarly descriptive . . .; I refer to the title "pragmatism".'[3]

The preference for pragmatic application rather than speculative insight is not of course an Anglican innovation. It appears with varying emphases in all the world's religions. Monotheism did not appear upon the world scene as a metaphysical theory, but was from the beginning a way of life. It was the central idea that animated the prophets and the later Talmudic sages. John reported that Jesus knew well that divine knowledge was possible only after the test of action: 'If any man will do his will he shall know the doctrine, whether it be of God, or whether I speak of myself' (John 7.17). British temperament was especially hospitable to such biblical ideals, and some empiricists went so far as to claim that all knowledge came from experience. The motto scientists chose for the Royal Society was *Nullius in Verba*.

Pragmatic priority became a characteristic of British cultural history, and Anglican morality may be understood as its expression in religious form (see pp. 178–9). In the fourteenth century, William Langland's *Piers Plowman* pointed to the power of goodness resident in every human being, enabling him to do what he needed to do in order to be saved; in Langland's view even ploughing a field had spiritual significance. The theological unity of the feudal-monarchial world characteristic of the Middle Ages was never completely dissipated in England by the advent of bourgeois democracy and the industrial age. Churchmen thought that making a moral protest against the injustice of secular society was not irrelevant to Christian theology, but instead was derived directly from it. Reinhold Niebuhr concluded that: 'From Gerald Winstanley, the leader of the Diggers in the seventeenth century, through Keir Hardie, Robert Smillie, Arthur Henderson, George Lansbury, Stafford Cripps, and Acland in the past decades, British Christianity, whether sectarian or state church, has generated prophets of religio-social criticism.' Niebuhr offered a plausible guess: 'It may be that the unbroken character of the Christian ethos in Britain is also the cause of the unbroken sociopolitical history since 1688.'[4] What Niebuhr describes is the distinctive Church–world relationship of what Ernst Troeltsch called the *church-type*, in comparison with the *sect-type*. In the former the organizational structure of the Church is formally related to the political power of the society, and so is 'established', and seeming to be, in the eyes of Free-Church people, 'worldly'.

Theology which expressed itself not as concept but as deed was a favourite seventeenth-century Anglican theme. Illustrations can be chosen almost at random. The comment of John Smith, one of the Cambridge Platonists, may serve as typical. Christ, he said, did not spell out canons, articles of belief, and codes of conduct. The reason is that he was 'not so careful to stock and enrich the World with Opinions and Notions, as with true Piety, and a Godlike pattern of purity, as the best way to thrive in all spiritual understandings. His main scope was to promote an *Holy Life*.'[5] George Herbert's 'The Elixir' is perhaps the best known poetical example of the Caroline translation of theory into praxis:

> Teach me, my God and King,
> In all things thee to see,
> And what I do in any thing,
> To do it as for thee . . .
>
> A servant with this clause
> Makes drudgerie divine;
> Who sweeps a room, as for thy laws,
> Makes that and th' action fine.

Jeremy Taylor's *The Rule and Exercise of Holy Living* (1650) may be considered the paradigmatic Anglican theological statement for the Christian morality of the period. It may be that the period of the interregnum, which turned the Church of England into a conclave and made formal priestly guidance impossible, was the immediate occasion of Taylor's book. There was widespread Anglican scorn for Puritan theology, which could express itself as regicide. But this very occasionalism is one of the aspects of the continuing Anglican reference of theological reflection to life structures. *Holy Living* carried on the tradition prominent since the English Reformation, and stressed by Colet, Erasmus, and More; that morality should be in the foreground of the Church's attention, while dogma was kept in the shade.

The insistence that practice determine the soundness of doctrine carried with it certain risks. For example, Jeremy Taylor was hostile to the doctrine of original sin, not because it was theologically unsound, but because it could be used to justify evil living. Such Pelagianism may have cost him a bishopric in England. The Caroline ethicists were hostile to the Roman Catholic doctrine of deathbed repentance, in our time illustrated in Evelyn Waugh's novel *Brideshead Revisited*. The Carolines would have said that Sebastian's reliance on a last-minute forgiveness leaned too heavily on the example of the thief on the cross. It wiped out the sinner's need for a reformed life, and so represented imperfect contrition. Taylor was sure that immorality was proof of heresy: 'Because faith is not only a precept of doctrine but of manners and holy life, whatsoever is either opposite to an article of Creed, or teaches ill life, that's heresy.'[6]

Critics have not been wanting, even among Anglicans, who claim that this preference for morality over doctrine had disastrous consequences, leading, as Bellarmine claimed, to 'nipping at the name of Christ'. The charge has been that the teaching of such radical immanence led to the Deism of the eighteenth century, and to the secularism of the twentieth. But the benefits of this dominant morality were also visible. Casuistry became most important, and the necessity of a good life, especially of sound social conduct, had the effect of vivifying the gospel. When dogma had a diminished role, tolerance became more common. In any case, Anglicanism developed its distinctive moral style, a kind of sober ecstasy, a way in which rational men and women could lead a 'godly, righteous, and sober life' (Book of Common Prayer). The recognition of the incarnation, the point where the Word became enfleshed, required a union between asceticism and morality, turning the model from a juristic to a pastoral form, and serving to enliven both sermons and the spread of lay vocations.

Of course the recommendation that Christians should live their faith rather than simply to profess it called immediately for a supplementary guide. Missing from this formula was elucidation on what constituted a Christian life, and some form of criteria for evaluating whether or not that goal was achieved. What after all was the distinctive character of a holy deed? After Plato, how could any particularity adequately reflect the holy will of God? From such questions the Middle Ages developed the science of moral theology, deductive, rational, Aristotelian-Thomistic. As H. R. McAdoo has pointed out in this primary account, *The Structure of Caroline Moral Theology* (1949), Caroline moral theory was both derivative and innovative in regard to Roman Catholic antecedents. Thomas Aquinas suited exactly an essential Anglican need, that of recognizing the presence of divine grace without at the same time denying efficacy of created nature and natural laws. In Aquinas' wide embrace the order of creation bedded happily with the order of redemption. The formal cause was man, a rational animal, finding himself a part of the cosmic order which had been laid down by God, and expected to take his appropriate place in the march toward fulfilment and perfection. The literary world reflected the basic anthropology. The Shakespearean plays turn on the assumption of a cosmic order which could be denied, but only at the cost of chaos and death. If one challenged that intimate connection, as Ulysses said in *The Tragedy of Troilus and Cressida*,

> Strength should be lord of imbecility,
> And the rude son should strike his father dead.[7]

That mysterious stay against chaos called Order was not thought to be a human contrivance, but a divine plan. Despite minor differences, detected by any close study in the moral theory of Richard Hooker, Jeremy Taylor, Robert Sanderson, and Joseph Hall, it was a major theme of the seventeenth century. The question of one's exact status in the Order remained unanswered. In the absence of any announced hierarchy, and without a developed casuistry supported by authoritative ecclesiastical rewards and punishments, the way in which *synderesis* (cosmic order) related to *syneidesis* (application to concrete cases) remained uncertain, and Anglicans were forced to rely on the conscience as the instrument of moral decisions. Three important Anglican works dealt with the problem: Sanderson's *De Obligatione Conscientiae* and Taylor's *Ductor Dubitantium* (both published in 1660); and Kenneth Kirk's *Conscience and Its Problems* (1927).

The Caroline period was not only produrtive in casuistry and in metaethical reflection, but also in a fruitful penetration of political structures by the clergy. Richard Bancroft, an early Bishop of London, licensed books, watched ports for seditious literature, and led a mission which negotiated a treaty with the Dutch. William Juxon, a later Bishop of London, had the care of the nation's treasury as part of his charge. William Laud was Archbishop of Canterbury, but he was also Chancellor of the University of Oxford and a member of the Privy Council, High Commission, and Star Chamber. The line which separated sacred from secular activity was indistinct.

The eighteenth century was very concerned with the role that reason should play in determining Christian theology and lifestyle. Anglicans since Richard Hooker had challenged a naive bibliolatry, and had insisted that divine truth was accessible to man not only by revelation, but, as Aquinas had said, by the very nature of law. This law could be grasped by natural reason. Bishop Joseph Butler (1692–1752) played a leading role in demonstrating that moral obligation is an essential feature of the rational universe. But he was not a Deist, and had no confidence in the use of reason which was unrelated to divine law. In sermons preached at the Rolls Chapel in Salisbury between 1718 and 1726, and in a crucial essay, 'On the Nature of Virtue' appended to his *Analogy of Religion* (1736), he argued that rules of nature and supernature, body and spirit, self-love and benevolence, were not opposed polarities but were supplementary to each other. Something primal and self-evident in human nature, which was created by God, provided the grounds on which the morality of an action must be judged. 'Man', he said, 'hath the rule of right within; what is wanting is only that he honestly attend to it.'[8]

The seventeenth and eighteenth centuries made notable strides in the direction of a reasonable faith, but some people judged Anglicanism to be too earthbound, a victim of its own formal theory. It could not match sectarians in the areas of doctrinal conviction, emotional warmth, and personal salvation. The Church, some thought, needed to recapture its ancient authority, and if the world were again to be shaken by what William Wilberforce called 'vital Christianity', it would surely not be by appeals to common sense. Two forms of the revisionary mood in the nineteenth century were the Evangelical Revival and the Oxford Movement.

The sustained supranaturalism of Evangelicalism, its concern for inward feeling and personal holiness and its goal of individual salvation in the next life, seemed to promise few resources for healing the social illnesses of the new century, or even recognizing that they existed. There was suffering in the cities following the Industrial Revolution, and neither casuistry nor conversion promised social reform. Fortunately, the Anglican concern for life structures, surviving from an earlier methodology, remained strong, even in sectarian circles. *The Christian Observer*, the Evangelical trade journal, and the Cambridge Evangelicals were very clear that conversion indeed meant love, but love informed with knowledge, and knowledge translated into deed. The theology led to a renewed social concern, exactly as it had done to the fourteenth-century *Devotio moderna*, the Brothers of the Common Life. Very like too, the Jewish Hasidim, founded as a reaction to the excessive rationalism of the Torah, and emerging in the eighteenth century as a transfiguration of common activities. Thomas Scott's *Commentary on the Bible* (1792), which served as a primary reference text for the Clapham Sect, is proof enough that early Evangelicalism did not neglect social duties. From these foes of the Enlightenment emerged in brilliant succession the beginnings of public education and the attacks on the slave trade. Regardless of their concern for a personal ethic of holiness rather than for communal obligations of love, it was the Evangelicals who reformed prisons, supported factory laws, and started charities aimed at cushioning blows suffered by the victims of the new urban slums.

The Oxford Movement had its own seriousness, but it was in the beginning more concerned with the authority of the Church and the recovery of ritual. There was at first little understanding that the function of liturgy is to send people into the world to practice love. Keble praised Hooker's 'practical good sense' when he observed that 'the poor should be good at fasting. Since their perpetual fasts are necessary, [they] may with better contentment endure the hunger, which virtue causes others to choose.'[9] But the second generation Tractarians were a different breed, interested in ritual, but only because it reinforced charity. Father A. H. Mackonochie of St Albans, Holborn, went together with another East Londoner, Charles Lowder, to Keble's funeral in 1866. R. W. Church, the historian, wrote to another first-generation Tractarian, John Copeland, that the younger crowd seemed like good fellows, but looked at him darkly.

One of the many benefits of the Oxford Movement was a recovery of the Caroline tradition of moral theology. It began with James Skinner, *Synopsis of Moral and Ascetical Theology* (1870), and reached its full flowering in the 1920s, under the inspiration of Kenneth Kirk, the Bishop of Oxford. He produced a series of primary books describing the concern for social conduct which had its roots in divine revelation: *Some Principles of Moral Theology* (1920), *Ignorance, Faith and Confession* (1925), *Conscience and Its Problems* (1927), and the climactic *Vision of God* (1931). His successor, Robert C. Mortimer, Regius Professor of Moral and Pastoral Theology at Oxford, was rather less critical of formalism and code morality, and was a more devoted Thomist; but he was also a primary Anglican moral theologian.

During the twentieth century the mood of Anglican moral theology, following a similar trend in world Christianity, has been away from identifying code principles as immutable and objective, though many continued to think of them as such imitating Aristotle, the followers of Thomas Aquinas, and Kant. The new impulse was to find moral guidance from history and evolving experience. Morality continued to be pragmatic, and the accepted trade terms were such words as empiricist, relativistic, personalistic, and dialogical. Even Kirk pronounced a requiem for the older moral theology: 'The clear-cut classification of scholastic theology about virtue, vice, stages of progress, operations of grace and the like, proved inadequate to the delicate phenomena they were intended to define; today they are half-forgotten and wholly inoperative.'[10]

Running parallel with the Tractarians' plea for the authority of the Church, new voices challenged Establishment shibboleths and began asking embarrassing questions about the relationship of the Church to property and wealth. Actually closer to Cardinal Manning than to the early Tractarians, the Christian Socialists were a new breed of pragmatists. J. M. Ludlow had experienced personally the cruel suffering of the poor in the early nineteenth century, and he was sure that society needed to be remade rather than rehabilitated. His companion, F. D. Maurice, was rather less radical than Ludlow, but he too chose the same usable element from the Anglican past, and called for social reform based on Christian principles. He founded Producers' Cooperatives and the Working Men's College.

According to M. B. Reckitt, 'Maurice's capacity to be what he was and to lead as he did arose from no special interest or knowledge of social questions, but from a profound grasp of the answers which God in Christ had already given.'[11] Other stalwarts, such as Charles Kingsley and E. Vansittart Neale, followed Maurice's lead, defining each in his own way a renewed Christianity which could be called muscular. Various kinds of churchmanship were engaged in this renewal. The Anglo-Catholic, Charles Gore, thought it obvious that social justice was not an adventitious addition to the gospel, but was its essential element. In his report to the Church Congress in 1896, he said that the principle of the incarnation was denied unless the Christian spirit could be allowed to concern itself with everything that interests and touches human life. He thought that *Catholicism* should be defined as the religious term for *brotherhood*.

The way had been cleared for the Conference on Politics, Economy, and Citizenship (COPEC) which met in Birmingham in 1924. It had been sponsored by a vigorous ecumenical group called the Collegium, and its chairman was William Temple, the Archbishop of York. Fifteen hundred delegates, many from foreign countries, met to give formal attention to the claim of Jesus Christ that he was the Way, the Truth, and the Life. COPEC asserted the social relevance of the gospel, and brought cultural, economic, and political problems under Christian scrutiny. It had lasting influence, though perhaps its more important contribution was to the new ecumenical movement.

Two decades later, at the beginning of World War II, the time seemed ripe for the recovery of the COPEC vision. According to William Temple, 'Few of the younger generation have heard of C.O.P.E.C.; fewer still know what was said there. They do not know of the great tradition of Christian social teaching associated with the names of Ludlow, Maurice, Kingsley, Westcott, Gore, Scott Holland.'[12] The intention at Malvern was also to pay more attention to the theological reference of ethical decisions, the divine intentions as visible in the natural order. 'Our concern', said Temple, 'was to find a Christian remedy for specific evils rather than to examine the whole order of existing society in the light of the intrinsically right relation of the various functions of society— financial, productive, distributive, cultural, spiritual—to one another.'[13] All were to be addressed with one purpose—the way in which God's kingdom might best be served.

The difficulty at Malvern did not arise out of the contention that political questions are primarily theological, but rather with the question of which political formula would best serve the coming Kingdom. All agreed on the goal of a more just order in society, but the fundamental means of establishing such an order was questionable. At Malvern there were conservatives such as T. S. Eliot, ardent socialists such as Sidney Dark, editor of the *Church Times*, and common ownership advocates such as Sir Richard Acland. The latter invented a new word: 'The private ownability of the major resources of our country is indeed the stumbling block which is making it harder for us to advance towards the Kingdom of God on earth.'[14]

Temple was able to get all the delegates to approve the *Malvern Manifesto* which came out of the conference, though there were some abstentions, and some, like T. S. Eliot and Alec Vidler, repudiated it later. Temple used what he called his 'parlour trick', but which was really the use of 'middle axioms' first used by J. H. Oldham in 1937. Oldham had defined them as compromises 'between purely general statements of the ethical demands of the gospel and the decisions that have to be made in concrete situations ... They are not binding for all time, but are provisional definitions ...'[15] Temple changed Acland's private ownership 'is indeed the stumbling block' to 'may be such a stumbling block.' He had found the uneasy middle ground between the concrete decision which would offend some well-meaning Christians, and Thomas Aquinas' primary natural law: that good must be sought for and evil avoided. After Malvern the Church could still retreat into its normal enclave, wasting its energy on such topics as the wording of the Prayer Book, or the sex of its priesthood; but after Malvern, it could not do so gracefully. It could not forget the deep Anglican tradition of a firm biblical faith which expressed itself in historical concern. And Temple's conclusion after Malvern seems more than ever decisive:

The Church must announce Christian principles and point out where the existing social order at any time is in conflict with them. It must then pass on to Christian citizens, acting in their civic capacity, the task of reshaping the existing order in closer conformity to the principles.[16]

In the United States, Christian Socialism had no such charismatic leader as William Temple, and it confronted a more resolute opposition. But here also there were brave priests willing to pay the price for challenging an entrenched capitalism. In the late nineteenth century, at New York City's Grace Church, Henry Codman Potter set out to serve as many as possible of his parishioners' needs, whether they be physical, social, intellectual, or more familiarly, spiritual. There were others: George C. Hodges at Calvary Church, Pittsburgh (later Dean of Episcopal Theological School), Philo W. Sprague, William D. P. Bliss, Frederic Dan Huntington, Henry S. Nash, William Scarlett, and several others whose names are recorded in the Book of Life. Reinhold Niebuhr said that his interest in the relevance of theology to industrial injustice was given its early impetus by the teaching and example of the Bishop of Michigan, Charles D. Williams. Nevertheless the main impetus of the Social Gospel movement in America came from such non-Episcopalians as Washington Gladden and Walter Rauschenbusch.

The social movement in the Church has of course been subject to criticism by persons profiting from established privilege, but also from some who used more sophisticated epistemological grounds. D. N. Munby called attention to the socialists' lack of detailed consideration for concrete reality, which he called 'unrepentant Platonism'. Perhaps the religious mind has always been tempted to supply *a priori* resolutions to complex socio-economic questions. 'The Christian prophetic witness has failed', according to Munby, 'because it has been misinformed, cocksure, and too ready to assure that theological correctitude was a sufficient substitute for theoretical knowledge.'[17] The clue may be the Church's penchant for do-goodism, a reliance on a supposed omnipotence of mind not challenged by actual conditions of everyday life. When someone said to Charles Kingsley that there were no such things as water babies, he replied, 'How do you know that? Have you been there to see? And if you have been there to see, and had seen none, that would not prove that there were none.'[18]

During the 1960s a new development in Anglican moral thought caught the attention of the Western world: situation ethics. Some of its initial advocates were Anglicans. It was a modernized version of the Caroline insistence on holy living, though it claimed more ancient roots, a recovery of biblical patterns. Like the recommendation of love, the new morality was methodological rather than substantive, and thus incorporated by design a vagueness of outline which proved costly. Taking a cue from philosophical Existentialists, the situationists claimed that the tradition of Christian morality through most of Christian history had been gravely distorted by an unwarranted legalism. Each situation was said to be unique, and the agent had for reference only one unchangeable law, the law of love.

333

Though critics and also supporters of the new method sometimes spoke of themselves as innovative and even radical, the movement relied heavily on such traditional Anglican themes as holy living and the *via media*. 'The thing to note,' said Joseph Fletcher, 'is that situation ethics is in the middle, between moral law and ethical extemporism.'[19] Though the point was missed by some outraged conservatives, the new method was intended to turn away from both authoritative legalism on the one hand, and antinomian freedom on the other, so preserving the tried wisdom of nothing too much.

In England the new ethicists were led by a bishop, John A. T. Robinson, a New Testament scholar who seemed most at home in the *Sitz im Leben* of the contemporary world. His popular *Honest to God* (1963) was determined not to conceal from God the truth about modernity. Ironically this implied an abandonment of a 'supernaturalist' way of thinking. In the new Reformation for which the Bishop played the Anglican Luther, doctrine was not to play the role which it played in the fourteenth century, but was rather to yield the dominating role to practice. The reason given is that times have changed, and most 'doctrinal questions today, in contrast with the previous Reformation, present themselves in the first instance as moral questions'.[20] Behind the drive for social relevance was the concern for the intelligibility of the gospel to the modern world.

Another strong British voice supporting the new Reformation in the 1960s came from Douglas Rhymes. Like Robinson, he was an eager immanentist. For him, prayer, which might seem at first to involve speaking to a God who is 'out there', turns out to be nothing of the sort. Prayer is really 'the inChristness which lights up all our actions in daily living from within'. Rhymes plays the Anglican Brother Lawrence, conversing with God, not on his knees, but absorbed in kitchen work, amidst the clatter of pots and pans. 'If you say to me, "But this is not prayer, this is Christian living," I shall reply, "There is no difference." What makes it prayer is that it is Christian living *consciously thought out and consciously motivated for Christ's sake*.'[21]

In the United States a professor at Episcopal Divinity School, Joseph Fletcher, was the early prophet of situation ethics. He thought of himself as in truth traditional, and was surprised at the hostility which greeted the new method. Was it not obviously biblical? St Paul had 'replaced the precepts of Torah with the living principle of *agape*—*agape* being goodwill at work in partnership with reason'.[22] There was of course no capitulation to traditional dogma. 'I believe,' he wrote, 'that the only sin of which we can meaningfully speak is personal sin, not original sin.' And again, 'I see no viability in any objective theory of the atonement.'[23] Similar views about the Church's 'excess baggage' of inapplicable doctrine were expressed in the turbulent 1960s by other situationalists such as Norman Pittenger and James Pike.

Situation or contextual ethics did not have a long life of prominence in Anglican history, but there can be little question that it has left lasting marks.

Mainline Anglicanism responded gladly to the reminder that one does not accept something as true simply because some authority has declared it to be so. Ideals must be tested in the crucible of living. Valuable insights were offered on the New Testament theme of Christian freedom under the tutelage only of love. But there were also some elements which would give pause even to Anglicans who were not always tutiorists. There was in the method a tendency towards autonomy, a message little needed in an undisciplined modern world. And there seemed also something smug about paying only polite attention to the moral guidelines of the past, and no attention at all to deontological factors, nor to the effect of future consequences as a cost for such radical freedom. If one were to identify a flaw, it probably would be an error precisely opposite to that which spelled the doom of Christian Socialism. The socialists were armed with an admirable ideal, but they took little cognizance of the texture of the concrete world in which their fragile ideal would be invited to live. The Existentialists seemed exquisitely aware of life structures, but were cavalier about the doctrinal principles which they proposed to enflesh in society.

The cunning of the Absolute Mind seems to be leading Western Christendom into a larger calling than we have known before. The religious world today is bristling with a kind of theological pragmatism which is much like that proposed by the Caroline Anglicans: a vital Christological theology which has as a chief category the necessity of action. There are of course stubborn transcendentalists who are reluctant converts, but immanence seems to be carrying the day as it has not been able to do since its primal event, the incarnation. The Vatican Document 'Christian Freedom and Liberation' defends the right of the poor to struggle against injustice. South American liberation theology confronts both a surprised world and the tendency in the Church to be aloof and serene, *au-dessus de mêlée*. Right-wing Protestantism has claimed for itself a moral majority, and has turned some of its concern from personal salvation and rules about drinking, dancing, gambling, and smoking to problems such as abortion, war, drugs, and racial hatred.

Anglicans, recognizing their traditional patronage of this morality, as well as their share in allowing the Church to be distracted by lesser themes, have with enthusiasm recognized the new development and the possibility of a revitalized Christian mission. At the most recent General Convention (of the Episcopal Church in the United States) in California, the concern for piety expressing itself by concerns for life forms was everywhere in evidence, and the new Presiding Bishop announced *compassion* and *service* as two of his controlling themes. Paul Van Buren uses linguistic analysis to show that biblical categories must be expressed in empirical and ethical terms if the Church would communicate with a scientific, technological society (*The Secular Meaning of the Gospel*, New York, 1963). David Jenkins argues that a doctrine of God useful to the contemporary world must be 'clearly related to a spiritual discipline and discipleship which is experiential and experimental in relation both to the tradition and to the current situation'.[24]

Much remains to be done. In order to recover the full power of its traditional moralism, Anglicanism must develop a more sophisticated and competent response to human need, and must not be satisfied with a liturgical sympathy and an allocation of funds. What seems clearly required is a more active lay involvement, and this in two directions: a more adequate programme of adult education; and a way of soliciting and using the knowledge of the world and its power structures which could be contributed by the lay mind. A traditional recovery of the priority of morals should also lead to a more successful ecumenicity, since agreement on an exemplary Christian deed can more easily be achieved than agreement on doctrinal, liturgical, or polity questions. Our seminaries should encourage a broader definition of practical theology, of the kind now being developed by such leaders as Don Browning, Hans Georg Gadamer, Richard Rorty, Robert Bellah, and David Tracy. They have been working out ways to correlate an interpreted theory of the Christian faith with the praxis of the contemporary situation.

It has often been observed that we are living in a new, secular society, in which the ultimate question no longer is how God's will may be satisfied. Though not dead, God has become obscure, allowing Rilke to cry, '*O du verlorener Gott! du unendliche Spur!* (O thou lost God! Thou infinite trace!)' We need to renew the search which Anglicans began two centuries ago, the search for the truth of ultimate being which includes the fullness of experience and the well-being of the whole created universe. The area of concern should include international crises such as war, as well as domestic crises such as poverty. There should be a free debate between churchgoing conservatives and the group which Harvey Cox called 'the New Breed'.[25] There should be room for the old breed, which confronted our various crises with a social service motif, and the new breed, which would give prior place to political motifs seeking structural change.

Of course the Church which refuses to be passive, but busies itself by actually being the instrument by which the Word of God penetrates and transforms existence, runs a risk of losing itself in the world and becoming simply an agency of social reform.[26] But the alternate risk is more frightening: a Church which is comfortable with its role as a cultic enclave, self-righteous and anachronistic, an archaic, dogmatic company, rightly ignored by the world. The remedy for such oblivion is surely that commonplace transcendence which was seen by Anglicans from the beginning, and is now widely recognized. We must learn anew to take seriously and then to act upon the claims of our Lord over the total existence of his creatures astride our whirling planet.

NOTES

1 *The Works of . . . Mr Richard Hooker*, ed. John Keble (Oxford University Press 1845), vol. i, p. 125.

2 Paul Elmer More and Frank Leslie Cross, eds., *Anglicanism* (SPCK 1962), p. xxii.

3 ibid., p. xxxii.

4 O. B. Robertson, ed., *Love and Justice* (Philadelphia, Westminster Press, 1977), p. 84.

5 'The True Way or Method of Attaining to Divine Knowledge', *Select Discourses* (London 1660), p. 9.

6 *The Liberty of Prophesying*, in *The Whole Works of the Rt Rev. Jeremy Taylor*, ed. Charles P. Eden (London 1853), vol. v, 409.

7 *Troilus and Cressida*, I, iii, 114–5.

8 Joseph Butler, *Sermons* (New York, Robert Carter & Bros., 1858), p. 48.

9 *Works*, V, ii, lxxii.

10 Kenneth E. Kirk, *Some Principles of Moral Theology* (Longmans, Green & Co. 1920), p. 5.

11 *Maurice to Temple: A Century of Social Movement in the Church of England* (Faber & Faber 1947), p. 19.

12 William Temple, *Malvern, 1941* (Longmans, Green & Co. 1941), p. 224.

13 ibid., p. 220.

14 ibid., p. 161.

15 W. A. Visser t'Hooft and J. H. Oldham, *The Church and Its Function in Society* (Chicago, Willett, Clark, 1937), pp. 193ff.

16 William Temple, *Christianity and Social Order* (Penguin Books 1942), p. 35.

17 D. L. Munby, (The Importance of Technical Competence', D. M. Paton, ed., *Essays in Anglican Self-Criticism* (SCM 1958), p. 49.

18 Charles Kingsley, *The Water Babies*. ed. J. H. Stickney (Boston 1916), p. 63.

19 *Situation Ethics. The New Morality* (Philadelphia, Westminster Press, 1966), p. 26. I have been helped in my discussion of the New Morality by Edwin G. Wappler, 'Four Anglican Situationists and their Tradition,' unpublished Ph.D. Dissertation, Duke University, 1972.

20 *The New Reformation* (Philadelphia, Westminster Press, 1965), p. 38.

21 *Prayer in the Secular City* (Lutterworth Press 1967), pp. 48–9.

22 *Situation Ethics*, p. 69.

23 Joseph Fletcher and Thomas Wassmer, *Hello Lovers! An Introduction to Situation Ethics* (Washington, Corpus Books, 1970), pp. 108, 125.

24 David Jenkins, 'Whither the Doctrine of God Now?' *New Theology No. 2*, Martin E. Marty and Dean G. Peerman, eds. (New York 1965), p. 73.

25 Harvey G. Cox, 'The "New Breed" in American Churches: Sources of Social Action in American Religion' *Religion in America*, W. G. McLoughlin and R. N. Bellah, eds. (Boston, Beacon Press, 1968), pp. 368–83.

26 See Langdon Gilkey, *How the Church Can Minister to the World Without Losing Itself* (New York, Harper & Row, 1964).

3 Anglican Pastoral Tradition

O. C. EDWARDS JR

Addison, W., *The English Country Parson.* J. M. Dent 1947.
Anon., *The Clergyman's Instructor or A Collection of Tracts on the Ministerial Duties.* 6th edn, Oxford University Press 1855.
Clebsch, W. A., and Jaekle, C. R., *Pastoral Care in Historical Perspective.* Harper & Row 1964.
Edwards, O. C. Jr, 'Preaching and Pastoral Care', in *Anglican Theology and Pastoral Care*, ed. J. E. Griffiss. Morehouse-Barlow 1985.
Hammond, P. C., *The Parson and the Victorian Church.* Hodder & Stoughton 1977.
Herbert, George, *The Country Parson (1652), The Temple*, ed. John N. Wall Jr. Paulist 1981.
Lloyd, R., 'The Book of Common Prayer and Pastoral Ministry'. SPCK 1949; and *The Anglican Digest* Transfiguration, Michaelmas, and Advent 1984 and Lent 1985.
McNeill, J. T., *A History of the Cure of Souls.* Harper & Row 1951.
Russell, A., *The Clerical Profession.* SPCK 1980.

INTRODUCTION

In pastoral tradition, as in most matters, the way to discover what is distinctively Anglican is to study the Book of Common Prayer. In the present case the most relevant document is the Ordinal (see pp. 143–51). Thus in the Exhortation for the Ordering of Priests (1662) we read:

> We exhort you, in the name of our Lord Jesus Christ, that you have in remembrance, into how high a Dignity and to how weighty an Office and Charge you are called: that is to say, to be Messengers, Watchmen, and Stewards of the Lord; to teach, and to premonish, to feed and provide for the Lord's family; to seek for Christ's sheep that are dispersed abroad, and for his children who are in the midst of this naughty world, that they may be saved through Christ for ever.

This duty is further specified in the next paragraph:

> See that ye never cease your labour, your care, and diligence, until ye have done all that lieth in you, according to your bounden duty, to bring all such as are or shall be

committed to your charge, unto that agreement in the faith and knowledge of God, and to that ripeness and perfectness of age in Christ, that there be no place left among you, either for error in religion, or for viciousness of life.

The means for performing this ministry are 'doctrine and exhortation taken out of the holy Scriptures' and 'a life agreeable to the same'. The ordination formula itself describes 'the Office and Work of a Priest in the Church of God' as being that of 'a faithful Dispenser of the Word of God, and of his holy Sacraments'.

Not all of the pastoral duties of parochial clergy are mentioned in the rite for ordaining priests, however. Some are in the form for making deacons. The duties of the diaconate, though, are not lost when the deacon becomes a priest because the priest continues to be a deacon. Thus it takes the two rites to list all of the pastoral duties of parochial clergy.

> It appertaineth to the Office of a Deacon, in the Church where he shall be appointed to serve, to assist the Priest in Divine Service, especially when he ministereth the holy Communion, and to help him in the distribution thereof; and to read holy Scriptures and Homilies in the Church; and to instruct the youth in the Catechism; in the absence of the Priest to baptize infants; and to preach, if he be admitted thereto by the Bishop. And furthermore, it is his Office, where provision is so made, to search for the sick, poor, and impotent people of the Parish, to intimate their estates, names, and places where they dwell, unto the Curate, that by his exhortation they may be relieved by the alms of the parishioners, or others.

There are many ways in which the duties of clergy listed in the ordinals can be specified in more detail. In another context I have tried to enumerate the duties of contemporary clergy of the American Episcopal Church. They included: officiating at liturgy, preaching, evangelization and missionary activity, catechesis and Christian education, parochial administration, spiritual direction, Christian social action, moral guidance, the incorporation of new members into the parochial community, theological explanation, leadership in stewardship, spiritual renewal in the parish, enablement of the ministry of the laity, ministry to the sick and bereaved and to families in crisis, pastoral counselling, denominational duties, ecumenical involvements, and community activities.[1] A more compact list, however, has been drawn up by Anthony Russell in *The Clerical Profession*: leader of public worship (Sunday worship), leader of public worship (surplice duties), preacher, celebrant of the sacraments, pastor, catechist, clerk, officer of law and order, almoner, teacher, officer of health, and politician.[2] While Russell is more concerned with the sociological description of the duties of a profession than with a theological listing of the responsibilities of clergy, his categories offer a convenient way to analyse the activities that have made up the Anglican tradition of pastoral care.

VARIABLES WITHIN THE TRADITION

Before an analysis of the Anglican pastoral tradition can be undertaken, there are certain variables that need to be noted. The first of these is to recognize that the ministry of clergy in the Church of England has always been that of the representatives of an established Church. This has not always been true of the work of clerics in other national branches of the worldwide Anglican Communion. In the Episcopal Church in the USA, for instance, parish clergy function in many ways as chaplains to the people who have voluntarily associated themselves with the local community which practises the Christian faith as this communion has received it. Their conception of their responsibility is very different from that which Church of England priests have for certainly the spiritual and to an extent the physical welfare of all who live within the bounds of their parishes. And, of course, Anglican clergy in some parts of the world exercise their ministry in cultures far more radically pluralistic than even that of the United States. In Nigeria, for instance, the spectrum of Christian Churches includes the indigenous churches, making it far more variegate than American Christianity. But Christendom also exists there in a marked pluralism of religions which includes an Islamic community which is still probably larger than the Christian one, and devotees of African traditional religion with various degrees of commitment. This means that the whole style of ministry exercised in the classic pattern of Anglican ministry has been greatly adapted to cultures with a wide diversity of religious situations.

A second factor which must be taken into consideration when attempting to understand the differences between the way that pastoral care was administered in the Church of England until recently and the way that it is administered in other Anglican Churches is the system of patronage. At the time of the Reformation the parishes of the English Church had provisions to supply income to their clergy. Very often the right to decide which priest would be appointed to a parish and receive that income was in the hands of a religious order. Thus when the monasteries were dissolved and the Crown transferred their assets to favoured persons, this right of presentation (as it was called) was one of the assets transferred. Thus lay people such as the local squire received the right of naming who would serve in those parishes. Other parishes were in, or came into, the presentation of the Crown or the local bishop.

Presentation, however, was to the benefice or 'living', which is to say, to the right to receive the income rather than to the duty to perform the services of a priest. This meant that both conceptually and practically the compensation became separated from the work. Two results of this distinction between receipt of pay and performance of duties were absenteeism and pluralism. The person presented to a benefice would often hire a curate to do his work for him and thus feel free to live outside the parish. And it was as easy to live outside several parishes as it was to live away from one, so some clergy came to be preferred to several livings, to receive the income of all of them, and to serve in none of them. The extent of these practices and their effect on the life of the Church of England has been discussed at length elsewhere and need not be considered here. It is enough to remember that a significant factor in the way that the Anglican tradition of pastoral care developed was influenced by this less-than-ideal system for the deployment and payment of clergy.[3]

It should be noted here that the present essay is more concerned with ideals than with practice, with how the pastoral duties of Anglican clergy have been conceived than how they have been discharged. Yet such a discussion must take place in a context of awareness that the ideals have seldom been totally realized and that the mere statement of a standard does not mean that it has always been executed punctiliously.

This observation is relevant to the third factor that should be remembered in distinguishing between the English and other manifestations of the Anglican pastoral tradition: the historico-sociological development discussed in the work by Anthony Russell already cited. His study is an 'attempt to show that the clergyman's role, as it is currently structured, resulted from processes of change in English society in the late eighteenth and the nineteenth century, and in particular, that of professionalization' (p. 305). This is to say that in the nineteenth century, clergy took the professions that were emerging at the time as their 'model and reference group'. Prior to that, the role of the clergy was that of 'an occupational appendage of gentry status' (p. 6). While his argument as presented is reductionistic in seeing exclusively social reasons for the evolution of the Anglican pastoral tradition and in failing to note that theological, spiritual, and benevolent motives were also involved, Russell does perform a service in reminding us that such social factors are always involved in the life of the Church and that it never has any existence that is exclusively religious. But the social factors which shaped the development of the English pastoral tradition are different from those which shaped the development of other branches of the Anglican Communion.

One other aspect of the historical context in which the Anglican pastoral tradition developed must be noticed before we begin an examination of the individual elements of that tradition. This aspect has influenced the other countries into which Anglicanism has spread as well as England. It is the shift from a predominantly rural setting for parochial ministry, to an urban setting for much of it that occurred in the nineteenth century. Such a change of the social conditions under which ministry was practised required adjustments of the tradition of pastoral care to fit the new situation.

The final contextual aspect which must be borne in mind is the internationalization of that pastoral tradition as the communion has spread around the world. Attention has been called to this element incidentally in the discussion of the first variable, establishment, but more changes were involved in the transplanting of Anglicanism into other lands than just that of moving from establishment to disestablishment. The issue becomes one of discovering what, to change the metaphor, was lost or at least altered in the translation.

THE ESSENTIAL CHARACTERISTIC

With all of that out of the way, it is now possible to identify what is really most distinctive about the Anglican pastoral tradition. It is that its ministry is given its form by the Book of Common Prayer (see pp. 121–33). As Roger Lloyd said:

> The common property of all Churches of the Anglican Communion is the Book of Common Prayer; and that more than anything else binds them together. It is therefore in the Prayer Book that we find the heart of Anglicanism laid bare, and the Prayer Book is the manual of the art of ministering as Anglicans have understood it down the ages and practise it today.[4]

By that is meant far more than that the Prayer Book furnishes us with the forms of our corporate worship, although this 'praying from a book' is one of the most distinctive things about the worship of Anglicans. The point instead is that beyond supplying our liturgy, the Prayer Book makes provision for the total life of the Church and therefore furnishes the shape of ministry in all of its aspects. After presenting the basic regular liturgy of Morning and Evening Prayer, Litany, and the Holy Communion, the 1662 English book, for instance, moves into cradle-to-grave care of Christians at all of the 'wonder moments' of life: baptism at birth, catechesis for the young, confirmation for those ready to take on adult responsibility, matrimony for those who will start families of their own, visitation for those who are ill, and burial for the dead. These rites are followed by the Thanksgiving for women after childbirth (out of order and as an afterthought), the Commination against sinners, the Psalms, a form of prayer to be used at sea, the Ordinal by which persons are provided to engage in ordained ministry, a form for celebrating the anniversary of the sovereign's accession, and the Articles which state the Church's position on issues of theological controversy.

Against this list must be placed the list of forms of pastoral care borrowed from Russell: leader of public worship (Sunday worship), leader of public worship (surplice duties), preacher, celebrant of sacraments, pastor, catechist, clerk, officer of law and order, almoner, teacher, officer of health, and politician. There can be no doubt that the first six of these duties are expected by the Prayer Book. Some of the remaining six are almost as easy to account for. Duties as a clerk grow out of the necessity to record baptisms, weddings, and burials, for instance. The mandate for the almoner could come from the form for making deacons if the duty were not already so explicit in the New Testament as to be a basic Christian activity. The sympathy shown for the sick in the provision for spiritual care is naturally expressed in their physical care as well; then, too, the Lord's example is ready at hand. One of the reasons that Evangelical clergy, at any rate, kept schools was to teach poor children how to read the Bible; thus this teaching could be considered an extension of catechesis.[5] The Accession Service, accompanied (until Queen Victoria intervened) by the inclusion in the calendar of commemorations for King Charles the Martyr, Charles II's birth and accession, and the 'Papist's Conspiracy', shows some involvement of the Church with the civil government and thus with law and order. Only the activity of the politician seems not to have a degree of authorization from the Prayer Book table of contents, although many clergy today feel that their ordination vows to care for the suffering impel them into political activity. The total vision of pastoral care in the Anglican Communion is thus shaped by the Book of Common Prayer.

There is probably no other communion that has its life so shaped by one book. Of course many Evangelical groups claim to be based on the Bible in this thoroughgoing way, but the Bible is so large and diverse that all Churches claim to be based on it and none can document its claims in an exclusive way. Among the non-liturgical Churches and even some liturgical ones the amount of space needed to print forms of worship can be small enough for the end-matter of hymnals to be adequate. Roman Catholics, on the other hand, need a number of books for their liturgical materials. And for Anglicans the Prayer Book comprehends much more than the rites of corporate worship; it shapes every aspect of our life as a Christian community. The situation was caught very well by C. S. Lewis when he quoted from *Tristram Shandy* in order to specify what his own faith added to *Mere Christianity*: 'About [my own beliefs], as I said before, there is no secret. To quote Uncle Toby: "They are written in the Common-Prayer Book."'[6]

MINISTRY IN THE PRAYER BOOK WORLD VIEW

The Ordinal, as quoted in the opening paragraph of this essay, implies an understanding of the universe and the place of human beings in it. God created the world so that human beings can enter into relationship with him and enjoy the blessings that he has prepared for them both here and hereafter. The purpose of human life is to enter into that relationship; the only real good consists in doing so and the final evil consists in failing to do so. Clergy exist in order to assist people in entering and remaining within that relationship. Thus they are of vital importance to the whole human enterprise. It is this which makes their office and charge 'weighty'. As messengers they are to inform men and women of this state of affairs, of what God has prepared for them through Christ. They are watchmen to protect those who have heard and accepted this message. And they are stewards to care for that which belongs to God. They must teach, premonish, feed, and provide for their flocks. Implied in this are two assumptions: (1) that clergy have responsibility for the people of their cures both individually and corporately, and (2) that their task is by no means easy nor its results assured. The world is 'naughty', but eternal salvation is at stake.

Thus the duty of clergy is to bring the people for whom they are responsible to mature Christian faith so that no place is left in the entire community 'either for error in religion or for viciousness of life'. The technique for discharging this ministry has not changed since the time of Chaucer's Poor Parson:

> Christes lore and his apostles twelve
> He taughte, but first he folwed it himselve.

Or, as the Ordinal puts it: 'doctrine and exhortation taken out of the holy Scriptures' and 'a life agreeable to the same'.

This world view is presupposed by the Prayer Book as a whole. Its understanding of the purpose of human life, for instance, comes out in the Catechism's specification of what is prayed for in the Lord's Prayer:

I desire my Lord God our heavenly Father, who is the giver of all goodness, to send his grace unto me, and to all people; that we may worship him, serve him, and obey him, as we ought to do. And I pray unto God that he will send us all things that be needful both for our souls and bodies; and that he will be merciful unto us, and forgive us our sins; and that it will please him to save and defend us in all dangers ghostly and bodily; and that he will keep us from all sin and wickedness, and from our ghostly enemy, and from everlasting death. And this I trust he will do of his mercy and goodness, through our Lord Jesus Christ. And therefore I say, Amen, So be it.

Clergy are those appointed by the Church and enabled by God to be channels by which all those prayers are granted. That is the Prayer Book view of minstry.

Some of the implications of that view have been spelled out in the essay of Roger Lloyd to which attention has already been called. He finds 'five principles drawn from the Book of Common Prayer which govern the whole range of an Anglican ministry and give to it its particular colour among the several ministries of the Church Universal':

1. The refusal to accept any barrier between what is done in church and the life lived outside it.
2. As its very title, Book of *Common* Prayer, suggests, it is strongly and radically communal.
3. ... It envisions the whole congregation as the unit of pastoral and evangelistic work of the parish.
4. At the same time the Prayer Book is very personal in the sense that it rates the responsibility of the individual worshipper very high.
5. ... The pastoral responsibility of priest and people is unlimited. They have a charge before God for every soul in the parish, not merely those who worship in the parish church.[7]

The essentials of this view have been maintained in the revisions the Prayer

Book has recently undergone, although what Marion Hatchett has said of the Ordinal of the American book of 1979 is essentially true for the English *Alternative Service Book* of 1980: 'The old form emphasized the teaching, preaching, and pastoral roles. The revised form incorporates emphasis upon the liturgical and sacramental roles of the priest, and the role of the priest in the councils of the church.'[8] He also points out that the exhortation of the older forms was essentially a translation of Bucer's treatise *De ordinatione legitima* and that it views the laity as 'a passive and helpless body'. The latter interpretation is obviously one with which Lloyd would have disagreed, at least as far as the understanding of ministry in the Prayer Book as a whole is concerned. In any case, it can still be maintained that the Anglican understanding of the nature of ministry comes from the Book of Common Prayer and the shape of that ministry is given by the entire Prayer Book.

Another point to be made about this Prayer Book understanding of ministry is that it contains no assumption that anything new was being established at the time of the Reformation, as the preface to the Ordinal indicates. This sense of continuity was so strong that when the American Episcopal Church drew up a Course of Ecclesiastical Studies in 1804 to be pursued by those who were 'reading for orders', along with Gilbert Burnet's *Discourse of the Pastoral Care* and Thomas Wilson's *Parochialia* was included St John Chrysostom's *Christian Priesthood* as a textbook in pastoral care.[9] How widely this sense was shared may be seen by the fact Wilson said in his cover letter for his handbook that his clergy already had two excellent books on the subject of pastoral care, Gregory the Great's *Pastoral Care* and George Herbert's *Country Parson*.

Finally, it can be seen that in this Anglican world view taken from the Prayer Book the understanding of the purpose of pastoral care is that the priest should be involved in the nourishing of a community of the faithful in which individuals and the community as a whole can grow in holiness and enjoy the salvation Christ made available here and hereafter. That is to say, the object of Anglican pastoral ministry is the sanctification of the people of God. Thus it is very appropriate that this chapter on pastoral care should appear in the section of this book devoted to Sanctification.

THE COMPONENTS OF PASTORAL CARE

In the short space that remains brief notice will be given to each of the areas of pastoral care listed by Russell.

Leader of Public Worship (Sunday Duties)

This is obviously the most characteristic work of the priest. Isaac Walton has made the world familiar with the practice of George Herbert in the public recitation of the daily offices in a way that 'brought most of his Parishioners, and many Gentlemen in the Neighbourhood, constantly to make a part of his congregation twice a day' and so affected workers in the field that they 'would let their Plow rest when Mr. *Herberts Saints-Bell* rung to Prayers, that they might also offer their devotions to God with him.'[10] Not all clergy have been able to maintain so high a standard, but, as Russell has shown, even during the worst part of the eighteenth century Sunday duty was usually performed, even if it was done by curates who came to be called 'gallopers' from their practice of living in a market town and hurrying around to conduct services in several surrounding churches every Sunday.[11]

Most churches expected Morning Prayer, Litany, AnteCommunion, and sermon in the morning and Evening Prayer with or without a sermon in the afternoon. As indicated in the quotation from Hatchett above, the tendency to place more emphasis on the sacraments since the Oxford Movement has caused the Eucharist to become the most common Sunday service. In 1887 the Lower House of Convocation in the province of Canterbury drew up an extension of the Catechism which, although never approved by the Upper House, appeared in the Second Office of Instruction in the American Prayer Book of 1928. In it the people say: 'My bounden duty is to follow Christ, to worship God every Sunday in his Church; and to work and pray and give for the spread of his kingdom.' With the duty of attending Sunday worship so important for laity, it is small wonder that leading Sunday worship should be so prominent among the duties of the clergy.

Leader of Public Worship (Surplice Duties)

By this category Russell referred to *rites de passage* conducted by clergy, such as Churching of Women, Marriages, and Burials (p. 76). Baptism is not included in this category because he treats it under Celebrant of the Sacraments, and preparation for confirmation is discussed as one of the priest's duties as a catechist. This involves a certain amount of question-begging about the number of sacraments, but in any such analysis, arbitrary lines have to be drawn. Surplice duties, then, are the actions for which some American clergy are accustomed to say that they receive 'stole fees'. Russell tells us that even resident clergy in the eighteenth century liked to crowd as many of these as possible in between the morning and afternoon services on Sunday. These services are related to the 'cradle to grave care of Christians at all of the "wonder moments" of life' referred to above. Thus they reflect the creational, incarnational, sacramental view of life that is so characteristic of Anglicanism and its view of ministry.

Preacher

The Prayer Book world view described above involves a very propositional understanding of knowledge, including theological knowledge. It assumes that there are 'truths' that one must know, believe, and act on—truths that are revealed in the Bible—in order to have a fulfilled life both here and hereafter. Preaching is regarded as one of the most effective ways of communicating these truths and thus has usually been regarded as a duty closely linked and on a par with conducting public worship. Thus George Herbert was able to say: 'The Country Parson preacheth constantly, the pulpit is his joy and throne' (*The Country Parson*, ch. vii). In twelve pages of his *Discourse Of the Pastoral Care* (ch. ix), Gilbert Burnet is able to offer advice about preaching from which many clergy today could still profit, even though he so much admired the sermons of Archbishop Tillotson in whom Archbishop Brilioth finds concentrated the moralism that he considers the bane of Anglican preaching.[12] By the time that John Henry Blunt produced his *Directorium Pastorale* in 1864, however, the partisan spirit that grew out of the Evangelical and Catholic awakenings had begun to be reflected in attitudes toward preaching. Thus the author of the Eighty-ninth Tract could be quoted as saying: 'We would not be thought entirely to depreciate preaching as a means of doing good. It may be necessary in a weak and languishing state; but it is an instrument which Scripture, to say the least, has never recommended.' And an Evangelical spokesman can be cited to the opposite effect.[13] Even though John Henry Newman is generally conceded to have been one of the greatest preachers that the Church of England has produced, it must be admitted that clergy in general have placed less emphasis on their preaching duty since the Oxford Movement. May this soon change!

Celebrant of the Sacraments

Enough has probably seen said about this role in the discussion of the leadership of public worship with the exception that the impression could have been left that infrequent celebrations before the middle of the nineteenth century indicated a low esteem of the sacraments. To see how misleading such an impression is, one need only to look at what Herbert says about the Eucharist:

> The Country Parson being to administer the Sacraments, is at a stand with himself, how or what behavior to assume for so holy things. Especially at Communion times he is in a great confusion, as being not only to receive God, but to break and administer Him. Neither finds he any issue in this, but to throw himself down at the throne of grace, saying, Lord, thou knowest what thou didst when thou appointedst it to be done thus; therefore do thou fulfill what thou didst appoint; for thou art not only the feast, but the way to it (ch. xxii).[14]

Catechist

The propositional view of religious knowledge mentioned above has led to great emphasis on teaching the Catechism (see pp. 154–62). In this as in so many things, Herbert set a high example, both requiring all his parishioners to be present for catechesis and taking great effort to see that words were not only memorized but also understood (chap. xxi). Even he did not go so far as Richard Baxter, whose *The Reformed Pastor* was written after he had left the Church of England but in an effort to secure ecumenical co-operation in a programme of examining every family in the parish on its knowledge of the Christian faith by a system of hourly appointments.[15] The sad state from which Confirmation began to emerge under the Catholic revival and the improvement of transportation has been well reported by Peter C. Hammond in *The Parson and the Victorian Church*.[16]

Pastor

One of the ways in which the difference between Anglican attitudes toward pastoral care and that of Protestants can be seen is the way that historians of the subject have limited pastoral care to ministry to individuals, especially in times of crisis. For John T. McNeill, pastoral care is 'the sustaining and curative treatment of persons in those matters that reach beyond the requirements of animal life.'[17] For Clebsch and Jaekle it is:

> helping acts, done by representative Christian persons, directed toward the healing, sustaining, guiding, and reconciling of troubled persons whose troubles arise in the context of ultimate meanings and concerns.[18]

In his history of pastoral care in America, E. Brooks Hollifield confines his attention to the 'private interchange (of clergy) with parishioners seeking counsel'.[19] This is to say that all of the clerical duties treated above would not have been regarded as pastoral care by the definitions used by these histories.

While Anglicanism thus has a far wider understanding of what pastoral care is, this sort of concern for the spiritual, psychological, and physical welfare of individuals has never been lacking in our tradition. It has usually been discussed in the textbooks under the rubric of 'Visitation'. Such visitation was often with the express purposes of ascertaining the spiritual health of the family visited and exhorting its members to higher achievements.

A continuing aspect of this in every period since the Reformation has been a concern with the sort of spiritual direction that has been so much in vogue generally in recent years. The concern for sanctification has never been absent. A special aspect of this concern has been the practice of private confession. Explicit provision for it has been made in every Prayer Book and while, from time to time, there have been Anglicans who have opposed its use, the permission of the Church for it has always been clear. There has been argument over whether the absolution pronounced was precatory, declaratory, or authoritative, and theologians have differed over whether the provision was for ordinary or exceptional use, but the possibility of private confession was always there.[20] Indeed, McNeill says: 'No other great communion has given greater attention to the cure of souls, either in theory or in practice' (p. 246).

In the United States especially, the rise of modern psychology has permitted a reduction of pastoral care to pastoral counselling, as is indicated in the subtitle to Hollifield's history of American pastoral care: 'from salvation to self-realization.' So characteristic of American culture has this psychologism become that Philip Rieff has suggested that psychology has replaced theology as America's 'unitary system of common belief'.[21] At times it has been hard to distinguish between pastoral counselling and psychotherapy, and the competence of many clergy to do such counselling has been a cause of concern. This is not to deny the immense contribution of psychological insight to pastoral care. In any case, Episcopal clergy have not been so inclined as some others to this reductionist approach to pastoral care.[22]

Clerk, Officer of Law and Order, Almoner, Teacher, Officer of Health, and Politician

Russell astutely distinguished between the 'charter' elements of the clerical role that were authorized by the Ordinal and the ancillary elements that had accrued to the role in traditional society (p. 38). Most of the elements listed in the title for this paragraph are not charter elements and can bear omission from this discussion.[23] Only two points need to be made here. The first is to recall what has been said above about how the work of an almoner is a charter element of the duties of a deacon and is intrinsic to any concept of Christian ministry, lay or ordained. The second is to point out how clergy have continued to organize schools wherever the Anglican Communion has spread. Often in Third World countries church schools are the best available. Also the popularity of parochial schools in the American Episcopal Church suggests that teaching may be more than a traditional accretion to Anglican ministry; it may belong to the nature of the work.

CONCLUSION

Clebsch and Jaekle have said:

> Among the helping professions upon which modern society so heavily relies—medicine, social work, teaching, law, psychiatry, and so forth—the ministry or priesthood is the least specialized, though by no means the least helpful. It is not too much to say that the parish parson . . . is the last remaining genus of the general-practitioner-at-helping-people (p. xv).

They say this from their limited perspective of restricting pastoral care to ministry to individuals in crisis. When one considers how much more inclusive the understanding of pastoral care is that the Anglican tradition has maintained, one can realize what a glorious calling it envisions. While the ways in which this ministry will be exercised in the future are beyond our present knowledge,[24] we see what an impoverishment of the Church it would be for this tradition of pastoral care in its basic shape to vanish. Its contribution to the sanctification of the people of God would be sorely missed.

NOTES

1 'Preaching and Pastoral Care,' in *Anglican Theology and Pastoral Care*, ed. James E. Griffiss (Wilton, CT, Morehouse-Barlow, 1985), pp. 133–58.

2 Anthony Russell, *The Clerical Profession* (SPCK 1980).

3 Russell, op. cit., pp. 28–41. Cf. Rosemary O'Day, *The English Clergy: The Emergence and Consolidation of a Profession 1558–1642* (Leicester University Press 1979); and Peter C. Hammond, *The Parson and the Victorian Parish* (Hodder & Stoughton 1977). Roughly half of Gilbert Burnet's *A Discourse of the Pastoral Care* (1692) is directed against the evils of this system.

4 Roger Lloyd, 'The Book of Common Prayer and Pastoral Ministry' (SPCK 1949; repr. in *The Anglican Digest* in the issues for Transfiguration, Michaelmas, and Advent 1984 and Advent and Lent 1985) Transfiguration 1984, p. 25.

5 Russell, op. cit., p. 188.

6 C. S. Lewis, *Mere Christianity* (Macmillan 1943, 1945, 1953; edn cited is that of Macmillan Paperbacks of 1960), p. 8.

7 Lloyd, op. cit., Michaelmas 1984, pp. 20–23. This article, written in 1949, is remarkably prophetic in its view of what today would be called 'mutual' or 'total' ministry.

8 Marion J. Hatchett, *Commentary on the American Prayer Book* (Seabury 1980), p. 521.

9 Powell Mills Dawley, *The Story of the General Theological Seminary* (Oxford 1969), p. 22.

10 Isaac Walton, *Life of George Herbert* (1670; rcpr. Oxford 1973), p. 302.

11 Russell, op. cit., pp. 54, 55. Some clergy did resort to strategems to make this conducting of services unnecessary as William Addison shows in the chapter on 'Sporting Parsons' and elsewhere in his delightful book on *The English Country Parson* (J. M. Dent 1947).

12 Yngve Brilioth, *A Brief History of Preaching* (Philadelphia, Fortress, 1965), p. 179.

13 John Henry Blunt, *Directorium Pastorale: Principles and Practice of Pastoral Work in the Church of England* (London 1864), p. 99.

14 Cf. Jeremy Taylor, *Rules and Advices to the Clergy of Down and Connor* (1661; edition used that published in *The Clergyman's Instructor, or A Collection of Tracts on Ministerial Duties* (Oxford 1855), lxxix.

15 Edition used was that of Hugh Martin (Atlanta, GA, John Knox, 1956).

16 Peter Hammond, op. cit., pp. 169–75.

17 *A History of the Cure of Souls* (New York, Harper & Row, 1951), p. vii.

18 William A. Clebsch and Charles R. Jaekle, *Pastoral Care in a Historical Perspective* (New York, Harper & Row, 1964), p. 4.

19 *A History of Pastoral Care in America: From Salvation to Self-Realization* (Nashville, TN, Abingdon, 1983), p. 12.

20 For an excellent concise summary of the history of private confession in Anglicanism see McNeill, op. cit., pp. 218–46.

21 *The Triumph of the Therapeutic: Uses of Faith after Freud* (New York, Harper & Row, 1966).

22 For an extensive consideration of this whole issue, see my article, 'Preaching and Pastoral Care'.

23 Something of the range of possible duties of clergy can be ascertained by looking at the Table of Contents for *A Manual of Parochial Work for the Use of Younger Clergy*, ed. John Ellerton (SPCK 1892).

24 For an interesting but by no means exhaustive consideration of the possibilities, see Russell, op. cit., pp. 289–306.

4 Church–State Relations

PETER HINCHLIFF

Butler, Perry, *Gladstone: Church, State and Tractarianism*. OUP 1982.

Clarke, W. K. Lowther, *Constitutional Church Government in the Dominions Beyond the Seas and in other parts of the Anglican Communion*. SPCK 1924.

Coulson, John, *Newman and the Common Tradition: A Study in the Language of Church and Society*. OUP 1970.

Dibdin, L., *Establishment in England*. Macmillan 1932.

Elton, G. R., *The Tudor Constitution*. CUP 1960.

Figgis, J. N., *Churches in the Modern State*. Longmans Green 1913.

Hinchliff, Peter, *The One-Sided Reciprocity: A Study of the Modification of the Establishment*. DLT 1966.

Jackson, M. J. and Rogers, J., eds., *Thomas Arnold: Principles of Church Reform*. SPCK 1962.

Jordan, W. K., *The Development of Religious Toleration in England*, 4 vols. George Allen & Unwin 1932.

Kemp, E. W., *Counsel and Consent: Aspects of the Government of the Church as exemplified in the History of the English Provincial Synods*. SPCK 1961.

McGrade, A. S., 'Introduction to Book VIII, *Of The Laws of Ecclesiastical Polity*', in W. Speed Hill (ed.), *The Folger Library Edition of the Works of Richard Hooker*, 6. Harvard University Press 1988.

Moyser, George, ed., *Church and Politics Today: The role of the Church of England in Contemporary Politics*. T. & T. Clark 1985.

Nicholls, David, *Church and State in Britain since 1820*. Routledge Kegan Paul 1967.

Thompson, K. A., *Bureaucracy and Church Reform*. OUP 1970.
Warren, M. A. C., *The Functions of a National Church*. Epworth Press 1964.

It has never been easy to relate the ideals of the Christian life to political structures. There are, perhaps, two reasons in particular why this is the case.[1] In the first place, moral principles which may seen clear and obvious in relation to the private life of individuals can be complex and difficult to apply to the corporate life of a society. Secondly, since politics is about the exercise of power, the considerations which govern political action are often directly opposed to those qualities which the New Testament regards as the marks of the Christian life—gentleness, humility, patience and love.

Moreover, in the nineteen centuries since the New Testament was written, there have been significant changes in both the position of Christians in relation to government and in at least the theoretical structure of those governments under which most Christians live. Romans 13.1–3 and 1 Peter 2.13, urging simple obedience to government as a 'given', were written at a time when no Christian participated in the exercise of power or had any say in how government was constituted or in what policies it chose to pursue. But by the fourth century, Christians had begun to be both makers of policy and exercisers of power. For such people, simple obedience to a government of which they were an important constituent was no longer a sufficient moral principle. In more modern times, in democracies where Christians are voters sharing in the creation of government and yet at the same time subjects of those governments, the position is even more confusing. When one has a responsibility (however indirect) for the very existence of government, one cannot simply take refuge in the belief that God has put it there and that one's moral duty is exhausted by obedience.

Shifts in the nature of government have been particularly important in the history of the religious establishment in England—from which, in a sense, all Anglican thinking about Church and State has begun. The Church of England is often said to be a part of the British constitution. But Britain has no written constitution: what is called 'the British constitution' is simply a name for the way in which British government happens to work at any given time. Some of it is enshrined in statute. Some of it is merely convention. None of it is entrenched or protected in any special way.

Moreover, the English religious establishment of the sixteenth century was built upon the relationship between Church and state that had already existed in the Middle Ages. Some aspects of that relationship—tithes, endowments, educational institutions—continued virtually unchanged. Others were modified or adapted, in varying degrees, to take account of the new situation. Others again were drastically altered by law to express a particular theory of the relationship between Church and state. Therefore the establishment was not a single relationship, neatly embodied in a fundamental constitutional document, but a complex of relationships often regulated by nothing more definite than tradition and custom.

The theory of the establishment under Henry VIII was, however, clear and simple. It is set out in the preamble to the Act in Restraint of Appeals (1533) which saw the realm as consisting of two parts, a temporalty—secular and lay persons—and a spiritualty—ecclesiastical and clerical persons. At the head of each of these two parts, and uniting them, was the Crown. The Act was not about the Church of England as 'the nation at prayer'; that would hardly have been a point worth making in the sixteenth century. It asserted the king's control over a single administrative structure of government and abolished the independent jurisdiction of the medieval church. For all that the Act seems to describe a symmetry of temporalty and spiritualty, it was an Act of *Parliament* and therefore contrary to its own theory. The imbalance was made even more clear by Henry's forcing the clergy to submit publicly to his authority. That submission, too, was embodied in an Act of Parliament which forbade the clergy to meet in convocation or to enact canons without royal approval. What the legislature of the spiritualty might do, in other words, was limited by the legislature of the temporalty.

The Henrician establishment did not assume that a new Church was being created. Henry himself was theologically conservative, though his system could probably not have been put into effect without the assistance of the many who desired reform for theological and religious reasons. But no one really thought in terms of introducing a new Church: the Church was being reformed. For the most part it continued to use the old forms of service and to act administratively as it had always done. Even when, in the reign of Henry's young son Edward VI, an English Prayer Book was introduced and a more Protestant theological stance adopted, a great deal remained unaltered.

The settlement of religion achieved by Elizabeth I strove for a balance which would bring as many people as possible within the English Church. For Elizabeth inherited a sharply polarized situation. Her predecessor and half-sister, Mary Tudor, had restored the jurisdiction of the papacy in England and had driven Protestants into exile. Elizabeth was, therefore, faced with papalists in power and returning exiles anxious to obtain control. She was no more willing than any other ruler of her time to tolerate a variety of religious denominations within her kingdom. The only alternative was a Church which would encompass as wide a range of opinion as possible.

At the same time, her solution was more radical than her father's. It was founded upon two Acts of Parliament which date from very early in her reign. The Supremacy Act revived a string of statutes from the reign of Henry VIII and Edward VI, forbidding appeals and the payment of taxes to Rome; and re-enacting the submission of the clergy, the method of appointing bishops, and the Crown's jurisdiction over the Church. And it also imposed upon all who held office in Church or state an oath recognizing the supremacy. While Elizabeth took the title of supreme governor, rather than revive Henry's title of supreme head of the Church, this was a change in name rather than in fact. There was no diminution of the powers that her father had claimed. Moreover, by incorporating some of the legislation of Edward VI's reign, the Act authorized a more Protestant theological position than Henry had ever been willing to tolerate. Even more important, a schedule of provisos annexed to the Act defined heresy as what could be proved to be contrary to Scripture or the decisions of the first four general councils of the early Church or had been declared to be heresy by Act of Parliament with the assent of convocation. It was a new and radical departure for Parliament to claim the right to determine what constituted heresy. (see pp. 6–15 and pp. 189–93).

The other Act which brought in the Settlement was the Act of Uniformity legalizing a new Prayer Book. It was substantially the second Prayer Book of Edward's reign, but softened and modified at many points so as to make it less obviously Protestant.

It would seem that Elizabeth had not originally intended to move so quickly in the matter of the Prayer Book, but the House of Commons contained a substantial number of members sympathetic to the viewpoint of the returning Protestant exiles. They attempted to turn the Act of Supremacy into an Act of uniformity also, by annexing Edward's Prayer Book to it. Since this would have alienated the more conservative, the Queen was virtually forced to devise her own alternative. Convocation had no hand in framing the Prayer Book, and it was authorized simply by Act of Parliament.

The new Settlement did not prevent continuing unrest and division. The Puritan party continued to resist it throughout Elizabeth's reign and radical opinion began to oppose the very principles of royal supremacy and a national Church. From 1566 onwards, having been defeated in convocation on the matter of the use of vestments, dissidents worked through Parliament, introducing into the Commons a whole series of bills which would have radically altered the Settlement. Elizabeth opposed them by arguing that it was intolerable for Parliament to intervene between herself and the convocations, a device which—however inconsistent with her earlier actions—did something to restore the theoretical equality of the partnership between Church and state.

Puritans continued to demand further reform, and had to be kept under tight control. Recusants—Roman Catholics who refused to accept the Settlement—remained outside it and were persecuted for doing so. But there remained only one legally recognized church in England and, as a new generation grew up, the established Church came to be regarded no longer as a compromise but as a thing in itself.

Towards the very end of Elizabeth's reign, Richard Hooker embodied this new view of the Church of England in his famous *Laws of Ecclesiastical Polity* which maintained that the Church and the state were two inseparable aspects of the one commonwealth. He argued, against the Puritans, that it was 'a gross error to think that regal power ought to serve for the good of the body, and not of the soul; for men's temporal peace and not for their eternal safety; as if God had ordained kings for no other end and purpose but only to fat men up like hogs...'[2] But he was not merely concerned to defend on pragmatic grounds what happened to be there. He may, indeed, have intended to transform as much as to defend the Settlement. He stood for a genuinely Christian society where the monarch's authority, limited by law and custom, would reflect the spirituality of the people as a whole. It is really from Hooker that the idea derives that the Church of England should be the nation at prayer (see pp. 224–6).

Puritans became less and less willing, however, to remain quiescent in the latter part of Elizabeth's reign and in that of her successor, James I. In the civil war with Charles I, the parliamentary party embraced the Puritan cause and by 1643 had begun to make the Church of England presbyterian. It is, again, important to realize that Parliament did not think of itself as substituting a Presbyterian denomination for an Anglican one. It was, rather, taking the reform of the national Church further than before. It abolished episcopacy in 1643 and in the same year created the Westminster Assembly.

This body was set up to advise Parliament on a new form of government for the Church. Its clerical members had, of course, been ordained and licensed in the Church of England but were Puritan by conviction. The few convinced episcopalians who had been nominated to it boycotted the meetings. There was a vigorous and vociferous minority of Independents, who believed that each local congregation had the right to determine its own affairs, its own doctrine and ministry. But the majority was committed to Calvinist doctrine and to a presbyterian pattern of church government.

Before Parliament and the Assembly could really contrive to make England presbyterian, however, differences developed between the House of Commons and its army. Eventually the triumph of the army under Cromwell led to the victory of Independency over presbyterianism. The Puritans were divided and were used to exercising private judgement in matters of religion. It was too late to insist that the essence of a presbyterian polity was a strict system of discipline designed to maintain uniformity in doctrine and polity.

Cromwell's Commonwealth is a period of particular importance in the history of relations between Church and state. All real power was in the hands of the army, but it did not wish to govern directly. The constitution-making which went on at intervals throughout the Commonwealth was a series of attempts to achieve an effective but compliant parliamentary government, none of which succeeded. Similarly the religious Settlement of the Protectorate was an attempt to establish Independency, itself almost a contradiction in terms. Independency stood for the sovereignty of the local congregation.

355

Toleration under the commonwealth was far from complete. Episcopalians and papists were never tolerated—though a blind eye was sometimes turned on their activities. Unitarians and some of the more radical sectarians were also, from time to time, excluded. But the basic design of Cromwell's Settlement was to take the unfinished presbyterian pattern of the Westminster Assembly and to broaden it. A commission selected ministers, whose views were generally Independent, Presbyterian or Baptist and who became part of the new establishment. Another commission weeded out of the Church those unsuitable clergymen who survived from Charles I's time. But in addition to the comprehensive and variegated establishment that resulted considerable toleration was allowed to others, so that a wide range of denominations flourished for the first time and acquired an organization and a form.

The effect of this policy was to ensure that there existed in England a variety of Christian denominations, too large and too firmly rooted to be eradicated again when the monarchy was restored. The return of Charles II in 1661 was expected to produce a new Settlement of the Church on Elizabethan lines and, indeed, a new Act of Uniformity and a new Prayer Book in 1662 were the outcome of that expectation. Once again there was a body of returning exiles, but this time they were High Churchmen and monarchists who wanted an 'Anglican' and episcopal establishment headed by the king. The presbyterian Puritans within the Commonwealth establishment hoped that any new Settlement would include themselves but not the more radical sectaries or Independents. The king himself, by the declaration of Breda issued before his return, had promised 'liberty to tender consciences'. He made a further declaration after his return, which appeared to promise a Settlement acceptable to presbyterians, and at the so-called Savoy Conference an attempt was made to devise such a compromise. It failed and the new Settlement was, in fact, imposed by a Parliament which was full of enthusiasm for the restoration of the old order. But it was equally determined to prevent ultimate control of the Church from passing out of lay hands. Nevertheless the convocations revised the Prayer Book and episcopacy was made an essential part of the Church of England.

The so-called Clarendon Code imposed limitations on those who were not members of the established Church. Holders of municipal office were required to receive the sacrament in the Church of England by the Corporation Act. An act of 1664 made attendance at services other than those of the Church illegal. The Five Mile Act made it an offence for dissenting clergymen to come within that distance of any town or city. But non-conformity did not disappear. For the first time in English history there were large denominations outside the established Church, which could not be destroyed however much they might be made subject to a variety of penalties.

The king, perhaps because of his sympathies with Roman Catholicism, continued to try to make things easier for those who would not conform. In 1663

356

he issued a Declaration of Indulgence which would have relieved dissenters from some of their disabilities. Opposition in Parliament rendered the attempt fruitless. In 1668 he again attempted to bring Presbyterians into the Settlement and again Parliament refused to agree. In 1670 he tried once more to use the royal prerogative to dispense with some of Parliament's laws. The Church of England would have been protected in its privileges but all penal religious laws against those who did not conform were to be suspended. Parliament refused to recognize the king's Declaration of Indulgence and in 1673 passed the Test Act, which required all office-holders under the Crown to take the oath of supremacy, forswear transubstantiation and receive the sacrament in the Church of England.

Perhaps the most radical changes in the establishment took place in the eighteenth and nineteenth centuries because the unwritten constitution of England was itself changing drastically in the period. Constitutional monarchy, parliamentary government and cabinet responsibility all began to develop. Though the Crown continued for a time to have some freedom in their choice, ministers gradually became primarily responsible to Parliament. A cabinet had also begun to emerge, though it was a long time before collective cabinet responsibility was established. Even when Victoria became Queen, the political control of the House of Commons over the government had not yet excluded the Crown entirely. But real power was passing into the hands of the Commons and an embryonic party system began to take shape. Those who could control the majority of seats in the Commons were those entitled to govern. The royal prerogative came to be exercised less by the sovereign acting on his or her own responsibility: it became an accepted convention that the Crown must act on the advice of its ministers.

At the beginning of the nineteenth century the establishment was taken for granted. It was regarded as the symbol of England's character as a Christian country. Politicians no less than churchmen regularly described the Church as 'part of the constitution'. That seems to imply a clearly defined, solid structure, enshrined in the nation's legal system, whose place and function could be easily understood. Yet in 1888, when Edward King, Bishop of Lincoln, was accused of illegal ritualist practices, the Archbishop of Canterbury had to revive a court which had only functioned once since the Reformation, which really owed its existence to the fact that in the Middle Ages the archbishops had also been papal legates, and which was of doubtful legality.[3] No one knew whether it really existed. No one knew whether one could appeal from its decision to the Privy Council—the final court in ecclesiastical causes—because no one knew what its authority was.

It was apparent, then, by the end of the century that the establishment was a confused and incomprehensible thing. What had happened was that the constitution had changed, partly because of legislation such as that which gave political rights to Roman Catholics or repealed the Test and Corporation Acts in 1828 and 1829, and partly because of changes in the conventions of government. Yet the significance of the changes had not really been perceived. Moreover, the Church of England was no longer the Church of the nation. It was one Christian body among many. It had certain privileges, but it was also tied to an uncertain and fluid legal system which was changing all the time.

Not surprisingly there was much opposition to the establishment. This came, initially, not only from dissenters who claimed that, in matters such as tithe, church rate and education, the privileges of the establishment were unjust; it also came from those who thought that the whole idea of a religious establishment was archaic and inefficient. *The Extraordinary Black Book* of 1831, for instance, argued that the ecclesiastical revenues of England and Ireland were greater than those of the rest of Europe put together, and were so inefficiently used that the ministry for which they paid catered for only about one-third of the population. The answer to charges of inefficiency was largely provided by Charles James Blomfield, Bishop of London 1828–56, and the Ecclesiastical Commission.[4] The Commission limited the size and incomes of cathedral chapters, evened out episcopal revenues and made provision for the creation of additional bishoprics. It also established a central fund from which the stipends of poorer clergy could be augmented. It thus created the first element of central administrative machinery in the Church of England.

It is not surprising, either, that the nineteenth century was also a period of much discussion of the theory of establishment. The Oxford Movement, because of its clear understanding of the nature of the Church, influenced much of this thinking. It is sometimes pointed out that Tractarians appeared at first to be defenders of the status quo and only became critical of the state connection subsequently. In fact, as is clearly shown by John Keble's famous 'National Apostasy' sermon of 1833, it was an ideal relationship with the state which they were concerned to defend. Indeed much Tractarian writing was concerned with attempting to identify the 'ideal Church'.

Other significant works on the idea of establishment from the period are Samuel Taylor Coleridge's *The Constitution of Church and State* of 1820, Thomas Arnold's *Principles of Church Reform* of 1833 and W. E. Gladstone's *The State in its Relations with the Church* of 1838.

Coleridge's position is important because he recognized that religion and politics each had its own proper concern, different from that of the other. These concerns he called 'ideas', necessary regulative conceptions, which may never have been fully actualized in historical event. The state is concerned with citizenship: the Church with nothing less than the promotion of the harmonious development of those qualities and faculties which characterize humanity. But the 'church' in Coleridge's writing was neither the transcendent theological concept of the ideal Church nor the actual Church of England. It was the sum of all the nation's spiritual resources, including art, science, literature, and scholarship. Though his thought influenced the ideas of many, including Newman, it did not, therefore, have much direct bearing upon the development of the actual establishment.

Thomas Arnold's *Principles of Church Reform* was much more concerned with practicalities. His fundamental premise was that it is impossible to demonstrate, beyond all question, the truth of theological propositions. Doctrinal disagreement was therefore inevitable. From this he drew the conclusion that the national Church should be as inclusive as possible, not based on dogmatic formularies nor uniformity of practice. Such a Church, he believed, would once more be an established Church which was truly national.

Gladstone's book, written while he was still a relatively young man, a junior politician and a Tory, was very much a defence of the establishment more or less in the form in which it existed. Where his work differed from the conventional defence of establishment was that it did not ask why it might be proper for the Church to accept the state connection. Instead it asked why it was proper for a state to establish a Church. There were two aspects to his answer to that question. On the one hand he insisted that politics and government must have a moral dimension, that there were things that the state must do because they were right, irrespective of whether they were expedient. Therefore it was important that the state should proclaim—by establishing a Church—that it accepted particular beliefs. Secondly, and as a necessary consequence of this, he believed that the state had a duty to defend the *true* Church.

This theory became increasingly difficult for Gladstone to maintain. By 1840, when he wrote a second work on the topic, *Church Principles Considered in their Results*, he had begun to insist far more firmly upon the divine authority of the Church. But as a Liberal, dependent, in part, on the electoral support of Free Churchmen, it was politically difficult to insist that the Church of England was the only true Church; and when he found himself responsible for the government of Ireland, where hardly any of the people were Anglican and where it was almost impossible to justify the establishment of an Anglican Church, it became morally difficult. Moreover, as England became more and more secular, Tractarian ideas of what constituted the truth became more difficult to maintain in society and uphold by law.

Some of the difficulties and anomalies of establishment were revealed most clearly in the colonies. Since the Elizabethan Act of Supremacy asserted the Crown's jurisdiction over all ecclesiastical persons and causes in all its territories, the establishment was automatically extended to the colonial empire as it came into existence. This was something different from the idea that the state should subsidize religion, for subsidies were often given to all denominations in a colony, including Roman Catholics. Indeed, as a dispute over clergy reserves in Canada showed, financial support from government was sometimes an alternative to establishment.[5]

Establishment existed in the colonies as part of the prerogative power of the English Crown. It was a personal nexus between the supreme governor of the English Church and his or her Anglican subjects. This is shown by the fact that the Church of Scotland was not similarly assumed to be established in British colonies: the Scottish religious Settlement did not recognize any ecclesiastical authority vested in the sovereign. Further evidence that establishment was as much concerned with persons as with territory is that in some colonies there could be more than one established Church. In the Cape Colony, which was captured from the Dutch during the Napoleonic wars, the Dutch Reformed Church was guaranteed all the privileges it had formerly possessed without this in any way affecting the assumption that the Church of England was 'by law established' in the colony.

By an order in council of the reign of Charles I, the Bishop of London had exercised episcopal jurisdiction in the colonies, but this could obviously not be very effective. Bishops were consecrated for India and various colonies and, indeed, after some difficulties, for America also. Bishops in British territory needed letters patent from the Crown to make their consecration lawful, just as English bishops did, and it was assumed that their legal status was exactly that of bishops in the Church of England. But when colonial bishops reached their dioceses and needed to issue regulations, adapt English customs to local conditions or put diocesan finances on a proper footing, they found that some kind of synodical body was desirable. Several colonial bishops tried to summon such bodies, but Henry VIII's Act for the submission of the clergy had specifically forbidden the holding of any synod without royal permission. And it would have been absurd for the Crown to create ecclesiastical legislatures exercising an authority independent of the local civil power.

The alternative might have been to persuade the British Parliament to pass an Act permitting the Church in the colonies to hold synods. In 1853 the Archbishop of Canterbury actually introduced a bill into the Lords which would have allowed this, but it was rejected by the Commons. Indeed, some of the colonial bishops were uneasy about the proposal because it seemed to them that it would have subjected the Church too firmly to the state. It proved, in fact, extremely difficult to transfer the delicate concept of establishment to the colonies. And if English colonists saw nothing incongruous in the existence of a 'Church of England' in Africa, North America, Asia or Australasia, not all colonies were colonies of settlement. Much British territory overseas was ruled rather than settled by the English. In black Africa it must have seemed odd to be required to subscribe articles of religion which included the proposition that 'the Bishop of Rome hath no jurisdiction in this realm of England'. Yet the anomaly was not thought disturbing (see pp. 395–8).

The 'Eton College' judgement of 1857 first raised doubts about the existence of the establishment in those colonies where the Crown, by creating an independent colonial legislature, had limited its own prerogative powers. By this time some parts of the Church overseas had already begun to experiment with synodical government and there followed a period in which even those overseas dioceses which had no reasons of their own for desiring it, were virtually compelled to devise a form of organization and discipline for themselves. The first Lambeth conference drew up a prototype constitution, which was one of three models upon which the emerging Anglican provinces based their own forms of government. The others were the Archbishop's draft bill of 1853 and the constitution of the American Church.

The question of establishment had come to a crisis in a series of legal cases related to the Church in Southern Africa[6] and arising directly or indirectly from an attempt to prosecute Bishop Colenso for heresy on account of his critical approach to the Old Testament. He was tried before a court set up by the Bishop of Cape Town who claimed the jurisdiction of a Metropolitan. Colenso was found guilty, excommunicated and removed from office.

But the Bishop of Cape Town, Robert Gray, had already run into problems over summoning a synod and, like other colonial bishops, had been given conflicting advice by the law officers of the Crown. Bishops in Canada and New Zealand had, however, been told by these same officers that there was no legal bar to their holding synods if they wished. Gray had therefore summoned a synod in Cape Town in 1856. One of his clergymen refused to attend, and the judicial committee of the Privy Council held that the Bishop and his synod could only exercise authority over those who voluntarily accepted it. It also held that the letters patent issued to the Bishop were invalid because the Cape had acquired its own legislature. The Bishop had no authority over the recalcitrant clergyman.

By the time this judgement was delivered, Gray had tried Colenso for heresy. He believed that his authority in this matter was unassailable because Colenso had taken an oath of canonical obedience to him, thus apparently voluntarily accepting his jurisdiction. But the judicial committee held that, because the letters patent were invalid, Colenso ought not to have taken the oath at all. It was also held that although neither bishop possessed valid letters patent, both had been created ecclesiastical persons by the Crown and only the Crown could unmake them.

Colenso then sued the Colonial Bishoprick's Fund for the payment of his stipend, which the Fund had been witholding since this excommunication. The Master of the Rolls, Lord Romilly, heard the case and declared that ecclesiastical persons, created by the Crown, were corporations capable of holding property in the name of the Church of England and that, in that sense, the Church of England as by law established could exist in the colonies in spite of all the Privy Council judgements since the Eton College case.

The South African Church, smarting under the tangle created by the courts, adopted a constitution which rejected the jurisdiction of the Privy Council. But in 1882 there was a further case from South Africa in which it was held that any Church which did not recognize that jurisdiction could not be the same as the Church of England.

Nevertheless it was clear that most parts of the Anglican Communion could not be legally established Churches and they adopted constitutions which based their corporate life upon a voluntary compact rather than upon establishment. The Church in the United States was not, in any case, established—nor was the Episcopal Church in Scotland. All these Anglican provinces were in a relationship with the state exactly like that of the Free Churches in England. The secular courts—if appealed to—would regard their disciplinary procedures as being analogous to those of, for instance, the Jockey Club.

The number of such provinces has grown continually. The Church of Ireland was disestablished in 1871 and the Church in Wales in 1920. Since World War II the vast majority of the overseas territories ruled by the British crown have become independent. There is now no part of the Anglican Communion outside England where the Church is certainly established.

Even in England itself the establishment continued to be modified. In 1903 a Representative Church Council was brought into being as part of a process, initiated a decade earlier, to reform the convocations and give laymen some part in their proceedings. In 1917 William Temple launched the Life and Liberty Movement to press for some degree of ecclesiastical autonomy, and in 1919 an enabling Act was passed by Parliament which created the Church Assembly. It had become plain that Parliament simply had not the time to give to ecclesiastical business. But the cumbersome character of this new machinery was very clearly revealed by the revision of the Prayer Book in the 1920s. Each stage in the lengthy business had to be considered by both convocations and the Church Assembly, and it was still subject to parliamentary approval. The proposed book, having been approved by the convocations and the Assembly, was sent to Parliament in 1927. It was passed by the Lords but rejected by the Commons. It was revised again in certain respects by the ecclesiastical legislatures and again rejected, provoking from the bishops of the province of Canterbury what amounted to a declaration that they would treat the revised Prayer Book as though it had been authorized.

Disestablishment was for a time a hotly debated issue; and the relationship between Church and state has, in one way or another, been under discussion during most of this century. There have been three commissions to report on possible modifications of it. The General Synod of the Church of England, with a substructure of diocesan and deanery synods, replaced the Church Assembly in 1969. The system of canon law has been revised, the alternative Services Book authorized and a new method of appointing bishops put into effect. The Synod has established a right to autonomy in matters of doctrine and worship. But it is, in the last resort, a creation of Parliament; and there have been several occasions since it came into existence when it has seemed that there might be confrontation between the two bodies. Crises have been evaded rather than resolved, and there has been no final trial of strength like the controversy over the 1928 Prayer Book (see pp. 42–4).

Historically, establishment has tended to make the Church, at least in some respects, the servant of the state. It might be thought, then, that the Anglican tradition would have been one which was conservative politically and disinclined to challenge the government. This has not, however, been the universal pattern. In some parts of the Anglican Communion, as in South Africa or Uganda, there has been outright condemnation of the policies and actions of governments. And even in England itself in recent years the Church has been prepared to criticize the political party in power. In part this is, no doubt, a consequence of a growing awareness of the points made at the very beginning of this chapter about the nature of power and about the new patterns of relationship between government and Christian citizens. But it may also be that living with a tradition of establishment has given Anglicans a sense that religion is something which belongs in the public domain. A long history of being involved with government has meant that the Church has been consulted about a variety of issues in which political action is to be taken. It has become accustomed to expressing a view on such matters. It has had to realize that political actions have a theological, religious and moral dimension.

NOTES

1 For an extended discussion of the problems see P. Hinchliff, *Holiness and Politics* (DLT 1982).

2 *Of The Laws of Ecclesiastical Polity*, VIII. iii. 2. (Book VIII was published in 1651.)

3 For an account of the trial see A. C. Benson, *Life of Edward White Benson*, 2 vols. (Macmillan 1899, 1900), vol. ii, pp. 319ff.

4 For an account of the commission see G. F. A. Best, *Temporal Pillars* (CUP 1964).

5 P. Burroughs, 'Lord Howick and Colonial Church Establishment', *Journal of Ecclesiastical History*, XXV (1974), pp. 381–405.

6 P. Hinchliff, *The Anglican Church in South Africa* (DLT 1963), pp. 48–53, 87–103, 111–29.

5 Sociology of Anglicanism

W. S. F. PICKERING

Barrett, D. B., 'The Anglican World in Figures', in *Lambeth Conference. Preparatory Information. Statistics: Documentation: Addresses: Maps.* London, CIO, 1978.

Barrett, D. B., *World Christian Encyclopedia.* Oxford and New York, OUP, 1982.

Barrett, D. B., 'Annual Statistical Table on Global Mission: 1986', *International Bulletin of Missionary Research* (January 1986), pp. 22–3.

The Church of England Year Book. London, CIO, annual.

Inter-Anglican Theological and Doctrinal Commission (IATDC) *For the Sake of the Kingdom.* London, Anglican Consultative Council, 1986.

Mehl, R., (ET) *The Sociology of Protestantism.* London, SCM, 1970.

Pickering, W. S. F., 'Protestantism and Power: Some Sociological Observations', *Social Compass* 32.ii/iii, 1985, pp. 163–74.

Sykes, Stephen W., *The Integrity of Anglicanism.* Oxford, Mowbray, 1978.

Sykes, Stephen W. and others, *Four Documents on Authority in the Anglican Communion.* London, Anglican Consultative Council, 1981.

Wand, J. W. C., ed., *The Anglican Communion: A Survey.* Oxford, OUP, 1948.

QUESTIONS OF IDENTITY AND ORGANIZATION

The Anglican Communion, or Anglicanism viewed as a global phenomenon, is not, as the name implies, a unified Church or even a number of Churches controlled by an authoritative body. It is made up of a loose federation of Churches which are in communion with the see of Canterbury. The constituent Churches acknowledge the fact that they have emerged from the Church of England, and the Christian doctrines and practices they exemplify proximate closely to those of that Church.[1]

The Anglican Communion as a social entity may be said to have come into existence in 1867 when C. T. Longley, Archbishop of Canterbury, called together Anglican bishops throughout the world. This gathering, the first of what were to be called Lambeth Conferences, was initially requested by bishops of Canada. Subsequent conferences have continued to be held approximately one every decade. They have been called by the Archbishop of Canterbury, who is very much the figure-head—the *primus inter pares*—and who has a bestowed status which makes him the point of union of the Anglican Communion. In 1968 machinery was set in motion to create an Anglican Consultative Council which would act as a more permanent advisory body.

The Lambeth Conferences are an official recognition of the growth of various branches of the Anglican Church throughout the world. Such conferences, however, have always been consultative. They do not legislate, make binding decisions, or exert power in the name of a universal Anglican Church. Strictly speaking there is no such body as the Anglican Church, unless the name is taken to mean, as it usually is, the Church of England and nothing more. Different Anglican Churches exist in various parts of the world. They are autonomous and are not subject to direct controls from other Churches, even the Church of England.

Quite apart from its relative smallness in following, the social organization of the Anglican Communion is far removed from that of the Roman Catholic Church, which is an international, autonomous Church with a centralized legislative base in Rome, and where power is ultimately exercised by one man, the pope.

The Anglican Communion has spread around the world through the agency of several factors. Initially, the Church of England extended itself beyond the British Isles to other parts of the globe through immigrants who, as members of the Church, settled in such places as North America, the West Indies, Australia, and so on. Outposts continued to grow as fresh waves of immigrants came from the mother country (see pp. 37–9). The second agency has been in the form of missionary societies, once again originating in England, which have been active in converting non-Christians within the boundaries of the fast-expanding British Empire, particularly in the nineteenth century (see pp. 430–7). The most obvious examples are India, Africa and parts of the Far East. The work of missionaries from the Church of England was in some cases supplemented by that of missionary societies formed in immigrant Churches. For example, the Church in Japan, the Nippon Sei Ko Kai, was founded through missionaries from Anglican Churches in the United States and Canada, as well as the Church of England. Today, among the Churches of the Anglican Communion, that in England remains by far the most missionary-inclined, as two-thirds of those working in missions abroad are from it.[2] Another factor in the growth of various Churches has been the natural increase of families who are members of them. Again, growth has come through conversions without any missionary agency, sometimes through mixed marriages involving Christians of other denominations, as well as those of other religions. It is said of the Episcopal Church in the United States that half its members are converts from other Churches and from none.

Either through problems arising from geographical distance or theological conviction (it is not clear which), the immigrant Churches during the nineteenth century, at a time when growth was most marked, were in some cases accorded a high degree of independence. In this respect, Anglicanism has veered towards a Protestant rather than a Roman Catholic ideal in supporting the concept of national Churches. Various Anglican Churches have been able to forge their own independence and develop particular paths of expression, while at the same time holding on to the overall doctrine and ethos of the Church of England. This has allowed for the possibility of indigenization, but at the same time let it be noted that many Churches did not in fact utilize such possibilities. Some of them developed a fixation on all things English and therefore tended to follow slavishly the ethos of the Church of England and the English nation (see pp. 395–8). For example, the Anglican Church in Canada always prided itself on its ties with England; its original name, the Church of England in Canada, was not changed until as late as 1958, and that in the face of six years of opposition. In Australia similar changes were adopted even later, and the Church of England in Australia became known as the Anglican Church of Australia only in 1981. In Ontario the Church rejected the state interference which the Church of England experienced, but wanted to retain all else; it created its own synod in 1851. In New Zealand synodical government came in 1857. The dominance of the Raj meant that bonds with England were particularly close in India, not least in the concept of the Indian Ecclesiastical Establishment, which ministered only to the British population. The Church in India was particularly slow in appointing Indian bishops and in establishing synodical government. The latter came in 1930.

What happened in the United States really set the pattern for the possibility of indigenization and freedom from British control. As a result of the War of Independence (1773–76), it became politically expedient for those American citizens who were of the Anglican faith to form a group totally cut off from the Church of England. Further, it would seem that the church authorities in England were of the opinion that there was no theological reason why the affairs of Anglicans in the United States should be controlled directly by the Archbishop of Canterbury and the British Parliament. Once the Anglican Church in the United States had obtained autonomy, a way was open for other Anglican Churches to follow suit. At least, there was no reason why they should not. Immigrants, as they developed new colonies, found themselves for religious purposes directly within the province of the Church of England. Only as a result of time and historical circumstances did they gradually sever their links with the mother Church.

Freedom given to member Churches has in certain instances meant that they have left the Anglican Communion altogether. This happened to the Anglican Church of India, Pakistan and Ceylon, when as a champion of church unity, the Church became at various stages part of the Church of South India (1947) and the Church of North India (1970). These might be called sanctioned losses, and mean that care has to be used in comparing statistics for certain years. A different case is where Anglicans have formed themselves into schismatic denominations or sects. There are two kinds. In those involving whites, it is estimated that over the past century or so 200,000 Anglicans have formed themselves into 16 schismatic bodies. Larger have been defections amongst non-whites, particularly in Africa, but also Asia, where, according to Barrett, 3.9 million members have created and become members of 850 schismatic groups.[3] Of course the Anglican Communion has also been weakened by conversions of individuals and small groups to other denominations, as well as a withdrawal into 'no religion' (see below). In the Barbados, which by tradition has been strongly Anglican, it is now said that there are more Pentecostal members than there are Anglicans; doubtless such a growth in Pentecostalism has been in part at the expense of the Anglican Church.

Thus, the Anglican Communion as an autonomous federation of Churches has no authoritative power to determine doctrine, ritual and policy, which is in any way binding on its members. Each Church is responsible to itself and governs itself in its own particular way according to a great variety of constitutions. The only factor which binds the Churches together is loyalty to a heritage which is bound up with the Church of England.

All Anglican Churches have accepted a Catholic concept of church order, namely, one based on the historic episcopacy (see pp. 296–308). The claim of apostolic succession means that the Church of England traces its ecclesiastical formation back to the early Church. Episcopalianism defined this way is what theologically marks off Anglican Churches from others, and such a characteristic makes Anglicanism unique amongst Reformed Churches.

DEMOGRAPHIC AND OTHER CONSIDERATIONS

It is difficult to give precise and at the same time meaningful statistics about any large religious group. In the case of world-wide Anglicanism the problems are compounded by the fact that in some countries, not least in England, the gathering of statistics, until perhaps very recent times, has never been seen to be a worthwhile occupation. On the other hand, some Churches, such as the Anglican Church of Canada, have taken the task more seriously. Another problem is the common enough one of creating statistical categories for membership, practice and belief which have generally accepted significance. The recent pioneering work of David B. Barrett, with limited help from certain dioceses and Provinces, offers the most reliable statistical picture of the Anglican Communion so far to emerge.

According to Barrett there were, in 1980, 49.8 million baptized Anglicans. The absolute number has been increasing since 1900 when it was 30.6 million and in 1970 it was 47.6 million, but as a proportion of the world's population it has been declining from 1.8% in 1900 to 1.3% in 1970 and 1.1% in 1980.[6] If one employs a somewhat vaguer category of professing membership, which includes those not known to the Churches, the number rises to just under 60 million in 1970, which represents 1.7% of the world's population.

In 1970 the number of adult, affiliated or baptized members was 16.4 million, which means that of total membership figures for all ages, only a third are adults (see Table 1). Thus globally on any reckoning the Anglicans constitute a tiny religious body. To be sure, over 160 countries have Anglican Churches; but one country, England, has more than half the total Anglican membership, depending

367

TABLE 1 *Anglican Communion*. Global figures of affiliated membership for 1970 according to region[10]

Region	Total affiliated (millions)	(baptized) members % of total	Adult members (millions)	(15 years and over) % of total
Africa	7.8	16.4	1.9	11.6
East Asia	0.1	0.2	0.1	0.6
Europe	29.4	61.9	10.3	62.8
Latin America	0.8	1.7	0.3	1.8
North America	4.4	9.3	2.8	17.0
Oceania	4.8	10.1	0.9	5.5
South Asia	0.2	0.4	0.1	0.6
USSR	—	—	—	—
Total	47.6	100.0	16.4	100.0

on the category of membership selected. In every other country Anglicans form a minority and are outnumbered by other Christians.[8] In ten Churches or other bodies, Anglicans are less than one per cent of the total population (ibid.).[9] About two-thirds of the Churches are located in the Third World; the total number of Churches is just under 30.

Each year about eight dioceses are created throughout the world.[11] The emergence of more dioceses might well reflect an increasing membership but, on the other hand, more dioceses might be created by a growing, practical policy of making smaller units of episcopal administration.

Although the Communion as a world-wide organization continues to grow in absolute numbers, its position now seems less convincing than it was in the 1920s and 30s, when the British Empire was at its zenith in the wake of the enormous expansion in the nineteenth century. Since the breakup of that empire the authoritative claims of Anglicanism have considerably weakened. Indeed many of the tensions in the contemporary Anglican Communion seem analogous to those in the British Commonwealth.

In the face of secularization in Western industrial society, those countries where Anglican membership is declining are Britain, the United States, Canada, Australia and New Zealand.[12] Membership is now growing mainly in African countries and in Papua New Guinea. In projected figures, Barrett has calculated that baptized members in Africa have grown from 7.8 million in 1970 to probably 12.3 million in 1985, and so their percentage of total membership in that period has risen from 16 per cent to 24%.[13] According to Barrett's figures for 1985 the percentage of non-whites amongst baptized Anglicans was 19.6%. Thus eight out of every ten were white.

England is experiencing the greatest falling away, but the general sentiment remains strong for the Church and polls have indicated that a very large proportion of the population thinks the Church of England is 'a good thing'. There is no strong desire to change its establishment status. When it comes to practice, it is a different matter. On an average Sunday less than 2% of the adult population attend an Anglican Church in England, and the level does not rise much more at Easter. For the Anglican Communion the number of Easter communicants is put at 5.8 million;[14] and the number of communicants is given as 16.2 million. This represents a great gap between professing membership and practice, and that gap is largely due to the position in England—9.3 million communicant members and only 1.7 million communicants at Easter.[15] It is probably not too strong to say that the enfeeblement of the mother Church has caused distress and even a lack of self-confidence amongst her daughters who have always had such a high regard for her. Similar enfeeblement, however, can be found in other parts of the world. For example, a recent survey in the diocese of Toronto showed that three-quarters of the Anglican population were inactive, although such people gave high value to their 'dormant' membership. It should also be noted that 90% claimed to have British roots.

Characteristics relating to social class vary enormously between the various Churches within the Anglican Communion and most likely between the parish churches of any one country or province. In some areas such as India, Central Africa and South Africa, the majority has been derived from the economically disadvantaged classes—outcasts and Blacks. In South Africa, the Church has been particularly influential amongst those who have suffered from the apartheid system, Coloureds as well as Blacks. Bishop Trevor Huddleston and Alan Paton have been leaders of those who have been oppressed. And recently Desmond Tutu, as Bishop of Johannesburg and now Primate of South Africa, has become foremost amongst black leaders seeking the alleviation of the sufferers of white domination. In India, Anglo-Indians have been a group much influenced by the Anglican Church.

By contrast, one might point to the United States, where the Episcopal Church has a following which, on a per capita basis, makes it very much the Church of the wealthy and the status-seeking.

In England, the Church has relatively few members who might be designated working-class. At the same time it is not strongly supported by the upper middle classes and nobility. Its main strength is derived from the upper-working classes, the lower-middle classes and professional groups, which are proportionally more in the churches than in society at large.

The age-structure of Anglican congregations inevitably varies from province to province and from parish church to parish church. As Barrett demonstrates, Churches in the Third World have a much younger age-structure than those Churches set in predominantly white countries.[16] Kenya in particular is a young

369

Church. Nevertheless, in Australia and Nort] America congregations are relatively younger than they are in the United Kingdom. In part it is due to the younger age-structure of the societies in which the congregations are set. But it is frequently the case that even in the 'newer' countries, the age-groupings in Churches are more weighted towards the elderly than they are in society. The Church of England has lamentably failed to influence the young. The exception perhaps is in the Evangelical wing of the Church, which in recent times has gained considerable strength particularly amongst young adults. Further, in England and in many places elsewhere, there is a predominance of females over males: the ratio of females to males is often in the order of 2 to 1.

UNIQUENESS: A COMBINATION OF TRADITIONS

The Anglican Communion cannot be understood ecclesiastically and socially apart from a thorough comprehension of the Church of England, its mother. Various Churches within the Communion thoroughly reflect the Church of England in many matters and yet in others significantly differ from it. What is important is to come to terms with and to appreciate the body which has given rise to the world-wide Communion. One must always start with the Church of England, because its reflection in other Churches has to be grasped before divergencies can be appreciated.

To the outsider who has some acquaintance with the development of Christianity, the Anglican Communion appears to be an extraordinary mixture of Christian traditions, something akin to what the French would call a *mélange*. Such a characteristic, which is sometimes proudly identified with comprehensiveness,[17] embraces some aspects of the two major Western traditions of Christianity from the sixteenth century onwards—Roman Catholicism and Protestantism. Both (and, within Protestantism, Calvinism in particular) have coherent theological systems. Not so Anglicanism. It has turned out to be an amalgam of the two systems, plus later liberalizing elements, which seems difficult to accept by those not brought up as Anglicans, or those who do not appreciate a *via media* position. Such a stand aims to obtain the best of both worlds—a biblically-based faith, expressed in the early creeds, which also allows for some degree of personal interpretation, as well as the use of Catholic forms of worship and church order. Today, many Anglicans do not see themselves as being just Protestant. Rather, they want to be understood as Catholic and Reformed. They like to see Christendom itself as comprising four major groups— Roman Catholic, Eastern Orthodox, Protestant and Anglican. That the last of these categories is an amalgam of the first and third does not create in their own minds ambiguities which others brought up in either one of them might see. The point of self-congratulation rests not on the establishment of a logically derived religious system but on a vague pragmatism. The Church holds together many who want to be neither Protestant nor Catholic: their reasoning therefore tends to be negative rather than positive. 'It's what we are not, rather than what we are.'

What is difficult to comprehend in Anglicanism is the existence of ecclesiastical parties all claiming to be loyal to its principles. Such parties in the Church of England, for example, are very removed from each other despite declarations of loyalty. Revivals in the eighteenth and nineteenth centuries—the Evangelical Revival and High Church movements—eventually became accepted as legitimate or semi-legitimate components of the Church (see pp. 32–7). It may well be that comprehensiveness, that is, the ability to absorb extremes and at the same time be the milieu for debate without giving rise to disunity, is the overriding virtue of Anglicanism. It is in a special position of acting as a bridge between Protestantism and Roman Catholicism. But it can be argued that virtue has arisen out of necessity. Why necessity? Because the Church of England as an autonomous body had no power to exclude members of movements which were initially held to be undesirable. It had no alternative but to accommodate Liberals, Evangelicals and Anglo-Catholics. All these groups—and others—have made great contributions to the theological, pastoral and spiritual life of the Church.

The internal tensions brought about by the presence of these parties within Anglicanism, which first arose in England, may not be as fierce in other parts of the Communion as they have been, and to a large extent still are, in England. There are many reasons for this. In certain Churches or provinces, dioceses and parishes of contrasting churchmanship are often well separated geographically compared with England, where parishes of radically difference churchmanship are often contiguous and therefore people are well aware of such differences. Another reason is that church parties, in establishing their own missionary societies—for example, the British Churchman's Missionary Society or the Universities' Mission to Central Africa—were able to agree that each society would operate in territories which were generally widely separated from each other. In this way they did not act as local rivals. Such an agreement seemed sensible, in the light of the enormous task which evangelism in the nineteenth century faced. Religious orders which undertook work overseas, such as the Society of St John the Evangelist and the Community of the Resurrection, also accepted this gentleman's agreement. Thus, converts to Anglicanism and their successors, growing up under the aegis of different societies, were in numberless cases unaware of the existence of a different type of churchmanship to that of their own. A contrast for ordinary churchgoers only became apparent when they moved from place to place, or when they came to England.

So the issue of churchmanship in particular Churches has varied according to regions. Many Anglican Churches, such as the Anglican Church of Canada, have never experienced extremes of churchmanship which have occurred in England.

371

Sometimes a more balanced position has emerged due to the presence of Low Church influences (not necessarily Evangelical), rather than the fact that in Canada and Australia, Anglo-Catholics of a more extreme kind were never able to make extensive gains. In Canada such extremes never developed, because parish ministers were partly answerable to a parochial, lay governing body. In some Churches, such as that of the United States, historical reasons have made certain dioceses uniformly Anglo-Catholic and others not so. Areas such as South America and the Middle East, because of the initial missionary influence, have been generally recognized as Evangelical or Low Church spheres of influence. On the other hand, the West Indies, Papua, Korea, Japan and Ghana are predominantly Anglo-Catholic (or High Church) because of corresponding missionary activity. In South Africa, Anglo-Catholic congregations are found amongst the Africans and Coloureds.

The Church of England did not undergo the radical changes which Churches on the Continent experienced in the sixteenth and seventeenth centuries. It reserved episcopacy as the linchpin of church order, but English bishops were placed in such a position that they governed their flocks and clergy in quite a different way from their predecessors of the Middle Ages. In the Church of England, the absence of a workable canon law and the tenure of parish priests (freehold) which still exists today, has meant two things.[18]

First, a remarkable combination of two components which has facilitated the establishment of extreme parties—the combination of an ideological position, which came early in the history of the Church, namely that of avoiding extremes, and which later turned into the notion of comprehensiveness; and the tenure of clergy who could be removed from their livings only on very limited counts. This association was particularly effective from the nineteenth century onwards in the emergence of a fast-accelerating religious pluralism.

The other implication relates to the role of bishops. As they became less involved in the affairs of state and more concerned with their dioceses they found their powers of administration were seriously limited. They were responsible for their sees yet they could not move their clergy from parish to parish, either to try to stem a growing secularization, or to remove a priest on account of his religious extremism or pastoral incompetence. By contrast, bishops in countries outside England found they could function in a much more authoritarian manner and more like bishops 'of old'. For example, they could exert some control over clergy who were without the protection of tenure. Further, bishops often had the authority of synod behind them and could employ, but at the same time be subject to, an effective canon law.

Anglicanism, as a world-wide religious phenomenon, displays one severe limitation, which another contributor has called 'the Anglo-Saxon captivity' (see p. 395). With English the foremost international language, a danger exists that Church leaders, with access to jet travel, falsely imagine that the Anglican

Communion is representative of cultures around the world. It is true that fourteen Churches and similar bodies have titles which are non-English. Everywhere the vernacular is employed for services of worship and for preaching, and the proceedings of the 1978 Lambeth Conference required simultaneous translation into French, Japanese and Spanish. Nonetheless some 90% of Anglicans live in countries of which the official language is English, nearly two-thirds of them in Western Europe.[19] And this limited internationalism is compounded by the fact that, despite later encouragement to indigenization, nearly all the Churches have adopted ecclesiastical terms unique to the Church of England, or at least rarely found in other Churches. Amongst these are archdeacon, rural deanery, church warden, rector, (vicar, however, is not so common), suffragan bishop, House of Bishops (after the Houses of Parliament), together with organizations such as the Girls' Friendly Society, the Mothers' Union, the Guild of the Servants of the Sanctuary. The way clergy dress, or used to dress, has been taken from English patterns.

THE FUTURE

The genius of Anglicanism is frequently said to lie in its blending of Christian traditions—its comprehensiveness. It can be seen as a living witness to the parable of the wheat and the tares. Great variety is allowed in the matter of belief and practice. Divergent elements grow side by side, and the final judgement rests in the hands of Someone transcending the human predicament. The Anglican Communion can also be said to reflect the divergencies and conflicts that existed within the primitive Church. Anglican Churches remain spiritual homes for the devout and committed; shelters for doubters and the perplexed; debating chambers for the unbelieving, the arrogant and the suspicious. Expressed in more institutional terms, Anglicanism claims to preserve the old, the traditional, the Catholic. Its inevitable appeal is to history: it stakes everything on what has happened in the past—a past that goes back to the beginning of Christianity. Yet at the same time it is prepared to change and to reform itself. Liturgies of today have developed extensively from those of Cranmer (see pp. 42–4 and 130–3); most Churches have synodical government and there is a greater involvement of lay people in every area of its life; and in some Churches women are now ordained to the priesthood with little or no opposition.

Yet its strength harbours its weakness. The flabbiness that many see in Anglicanism is a sufficient reason for some to forsake it and embrace another denomination. It has been the case in the past: it is true also today. In some instances Anglicans of a High Church persuasion have left to join the Church of Rome or the Orthodox Church; the exit or partial exit of certain Evangelicals, on the other hand, has been into non-denominational house-churches. Joining another Church is not the only solution to being free of the alleged flabbiness of

Anglicanism. Continuing Churches can be established, and certainly that has been the case in the United States and Canada where there are the Anglican Catholic Church; the American Episcopal Church; the United Episcopal Church; the Anglican Rite Jurisdication of the Americas; and the Anglican Catholic Church of Canada. The membership of all these groups together is estimated to be in the order of 50–60,000. Such groups maintain links with various Anglo-Catholic bodies in Anglican Churches around the world. These continuing Churches by their very limited size and mentality indeed become sects. And if the larger Churches of the Anglican Communion are seriously weakened by the exodus of groups dissatisfied with present doctrine and practice, such Churches would in fact become sects, or if they already possess sectarian qualities, these would become more accentuated.

Is Anglicanism, as a unique component of Christianity, destined to survive? The question invites two kinds of response. The first is to ask whether the doctrines, practices, and ethos of Anglicanism, despite local variations, will continue in the face of church reform, liturgical change, charismatic enthusiasm, the influences of ecumenism, and a desire on the part of many young Christians to blur—even to the point of extinction—differences between denominations. Indeed, one might ask how far does the Anglican in the pew want to keep the distinctive characteristics of Anglicanism? This issue needs to be researched and cannot be explored here. The second response focuses on the existence of the Anglican Communion as a concrete social expression of Anglicanism. Will this survive? It is impossible to predict, and in any case sociologists in general hold that futurology is not part of their trade. None the less the question of the Anglican Communion in the years ahead is more pressing now than heretofore.

In one sense it would seem that the future of the Anglican Communion is assured. As has been shown, its overall growth continues and expansion in one part of the world offsets losses in another. The general state of Anglicanism will depend on how it can cope with a rising secularization, strongly evident in the West, but emerging in all societies influenced by it. Growing affluence is so often the enemy of religious belief and practice. Some would doubt whether the comprehensiveness, and what has been called the flabbiness, of Anglicanism can stem the tide of universal secularizing processes.

Another factor relates directly to internal tension and dissatisfaction, with what appears to be the ever-widening parameters of diversity within which unity is extended. Are there no clear limits beyond which tolerance is exhausted (see pp. 208–13)? Among sociologists there is no consensus that only one component, be it belief, practice or culture, is the *sine qua non* of the unity of a social entity such as a Church. Unity itself is not a unitary concept, but open to variability and diversity. Something more decisive than 'live and let live' is required when issues of the gospel and the Church are at stake. Yet any attempt to create new formulae to draw sharper boundaries of membership goes against the grain of an important strand of historic Anglicanism. Herein lies its dilemma.

NOTES

1 The present list of Churches, Provinces and councils is found in *The Church of England Year Book* (London 1986), p. 179. See also D. B. Barrett, 'The Anglican World in Figures', in *Lambeth Conference. Preparatory Information. Statistics: Documentation: Addresses: Maps* (London 1978), p. 8.

2 Barrett, op. cit., p. 34.

3 Barrett, op. cit., p. 15.

4 J. W. C. Wand, *The Anglican Communion: A Survey* (Oxford, OUP, 1948), p. 23.

5 See Barrett, op. cit., hereafter cited as Barrett (1978). See also D. B. Barrett, *World Christian Encyclopedia* (Oxford and New York, OUP, 1982), hereafter cited as Barrett (1982); and D. B. Barrett, 'Annual Statistical Table on Global Mission: 1986', *International Bulletin of Missionary Research* (January 1986), pp. 22–3, hererafter cited as Barrett (1986).

6 Barrett (1986), p. 23.

7 Barrett (1978), p. 14.

8 Barrett (1978), p. 15.

9 ibid.

10 Based upon Barrett (1982), p. 791.

11 *The Church of England Year Book* (London 1985), p. 246.

12 Barrett (1978), p. 14; (1982), p. 791.

13 Barrett (1982), Table 26.

14 Barrett (1978), p. 16.

15 ibid.

16 Barrett (1978), p. 20.

17 S. W. Sykes, *The Integrity of Anglicanism* (Oxford, Mowbrays, 1978), contains an analysis of the notion of comprehensiveness.

18 W. S. F. Pickering, 'Protestantism and Power: Some Sociological Observations', *Social Compass* 32.ii/iii (1985), p. 171.

19 Barrett (1978), p. 9.

PART SEVEN

Prospects

1 The Ecumenical Future

MARY TANNER

Bell, G., *Documents on Christian Unity* 1920–57, 4 vols. OUP 1924–58.
Boegner, M., *The Long Road to Unity*. Collins 1970.
Crow, P. *Christian Unity: Matrix for Mission*. New York, Friendship Press, 1982.
Davies, R., *The Church in Our Times*. Epworth Press 1979.
Fey, H., *A History of the Ecumenical Movement Vol ii, The Ecumenical Advance, 1948–1968*. SPCK 1970.
Goodall, N., *The Ecumenical Movement*. 2nd edn, OUP 1964.
Neill, S., *The Church and Christian Union*. OUP 1968.
Neill, S., Rouse, R. (ed.) *A History of the Ecumenical Movement*, Vol i, *1517–1954*. SPCK 1970.
Runciman, S. *et al.*, *Anglican Initiatives in Christian Unity*. SPCK 1967.
Till, B., *The Churches Search for Unity*. Penguin Books 1972.

Anyone reviewing the history of Christianity in the twentieth century will be struck by the fact that this has been the century of ecumenism. Although there have been few signs of success in terms of the coming together of denominations, with such notable exceptions as the Church of South India, the Church of North India and the Church of Pakistan, yet the advances in mutual understanding and the commitment to joint action in life have been dramatic. The years that have seen such changes in the relation of the Churches to one another have also witnessed great changes in the Anglican Communion and in Anglican self-understanding. These have been in part affected by Anglican involvement in the Ecumenical Movement. The eve of the Twelfth Lambeth Conference is an appropriate time to ask, where are we and where are we going as Anglicans in the ecumenical future? In what follows, some of the developments that have brought us to the ecumenical present will be charted. Only then will an assessment of Anglicans and the ecumenical future be attempted.

THE DEVELOPMENT OF THE ECUMENICAL MOVEMENT

In writing about the Ecumenical Movement at the turn of the century Stephen Neill emphasizes the commitment of individuals and of like-minded groups rather than the commitment of churches.[1] Certainly groups like the YMCA (founded in 1844), the Evangelical Alliance (1846) and the Student Christian Federation (1880) provided opportunities for young Christians to form deep and lasting friendships and to develop a shared vision of unity. It was, however, the meetings of the missionary societies in 1888 and 1900 and finally the Edinburgh Conference in 1910 that gave birth to the modern Ecumenical Movement. The participants at Edinburgh saw clearly that the scandalous divisions were a grave hindrance to the mission of the Church: mission and unity belong together. It was, more than anyone else an Anglican, Bishop Charles Brent of the Episcopal Church of the USA, who discerned at Edinburgh that unity would only be brought about on the basis of agreement in faith. He determined to bring together bishops, church leaders and theologians to begin the task of studying the reasons for the divisions of the Church. After many setbacks, not least the ravages of the First World War, the theological arm of the Ecumenical Movement was set up and the First World Faith and Order Conference met in Lausanne in 1927. Here Orthodox, Anglicans and Protestants began to face divisive questions and set an agenda of work, a part of which matured sixty years later in the agreed statement, *Baptism, Eucharist and Ministry*.[2] The theologians at Lausanne agreed with Bishop Brent's concern that there would never be any true unity without communion in faith and the acceptance of a common doctrine of the ministry. The four points of the Lambeth Quadrilateral—covering the normative authority of Scripture, the witness of the primitive creeds, the sacraments of baptism and Holy Communion and the ministry—which had formed the basis of the Anglican 'Appeal to all Christian People' in 1920, were acknowledged as having had a formative effect upon the agenda set by Lausanne.

Two years prior to Lausanne another ecumenical group had gathered to consider problems of war and peace, race, education, capital and labour and the social order facing the Churches; and so the second arm of the Ecumenical Movement, Life and Work, was born. A decade later the two movements that were eventually to merge to form the World Council of Churches met: Faith and Order under the chairmanship of Bishop William Temple, and Life and Work under Bishop George Bell. These conferences raised questions that continue to engage the Ecumenical Movement: the relation of Scripture and tradition; the nature of the sacraments; apostolic succession and a sacramental episcopate; the nature of the Church. Underlying many of the debates was a tension between a Western intellectual approach and logic, and an Eastern sacramental approach. However, the experience of daily shared worship had a profound influence upon the movement, and the decision by the Archbishops of York and Canterbury to extend eucharistic hospitality was both a foretaste of the unity that lay ahead and a bitter reminder of the pain of continuing divisions.

The merging of Faith and Order and Life and Work, together with Christian Aid, had to wait another war-torn decade. The First Assembly of the World Council of Churches met in Amsterdam in 1948. Another Anglican, Archbishop Geoffrey Fisher, was in the chair when the formal decision to set up the Council was approved by representatives from over a hundred Churches, Orthodox, Anglican and Protestant. Although Anglicans played a major part in the history leading up to the formation of the Council, their voice was not always uncritical. Bishop Charles Headlam prophetically warned of the inevitable tension between the interests of Faith and Order and Life and Work, and the danger of political involvement of the Council foreshadowed in the capitalist-communist confrontation at Amsterdam. He asked, too, whether the setting up of a council pointed to a goal of church unity which was a federal model and not that to which he was himself passionately committed, a truly united Catholic Church. The First Assembly of the Council in 1948 marked a turning point in the Ecumenical Movement. At Amsterdam the Churches, as Churches, committed themselves to a common search for unity. Anglicans had played a leading role in setting up and directing the movement.

It is not possible to do more than indicate some key developments in the World Council of Churches and its agenda from Amsterdam to the Sixth Assembly in Vancouver in 1983. First, the Council has become much more representative: over 400 churches were represented at Vancouver. The growing number of Orthodox churches have significantly affected the Council's work and its spirituality. Following on from Vatican II, the Roman Catholic attitude has changed from one of hostility to partnership. Official observers from the Roman Catholic Church play an important part in Assemblies, and even more significant, the Roman Catholic Church is a full member of the Faith and Order Commission, and so is fully participant in the theological reflection of the Council. It is not only the ecumenical representation that has changed the face of the Council. What began as a white, Western, largely male gathering of church leaders now embraces women and men, clergy and laity from every part of the world, representing many cultures.

Secondly, as the community of the Council has widened, the members have added new concerns to the agenda. The pragmatic agenda that was once the concern of the Life and Work movement has sometimes seemed to be in opposition to the cerebral, academic work of the Faith and Order Movement. This tension has been felt equally within the Faith and Order Commission itself. However, the Commission has struggled in its own programmes on racism, the handicapped and women and men to show that the two agendas are interrelated. The search for agreement in faith, seen so clearly by Bishops Brent and Headlam as necessary for the visible unity of the Church, may not be surrendered; but the unity of the Church is not a matter of cerebral agreement or ecclesiastical joinery but is about a life of unity expressed in a community which is itself constantly being renewed in its own life. The early movement saw that unity and mission belong together; developments in the seventies highlighted unity and renewal. The Faith and Order Commission struggles still to articulate the theological undergirding of unity and renewal in its current programme on 'The Unity of the Church and the Renewal of the Human Community'. This is vital for the effect on its own agenda and for the foundation of the work of the entire Council.

A third development has come in the style and method of work. An attempt is made to ground the work of the Council in the lives of Christians in the member

Churches. Not only are agendas prepared for in various parts of the world but statements and reports are 'received' by member Churches and local congregations. The multilateral work is no longer tightly in the control of a few towering ecumenical giants, but is shared by an ever wider community. This change is still in its infancy but it is testimony to a developing ecclesiological understanding of the Church as the whole people of God, a community of interpretation, of faith and of life.

A fourth contribution lies in the developing and deepening vision of the goal of unity which has emerged in successive Assembly statements. An important contribution to this developing goal has been made by Faith and Order's work on sacraments and ministry, in its present work on a common confession of the apostolic faith, and on structures of decision-making and teaching authoritatively.

A final development is the way all of this is carried by a growing life of shared worship. The gradual discovery of the richness of the different spiritualities bore fruit at the Vancouver Assembly, where it was recognized that it is possible to preserve a rich variety of spirituality in a visibly united Church. Moreover, the Lima Liturgy presided over at Vancouver by the Archbishop of Canterbury, assisted by a Lutheran woman minister and a presbyter from the Church of South India, marked a significant moment in eucharistic sharing and was a foretaste of a shared sacramental life.

While the twentieth century has seen the development of the multilateral search for the visible unity of the Church, relations have developed between two or more partners. One of the earliest bilateral conversations between Anglicans and Roman Catholics, the Malines Conversations, began in 1921. The aim was to see whether, and on what conditions, Anglicans could be reunited with the Church of Rome, 'united, not absorbed'. The talks were closed by Pope Pius XI in 1928. The Bonn agreement of 1931 established a relationship of intercommunion between Anglicans and Old Catholics. A similar concordat was reached between some Anglican provinces and the Philippine Independent Church. To these can be added the close ties of intercommunion between the Lutheran Church of Sweden and the Church of Finland and the Church of England.

It has, however, been on the sub-continent of India that the greatest advance has been made. The Church of South India, founded in 1947, joined for the first time episcopal and non-episcopal Churches in an episcopally ordered Church. The union brought together Anglican, Methodist and Reformed traditions in an independent regional Church. Now, some thirty-five years after its inauguration, there remains a lack of clarity about the precise nature of the relationship with the Anglican Communion. The General Synod of the Church of England in 1985 refused to declare itself in full communion with the Church of South India, partly because there are still a few non-episcopally ordained presbyters in the Church and partly because the notion of full communion has developed since

1947 and is now seen by many to involve sharing together in universal structures of decision-making and teaching authoritatively. Whatever the verdict of the Church of England, the Church of South India has been important for its example in uniting episcopal and non-episcopal ministries; for developing an autonomous regional Church rooted in the local culture which can hold together differing denominational traditions; and for struggling latterly to understand what organs can best link the regional to the universal manifestations of the Church. The Church of South India also provided an example which was followed by the Church of North India and the Church of Pakistan in 1970. The success of union schemes involving Anglicans on the sub-continent of India have not, however, been matched in other parts of the world. In England, the failure of the Anglican-Methodist scheme and later the Covenant Proposals have their counterparts in failures in South Africa, Tanzania, New Zealand, the States and elsewhere.

A more hopeful sign, however, can be seen in the area of theological conversations. Bilateral dialogues at the international level proliferated as a result of the commitment of the Roman Catholic Church to unity following Vatican II. The texts of four bilateral dialogues are before the Anglican Communion for official response in the mid-eighties. The Anglican-Lutheran, Anglican-Orthodox, Anglican-Reformed and Anglican-Roman Catholic dialogues, while pursuing agendas relating to the specific cause of division between the partners, show remarkable convergences in understanding, particularly on the sacramental agenda of baptism, Eucharist and ministry. They have learnt to take into account each other's work as well as to build upon the convergences of understanding reached in the multilateral text, *Baptism, Eucharist and Ministry.* Some dialogues go further towards reaching consensus than others. The Anglican-Roman Catholic dialogue claims 'substantial agreement' for its work on Eucharist and ministry and remarkable convergence in its understanding of authority and primacy.[3]

The Anglican-Reformed dialogue, more than any other, has held together the search for the unity of the Church within the perspective of mission and the eschatological fulfilment; and within this broad perspective it has sought creatively to understand those areas of faith and order which continue to keep the Churches apart.[4] The Anglican-Orthodox dialogue has deepened the understanding of the inner reality of the Church.[5] The almost simultaneous publication of these texts helps to show that they are not rival ecumenisms but each belong within the one search for the visible unity of the Church which must be grounded in agreement in faith.

The picture of the Ecumenical Movement involving Anglicans would be incomplete without reference to the essential growing together of Christians at the local level. Regional councils of churches and local councils have encouraged the denominations to get to know one another, to reconcile memories of past divisions and hatred and, on the basis of the Lund Principle, to do only on their own what cannot yet be done together.[6] The Week of Prayer for Christian Unity, established in 1946, has helped to ground the movement in prayer. In some parts of the world, in New Zealand, in England and in Wales, Anglicans share with others in Local Ecumenical Projects, sharing buildings, worship and life, and with an increasing degree of shared ministry. In the United States of America Anglicans and Lutherans have entered into an agreement of 'interim eucharistic sharing' which acknowledges a degree of agreement in faith and a commitment to shared life. The theological convergences of the international dialogues, particularly the *Lima Text*, provide 'a charter' which gives a doctrinal basis for advances in shared life. Closer relationships at the local level are, in some places of the world, now involving Roman Catholics. Local covenants between Anglicans, Roman Catholics and the Free Churches in England, for example, provide a formal commitment to the sharing of life and witness. Another hopeful sign is an increase in sharing at the level of episcopal oversight, providing opportunities for joint witness to the world. And the facing and overcoming of divisions by individuals in 'mixed marriages' is an important sign of the ecumenical advance.

Against all of these advances in the way Christians relate to those of other denominations there remain the places of bitter divisions and polarization. The division between Roman Catholics and Protestants in Northern Ireland is an example and even in England, where so much can be recorded in ecumenical advance, the voices of a few raised in angry protest at the work of the Anglican-Roman Catholic International Commission testify to the need for greater determination in overcoming the entrenched positions and commitment to outmoded categories which go back to the Reformation.

THE ECUMENICAL FUTURE

The ecumenical scene in the mid-eighties is thus a complex one. It is difficult to hold together the multilateral and bilateral conversations, the regional schemes for unity and the many local initiatives which make up the one Ecumenical Movement. Against such a complex background it is appropriate to ask: what are the directions for the Ecumenical Movement? Is it possible to detect emerging a vision of unity to which Anglicans, together with others, can commit themselves, and what are the next steps that might be taken towards such an end?

The World Council of Churches is concerned to call all churches to the goal of visible unity. The Uppsala Assembly (1968) described this goal as 'conciliar fellowship'. This refers not only to outward structures which hold Christians who are united in each place together, but is a quality to be displayed by the

Church in each given situation. That quality has its model—more than that, its source—in the life of the Triune God and in the self-giving love of the incarnate Christ. The Nairobi Assembly (1975) recognized at least three basic marks of 'conciliar fellowship': consensus in the apostolic faith; mutual recognition of baptism, Eucharist and ministry; and conciliar gatherings for common deliberations and decision-making. In spite of the fact that the Nairobi Statement made quite clear that 'conciliar fellowship' does not describe any present reality, certainly not the World Council itself, and the repeated attempts by Faith and Order theologians to show that 'conciliar fellowship' is not an alternative to organic union, the concept has yet to gain widespread reception. More recently the Vancouver Assembly (1983) underlined the three 'marks' of the Church, while re-emphasizing that the Church is called to be a prophetic community through which and by which the transformation of the world can take place.[7] It can only be such a sign as long as it is itself being renewed in its own life.

The emerging goal in the multilateral dialogue is being further developed by the work of the Faith and Order Commission. The *Lima Text* has deepened the understanding of the second 'mark', the Church's sacramental life: the latest programme, 'Towards a Common Expression of the Apostolic Faith Today', has made a start on what a shared confession of the apostolic faith in word and in life might be when the faith is authentically expressed in different cultural contexts; preliminary work has begun on common structures of decision-making and teaching authoritatively. In developing these basic 'marks' or characteristics of the Church, the work of the multilateral dialogue will sharpen the picture of a Church living in unity, confessing a common faith, sharing in the Eucharist, served by a single ministry and held together by structures of decision-making. Anglicans will have a contribution to make to this reflection from their own experience, as well as insights to receive from the wider community.

The vision emerging from the bilateral dialogues in the coming years will need to be considered against the work of the multilateral forum. It is the Anglican-Reformed dialogue that resembles most closely the vision of the World Council. This dialogue holds together the universal aspect of the Church with the manifestation of unity at the local level. The aim is for reconciled local communities, each of which is recognizable as 'church': that is, 'communities which exhibit in each place the fullness of ministerial order, eucharistic fellowship, pastoral care and missionary commitment and which, through mutual communion and co-operation, bear witness to the regional, national and even international levels'.[8] While providing the most impressive overall ecclesiological vision set within the context of mission and the eschatological purpose of God, there are many points at which Anglicans may wish to deepen the convergence with the Reformed: the understanding of the Eucharist and sacrifice, the relation of personal, collegial and communal aspects of ministry, the exercise of personal oversight and a universal personal focus of unity and continuity.

Relations between Anglicans and Lutherans have been especially close. It is therefore of great interest to reflect in the eighties on how this relationship might develop in the light of the results of the bilateral dialogue. The expressed aim has been to move towards 'full communion'. 'Full communion' is taken to imply that members may receive the sacraments of the other; bishops of one Church may take part in the consecration of bishops of the other; when invited, an ordained minister may exercise liturgical functions in a congregation of the other body and that there would be regular organs of consultation.[9] The emphasis is upon 'interdependent while remaining autonomous', upon 'reconciled diversity' which takes into account the legitimacy of confessional differences and the need to preserve them.[10] Whether this points in the direction of a goal compatible with 'conciliar fellowship' remains to be assessed in the next stage of the dialogue as Anglicans move forward with Lutherans within the wider context of the ecumenical fellowship. But, at first sight, the emphasis upon 'interdependent while remaining autonomous' would seem to imply something less than the vision of organic union expressed by, for example, Bishop Charles Headlam when the World Council was set up in the 1940s.

The Anglican-Orthodox dialogue in 1977 expressed the goal of unity as 'the union of all Christians in one Church'.[11] This, however, has to be seen in the context of the statement that 'Anglicans ... see our divisions as within the Church ... Orthodox believe that the Orthodox Church is the one Church of Christ which, as his body, is not and cannot be divided'.[12] Here we are back at the ecclesiological difference that has reverberated throughout unity discussions since Lausanne. The resolution of this fundamental difference lies in the future. It may be, as one Orthodox theologian recently suggested, that in receiving the convergences of the sacramental agenda of the *Lima Text*, some implications will be realized for the reconciling of apparently conflicting ecclesiologies.[13] Whether or not this is a possible way forward in future, Anglicans, in dialogue with the Orthodox, will continue to develop an understanding of the inner reality of the Church grounded in the life of the holy and undivided Trinity.

The most developed dialogue, that between Anglicans and Roman Catholics (ARCIC), began with the intention of working towards 'full visible unity', 'full organic unity of our two communions'.[14] The concept of the Church which underlies this dialogue is that of *koinonia*, communion: the Eucharist is the effectual sign of *koinonia*, *episkope* its servant, and primacy its focus. *Koinonia* is both the goal and the way. One of the most welcome things to emerge from this dialogue is what unity and proper diversity might mean in a united Church. Unity must be focused in persons and in structures, transcending the local. A Church that has a universal primate who is never divorced from the wider collegiality of bishops, a servant figure, should be able to tolerate and sustain more, not less, diversity. In this dialogue, as in the dialogue with Lutherans, there appears some ambiguity. The quotation of Pope Paul VI's assurance that there will be no seeking to lessen the legitimate prestige and patrimony of piety and usage proper to the Anglican Church, while being a comfort to some who fear being 'swallowed up' by a larger body, might be thought to hint at an Anglican rite or jurisdiction within a reunited Church which would basically retain its own liturgy and canon law. This might seem to some a different perspective from one which holds together local and regional churches shaped more by the variety of their local history, cultural context and immediate missionary task than by old denominational loyalties. The future work of ARCIC II will be important in clarifying the notion of *koinonia*, the goal to which the two communions are committing themselves.

Bishop Lesslie Newbigin has written: 'A sincere intention to seek unity is incompatible with an intention to remain permanently uncommitted to any particular form of unity.'[15] Future work in both the multilateral and bilateral conversations will need to develop the remarkable convergences emerging in the sacramental agenda. But perhaps the most significant contribution of the next years will be to develop, using the convergences already achieved, a vision of a united Church. The goal can only be provisional, for new things are perceived as the Ecumenical Movement progresses, but the articulation of a vision would provide the Ecumenical Movement with a new impetus, and without a desire and a longing for unity the movement will achieve nothing. A vision would also help to set local initiatives and schemes in a wider context, thus ensuring a proper relation between the local and universal aspects of the Church.

In the future work of developing the vision of unity, Anglicans may have some special contributions to make from their own emerging self-understanding. The century that has seen the rise of the Ecumenical Movement has also seen dramatic changes within the Anglican Communion and, perhaps most significant of all in the last few years, a discovery of what it is that holds the Anglican Communion together. It is no accident that in the reports of the last three Lambeth Conferences attempts to deepen the understanding of Anglican identity are to be found in section reports on unity and renewal. It is often in dialogue with others that self-perception is sharpened. The ecumenical debates on apostolic succession, for example, have helped to free Anglicans from a narrow view of tactile succession and to concentrate rather on faithfulness to the apostolic teaching and mission symbolized in the succession of bishops. The four principles of the Lambeth Quadrilateral, embodied in the 1920 'Appeal to All Christian People', are acknowledged to have played a formative part in the development of the early ecumenical agenda. Now, Anglicans have come to recognize that these principles express not only the gifts of God which hold their own communion together, but that they also point towards that which God is calling the whole Church in unity more fully to become. The Quadrilateral thus describes both 'that vision which God has given, and that to which he calls'.[16] In dialogue with others, Anglicans will come to understand how to embody these principles more fully in word and life.

There are further aspects that might be offered by the Anglican Communion to the Ecumenical Movement. The Communion is held together by a theological method in which Scripture, tradition and reason are characteristically interrelated and also by a characteristic piety. The latter is no longer narrowly understood as worship according to the Book of Common Prayer. The 1978 Lambeth Conference emphasized the central position which the ordered worship of the Church occupies in the distinctive basis of the Anglican Communion. This worship 'patterns and limits the diversity which has characterised Anglicans from the first'.[17] The new forms of liturgy in almost every Province resemble each other in main outline and witness to the unity, not uniformity, of the Communion. This may point to that legitimate diversity which will be a proper mark of the universal Church. In a speech to the General Synod of the Church of England in 1985, the Archbishop of Canterbury brought the four principles of the Quadrilateral together with the shared piety of Anglican worship as he described what holds Anglicans together. The Quadrilateral is not a kind of ecclesiastical check-list:

> It is rather a description of the common life of the body of Christ. We share the Gospel of God when the Creeds are recited. We share the life of the crucified and risen Christ when Baptism and Eucharist are celebrated ... Having this common life is what communion means. It is deeper than denominational and confessional constitutions. It is about the participation of human beings in God and in each other.[18]

The identity of Anglicanism lies in communion in faith, maintained and built up in sacramental living and ministered to by an ordered ministry. A further aspect is developing as the Communion moves away from perceiving itself as the Church of England on a world scale to a fellowship of twenty-five autonomous Provinces drawing together the world's races, cultures and social conditions. 'Bonds of affection' in terms of persons and structures are emerging to maintain and nurture the internal unity of the Communion. The collegiality of bishops has been focused since 1886 in Lambeth Conferences; in 1954 the Anglican Consultative Council was set up, bringing together clergy and laity from every Province and thus providing for inter-Anglican solidarity; and more recently a meeting of Primates has been formed as well as an Inter-Anglican Doctrinal Commission. These various structures of consultation provide an arena for listening to the concerns of the various parts of the world and carrying those concerns back to different regions. They provide also an arena for helping the Provinces to take common decisions. The Archbishop of Canterbury has emerged as the senior bishop of the Communion, 'the eldest brother in a family' with a role 'to nurture the churches and not to rule them'. This development means that universal primacy, of which the Anglican-Roman Catholic dialogue speaks, is already a part of Anglican experience.

These 'bonds of affection' in terms of both structures and persons may be one contribution Anglicans have to make to an ecumenical vision of the unity of the Church in which local and regional manifestations of the Church are held together and embodied at the universal level. However, as these structures have emerged, so also have new and difficult questions: is it possible to ensure in a communion of such diversity that all the voices are heard and a genuine community of interpretation brought into being; what is the proper place and role of the episcopal voice in the oversight of any communion; where and how can the laity take their proper place in decision-making and teaching authoritatively; how can the voice of women be heard in the structures of a Church in which oversight still remains with men; what are those areas of faith and order which may properly be decided upon by autonomous provinces, and what must wait for the emergence of a common mind of the whole Communion, or indeed, of a truly ecumenical council; and what place is to be afforded to the process of receiving the decisions of councils by the local churches? In the past this last question was often focused in debates over eucharistic sharing and whether one province might proceed contrary to the mind of other parts of the Communion.[19] Currently, the question of unity and legitimate diversity has been focused in the (as yet) unresolved matter of the ordination of women to the priesthood and of the consecration of women to the episcopate. The matter is urgent, involving not simply a matter of order, but what is believed about the nature and being of God, of women and men created in God's image and the nature of the Church. It is a matter which affects the internal unity of the Anglican Communion. Can the communion between Anglicans remain unimpaired where priests from one province are not recognized by another province? How Anglicans proceed with this has implications for their own internal unity: it also has implications for the whole Ecumenical Movement, as those Churches who do already ordain women look for an affirmation of their decision, and those who do not ordain women look to the Anglicans to maintain the unbroken tradition. Clearly the Anglican Communion is being tested by this issue.

It is perhaps, paradoxically, in the development, during the last years of this century, of an understanding of what holds the Anglican Communion together, that Anglicans will make their most significant contribution to the Ecumenical Movement. It could be that, in expanding the Lambeth Quadrilateral to embrace the 'bonds of affection' that hold the Communion together, Anglicans would in turn develop the understanding of that third 'mark' of the Church which the Vancouver Assembly determined as necessary for the visible unity of the Church.

So far, emphasis has been placed upon the contributions Anglicans may make to the Ecumenical Movement in the future. The Ecumenical Movement calls equally for changes to be made in the lives of single denominations now. The World Council of Churches has invited those Churches which recognize the

389

'faith of the Church through the ages' in the *Lima Text* to consider what changes are appropriate in their own lives are appropriate on the basis of such agreement in faith, and what changes are appropriate in their relations with one another. By making changes in their own life on the basis of an affirmation of the theological convergences in the theological dialogues, Anglicans would signify a serious recommitment to the Ecumenical Movement. The *Lima Text* challenges Anglicans, for example, to review an apparently indiscriminate baptismal policy; to look at their exercise of episcopacy with the existence of unwieldly dioceses and the anomaly of suffragan bishops; to discover ways of reconstituting the third order of ministry; to reconcile seemingly opposing understandings of the priesthood of the ordained ministry that exist amongst Anglo-Catholic and Evangelical Anglicans; and to resolve the growing tensions over the ordination of women to the priesthood and the consecration of women to the episcopate. Lying behind a number of issues is the challenge to Anglicans to reaffirm a theological method based upon a proper relation of Scripture, tradition and reason which understands the place of a dynamic tradition and is not tempted to elevate Anglican formularies to rigid confessional statements (see pp. 410–22). By working at these issues in their own lives Anglicans would show that they are concerned with more than mere assent in word to ecumenical agreements, and that they are prepared for costly change in their own life for the sake of the unity of the Church.

In relations with others there are steps that can be taken in the immediate future. An interim eucharistic sharing agreement has already been made in the USA between Episcopalians and Lutherans on the basis of their bilateral dialogue. A similar agreement might be the next appropriate step between Anglicans and Lutherans in other parts of the world. The Church of England is currently considering new ecumenical canons to make closer relations legal with other denominations on the basis of the theological convergences expressed in the ecumenical texts. Now may well be the time to consider a greater degree of sharing of oversight at local and regional levels, the establishment of more officially recognized ecumenical projects and local covenants, and a greater determination to live according to the Lund Principle of never doing alone what can already be done together.

Finally, Anglican-Roman Catholic relations will need special consideration after the official response is given by both Churches to the Final Report in 1988. Both Churches have been asked to consider in advance what are the next 'concrete steps' that might be taken on the basis of the substantial agreements and convergence of the texts. Should these advances be affirmed, then two particular issues will need to be faced: the degree of eucharistic sharing that is appropriate on the basis of such agreement, and the possibility of the Roman Catholic Church recognizing future Anglican ordinations. The letter of Cardinal

Johannes Willebrands to the Co-Chairman of ARCIC II in July 1985 holds out promise for future progress in this second area.[20]

It is not easy to do justice in such a short essay to the rise of the Ecumenical Movement and to Anglican involvement in that movement. It is a complex movement involving relations between many partners at many different levels: between members of a single family, between Churches at local, regional and international levels, sometimes bilateral relations, sometimes multilateral. The agenda covers theological dialogue as well as the facing together of the common problems of the contemporary world and the discovery of ways of worshipping together. Anglicans have, undoubtedly, played a significant and often leading part from the beginning of the movement. The criticism heard so often—that Anglican involvement has been full of promise but short on achievement—is not easy to assess. The undoubted failure, all too obvious in the 1980s, to bring about more united Churches like South India and North India has in many instances been the result of Anglican withdrawal from negotiations at a damagingly late stage in the process. It may prove in the long run to be a temporary and short-lived failure. It may prove to have been an attempt to safeguard and bring about that real and costly agreement in faith necessary for the confident acceptance of one another. We have to recognize one another as sharing one faith in word and life if we are credibly to celebrate that common faith, hope and love together in the face of a broken and divided world. If such a charitable verdict is right, Anglicans will need to recommit themselves with even more determination and devotion to the Ecumenical Movement in the future. The search for the visible unity of the Church, grounded in the life of the holy Trinity, focused in a common confession of the apostolic faith in word and life, in shared sacraments and ministry and in bonds of affection, is not an optional extra but an essential part of our Christian obedience. It is our fidelity to the prayer of Jesus that those who follow him might be one.

In the search for the visible unity of the Church, commitment to the development of Anglican self-understanding and identity ought not to be set against the advance of the Ecumenical Movement. The heightened awareness of being a part of a world-wide Anglican Communion, with all the gifts and riches of cultural diversity that offers, ought itself to be a marvellous preparation for being a part of a truly universal Church. Anglicans need to preserve a balance by being open to receive the riches safeguarded in other traditions as well as preserving those things in their own life which can be contributed to the whole, but always ready to surrender that which is outdated for the sake of richer and better gifts that God desires to give to his Church. There will always be diversity in the Church, but what part denominational traditions will have to play in the rich diversity held together in unity in the Church of the future is a question still to be answered. At least some Anglicans are ready to believe that 'Anglicanism is not a confession: and is not primarily interested in Anglicanism'[21] (see pp. 219–231).

Even this agenda of ecumenism looks narrow when set against what some are bold enough to call 'the wider ecumenism' of the 1980s, namely the relations between Christians and those of other faiths. What we have learned about the principles of dialogue amongst Christians, about listening attentively to others and only then responding, about searching together, believing that each has something to communicate and that no one person, no single system is the depository of the whole truth, are equally important in this dialogue. The wider framework of inter-faith dialogue is a necessary and proper context for the Christian search for the visible unity of the Churches. As Christians together engage in dialogue with those of other faiths, they will be led to perceive new things in the gospel they share and are commanded to share with the world. It is those who, in ecumenism and inter-faith dialogue, show the characteristics of openness to others as well as a commitment to safeguard the 'jealousies' of their own tradition as they see it, who will be able to overcome the blind a rigid fundamentalism that threatens everywhere the contemporary world.

NOTES

1 Neill, S. *The Church and Christian Union.* OUP 1968.

2 *Baptism, Eucharist and Ministry,* (The Lima Text), Faith and Order Paper 111. Geneva, WCC, 1982.

3 *The Final Report of the Anglican-Roman Catholic International Commission.* London, CTS/SPCK, 1982.

4 *God's Reign and Our Unity,* The Report of the Anglican-Reformed International Commission. SPCK 1984.

5 *Anglican-Orthodox Dialogue,* The Dublin Agreed Statement. SPCK 1984.

6 'Should not our Churches ask themselves whether they are showing sufficient eagerness to enter into conversation with other Churches and whether they should not act together in all matters except those in which deep differences of conviction compel them to act separately?' *The Report of the Third World Conference on Faith and Order* (Lund 1952), p. 34.

7 *Gathered for Life,* Report of the Vancouver Assembly (WCC 1983), Section 2 p.

8 *God's Reign and Our Unity,* para. 110.

9 *Anglican-Lutheran Dialogue,* The Report of the European Commission (SPCK 1983), para. 62.

10 *Anglican-Lutheran Relations,* Report of the Anglican-Lutheran Joint Working Group (ACC 1983), para 25.

11 *Anglican-Orthodox Dialogue,* The Moscow Agreed Statement. SPCK 1977.

12 *Anglican-Orthodox Dialogue*, The Dublin Agreed Statement. SPCK 1984.

13 Nissiotis, N. *A Credible Reception of Baptism, Eucharist and Ministry*, to be published by the Conference of European Churches, Geneva, 1986.

14 Clark, A. and Davey, C. *Anglican-Roman Catholic Dialogue*, OUP 1974. The Common Declaration by Pope Paul VI and the Archbishop of Canterbury, pp. 1–3.

15 Newbigin, L. *All in Each Place*. WCC 1981.

16 *The Report of the Lambeth Conference 1968*. London, CIO, 1968.

17 *The Report of the Lambeth Conference 1978*. London, CIO, 1978.

18 *Report of Proceedings*, General Synod November Group of Sessions, 1985, Vol. xvi. no. 3, pp. 1035–42.

19 cf. Neill, S. above p.203.

20 Correspondence between Cardinal Johannes Willebrands and the Co-Chairmen of ARCIC II, in *Women Priests: Obstacle to Unity?* London, CTS, 1986.

21 Paton, D. *Anglicans and Unity*. Oxford, Mowbray, 1962.

2 Newer Dioceses of the Anglican Communion—Movement and Prospect

JOHN S. POBEE

PROLEGOMENON

At the beginning of this century *ecclesia Anglicana* was largely Anglo-Saxon. It comprised what may be termed the older provinces: i.e. Australia, Canada, England, Ireland, New Zealand, Scotland, the United States of America, and Wales. Today, the majority of the dioceses are not Anglo-Saxon, and the majority of Anglicans are either non-native-speakers of English or non-speakers of English. Out of the twenty-seven Provinces of the Communion, fourteen have grown up since 1950: West Africa (1951), Central Africa (1955), Uganda (1961), Brazil (1965), Kenya (1970), Burma (1970), Indian Ocean (1973), Iglesia Americana del Cono Sur (1974, 1982), Melanesia (1975), Jerusalem and the Middle East (1976), Sudan (1976), Papua New Guinea (1977), Nigeria (1979) and Burundi, Rwanda and Zaire (1980). Before 1950 the other non-Anglo-Saxon Provinces were Chung Hua Sheng Kung Hui (Holy Catholic Church in China) and Diocese of Hong Kong,[1] Nippon Sei Ko Kwai (Holy Catholic Church in Japan) and West Indies. We may also mention two other Provinces which are neither Anglo-Saxon nor exactly 'Third World': the Lusitanean Church of Portugal (1980) and the Spanish Reformed Episcopal

Church (1980). Thus more than half the dioceses of the Communion are not in the British Commonwealth and, therefore, more and more Anglican Churches do not have a living association with British history (see pp. 367–70).

The foregoing set of facts tells a significant story. The word 'Anglican' which in origin is so wedded to the English culture and is, therefore, not exactly a term the non-Anglo-Saxon members are fond of, 'no longer means simply English, but has come to be a term for the particular embodiment of the historic faith, order and worship of the Catholic Church that is the heritage of this Communion'.[2] In any case, the word is too entrenched in history and many minds that it is difficult to avoid it. So one retains the word Anglican in one of its forms in this essay as a matter of convenience, and in no way ignores what will be said later about the Anglo-Saxon captivity of *ecclesia Anglicana* (see pp. 424–428).

In India, Bangladesh and Pakistan Anglicans have gone into union schemes, so that one may not exactly speak of them in Anglican terms (see pp. 379–83). On the other hand, the United Churches of North India (born in 1979), South India (born in 1947) and Pakistan (born in 1970) have membership in the Anglican Consultative Council.

This essay is addressing the parts of the Communion that in other areas of life are termed 'Second and Third World'. The 'Second World' is normally used of the Communist world from China westwards, plus perhaps Cuba in the western hemisphere.[3] With the exception of Cuba,[4] where there are some 7,000 Anglicans out of the Christian population of 4,434,000 in mid-1980, and possibly China, which is just beginning to open up again, there is hardly any *ecclesia Anglicana* in the Second World that is worth writing about. So one is left with the so-called 'Third World'.

The 'Third World' is such a vast and diverse world taking in black Africans, brown and yellow Asians, Oceaneans and Latinos that not only is it unlikely for one person to know them all sufficiently well to have the confidence to pontificate on them, but also incoherence and sweeping generalization could be the only consequence of such an attempt. In any case, the very expression 'Third World' generates so much heat in Africa and Asia, where it is said to have negative judgemental overtones, that it is best to avoid it. Such is the rationale for writing on 'the newer dioceses of the Anglican Communion'.

One more comment may be offered on 'Third World' and its synonym 'the developing world'. Whether we retain the phrases or replace them with some other word, they usually speak of poor peoples outside Europe, America, Australasia. But there are pockets of so-called 'Third World' in the northern hemisphere, which may not be ignored. A report on the Church in the inner city areas of England demonstrates convincingly that, although people may not be starving like peoples in the southern hemisphere, 'many residents in the Urban Priority Areas are deprived of what the rest of society regard as the essential minimum for a decent life'. The degree of inequality in society 'exceeds the limits that could be thought acceptable by most of their fellow citizens'.[5] Thus more and more we are hearing of 'Afro-Anglicanism' and 'black Anglicanism' which takes in not only those from so-called Third World, but also from the pockets of 'Third World' in the northern hemisphere.[6]

Again, the membership of *ecclesia Anglicana* has been falling in Australia, England, Ireland, Scotland, the United States of America and Wales—that is, in the older Churches of the Communion. In the younger dioceses of China (Hong Kong), Brazil, Japan and South America the growth has been static for some time. On the other hand, in the younger dioceses of Africa, particularly Central Africa, Kenya, Sudan, Tanzania and Uganda as well as Papua New Guinea, *ecclesia Anglicana* is enjoying tremendous and fast growth; indeed, the fastest in the Communion. Whatever questions there may be about statistics, the foregoing picture is of a piece with the general picture that by the year AD 2000 the overwhelming majority of self-professed Christians will be living in the southern continents, particularly Africa.[7]

THE ANGLO-SAXON CAPTIVITY OF ECCLESIA ANGLICANA

Ecclesia Anglicana by virtue of its provenance is English in texture and fibre. This is perfectly natural, because when 'God becomes flesh', he takes the form and shape of the locus. Anglicanism in the southern hemisphere came *principally* through agents from the British Isles, the others being from USA and Australia. They naturally brought what they had and knew. Thus Anglicanism in Africa, for example, was born in the matrix of Anglo-Saxon culture and the 'daughter' Churches can be said to be in Anglo-Saxon captivity. Lambeth Palace, the London residence of the Archbishop of Canterbury, is the spiritual home of most dioceses. But in practical terms the spiritual home often works out as captivity to Lambeth, through no fault of Lambeth. For although juridically autonomous, these African Churches almost always want to follow Canterbury's line. They doggedly use the Book of Common Prayer (BCP) which indisputably bears the marks of English culture. Of BCP Shepherd writes: 'Into a texture of liturgical prayer retained from the medieval services, Cranmer skilfully interwove many phrases drawn from many sources, ancient and contemporary, with occasional touches of his own creation. The result was a fabric conceived as a consistent whole, with an integral blend of old and new trends and colours.'[8] Despite the manifest contextual nature of BCP, the younger Churches hold on to it. The best they have done is to translate BCP into its vernaculars, presuming that such translations constitute indigenization of worship.[9] Frequently *Hymns Ancient and Modern* or the *English Hymnal*, despite the foreign rhythm and idiom, is held to tenaciously, as if it were tradition once-for-all delivered to the saints; and native compositions which are really heart-throbbing are ignored.

Church structures, likewise, have tended to be imitated from those of the north. All too often the bishop has become a carbon copy of the English bishop whose office and style have been accommodated to the English culture, particularly the upper-class culture. A classic example is the African bishop being addressed as the Lord Bishop of Cape Coast or Tamale or Freetown. The title reflects an English culture and social structure which are irrelevant to the African situation. Thus a major task before the younger dioceses of the Anglican Communion is to work their way out of the captivity, so that the Anglican apprehensions of Christ may become authentically 'enfleshed' in Africa. Two major aspects of this task are (a) the question of how to treat tradition and (b) clarifying the identity of the African Churches themselves.

While African or Asian or Pacific Anglicans contribute to their own captivity to the Anglo-Saxon *ecclesia Anglicana*, the captivity is also imposed from outside. The younger Churches came into being through the agency of various Mission Societies, for example the Church Missionary Society, Society for the Propagation of the Gospel, Universities Mission to Central Africa, etc. These missionary societies have done a good job (see pp. 430–37). But, as the Akan of Ghana put it in a proverb, 'It is the one whose duty it is to fetch water, who may break the pot for fetching the water.'

In other words, in going about a good job, one risks causing some damage or making some mistakes. They were sometimes paternalistic and consequently contributed to the Peter Pan syndrome in which non-Anglo-Saxon dioceses are held.[10] The relationship is further complicated by the power of the purse, since several dioceses depend on funds from Europe, America or Australia. It is thus obvious that the growth of the younger Churches to maturity is as much their responsibility as that of the older Churches. A healthy relationship between mother Churches and daughter Churches should be one of love which respects the integrity of the other partner. Basic to that relationship of love is the question, 'What is the true shape of selfless and self-sacrificing devotion and service to the other person?' And the daughter Churches need to ask: 'What do we, youthful and poor as we are, bring to the family?' It should be a relationship of giving and receiving.

An aspect of the linking of Anglicanism and Englishness is the phenomenon of the Establishment. The English Reformation which brought into being the Anglican Church was the tip of an iceberg of discontent with corrupt ecclesiasticism, fuelled by English nationalism (see pp. 3–10 and pp. 352–354). The *submission of the clergy* of 15 May 1532, which stripped the Church of England of the right of legislation independently of the State, was itself one expression of the Renaissance conception of the absolute unitary sovereignty which could tolerate no rivals. That tradition was brought to its logical conclusion when in 1534 the King of England was declared to be the head of *ecclesia Anglicana*. The Church of England became the established Church in the realm of England. By the Establishment the Church of England was declared English, in body and soul and mind. The question came up, and had to be resolved, of how it was possible for *ecclesia Anglicana* to exist in a situation where there was no *de jure* establishment. In any case, it is not possible for such Englishness of the Church to be transplanted outside England to Africa or elsewhere in the non-English world.

In the former British colonies Anglican missions generally followed British political and economic interests, even though Anglicanism was not officially established.[11] The mission was often in the vicinity of the castle; the Anglican clergyman was often a kind of religious department of the British administration. In Accra, where Anglicans continued to behave as if they were the established Church, when the governor opened the Legislative Council, the Anglican bishop sat with him on the dais. Until about 1950 the Anglican diocese of Accra, for example, was called the *English* Church Mission, or as the vernacular put it, *aban mu asor*—that is, the Church that was most closely associated with the colonial government.

Non-Anglo-Saxon dioceses have the English albatross around their necks and they need to free themselves of it. If they fail to divest themselves of the English baggage, they will be irrelevant promontories in politically independent African landscapes. I dare to suggest that in freeing themselves of the English albatross, they will be helping to free the Church of England, for which also the English cultural heritage is so often today an unhealthy drag. To the question of how to free themselves we shall return a little later.

The quasi-establishment does not appear to have done *ecclesia Anglicana* much good in most of Africa. In most places Anglicanism is numerically eclipsed by other denominations. For example, in Ghana in 1970 the historic Churches are grouped as follows: Roman Catholics 15.77%; Presbyterians 12%; Methodists 11.37%; Anglicans 2.2%.[12]

The Rt Rev. John Orfeur Aglionby, Bishop of Accra 1925–49, addressed a diocesan conference in Accra on 14 January 1925 as follows: 'As long as people believed—as they did—that we were the Government Church supported by Government funds, it is no wonder that they were content to fold their hands and open their mouths to see what would drop into them.'[13] Clearly the quasi-establishment was not necessarily healthy for the Church.

Is it possible for *ecclesia Anglicana* to be other than the Anglo-Saxon at prayer? I believe on the basis of the experience of the Old Catholics (especially those in Geneva) and of the Episcopal Church of Scotland, that it is possible. But a prerequisite is to be clear on the non-negotiables of the Anglican ethos. To that we shall return later. A related question is, what are the legitimate limits of the welding of Anglicanism to the English culture—and for that matter, the Anglo-

Saxon culture? To put it theologically, the story of *ecclesia Anglicana* in Africa or Oceania is a matter of the nature of the incarnation in a plural world.

Again to be able to free themselves from the Anglo-Saxon albatross, the younger dioceses must themselves search for an indigenized theology, spirituality and worship. Loved as Hooker, Gore etc. are, their theologies are contextual, emerging out of a particular situation. If the younger dioceses are to be living, they too must develop their own contribution and bring it into the Anglican pool. Spirituality, like worship, is contextual and cannot be meaningfully and satisfyingly appropriated *en masse* from another culture. It comes from the wrestling of real living bodies with that same revelation of God. That wrestling cannot be done for one by another; the revelation of God demands engagement with it in one's own context, if it is to be understood.

THE NON-NEGOTIABLES OF THE ANGLICAN ETHOS

In arguing for liberation from the Anglo-Saxon captivity of the younger dioceses, one is not exactly arguing for iconoclasm. So let us address ourselves to the Anglican non-negotiables that will guide the debate.

(i) *Catholic*

The story of the English Reformation which brought into being the Church of England has been encapsulated in the phrase 'Catholicism without the pope'. Anglicans claim to retain the Catholic tradition shorn of its medieval accretions and abuses. One side of it is that *ecclesia Anglicana* claims to preserve the tradition of the ancient Church.

The pegs of that tradition have been defined in the Chicago-Lambeth Quadrilateral as Scripture, Creeds, sacrament, and ministry. But in the best Anglican tradition, tradition is seen not in static terms but rather as something representing the responses of particular Churches to specific situations, challenges and problems. Tradition is a dynamic process which is also an aid to a sense of history and a guide to the present in its various components of Scripture, creeds, decisions of Councils, liturgical order, canon law, etc.

In the younger Churches there has been a danger and a tendency to treat the received tradition in fixed terms. But that is not truly Anglican. It is thus heartening that Declaration 20 of the 1930 Constitution of the Church of India, Burma and Ceylon stated: 'As the Church of England, receiving Catholic Christianity from the undivided Church, has given characteristically English interpretation to it, so the Church of this Province aspires to give characteristically national interpretation of that same common faith and life.' That aspiration is what the younger Churches must never lose sight of, if they are to be relevant to their varying contexts. And they should do so without any sense of betraying the

Anglican tradition. Bishop Prince E. S. Thompson of Freetown, Sierra Leone, West Africa, responding to the first draft of this essay, comments:

> Emphasize that there is no one tradition to which all Anglicans must conform. You need only refer to the different shades of eucharistic theology and practice, different approaches to the Bible (from rabid fundamentalism to excellent scientific study) to be convinced that there is in fact no one tradition. Such tradition as is created becomes the context of growing into Christ. And yet all of these also reflect a certain fidelity to the traditions.

(ii) *Episcopal*

The Anglican tradition is committed to the threefold ministry of bishops, presbyters and deacons which is earliest attested by Ignatius of Antioch (Trallians 3) as essential for a community qualifying to be called a Church. But:

> the early Church learnt by experience that the diocesan family needs to have one man rather than a committee as the focus of unity both in the local church and in his fellowship with the college of bishops. Despite the strong language of Ignatius of Antioch, the 'monarchical' character of the episcopate is not, as such, a matter of fundamental juridical dogmatic principle, essential to the church in the sense that if the episcopacy were shared and not monarchical the church would be amputated, but is a practical need for the expression of unity. Nevertheless, Ignatius is surely right in seeing the bishop's central authority as linked to his presidency at the eucharist, in which he stands in a sacramental relation to Christ. He is the focus of the harmony . . . in the family of God.[14]

However, the Catholic emphasis on episcopacy needs to be liberated from the Anglo-Saxon trappings by the younger dioceses. The concept and practice, as was mentioned earlier, have been assimilated to the Anglo-Saxon cultures,[15] which are not exactly relevant to an African context marked by poverty and degradation. A task before the non-Anglo-Saxon Catholic episcopal movement is to rehabilitate episcopacy. There is need to examine theologically, sociologically, empirically and practically in the African context, for example, what it means to exercise *episcope*. The structures that relate to *episcope* must be seen in terms of wholeness of ministries which bring wholeness to the people of God, as to humanity.

(iii) *And yet Protestant*

Anglicans everywhere love to appropriate the phrase 'the *via media*'—the middle way. It is a phrase that captures Anglicanism as an institution that is at once Catholic, episcopal and Protestant. As originally enunciated, the Anglican divines claimed Anglicanism to represent the middle ground between the extremes of medieval Roman Catholicism and Anabaptism. It was the middle ground between 'Roman superstition' and licentious heresy. When the Scottish Episcopalians and the Dutch and Swiss Old Catholics affirmed the *via media*, they claimed to be minorities between large blocks of Calvin-inspired Reformers and 'Counter-Reformed' Roman Catholics. Anglicanism sees itself also as Reformed, in the sense of disavowing the doctrinal and practical innovations of the Middle Ages.

Whatever its precise shape on the ground, the *via media* is a catch-phrase for a number of related things: (a) spiritual freedom illustrated by the refusal to lay down rigid lines; (b) the willingness to accept each other across the board; and (c) order and propriety which are not too loud. In theory, at any rate, this means that there is room for a relative degree of diversity in holy chaos and the recognition of each member of the Church. Diversity does not necessarily compromise essential Anglicanism. This is worth recall when the younger Churches discuss with the older Churches what the sense of communion and ecumenism should be. In this regard, the *via media* commits Anglicans to excluding limited interpretation and to seeing the Communion as a family in which there is free association, discussion and mutual esteem of the whole. It should also be a key to the liberation of the younger Churches from their Anglo-Saxon captivity. It means the freedom to devise theology and worship consonant with African ethos and usage. For example, in a society that is notoriously communalistic, how may the *pax* be used to express the sense of belonging to a group?

The implications of the *via media* principles and method should embolden non-Anglo-Saxon dioceses to work from the local ground an authentic theology, spirituality and worship which are nevertheless faithful to the Bible, Creeds, sacraments and ministry. It means mutual acceptance of Evangelicals and people of High Church persuasion, an attitude which in some provinces, such as Tanzania, is far from easy. There, when one from the High Church tradition goes on transfer to a Low Church area, he or she would rather join the Roman Catholics than the Low Church Anglicans for worship. Similarly the Low Church would rather worship with the Lutherans than with the High Church Anglicans. This situation is contrary to the Anglican ethos.

As a Protestant movement the non-Anglo-Saxon diocese takes seriously the Bible, probably in the appropriate vernacular, in its liturgy and devotional life. The underlying conviction is that Scripture contains that life-giving message which can most effectively engage people in their own language and, therefore, on their wavelength. The people of God are expected to learn to use the Bible and to relate it to their life-salvation through a critical engagement with the text and situation. That is part of what Anglicans call 'probable reason'. Scripture should now also be read through the African spectacles, in the way in which the English divines read it through their English spectacles. The African's spectacles bear the marks of culture and poverty, and can help to unearth insights which it should put into the pool of the Communion for mutual affirmation and correction.

The development of African, Asian and other theologies in the non-Anglo-Saxon dioceses becomes an urgent task of the Church.

A NON-ANGLO-SAXON PERSPECTIVE: THE AFRICAN EXAMPLE

What are the elements of the African perspective? In the first place Africans are yet another specimen of God's creation, human like any other human of whatever colour. They are not some exotic creatures to be pitied and fawned upon. They are identifiable members of a world of human beings with their own identity and integrity. There is no room for romanticization of Africa, special pleading and condoning or sanctifying of wickedness and false human values. All this means that the Anglican Church should be concerned with human, political and religious issues of human dignity. They must be concerned about multinational organizations that contribute to the pauperization of Africans. Then, secondly, Africans bring cultures of which they are proud and which are different from the Anglo-Saxon cultures. That is the significance of such phrases as 'African Personality' (Nkrumah of Ghana), 'negritude' (Senghor of Senegal), 'authenticité' (Mobutu of Zaire), *Nkosi Sikelel! Afrika* ('God bless Africa', which is now known as the African National Anthem), self-reliance. All of these, whatever else they may be, also speak of self-authenticity of Africans and pride in their culture. The classic statement of it is that of the Asante King to Rev. T. R. Picot:

> You must understand that we will not select children for education, for the Ashanti children have better work to do than to sit down all day idly to learn 'Hoy! 'Hoy! 'Hoy! ... The Bible is not a book for us. God at the beginning gave the Bible to the White Peoples, another to the Cramos [Muhammadans?], and fetish to us ... We know God already ourselves ... We will never embrace your religion, for it would make our people proud. It is your religion which has ruined the Fanti country, weakened their power and brought down the high man on a level with the low man.[16]

They delude themselves who think Africans have no culture or are ashamed of their cultures.

Three aspects of the African culture are important for the tasks of theology and worship.

(a) Africans, despite some secularism, have a religious ontology and epistemology. To be is to be religious. That is why the most rabid Marxist African politicians not too infrequently resort to religion in their personal life. This means that theologizing starts from already religious premises and only sometimes from secularist presuppositions. Rather, theology has to relate to religious pluralism. The subjects of the absoluteness of Christ in a religiously plural society and of ecumenical perspectives become crucial in engaging the society. Besides, Anglo-Saxon theologies with their dose of the Enlightenment mentality with its inbuilt humanism and agnosticism will need to learn to see how it relates to a culture which decidedly has a religious ontology and epistemology. And that will help liberate the scientific society from an arid life.

(b) A contemporary African's epistemology and ontology is *cognatus sum, ergo sum*, or, 'I am because I have relatives.' A sense of community as opposed to a very individualistic culture, is of the essence of being human. The individualism of Anglo-Saxon societies leaves much to be desired, when one only considers the suicide rate within the societies with decent welfare state systems. A theologizing that is community-conscious, if not community-based, is what Africa's Church can contribute to the world Church as it struggles to realize the Church as the People of God.

(c) Africans have their own concepts of art and beauty. This is crucial for music, the shape of the liturgy, and liturgical colours. Cranmer's liturgy is, at the end of the day, very Anglo-Saxon and particularly English in texture. Beautiful as it may be, it may not speak to many Africans. I wish to suggest that if Christianity, and for that matter Anglicanism, is to be authentic in Africa, art and beauty need to be carefully engaged.[17] Theologically speaking, this is a question of local concepts of art and beauty being vehicles for capturing insights of Anglicanism and Christian faith. It is as a matter of the contextuality and universality in the expression of the Christian faith.

The African context, thirdly, is one of poverty and pain, suffering and degradation. Part of it is self-induced; part inflicted by an unjust social order. Now, Anglicanism as one expression of Christianity is ultimately about good news. If Anglicanism is to be about good news, then the question is: How can Anglicanism truly be experienced as good news, especially as other denominations and religions are seeking to bring relief to embattled peoples of Africa? In the face of stark poverty, suffering and brutality, the issue is how we show solidarity with the suffering peoples from our little corners. As the Archbishop of Canterbury, Robert Runcie, put it in his Christmas message of 1985: 'We are learning in the Communion that when one member suffers, we all suffer. And we are learning to express our common sympathy in ways which build up the common good.' *Ecclesia Anglicana* in Africa cannot but affirm the preferential option for the poor and work out its practical implications. The model of the Church there cannot be the prestigious, rich Solomonian temple, but a tent.

Anglicanism is respectable. But looking at it in terms of the Christian faith itself, one may dare to say there is no special virtue in being an Anglican. To be an Anglican is only a half-way-house to the kingdom of God. Besides, to revel in denominationalism is to undermine the credibility of the Church as the reconciler of all things in Christ. In an Africa plagued by divisions of tribes, race, and sexes, denominationalism only exacerbates the problem. So the ecumenical task is an urgent one before the African Churches. Unfortunately, the African Churches have learnt their European lessons all too well, so that they are not exactly on the way to structural reconciliation. In Ghana, where Anglicans initially made a tremendous input in the Church Union negotiations, the Anglicans of the Accra diocese pulled out of the negotiations in 1973–4. Part of the problem is the arrogance of the denomination. But it is also a fear of falling out of communion with the mother Church. It thus behoves the older parts of *ecclesia Anglicana* to take seriously their ecumenical task. In any case, the model of the *via media* logically leads to ecumenism, a diversity in unity.

The stress on ecumenism is closely linked with mission. The goal of mission is not to create a denomination but the people of God, the community reconciled to God and to one another. The point has been made that the Anglican Church like all denominations is growing fastest in the southern hemisphere, particularly Africa. But, as Tom Tuma has shown,

> although the Church in Africa is growing steadily, this growth has been both encouraged and facilitated more by the prevailing situation than by a developed and systematic policy of discipling which the Church does not have the machinery to sustain. It may well be advisable to start developing a systematic policy of discipling before Islam, which is gradually increasing its influence in Africa, becomes a major threat to the Churches there.[18]

When the foregoing comment is applied to Anglicanism in Africa, one has much to worry about. In its history it is debatable whether the Anglican Church as such has ever had a sense of mission. Its mission was often carried on by missionary societies which were not exactly the responsibility of the Church. In some cases chaplaincy was confused with mission. Besides, the structure of the mission agencies produced effects which would have been undesirable in any business; for example, promotion of uniform product, the temptation to side-step the national Churches, the temptation to control the process. I suspect that the local Churches have imbibed this example of the mother Churches and need to grow out of it, if they are not to lose out in the end. Moreover, in Africa the Church is in such a stiff race with ideologies and other religions for the hearts and minds of people that it cannot afford the luxury of a faulty mission sense. At the end any Church exists for mission, God's mission to create a people of God who would be agents of God to achieve his purposes in this world, to bring liberty to all and to sum up all things for Christ.

NOTES

1 When China was closed to the rest of the world, the only Chinese Church that was in touch with the ACC was the diocese of Hong Kong.

2 Howe, John, *Highways and Hedges. Anglicanism and the Universal Church* (CIO 1985), p. 81.

3 Barrett, David B., ed., *World Christian Encyclopaedia. A Comparative Survey of Churches and Religions in the Modern World AD 1900–2000* (OUP 1982), pp. 252–5.

4 There are the cases of Korea, Taiwan, Hong Kong and Singapore which may be called non-Communist Second World.

5 *Faith in the City: A Call for Action by Church and Nation. The Report of the Archbishop of Canterbury's Commission on Urban Priority Areas* (Church House Publishing, 1985), p. xv.

6 In June 1985 there was a meeting in Barbados, West Indies which brought together Blacks from mainland Africa and the diaspora to reflect on 'Afro-Anglicanism, Present Issues and Future Tasks'. Out of that emerged the Codrington Consensus which may well prove an important landmark in the history and development of non-Anglo-Saxon Anglicanism.

7 Barrett, M. David B., 'A.D. 2000: 350 million Christians in Africa' in *International Review of Mission* 59 (1970) pp. 39–54; Winter, Ralph D. *The Twenty-Five Unbelievable Years* (South Pasadena 1970); Walls, Andrew F, 'Africa's Place in Christian History' in *Religion in a Pluralistic Society*, ed. Pobee, John S. (E. J. Brill 1976), pp. 180–9.

8 Shepherd, Massay, H. Jr, 'Our Worship' in *Anglican Congress* (1954) p. 74.

9 Even the liturgy of the Church of South India (1950; rev. 1954, 1962, 1972) and the *Liturgy for Africa* (1964) remained close to Cranmerian models, though the former included several features from the ancient Syrian tradition of India.

10 Pobee, John S., 'Mission, Paternalism and the Peter Pan Syndrome' in *Crossroads Are For Meeting: Essays on the Mission and Common Life of the Church in a Global Society*, eds. Turner, P. and Sugeno, F. (SPCK 1986), pp. 177–87; Samuel, V. K. 'Christian Mission in the Eighties—A Third World Perspective' in *Asian Partners in Mission* (1981): Taber, C. R., 'Contextualization' in *Exploring Church Growth*, ed. Shenk, Wilbert (Wm. Eerdmans 1983), p. 28.

11 This much recalls the situation in Geneva in 1986. Holy Trinity Church is known as the English Church and its General annual meeting is called the Society of the English Church. Generally the Church is organized as a chaplaincy to the English resident in Geneva and non-English are really addenda to the whole show. Warren, Max A.C., *Social History and Christian Mission* (SMC 1967), pp. 33–4; Hastings, Adrian A., *A History of African Christianity 1950–1975* (CUP 1979), pp. 19–20.

12 *Post-Enumeration Survey* (Government Printer 1970).

13 *Golden Shore* 1. vii (January 1926), pp. 177–8.

14 Chadwick, Henry, 'Episcopacy in the New Testament and Early Church' in *Today's Church and Today's World*, ed. Howe, John (CIO 1977), pp. 211–12.

15 Howat, G. M. D., 'Sociological Factors That Have Shaped Episcopacy' in *Today's Church and Today's World*, pp. 215–20.

16 Findlay, George C. and Holdsworth, W. W., *The History of the Wesleyan Methodist Missionary Society* (Epworth 1922), vol. iv, p. 175.

17 Pobee, John S. 'The Skenosis of Christian Worship in Africa' in *SL* 14. i (1980–1), pp. 37–52, esp. pp. 47f.

18 Tuma, Tom, 'Directions on Church Growth' in *Today's Church and Today's World* (CIO 1977), p. 99.

3 What is 'Anglicanism'?

PAUL AVIS

Avis, P. D. L., *The Church in the Theology of the Reformers*. London, Marshall, Morgan & Scott; Atlanta, John Knox, 1981.

Avis, P. D. L., *Ecumenical Theology and the Elusiveness of Doctrine*. SPCK 1986 (= *Truth Beyond Words*. Cambridge, Mass., Cowley, 1986).

Avis, P. D. L., *Anglicanism and the Christian Church: Theological Resources in Historical Perspective*. Forthcoming.

Fallows, W. G., *Mandell Creighton and the English Church* (OUP 1984), ch. 4.

Garbett, C., *The Claims of the Church of England*. Hodder & Stoughton 1947.

Henson, H. H., *The Church of England*. CUP 1939.

McAdoo, H. R., *The Spirit of Anglicanism*. A. & C. Black 1965.

More, P. E., and Cross, F. L., eds., *Anglicanism*. (SPCK 1935), ch. 1.

Neill, S., *Anglicanism*. Penguin 1958.

Ramsey, A. M., *The Gospel and the Catholic Church* (London, Longmans, 1938), ch. 13.

Sykes, S. W., *The Integrity of Anglicanism*. London and Oxford, Mowbray, 1978.

Temple, W., 'The Genius of the Church of England', in *Religious Experience and other Essays and Addresses*. James Clarke 1958.

Van der Pol, W. H., *Anglicanism in Ecumenical Perspective*. Duquesne University Press 1965.

Vidler, A. R., *Essays in Liberality* (London, SCM, 1957), chs. 7 and 8.

Wand, J. W. C., *Anglicanism in History and Today*. Weidenfeld & Nicolson 1961.

Woodhouse, H. F., *The Doctrine of the Church in Anglican Theology 1547–1603*. SPCK 1954.

What is 'Anglicanism'? As a provisional definition we may say that Anglicanism is the faith, practice and spirit of the Churches of the Anglican Communion. But the crucial underlying question is: are the faith, practice and spirit of the Churches of the Anglican Communion merely a product of the accidents of history, an expedient legitimation of the way things have turned out, and destined to be dissolved into its constituent elements by equally contingent and irrational historical forces in the future? Or are they the embodiment of some genuine theological truth or principle, with some degree of abiding relevance and with something of value to offer to the whole Church? To sharpen the question: is Anglicanism merely the decadent legacy of unprincipled Anglo-Saxon religious imperialism? Or is it able to take its stand on, and find its justification in, the reality of essential Christianity, the Christian gospel?

The ambiguity of posing the dilemma of Anglican ecclesiology in this way is brought out in William Temple's remark that nowhere was the Reformation accomplished with so little assertion of abstract principles as in England. From the point of view of a Church committed to a developmental, progressive view of Christian truth and committed to respect for the claims of individual conscience, it was a matter for profound thankfulness that the English Reformation was primarily a political rather than a religious movement and consequently tied the Church to dogmatic definitions less than anywhere else.[1] But the fact remains that the political, social and cultural context can only provide the *occasion* for a Church and contribute to the shaping of its outward form: it cannot provide a *definition* of a Church or its *raison d'être*.

THE TERMS 'ANGLICAN' AND 'ANGLICANISM'

Like the words 'Christian', 'Catholic' and 'Protestant', the words 'Anglican' and 'Anglicanism' present what the theological polemic of past centuries used to call 'a nose of wax', in other words, something that could be shaped to suit one's requirements. Certainly the concept of Anglicanism offers a field day for tendentious interpretations and definitions. What is not controversial is that the terms 'Anglican' and 'Anglicanism' derive etymologically from the Latin *anglicanus* = English. The expression *ecclesia Anglicana* was commonly used to refer to the medieval English Church, and *Anglicana ecclesia* occurs in Magna Carta (1215): *Quod Anglicana ecclesia libera sit* ('that the English Church shall be free') (see pp. 424–8).

At the Reformation this precedent was invoked to emphasize the Reformers' twofold claim of continuity with the ancient Church and independence of foreign (papal) jurisdiction. In times past, as 'divers sundry old authentic histories and chronicles' testified, the English Church had enjoyed a primitive freedom and independence latterly curtailed by the 'usurpations' of the Bishop of Rome. Thus the Act of 1534 confirming the royal supremacy spoke of the sovereign as 'the only supreme head in earth of the Church of England called *Anglicana Ecclesia*'.[2] John Jewel, Bishop of Salisbury, entitled his defence of the English Reformation *Apologia Ecclesiae Anglicanae* (1562). In Hooker, who conducted his argument in the vernacular, this becomes 'the Church of England'.

In the eighteenth and nineteenth centuries the word 'Anglican' began to shed its national connotations and to refer more specifically to a distinct theological position. Thus Burke refers to 'Catholicks, Anglicans or Calvinists', Macaulay to Anglican doctrine and discipline, and Gladstone to Anglican orders. By means of this development the ground was prepared for the adoption of the title 'Anglican' for the colonial Churches who looked both morally and canonically to Canterbury, and ultimately a term was at hand to describe the family of Churches of the emerging 'Anglican Communion', even when they had become legally emancipated from the mother Church in England.

The French form *anglicanisme* occurs, perhaps for the first time, in Lamennais in 1817, presumably by analogy with *gallicanisme*, and 'Anglicanism' was employed from 1838 by Newman (see pp. 424–8), who of course had little sympathy with the national aspects of English religion by this time. In the 1840s the term 'Anglican' or 'mere Anglican' was used pejoratively by the Tractarians to refer to the old High Churchmen who resisted Tractarian radicalism. The first Lambeth Conference was referring to the 'Anglican Communion' in 1867 (the term had first appeared in 1851),[3] but Anglicanism as a *concept* is a preoccupation of a later generation, when national ties had been much weakened, pluralism of religious expression was becoming an issue, and the social and political aspects of religious belief and practice were forcing themselves on the attention of theologians. The situation was then ripe for the common faith and life of the diverse Church of England and the equally diverse Churches of the Anglican Communion to be evaluated as an *ideology* (the term is not pejorative here), by analogy with Catholicism, Marxism, capitalism and so on.

The dilemmas of modern Anglicanism with regard to, for example, the role of women in the church, ecumenical rapprochement, and the reconstruction of doctrine stem from the application of theological analysis informed by the methods of ideological criticism, the inevitably corrosive effects of which are being felt throughout Christian theology, not least in ecclesiology. To avoid these unpleasant effects, the study of Anglicanism would have to be detached from the theological category of ecclesiology, that is, from the scrutiny of theology as such. Anglicanism would then be entirely free to develop unhampered by theological assessment and criticism. Free reign would be given to groups and individuals to operate in pursuit of their ends by direct political manipulation, untramelled by theological principles which ground the Christian Church in the person and destiny of Jesus Christ. Here we would see the naked pursuit of self-interest, power and prestige and the gratification of unreconstructed psychological fantasies. That would indeed be blatant ideology in the pejorative sense; and the answer to our initial question—whether Anglicanism merely expresses human interests or whether it can claim to be the embodiment of theological principle— would be abundantly clear. This being the case, I doubt whether most Anglicans, on reflection, would wish their Church or Communion to escape the searching enquiry of critical ecclesiology.

ANGLICAN APOLOGETIC

The claims of Anglicans for their Church have not, needless to say, been articulated in a timeless realm of abstract truths but in response to the challenge or threat of the moment—over against Rome, or the Puritans, or modern science, or the Ecumenical Movement, or the chronic pluralism of the contemporary world. In responding to these challenges or threats, various aspects of the Anglican synthesis have been singled out for emphasis.

In the sixteenth and seventeenth centuries Anglicans defended their continuity with the pre-Reformation Church, refuted charges of schism and rebutted the claims of the papacy (see pp. 10–18). They thus emphasized the 'Catholicity' of the Church of England. At the same time, however, they had to contend with the threat from the Puritans, who maintained that reform had not gone far enough and even that the Church of England was no true Church. In response, Anglican apologists such as Hooker and Whitgift upheld the fully Reformed and Protestant character of the Church of England, to which no essential aspect of a Reformed Church was lacking.

In these battles the weapons of controversy were those of theological, historical and biblical scholarship (which is certainly not to imply that this scholarship was never deployed tendentiously and the evidence never distorted). The Church of England took its stand on the new humanist learning of the Renaissance and the accumulation of erudition in the seventeenth century. The appeal to sound learning was therefore already a significant factor in Anglican apologetic. Furthermore, this appeal was imbued with a certain philosophical and ethical spirit, marked by moderation, caution, pragmatism, philosophical probabilism, moral insight and a sense of the limits of human speculation. In the hands of Hooker, Locke and Butler, arguments characterized by these modest qualities were not merely ineffectual gestures, as we might be inclined to suppose, but devastating cumulative arguments that successfully defended Anglican ideology (see pp. 108–11).

In the second half of the nineteenth century Anglican thought began to grapple—not without trauma—with developments in modern thought: biblical criticism, evolutionary theory and immanental philosophy. The appeal to sound learning entered a new phase which came to fruition in 1889 in *Lux Mundi*, the volume of essays edited by Charles Gore. The aim of the contributors, Oxford Anglo-Catholic clerical dons, was ' "to succour a distressed faith" by endeavouring to bring the Christian creed into its right relation to the modern growth of knowledge, scientific, historical and critical, and to modern problems of politics and ethics.'[4]

In the twentieth century Anglican apologetic began to respond to the vision of the emerging Ecumenical Movement, and the claim began to be heard that the combination of Catholic, Protestant and Liberal factors in Anglicanism qualified it to serve as a paradigm of Christian unity. The Anglo-Catholic document *Catholicity* (1947) suggested that Anglicanism's success in holding together living principles that in other traditions had been torn asunder opened the way for 'the Church of England [sic] to be a school of synthesis over a wider field than any other church in Christendom'. Anglicanism, it was claimed, had maintained a special witness to the Christian tradition in its fullness: 'The history of Anglican theology shows that it possesses a power of construction which has made for synthesis rather than for division.'[5]

However, the example of the Church of England's failure to rise to the challenge of the ecumenical vocation by the persistent blocking of initiatives in the Church's synodical machinery of government leads us to conduct a searching questioning of Anglicanism's supposed 'synthesis' (see pp. 379–84). The reality of the theological life of the Church of England (members of other Churches of the Anglican Communion must make their own assessment of their own Churches) gives little grounds for self-congratulation. The domestic traditions of churchmanship—the so called ecclesiastical parties, High, Low and Broad as they were once known: now Catholic, Evangelical and Liberal—would seem to have largely gone their own way, taking care to reinforce their prejudices through party patronage of livings, partisan theological colleges, newspapers and journals. Internal ecumenism has been minimal. Compromise may have occurred, but not synthesis. There is little we can do to bring about synthesis and integration at the tacit level of the symbolic life of a religious communion, but there is much we can do to enhance theological enquiry, criticism and awareness. Theologies that are ideologically dubious and critically incoherent can be banished from the scene by criticism and education, and theological obstacles to the realization of at least one aspect of the Anglican vocation—the welcome to new knowledge and insight—thus demolished.

Finally, the feminist movement—as momentous a revolution as the Reformation or the Enlightenment—presents the latest challenge to Anglican Christianity. Once again secular knowledge contributed by the disciplines of psychology and sociology, as well as human biology, compel us to reassess the assumptions as to gender identity that underlie virtually every aspect of Christian theology, including the doctrine of God, Christology and ecclesiology. Theology may be brought into line with what we know about the human world, but once again we do not have the same power over the subliminal archetypal projections and images that pervade our perception of the realm of gender identity. It is these unacknowledged, unreconstructed psychological inhibitions that present the real obstacle to the progress of Anglican thought in its dialogue with contemporary knowledge and insight, rather than inadequate theologies which are often so patently implausible that their true status as the rationalization and legitimation of psychological and sociological factors is concealed from no one. The legitimate claims and valid insights of the feminist movement constitute the latest challenge to Anglicanism's appeal to sound learning, its drawing on all the resources of truth and understanding, its intellectual 'Catholicity'. But in this respect it is apparent that at last the torch of moral leadership and initiative has passed from the mother Church to the younger Churches of the Anglican Communion.

ANGLICAN SELF-DEFINITION

One approach to the question, 'What is "Anglicanism"?' is to look at various formulations of Anglican self-definition through the centuries, bearing in mind the particular circumstances in which they were made and the audiences to which they were addressed. Anglican exercises in self-definition fall into two categories: those that focus on the material ingredients of the Anglican synthesis—Scripture, tradition, reason and so on—and those that claim a distinctive method, ethos or praxis for the Anglican way. The former hark back to the formation of Anglicanism in the sixteenth and seventeenth centuries. Between the English Reformation and the Oxford Movement there existed a consensus as to the identity of Anglicanism as a Reformed Church confessing with all the Reformers the supreme authority of Scripture, justification by faith, the legitimate role of the laity (embodied in the sovereign and Parliament) in the government of the Church, and a particular national identity and integrity. The latter—the appeal to an elusive ethos—belongs to the period since the Oxford Movement, for the Tractarians successfully challenged this consensus by asserting the decisive authority of tradition ('The Church to teach, the Bible to prove'), compromising the doctrine of justification by faith with a supplementary notion of infused sacramental grace, clericalizing the government of the Church and repudiating the stake that the (admittedly by now partly secularized) state has in the Church. The Church of England, and by implication the wider Anglican Communion of the day, derived its claims, its authority and its integrity, according to the Tractarians, from its apostolic foundation rather than from the preached word of the gospel or the recognition of the state.

The earlier consensus which, with whatever variations of emphasis and reservations on the part of individuals, upheld the Protestant character of the Church of England, and to which all parties of churchmanship subscribed, was effectively undermined. The Protestant elements in Anglicanism, detached however from the high ecclesiology of the High Church tradition and from the liberal humanism of the Latitudinarian or Broad Church tradition, became the special preserve of the Evangelicals. Appeal could now be made only to a consensus that remained extremely vague and elusive, a matter of ethos, approach, tacit rather than explicit, an unwritten understanding between members of a common fellowship.[6]

To define the distinctiveness of Anglicanism in this way is certainly to make a virtue of necessity. The notion of a tacit consensus residing in a common ethos is a *post factum* accommodation to the demise of doctrinal accord within the

410

Church. To say that is not by any means to reject the concept of a tacit consensus subsisting in the realm of praxis, but simply to make it abundantly clear that what we are talking about is not the timeless essence of Anglicanism but a pragmatic adjustment to the facts of history.

Now let me bring forward some witnesses to Anglican self-definition—first as to the threefold composition of the Anglican synthesis.

THE ANGLICAN SYNTHESIS

'I am such a catholic Christian,' maintained King James I in 1609, 'as believeth the three creeds, that of the apostles, that of the Council of Nice, and that of Athanasius ... And I believe them in that sense as the ancient fathers and councils that made them did understand them ... I reverence and admit the four first general councils as catholic and orthodox ... As for the scriptures, no man doubteth I will believe them' (More and Cross, p. 3). King James mentions the Scriptures last, not as the least important, but because their paramount authority can be taken for granted. The Thirty-nine Articles had already affirmed: 'Holy scripture containeth all things necessary to salvation: so that whatsoever is not read therein, nor may be proved thereby, is not to be required of any man, that it should be believed as an article of the faith, or be thought requisite or necessary to salvation' (Article VI). Implicit in the Articles is a notion of primary and secondary truths, things necessary to salvation and things indifferent, a hierarchy of truths (to use the phrase of the Second Vatican Council) (see pp. 233–8). The creeds themselves derive their authority from the fact that 'they may be proved by most certain warrants of holy scripture' (Article VIII). The same inequality between Scripture and tradition is reflected in the Church of England's canon law: 'The doctrine of the Church of England is grounded in the holy scriptures and in such teachings of the ancient fathers and councils of the church as are agreeable to the said scriptures' (Canon A5). This combination of Scripture and tradition, with Scripture in the dominant position, represents Anglicanism's Reformed Catholicism (see pp. 189–93).

When, in the nineteenth century, it became necessary to stretch the fabric of the Anglican synthesis to accommodate the findings of biblical scholarship, scientific discoveries and immanental worldviews, this reformed Catholicism became metamorphosized into '*Liberal* Catholicism' of which Charles Gore (1853–1932) was the outstanding exponent. Not that Gore intended in any way to play down the scriptural component in Anglicanism. 'The character of the Anglican church,' he wrote, 'has been from the first that of combining steadfast adherence to the structure and chief formulas of the church catholic with the "return to scripture" which was the central religious motive of the Reformation.' Anglicanism therefore bears witness to a scriptural Catholicism, 'a catholicism

411

in which scripture is enthroned in the highest place of controlling authority in the church'. But the revival of learning at the Renaissance had introduced a third participant in the Anglican synthesis, the appeal to scholarship:

> It is the glory of the Anglican church that at the Reformation she repudiated neither the ancient structure of catholicism, nor the new and freer movement. Upon the ancient structure—the creeds, the canon, the hierarchy, the sacraments—she retained her hold while she opened her arms to the new learning, the new appeal to scripture, the freedom of historical criticism and the duty of private judgement.

At the beginning of his public career, in 1889, Gore affirmed not only the Reformed but also the Liberal character of Anglican Catholicism—'a catholicism ... which is scriptural and represents the whole of Scripture; which is rational and can court the light of all genuine enquiry; which is free to deal with the new problems and wants of a new time'. At the height of his influence, as Bishop of Oxford in 1914, Gore reiterated this position. Anglicanism has stood since the Reformation for a 'liberal or scriptural catholicism' in which Scripture constituted 'the sole final testing ground of dogmatic requirement'.[7] The characteristically assured way in which Gore attempted to freeze this synthesis so as to prevent further development—in particular to inhibit intercommunion with non-episcopalians and critical positions that went beyond *Lux Mundi* (1889), as well as Romanizing tendencies among the Anglo-Catholic clergy—is not our concern here.[8] But in his threefold appeal to Catholic, Protestant and Liberal elements—to Scripture, tradition and reason—Gore is representative of classical Anglican self-definition.

This conception of Anglican identity and the Anglican vocation received the 'imprimatur' of the whole Anglican Communion at the Lambeth Conference of 1930 which declared, in a statement drafted by William Temple:

> Our special characteristic and, as we believe, our peculiar contribution to the universal church, arises from the fact that, owing to historic circumstances, we have been enabled to combine in our one fellowship the traditional faith and order of the catholic church with that immediacy of approach to God through Christ to which the evangelical churches especially bear witness, and freedom of intellectual enquiry, whereby the correlation of the Christian revelation and advancing knowledge is constantly effected.

Anglican apologists have sung the same song until very recently. In 1965 Archbishop Michael Ramsey, writing for a Roman Catholic audience, played down the liberal ingredient in the Anglican synthesis but stressed its Reformed Catholicity. 'Our church has two aspects,' he explained:

> On the one hand we claim to be a church possessing catholic tradition and continuity from the ancient church, and our catholic tradition and continuity includes the belief in the real presence of Christ in the blessed sacrament; the order of episcopacy and the priesthood, including the power of a priestly absolution. We possess various institutions belonging to catholic Christendom like monastic orders for men and women.

Nevertheless, Archbishop Ramsey went on:

> Our Anglican tradition has another aspect as well. We are a church which has been through the Reformation, and values many experiences derived from the Reformation, for instance the open Bible: great importance is attached to the authority of the holy Scriptures, and to personal conviction and conversion through the work of the Holy Spirit.[9]

Let me add a few words of assessment at this point. To describe Anglicanism as a synthesis of Catholic, Protestant and Liberal elements is sound, but it does not get us very far. It is not enough to bring out the distinctiveness of Anglicanism. On the one hand, bilateral dialogue with the Churches of the Reformation has made Anglicans more aware of the extent to which these Churches also appeal to the undivided Church and to the classical doctrines of patristic Christianity (see pp. 384–92). Neither are these Churches short of 'sound learning' or spiritual liberty. On the other hand, the process of reform within the Roman Catholic Church, initiated by the Second Vatican Council, while they by no means neutralize Anglican objections to Roman Catholic claims, go some way towards muting the traditional anti-Roman stance of Anglican apologetic. The common ground achieved in the area of doctrine by the Anglican-Roman Catholic International Commission (ARCIC), while open to criticism as far as its method is concerned (*cf.* Avis, *Ecumenical Theology*) and lacking the imprimatur of the Vatican, nevertheless serves to mitigate further the aspect of Anglican apologetic that has traditionally served to distinguish Anglican identity from Roman Catholicism.

All shades of Anglican churchmanship can be found subscribing to the view that the Anglican faith is both Catholic and Reformed and at the same time hospitable to intellectual enquiry. But the conclusions they draw are rather different. To some this threefold appeal will mean ordaining women, to others not on any account doing so. To some it will follow that there is no theological obstacle to intercommunion with Lutherans, to others no such conclusion follows. To some it will entail adopting a tolerant and sympathetic attitude to doctrinal radicals within the Church, to others this would be a betrayal. This situation might lead us to consider the view that the distinctiveness of Anglicanism lies not in the ingredients—which are not unique to Anglicanism—but in the nature of the mixture.

THE DISTINCTIVENESS OF ANGLICANISM

Is Anglicanism then ultimately an ethos, a method of approach, an attitude of mind? If the 'static' view of the Anglican synthesis that we have been considering represents an attempt at a *via media*, a balancing act between various factors based on compromise and concession, this more mystical view of Anglicanism sees it as an attempt to reconcile opposites and to transcend conflicts. If the first stands for 'the love of balance, restraint, moderation, measure' (More and Cross, p. xxii), the second invokes vision, passion and risk. The first is conservative in tendency, the second progressive; the former defensive, the latter innovatory.

As Michael Ramsey has written, Anglican theology is not a system or a confession, but 'a method, a use and a direction'. Though appeal is made to the gospel, the Catholic tradition and sound learning, these do not run side by side but are fused together creatively. Ramsey's *The Gospel and the Catholic Church* (1936) is a notable attempt to achieve this. Both Ramsey and Vidler have found such an approach in the thought of F. D. Maurice with his insistence on digging beneath competing systems to discover the living principles of which they were at the same time rationalizations and distortions. It was inconceivable to Maurice that those principles, born of encounter with 'the divine order', could be ultimately incompatible.[10] Thus Vidler too insists that what is distinctive of Anglicanism is not a theological system but 'a theological method or direction':

> Anglican theology is true to its genius when it is seeking to reconcile opposed systems, rejecting them as exclusive systems, but showing that the principle for which each stands has its place within the total orbit of Christian truth, and in the long run is secure only within that orbit or ... when it is held in tension with other apparently opposed, but really complementary principles (pp. 166f).

In his useful study of seventeenth-century Anglican writings, H. R. McAdoo has claimed to detect this principle at work. Drawing attention to the 'polarity or quality of living tension' which is 'an overall characteristic of Anglican theological method', McAdoo regards the Caroline divines (together with the *Lux Mundi* group) as its most authentic exponents. Of this approach, from Hooker onwards, he writes:

> Beneath the surface was the feeling for the *via media* which was not in its essence compromise or an intellectual expedient but a quality of thinking, an approach in which elements usually regarded as mutually exclusive were seen to be in fact complementary. These things were held in a living tension, not in order to walk the tight-rope of compromise, but because they were seen to be mutually illuminating and to fertilise each other.

Scripture and tradition, revelation and human reason, 'credal orthodoxy and liberty in non-essentials, the appeal to antiquity and the welcome to new knowledge, the historic continuity of the church and the freedom of national churches'—all were held together to form the distinctive spirit of Anglican theology (pp. 312f). Setting aside the question of whether this is perhaps a rather idealized view of what was going on in the seventeenth century McAdoo's thesis is a valid and significant interpretation of Anglicanism.

Something similar was being advocated at the 1930 Lambeth Conference. The conference committee set out, without specifying doctrines, the 'ideals for which the Church of England [sic] has always stood'. These ideals are not unique: 'they are the ideals of the church of Christ. Prominent among them are an open Bible, a pastoral priesthood, a common worship, a standard of conduct consistent with that worship and a fearless love of truth'.[11] Here it is the qualifiers that are significant. The Bible is 'open', available, unchained, not subject to control, monitoring and binding interpretation by ecclesiastical authority. The Anglican priesthood is a 'pastoral' one, neither a sacerdotal caste serving to restrict the spiritual privileges of the laity, nor a didactic, scribal, judicatory order that lays down the law as to belief and practice and is entrusted with the task of policing its enforcement. Worship is 'common', that is to say not performed on behalf of a liturgically unqualified laity by a vicarious priesthood, but shared by the whole priestly body of the Church. Here is a tacit egalitarian principle grounded in the nature of worship. Finally, Anglicanism's love of the truth is to be 'fearless'.

There is, of course, a valid distinction to be made between descriptive and prescriptive definitions of Anglicanism, though it is certainly not a distinction that is consistently observed; all too many interpreters of Anglicanism have spoken as though the ideal and the actual were one. Charles Gore could not be accused of making this mistake. He knew that his version of the Anglican vocation was one that had rarely, and never fully, been realized. The history of the Anglican Church, he confessed, 'fills me with a profound humiliation'. 'I find its continuous Erastianism, its complacent nationalism, its frequent deafness to the most urgent and obvious moral calls, its long-continued identification of itself with the interests and tastes of the "upper classes" ... depressing and humiliating.'[12]

The Anglican ideal is a noble one, though one that remains to be attained. It is focused in a particular view of the role of authority in the sphere of religion. It appeals to Scripture, tradition and reason, but does so in the acknowledged context of our modern pluralistic situation. As a result, Scripture, tradition and reason are combined in a particular way, slanted to serve as mutual qualifiers, checks and balances, to restrict and relativize each other. The result is a muted— some would say emasculated—notion of authority, but it is one that is eminently suited to our condition.

The question of the distinctiveness of Anglicanism is a legitimate one, but it is not our prime concern. The problem of identity is important both to individuals and to institutions, including Churches, but to become obsessed by it is neurotic. Identity is not an end in itself but is a corollary of integrity. While Stephen Sykes has suggested that there is no integrity without identity, I would prefer to see the problem the other way round. A distinctive identity does not necessarily bring integrity. Identity can be contrived by dubious means, but there is no short cut to integrity. Pursue integrity and identity will take care of itself. Anglicanism exists. Its political, social and cultural parameters are set. We should not fret about them. Anglicanism's vocation is to express the gospel of Christ within those parameters, appealing—as is its wont—to all sources of information and insight, and to spend itself in the service of the gospel and the redemption of humanity. As Michael Ramsey wrote more than fifty years ago:

> While the Anglican church is vindicated by its place in history, with a strikingly balanced witness to gospel and church and sound learning, its greater vindication lies in its pointing through its own history to something of which it is a fragment. Its credentials are its incompleteness, with the tension and travail in its soul. It is clumsy and untidy, it baffles neatness and logic. For it is sent not to commend itself as 'the best type of Christianity', but by its very brokenness to point to the universal church wherein all have died (p. 220).

A CATHOLIC FAITH?

Anglicanism aspires to be a *Catholic* faith. Charles Gore used to speak of 'catholicism without the pope', and Garbett described the Church of England as 'the catholic church in this land, set free from subjection to the Church of Rome'. This was indeed not the language of the English Reformers, but it aptly expresses their claims. They appealed to the antiquity of the British Church, an autonomous Church that long antedated the mission of St Augustine of Canterbury in 597 and had had its bishops at the Council of Arles in 314. The claim was made (for example by Archbishop Parker) that the English episcopate derived from the mission of Joseph of Arimathea to the British Isles in the apostolic age itself. Bishop Jewel insisted that the Church of England had departed not from the Catholic Church but from the errors of Rome. Fulke likewise affirmed that the separation was not on account of the corruption of life of the leaders of the Roman Church but because of false doctrine (here he was echoing Luther himself). Whitgift pointed out that the Church of England was 'reformed' not 'transformed' because 'we retain whatsoever we find to be good, refuse or reform that which is evil'.[13]

The Catholicity of the Anglican Church (or Churches) rests upon its continuity of worship, employing ancient forms purged of medieval accretions, and of pastoral care in the parishes and parish churches whose origins go back to time immemorial. It rests also upon the retention of the threefold ministry of bishops, priests and deacons (though the Reformers do not share the insistence of the old High Church divines and the Tractarians, that a particular theory of the historical transmission of orders through 'apostolic succession' is the indispensable condition of the ministry—the view that has come to prevail in modern Anglicanism, though without receiving canonical formulation). Above all, the catholicity of Anglicanism is revealed in its adherence to the Scriptures, the creeds and the councils of the undivided Church (canonically, the first four) which provide orthodox Christianity with its Christological and Trinitarian

416

doctrines (though, as Shriver has pointed out above, this does not distinguish the Anglican Churches from the Lutheran and Reformed). However, among this constellation of authorities the Scriptures are supreme.

The 'Catholic' character of the Anglican faith is evidenced by its acknowledgement of the authority of the Church in disputed matters of faith (this goes beyond Calvin's permission for the Church to make laws to regulate its life), though this discretion, affirmed in Article XX, is always subject to the control of Scripture (see p. 92). The authority of a pan-Protestant council was mooted in correspondence between English and Reformed divines. Together with the continental Churches of the Reformation, Anglicanism invoked a conciliar, as opposed to a monarchical Catholicism. As Shriver has remarked above, 'The "conciliar" nature of the Anglican Communion is perhaps one of the least recognised, and yet most characteristic, features of modern Anglicanism'—though he justly adds that this is an attribute shared with most other Christian communions (see pp. 197–99).

A REFORMED FAITH?

Anglicanism aspires to be a *Reformed* faith. If some Anglicans seek a 'catholicism without the pope', others, it might be claimed, desire a Protestantism without a Luther, a Calvin, a Knox or a Wesley. The essentially Protestant character of Anglicanism is evidenced above all in the place it gives to Scripture as 'the norm of faith and the norm by which other norms (creeds, tradition, confessions of faith) are judged' (see pp. 79–85). It was by comparison with the touchstone of Scripture that the Reformers rejected aspects of medieval Catholicism: the papacy, the mediatory office of the priesthood, the propitiatory sacrifice of the Mass, communion in one kind, the liturgy in a foreign tongue not 'understanded of the people' and clerical celibacy. It was on the authority of Scripture—at least the Old Testament—that they upheld the role of the 'godly prince', the magistrate, as the supreme governor in both Church and state. Again it was by appeal to Scripture that the English Reformers maintained the doctrine of justification by faith alone, without merit accruing to good works, and furthermore insisted on this doctrine as the article of a standing or falling Church (*articulus stantis aut cadentis ecclesiae*), as Luther put it.[14]

It is sometimes said that Anglicans have protestant Articles but a Catholic liturgy. This is a misleading oversimplification. It is true that the *Thirty-nine Articles of Religion* are concerned mainly with points of contention in the aftermath of the Reformation. But they are directed as much against the radical views of the Anabaptists as against the corruptions of Rome. Furthermore, as F. D. Maurice used to point out, these polemical articles are prefaced by, and thus set in the context of, an affirmation of Trinitarian and Christological

417

doctrine. To do this was to set forth common ground with Rome against Socinians and spiritualists who rejected the dogmas of a Church which had fallen into apostasy, they believed, soon after the death of the Apostles. The Articles were apparently intended to provide a basis for the comprehension in a national Church of the various shades of mainstream Protestantism. The only exclusions were 'papists' or recusants, whose loyalty was deemed to be primarily to the pope as a temporal as well as a spiritual sovereign, and radicals who equally rejected the Church-state nexus, and claimed a liberty to interpret the Scriptures according to their lights and to implement that interpretation; their claim culminating in a scarcely veiled threat (based on an appeal to the judicial laws of the Old Testament) to take into their own hands the execution of the vengeance of God against the ungodly—the bishops and clergy of the Church of England whom they had already anathematized.[15] Thus the Articles were designed to exclude the extreme right and extreme left wings of sixteenth-century religious profession, whose challenge was alike to the commonwealth which existed in indissoluble unity with the Church established by the Elizabethan Settlement (see pp. 133–7).

On the other hand, a liturgy that was purged of sacrificial and sacerdotal language and invocation of the saints, that explicitly rejected adoration of Christ in the sacramental elements, that offered communion in both kinds and was in the vernacular, could hardly be described as 'Catholic' in the medieval sense. It was in fact a Reformed liturgy, but reformed in accordance with the pattern of primitive worship as then understood (see pp. 273–7).

The picture today is much less clear-cut. The tacit consensus as to the Protestant character of the Church of England and hence of wider Anglicanism, that undoubtedly pertained until the Oxford Movement began to make its influence felt, and resided in acceptance of the doctrines of the supremacy of Scripture, justification by faith, and the national connection, together with the role of the sovereign (a lay person) in the government of the Church, has faded. The Articles have only a nominal, token authority and cannot be invoked against doctrinal deviations (though from this state of disciplinary paralysis all shades of churchmanship actually benefit). The revised liturgies contain so many options and such a mass of material that they cannot function as a standard of orthodoxy as the Book of Common Prayer did. Biblical criticism has weakened the authority of Scripture in practice, to the extent that the Anglican members of the Anglican-Roman Catholic Internation Commission (ARCIC I) could sponsor the view that though the universal primacy of the Bishop of Rome could not be derived from Scripture, it ought nevertheless to be accepted as God's will for the Church.[16]

There is of course one glaring anomaly in the picture of Anglicanism as a Reformed faith, and that is the requirement for episcopal ordination to constitute a valid ministry and, consequently, valid sacraments (see pp. 296–308). In the charter documents of Anglicanism, the threefold ministry is accepted as the practice of Catholic Christendom since the earliest times (the 1662 Preface to the Ordinal rashly claims the authority of Scripture and the practice of the Apostles for this), but it is not undergirded by any theory—least of all a mechanical 'pipeline' theory of the transmission of sacramental grace through the historic episcopate. This latter theory was the product of Tractarian ecclesiology, though the ground was prepared for it by developments in the late sixteenth century and by administrative practices in the seventeenth.[17] As Hensley Henson wrote: 'The Church of England had always been episcopal, it now became episcopalian, that is, what had been a matter of practical policy became the requirement of religious principle' (p. 123).

The inflexible insistence of the Church of England, and to a lesser extent her sister Churches of the Anglican Communion, on the historic episcopate or apostolic succession as a condition of a true Church is certainly incompatible with a genuine Reformation ecclesiology, according to which word and sacrament suffice for the full integrity of ecclesial life since through their means Christ has promised to be present with his people (cf. Avis, *Church in Theology of Reformers*, pt. 1). Not only has this insistence proved a perennial stumbling block to hopes of reunion with other Protestant Churches, but it contains a supreme irony in that Anglican orders are not recognized by Rome.

While the principle of transmitted authority can indeed be derived from Scripture, the threefold ministry cannot be reconstructed from the complex picture of various *ad hoc* forms of ministry to be found in the New Testament. To this extent the 1662 Preface to the Ordinal is relying on a broken reed. But even if the threefold ministry could be projected into the Apostolic age, by invoking the evidence of the epistles of Ignatius of Antioch, this is still a far cry from the sacramental conception of ordination at the hands of a bishop within the historical line of succession. At this point we are confronted with an irreconcilable contradiction of the claim of the Church of England to be a Reformed Church. As Stephen Sykes as trenchantly put it: 'Anglicanism as it now exists is founded on an incoherent doctrine of the church, and ... its attempts to resolve or conceal this gross internal antinomy has repeatedly led it into a series of chronic conflicts from which it barely escapes with any integrity.'[18]

A RATIONAL FAITH?

Anglicanism aspires to be *rational* faith (see pp. 105–17). Its tradition of offering hospitality to scholarly enquiry pre-dates the Reformation, and many a scholar persecuted by stricter regimes has found sanctuary in the Church of England. Anglicanism can sustain criticism of its claims and beliefs as few Churches can. It is tolerant of the clash of opinion within its ranks. Provided outward forms are observed—and let us remember that these are the tacit, symbolic expression of the Church's most fundamental convictions—she is satisfied. A principle of spiritual liberty gradually emerged from the power struggles of Anglican history. Anglicanism is now committed to liberty of prophesying. If, as Karl Popper insists, rationality consists in openness to rational criticism, Anglicanism may fairly claim to be a rational faith.

As Wand observes, 'On the evidence of friend and critic alike the three most obvious features of Anglicanism are tolerance, restraint and learning' (p. 241). Garbett calls the Church of England 'the most liberal-minded church in the world', adding, 'perhaps we might say it is the most charitable of all churches' (p. 28). However, just as Ramsey (op. cit.) has attempted to ground Catholic order in the gospel itself, so Anglicans need to ground their claims for liberty, toleration and rationality on the gospel of Christ. This is a challenge that awaits the attention of contemporary Anglican theologians.

It must be admitted that two of the most 'notorious' of liberal English bishops, Barnes of Birmingham and Jenkins of Durham, have actually stood out as passionate advocates of the Christian gospel of redemption. Barnes wrote in 1915, 'My ideal is a liberal Christianity in which liberalism is not a cloak for unbelief but an attitude of sympathy to all Christian religious experience and a positive formulation of Christian values, principles and facts.'[19]

Mandell Creighton laid it down that 'the formula which most explains the position of the Church of England is that it rests on an appeal to sound learning'.[20] The great intellectual movement of the Renaissance that had its theological payoff in the Reformation was 'accentuated in England by being more frankly accepted there than elsewhere'. As Garbett claims, 'Alone among the ancient churches, the Church of England has consistently made this appeal to sound learning' (pp. 25f). Creighton calls the post-Reformation English Church 'the church of the new learning'.[21] It fostered, according to Creighton—and here we have to make allowances for the so-called Whig interpretation of history making itself strongly felt—the pure, disinterested enquiry after truth. For where, he asks, in either Rome or Geneva, 'was there a place for the aspirations of the devout scholar, of the man who reverenced liberty, who believed in progressive enlightenment, who longed for an intelligent order of things in which the Christian consciousness should seek for spiritual truth?'[22]

Such claims obviously need to be qualified. As Hensley Henson pointed out: 'Something very different from a zeal for sound learning covered England with ruined monasteries, raised no less than three revolts, and added to our national history a long list of judicial murders.' 'Neither sound learning nor a zeal for true religion swayed the Tudor sovereigns, but their personal predilections and the cold sagacity of their cynical statecraft' (pp. 58f). The operative principle in the formation of the Anglican synthesis was not mere learning, but a critical application of it that blunted the edge of uncompromising claims on behalf of any single source of authority. Both 'papists' and Puritans claimed divine right for tradition and Scripture respectively. As Henson put it: 'Against the traditionalism of the papist, the Anglican apologist made appeal to the supreme authority of scripture interpreted by the primitive undivided church. Against the unintelligent literalism of the puritan, he urged a more reasonable application of the sacred text' (ibid.).

By such means, Jewel, Whitgift and Hooker defended the *status quo*; the so-called 'Elizabethan Settlement' was meant to be final. Here, we must concede, was no application of a moral and aesthetic ideal of 'moderation', but a theological legitimation of the cold compromises of Tudor statecraft. But it *looked* like moderation; it had the appearance of tempering the excesses of spiritual authority and could be reinterpreted into a principle of toleration which respected dissent on secondary matters.

It was no doubt for reasons of political expediency that Elizabeth I declined 'to make windows into men's souls', but that policy came to acquire theological legitimation as the expression of a principle of spiritual reticence. The same theological intuition informed the ecclesiology of Richard Hooker. In grounding the ecclesial integrity of Churches on their 'outward profession of those things which supernaturally appertain to the very essence of Christianity and are necessarily required in every particular Christian man', namely the baptismal faith, Hooker was refusing to unchurch both Rome for her corruptions and the Churches of the continental Reformation for their deficiencies, and was at the same time asserting for the Church of England that it possessed all that could be required for its ecclesial integrity. But he was also, wittingly or unwittingly, curtailing the scope of ecclesiastical authority by implying that it could rest content when outward profession was satisfied.[23] Thus, the reality of political manipulation could become transposed into the rhetoric of spiritual liberty. And why not?—as Vico and Freud have taught us, many of our highest aspirations have their historical or evolutionary origins in somewhat unedifying earthly and fleshly needs.[24]

As Henson points out against Creighton, what emerged from this process by the end of the seventeenth century was not merely an appeal to sound learning in general but an acceptance of the role of criticism in particular. 'The principle of the English Reformation was not so much sound learning as such—for every Christian apologist claimed for his own church the support of sound learning— but a frank acceptance of sound learning as competent to revise the current tradition, both by interpreting afresh the sacred text, and by certifying through independent research the true verdict of Christian antiquity' (p. 59). The claims of learning implied the rights of criticism and they in turn rested upon a principle of spiritual liberty.

For all its lack of definition, its pragmatism, muddle and inconsistency, its hospitality to lost causes, unreconstructed prejudice and unenlightened views, its apathy and inertia, Anglicanism nevertheless offers an environment for the fearless pursuit of the truth without let or hindrance by ideologically motivated ecclesiastical authority, whose remit is not to seek 'the truth as it is in Jesus' but to defend the structures that give some individuals power over the souls of others. As Henson put it:

> The doctrinal incoherence of the Church of England, though it is unquestionably perplexing, practically embarrassing and not infrequently actually scandalous, has its roots in something far more respectable than an indolent acquiescence in undiscipline or a reprehensible indifference to truth. It reflects the reluctance of considering and responsible English churchmen to thrust the rough hand of authority into the sphere of religious opinion. Not an indifference to truth, but a juster perception of the conditions under which truth must be sought and defended, leads them to shrink from discouraging individual efforts to discover a solution of the problem which now confronts, in various measures of urgency, every section of the Christian church, namely, how to reconcile the theological tradition expressed in creeds and immutable in theory, sacrosanct by time, and the ever-growing knowledge of mankind (p. 108).

Anglicanism is committed historically to a distinctive approach to the question of authority. Its sources of authority, dispersed as they are through many channels, are mutually restricting, mutually illuminating. In the modern intellectual situation this is beneficial, since it inhibits the enunciation of dogma, the articulation of absolutes and the exercise of ecclesiastical authority. Though all these might bring a temporary sense of satisfaction to those who are frustrated by the dilemmas of contemporary theology, in a longer perspective they are likely to prove, as they have proved in other Churches, a millstone round our necks. The Anglican vocation is to create the climate of spiritual liberty in which individuals may bear witness to the truth as they see it, submitting themselves to the criticism of their peers without fear of ecclesiastical censure or censorship, the only condition being their continued voluntary participation in the worshipping life of the Church and outward profession of the fundamental baptismal faith. On this interpretation the distinctive identity of Anglicanism is understood in theological, rather than liturgical, pastoral, devotional or hierarchical, gubernatorial, terms. Anglicans are intellectually privileged; their theological tradition is a noble one; their theological resources are ample. If at the present time they deserve to be chastised for a nerveless failure to grapple with Christian truth rigorously and systematically, that indicates a departure from the tradition, a decline, and one that needs to be reversed.

NOTES

1 Iremonger, F. A., *William Temple* (OUP 1948), p. 487.

2 Elton, G. R., ed., *The Tudor Constitution* (CUP 1972), p. 355.

3 Stephenson, A. M. G., *Anglicanism and the Lambeth Conferences* (SPCK 1978), p. 7f.

4 Gore, C., ed., *Lux Mundi*, (10th edn, London, Murray, 1904), preface.

5 *Catholicity: A Study in the Conflict of Christian Traditions in the West, being a report presented to His Grace the Archbishop of Canterbury* (London, Dacre, 1947), p. 49.

6 Avis, P. D. L., 'The Tractarian Challenge to Consensus and the Identity of Anglicanism', *King's Theological Review*, 9.1 (1986), pp. 14–17. c.f. McManners, J., 'The Individual in the Church of England', in *Christian Believing*, The Doctrine Commission of the Church of England, (SPCK 1981), esp. pp. 222ff.

7 Gore, C., *Dissertations on Subjects connected with the Incarnation*, (2nd edn, London, Murray, 1896), p. 196; *Catholicism and Roman Catholicism* (London, Mowbray, 1923), p. 48; *Orders and Unity* (London, Murray, 1909), p. 198f; *The Mission of the Church* (London, Murray, 1892), p. 36f; *The Basis of Anglican Fellowship in Faith and Organisation* (London, Mowbray 1914), p. 4f. Carpenter, J., *Gore: A Study in Liberal Catholicism* (London, Faith Press, 1960), pp. 42ff.

8 cf. Avis, P. D. L., *Gore: Construction and Conflict* (Worthing, Churchman Publishing, 1988).

9 Cited Fouyas, M., *Orthodoxy, Roman Catholicism and Anglicanism* (OUP 1972), p. 86f.

10 Maurice, F. D., *Moral and Metaphysical Philosophy* (London, Macmillan 1872), vol. ii, p. 138f; *The Kingdom of Christ*, ed. Vidler, A. R. (London, SCM, 1958), vol. ii, p. 323; cf. Christensen, T., *The Divine Order* (Leiden, Brill, 1974); Ramsey, A. M., *F. D. Maurice and the Conflicts of Modern Theology* (CUP, 1951), ch. 2.

11 Cited Thomas, P. H. E., 'The Lambeth Conferences and the Development of Anglican Ecclesiology 1867–1978' (Ph.D. thesis, Department of Theology, University of Durham 1982), p. 82.

12 Gore, C., *Catholicism and Roman Catholicism*, p. 45.

13 *The Works of the English Reformers* (Cambridge, Parker Society, 1940–): Bale, p. 188; Fulke, vol. ii, pp. 7, 20, 175; Whitgift, vol. i, p. 3; vol. ii, p. 439; Jewel, vol. iii, p. 79.

14 cf. McGrath, A. E., 'The Article by which the Church stands or falls', *Evangelical Quarterly*, 58. iii (1986), pp. 207–28.

15 Carlson, H. L., ed., *The Writings of Henry Barrow 1587–1590* (London, Allen and Unwin, 1962), p. 75; Avis, P. D. L., 'Moses and the Magistrate', *Journal of Ecclesiastical History*, 26 (1975), pp. 149–72, esp. p. 169f.

16 *The Final Report* of the Anglican-Roman Catholic International Commission (SPCK 1982), pp. 83ff; cf. Avis, *Ecumenical Theology*, pp. 103ff.

17 cf. Sykes, N., *Old Priest and New Presbyter* (CUP 1956); Avis, *The Church in the Theology of the Reformers*, ch. 8.

18 Sykes, S. W., 'Anglicanism and Protestantism', in Sykes, ed., *England and Germany: Studies in Theological Diplomacy* (Frankfurt am Main & Bern, P. D. Lang, 1982).

19 Barnes, J., *Ahead of his Age: Bishop Barnes of Birmingham* (London, Collins, 1979), p. 79.

20 Creighton, M., *The Church and the Nation* (London, Longmans, 1901), p. 251.

21 Creighton, M., *Historical Lectures and Addresses* (London, Longmans, 1903), p. 150; see Fallows, ch. 4.

22 ibid. p. 176.

23 Hooker, R., *Of the Laws of Ecclesiastical Polity* (ed. Keble J.), (OUP 1845), vol. iii, i.3–4.

24 cf. Avis, P. D. L., *Foundations of Modern Historical Thought: From Machiavelli to Vico* (Bromley, Croom Helm, and Buffalo, Croom Helm US, 1986), pp. 147–151.

4 Anglicanism, *Ecclesia Anglicana*, and Anglican: An Essay on Terminology

J. ROBERT WRIGHT

At what historical point can and should the study of Anglicanism begin? One logical answer would be to begin at the earliest point at which something called 'Anglicanism' is acknowledged to exist in recorded thought. Admitting that oral usage frequently antedates to some extent the written word, and holding to conservative principles of editing, the *Oxford English Dictionary* in 1933 recorded the earliest written occurrence of the term 'Anglicanism' as being in 1846 by Charles Kingsley,[1] and in its 1972 supplement moved this point back to John Henry Newman in 1838.[2] So in one real sense, the sense in which contemporaries would have acknowledged the existence of the term, the study of 'Anglicanism' can only begin with the nineteenth century. Yet most people today believe the term must represent a meaning that is broader and deeper than this. After all, the term 'Anglican Communion' would soon originate, on both sides of the Atlantic, first in 1851;[3] and certainly by this time the adjective 'Anglican' had come to mean not simply 'English' or 'pertaining to the Church of England', but also, ecclesiastically and more broadly, 'historically descended from the Church of England'.[4]

An early projection of Anglicanism back in time was recorded by Newman himself in his *Apologia* (1864): 'Anglicanism claimed to hold that the Church of England was nothing else than a continuation in this country ... of that one Church of which in old times Athanasius and Augustine were members.'[5] And so also modern Anglican writers characteristically reverse their chronological perspective for the concept 'Anglicanism', even if they can not do this for the factual use of the word itself. Professor John Macquarrie, probably the most eminent of modern Anglican theologians, writes (1970), 'Anglicanism has never considered itself to be a sect or denomination originating in the sixteenth century. It continues without a break the *Ecclesia Anglicana* founded by St. Augustine thirteen centuries and more ago, though nowadays that branch of the Church has spread far beyond the borders of England.'[6] And Bishop H. R. McAdoo, a leading exponent of what is thought by many to be a, or the, characteristic Anglican method in theology, states (1965):

> Anglicanism is not a theological system and there is no writer whose work is an essential part of it either in respect of content or with regard to the form of its self-expression ... The absence of an official theology in Anglicanism is something deliberate which belongs to its essential nature, for it has always regarded the teaching and practice of the undivided Church of the first five centuries as a criterion.[7]

At first such a disclaimer of 'an official theology' seems in conflict with the OED definition of Anglicanism itself, 'Adherence to the doctrine and discipline of the reformed Church of England (and other churches in communion therewith) as the genuine representative of the Catholic Church';[8] but in fact the OED definition is consistent with what is now widely claimed. Macquarrie, for example, continues,

> It is often claimed that Anglicanism has no special doctrines of its own and simply follows the universal teaching of the Church. When one considers the nature of the English Reformation, one sees that there is strong support for the claim. In England there was no single dominant figure, such as Luther or Calvin, who might impress upon the Church his own theological idiosyncrasies. The conscious aim of the English Reformation was to return, so far as possible, to the Catholic Christianity of the undivided Church of the first five centuries.[9]

And the late Bishop Stephen Neill, in his best-selling paperback *Anglicanism* (1958) even asserted, 'There are no special Anglican doctrines, there is no particular Anglican theology ... In the strict sense of the term there is, therefore, no Anglican faith.'[10] At the more official level, there is the Report to the Lambeth Conference of 1930 on 'The Anglican Communion', commended in Resolution 48 of the Conference itself, which at first seems to suggest that there is something essentially new and distinct about Anglican doctrine, but then defines it in essentially the same way as Macquarrie, McAdoo, and Neill:

> We desire emphatically to point out that the term 'Anglican' is no longer used in the sense it originally bore. The phrase 'Ecclesia Anglicana' in Magna Carta had a purely local connotation. Now its sense is ecclesiastical and doctrinal, and the Anglican Communion includes not merely those who are racially connected with England, but many others whose faith has been grounded in the doctrines and ideals for which the Church of England has always stood.
> What are these doctrines? We hold the Catholic faith in its entirety: that is to say, the truth of Christ, contained in Holy Scripture; stated in the Apostles' and Nicene Creeds; expressed in the Sacraments of the Gospel and the rites of the Primitive Church as set forth in the Book of Common Prayer with its various local adaptations; and safeguarded by the historic threefold Order of the Ministry.[11]

The Report on 'The Anglican Communion' for 1948 Lambeth repeated the same theme: 'The English Reformers were not trying to make a new Church. It continued to be the Church of England, the *Ecclesia Anglicana*, as Magna Carta described it in 1215. For this reason, the Anglican Communion is not a sect. It is a true part of the Church Catholic.'[12]

And so we come to a preliminary conclusion, that the study of Anglicanism must begin much earlier than the first occurrence of the term in 1838 or thereabouts; but now the question is, how much earlier? It must be observed that the continuity being asserted by Macquarrie and McAdoo, as well as by the Lambeth Reports of 1930 and 1948, projects an understanding of Anglicanism in essentials that extends not only prior to the nineteenth century but prior to the Reformation as well, even back to the patristic period historically and to the New Testament doctrinally. Of course recent years have seen the discovery of much archaeological evidence from Britain in the patristic period, such as the Silchester basilica, the Lullingstone villa, the Hinton-St Mary mosaic, the Walesby and Icklingham lead baptismal tanks, the Water Newton and Mildenhall silver treasures, the 'Pater Noster' word-squares, and other things, all of which indicate the widespread historical origins of British Christianity in the second, third, and fourth centuries.[13] But can we agree, in common with the authorities cited above, that the Anglicanism of today stands in essential continuity even with the Church of this early period? Or was there perhaps some essential change, most probably at the English Reformation, some new doctrine or emphasis that all Anglican authorites then and now would regard as essential, that allows a modern interpreter to trace his or her concept of 'Anglicanism' back beyond 1838 to the sixteenth century but not earlier? More specifically, did a 'Church *of* England' replace a 'Church *in* England' at the time of the Reformation?

One important view is that of Professor A. G. Dickens, a historian of distinction, who in 1964 wrote:

> The common medieval term *Ecclesia Anglicana* never meant 'Church of England' in the post-Reformation sense of an independent national Church claiming parity with that of Rome. Whatever its material reservations, the medieval English church acknowledged the spiritual overlordship and jurisdiction of the Papacy. It administered in its courts a body of law based upon papal decrees and upon the canons of international church councils. Only on its fringes, for example on matters concerning tithes and testamentary jurisidiction, had this law been modified by English national custom.[14]

Professor Dickens' view has not gone uncriticized,[15] but perhaps the sharpest contrast can be seen, from an official English/Anglican position, in the volume *Ecclesiastical Law* from Halsbury's *Laws of England* as edited for the Church Assembly (1957):

> In law the Church of England ... is that branch of the Holy Catholic and Apostolic Church which was founded in England when the English were gradually converted to christianity between the years 597 and 686 ... The accepted legal doctrine is that the Church of England is a continuous body from its earliest establishment in Saxon times ... When the statutes to exclude papal jurisdiction were passed in the reign of Henry

VIII, the Church of England was regarded as an existing church and there was no intention to vary from the congregation of Christ's Church, but the papal authority in England was regarded as a usurpation.[16]

In the contrast of these views one hears echoes of the late nineteenth-century Stubbs–Maitland controversy over the place of papal canon law in late medieval England. This classical debate can not be rehearsed in these few pages, but from some modern studies[17] related to it certain further observations can be made that bear upon the question of how early to begin the study of Anglicanism today. First there is the fact, now clearly established, that the common medieval phrase *ecclesia Anglicana* (meaning literally 'English Church') was normally translated 'Church *of* England' by Englishmen of the later Middle Ages: in Latin 'ecclesia de regno Angliae' from 1290, in French 'eglise Dengleterre' from 1341, and in English 'chirche of Engelond' from the later fourteenth century.[18] Second, the phrase *ecclesia Anglicana* was given definitional equivalents, confirming the same point, by Pope Alexander III in 1173 ('the archbishops, bishops, and other prelates and all the clergy and people constituted in England')[19] and by Archbishop Hubert Walter in 1195 ('that portion of the Western Church which the Most High has planted in England').[20] Third, *ecclesia Anglicana* was also understood, by about this time, to include Wales as well as England.[21] Fourth, that there were other Churches elsewhere roughly corresponding to the *ecclesia Anglicana* was acknowledged by (among many others) Archbishop Henry Chichele in 1434, who spoke of it as formerly 'excelling other churches'.[22] Fifth is the fact that the phrase *ecclesia Anglicana* came into common use around the middle of the twelfth century[23] (not, as has at times been erroneously supposed, in 1215 with Magna Carta), when it replaced synonymously such earlier phrases as *ecclesia Angliae* ('Church of England'), as in the letters of St Anselm,[24] and *ecclesia Anglorum* ('Church of the English'), as in the early twelfth-century *Historia Novorum* of Eadmer or earlier in the *Ecclesiastical History* of the Venerable Bede.[25] Sixth, the Latin adjective 'Anglicanus' obviously meant 'English' in medieval usage; for the Church it had a geographical reference and did not carry with it any doctrinal limitation or particularity. Returning finally to the *Oxford English Dictionary*, we find that the earliest sense given for the adjective 'Anglican', which translates the Latin *Anglicanus*, is exactly the same: 'of or peculiar to the English ecclesiastically', and even its second sense is defined as merely 'of the reformed Church of England, and other churches in communion therewith'.[26] No particular doctrinal definition is attached to it, but its geographical reference is also compatible with the multi-cultural and multi-racial diversity of membership that comprises the Anglican Communion today.

Just as the term 'Anglicanism' cannot be found in common usage before the nineteenth century, so the terms 'Anglican' and even 'Church of England' in their various translations can be shown to have a continuous and consistent non-doctrinal use that stretches from the modern era well back into the Middle Ages.

Where, then, should the study of 'Anglicanism' begin? Certainly not in 1838. If the term is to be used descriptively, and not narrowly or prescriptively, it must finally go back conceptually/doctrinally to the New Testament and historically/ geographically to the martyrdom of St Alban in the 'patristic' period of 'Anglican' church history.[27]

NOTES

1   *The Oxford English Dictionary*, vol. i, p. 327.

2   ibid., vol. i, p. 89.

3   R. S. Bosher, *The American Church and the Formation of the Anglican Communion 1823–1853* (Evanston, Illinois, 1962), pp. 12, 13, 21; A. M. G. Stephenson, *The First Lambeth Conference 1867* (SPCK 1967), pp. 55–6; A. M. G. Stephenson, *Anglicanism and the Lambeth Conferences* (SPCK 1978), pp. 5–8.

4   Borden W. Painter, 'Bishop Walter H. Gray and the Anglican Congress of 1954', *Historical Magazine of the Protestant Episcopal Church*, xlix: 2 (June 1980), p. 158.

5   OED, op. cit.

6   John Macquarrie, 'What Still Separates Us from the Catholic Church? An Anglican Reply', *Concilium* 54, *Post-Ecumenical Christianity*, ed. Hans Küng, pp. 45–46.

7   H. R. McAdoo, *The Spirit of Anglicanism* (New York, Charles Scribner's Sons, 1965), p.v. For this author's interpretation of 'the' Anglican method, cf. e.g. p. 49: 'the authentic note of Anglicanism which consistently rejected the idea that it had any specific doctrines of its own in that it demanded subscription to no confession other than the creeds, its aim being one of interpretation by means of a theological method which combined the use of Scripture, antiquity and reason'.

8   OED, op. cit.

9   Macquarrie, op. cit.

10   Stephen Neill, *Anglicanism* (3rd edn, Baltimore, Penguin Books, 1965), pp. 417–8.

11   *The Lambeth Conference 1930* (SPCK n.d.), pp. 54, 154.

12   *The Lambeth Conference 1948* (SPCK 1948), part ii, p. 83.

13   For a recent survey see Charles Thomas, *Christianity in Roman Britain to AD 500* (Berkeley and Los Angeles, University of California Press, 1981).

14   A. G. Dickens, *The English Reformation* (London, Batsford, 1964), pp. 86f.

15   Denys Hay, 'The Church of England in the Later Middle Ages', *History* vol. liii, no. 177 (February 1968), p. 35.

16   London, Church House Bookshop, 1957, pp. 33, 34, and note(s).

17   Hay, op. cit.; J. W. Gray, 'Canon Law in England: Some Reflections on the Stubbs-Maitland Controversy', *Studies in Church History*, vol. iii (1966), pp. 48–68; Charles Donahue Jr, 'Roman Canon Law in the Medieval English Church: Stubbs vs. Maitland

Re-examined after 75 Years in the Light of Some Records from the Church Courts', *Michigan Law Review*, lxxii: 4 (March 1974), pp. 647–716.

18 Hay, op. cit., p. 48. This usage is even continued in the Act of Supremacy, 1534: 'the Church of England, called *Anglicana Ecclesia*'.

19 Z. N. Brooke, *The English Church & the Papacy from the Conquest to the Reign of John* (CUP, 1931), pp. 11, 20: 'archiepiscopis episcopis et ... aliis ecclesiarum praelatis et universo clero et populo per Angliam constitutis'.

20 Brooke, op. cit., p. 13: 'hanc occidentalis ecclesiae portionem quam in Anglia plantavit Altissimus'.

21 C. R. Cheney, *Pope Innocent III and England* (Stuttgart, Anton Hiersemann, 1976), p. 168 n. 179.

22 Hay, op. cit., p. 48.

23 Charles Duggan, 'From the Conquest to the Death of John', in *The English Church and the Papacy in the Middle Ages*, ed. C. H. Lawrence (London, Burns & Oates, 1965), pp. 107–8.

24 Brooke, op. cit., p. 5.

25 Martin Brett, *The English Church under Henry I* (OUP 1975), p. 13. The examples cited from Bede are found at bk. i, ch. 27, 29, and bk. iii, ch. 29. Whereas Bede had used the Latin genitive plural for the Churches of the English and of the French, reserving the adjectival form for the Roman Church alone (Romana ecclesia, as in bk. i, ch. 27), later usages would commonly write of an ecclesia Scoticana, Hibernicana, and, of course, Gallicana.

26 OED, op. cit., which dates the earliest uses of the adjective 'Anglican' to 1635 and 1660. Further see Borden W. Painter, 'Anglican Terminology in Recent Tudor and Stuart Historiography', in *Anglican and Episcopal History*, lvi: 3 (Sept. 1987), pp. 237–49.

27 For a stimulating and provocative theological critique of this entire subject, see S. W. Sykes, *The Integrity of Anglicanism*. Mowbray 1978.

5 Anglicans and Mission

T. E. YATES

Neill, S. C., *A History of Christian Missions*. London 1964.
McCleod Campbell, J., *Christian History in the Making*. London 1946.
Thompson, H. P., *Into All Lands*. London 1951.
Dewey, M., *The Messengers*. London 1975.
Stock, E., *The History of the Church Missionary Society*, 3 vols., London 1899; vol. iv, London 1916.
Hewitt, G. H. G., *The Problems of Success*. London vol. i 1972; vol. ii 1977.
Murray, J., *Proclaim the Good News*. London 1985.

Gibbs, M. E., *The Anglican Church in India 1600–1970*. Delhi 1972.
Warren, M. A. C., *The Missionary Movement from Britain in Modern History*.
London 1965.

Anglicans have made a considerable contribution to the mission of the Church universal. Unlike the Roman Catholic Church, there is no body of theory to which the enquirer may turn for an understanding of the Church's mind. Since Vatican II, the study of such formative documents as the Dogmatic Constitution of the Church (*Lumen Gentium*), the Decree on the Missionary Activity of the Church (*Ad Gentes*) and the Declaration on the relationship of the Church to the non-Christian Religions (*Nostra Aetate*) have offered a rounded Roman Catholic perspective on the Church's missionary activity. By contrast, the Anglican contribution has to be pursued by study of its practice and the writings of individuals, with occasional references in official documents. Certain characteristic emphases can be discerned. First, there has been a stress on indigenization in terms of planting the Church and of drawing out an indigenous ministry. As early as 1765 Philip Quaque, an ordained African, ministered on the West Coast of Africa for fifty years. He was an isolated instance but was to be followed by the Indian Abdul Masih (ordained in 1825), the Canadian Indian Henry Budd (1850) and by the freed-slave and first African bishop, Samuel Crowther (consecrated in 1864). Secondly, there has been a strong emphasis on learning, whether it be to equip converts or the incipient ministry. Codrington College, Barbados, founded as a school in 1745 and reconstituted as a theological college in 1830; Bishop's College, Calcutta founded in 1820; Fourah Bay College in Sierra Leone, founded in 1827, of which Samuel Crowther was one of the first pupils; St John's College, Auckland, towards which SPG paid £5,000 on its foundation in 1847, were among many notable institutions which have been a mark of Anglican mission. With this dual emphasis there has been an accompanying stress on the translation of the Bible and the Anglican liturgy into the vernacular languages. Along with much heroism in the field, which has included martyr bishops like J. C. Patteson in Melanesia in 1872 or the boy martyrs of Uganda in 1884, there have been profound missionary thinkers and writers. The world Church is indebted to certain great Anglicans in this field. It suffices to mention, among the many, thinkers and missionary strategists such as Henry Venn, Roland Allen and Max Warren, with scholars like Bishop Stephen Neill and Bishop Kenneth Cragg.

BEGINNINGS: THE EIGHTEENTH CENTURY

The Book of Common Prayer of 1662 recognized the responsibility of Anglicans for the non-Christians among whom they lived. The office for the 'Baptism of such as are of riper years' 'may be always useful for the baptising of Natives of our plantations and others converted to the faith'. Nevertheless, the seventeenth century, which saw the formation by Rome of the Sacred Congregation for the Propagation of the Faith (Propaganda) in 1622 and such remarkable missionaries as the Roman Catholic Robert de Nobili (1577–1656) among Indian Brahmins and the Presbyterian John Eliot (1604–90) among the Iroquois Indians of North America, had no Anglican equivalent. Thomas Bray (1656–1730), Rector of Sheldon in Warwickshire, whose activities have been noticed in an earlier essay (see p. 37) was responsible by the end of the seventeenth century for the oldest Anglican missionary society, the SPCK (Society for Promoting Christian Knowledge, founded 1698) and for the foundation of the SPG (Society for the Propagation of the Gospel, 1701) at the beginning of the eighteenth century. By Royal Charter of William III, the SPG was to supply the 'want of learned and orthodox ministers' in the plantations, colonies and 'factories beyond the seas'. It was this limitation which meant that it was SPCK, rather than SPG, which supported the Danish mission at Tranquebar in India and employed German missionaries, some in Lutheran orders, in territories not administered by the Crown of England. Nevertheless, SPG accepted dual responsibility from the beginning, both to 'settle the State of Religion as well as may be for our *own People* . . . and then to proceed in the best methods they can towards the *conversion* of the *Natives*'.[1] As well therefore as providing chaplains to the colonies of North America (among whom was numbered John Wesley in Georgia in 1736), SPG began work among the Mohawk Indians in Albany, north of New York, in 1704, four of whom were presented to Queen Anne in London. The Queen gave them a set of silver communion plate for 'her Indian Chappell of the Mohawks'.

Work was also begun among the negro population of New York. One eighteenth-century plantation owner, Christopher Codrington, Governor of Barbados, was moved to leave his estate, with its negro slaves, to SPG in 1710. From this gift Codrington School developed in 1745 and, later, Codrington College, where many Anglican clergy have been nurtured. Finally, the plight of slaves prompted one of SPG's chaplains, Thomas Thompson, to visit the West Coast of Africa. Through his initiative three African boys were taken to be educated in England. From them the first non-European Anglican priest, Philip Quaque, was ordained in 1765.

The work of SPG received a crushing blow through the American War of Independence. After the surrender of English forces in 1781 the SPG mission came to an end; but not before the society had recorded eighty years of service to the American Church, during which 300 clergy had been supported, of whom 100 died while working in the American Church.

THE ERA OF VOLUNTARY SOCIETIES:
THE NINETEENTH CENTURY

Where SPG was a chartered society, owing much to the individual initiative of Thomas Bray but also limited by its royal patronage and charter, its sister society, the CMS (Church Missionary Society) was a voluntary association with no such limitations. The end of the eighteenth century had seen the rise of various missionary societies. Among them the inter-denominational London Missionary Society (founded 1795) provided both a model and a catalyst for Evangelical Anglicans. Members of the Eclectics Society, a clerical and lay discussion group, were sensitive to criticisms of lack of churchmanship to which involvement in societies like LMS and the inter-denominational British and Foreign Bible Society laid them open. This, as well as a genuine concern for the 'heathen', led Charles Simeon to ask, at a meeting in 1796: 'With what propriety and in what mode can a mission be established to the Heathen from the Established Church?' The foundation of the 'Society for Missions to Africa and the East' followed in 1799 and became the Church Missionary Society. From the same circle and again inspired by the LMS, the 'London Society for promoting Christianity among the Jews', which today is known as the Church's Ministry among the Jews, developed in 1809. The Colonial and Continental Church Society, now the Inter-continental Church Society, was also Anglican Evangelical in its origins.

There is some truth in the comment that, where SPG became the *Church* missionary society, CMS was the society for the propagation of the gospel. By this is meant that, whereas SPG had been at pains to emphasize that those supported by the society were agents of the Church (a policy which led in the nineteenth century to all candidates being required to sit the Archbishops' Board Examination) the CMS showed historically a greater independence. Again, where SPG laid great emphasis on Church planting, CMS stressed above all individual conversion.[2] Yet such judgements must be severely qualified. The founders of SPCK and SPG were in touch with the springs of Pietism in men like A. H. Francke of Halle and with the Pietist emphasis on conversion which he represented; and no one believed more firmly in Church planting than Henry Venn, the CMS secretary of the mid-nineteenth century. Some of the founder members of CMS were also members of SPG. One, Josiah Pratt, a CMS secretary, went so far as to commend SPG to the public for funding in an anonymous pamphlet of 1819. Flanked by SPG and LMS, however, the response of John Venn as a founder of CMS was typical of the Anglican Evangelicals: 'the Church principle but not the High Church principle'. The ordering of relationships between CMS and the developing Anglican episcopate overseas was to be one dominant theme of its history.

William Wilberforce professed as deep a concern for India as for the abolition of the slave trade. Both provided a missionary dynamic in the early nineteenth century. In the case of India, the East India Company's operations were, like SPG's, governed by Royal Charter. Wilberforce pressed long and hard for ecclesiastical provisions to be included in the charter, hoping to open India to missionaries. Other colonial models, such as the Danes at Tranquebar and the Dutch in their East Indies possessions, suggested official encouragement for missionaries when the charter was renewable in 1793. He had to be content with EIC chaplaincies, accepted by various godly men often influenced by Charles Simeon's ministry in Cambridge, of whom the brightest star of the galaxy was Henry Martyn (1781–1812) on account of his academic brilliance, piety and dedication, cut short by an early death. In 1813, the new charter secured the appointment of a Bishop of Calcutta in T. F. Middleton and Wilberforce's so-called 'Pious Clause' to facilitate missionary work passed after sustained and strenuous resistance.

This was one sign among many in the century that it was not always to the advantage of the missionary movement to be closely related to organs of influence, whether traders or colonial administrators. The new bishop held that his Letters Patent from the crown did not permit him to exercise any powers in relation to native Indians, and he was embarrassed by the presence of missionaries. His successor, Reginald Heber, felt less inhibited. He decided to ordain Henry Martyn's convert, Abdul Masih, in 1825. If this was a sign of an early Anglican determination to indigenize the ministry, Daniel Wilson's episcopate (1832–58) was to demonstrate the continuing tension between the established church structure of government by bishops and the voluntary missionary society. It was a tension known to the Roman Catholic communion as one experienced between the religious orders, with their capacity to initiate and develop in mission, and the central machinery of government in Rome. Eventually a concordat was hammered out between the bishop, a friend of CMS but determined to uphold order, and the committee in London in 1839.

Both CMS and SPG developed extensive missionary work in the Indian sub-continent during the century. They were joined by such bodies as the Cambridge Mission to Delhi (1877) and the Church of England Zenana Missionary Society (1880) who, in time, were to merge with SPG and CMS respectively.

The slave trade gave rise directly to the first CMS mission in Africa. Zachary Macaulay, father of the historian, had founded the Sierra Leone Company in 1791. It was to be a colony for liberated slaves, many of them re-captives of the British naval squadron, landed after rescue from the ships of slavers. The CMS mission there gave rise to the dream of men like T. F. Buxton that Africa could be civilized and transformed by the combined effect of commerce and Christianity. In his *African Slave Trade and its Remedy* (1839) Buxton wrote: 'Let missionaries and schoolmasters, the plough and the spade, go together ... civilisation will advance ... and Christianity ... as the proximate cause of this happy change'.[3] One of the early re-captives was Samuel Adjai Crowther. After schooling at Fourah Bay College he was ordained in 1834. He and others entertained another 'pleasing dream': the various tribes-people landed at Sierra Leone should become missionaries to their own tribes. He himself became a CMS missionary to the Yoruba in modern Nigeria in 1843.

After the loss of the American colonies the government were faced with finding an area for the transportation of convicts. They decided on Botany Bay. William Wilberforce's ubiquitous philanthropy found a chaplain, Richard Johnson, willing to sail to Australia in 1786. Both SPG and SPCK helped with his payment and equipment. He was joined later by Samuel Marsden, whose eyes turned to New Zealand as a mission field. Marsden persuaded CMS to launch a mission, which was to be first civilizing and then missionary. Among Anglican missions, perhaps only the mission to the Arctic, where some 80% of Esquimaux became Anglican Christians, is more remarkable than the early Maori missions. Here a cannibalistic and warlike people showed itself highly responsive to the Christian message and capable of spreading it rapidly and spontaneously in the 1830s and 1840s. Once again, relationships between Selwyn, a heroic pioneer bishop, and CMS were not easy. Like Daniel Wilson, he maintained his rights as bishop and, in his case, tried to extend them further in regard to the placing of missionaries. His ideas on church government, synodical and free of the apparatus of legal establishment, also alarmed traditionalists in Salisbury Square, headquarters of the CMS.

Henry Venn, the controlling mind at Salisbury Square, must be regarded as the leading Anglican missionary strategist of the century. He was son of one of the founders of CMS and became honorary secretary from 1841–72. He coincided with his great SPG counterpart, Edward Hawkins, (SPG secretary 1843–64), with whom he kept in close contact. Venn did his best to relate CMS, as a voluntary society, to the episcopate at home and the developing overseas episcopate, which grew in his time from nine to over fifty. Venn's real claim to greatness lay in his vision for, and implementation of, indigenous Churches. He developed his ideas in a series of papers written for CMS. First, indigenous Churches should be developed 'from the bottom upwards' rather than created by organizational fiat from above. Small groups of 'native Christians' would coalesce into native pastorates, which would become 'self-supporting, self-governing and self-extending'. The role of the mission was to be the scaffolding, to be removed in due course, so leading to the '*euthanasia* of the mission'. The indigenous Church could then be left to itself; and the missionaries, often European exotics, would move on to the 'regions beyond'. As the native pastorates developed, they would group into a diocese. The 'crown' of this indigenous church edifice would be the native bishop.

Underlying Venn's thinking was a sharp distinction between the evangelist, whose function was to preach the gospel in the 'regions beyond', and the pastor, whose role was to build up the 'settled Church'. When, however, Venn first realized his vision in Sierra Leone in 1861 the European bishop remained, partly on account of the presence of Europeans in the colony. When he persuaded Samuel Crowther to become a bishop, Crowther became, in fact, not the bishop of a settled Church, the 'crown' of Venn's plan, but an evangelist in episcopal orders as Bishop on the Niger. It was in part due to failure to follow through Venn's own logic that, sadly, a great Christian pioneer, translator and pastor became, not so much the sign that Africans were ready for leadership (as Venn had intended), as a 'symbol of the supposed failure of African leadership'.[4] Even so, it was a sign of Venn's vision that an African bishop should have been envisaged in 1864, sixty years after CMS entered West Africa. It was another example of the Anglican desire for an indigenous Church and ministry.

By its jubilee in 1849, CMS had sent out 350 missionaries to India, East and West Africa, New Zealand, Canada and China. SPG had entered the fields of the West Indies (1712), West Africa (1752), Canada (1759), Australia (1793), India (1818), South Africa (1820), New Zealand (1841) and Borneo (1847).

FROM THE INDIAN MUTINY TO THE END OF THE CENTURY

In Anglican missionary history the year 1857 is a turning point. It was the year of the Indian Mutiny, after which the government replaced the East India Company as the controlling power. For Africa, there were to be special developments after David Livingstone's addresses at the ancient universities of Oxford and Cambridge in that year. In his speech at the Senate House in Cambridge he had said: 'I beg to direct your attention to Africa. I know that in a few years I shall be cut off in that country which is now open. Do not let it be shut again! I go back to Africa to try to make an open path for commerce and Christianity. Do you carry on the work which I have begun. I leave it with you!'.
A strange result of Livingstone's eloquence was that a Scottish Presbyterian, who had been in the employment of the LMS but had exchanged the life of a missionary for that of an explorer, was instrumental in founding a great Anglo-Catholic mission in 1858. Originally the title had been the 'Oxford and Cambridge Mission to Central Africa'. The advent of Durham and Dublin universities changed this to the 'Universities' Mission to Central Africa'. UMCA had anything but an auspicious beginning. C. F. Mackenzie, consecrated in 1867 as 'bishop to the mission and the tribes dwelling in the neighbourhood of Lake Nyassa and the River Shire' personified the dream of certain Tractarians that the bishop should be the pioneer evangelist and missionary leader. Mackenzie soon died of malaria but his successors, Bishops William Tozer and Edward Steere, consolidated the work of UMCA. Tozer moved the mission's base to

Zanzibar, and Steere had the satisfaction of building Christ Church Cathedral with his own hands on the site of the Arab slave market. A later bishop, John Hine, expressed the aim of UMCA as 'the building up of a Native Church ... the Church of the people of the land, irrespective of European influence, adapting itself to the special circumstances of the race and country in which it exists'.[5]

The South American Missionary Society was founded in 1844 by Captain Allen Gardiner, a retired naval officer like another great pioneer of the Maori mission, Henry Williams. It was not until after his tragic death by starvation in Tierra del Fuego in 1851 that the mission really developed. During the century the mission entered Paraguay (1888) and Chile (1895) and after 1900 Argentina (1911) and Peru (1974). Again there has been an emphasis on developing an indigenous ministry. The first Mapuche Indian was ordained in 1937 and a group of seven Mataco Indians in 1966. The society has now developed branches in other parts of the Anglican Communion, for example in the Church of the Province of South Africa and the Episcopal Church of the United States. It goes today by the name SAMS International. A feature of the Anglican Communion is that missionary societies, founded within the Church of England, have established themselves in sister Churches overseas, as, for example, Australian and New Zealand CMS, each independent missionary bodies.

Space forbids a full account of Anglican missions in the second half of the nineteenth century in all their exuberant vitality. The opening of the Far East to missionary activity, however, deserves special notice. First, it was an example of the doubtful advantages to the Christian mission of Western gun-boat diplomacy and commercial pressure. China was pressed by Britain, first, into a treaty to open certain 'treaty ports' to trade in 1842 and then in 1858 to permit access to the interior. One result of the treaties was the import of opium as part of British policy in China. Japan, a parallel case of isolation, was forced by American pressure to open her ports in 1854. Secondly, both these fields were reminders that Anglican mission was no longer the preserve of the English-based societies. American and Canadian Anglicans were a growing force to be reckoned with. In China, W. J. Boone, a missionary of the American Episcopal Church, established a mission of his Church in Shanghai in 1840 and was consecrated bishop in China in 1844. This was to raise questions of ecclesiastical jurisdiction among English Anglicans with the CMS. Boone was joined later by one of the greatest of all Anglican missionaries, linguists and translators in the Jewish convert S. I. J. Scherewschewsky in 1859, who was consecrated bishop in 1877. Despite nearly total paralysis of body after 1881 he added to his mandarin translations of the Bible and the Book of Common Prayer further renderings of both into another Chinese form, 'easy *Wenli*'.

Japan was a field in which Americans of the Episcopal Church and later Canadians of the Anglican Church of Canada served with missionaries of both the SPG and the CMS. Each had oversight in different geographical areas.

Channing Moore Williams, one of the early American missionaries, became Bishop of China and Japan in 1866 and was resident in Osaka and Tokyo from 1869. The arrival of Edward Bickersteth, who had served with the Cambridge Mission to Delhi noted above, as bishop in 1886 led to his vision of an indigenous Japanese Anglican church, *Nippon Sei Ko Kai*, being realized in 1887, in which all the various Anglican components were represented. At least one notable Anglican institution, St Paul's School, Tokyo (founded 1874), now Rikkyo University, was and is an example of the Anglican approach to mission through educational institutions. Bishop Williams was its founder. An equally notable medical institution, St Luke's Hospital, Tokyo (founded 1900) was established by another American, also from Richmond, Virginia, in Dr Rudolf Teusler. It was a Virginian missionary and bishop, Henry St George Tucker, Bishop of Kyoto, who was to encourage self-government in NSKK in the early twentieth century. Although the Anglican body remained very small by reference to the whole population of Japan (some 50,000 only to-day), cultural penetration was achieved through these and other educational and medical foundations.

THE TWENTIETH CENTURY: FROM MISSIONS TO MISSION

Although there had been earlier international missionary conferences in Liverpool (1860), London (1888) and New York (1900) the World Missionary Conference at Edinburgh in 1910 was of special significance. For the Anglicans this was symbolized by the presence of the Archbishop of Canterbury, Randall Davidson. In common with the leaders of SPG, he had hesitated to attend a conference which might not be fully representative of all views. In fact, a very broad selection of Anglican opinion was represented. Bishop Charles Gore, Father H. H. Kelly of the Society of the Sacred Mission (now charged with training candidates for the Anglican mission in Korea), Bishop Montgomery, the secretary of SPG, Temple Gairdner, CMS missionary and Arabic scholar, who was to write a widely read account of the conference, and, as a young man and steward, William Temple. Among the leaders of the 'younger Churches' was V. S. Azariah, later Anglican Bishop of Dornakal in India. Davidson, in his address to the conference, underlined that for him, as a representative figure in the Anglican Church, 'the place of missions in the life of the church must be the central place'. Azariah gave voice to the new relationship needed between the national leaders and the expatriate missionaries: 'through all ages to come the Indian church will rise up in gratitude to attest the heroism and self-denying labours of the missionary body. You have given your goods to feed the poor. You have given your bodies to be burned. We ask for *love*. Give us FRIENDS'.[6]

Another prophetic voice raised against received missionary practice was that of Roland Allen (1868–1947), SPG missionary in China and writer. In 1912

Allen published *Missionary Methods: St Paul's or Ours*. He asked whether the aim was to plant Churches or to perpetuate missions. In contrast to St Paul, Western missionaries had failed to give the local church the full spiritual authority needed for its healthy development. Allen was equally suspicious of missions and large 'national' Churches. Both stifled the development of God's gifts to the local body. He called for a greater trust in the Holy Spirit, over against imposed orthodoxies and external administration by societies or national Churches. His charge that missionaries made converts over-dependent on themselves recalls the Sierra Leonean convert's comment on the death of the great missionary, W. A. B. Johnson: 'We looked more to Mr Johnson than to Jesus.'[7] To Allen, this was the ultimate indictment, a fault from which St Paul was free because he moved on, devolving leadership on local elders.

It is not possible here to do more than notice the profound questions raised to all non-Christian peoples by the World War of 1914–18, which led to the disillusionment of many with the so-called Christian nations. Between the wars, the Bible Churchmen's Missionary Society was added to the societies in England, after alarm among certain CMS supporters at what was regarded as a drift into liberalism by its leadership. The split came in 1922. BCMS has worked in Burma, China, Iran, India, the Arctic, Canada, East Africa and Morocco. It has also been a notable example of the Anglican tendency to wish to revive ancient Christian bodies rather than proselytize or divide. This was true of CMS in South India among the Syrian Malabar Church in the 1820s and 1830s. It was now true of BCMS in Ethiopia with the ancient Coptic Church. Alfred Buxton of BCMS visited Ethiopia in 1931 and judged that 'it would be sound policy to stimulate and help this ancient church . . . to carry out . . . her own proper share in the work of evangelisation'.[8] This policy was followed. In East Africa, spiritual revival brought fresh, invigorating renewal to church life. The *balokole* or 'saved ones' spread this influence throughout East Africa and beyond during the 1930s. The Ruanda mission, of which Dr J. E. Church was a prominent member, remained in association with CMS but was known for supporters as CMS Ruanda.

When Archbishop William Temple was enthroned in Canterbury Cathedral in 1942 he referred to the 'great new fact of our era', a reference to the existence of the Church of Christ in every major ethnic group in the world. It was a fitting tribute to the missionary movement. It also pointed to the new future, expressed at the Lambeth Conference of 1958 as 'mission to the whole world (with) no frontiers between "Home" and "Foreign".'[9] In 1963 at the Anglican Congress in Toronto, Archbishop Michael Ramsey went further: 'We must plan our mission together and use our resources in the service of a single task. The word 'missionary' will mean not colonialism of any kind but going to one another to help one another. Let African and Asian missionaries come to England to help convert the post-Christian heathenism in our country and convert our English church to a closer following of Christ'.[10]

An aspect of this 'one world' was the growth of awareness of the other great religious traditions and the confidence of Islam, Hinduism and Buddhism often associated with nationalist aspirations after 1950. Later, in addition to this, there was a growing presence of people of other races and religious traditions among the 'sending' nations. A pioneering study in the realm of inter-faith relations was made by the Anglican scholar and profound student of Islam, Bishop Kenneth Cragg, in his *Call of the Minaret* (1956). This book impressed the secretary of CMS, Max Warren, very deeply. He himself edited the *Christian Presence* series of studies by Anglican scholars of the great religious traditions, where he espoused Cragg's way of dialogue in his general preface as the proper approach to those of other faiths: the first need is to 'take off our shoes ... else we may find ourselves treading on other men's dreams ... to ask what is the authentic religious content in the experience of the Muslim, the Hindu, the Buddhist or whatever he may be ... to be 'present' with them'.[11] It was a decade when the Roman Catholic Church was to see dialogue as a means for Catholics to 'preserve and promote the spiritual and moral goods found among these men' (*Nostra Aetate*). In an England confronted by a World Festival of Islam in 1976, Bishop David Brown, like Cragg an Arabic scholar and student of Islam, produced a widely received monograph, *A New Threshold* (1976), which sought to guide those perplexed by manifestations of the Muslim presence in a traditionally Christian context. The missionary societies responded by setting up the BCMS/CMS Other Faiths Theological Project, with Bishop Stephen Neill as its first chairman in 1979. A series of Lambeth Inter Faith lectures also pointed to the importance of this issue.[12]

A new organ of consultation for the whole Anglican Communion, the Anglican Consultative Council, met at Limuru, Kenya in 1971, with the Archbishop of Canterbury as President and representatives from all Anglican provinces. This meeting too commended dialogue, emphasizing that it 'will not be simply another form of evangelism' but 'each ... will lay himself open, not only to his partner but to the Spirit of God'.[13] Successive meetings of the ACC at Dublin (1973), Trinidad (1976), Ontario (1979), Newcastle on Tyne (1981) and Badagry (1984) have set up 'Partners-in-Mission' consultations, have carried mission on their agendas but have emphasized the changed nature of mission in the twentieth century. In the words of the Dublin report 'there is but one mission in all the world ... the responsibility for mission in any place belongs *primarily* to the Church in that place'.[14] As Bishop Stephen Neill wrote in 1964: 'The age of missions is at an end; the age of mission has begun.'[15]

439

ISSUES FOR THE FUTURE

This essay has been concerned with the history of the great Anglican missionary societies. Throughout their history there have been calls for their integration into the Church in, perhaps, a board of mission. Bishop Samuel Wilberforce was a nineteenth-century advocate of this policy, and he has had a number of twentieth-century followers. The creation of the Partnership for World Mission in 1978 with a secretariat in London has been an attempt to hold together the strengths of the voluntary society with the need for a representative body which is recognized as, for example, corporately representing the societies to overseas member Churches, who may prefer to deal with such a body than with individual societies. In the words of the Partners in Mission consultation in England of 1981, 'voluntary societies should be integrated with the structures of the church but without losing their identity and flexibility' because 'voluntary societies encourage enthusiasm and personal engagement at parish level. We must not lose this.'[16] Some unification has been noticed above as between CMS and CEZMS and between SPG, CMD and now UMCA. Since 1965 SPG and UMCA have merged to become USPG. In 1986, CMS, USPG and PWM are to be housed in the same building in London.

The issue of the voluntary society and the structures of the Church remains and now has an international dimension, not only in the case of SAMS noticed above, but now also with the Church's Ministry to the Jews. As a result of the Partners in Mission consultation set up by the ACC, the General Secretary of Board of Mission of the Episcopal Church has invited the society to form CMJ/USA in 1982, based in Fairfax, Virginia. It remains to be seen how far those parts of the Anglican Communion which have been used to handling mission through central boards like the Episcopal Church of the United States, in common with a British Church like the (presbyterian) Church of Scotland, will relate to new initiatives by the societies. The societies themselves may develop a function and role as organs of response to the mission needs of the whole Anglican communion, holding the whole Church to its missionary vocation in word and deed by promoting the interchange of personnel, funding and ideas. A recent example which may provide a model was a programme for renewal mounted by the diocese of Hokkaido, with East African Anglican church leaders as missioners, funded by the CMS from London. The use of a near-universal language as a means of communication in English is no negligible factor at the disposal of Anglicans in mission.

Two further issues may be considered in conclusion. First, it is likely that mission will remain on the agenda of the Anglican communion in a world which, as the Vatican II document *Ad Gentes* pointed out, two billion remain unevangelized. Here the original insight of the BCP with which this essay began remains valid: missionary responsibility is present in the persons of those who are unattached or ignorant or unconvinced among whom Anglicans live. This is but another way of saying that the Church is missionary in its being: that, in Emil Brunner's words, 'the Church lives by mission as a fire lives by burning'. Secondly, the Anglican Church, with the Church Universal, faces a sharp change of perspective. Much of the liveliest Anglican life exists in Africa south of the Sahara, in Asia and in Latin America. These voices will claim a hearing increasingly in Anglican consultations and may act as a healthy corrective to the Anglicanism of the comparatively settled, wealthy and arid north, arid in the view of many of these communities because of what is perceived as an over-intellectualized theological tradition and a weakened spirituality. As Archbishop Michael Ramsey suggested at Toronto, may it be that the vitality of the younger Churches in the Anglican communion is needed to renew the older Churches in their mission?

NOTES

1 SPG First Annual Sermon quoted in H. P. Thomson, *Into All Lands* (1951), pp. 20–21

2. This is still the case. See the remarks of the then President of CMS, Dame Diana Reader Harris, in 'What we hold dear' USPG/CMS Consultation 8–10 February 1973; 'We have great unanimity over the centrality of conversion in Christian experience.'

3 T. F. Buxton, *The African Slave Trade and its Remedy* (1839), pp. 282, 511.

4 B. G. M. Sundkler, *The Christian Ministry in Africa* (1960), pp. 46–7.

5 M. Anderson-Morshead, *History of the Universities' Mission to Central Africa* (1955–62) vol. i, p. 220.

6 *Edinburgh World Missionary Conference Report* (1910), vol. ix, pp. 150, 315.

7 E. Stock, *History of the Church Missionary Society* (1899), vol. i, p. 118.

8 S. F. Russell, *Full Fifty Years* (1972), p. 45.

9 *Lambeth Conference Report* (1958), resolution 58.

10 *Anglican Congress, Toronto Report* (1963), p. 16.

11 Editor's preface for series by M. A. C. Warren as found in P. Schneider, *Sweeter than Honey* (1966), p. 12.

12 For an acute Anglican mind grappling with these issues from a context of religious pluralism see Bishop Lakshman Wickremesinghe, then Bishop of Kurunugala in Sri Lanka, in *Crucible* Oct–Dec 1979, the Second Lambeth Inter-faith Lecture.

13 ACC Limuru Report *The Time is Now* (1971), p. 44.

14 ACC Dublin Report (1973), p. 53.

15 S. C. Neill, *History of Christian Missions* (1964), p. 572.

16 Report, *To a Rebellious House?* (1981), p. 33.

GLOSSARY

ACC: the Anglican Consultative Council, established after the 1968 Lambeth Conference. Its membership drawn from each province of the Anglican Communion and inclusive of bishops, priests, deacons and lay people, the Council provides a continuity of consultation and guidance on policy. The permanent secretariat is based in London, and meetings are held in different parts of the world at two to three year intervals.

Act in Restraint of Appeals (1533): asserted that England was an empire to whose supreme head and king all in the realm, both temporal and spiritual, owed obedience. By removing England from the authority of Rome and restricting the power of the English Church to spiritual matters this Act enabled the annulment of Henry VIII's marriage to Catharine of Aragon and made possible his marriage to Anne Boleyn.

Acts of Supremacy: the Act of 1534 summed up the claims of Henry VIII to be supreme head of the Church of England, and claimed for the king both spiritual and temporal jurisdiction over the realm. It made England an ecclesiastically sovereign state, though it did little more than ratify what had already been accomplished. The Act of 1559 was part of the Elizabethan Settlement, and used the term 'supreme governor' in reaffirming the Crown's spiritual authority in England—a terminology which placated some opponents (See also Royal Supremacy).

Acts of Uniformity: the first Act of Uniformity (1549) commanded the use of English in all services except in universities and in private, and made use of the First Book of Common Prayer compulsory in English churches, subject to increasingly severe penalties. The second Act (1552) enforced the use of the revised Prayer Book, and increased the strictures of the first Act. Both were repealed by Mary Tudor in 1553. The Act of Uniformity (1559) enforced the Elizabethan Settlement, repealed the Roman practices of Mary Tudor, established regulations for church discipline, and contained seeds of future controversy with the Puritans. The Act of 1662 followed the Restoration (qv) of Charles II, and was the first of a number of restrictive measures known as the Clarendon Code (qv). It commanded the use of the 1662 Prayer Book and demanded that all ministers publicly assent to it and, if not ordained, be ordained. As a result of this Act the Great Ejection (in which 2,000 Presbyterian, Baptist and Independent ministers left the Church), and an irretrievable division between Anglicans and Puritans, marked the beginning of English non-conformity.

Andrewes, Lancelot (1555–1626): Bishop of Winchester, a notable scholar and apologist for Anglicanism, and an outstanding preacher. He was involved as a translator in the 1611 Authorized Version of the Bible. His sermons and posthumous *Preces Privatae* have attracted much modern interest, chiefly due to the championship of T. S. Eliot (See also Caroline Divines).

Anglican Communion, the: the fellowship of Churches in communion with the see of Canterbury, sharing a common theology and liturgical tradition with the mother Church; focused since 1867 in the Lambeth Conferences (See Lambeth Conferences), the Anglican Consultative Council (See ACC), and the meetings of the Primates of the Communion (See Primate Meeting).

Anglicana Ecclesia: the term describing the Church of England in the 1534 Act of Supremacy.

Anglo-Catholicism: a dogmatic and sacramental position within Anglicanism emphasizing the continuity of links with the early Church, displaying an affinity with medieval Christianity, and rejecting the label 'Protestant'. Its immediate forebear was the Oxford Movement (qv), of which it was a late phase.

Archbishop of Canterbury: Augustine's first church in Britain (597) was at Canterbury, which therefore became the centre of the English Church. By the fourteenth century the Archbishop of Canterbury had the rank of Primate of All England, to which today is added his accepted role as leader and head of the Anglican Communion (qv).

ARCIC: the Anglican–Roman Catholic International Commission. The first Commission was set up in 1970 following the Archbishop of Canterbury's visit to Pope Paul VI, and the second in 1983. One of several post-Vatican II ecumenical initiatives, its conclusions have envisaged a future reunion of the two Churches, subject to much further discussion.

Articles: the Thirty-nine Articles reached their present form in 1571, and were preceded by the Ten Articles (1536), the Bishops' Book (1543), and the Forty-Two Articles (1553). They form a statement of the doctrinal position of the Church of England with respect to various theological issues of the sixteenth century and have been variously interpreted and used in the Anglican Communion since.

Bangorian Controversy (1717): the crisis precipitated by a sermon preached by Bishop Hoadly of Bangor before George I. The Lower House of Convocation accused Hoadly of erroneous teaching on the nature of the Church and the work of the Holy Spirit, and appealed to the Upper House to censure him. The conflicts which existed between the upper and lower clergy were thereby aggravated, and the consequent war of words led to the King's proroguing of Convocation. It was not to meet again for 135 years.

Bell, George Kennedy Allen (1883–1958): Bishop of Chichester 1929–58 and elected honorary president of the WCC in 1954, Bell was a significant figure in the Ecumenical Movement. He was chaplain to the Archbishop of Canterbury 1914–24, and while at Lambeth was involved in several early ecumenical initiatives; later he was influential in Life and Work 1937–48.

Book of Common Prayer: see Prayer Book

Broad Church: an imprecise term sometimes used to denote the loose 'party' of the Cambridge Platonists and Latitudinarians in the seventeenth century. Used in the nineteenth century of those who objected to what they saw as the dogmatic rigidity of Evangelicals (qv) and Anglo-Catholics (qv). They affirmed that God has given reason to human beings for the verification of revelation, and sought for a larger freedom for the interpretation of revelation in contemporary culture. The contributors to *Essays and Reviews* (qv) can be regarded as Broad Churchmen.

Butler, Joseph (1692–1752): Bishop, apologist and moral philosopher. Butler's major work was the *Analogy of Religion* (1736), which was a major weapon against Deism and a book of enduring influence. Against the Deists' argument from design, Butler argued that nature and revelation are both characterized by order and also by difficulties. The former he attributed to a divine Creator, the latter to human finiteness. He emphasized the weight of probability in evidences.

Cambridge Platonists: rejecting the doctrine of total depravity taught by the Calvinistic Puritans, the Platonists (who were based on Emmanuel College, Cambridge) held that human reason was an inner light and that good and evil, and an awareness of the infinite, were ineradicably part of human nature.

Canons: The *Book of Canons* (1604–6) adopted by James I was a manual of church law, essentially preserving the Elizabethan Settlement and making few concessions to Puritanism. It remained little changed until 1939, with the establishment of a canon law commission. Since then canon law has been continuously revised, such revision now being in the hands of a commission of the General Synod of the Church of England. Each Province of the Anglican Communion (qv) has its own canon laws, all related to but all different from the canon law of the Church of England.

Caroline Divines: the name given to a group of theologians, many of them bishops, of the seventeenth century, represented by Lancelot Andrewes (qv) and William Laud (qv), opposed to extreme Calvinism and Latitudinarianism (qv).

Catechism: instruction by question-and-answer. Used extensively by the Reformers, both because of its significance for the young and its suitability for teaching the poorly educated. Major catechisms were Luther's *Small Catechism* (1529), the Heidelberg Catechism (1563), the catechism before confirmation in the Prayer Book (added 1604) and the Westminster *Larger Catechism* (1658).

Chicago-Lambeth Quadrilateral: see Lambeth Quadrilateral.

Clarendon Code: a series of restrictive statutes passed by the Cavalier Parliament 1661–5. The intention was to strip those not conforming to the Church of England of all spiritual and secular leadership (See also Acts of Uniformity; Five Mile Act).

Commonwealth: following the execution of Charles I and the abolition of the House of Lords, England was declared a 'Commonwealth or Free State'. Government was by a Council of State and the drastically purged Rump Parliament. The Commonwealth saw the abolition of episcopacy and the Prayer Book, and the Church of England was proscribed.

Comprehension: the character of the English Church prior to the reign of Charles I, whereby a refusal to narrow doctrinal boundaries ensured that many not entirely happy with the Anglican Church nevertheless felt able to remain within it. 'Comprehensive' is a term often used today to indicate the element of inclusiveness thought to be integral to the definition of Anglicanism.

Convocation: regional gatherings of clergy in Canterbury and York, predating Parliament. The bishops formed the Upper House, the rest of the clergy the Lower. Conflicts between the two led to the suspension of Convocation for 135 years (See Bangorian Controversy). In 1920 the Church Assembly was created as a parallel body, and in 1969 functions of both were combined in the creation of the General Synod. Convocation still exists, though with greatly reduced powers.

Cranmer, Thomas (1489–1556): Archbishop of Canterbury 1533–55, Cranmer was the architect of English liturgy. He produced the vernacular liturgy of 1544, and in 1549 his first Book of Common Prayer. Other writings included *The True and Catholic Doctrine of the Lord's Supper* and a revision of canon law. Having joined the cause of Lady Jane Grey at the death-bed wish of Edward VI, he was condemned to death with the accession of Mary in 1553, though he was not executed until 1556.

Ecclesiastical Commission: Elizabeth I's chief instrument of governing of the Church, authorized by the 1559 Settlement.

Edward VI (1537–53): while still in his minority, Edward succeeded his father, Henry VIII (qv) on the throne, and under the guidance of a Protestant-minded protector, forwarded the Reformation in England. The English Bible returned to authorized use,

Prayer Books (qv) in English were provided, Articles of Religion (qv) were devised, and these and other instruments of reform were enforced through Articles and Injunctions of Visitation.

Elizabeth I (1533–1603): Elizabeth's reign was marked by increased toleration and adroitness. The Elizabethan Settlement (1559) displayed both qualities, and was opposed by Roman Catholics and Puritans. The Settlement established the monarch as 'supreme governor' of the Church, and sought for religious uniformity through the enforced use of the 1552 Book of Common Prayer, conservatively revised. The Settlement was further defined during the Queen's reign in process of the conflict emerging between its defenders and those who were opposed to it.

Erastianism: the doctrine, named after the Swiss theologian Thomas Erastus (1524–83), that the state has the right to intrude upon the affairs of the Church and overrule decisions. In a limited sense the Church of England is an Erastian Church. The doctrine was opposed by Gore (qv) and others.

Essays and Reviews (1860): a collection of seven essays, radical and sometimes sceptical in nature, demanding an openness from the Church to the findings of modern criticism. It provoked a bitter controversy, which confirmed that liberal theology had a significant following.

Establishment: technically, the instituting of a Church system by law; in wider use, the term embraces the identification of Church and state and the supremacy of the sovereign as spiritual head of the Church—both concepts affirmed by the English Reformation (See also Act of Supremacy; Royal Supremacy).

Evangelical: a term derived from the German 'evangelisch', used by Luther to signify the character of the Christian Church as renewed by the gospel. It achieved greater prominence in English religious usage after the Evangelical Revival (qv). Anglicans who identify themselves as Evangelicals are generally characterized by commitment to the mission of the Church, often inclusive of social action, by stress on the atoning work of Christ and the necessity for conversion, and by use of the Scriptures as alone normative for faith and life. They are sometimes referred to as 'Low Church', in contrast to High Church (qv), for their comparative lack of concern for ceremonial and tradition, and for their ready association with Evangelicals of other Churches.

Evangelical Revival: often called the 'Wesleyan' Revival because of the crucial role of John Wesley (1703–91). The movement in England which began with the field-preaching of Wesley and George Whitefield (1714–70) was closely related both to the Moravian movement on the continent of Europe and the First Great Awakening in New England. Hymns were a feature of the Revival, and Charles Wesley (1707–88) was one of the most gifted of all English hymn-writers. The Evangelical Revival, with its emphasis on the value and worth of the individual, was responsible for extensive social reform and education.

Field, Richard (1561–1616): a close friend of Richard Hooker, Field was one of the outstanding theologians of his day. His major work, *Of the Church* (1606), was an affirmation of the Church of England against Rome. He maintained that Anglicanism was a continuation of old (pre-Trent) Catholic conciliar tradition and that modern Catholicism was echoing the errors of Donatism in its claim to exclusive purity.

Five Mile Act (1655): one of the rigorous measures of the Clarendon Code against those not assenting to the beliefs and practices of the Church of England, the Act made it an offence for Non-conformist ministers or teachers to approach within five miles of any city, town or borough.

Glorious Revolution, the: the revolution of 1688 which deposed James II and inaugurated the reign of William and Mary. Its cause was the widespread belief that James intended to implement a thorough-going Catholic state (as indicated by e.g. his preferment of Catholics to high office), and the fact that the birth of the Prince of Wales indicated that a Catholic dynasty was now secured. Early legislation of William and Mary dismantled much of the Clarendon Code.

Gore, Charles (1853–1932): Anglo–Catholic bishop who exerted a liberalizing influence on the Oxford Movement (See *Lux Mundi*). Gore was associated with the Christian Socialist movement, the Community of the Resurrection, and the Worker's Educational Association. A gifted scholar, he wrote numerous books and had a wide ministry and influence. He was an opponent of Erastianism (qv).

Henry VIII (1491–1547): although the head of the Reformed Church of England, Henry's sympathies remained Catholic. The dissolution of the monasteries was arguably an economic rather than a spiritual act, and the breach with Rome was inextricably implicated with his need for a male heir (See also Act of Supremacy; Royal Supremacy).

High Church: Laudianism; also more generally, any emphasis on ritual, order, and pre-Reformation church practice within the Protestant Churches (See also Laud).

Hooker, Richard (c. 1554–1600): preacher and minister, but more notably scholar and theologian. A landmark both in the history of English prose and also that of the English Church, Hooker's *Laws of Ecclesiastical Polity* (1593 and 1597) is a masterly defence of reason and order in ecclesiastical practice, which became a profoundly influential defence of Anglicanism and a strong argument against the Puritan case.

Huntington, William Reed (1838–90): American Episcopalian priest who in 1870 framed the four principles which were adopted in 1886 as the Chicago Quadrilateral and in 1888 as the Lambeth Quadrilateral (qv).

Inter-Anglican Theological and Doctrinal Commission: this commission was established in 1980 on the recommendation of the first meeting of the Anglican Consultative Council in 1980.

Jewel, John (1522–71): Bishop of Salisbury 1560–71. Jewel was deeply influenced by, and involved with, continental Reformers. A refugee in Mary's reign, shortly after his return to England he wrote *Apologia Pro Ecclesia Anglicana* (1562), a major defence and justification of the English Reformation. He supported the Elizabethan Settlement and opposed the Puritans.

Keble, John (1792–1866): hymnwriter and author of *The Christian Year* (1827). Keble's Oxford Assize Sermon of 1833 against Erastianism (qv) was held by Newman to be the beginning of the Oxford Movement (qv), of which, with Pusey, he was a prominent leader.

'King-in-Parliament': the concept that the king ruled surrounded by his subjects, present either in person or by representation. Henry VIII's laws gave the Crown powers which extended over canon law and the church courts. Nevertheless there was a tacit assumption that the king and the law were not the same thing; a tension which by the reign of James I had become a major constitutional issue.

Lambeth Conference: the first Lambeth Conference met in 1867, at the suggestion of C. T. Longley the Archbishop of Canterbury, and was attended by 67 bishops. Longley's proposal was that an informal gathering of bishops should meet at his invitation to discuss Anglican problems. The Conferences have continued approximately every ten years, attended by most Anglican bishops. Issues discussed include theological, domestic, church unity and social issues. The statements of the Lambeth Conferences are not binding on member Churches, being only expressions of the bishops' opinion, though they are of great influence.

Lambeth Quadrilateral: the 'Chicago-Lambeth Articles': four Articles adopted by the American Episcopal Church in Chicago in 1886 and by the 1888 Lambeth Conference. They cover Scripture, the creeds, the two sacraments and the historic episcopate, and attempt to establish common ground in discussions on church unity. The Articles have been influential in the Ecumenical Movement.

Latitudinarians: seventeenth-century divines, often very influential, who appealed to reason as well as to Scripture and the Church. Many had been students of the Cambridge Platonists. Their faith in reason led many to become interested in science, and some became members of the Royal Society. They emphasized moderation, morality and a distrust of extremes such as Puritanism and Deism.

Laud, William (1573–1645): Archbishop of Canterbury 1633–45. Laud was an opponent of Puritanism and a champion of order and external uniformity, pre-Reformation liturgy, and episcopacy. He initiated a campaign to reintroduce ritual, ornament and genuflection into the churches, and his influence extended into all sectors of English life. Out of the Laudian programme emerged the High Church party, which emphasized Arminianism over Calvinism and shared Laud's views on worship and church life. Laud, who had become identified with the despotism of Charles I, was executed for treason in 1645 during the Civil War.

Liberal Catholicism: a term coined by Charles Gore to describe the synthesis of incarnational theology and evolutionary thought of the authors of *Lux Mundi*. He maintained that its combination of Catholic doctrine, critical method and social concern was the authentic Anglican vocation. Later liberal Catholicism was more experiential and critical, and is represented by *Essays Catholic and Critical*, ed. E. G. Selwyn (1926). To be distinguished from the eclectic and theosophical Liberal Catholic Church, founded 1918.

Locke, John (1632–1704): a father of deism, Lock argued that the mind is a *tabula rasa*, and knowledge is the result of ideas derived from sense-experience and awareness of self. For Locke, faith was the result of proof. He opposed Enthusiasm, and in *The Reasonableness of Christianity* (1695) he demonstrates a very high view of reason—a view which had considerable influence on subsequent theology. He discarded most dogma, was an advocate of toleration, and accepted that high moral and ethical imperatives must follow from his rationalism.

Lux Mundi: a Series of Studies in the Religion of the Incarnation (1889): collection of essays from a position of liberal Catholicism (qv) edited by Charles Gore, critiquing the Anglo-Catholic movement and arguing for a more socially aware and contemporary Catholicism in the Church of England. It was an attempt to unite Tractarian theology with critical scholarship and sound learning.

Maurice, F. D. (1805–72): a leading Anglican theologian and founder member, with Charles Kingsley and J. M. F. Ludlow, of the Christian Socialist movement. A prolific and influential writer, his works included: *The Kingdom of Christ* (1838), his major work in which he addressed the issue of unity between Christians in the light of the incarnate Christ; and *Theological Essays* (1853), which contained unorthodox and controversial views on eternal punishment.

Modernism: in general, used of theological developments showing accommodation to scientific, historical and philosophical argument. In Roman Catholicism of the early twentieth century, a heterogeneous movement represented by A. Loisy, F. von Hügel and G. H. Tyrrell; they were sceptical of dogma and endorsed higher criticism. Anglican Modernism was roughly contemporary, influenced by continental liberal Protestantism, was the heir to the Broad Church movement and focused, in the 1920s, in the Modern Churchman's Union. Unorthodox and radical views expressed by the Modernists provoked controversy.

Newman, J. H. (1801–90); of Evangelical upbringing, Newman became in 1828 vicar of St Mary's, Oxford. He was an early Tractarian (qv), but moved from advocacy of the *via media* to a controversial Catholic interpretation of the Thirty-nine Articles in Tract XC (qv). In 1843 he resigned his living and in 1845 converted to Roman Catholicism. He published *Apologia Pro Vita Sua* in 1864, *Grammar of Assent* (an apologetic work) in 1870, and became a cardinal in 1879.

Non-conformist: a term originating after the Restoration to describe those not conforming to the doctrine and practice of the Church of England.

Non-jurors: those of the Church of England who did not take the Oath of Allegiance to William and Mary (See Glorious Revolution). Also, from 1714, used of those who did not swear allegiance to George I.

Oxford Movement: a nineteenth-century movement within the Church of England against Erastianism (qv) and liberalism. Deriving from the High Church party. Generally regarded as dating from Keble's 1833 sermon (See Keble), it soon acquired the name 'Tractarianism' (qv). When its anti-Reformation leanings were perceived it aroused hostility. From 1840, part of the movement shifted towards Rome under the leadership of Newman (qv; See also Tract XC). In 1845 Newman converted to Rome, and the movement lost its Oxford base and acquired the label 'Anglo-Catholic' (qv). The Oxford Movement emphasized High Church practices and the traditions of Old Catholicism.

Prayer Book: the 1549 Book of Common Prayer followed the 1544 English liturgy and the 1548 *Order of Communion*. A new, vernacular liturgy, Cranmer's Prayer Book was a replacement for its Latin equivalents, based substantially on the old Sarum rites but significantly Protestant—a characteristic strengthened in the 1552 Prayer Book, produced in response to demands from English and continental Reformers. The 1552 book was abolished by Queen Mary, was restored in 1559 by Queen Elizabeth with few but significant changes, resisted appeals for change from e.g. Puritans, was again lightly revised in 1604, and was abolished in 1645. The Prayer Book as enforced by the 1662 Act of Uniformity was essentially unchanged, though with some additions and many minor revisions. Other Prayer Books appeared as the Anglican Communion expanded, including the 1789 book of the Episcopal Church in the United States.

In England in 1927 there was a revision in response to developments that had begun in the late nineteenth century, to include e.g. reservation of the sacrament. This was perceived by Parliament as an attempt to shift the doctrinal emphases of the Church of England, and rejected. Although revised Prayer Books have been introduced in various Provinces, no further revisions to the 1662 Prayer Book have been authorized in England, and it remains the official service book, the work produced in 1980 being strictly therefore an *Alternative Service Book*.

Primates Meeting: a group composed of the presiding or senior bishops of the autonomous Provinces of the Anglican Communion. Given a more prominent status at the 1978 Lambeth Conference, it has met on a regular basis since 1979 and constitutes one of several recent moves to strengthen communication and consultation within the Anglican Communion.

Puritan: originally a movement within the English Church, Puritanism in the reign of Elizabeth argued for a more complete reformation than was achieved under Henry VIII. The first Puritans in the accepted sense were Marian exiles, returning to England intent on purifying the Church on the basis of the supremacy of Scripture, the right of individual access to the Bible and the importance of teaching it to the people, and a Calvanistic perspective drawn from continental Reformed Churches. The Puritans were disappointed with the Elizabethan Settlement and their demands to James I met with only limited response. By 1640 they were the dominant force behind Parliament in the Civil Wars, but by the time of Cromwell were divided among themselves. Puritanism, which began within the Church, was forced outside it by the Clarendon Code, and thereafter the Puritan ideal of a total reformation of Church and state withered.

'Puritanism', in both learned and popular forms, was often misused as a term, a practice which began in Elizabeth's reign. Modern usage is a reminder that historic Puritanism was identified by a distinct lifestyle and discipline.

Queen Anne's Bounty: a fund established by Queen Anne in 1704 to redistribute clerical taxes in a more equitable system of clerical incomes.

Recusant: a Roman Catholic who refused to accept the Elizabethan Settlement, specifically the provisions of the 1559 Act of Uniformity (qv). Increasingly harsh penalties against recusants culminated in the years after 1688. The Catholic Emancipation Act (1829) finally removed most of the penalties.

Restoration: the return of Charles II to the English throne in 1660 and the restoration of the Stuart dynasty. It meant the re-establishment of the Church of England (See Savoy Conference).

Royal Supremacy: in contradistinction to papal supremacy, describes the process whereby Henry VIII progressively, and conspicuously in legislation of 1529–34, removed from the pope jurisdiction, prerogatives and revenues previously his due from England. The process culminated in the Act of Supremacy (1534) (qv), which gave Henry supreme headship of the English Church.

Savoy Conference (1661): a conference comprising twelve bishops and twelve Puritan divines, convened after the Restoration (qv) to resolve disagreements over the nature of the restored Church. The Puritans argued strongly for satisfaction of grievances extending back to the Elizabethan Settlement, but the result was only minor revision of the Prayer Book and numerous Puritan secessions following the 1662 Act of Uniformity (qv).

Simeon, Charles (1759–1836): leading Evangelical, influential in Cambridge, a noted preacher and involved in many Evangelical enterprises. Founded the Simeon Trust to promote Evangelicalism in the parishes.

Supreme Governor: see Acts of Supremacy

Synod: in general church usage, a council of senior clergy to discuss doctrine, policy etc. In England such assemblies have had various titles (See Convocation). The needs of Scottish Episcopalians after the 1690 establishment of the (Presbyterian) Church of Scotland led to the first example of constitutional and synodical government known in the history of Anglicanism. The first post-revolutionary American General Convention was held in 1785 in Philadelphia, and contained both clerical and lay members. From the mid-nineteenth century the term 'synod' was regularly used for gatherings of bishops, clergy and lay persons to govern the corporate life of an Anglican Church outside England, by common consent.

Temple, William (1881–1944): Archbishop of York 1929–42, Archbishop of Canterbury 1942–44, and chairman of the Archbishops' Commission on Christian Doctrine (1922–37). A leader in the Ecumenical Movement, he presided at the inaugural meeting of the British Council of Churches, and was instrumental in the founding of the World Council of Churches. He was a distinguished theologian and apologist who espoused, notably in *Nature, Man and God* (1934), a metaphysical philosophy in which Christ is the highest realization of the world process.

Test Act (1673): passed by Parliament in opposition to Charles II's 1672 Declaration of Indulgence, the Test Act required all office-holders under the Crown to, in effect, publicly and legally embrace membership of the Church of England. The Act made many enemies for the Church, and committed Dissenters to active opposition.

Tractarianism: the period of the Oxford Movement that saw the publication of the *Tracts for the Times*. Written by e.g. J. H. Newman, E. B. Pusey, R. H. Froude, R. W. Church and J. B. Mozley, the Tracts, which were widely distributed, expounded the credal statement, 'I believe in one holy, Catholic and Apostolic Church.' Tract I, by Newman, urged the reclamation of the doctrine of apostolic succession. In all, 90 Tracts were issued.

Tract XC (1841, J. H. Newman): Tract in which Newman argued that the Thirty-Nine Articles did not, as had been wrongly supposed, condemn many Roman Catholic practices. Its hostile reception indicated to Newman that Anglicanism's claims to be a *via media* (qv) were not tenable.

Tyndale, William (*c.* 1494–1536): English Reformer, popularly known as 'the English Luther'. Tyndale's vernacular English Bible was printed on the continent in difficult and fugitive circumstances. Opposed by Thomas More and other English churchmen, Tyndale was given help by expatriate English sympathizers. When it appeared in England, Tyndale's New Testament was publicly burned in London.

Author of several theological works as well as a prolific translator, Tyndale is a significant literary figure besides a seminal contributor to the English Reformation. He was executed at Vilvorde, near Brussels, in 1536.

Via Media: 'the middle way', a designation for the stance of Anglicanism between Roman Catholicism and one form or another of Protestantism. The significance of the term is ambiguous, since on occasions extreme or radical Protestantism (Anabaptism) is taken as one pole, in which case Anglicanism shares the 'middle way' with e.g. Lutheranism; on other occasions the designation is intended to contrast Anglicanism with more central forms of Protestantism, e.g. Puritanism (qv), Presbyterianism, and what J. H. Newman called 'popular Protestantism'.

Whitgift, John (*c.* 1530–1604): Archbishop of Canterbury 1583–1604, Whitgift was staunchly aligned with the Anglicanism of Queen Elizabeth and instituted numerous measures against Puritans, including the publishers of the *Marprelate Tracts*. His Calvinist revision of the Thirty-Nine Articles (the Lambeth Articles) was rejected by Elizabeth.

Wilberforce, William (1759–1833): Anglican Evangelical (qv) at the core of the Clapham Sect, Wilberforce was a social reformer most notably committed to the abolition of the slave trade, which took place in 1807 as a result of his and his associates' work. His *Practical View of the Prevailing Religious System . . .* (1797) was an Evangelical challenge to nominal Christianity, and was highly influential; he and the Clapham Sect were also active in evangelizing the upper classes.

INDEX

The index is virtually exhaustive for names, but necessarily selective for subjects. Terms implicit throughout the book such as 'Anglican Communion' are indexed only when important references are made to them.

Books mentioned in the text are indexed by author. Short titles are used. The Preface and Notes are indexed only where they add something substantial to the main text. The Glossary and biblical references are not indexed.

Page numbers of sections where a subject is comprehensively treated are in italics.

Index

Index

Index

Index

Grotius, Hugo 100, 236f., 238f.
Guild of the Servants of the Sanctuary 373
Gunpowder Plot, special service commemorating deliverance from 100
Gutenberg, Johann 5

Hackney Phalanx 34
Halifax, Lord 45
Hall, Joseph 164, 328: *The Divine Arte of Meditation* (1606) 167
Halsbury, Lord *Laws of England: Ecclesiastical Law* (as edited for the Church Assembly 1975) 426–7
Hammond, Peter C.: *The Parson and the Victorian Church* (1977) 348
Hammond, Henry 102, 237, 241
Hampden, R.D. 226
Hampton Court Conference (1604) 9
Hanson, R.P.C. 89n.3
Hardie, Keir 326
Hare, Julius 36
Harmony of the Confessions of Faith of the Orthodox and Reformed Churches (1581) 142
Harperfield, John 138
Harrison, Benjamin 240f.
Harvey, A.E. 90n.16
Hasidim 330
Hatch, Edwin 292
Hatchett, Marion J. 345
Hawkins, Edward 434
Headlam, A.C., Bp 44f., 380f., 386: *Doctrine of the Church and Reunion* (1920) 45
Heber, Reginald, Bp 433
Hebert, A.G. 41: *Liturgy and Society* (1935) 43, 280; *The Parish Communion* (1937) 43
Heidegger, Martin 114
Heidelberg Catechism (1563) 157
Henderson, Arthur 326
Henry II 178
Henry VIII 134, 156, 248, 296f., 353f., 397: responses to reform 3–6, 11; marriage problems 221: *Assertion of the Seven Sacraments* (1521) 234
Henry's Primer 122
Henson, Hensley, Bp 84f., 419–22
Herbert, George 107, 155, 159f., 164, 315, 322, 346: *Country Parson* 345; 'The Elixir' 327
High Church movement 34–5, 305, 371, 409f., 416: Laudianism 22f.; outside England 400
Hildebrand *see* Gregory VII
Hilsey's Primer 122
Hine, John 436
'Historic episcopate' (Huntington's term) 40, 52, 367
Hoadly, Benjamin, Bp 31
Hobart, John Henry, Bp 171
Hodges, George C. 333
Hokkaido, Diocese of 440
Holiness 314

Holland, Henry Scott 332
Hollifield, E. Brooks 348f.
Holmes, Urban T. 252
Holy Communion *see* Eucharist
Homilies *133–43*
Homilies, Book of *see Book of Homilies*
Homily on the Peril of Idolatry (1571) 103; Against Disobedience and Wilful Rebellion (Abp Parker, 1571) 139, 248; Of the Worth Receiving and Reverent Esteeming of the Body and Blood of Christ 288
Homoousion 114,191
Hong Kong, Diocese of 393, 403n.1
Hooker, Richard 11, 13ff., 16f., 23f., 26, 67–73 *passim*, 80, 100f., 108, 114, 164–8, 172, 173, 175, 224ff., 231, 235f., 239, 242, 251, 258, 274ff., 287, 289, 299, 301, 303, 307, 315, 325, 328, 330, 398, 406, 408, 414, 421: on justification 67ff., *Discourse of Justification* 67, 165; *Of the Laws of Ecclesiastical Polity* (1594, 1597 seq.) 106, 164ff., 201f., 224ff., 254, 302, 319, 354f.: discussed by Loyer 318–20
Hooper, John, Bp 127
Horne, George 34
Horsley, Samuel, Bp 34
Hort, F.J.A. 169, 292: Hulsean Lectures *The Way, the Truth and the Life* 40, 170; *Christian Ecclesia* 170
Hoskyns E.C. 41, 83
House of Bishops (USA) adoption of Chicago Quadrilateral (1886) 209
House of Laymen, House of Laity (Convocation initiative) 253
Howe, John, Bp x, 196
Huddleston, Trevor, Abp 369
Humanism, Renaissance 4
Hunnius, Nicholaus 236
Huntington, Frederic Dan 333
Huntington, James, biography by Scudder 173
Huntington, William Reed 40, 219ff., 228, 229ff.: *The Church Idea* (1870) 219
Hutchinsonians 34
Hymns Ancient and Modern 395–6

Iglesia Anglicana Del Cono Sur 212, 393
Ignatius of Antioch, St 88, 102, 303, 399, 419
Illingworth, J.R. 113, 255
Images 103
Incarnational theology *see* Liberal Catholicism
Independents 355–6
India, Burma and Ceylon, Church of 398, 366
India 366: United Churches of South and North India 30, 38, 45, 230, 366, 379f., 382f., 391, 394: Anglican reluctance to enter into communion with Church of South India 290; Ordination rites for Church of South India (1958) 153; catechism revision 154; liturgy of Church of South India 404n.9

Index